Compendium on the Family and Human Life

LIBRERIA EDITRICE VATICANA

First printing, April 2015

ISBN 978-1-60137-369-4

Contents

PART I

Papal Documents
and Teachings of
Pope John Paul II

CHAPTER I

To the Plenary Assemblies of the Pontifical Council for the Family

Address to the Plenary Assembly of the Pontifical Council for the Family

"Pastoral care of the family and of couples in difficulty"

October 18, 2002

Your Eminences,
Brothers in the Episcopate,
Dear Married Couples,

1. I am happy to welcome you for the Fifteenth Plenary Assembly of the Pontifical Council for the Family. To everyone a cordial greeting. I thank Cardinal Alfonso López Trujillo, President of the Pontifical Council, for the kind words he addressed on behalf of everyone who is present. I wish to thank each of you and also those who are on the staff of the Council for carrying out with generosity and competence such an important mission for the Church and for society to serve the family, the domestic church and the cradle of life.

Much has been done in these years, much remains to be done. I encourage you not to be discouraged by the immensity of the challenge today, but continue without hesitation to fulfill the duty of safeguarding and promoting the immeasurable good of marriage and the family. On this endeavor, to a great extent, depend the destiny of society and the future of evangelization.

The theme of your plenary meeting is very timely: *The Pastoral Care of the Family and of Couples in Difficulty*. This is a broad and complex topic; you will deal with only a few aspects since you have had the opportunity to examine it on other occasions. In this regard, I would like to offer you a few starting points for your reflection and guidance.

2. In a world that is becoming ever more secularized, the great task of the believing family is to become conscious of its own vocation and mission. In every circumstance, the starting point for this work is to safeguard and inten-sify *prayer, an unceasing prayer to the Lord* to increase one's faith and make it more vigorous. As I wrote in the Apostolic Letter *Rosarium Virginis Mariae*: "The family that prays together, stays together" (no. 41).

It is true that, when one goes through difficult times, the support of sci-ence can be of great help, but nothing can replace an ardent, personal and confident faith that is open to the Lord, who said, *"Come to me, all you labor and are heavy burdened and I will give you rest"* (Mt 11:28).

The indispensable source of energy and renewal, when frailty and weak-ness increase, is the encounter with the living Christ, Lord of the Covenant. This is why you must develop an intense spiritual life and open your soul to the Word of life. In the depths of the heart the voice of God must be heard, even if at times it seems to be silent, in reality it resounds continually in the heart and accompanies us along the path that can have its burden of sorrow as happened to the two travelers of Emmaus.

Special care must be shown to young spouses so that they do not surrender in the face of problems and conflicts. Prayer, frequent recourse to the sacra-ment of reconciliation, spiritual direction, must never be abandoned with the idea that one can replace them with other techniques of human and psycho-logical support. We must never forget what is essential, namely, to live in the family under the tender and merciful gaze of God.

The richness of the sacramental life, in the life of the family, that partici-pates in the Eucharist every Sunday (cf. *Dies Domini*, no. 81) is undoubtedly the best antidote for confronting and overcoming obstacles and tensions.

3. This is even more necessary when there abound lifestyles, fashion and cul-tures that bring into doubt the value of the marriage, even reaching the point of holding that it is impossible to realize the mutual gift of self in marriage until death in joyful fidelity (cf. *Letter to Families*, no. 10). Human frailty grows if the divorce mentality dominates, something that the Council denounced with such vigor because it leads so often to separations and definitive break-ups. Even a bad education for sexuality harms the life of the family. When there is lacking an integral preparation for marriage that respects the grad-ual stages of the maturation of the engaged couple (cf. *Familiaris Consortio*, no. 66), in the family this lessens the possibility of defense.

There is no difficult situation that cannot be adequately confronted when one cultivates a genuine atmosphere of Christian life. Love itself, wounded by sin, is still a redeemed love (cf. *The Catechism of the Catholic Church* [CCC], no. 1608). It is clear that, if sacramental life is weak, the family yields more easily to snares because it is deprived of any defenses.

How important it is to foster family support for couples, especially young couples, by families who are spiritually and morally solid. It is a fruitful and necessary apostolate at this time in history.

4. I would like to offer a reflection on the dialogue that should go on at home in the formation of the children. Often there is no time to live and dialogue in the family. Many times parents do not feel prepared and even fear to assume what is their duty, the task of the integral education of their children. It might be that, due to the lack of any dialogue, the children feel serious obstacles when it comes to seeing in their parents genuine models to imitate, and look elsewhere for models and lifestyles that are often false and harmful to human dignity and to genuine love. The *trivialization of sex* in a society that is saturated with eroticism, and the lack of any reference to ethical principles, can ruin the life of children, adolescents and youth, preventing their being formed in a responsible, mature love and in the harmonious development of their personality.

5. Dear Brothers and Sisters, thank you for the attention that you dedicate in your plenary assembly to such a timely topic that I have very much at heart. May God help you to focus on what is most useful for families today. Continue to prepare with enthusiasm for the World Family Day that will be held in Manila in January of the coming year.

I heartily hope that the convention that I convoked during the observance of the Jubilee of the Family and for which I assigned the theme: *The Christian Family: Good News for the Third Millennium*, might foster the missionary zeal of families around the world.

I entrust all of this to Mary, Queen of the Family. May she accompany and protect you always. With affection I bless you and those who collaborate with you in the service of the true good of the family.

Address to the Participants in the Plenary Assembly of the Pontifical Council for the Family

"The mission of mature and experienced couples to engaged and young married couples"

November 20, 2004

Your Eminence,
Venerable Brothers in the Episcopate and in the Priesthood,
Dear Brothers and Sisters,

1. I am pleased to receive you on the occasion of the Plenary Assembly of the Pontifical Council for the Family. I address my cordial greeting to you all. In particular, I greet Cardinal Alfonso López Trujillo, whom I thank for the sentiments he has expressed.

I know that the Dicastery is working hard to spread the "Gospel of the family." The expression is an appropriate one, for to proclaim the "wonderful news" of the family that is rooted in the Heart of God the Creator is a noble and crucial mission. The family founded on marriage is an irreplaceable natural institution and a fundamental element of the common good of every society.

2. Those who destroy this fundamental fabric of human coexistence by failing to respect its identity or distorting its tasks injure society deeply and often cause irreparable damage. You rightly intend, therefore, to reflect on various national and international aspects that affect the family. In this context too the Church cannot disregard the norm pronounced by the Apostle Paul: "We must obey God rather than men" (Acts 5:29).

In the Apostolic Exhortation *Familiaris Consortio*, I already gave prominence to "the unique place that, in this field, belongs to the mission of married couples and Christian families by virtue of the grace received in the sacrament," and I recalled that this mission must be "placed at the service of the building up of the Church" and "the establishing of the Kingdom of God in history" (no. 71). This mission has lost none of its timeliness; on the contrary, it has become exceptionally urgent.

3. Coming to the main theme of your Plenary Meeting, *"The mission of mature and experienced couples in regard to engaged couples and young married couples,"* I would like to encourage you to renew your commitment to young families.

As I said in *Familiaris Consortio*, "in her pastoral care of young families, the Church must also pay special attention to helping them to live married love responsibly in relationship with its demands of communion and service to life. She must likewise help them to harmonize the intimacy of home life with the generous shared work of building up the Church and society" (no. 69).

Moreover, in that Document I pointed out that young families, "finding themselves in a context of new values and responsibilities, are more vulnerable, especially in the first years of marriage, to possible difficulties, such as those created by adaptation to life together or by the birth of children" (no. 69). I therefore urged young couples to accept warmly and evaluate intelligently the discreet, delicate and generous help of other couples who have had a long experience of marriage and the family.

4. In this regard, I am pleased to point out the increasing presence throughout the world of pro-family and pro-life movements. Their dynamism, placed at the service of those setting out on the path of recently contracted marriage, guarantees valuable assistance in inspiring the appropriate response to the riches of the vocation to which the Lord is calling them.

Ten years ago, in my *Letter to Families*, I stressed how important the rich experience of other families can be, especially when the "we" of the parents, of husband and wife, develops in the "we" of the family with the most precious gift of children (cf. no. 16). It is in this way that the domestic Church, the sanctuary of life and the true pillar of humanity's future, is built.

5. To conclude, my thoughts go to the Fifth World Meeting of Families, which will take place in 2006 in Valencia, Spain. I know that your Pontifical Council is preparing that event jointly with the Archdiocese of Valencia. I greet Archbishop Agustín García-Gasco who is present here, and send a warm greeting to the beloved Land of Spain that will have the honor of hosting this event.

As I invoke continuous divine assistance upon your work, I entrust you to the special intercession of the Holy Family of Nazareth and bless you with all my heart.

CHAPTER II

To the Pontifical Academy for Life

Message on the Tenth Anniversary of the Establishment of the Pontifical Academy for Life

February 17, 2004

Venerable Brothers,
Distinguished Ladies and Gentlemen,

1. With pleasure I send you my Message on the occasion of the day on which you are commemorating the *tenth anniversary of the foundation of the Pontifical Academy for Life*. Once again I express my gratitude to each one of you for the Academy's high-quality service of spreading the "Gospel of life." I greet in particular Prof. Juan de Dios Vial Correa, President, Bishop Elio Sgreccia, Vice-President, and the entire Administrative Council.

First of all, I thank the Lord with you for your useful Institution which was added ten years ago to the others created after the Council. The *doctrinal and pastoral Bodies of the Apostolic See* are the first to benefit from your collaboration with regard to the *knowledge and facts* that decisions in the area of moral norms regarding life require. This is the case with the Pontifical Councils for the Family and for Health Pastoral Care, as well as in response to requests from the Section for Relations with States of the Secretariat of State, from the Congregation for the Doctrine of the Faith and from other Dicasteries and Offices.

2. As the years have passed, the importance of the Pontifical Academy for Life has become more and more evident. However, while progress in the biomedical sciences gives us a glimpse of promising prospects for the good of humanity and the treatment of chronic and distressing diseases, it also

frequently presents *serious problems concerning the respect for human life and the dignity of the person.*

The growing control of medical technology in the process of human pro-creation, discoveries in the fields of genetics and molecular biology, changes in the therapeutic treatment of seriously-ill patients as well as the spread of currents of thought of a utilitarian or hedonistic inspiration are factors that can lead to aberrant conduct as well as to drafting laws which are unjust with regard to the dignity of the person and the respect that the inviolability of innocent life requires.

3. Your contribution is also invaluable to intellectuals, especially Catholics, "who are called to be present and active in the leading centers where culture is formed, in schools and universities, in places of scientific and technological research . . . " (Encyclical Letter *Evangelium Vitae*, no. 98). The Pontifical Academy for Life was set up for this purpose, with the specific task "to study and to provide information and training about the principal problems of law and biomedicine pertaining to the promotion and protection of life, espe-cially in the direct relationship they have with Christian morality and the directives of the Church's Magisterium" (Motu Proprio *Vitae Mysterium,* no. 4; *L'Osservatore Romano* English edition [ORE], March 9, 1994, 3).

In a word, your highly responsible role includes the complex subject known today as *"bioethics."* I thank you for your commitment to examin-ing specific issues of great interest and likewise for furthering the dialogue between scientific investigation and philosophical and theological reflection, guided by the Magisterium. Researchers, especially those who work in the field of biomedicine, must be made more and more aware of the beneficial enrichment that can derive from combining scientific rigor and the claims of anthropology and Christian ethics.

4. Dear brothers and sisters, may your service now with ten years of experi-ence continue to be increasingly appreciated and supported and provide the desired results in the field of the humanization of biomedical science and the convergence of scientific research and faith.

To this end, I invoke upon the Academy for Life continuous divine assis-tance through its Patroness, the Virgin Mary, and as I assure my remembrance in prayer to each one, I impart a special Apostolic Blessing to you all, which I willingly extend to your collaborators and your loved ones.

Address to the Members of the
Pontifical Academy for Life

February 21, 2004

Dear Brothers and Sisters,

1. I am pleased to be able to personally meet all of you, members of the Pontifical Academy for Life, on this special occasion when you are celebrating the tenth anniversary of the Academy's foundation. You are commemorating all the people who contributed to its birth, with a special thought for the distinguished and meritorious Prof. Jérôme Lejeune, your first President, whose memory I cherish with gratitude and love.

I thank Prof. Juan de Dios Vial Correa, President, for his kind words, and I also greet the Vice-President, Bishop Elio Sgreccia, and the members of the Administrative Council, expressing to one and all my appreciation for the great dedication with which you support the Academy's activity.

2. You are now taking part in two "Study Days" devoted to the topic of artificial procreation. The subject is proving full of serious problems and implications which deserve careful examination. Essential values are at stake, not only for the Christian faithful but also for human beings as such.

What emerges ever more clearly in the procreation of a new creature is its *indispensable bond* with spousal union, by which the husband becomes a father through the conjugal union with his wife, and the wife becomes a mother through the conjugal union with her husband. The Creator's plan is *engraved in the physical and spiritual nature* of the man and of the woman, and as such has universal value.

The act in which the spouses become parents through the reciprocal and total gift of themselves makes them cooperators with the Creator in bringing into the world a new human being called to eternal life. An act so rich that it transcends even the life of the parents cannot be replaced by a mere technological intervention, depleted of human value and at the mercy of the determinism of technological and instrumental procedures.

3. Rather, it is the scientist's task to *investigate the causes of male and female infertility,* in order to prevent this situation of suffering in spouses who long to find "in their child a confirmation and completion of their reciprocal self-giving" (*Donum Vitae*, II, A, no. 1). Consequently, I would like *to encourage scientific research that seeks a natural way to overcome the infertility of the spouses,* and likewise to urge all specialists to perfect those procedures that

can serve this end. I hope that the scientific community—I appeal particularly to those scientists who are believers—may advance reassuringly on the road to true prevention and authentic treatment.

4. The Pontifical Academy for Life will not fail to do everything in its power to encourage every valid initiative which aims to avoid the dangerous manipulation that is part of the processes of artificial procreation.

May the community of the faithful itself strive to support authentic research channels and, when making decisions, resist technological possibilities that replace true parenthood and is therefore harmful to the dignity of both parents and children.

In support of these wishes, I cordially impart my Blessing to you all, which I willingly extend to all your loved ones.

Letter to the President of the Pontifical Academy for Life for the Study Congress on "Quality of Life and Ethics of Health"

February 19, 2005

To my Venerable Brother Bishop Elio Sgreccia,
President of the Pontifical Academy for Life,

1. I am pleased to send my cordial greetings to those who are taking part in the Study Congress that the Pontifical Academy for Life has sponsored on the theme: *"Quality of life and ethics of health."* I greet you in particular, venerable Brother, and offer you my congratulations and good wishes on your recent appointment as President of this Academy. I also extend my greetings to the Chancellor, Msgr. Ignacio Carrasco, to whom I also wish success in his new office. I next address thoughts of deep gratitude to eminent Prof. Juan de Dios Vial Correa, who has retired from the presidency of the Academy after ten years of generous and competent service.

Finally, a word of special thanks goes to all the Members of the Pontifical Academy for their diligent work, especially valuable in these times, marked by the manifestation of many problems in society related to the defense of life and the dignity of the human person. As far as we can see, the Church in the future will be increasingly called into question on these topics that affect the fundamental good of every person and society. The Pontifical Academy for Life, after ten years of existence, must therefore continue to carry out its role of sensitive and precious activity in support of the institutions of the Roman Curia and of the whole Church.

2. The theme addressed at this Congress is of the greatest ethical and cultural importance for both developed and developing societies. The phrases "quality of life" and "promotion of health" identify one of contemporary society's main goals, raising questions that are not devoid of ambiguity and, at times, tragic contradictions. Thus, they require attentive discernment and a thorough explanation.

In the Encyclical *Evangelium Vitae*, I said regarding the ever more anxious quest for the "quality of life" typical of the developed societies: "The so-called 'quality of life' is interpreted primarily or exclusively as economic efficiency, inordinate consumerism, physical beauty and pleasure, to the neglect of the more profound dimensions—interpersonal, spiritual and religious—of existence" (no. 23). These *more profound dimensions* deserve further clarification and research.

3. It is necessary first of all to recognize the *essential quality* that distinguishes every human creature as that of being made *in the image and likeness* of the Creator himself. The human person, constituted of body and soul in the unity of the person—*corpore et anima unus*, as the Constitution *Gaudium et Spes* says (no. 14)—is called to enter into a personal dialogue with the Creator. Man therefore possesses a dignity essentially superior to other visible creatures, living and inanimate. As such he is called to collaborate with God in the task of subduing the earth (cf. Gn 1:28), and is destined in the plan of redemption to be clothed in the dignity of a child of God.

This level of *dignity* and *quality* belongs to the ontological order and is a constitutive part of the human being; it endures through every moment of life, from the very moment of conception until natural death, and is brought to complete fulfillment in the dimension of eternal life. Consequently, the human person should be recognized and respected in any condition of health, infirmity or disability.

4. Consistent with this first, essential level of dignity, a *second*, complementary *level* of quality of life should be recognized and promoted: starting with the recognition of the right to life and the special dignity of every human person, society must promote, in collaboration with the family and other intermediate bodies, the practical conditions required for the development of each individual's personality, harmoniously and in accordance with his or her natural abilities.

All the dimensions of the person, physical, psychological, spiritual and moral, should be promoted in harmony with one another. This implies the existence of suitable social and environmental conditions to encourage this harmonious development. The *social-environmental context*, therefore, characterizes this second level of the quality of human life which must be recognized by *all people,* including those who live in developing countries. Indeed, human beings are equal in dignity, whatever the society to which they may belong.

5. However, in our time the meaning which the expression "quality of life" is gradually acquiring is often far from this basic interpretation, founded on a correct philosophical and theological anthropology.

Indeed, under the impetus of the society of well-being, preference is being given to a notion of quality of life that is both *reductive* and *selective:* it would consist in the ability to enjoy and experience pleasure or even in the capacity for self-awareness and participation in social life. As a result, human beings who *are not yet* or *are no longer* able to understand and desire or those who can no longer enjoy life as sensations and relations are denied every form of quality of life.

6. The *concept of health* has also suffered a similar distortion. It is certainly not easy to define in logical or precise terms a concept as complex and anthropologically rich as that of health. Yet it is certain that this word is intended to refer to all the dimensions of the person, in their harmony and reciprocal unity: the *physical, the psychological,* and *the spiritual and moral* dimensions.

The latter, the moral dimension, cannot be ignored. Every person is responsible for his or her own health and for the health of those who have not yet reached adulthood or can no longer look after themselves. Indeed, the person is also duty bound to treat the environment responsibly, in such a way as to keep it "healthy."

How many diseases are individuals often responsible for, their own and those of others! Let us think of the spread of alcoholism, drug-addiction and AIDS. How much life energy and how many young lives could be saved and kept healthy if the moral responsibility of each person were better able to promote prevention and the preservation of that precious good: health!

7. *Health is not,* of course, *an absolute good.* It is not such especially when it is taken to be merely physical well-being, mythicized to the point of coercing or neglecting superior goods, claiming health reasons even for the rejection of unborn life: this is what happens with the so-called "reproductive health." How can people fail to recognize that this is a reductive and distorted vision of health?

Properly understood, health nevertheless continues to be one of the most important goods for which we all have a precise responsibility, to the point that it can be sacrificed only in order to attain superior goods, as is sometimes demanded in the service of God, one's family, one's neighbor and the whole of society.

Health should therefore be safeguarded and looked after as the *physical-psychological and spiritual balance* of the human being. The squandering of health as a result of various disorders is a serious ethical and social responsibility which, moreover, is linked to the person's moral degeneration.

8. The ethical relevance of the good of health is such as to motivate a strong commitment to its *protection* and *treatment* by society itself. It is a duty of solidarity that excludes no one, not even those responsible for the loss of their own health.

The ontological dignity of the person is in fact superior: it transcends his or her erroneous or sinful forms of behavior. Treating disease and doing one's best to prevent it are ongoing tasks for the individual and for society, precisely as a tribute to the dignity of the person and the importance of the good of health.

Human beings today, in large areas of the world, are victims of the well-being that they themselves have created. In other, even larger parts of the world, they are victims of widespread and ravaging diseases, whose virulence stems from poverty and the degradation of the environment.

All the forces of science and wisdom must be mobilized at the service of the true good of the person and of society in every part of the world, in the light of that basic criterion which is the *dignity of the person*, in whom is impressed the image of God himself.

With these wishes, I entrust the work of the Congress to the intercession of the One who welcomed the Life of the Incarnate Word into her life, while as a sign of special affection, I impart my Blessing to you all.

CHAPTER III

To the Tribunal of the Roman Rota

Address to the Tribunal of the
Roman Rota at the Start of the Judicial Year

January 29, 2004

Dear Members of the Tribunal of the Roman Rota,

1. I am delighted to have this annual meeting with you for the inauguration of the Judicial Year. It offers me a favorable opportunity to reaffirm the importance of your ecclesial ministry and the need for your legal work.

I cordially greet the College of Prelate Auditors, starting with the Dean, Msgr. Raffaello Funghini; I thank him for expressing his profound thoughts on the meaning and value of your work. I then greet the Officials, the Advocates and the other Collaborators of this Apostolic Tribunal, as well as the Members of the *Studium Rotale* and all who are present here.

2. At our meetings in recent years I have addressed certain fundamental aspects of marriage: its nature ordered toward the good, its indissolubility, its dignity as a sacrament. Actually, various other types of appeal also reach the Tribunal of the Apostolic See on the basis of the norms established by the *Code of Canon Law* (cf. cc. 1443-1444) and the Apostolic Constitution *Pastor Bonus* (cf. nos. 126-130). The Tribunal is required first and foremost, however, to focus on marriage. Today, therefore, in response to the concerns the Dean has expressed, I would like once again to reflect on the matrimonial cases submitted to you and, in particular, on one pastoral and juridical aspect that emerges from them: I am alluding to the *favor iuris* (the favor of the law) that marriage enjoys, and to the associated presumption of its validity in case

of doubt, as declared in canon 1060 of the Latin Code and in canon 779 of the Code of Canons of the Eastern Churches.

Indeed, this has met at times with criticism. To some people, these principles seem to be anchored in social and cultural situations of the past, in which the request to marry in accordance with canon law would normally have implied that those engaged to be married understood and accepted the true nature of marriage. In the crisis that unfortunately marks the institution of marriage in so many milieus today, those people hold that often the very validity of the consent may be said to be jeopardized, due to various forms of incapacity or to the absence of the essential properties. With regard to this situation, the critics mentioned wonder if it might not be correct to presume the invalidity of the marriage contracted rather than its validity.

In this perspective, the *favor matrimonii*, they say, should give way to the *favor personae*, the *favor veritatis subiecti* or the *favor libertatis*.

3. *To evaluate these new attitudes correctly, one should first of all identify the foundation and limitations of the favor* in question. Indeed, this principle easily transcends the presumption of validity since it shapes from within all the canonical norms on marriage, both substantial and procedural. The *support* of marriage, in fact, must inspire the entire activity of the Church, of Pastors, of the faithful and of civil society: in a word, of all people of good will. This attitude is not based on a more or less debatable choice but rather on the appreciation of the objective good that every conjugal union and every family represents. It is precisely when the personal and social recognition of so fundamental a good is threatened that the depths of its importance for individuals and communities are discovered.

In light of these considerations, the holy Pastors' duty to defend and foster marriage is quite clear. However, this is also a specific responsibility of all the faithful, indeed, of all men and women and the civil authorities, each according to his or her own competency.

4. The *favor iuris* reserved for marriage implies the presumption of its validity until the contrary is proven (cf. *Code of Canon Law* [CIC], c. 1060; CCEO, c. 779). To grasp the significance of this presumption one should first remember that it does not represent an exception with regard to a general rule in the opposite sense. On the contrary, it is a matter of applying to marriage a presumption that constitutes a fundamental principle of every juridical disposition: human acts licit in themselves and that affect juridical relations are presumed valid, even if proof of their invalidity is obviously admissible (cf. CIC, c. 124 2; CCEO, c. 931 2).

This presumption cannot be interpreted as the mere protection of appearances or of the *status quo* as such, since the possibility of contesting the act is also provided for, within reasonable limits.

However, what appears outwardly to be correctly placed, to the extent that it is lawful, deserves initially to be considered valid and, consequently, to be upheld by law since this external reference point is the only one which the legal system realistically provides to discern situations which must be safeguarded. To hypothesize the opposite, that is, the obligation to provide positive proof of the validity of the respective acts, would mean exposing the subjects to a demand that would be almost impossible to achieve. Indeed, the proof must include the many presuppositions and prerequisites of the act, which are often long drawn out and involve a large number of persons and previous, interconnected acts.

5. Then what can one say to the argument which holds that the failure of conjugal life implies the invalidity of the marriage? Unfortunately, this erroneous assertion is sometimes so forceful as to become a generalized prejudice that leads people to seek grounds for nullity as a merely formal justification of a pronouncement that is actually based on the empirical factor of matrimonial failure. This unjust formalism of those who are opposed to the traditional *favor matrimonii* can lead them to forget that, in accordance with human experience marked by sin, a valid marriage can fail because of the spouses' own misuse of freedom.

Admission of true nullities should rather lead to ascertaining with greater seriousness at the time of the marriage the necessary prerequisites for matrimony, especially those concerning the consent and true disposition of the engaged couple. Parish priests and those who work with them in this area have the grave duty not to surrender to a purely bureaucratic view of the pre-matrimonial examination of the parties, specified in canon 1067. Their pastoral intervention must be dictated by awareness that at precisely that moment, people are able to discover the natural and supernatural good of marriage and consequently commit themselves to pursuing it.

6. The presumption of the validity of a marriage is truly set in a broader context. Often the real problem is not so much the presumption in words as the overall vision of marriage itself, hence, the process to ascertain the validity of its celebration. Such a process is essentially inconceivable apart from the context of ascertaining the truth. This teleological reference to the truth is what unites all the protagonists of the process, despite the diversity of their roles. In this regard, a more or less open skepticism has been inferred as to the human ability to recognize the truth about the validity of a marriage. In this area too, a renewed confidence in human reason is necessary with regard

both to the essential aspects of marriage and to the specific circumstances of each union.

The tendency to instrumentally broaden the causes for nullity, losing sight of the bounds of objective truth, involves a structural distortion of the entire process. In this perspective the preliminary investigation would lose its effectiveness since its outcome would be preordained. The search itself for the truth, to which the judge is seriously bound *ex officio* (CIC, c. 1452; CCEO, c. 1110) and for the attainment of which he seeks the help of the defender of the bond and of the advocate, would result in a series of empty formalities. The constitutive aspiration to the truth of the sentence would be lost or seriously minimized were it to be subjected to a series of preordained responses, as these would undermine its critical power of inquiry and analysis. Key concepts such as moral certitude and the free examination of the proofs would be left without their necessary reference point in objective truth (cf. CIC, c. 1608; CCEO, c. 1291), the search for which would be abandoned or considered unattainable.

7. Going back further, the problem concerns the concept of marriage seen in a global vision of reality. The essential dimension of the justness of marriage, which is based on an intrinsically juridical reality, is replaced by empirical viewpoints of a sociological, psychological, etc. kind, as well as by various forms of juridical positivism. Without in any way belittling the valid contributions of sociology, psychology or psychiatry, it cannot be forgotten that an authentically juridical consideration of marriage requires a metaphysical vision of the human person and of the conjugal relationship. Without this ontological foundation the institution of marriage becomes merely an extrinsic superstructure, the result of the law and of social conditioning, which limits the freedom of the person to fulfill himself or herself.

It is necessary instead to rediscover the truth, goodness and beauty of the marriage institution. Since it is the work of God himself, through human nature and the freedom of consent of the engaged couple, marriage remains an indissoluble personal reality, a bond of justice and love, linked from eternity to the plan of salvation and raised in the fullness of time to the dignity of a Christian sacrament. It is this reality that the Church and the world must encourage! This is the true *favor matrimonii!*

In presenting these ideas to you for reflection, I would like once again to express to you my appreciation of your sensitive and demanding work in the administration of justice. With these sentiments, as I pray for constant divine help for each one of you, dear Prelate Auditors, Officials and Advocates of the Roman Rota, I impart my Blessing to you all with affection.

Address to the Tribunal of the
Roman Rota at the Start of the Judicial Year

January 29, 2005

1. This annual appointment with you, dear Prelate Auditors of the Apostolic Tribunal of the Roman Rota, highlights the essential connection between your precious work and the judicial aspect of the Petrine ministry. The words of the Dean of your College have expressed your common commitment to full fidelity in your ecclesial service.

It is in this perspective that I would like to place certain considerations concerning *the moral dimension* of the activity of all who work at the ecclesiastical tribunals, especially the duty to *conform to the truth about marriage* as the Church teaches it.

2. The *ethical question* has always been asked very pointedly in any kind of judicial proceedings. In fact, individual or collective interests can induce the parties to resort to various kinds of duplicity and even bribery in order to attain a favorable sentence.

Nor are *canonical proceedings*, in which an attempt is made to discover the truth about whether or not a marriage exists, immune from this risk. The unquestionable importance of this for the moral conscience of the parties involved reduces the likelihood of acquiescence to interests alien to the quest for the truth. Nevertheless, cases can exist in which a similar acquiescence is expressed that jeopardizes the regularity of the proceedings. The firm reaction of canon law to such behavior is well known (cf. CIC, cc. 1389, 1391, 1457, 1488, 1489).

3. However, in the current circumstances there is also the threat of another risk. In the name of what they claim to be pastoral requirements, some voices have been raised proposing to *declare marriages that have totally failed null and void*. These persons propose that in order to obtain this result, recourse should be made to the expedient of retaining the substantial features of the proceedings, simulating the existence of an authentic judicial verdict. Such persons have been tempted to provide reasons for nullity and to prove them in comparison with the most elementary principles of the body of norms and of the Church's Magisterium.

The *objective juridical and moral gravity of such conduct*, which in no way constitutes a pastorally valid solution to the problems posed by matrimonial crises, is obvious. Thanks be to God, there is no lack of faithful people who refuse to let their consciences be deceived. Moreover, many of them, despite being personally involved in a conjugal crisis, are not prepared to solve it except by keeping to the path of truth.

4. In my annual Addresses to the Roman Rota, I have referred several times to the *essential relationship* that the process has with the search for objective truth. It is *primarily the Bishops*, by divine law judges in their own communities, who must be responsible for this. It is on their behalf that the tribunals administer justice. Bishops are therefore called to be personally involved *in ensuring the suitability of the members of the tribunals*, diocesan or interdiocesan, of which they are the Moderators, and in verifying that the *sentences passed conform to right doctrine*.

Sacred Pastors cannot presume that the activity of their tribunals is merely a "technical" matter from which they can remain detached, entrusting it entirely to their judicial vicars (cf. CIC, cc. 391, 1419, 1423 1).

5. *The criterion that inspires* the deontology of the judge is *his love for the truth*. First and foremost, therefore, he must be convinced that *the truth exists*. The truth must therefore be sought with a genuine desire to know it, despite all the inconveniences that may derive from such knowledge. It is necessary to resist the *fear of the truth* that can, at times, stem from the dread of annoying people. The truth, which is Christ himself (cf. Jn 8:32, 36), sets us free from every form of compromise with interested falsehoods.

The judge who truly acts as a judge, in other words, with justice, neither lets himself be conditioned by feelings of false compassion for people, nor by false models of thought, however widespread these may be in his milieu. He knows that unjust sentences are never a true pastoral solution, and that God's judgment of his own actions is what counts for eternity.

6. The judge must then abide by *canonical laws*, correctly interpreted. Hence, he must never lose sight of the intrinsic connection of juridical norms with Church doctrine. Indeed, people sometimes presume to separate Church law from the Church's magisterial teaching as though they belonged to two separate spheres; they suppose the former alone to have juridically binding force, whereas they value the latter merely as a directive or an exhortation. Such an approach basically reveals a *positivist mindset* which is in contradiction with the best of the classical and Christian juridical tradition concerning the law. In fact, the authentic interpretation of God's Word, exercised by the Magisterium of the Church (cf. Second Vatican Council, Dogmatic Constitution on Divine Revelation *Dei Verbum*, no. 10), *has juridical value to the extent that it concerns the context of law*, without requiring any further formal procedure in order to become juridically and morally binding.

For a healthy juridical interpretation, it is indispensable to understand *the whole body of the Church's teachings*, and to place every affirmation systematically in the flow of tradition. It will thus be possible to avoid selective and distorted interpretations and useless criticisms at every step.

Lastly, the *preliminary investigation of the case* is an important stage in the search for the truth. The very reason for its existence is endangered and degenerates into pure formalism when the outcome of the proceedings is taken for granted. It is true that the entitlement to timely justice is also part of the concrete service to the truth and constitutes a personal right. Yet *false speed* to the detriment of the truth is even more seriously unjust.

7. I would like to end this Meeting by offering *my truly heartfelt thanks* to you, Prelate Auditors, Officials, Advocates and all who work at this Apostolic Tribunal, as well as to the members of the Studium Rotale.

You know that you can count on the prayers of the Pope and of many people of good will who recognize the value of your work at the service of the truth. The Lord will repay your daily efforts with peace and joy of conscience and with the esteem and support of those who love justice, not only in the life to come but already in this life.

In expressing the wish that the truth of justice will shine out ever more brightly in the Church and in your lives, I cordially impart my Blessing to you all.

CHAPTER IV

Addresses and Messages

Message for the Twelfth World Day of the Sick

Shrine of Lourdes, France, February 11, 2004

December 1, 2003

To my Venerable Brother
Cardinal Javier Lozano Barragán,
President of the Pontifical Council for Health Pastoral Care,

1. The World Day of the Sick, an event held on a different Continent each year, takes on a singular meaning this time. Indeed, it will take place in Lourdes, France, site of the apparition of the Blessed Virgin on February 11, 1858, which since that time has become the destination of many pilgrimages. In that mountainous region, Our Lady wished to demonstrate her maternal love, especially toward the suffering and the sick. Since then, she continues to be present through her solicitude.

This Shrine was chosen because in 2004 is the 150th Anniversary of the proclamation of the Dogma of the Immaculate Conception. It was on December 8, 1854 with the Dogmatic Bull *Ineffabilis Deus* that my Predecessor, Bl. Pius IX of happy memory, affirmed that "the doctrine which holds that the most Blessed Virgin Mary, in the first instance of her conception, by a singular grace and privilege granted by Almighty God, in view of the merits of Jesus Christ, the Savior of the human race, was preserved free from all stain of original sin, is a doctrine revealed by God" (Denzinger-Schönmetzer, 2803). At Lourdes, speaking in the native dialect, Mary said: *"Que soy era Immaculada Councepciou"* ["I am the Immaculate Conception"].

2. With these words, did not the Blessed Virgin wish to express the link that unites her to health and to life? If death entered the world because of original

sin, by the merits of Jesus Christ, God preserved Mary free from every stain of sin, and salvation and life came to us (cf. Rom 5:12-21).

The Dogma of the Immaculate Conception introduces us into the heart of the mystery of Creation and Redemption (cf. Eph 1:4-12; 3:9-11). God wanted to give life in abundance to the human creature (cf. Jn 10:10), on the condition, however, that his initiative would be met by a free and loving response. Man tragically cut off vital dialogue with the Creator, refusing this gift with the disobedience that led to sin. To the "yes" of God, source of the fullness of life, the "no" of man was placed in opposition, motivated by proud self-sufficiency, harbinger of death (cf. Rom 5:19).

Entire humanity was heavily involved in this closure toward God. In view of Christ's merits, only Mary of Nazareth was conceived without original sin and was completely open to the divine design so that the Heavenly Father was able to accomplish in her the project that he had for mankind.

The Immaculate Conception introduces the harmonious interlacing between the "yes" of God and the "yes" that Mary pronounced without reserve when the angel brought the heavenly announcement (cf. Lk 1:38). Her "yes" in the name of humanity re-opened the doors of Heaven to the world, thanks to the Incarnation of the Word of God in her womb by the work of the Holy Spirit (cf. Lk 1:35). In this way, the original project of creation was restored and strengthened in Christ; the Virgin Mother also shares in this project.

3. The keystone of history lies here: with the Immaculate Conception of Mary began the great work of Redemption that was brought to fulfillment in the precious blood of Christ. In him, every person is called to achieve the perfection of holiness (cf. Col 1:28).

The Immaculate Conception is, therefore, the promising dawn of the radiant day of Christ, who with his death and Resurrection was to restore full harmony between God and humanity. If Jesus is the source of life that conquers death, Mary is the attentive mother who comes to meet the needs of her children, obtaining for them the health of soul and body. This is the message that the Shrine of Lourdes constantly re-proposes to the devout and to pilgrims. This is also the meaning behind the healings of body and spirit that take place at the grotto of Massabielle.

On that site, since the day of the apparition to Bernadette Soubirous, Mary has "healed" pain and sickness, also restoring many of her sons and daughters to health of body. She has worked much more surprising miracles, however, in the souls of believers, preparing them for the encounter with her Son Jesus, the authentic answer to the deepest expectations of the human heart. The Holy Spirit, who covered her with his shadow at the moment of the Incarnation of the Word, transforms the soul of countless sick people who turn to her. Even when they do not obtain the gift of bodily health, they are able to receive another that is much more important: the conversion of heart, source of peace and interior joy. This gift transforms their existence and makes them apostles of the Cross of Christ, standard of hope, even amid the hardest and most difficult trials.

4. In the Apostolic Letter *Salvifici Doloris* I noted that suffering belongs to the ups and downs of men and women throughout history, who must learn to accept and go beyond it (cf. no. 2: [February 11, 1984]; *L'Osservatore Romano* English Edition [ORE], February 20, 1). And yet how can they, if not thanks to the Cross of Christ?

In the death and Resurrection of the Redeemer human suffering finds its deepest meaning and its saving value. All of the weight of humanity's affliction and pain is summarized in the mystery of a God who, taking on our human nature, was humiliated "for our sake . . . to be sin" (2 Cor 5:21). On Golgotha he was burdened with the sin of every human creature, and in solitude and abandonment he called out to the Father: *"Why have you forsaken me?"* (Mt 27:46).

From the paradox of the Cross springs the answer to our most worrying questions. *Christ suffers for us.* He takes upon himself the sufferings of everyone and redeems them. *Christ suffers with us,* enabling us to share our pain with him. United to the suffering of Christ, human suffering becomes a means of salvation; this is why the believer can say with St. Paul: *"Now I rejoice in my sufferings for your sake, and in my flesh I complete what is lacking in Christ's afflictions for the sake of his body, that is, the Church"* (Col 1:24). Pain, accepted with faith, becomes the doorway to the mystery of the Lord's redemptive suffering; a suffering that no longer takes away peace and happiness since it is illuminated by the splendor of the Resurrection.

5. At the foot of the Cross Mary, made Mother of humanity, suffers in silence, participating in her Son's suffering, ready to intercede so that every person may obtain salvation (cf. *Salvifici Doloris*, no. 25; ORE, February 20, 1984, 6).

At Lourdes, it is not difficult to understand Mary's unique participation in the salvific role of Christ. The prodigy of the Immaculate Conception reminds believers of a fundamental truth: it is possible to reach salvation only through docile participation in the project of the Father, who wanted to redeem the world through the death and Resurrection of his only-begotten Son. Through Baptism, the believer becomes part of this design of salvation and is freed from original sin. Sickness and death, although present in earthly existence, lose their negative sense, and in the light of faith, corporal death, overcome by Christ's death (cf. Rom 6:4), becomes the required passage for entering the fullness of immortal life.

6. In our time, great progress has been made in the scientific understanding of life, a fundamental gift of God of which we are the administrators. Life is to

be welcomed, respected and defended from its beginning until its natural end; the family, cradle of each newborn life, must be protected with it.

Today, "genetic engineering" is spoken of, referring to the extraordinary possibility that modern science offers to intervene in the very sources of life. Every authentic progress in this field is to be encouraged, provided that it always respects the rights and dignity of the person from his or her conception. Indeed, no one can claim the right to destroy or indiscriminately manipulate the life of the human being. A specific duty of workers in the field of Health Pastoral Care is to sensitize those who work in this delicate sector so that they always engage to put themselves at the service of life.

On the occasion of the World Day of the Sick I wish to thank all of the members of Health Pastoral Care, especially the Bishops from the different Episcopal Conferences who help in this sector; the chaplains, parish priests and the other priests who are engaged in this field; the religious orders and congregations; volunteers and those who do not tire of offering a consistent witness to the death and Resurrection of the Lord in the face of suffering, pain and death.

I would like to extend my gratitude to health-care workers, medical and paramedical personnel, researchers—especially those dedicated to discovering new treatments—and to those employed in the production of medicines to be made available also to the poor.

I entrust all of you to the Most Holy Virgin, venerated at the Shrine of Lourdes as the Immaculate Conception. May she help every Christian to witness that the only authentic answer to pain, suffering and death is Christ our Lord, who died and rose for us.

With these sentiments, I willingly send to you, Venerable Brother, and to those participating in the celebration of the World Day of the Sick, a special Apostolic Blessing.

Post-Synodal Apostolic Exhortation *Ecclesia in Europa*, On Jesus Christ Alive in His Church, the Source of Hope for All Europe

June 28, 2003

The dimming of hope

8. This loss of Christian memory is accompanied by a kind of *fear of the future*. Tomorrow is often presented as something bleak and uncertain. The future is viewed more with dread than with desire. Among the troubling indications of

this are the inner emptiness that grips many people and the loss of meaning in life. The signs and fruits of this existential anguish include, in particular, the diminishing number of births, the decline in the number of vocations to the priesthood and religious life, and the difficulty, if not the outright refusal, to make lifelong commitments, including marriage.

We find ourselves before a widespread *existential fragmentation*. A feeling of loneliness is prevalent; divisions and conflicts are on the rise. Among other symptoms of this state of affairs, Europe is presently witnessing the grave phenomenon of family crises and the weakening of the very concept of the family, the continuation or resurfacing of ethnic conflicts, the re-emergence of racism, interreligious tensions, a selfishness that closes individuals and groups in upon themselves, a growing overall lack of concern for ethics and an obsessive concern for personal interests and privileges. To many observers the current process of globalization, rather than leading toward the greater unity of the human race, risks being dominated by an approach that would marginalize the less powerful and increase the number of poor in the world. . . .

Concern for vocations

40. To create a much-needed pastoral program of promoting vocations, it is beneficial to explain to the laity the Church's faith regarding the nature and dignity of the ministerial priesthood; to encourage families to live as true "domestic churches," so that in their midst the variety of vocations can be discerned, accepted and nurtured; and to engage in pastoral work aimed at helping young people in particular to choose a life rooted in Christ and completely dedicated to the Church (cf. *Propositio* 17). . . .

The truth about marriage and the family

90. The Church in Europe at every level must faithfully proclaim anew *the truth about marriage and the family* (cf. *Propositio* 31). She sees this as a burning need, for she knows that this task is integral to the mission of evangelization entrusted to her by her Bridegroom and Lord, and imposes itself today with unusual force. Many cultural, social and political factors are in fact conspiring to create an increasingly evident crisis of the family. In varying ways they jeopardize the truth and dignity of the human person, and call into question, often misrepresenting it, the notion of the family itself. The value of marital indissolubility is increasingly denied; demands are made for the legal recognition of *de facto* relationships as if they were comparable to legitimate marriages; and attempts are made to accept a definition of the couple in which difference of sex is not considered essential.

In this context the Church is called to *proclaim with renewed vigor what the Gospel teaches about marriage and the family*, in order to grasp their meaning and value in God's saving plan. In particular it is necessary to reaffirm that these institutions are realities grounded in the will of God. There is a need to rediscover the truth about the family as an intimate communion of life and love (cf. *Gaudium et Spes*, no. 48) open to the procreation of new persons, as well as its dignity as a "domestic Church" and its share in the mission of the Church and in the life of society.

91. According to the Synod Fathers, recognition is due to the many families who, in the simplicity of a daily existence lived in love, are visible witnesses of the presence of Jesus who accompanies and sustains them with the gift of his Spirit. In order to support their journey, it will be necessary to enrich the theology and spirituality of marriage and family life; to proclaim with firmness and integrity, and to demonstrate by convincing examples, the truth and the beauty of the family founded upon marriage and understood as a stable and fruitful union of a man and a woman; and to promote in every ecclesial community an adequate and integrated program of pastoral care for the family. At the same time the Church will need, with maternal concern, to provide assistance to those who are in difficult situations, such as single mothers, the separated, the divorced, and abandoned children. In all events it will be necessary to encourage, assist and support families, both individually and in associations, who seek to play their proper role in the Church and in society, and to work for the promotion of genuine and adequate family policies on the part of individual States and the European Union itself (cf. *Propositio* 31).

92. With respect to *young people and engaged couples*, particular attention must be given to providing *education in love* through special programs of preparation for the celebration of the Sacrament of Matrimony, as a means of helping them to live chastely as they prepare for this moment. In her educational activity the Church must also demonstrate a concern to provide guidance and support to newly-married couples after the celebration of their wedding.

93. Finally, the Church is also called to be present with maternal affection to those marital situations which could easily appear hopeless. In particular, "with regard to the large number of broken families, the Church feels called not to express a harsh, detached judgment, but rather to *let the light of God's word*, accompanied by the witness of his mercy, *shine deep within so many tragic human situations*. This is the spirit in which the pastoral care of families must also address the situation of *the faithful who are divorced and civilly remarried*. They are not excluded from the community; rather, they are encouraged to share in its life, while undertaking a journey of growth in the spirit of the Gospel's demands. The Church, while not concealing from them the truth about the objective moral disorder of their situation and its consequences

for sacramental practice, wishes to show to them all her maternal closeness" (John Paul II, *Address to the Third World Meeting with Families on the Occasion of their Jubilee* [October 14, 2000], no. 6).

94. If serving the Gospel of hope calls for giving adequate attention and priority to the family, it is equally the case that *families themselves have an irreplaceable responsibility* for the Gospel of hope. With confidence and affection, then, I renew my invitation to all Christian families living on this continent of Europe: "Families, become what you are!" You are *a living sign of God's love*: indeed, you have a "mission to guard, reveal, and communicate love, and this is a living reflection of and a real sharing in God's love for humanity and the love of Christ the Lord for the Church his Bride" (*Familiaris Consortio*, no. 17).

You are "*a sanctuary of life*: the place in which life—the gift of God can be properly welcomed and protected against the many attacks to which it is exposed, and can develop in accordance with what constitutes authentic human growth" (*Centesimus Annus*, no. 39).

You are the *foundation of* society, as the primary locus for the "humanization" of individuals and society (*Christifideles Laici*, no. 40), a model for the establishment of social relations lived out in love and in solidarity.

Be credible witnesses to the Gospel of hope! For you yourselves are "*gaudium et spes*" (cf. John Paul II, *Address to the First World Meeting with Families* [October 8, 1994], no. 7).

At the service of the Gospel of life

95. The growing age and declining population in various European countries cannot fail to be a cause of concern; the *falling birthrate* is in fact symptomatic of a troubled relationship with our own future. It is a clear indication of a lack of hope and a sign of the "culture of death" present in contemporary society (cf. *Propositio* 32).

Together with the decline in the birthrate, mention should be made of other factors that have obscured the sense of the value of life, and led to a kind of conspiracy against life. Sadly, among these factors must be numbered, first of all, the spread of *abortion*, also through the use of chemical-pharmaceutical preparations which make abortion possible without the involvement of a physician and in a way detached from any form of social responsibility. This is favored by the fact that the legal systems of many European countries contain legislation permitting an act which remains an "abominable crime" (*Gaudium et Spes*, no. 51) and which always constitutes a grave moral disorder. Mention must also be made of attacks involving "forms of intervention on human embryos which, although carried out for purposes legitimate in themselves, inevitably involve the killing of those embryos" or the incorrect use of prenatal diagnostic techniques, which are placed at the service not of early detection and possible treatment but of "a eugenic intention which accepts selective abortion" (*Evangelium Vitae*, no. 63).

We must also mention the presence of a tendency in certain parts of Europe to consider it permissible to make a conscious decision to end one's own life or that of another human being: the result is the spread of covert, or even openly practiced *euthanasia*, the legalization of which is often sought and, tragically, at times achieved.

96. Given this state of affairs, it is necessary to serve the Gospel of life through "a general mobilization of consciences and a united ethical effort to activate a great campaign in support of life. All together, we must build a new culture of life" (*Evangelium Vitae*, no. 95). This is the great challenge which we must accept as our responsibility, in the certainty that "the future of European civilization greatly depends on the resolute defense and promotion of the life-giving values which are the core of its cultural patrimony" (John Paul II, Address to the new Ambassador of Norway to the Holy See [March 25, 1995]). This means restoring to Europe her true dignity as a place where every person is affirmed in his or her incomparable dignity.

I gladly make my own these words of the Synod Fathers: "The Synod of European Bishops encourages Christian communities to become evangelizers of life. It encourages Christian couples and families to support one another in fidelity to their mission as cooperators with God in the generation and education of new creatures. It values every generous effort to react to a selfishness in the area of transmitting life encouraged by false models of security and happiness. It asks the States of the European Union to enact far-sighted policies aimed at fostering concrete conditions of housing, employment and social services suitable for favoring the establishment of families and enabling them to respond to the call to parenthood, and also to assure today's Europe of its most precious resource: the Europeans of tomorrow" (*Propositio* 32).

Chapter Six: The Gospel of Hope for a New Europe

> *"And I saw the holy city, new Jerusalem, coming down*
> *out of heaven" (Rv 21:2)*

The newness of God in history

106. The Gospel of hope resounding throughout the Book of Revelation opens our hearts to the *contemplation of the newness brought about by God*: "I

saw a new heaven and a new earth; for the first heaven and the first earth had passed away" (Rv 21:1). God himself says as much, in the words explaining the vision which has just taken place: "Behold, I make all things new" (Rv 21:5).

The newness of God which can only be fully understood against the back-drop of the old things, made up of tears, mourning, lamentation, travail and death (cf. Rev 21:4)—consists in leaving behind the state of sin and its con-sequences in which humanity finds itself; it is the new heavens and the new earth, the new Jerusalem, in contrast to the old heaven and earth, an obsolete order of things and an old Jerusalem, tormented by its rivalries.

The image of the new Jerusalem coming down "out of heaven from God, prepared as a bride adorned for her husband" (Rv 21:2) is a direct reference to the mystery of the Church and is not irrelevant for building the city of man. It is an image which speaks of an *eschatological reality* which transcends human possibilities and is a gift of God which will appear in the last days. Yet it is not a utopia: it is a *reality already in our midst*. This can be seen by the present tense of the verbs which God uses: "Behold, I *make* all things new" (Rv 21:5), and, as a further clarification: "It is done!" (Rv 21:6). God is already at work renewing the world; the newness of God is already found in Jesus' Pasch. It is this which brings the Church to birth, inspires her life, and renews and transforms her history.

107. This newness begins to take shape first of all *in the Christian community*, which is even now "the dwelling of God with men" (Rv 21:3), in whose midst God is already at work, renewing the life of all who yield to the Spirit's breath. The Church is for the world a sign and instrument of the Kingdom which comes about first in human hearts. A reflection of this newness can also be seen *in every form of human coexistence inspired by the Gospel*. It is a newness that speaks to society at every moment of history and in every place on earth, and in particular to European society, which for so many centuries has heard the Gospel of the Kingdom inaugurated by Jesus.

I. Europe's spiritual vocation

Europe as a promoter of universal values

108. The history of the European continent has been distinctively marked by the life-giving influence of the Gospel. "If we turn our gaze to the past centuries, we can only give thanks to the Lord that *on our continent Christianity has been a primary factor of unity among peoples and cultures* and of the integral promotion of man and his rights" (John Paul II, *Homily at the Conclusion of the Second Special Assembly for Europe of the Synod of Bishops* [October 23, 1999], no. 5).

There can be no doubt that the Christian faith belongs, in a radical and decisive way, to the foundations of European culture. Christianity in fact has shaped Europe, impressing upon it certain basic values. Modern Europe itself, which has given the democratic ideal and human rights to the world, draws its values from its Christian heritage. More than a geographical area, Europe can be described as "a *primarily cultural and historical concept*, which denotes a reality born as a continent thanks also to the unifying force of Christianity, which has been capable of integrating peoples and cultures among themselves, and which is intimately linked to the whole of European culture" (*Propositio* 39).

Today's Europe however, at the very moment it is in the process of strengthening and enlarging its economic and political union, seems to suffer from a profound crisis of values. While possessed of increased resources, it gives the impression of lacking the energy needed to sustain a common project and to give its citizens new reasons for hope.

The new face of Europe

109. In the process of transformation which it is now undergoing, *Europe is called above all to rediscover its true identity*. Even though it has developed into a highly diversified reality, it needs to build a new model of unity in diversity, as a community of reconciled nations open to the other continents and engaged in the present process of globalization.

To give new impetus to its own history, Europe must "recognize and reclaim with creative fidelity those fundamental values, acquired through a decisive contribution of Christianity, which can be summarized in the affirmation of the transcendent dignity of the human person, the value of reason, freedom, democracy, the constitutional state and the distinction between political life and religion" (*Propositio* 39).

110. The European Union continues to expand. All peoples who share its same fundamental heritage have a vocation to take part in it, on a short-term or a long-term basis. It is to be hoped that this expansion will come about in a way that respects all people, valuing their historical and cultural distinctions, their national identities and the great contributions which can come from new members. It should also take place in a way that puts into practice in an ever more fully developed manner the principles of subsidiarity and solidarity (cf. *Propositio* 39, 28). In the process of the continent's integration, it is of capital importance to remember that the union will lack substance if it is reduced to its merely geographic and economic dimensions; rather, it must consist above all in an agreement about the values which must find expression in its law and in its life. . . .

Promoting solidarity and peace in the world

115. The European institutions have as their declared purpose the defense of the rights of the human person. In carrying out this task they contribute

to the building of the Europe of values and of law. The Synod Fathers called upon the leaders of Europe in the following words: "Raise your voices in the face of the violation of *human rights* of individuals, minorities and peoples, beginning with the right to religious freedom; pay utmost attention to everything that concerns *human* life from the moment of its conception to natural death and to the *family* based on marriage: these are the foundations on which our common European home rests; . . . respond, with justice and equity and with a great sense of solidarity, to the growing phenomenon of *migration*, and see in it a new resource for the future of Europe; make every effort to guarantee young people a truly humane future with *work, culture,* and *education* in moral and spiritual values" (Synod of Bishops—Second Special Assembly for Europe, *Final Message,* no. 6: *L'Osservatore Romano,* October 23, 1999, 5).

Post-Synodal Apostolic Exhortation *Pastores Gregis,* On the Bishop, Servant of the Gospel of Jesus Christ for the Hope of the World

October 16, 2003

The Bishop's concern for the family

52. The Synod Fathers frequently spoke up in favor of the family, which is rightly called a "domestic Church," a space open to the presence of the Lord Jesus and a sanctuary of life. Founded on the sacrament of Matrimony, the family is seen to be a community of primary importance, since in the family both the spouses and their children live out their proper vocation and are perfected in charity. The Christian family—as was emphasized in the Synod—is an apostolic community open to mission (cf. *Propositio* 51).

It is the Bishop's particular task to ensure that within civil society the values of marriage are supported and defended by means of correct political and economic decisions. Within the Christian community he will not fail to encourage the preparation of engaged couples for marriage, the pastoral accompaniment of young couples and the formation of groups of families who can support the family apostolate and, not least, be in a position to assist families in trouble. The closeness of the Bishop to married couples and their children, expressed also by various initiatives on the Diocesan level, will prove a source of encouragement to them.

In considering the family's responsibilities in the area of education, the Synod Fathers unanimously acknowledged the value of Catholic schools for the integral formation of the younger generation, for the inculturation of the faith and for dialogue between different cultures. Bishops need to support and enhance the work of Catholic schools, seeking to establish them where they do not yet exist and, to the extent of his ability, calling upon civil institutions to favor effective freedom of instruction within the country (cf. *Propositio* 51). . . .

The Bishop's ministry in the field of health

71. Human concern leads the Bishop to imitate Jesus, the true "Good Samaritan," filled with compassion and mercy, who cares for others without discrimination. Health care represents one of the outstanding challenges of the present time. Tragically, many forms of sickness still persist in different parts of the world, and although science is making tremendous strides in the search for new solutions and better treatments, there are always new situations which pose a threat to physical and mental health.

Within his own Diocese each Bishop, with the help of qualified persons, is called to work for an integral proclamation of the "Gospel of life." When Christians try to humanize medicine and the care of the sick by showing personal concern and closeness to the suffering, they become for everyone a powerful image of Jesus himself, the healer of bodies and souls. Among the instructions which he gave to his Apostles, the Lord included an exhortation to heal the sick (cf. Mt 10:8) (cf. *Propositio* 57). The organization and promotion of adequate pastoral care for health-care workers should thus be a priority close to the heart of every Bishop.

In a special way, the Synod Fathers felt the need to give forceful expression to their concern for the promotion of an authentic "culture of life" in contemporary society: "Perhaps what most upsets us as pastors is the contempt for human life, from conception to death, as well as the breakdown of the family. The Church's 'No' to abortion and euthanasia is a 'Yes' to life, a 'Yes' to the fundamental goodness of creation, a 'Yes' which can move every person in the depths of his conscience, a 'Yes' to the family, the most basic community of hope, which so pleases God that he calls it to become a domestic Church" (Synod of Bishops, Tenth Ordinary General Assembly, *Message* [October 25, 2001], no. 12).

Message for Lent 2004

December 8, 2003

Dear Brothers and Sisters!

1. The evocative rite of the imposition of ashes marks the beginning of the holy season of Lent, when the Liturgy once more calls the faithful to radical conversion and trust in God's mercy.

This year's theme—"*Whoever receives one such child in my name receives me.*" (Mt 18:5)—invites us to reflect on the condition of children. Today Jesus continues to call them to himself and to set them as an example to all those who wish to be his disciples. Jesus' words call upon us to see how children are treated in our families, in civil society, and in the Church. They are also an incentive to rediscover the simplicity and trust which believers must cultivate in imitation of the Son of God, who shared the lot of the little ones and the poor. St. Clare of Assisi loved to say that Christ, "lay in a manger, lived in poverty on the earth and died naked on the Cross." (*Testament, Franciscan Sources*, no. 2841).

Jesus had a particular love for children because of "their simplicity, their joy of life, their spontaneity, and their faith filled with wonder" (*Angelus Message*, December 18, 1994). For this reason he wishes the community to open its arms and its heart to them, even as he did: "*Whoever receives one such child in my name receives me*" (Mt 18:5). Alongside children Jesus sets the "very least of the brethren:" the suffering, the needy, the hungry and thirsty, strangers, the naked, the sick, and the imprisoned. In welcoming them and loving them, or in treating them with indifference and contempt, we show our attitude toward him, for it is in them that he is particularly present.

2. The Gospel recounts the childhood of Jesus in the simple home of Nazareth, where he was obedient to his parents and "*increased in wisdom and in years, and in favor with God and man*" (Lk 2:52). By becoming himself a child, he wished to share our human experience. "*He emptied himself,*" writes the Apostle Paul, "*taking the form of a slave, being born in the likeness of men. And being found in human form he humbled himself and became obedient unto death, even death on a Cross*" (Phil 2:7-8). When at twelve years old he remained in the Temple in Jerusalem, he said to his parents who anxiously looked for him: "*How is it that you sought me? Did you not know that I must be in my Father's house?*" (Lk 2:49). Indeed, his whole life was marked by a trusting and filial obedience to his heavenly Father. "*My food,*" he said, "*is to do the will of him who sent me, and to accomplish his work*" (Jn 4:34).

In the years of his public life Jesus often insisted that only those who become like children will enter the Kingdom of Heaven (cf. Mt 18:3; Mk 10:15; Lk 18:17; Jn 3:3). In his teaching, young children become a striking image of the disciple who is called to follow the divine Master with child-like docility: "*Whoever humbles himself like this child, he is the greatest in the Kingdom of Heaven*" (Mt 18:4).

"To become" one of the least and "to receive" the little ones: these are two aspects of a single teaching which the Lord repeats to his disciples in our time. Only the one who makes himself one of the "least" is able to receive with love the "least" of our brothers and sisters.

3. Many believers strive faithfully to follow these teachings of the Lord. Here I would mention those parents who willingly take on the responsibility of a large family, mothers and fathers who, rather than considering success in their profession and career as the highest value, make every effort to pass on to their children those human and religious values that give true meaning to life.

With great admiration I also think of all those committed to caring for underprivileged children and those who alleviate the sufferings of children and their families resulting from war and violence, inadequate food and water, forced immigration and the many forms of injustice present in the world.

Together with such great generosity, however, a word must be said about the selfishness of those who do not "receive" children. There are young people who have been profoundly hurt by the violence of adults: sexual abuse, forced prostitution, involvement in the sale and use of drugs; children forced to work or enlisted for combat; young children scarred forever by the breakup of the family; little ones caught up in the obscene trafficking of organs and persons. What too of the tragedy of AIDS and its devastating consequences in Africa? It is said that millions of persons are now afflicted by this scourge, many of whom were infected from birth. Humanity cannot close its eyes in the face of so appalling a tragedy!

4. What evil have these children done to merit such suffering? From a human standpoint it is not easy, indeed it may be impossible, to answer this disturbing question. Only faith can make us begin to understand so profound an abyss of suffering. By becoming *"obedient unto death, even death on a Cross"* (Phil 2:8), Jesus took human suffering upon himself and illuminated it with the radiant light of his resurrection. By his death, he conquered death once for all.

During Lent, we prepare to relive the Paschal Mystery, which sheds the light of hope upon the whole of our existence, even its most complex and painful aspects. Holy Week will again set before us this mystery of salvation in the evocative rites of the Easter Triduum.

Dear Brothers and Sisters, let us set out with trust on our Lenten journey, sustained by fervent prayer, penance and concern for those in need. In particular, may this Lent be a time of ever greater concern for the needs of children, in our own families and in society as a whole: for they are the future of humanity.

5. With childlike simplicity let us turn to God and call him, as Jesus taught us in the prayer of the "Our Father," *"Abba,"* "Father."

Our Father! Let us repeat this prayer often during Lent; let us repeat it with deep emotion. By calling God "Our Father," we will better realize that we are his children and feel that we are brothers and sisters of one another. Thus it will be easier for us to open our hearts to the little ones, following the invitation of Jesus: *"Whoever receives one such child in my name receives me"* (Mt 18:5).

In this hope, I invoke upon each of you God's blessings, through the intercession of Mary, Mother of the Word of God made man and Mother of all humanity.

Address to the Ambassador of Italy Accredited to the Holy See

January 9, 2004

Mr. Ambassador, you have stressed the key role played by the family. Today, in many people's opinion, it is threatened by a misunderstood concept of rights. The Italian Constitution recalls and protects the central role of this "natural society founded on marriage" (art. 29). It is therefore the task of the Government Authorities to make laws that encourage its vitality. The unity of this primary and essential cell of society must be safeguarded; families also expect the social and financial assistance they need to carry out their mission. They are called to play an important educational role, forming mature persons equipped with moral and spiritual values and who are able to live as good citizens. It is important that the State help families without ever stifling the freedom of parents to choose an education, sustaining them and their inalienable rights and efforts to consolidate their nuclear family.

Message for the Thirty-Eighth World Communications Day

[May 23, 2004]

"The Media and the Family: A Risk and a Richness"

January 24, 2004

Dear Brothers and Sisters,

1. The extraordinary growth of the communications media and their increased availability has brought exceptional opportunities for enriching

the lives not only of individuals, but also of families. At the same time, families today face new challenges arising from the varied and often contradictory messages presented by the mass media. The theme chosen for the 2004 World Communications Day—"The Media and the Family: A Risk and a Richness"—is a timely one, for it invites sober reflection on the use which families make of the media and, in turn, on the way that families and family concerns are treated by the media.

This year's theme is also a reminder to everyone, both communicators and those whom they address, that all communication has a moral dimension. As the Lord himself has said, it is from the abundance of the heart that the mouth speaks (cf. Mt 12:34-35). People grow or diminish in moral stature by the words which they speak and the messages which they choose to hear. Consequently, wisdom and discernment in the use of the media are particularly called for on the part of communications professionals, parents and educators, for their decisions greatly affect children and young people for whom they are responsible, and who are ultimately the future of society.

2. Thanks to the unprecedented expansion of the communications market in recent decades, many families throughout the world, even those of quite modest means, now have access in their own homes to immense and varied media resources. As a result, they enjoy virtually unlimited opportunities for information, education, cultural expansion, and even spiritual growth—opportunities that far exceed those available to most families in earlier times.

Yet these same media also have the capacity to do grave harm to families by presenting an inadequate or even deformed outlook on life, on the family, on religion and on morality. This power either to reinforce or override traditional values like religion, culture, and family was clearly seen by the Second Vatican Council, which taught that "if the media are to be correctly employed, it is essential that all who use them know the principles of the moral order and apply them faithfully" (*Inter Mirifica*, no. 4). Communication in any form must always be inspired by the ethical criterion of respect for the truth and for the dignity of the human person.

3. These considerations apply in particular to the treatment of the family in the media. On the one hand, marriage and family life are frequently depicted in a sensitive manner, realistic but also sympathetic, that celebrates virtues like love, fidelity, forgiveness, and generous self-giving for others. This is true also of media presentations which recognize the failures and disappointments inevitably experienced by married couples and families—tensions, conflicts, setbacks, evil choices and hurtful deeds—yet at the same time make an effort to separate right from wrong, to distinguish true love from its counterfeits, and to show the irreplaceable importance of the family as the fundamental unit of society.

On the other hand, the family and family life are all too often inadequately portrayed in the media. Infidelity, sexual activity outside of marriage, and the absence of a moral and spiritual vision of the marriage covenant are depicted uncritically, while positive support is at times given to divorce, contraception, abortion and homosexuality. Such portrayals, by promoting causes inimical to marriage and the family, are detrimental to the common good of society.

4. Conscientious reflection on the ethical dimension of communications should issue in practical initiatives aimed at eliminating the risks to the well-being of the family posed by the media and ensuring that these powerful instruments of communication will remain genuine sources of enrichment. A special responsibility in this regard lies with communicators themselves, with public authorities, and with parents.

Pope Paul VI pointed out that professional communicators should "know and respect the needs of the family, and this sometimes presupposes in them true courage, and always a high sense of responsibility" (*Message for the 1969 World Communications Day*). It is not so easy to resist commercial pressures or the demands of conformity to secular ideologies, but that is what responsible communicators must do. The stakes are high, since every attack on the fundamental value of the family is an attack on the true good of humanity.

Public authorities themselves have a serious duty to uphold marriage and the family for the sake of society itself. Instead, many now accept and act upon the unsound libertarian arguments of groups which advocate practices which contribute to the grave phenomenon of family crisis and the weakening of the very concept of the family. Without resorting to censorship, it is imperative that public authorities set in place regulatory policies and procedures to ensure that the media do not act against the good of the family. Family representatives should be part of this policy-making.

Policy-makers in the media and in the public sector also must work for an equitable distribution of media resources on the national and international levels, while respecting the integrity of traditional cultures. The media should not appear to have an agenda hostile to the sound family values of traditional cultures or the goal of replacing those values, as part of a process of globalization, with the secularized values of consumer society.

5. Parents, as the primary and most important educators of their children, are also the first to teach them about the media. They are called to train their offspring in the "moderate, critical, watchful and prudent use of the media" in the home (*Familiaris Consortio*, no. 76). When parents do that consistently and well, family life is greatly enriched. Even very young children can be taught important lessons about the media: that they are produced by people anxious to communicate messages; that these are often messages to do

something—to buy a product, to engage in dubious behavior—that is not in the child's best interests or in accord with moral truth; that children should not uncritically accept or imitate what they find in the media.

Parents also need to regulate the use of media in the home. This would include planning and scheduling media use, strictly limiting the time children devote to media, making entertainment a family experience, putting some media entirely off limits and periodically excluding all of them for the sake of other family activities. Above all, parents should give good example to children by their own thoughtful and selective use of media. Often they will find it helpful to join with other families to study and discuss the problems and opportunities presented by the use of the media. Families should be outspoken in telling producers, advertisers, and public authorities what they like and dislike.

6. The media of social communications have an enormous positive potential for promoting sound human and family values and thus contributing to the renewal of society. In view of their great power to shape ideas and influence behavior, professional communicators should recognize that they have a moral responsibility not only to give families all possible encouragement, assistance, and support to that end, but also to exercise wisdom, good judgment and fairness in their presentation of issues involving sexuality, marriage and family life.

The media are welcomed daily as a familiar guest in many homes and families. On this World Communications Day I encourage professional communicators and families alike to acknowledge this unique privilege and the accountability which it entails. May all engaged in the field of communications recognize that they are truly "stewards and administrators of an immense spiritual power that belongs to the patrimony of mankind and is meant to enrich the whole of the human community" (*Address to Communications Specialists*, Los Angeles, September 15, 1987, 8). And may families always be able to find in the media a source of support, encouragement and inspiration as they strive to live as a community of life and love, to train young people in sound moral values, and to advance a culture of solidarity, freedom and peace.

Message for the International Convention on "Natural Regulation of Fertility and Culture of Life"

January 28, 2004

Illustrious Ladies and Gentlemen,

1. I am pleased to address my cordial thought to all of you, participants of the international Convention on "*Natural Regulation of Fertility and Culture*

of Life," being held in Rome in these days. To all and to each one I extend my warm greetings. I express my deep appreciation to those who have organized this meeting, most especially the Study Centers for Natural Regulation of Fertility; the Faculties of Medicine and Surgery of the various Roman Universities; the Italian Ministry of Health; the Italian Institute of Social Medicine and the Office for the University Apostolate of the Rome Vicariate.

This meeting deals with relevant themes concerning the development of relations between science and ethics. The Magisterium of the Church has followed with lively interest the development of what we could call the "culture of responsible procreation," and has promoted the knowledge and diffusion of the so-called "natural" methods of fertility regulation. My venerable Predecessors, from Pius XII to Paul VI, on many occasions encouraged research in these fields, so as to offer an ever more sound scientific basis for a regulation of births that respects the person and God's design for the human couple and procreation. In these years, thanks to the contribution of countless Christian couples in many parts of the world, the natural methods have been introduced and reflected on by family groups and movements and by ecclesial associations.

2. Today, we increasingly observe a mindset that, on the one hand, draws back from responsible procreation, while on the other, it would like to dominate and manipulate life. Therefore, it is urgent to intensify effective cultural action that would overcome in this regard commonly-held opinions and misinformation, very often exaggerated by a certain type of propaganda. At the same time, careful education and formation should be provided for married and engaged couples, young people in general, as well as for social and pastoral workers, to illustrate properly all the fundamental and motivational aspects of fertility's natural regulation as well as its practical application.

Centers of study and the teaching of these methods will be invaluable in promoting responsible motherhood and fatherhood, in such a way that every person, beginning with the child, will be recognized and respected for who they are, because every choice will be based on and guided by the criterion of the sincere gift of self.

Clearly, when one speaks of "natural" regulation, respect for biological rhythm alone is not what is meant. In a much more complete way, it entails upholding the truth of the person's profound unity of spirit, psyche and body, a unity that can never be reduced to a simple set of biological mechanisms.

It is only in the context of complete and limitless reciprocal love by the married couple that the act of procreation, on which the future of humanity itself depends, can be carried out in all of its dignity.

It is right, therefore, that not only doctors and researchers be called to offer their responsible contribution to this fundamental event, but also pastoral workers and political authorities in their respective areas of competence.

3. The fact that some Faculties of Medicine have promoted the Convention allows me to stress in a special way the role doctors have in this delicate field. Here I wish to renew the expression of respect the Church has always reserved for those in the world of health care who strive to fulfill their vocation at the service of life consistently. I am especially thinking of the men and women scientists involved in the research and diffusion of natural methods of fertility regulation who, enlightened by faith, also educate people in the moral values that the practice of these methods presupposes. The role and the responsibility of Universities are decisive for the promotion of research programs in this field, and for the formation of future professionals capable of helping young people and couples always to make conscious and responsible choices.

I hope that this meeting will be another step on this journey, offering deep insights into the theme in its many scientific, cultural, psycho-social and formative aspects. It will provide an updated report on the state of the teaching of natural methods at the international level, especially in the European Faculties of Medicine.

While assuring my spiritual closeness to each of those participating in the Convention, I wish your intense days of study a successful outcome. With these sentiments, as I invoke the special assistance of Mary Most Holy on your work, I willingly extend to all a special Apostolic Blessing.

Address to the Fifth Group of
French Bishops on Their *Ad Limina* Visit

January 30, 2004

6. The concern to promote and guide families is at the heart of your concerns as Pastors. The family is not one model of a relationship among others, but a type of relationship indispensable to the future of society. In fact, a society cannot be healthy if it does not foster the family ideal in order to build stable conjugal and family relationships and for a proper relationship between the generations. How should families be helped? Your Dioceses are always ready to offer the practical means to further their growth, enabling them to bear a credible witness in the Church and in society.

As some of your reports suggest, you are especially eager to offer guidance to newly-weds, enabling them to acquire the human and spiritual maturity they need for the harmonious development of their family. I am also thinking of the new generations of young people whom the Church has difficulty in reaching and who come to ask the Church *to prepare them for marriage*. I encourage the priests, deacons and faithful involved in this fine task to help them discover the profound meaning of this sacrament, as well as the tasks to which it commits them. In this way, they will present *a positive view of emotional relationships and sexuality* that will contribute to the growth of the couple and the family. As I previously asked at Sainte-Anne-d'Auray during my Pastoral Visit to France, I ask you once again to support families in their vocation to express the beauty of parenthood and nurture the culture of life (cf. Address at Meeting with Families, September 20, 1996, no. 7; ORE, October 2, 1996, 4).

I also recognize the *important work carried out under your supervision by the services and movements for the family apostolate.* The initiatives they promote are indispensable in helping young families to grow in human and spiritual vitality in their homes, as well as being a practical response to the phenomenon of the break-up of families. One cannot helplessly watch the family institution disintegrate. In this context, the Church wishes to bring about a real change of mindset and behavior, so that the positive values linked to married and family life may prevail and relationships may not be seen merely from the perspective of individualism and personal pleasure which distorts the deep meaning of human life that is primarily altruism and the gift of self. The commitment to marriage entails a certain number of tasks and responsibilities. These include maintaining and deepening the conjugal bond and caring for the children. In this spirit, it is right to offer help to parents who are the first educators of their children. Thus, they will be able, on the one hand, to deal with and solve marital crises that they may experience, and on the other, to bear witness to the young of the greatness of faithful, unique love and of the elements of a human, emotional and sexual education, challenged by the frequently destructive messages of contemporary society that give the impression that all forms of emotional conduct are acceptable, denying to human acts any moral qualification. Such an attitude is particularly harmful for young people since it involves them, at times in imprudent ways, in erroneous forms of behavior. As we often see, these leave deep scars on their psyche, mortgaging their future outlook and commitments.

Angelus

February 1, 2004

1. "There is no future without children." This is the theme of the Pro-Life Day being celebrated throughout Italy today. In their Message, the Italian Bishops highlight the many causes of the current demographic crisis. They

recall that all too often the cultural and social context does not promote the family or the role of parents.

Furthermore, many married couples would like more children but are forced, as it were, to abandon this because of *economic concerns*. Although public institutions provide considerable assistance, it is often insufficient. People are feeling the need for *a more concrete family policy*.

2. The nuclear family that develops from marriage is the basic cell of society. In it, as in a reassuring nest, life should always be nurtured, defended and protected, and today's Pro-Life Day reminds everyone of this fundamental duty.

Dear brothers and sisters, *we must not resign ourselves* to any attacks on human life, least of all abortion! I renew my appreciation for the courageous support that the Italian Pro-Life Movement offers to this cause, and I urge every Ecclesial Community to support its initiatives and the services it offers. Efforts must be redoubled so that the right to life of unborn children is *not affirmed against their mothers but with their mothers*.

3. Let us now turn to Mary Most Holy and call on her especially for families so that, trusting in divine help, they may carry out with joy and dedication their wonderful mission to give humanity a future rich in hope.

Address to the Bishops of Bordeaux and Poitiers, France, on Their *Ad Limina* Visit

February 13, 2004

2. . . . Society is marked by numerous inconsistencies that render young people particularly fragile: broken families, families reconstituted with different siblings, a rupture in social relations. How can we fail to think of those children and young people who suffer deeply from the break-up of their nuclear family or who are in unstable situations that often make them feel as if society rejects them? Likewise, the evolution of attitudes continues to be a cause of worry: an exacerbated subjectivity; an excessive distancing from customs that give young people the idea that any form of conduct is right because it is possible; a serious deterioration of moral awareness that leads to the conviction that objective good and evil no longer exist. You also mention social violence that gives rise to serious tensions, especially in certain urban or suburban neighborhoods, as well as the increase in suicidal tendencies and the use of drugs. Lastly, the growth of unemployment worries young people. . . .

4. Young people tend to form groups where they are recognized and loved. No child can live or be formed without love and the kindly watchfulness of adults; this is actually the mission of education. I therefore ask diocesan communities to pay *ever greater attention to the places of education*; first of all, the family, which it is right to support and help, especially in parent-child relationships and particularly during adolescence. The presence of adults other than parents is often beneficial.

Likewise, school is a privileged place for a fraternal and peaceful life where each person is accepted for who he is, with respect for his values and personal and family beliefs. . . .

6. I would also like to draw your attention to the support you should give to *young people preparing for marriage*. They have frequently known much suffering in their families and sometimes have repeated experiences of it. Society abounds with various types of relationships, devoid of anthropological or moral qualifications. For her part, the Church wishes to propose the path of progress in a loving relationship that passes through the engagement period and proposes the ideal of chastity; she recalls that marriage between a man and a woman as well as the family are founded first of all on a strong relationship and a definitive commitment, and not only on the purely emotional aspect which cannot constitute the sole basis of married life. Pastors and Christian couples should not be afraid to help young people reflect on these sensitive and essential matters through catecheses and lively, appropriate dialogue, making the depth and beauty of human love shine forth!

7. The Church has an *original word to add in the discussions on education*, on the social phenomena and especially on issues concerning the emotions and the moral and spiritual values. Formation cannot consist only in technical and scientific training; it aims principally at an education of the whole being.

Message to the Bishops, Friends of the Focolare Movement

February 18, 2004

"For the sanctity of people": this specification puts the accent precisely on the universal character of the Church's vocation to holiness, a truth that is one of the pillars of *Lumen Gentium*, the Constitution of the Second Vatican Council. Two general aspects should be appropriately emphasized. First of all is the fact that the Church is profoundly holy and is called to live and express this holiness in each of her members. Secondly, the phrase "sanctity of people" suggests ordinary life, that is, the need for all the baptized to be able to live the Gospel consistently in their daily lives: in the family, at work, in every relationship and occupation. It is precisely in the ordinary that one must live the extraordinary, so that the "standard" of living is directed "high," that is, "to the measure of the stature of the fullness of Christ," as the Apostle Paul teaches (cf. Eph 4:13).

Address to the Ambassador of Mexico to the Holy See

February 24, 2004

The widespread, painful problem of poverty, with its serious consequences for the family, education, health and housing, is a pressing challenge for Government and political Authorities responsible for public life. There is no doubt that its eradication will require technical and political measures aimed at ensuring that economic activities and production take into account the common good, and especially the most deprived groups. It should not be forgotten, however, that all these measures will prove futile unless they are motivated by authentic ethical values. Furthermore, I would like to encourage the efforts made by your Government and other Mexican public Authorities to foster solidarity among everyone, avoiding evils that derive from a system that puts gain before the person and unjustly victimizes the individual. A model of development that does not tackle social imbalances with determination cannot prosper in the future....

Another concern of the Church and society in Mexico is the high rate of Mexicans emigrating to other countries, especially to the United States. In addition to the uncertainty of those Mexicans who leave in search of a better life is the problem of their cultural uprooting and painful dispersion or separation from their family, not to mention the regrettable consequences of numerous illegal cases.

Address to the Priests of the Diocese of Rome for Their Annual Lenten Meeting

February 26, 2004

Your Eminence,
Venerable Brothers in the Episcopate,
Dear Priests of Rome,

1. I am delighted with this meeting that is once again taking place at the beginning of Lent, giving me an opportunity to see you, listen to you and

share your hopes and pastoral concerns. I offer an affectionate greeting to each one of you, thanking you for your service to the Church of Rome. I greet and thank the Cardinal Vicar, the Vicegerent, the Auxiliary Bishops and those of you who have addressed me.

We are meeting at a time when I am about to resume my encounters with the parishes of Rome in which most of you carry out your daily ministry. I have very much been looking forward to this direct contact with the parish communities I have not yet been able to visit, because this is part of my task as Bishop of this beloved Church of Rome.

2. The Cardinal Vicar's words and subsequently your addresses have shed light on the various aspects of the pastoral program centered on the family to which our Diocese is committed this year and the next, within the framework of that "ongoing mission" which, after the Great Jubilee and the positive experience of the "City Mission," constitutes the backbone of our pastoral activity.

Dear Priests, putting the family at the center, or rather, recognizing the centrality of the family in God's design for humanity and thus in the life of the Church and society, is an indispensable task that has motivated these twenty-five years of my Pontificate, and even earlier, my ministry as a Priest and Bishop and also my commitment as a scholar and university lecturer.

I therefore rejoice at sharing with you your concern for the families of our beloved Diocese of Rome on this happy occasion.

3. If it is to be authentic and fruitful, our service to families must always lead to the source, that is, to God who is love and who lives in himself a mystery of personal communion of love. In creating humanity in his image out of love, God has inscribed a vocation in the hearts of men and women, and hence, the capacity for love and communion and for bearing the responsibility they carry. This vocation can be fulfilled in two specific ways: through marriage and through virginity or celibacy. Both, therefore, are an actuation, each in its own way, of the most profound truth of man and of his being created in the image of God (cf. Apostolic Exhortation *Familiaris Consortio*, no. 11).

Marriage and the family thus cannot be considered a mere product of historical circumstances or a superstructure imposed from outside on human love. On the contrary, they are an inner need of this love to fulfill itself in its own truth and in the fullness of the reciprocal gift of self. Even those features of spousal union that today are all too often misunderstood or rejected, such as unity, indissolubility and openness to life, are instead requests for the authenticity of the covenant of love. It is in this very way that the bond which unites the man and the woman becomes an image and symbol of the covenant between God and his People, which finds its definitive fulfillment in Jesus Christ. Therefore, among the baptized marriage is a sacrament, an effective sign of grace and salvation.

4. Dear Priests of Rome, let us never tire of proposing, proclaiming and witnessing to this great truth about love and Christian marriage. Our vocation, of course, is not that of marriage, but the priesthood and virginity for the sake of the Kingdom of God. However, it is precisely in celibacy, joyfully welcomed and protected, that we in turn are called to live the truth about love in a way that is different though just as full, giving ourselves totally with Christ to God, to the Church, and to our brothers and sisters in humanity.

Thus, our virginity "keeps alive in the Church a consciousness of the mystery of marriage and defends it from any reduction and impoverishment" (*Familiaris Consortio*, no. 16).

5. I have very often stressed the fundamental and indispensable role of the family, both in the life of the Church and in civil society. But precisely in order to sustain Christian families in their demanding tasks, the pastoral solicitude of us priests is essential.

In the Apostolic Exhortation *Familiaris Consortio*, I therefore recalled that the Bishop is "the person principally responsible in the diocese for the pastoral care of the family" (no. 73). Likewise, dear Priests, your responsibility to families "extends not only to moral and liturgical matters but to personal and social matters as well" (ibid.). You are called in particular to "support the family in its difficulties and sufferings" (ibid.), caring for its members and helping them to live their lives as husbands and wives, parents and children in the light of the Gospel.

6. In fulfilling this important mission, many of us will be able to draw very valid help from the experience we have lived in our own families, from the witness of faith and trust in God, of love and dedication, of the capacity for sacrifice and forgiveness that we received from our own parents and relatives. The daily contact with Christian families entrusted to our ministry, however, offers us constantly renewed examples of life in accordance with the Gospel and thus stimulates and comforts us in turn to live our own specific vocation with fidelity and joy.

Therefore, dear Priests, we must consider our apostolate with families a source of grace, a gift that the Lord offers us even before we see it as a specific pastoral duty.

So do not be afraid to spend yourselves for families, to dedicate to them your time, energy and the spiritual gifts the Lord has given you. Be caring and trustworthy friends to them as well as pastors and teachers. Accompany them and sustain them in prayer; suggest to them the Gospel of marriage and the family with truth and love, without reservations or arbitrary interpretations. Be spiritually close to them in the trials life often holds in store, helping them to understand that the Church is always mother for them as well as teacher. Also teach the young to understand and appreciate the true meaning of love and thus to prepare themselves for forming authentic Christian families.

7. The erroneous and frequently aberrant forms of behavior that are publicly proposed, flaunted and exalted, and likewise the daily contact with the difficulties and crises that many families experience can also give rise in us to the temptation of distrust and resignation.

Dear Priests of Rome, it is exactly this temptation that we must overcome with God's help, first of all within us, in our hearts and in our minds. In fact, the plan of God who inscribed in man and woman the vocation to love and to the family is still the same today. The action of the Holy Spirit, the gift of the dead and risen Christ, is just as powerful. No error, no sin, no ideology and no human deceit can demolish the profound structure of our being, which needs to be loved and is in turn capable of true love.

Thus, however great the difficulties, our confidence in the present and future of the family is all the stronger and our service to families as priests must be all the more generous and zealous.

Dear Priests, thank you for this meeting. With this trust and with these hopes, I entrust each one of you and every family in Rome to the Holy Family of Nazareth, and I wholeheartedly bless you and your communities.

At the end of the meeting, the Holy Father spoke extemporaneously:

"*Est tempus concludendi*," especially looking at those of our brothers who have had to remain standing throughout because there was no seat for them, not one more seat: we are numerous.

I would like to thank the Cardinal Vicar and the Episcopal College of Rome for organizing this meeting. I would now like to sum it up.

In the first place, Rome: what does Rome mean? The Petrine City and every parish is Petrine. There are 340 parishes in Rome. I have visited 300 of them but still have forty left to visit. However, we will begin this Saturday to complete the number of visits. Let us hope everything will go well.

Next, Rome is not only parishes: it is seminaries, universities and different institutions. At this meeting, we have spoken directly or indirectly of all these institutions.

The theme is the family. Family means: "male and female he created them"; it means love and responsibility. From these two words spring all the consequences. We have heard a lot said of these consequences with regard to marriage, the family, parents, children, school.

I am deeply grateful to all of you because you have described these consequences, this reality. This concern certainly belongs to the parish. I learned long ago, when I was in Krakow, to live beside couples and families. I also followed closely the process that leads two people, a man and a woman, to create a family, and with marriage, to become spouses, parents, with all the consequences that we know.

Thank you for focusing your pastoral concern on families and for seeking to solve all those problems that the family can bring with it. I hope you will proceed in this most important area, because the future of the Church and of the world passes through the family. I hope you will be able to prepare this good future for Rome, for your Homeland of Italy and for the world. Many, many good wishes!

Here is the text that I had prepared, but I laid it aside! You will find it in *L'Osservatore Romano*.

Here are some phrases written in Romanesco [the Roman dialect]: "Dàmose da fà!" (let us keep busy), "Volèmose bene!" (let us love one another), "Semo Romani!" (we are Romans). I never learned Romanesco: does that mean that I am not a good Bishop of Rome?

Address to the Ambassador of Argentina to the Holy See

February 28, 2004

In carrying out her mission, the Church never ceases to strive to invite all men and women of good will to build a society based on basic and indispensable values for a national and international order worthy of the human being.

One of these is undoubtedly the value of human life. Lack of respect for it not only attacks the right to life of each human being from the moment of conception to natural death, which no one can claim the right to violate, but it also reduces the very foundation of all human coexistence. Indeed, it is fitting to ask what might be the meaning of the effort to improve the forms of social coexistence other than to guarantee life itself. This value therefore needs to be carefully safeguarded by reacting promptly to counter the many subtle plays to degrade the primordial good of life by objectifying it for other ends.

Another pillar of society is marriage, the union of a man and a woman who are open to life, which gives rise to the natural institution of the family. It is not only older but also more universal than any other form of human coexistence which it supports, since it constitutes the first fabric of intimate relationships woven by love, mutual support and solidarity. The family, therefore, has its own rights and duties that it must exercise in the context of its own autonomy. In this regard, it is incumbent upon the legislative and political bodies of the larger societies, in accordance with the principle of subsidiarity, to guarantee these rights scrupulously and to help families to discharge their duties when they cannot carry them out with their own means.

Here, it seems to me appropriate to recall that legislators, especially Catholic legislators, cannot contribute to formulating or approving laws contrary to "the primary and essential norms regulating the moral life," and consequently, to the loftiest values of the human person which ultimately come from God, the supreme legislator (cf. *Address to Government Leaders, Members of Parliament and Politicians*, November 4, 2000, no. 4; ORE, November 8, 2000, 7).

It is necessary to recall this at a time when many seek to reduce marriage to a mere individual contract with features very different from those of marriage and the family, and end by degrading it as though it were a superfluous association within the social body. More than ever, therefore, the Public Authorities must protect and assist in all its dimensions the family, the basic cell of society, aware that by so doing they are promoting a just, stable and promising social development.

Argentina has been and is particularly sensitive to these aspects, knowing that these are issues on which the whole of humanity's future depend. Consequently, I would like to express my appreciation for the efforts made in favor of marriage and the family at certain international meetings, while at the same time I ask that this course be pursued.

Homily at Mass with the
Communities of Four Roman Parishes

February 28, 2004

4. Dear brothers and sisters, the neighborhoods in which your Parishes are located are constantly expanding and it is mainly young families who live in them. Offer them an open and cordial welcome; foster their reciprocal knowledge, so that the communities may become increasingly "families of families" that can share their joys and difficulties together.

Involve parents in the preparation of children and young people for the sacraments and for Christian life, keeping in mind family schedules and needs; offer to organize prayer meetings and formation in their apartment block or in their own homes. Remember that families really are the first place for the Christian education of children.

Guide with tender concern those families in difficulty or in precarious conditions, helping them to understand and carry out God's authentic plan for marriage and the family.

5. Dear friends, I know that at present you have to make do with temporary structures for liturgical life and pastoral service. I hope that you will soon be able to use proper premises! In the meantime, however, be concerned to make your parishes genuine spiritual buildings that stand on the corner stone that is Christ! Christ and always Christ!

Address to the Bishops of the Netherlands on Their *Ad Limina* Visit

March 12, 2004

3. Clearly there is a need to proclaim the Good News of Christ's love particularly to the young people who are no longer guided by reliable reference points and live in a society more and more marked by moral relativism and religious pluralism. Parishes and Catholic schools, together with families, should do their part to assure the transmission of the Christian heritage, not only by providing children and young people with the knowledge they need to assimilate and understand Catholic doctrine, but also by offering them an example through daily witness of demanding Christian life, nourished by love of God and neighbor. In this perspective, I invite Catholic teaching to maintain and strengthen its proper identity by its harmonious adaptation to the ever new needs of education in a pluralistic society, with respect for others but without sacrificing what constituted its original wealth. It is your responsibility as Pastors to watch over this, by encouraging all teachers to work along these lines. . . .

6. . . . I am counting first of all on the young people of your Country so that, like Peter, they will hear the Lord's call: "Do not be afraid; henceforth, you will be fishers of men" (Lk 5:10), and respond generously. I also ask families to be places of faith and seedbeds for vocations, passing on dauntlessly the Lord's call to the young! . . .

7. Do not be afraid to recall the importance of the *witness of consecrated life*. It has left a deep mark on your Country; unfortunately, the communities which

live there today have aged considerably and, moreover, risk disappearing if an effort is not made to inspire new vocations. This implies parents in the home are careful to create true freedom for their children, without directing them too soon to purely social criteria of a successful career. Catholic schools must also contribute to this awakening and enable young people to discover, especially through the saints, the example of men and women who could respond to the Lord's call and witness to the beauty of a life given without reserve. This also implies that Christian communities know how to appreciate the variety and complementarity of vocations, and that the young discover that consecrated life is close to them and receptive to their questions. . . .

8. . . . I hope that all the children of the Church, especially the lay faithful, will truly have at heart to witness to their faith, bringing the light of the Gospel to the various social milieus. May they extol the greatness of marriage and the beauty of the family in a society tempted to renounce definitive commitments for more transient forms of union!

Address to the Participants
in the International Congress on
"Life-Sustaining Treatments and Vegetative State:
Scientific Advances and Ethical Dilemmas"

March 20, 2004

Distinguished Ladies and Gentlemen,

1. I cordially greet all of you who took part in the International Congress: *"Life-Sustaining Treatments and Vegetative State: Scientific Advances and Ethical Dilemmas."* I wish to extend a special greeting to Bishop Elio Sgreccia, Vice-President of the Pontifical Academy for Life, and to Prof. Gian Luigi Gigli, President of the International Federation of Catholic Medical Associations and selfless champion of the fundamental value of life, who has kindly expressed your shared feelings.

This important Congress, organized jointly by the Pontifical Academy for Life and the International Federation of Catholic Medical Associations, is dealing with a very significant issue: *the clinical condition called the "vegetative state."* The complex scientific, ethical, social and pastoral implications of such a condition require in-depth reflections and a fruitful interdisciplinary dialogue, as evidenced by the intense and carefully structured program of your work sessions.

2. With deep esteem and sincere hope, the Church encourages the efforts of men and women of science who, sometimes at great sacrifice, daily dedicate their task of study and research to the improvement of the diagnostic, therapeutic, prognostic and rehabilitative possibilities confronting those patients who rely completely on those who care for and assist them. The person in a vegetative state, in fact, shows no evident sign of self-awareness or of awareness of the environment, and seems unable to interact with others or to react to specific stimuli.

Scientists and researchers realize that one must, first of all, arrive at a correct diagnosis, which usually requires prolonged and careful observation in specialized centers, given also the high number of diagnostic errors reported in the literature. Moreover, not a few of these persons, with appropriate treatment and with specific rehabilitation program, have been able to emerge from a vegetative state. On the contrary, many others unfortunately remain prisoners of their condition even for long stretches of time and without needing technological support.

In particular, the term *permanent vegetative state* has been coined to indicate the condition of those patients whose "vegetative state" continues for over a year. Actually, there is no different diagnosis that corresponds to such a definition, but only a conventional prognostic judgment, relative to the fact that the recovery of patients, statistically speaking, is ever more difficult as the condition of vegetative state is prolonged in time.

However, we must neither forget nor underestimate that there are well-documented cases of at least partial recovery even after many years; we can thus state that medical science, up until now, is still unable to predict with certainty who among patients in this condition will recover and who will not.

3. Faced with patients in similar clinical conditions, there are some who cast doubt on the persistence of the "human quality" itself, almost as if the adjective "vegetative" (whose use is now solidly established), which symbolically describes a clinical state, could or should be instead applied to the sick as such, actually demeaning their value and personal dignity. In this sense, it must be noted that this term, even when confined to the clinical context, is certainly not the most felicitous when applied to human beings.

In opposition to such trends of thought, I feel the duty to reaffirm strongly that the intrinsic value and personal dignity of every human being do not change, no matter what the concrete circumstances of his or her life. A *man, even if seriously ill or disabled in the exercise of his highest functions, is and always will be a man,* and he will never become a "vegetable" or an "animal."

Even our brothers and sisters who find themselves in the clinical condition of a "vegetative state" retain their human dignity in all its fullness. The loving gaze of God the Father continues to fall upon them, acknowledging them as his sons and daughters, especially in need of help.

4. Medical doctors and health-care personnel, society and the Church have moral duties toward these persons from which they cannot exempt themselves without lessening the demands both of professional ethics and human and Christian solidarity.

The sick person in a vegetative state, awaiting recovery or a natural end, still has the right to basic health care (nutrition, hydration, cleanliness, warmth, etc.), and to the prevention of complications related to his confinement to bed. He also has the right to appropriate rehabilitative care and to be monitored for clinical signs of eventual recovery.

I should like particularly to underline how the administration of water and food, even when provided by artificial means, always represents a *natural means* of preserving life, not a *medical act.* Its use, furthermore, should be considered, in principle, *ordinary* and *proportionate,* and as such morally obligatory, insofar as and until it is seen to have attained its proper finality, which in the present case consists in providing nourishment to the patient and alleviation of his suffering.

The obligation to provide the "normal care due to the sick in such cases" (Congregation for the Doctrine of the Faith, *Iura et Bona,* p. IV) includes, in fact, the use of nutrition and hydration (cf. Pontifical Council "Cor Unum," *Dans le Cadre,* 2, 4, 4; Pontifical Council for Pastoral Assistance to Health Care Workers, *Charter of Health Care Workers,* no. 120). The evaluation of probabilities, founded on waning hopes for recovery when the vegetative state is prolonged beyond a year, cannot ethically justify the cessation or interruption of *minimal care* for the patient, including nutrition and hydration. Death by starvation or dehydration is, in fact, the only possible outcome as a result of their withdrawal. In this sense it ends up becoming, if done knowingly and willingly, true and proper euthanasia by omission.

In this regard, I recall what I wrote in the Encyclical *Evangelium Vitae,* making it clear that "by *euthanasia in the true and proper sense* must be understood an action or omission which by its very nature and intention brings about death, with the purpose of eliminating all pain"; such an act is always "a *serious violation of the law of God,* since it is the deliberate and morally unacceptable killing of a human person" (no. 65).

Besides, the moral principle is well known, according to which even the simple doubt of being in the presence of a living person already imposes the

obligation of full respect and of abstaining from any act that aims at anticipating the person's death.

5. Considerations about the "quality of life," often actually dictated by psychological, social and economic pressures, cannot take precedence over general principles.

First of all, no evaluation of costs can outweigh the value of the fundamental good which we are trying to protect, that of human life. Moreover,
to admit that decisions regarding man's life can be based on the external
acknowledgment of its quality, is the same as acknowledging that increasing
and decreasing levels of quality of life, and therefore of human dignity, can be
attributed from an external perspective to any subject, thus introducing into
social relations a discriminatory and eugenic principle.

Moreover, it is not possible to rule out *a priori* that the withdrawal of nutrition
and hydration, as reported by authoritative studies, is the source of considerable
suffering for the sick person, even if we can see only the reactions at the level of
the autonomic nervous system or of gestures. Modern clinical neurophysiology
and neuro-imaging techniques, in fact, seem to point to the lasting quality in
these patients of elementary forms of communication and analysis of stimuli.

6. However, it is not enough to reaffirm the general principle according to
which the value of a man's life cannot be made subordinate to any judgment
of its quality expressed by other men; it is necessary to promote the *taking of
positive actions* as a stand against pressures to withdraw hydration and nutrition as a way to put an end to the lives of these patients.

It is necessary, above all, *to support those families* who have had one of their
loved ones struck down by this terrible clinical condition. They cannot be left
alone with their heavy human, psychological and financial burden. Although
the care for these patients is not, in general, particularly costly, society must
allot sufficient resources for the care of this sort of frailty, by way of bringing
about appropriate, concrete initiatives such as, for example, the creation of a
network of awakening centers with specialized treatment and rehabilitation
programs; financial support and home assistance for families when patients
are moved back home at the end of intensive rehabilitation programs; the
establishment of facilities which can accommodate those cases in which
there is no family able to deal with the problem or to provide "breaks" for
those families who are at risk of psychological and moral burn-out.

Proper care for these patients and their families should, moreover, include
the presence and the witness of a medical doctor and an entire team, who
are asked to help the family understand that they are there as allies who are
in this struggle with them. The participation of volunteers represents a basic
support to enable the family to break out of its isolation and to help it to realize that it is a precious and not a forsaken part of the social fabric.

In these situations, then, spiritual counseling and pastoral aid are particularly important as help for recovering the deepest meaning of an apparently desperate condition.

7. Distinguished Ladies and Gentlemen, in conclusion I exhort you, as men and women of science responsible for the dignity of the medical profession, to guard jealously the principle according to which the true task of medicine is "to cure if possible, always to care."

As a pledge and support of this, your authentic humanitarian mission to give comfort and support to your suffering brothers and sisters, I remind you of the words of Jesus: "Amen, I say to you, whatever you did for one of these least brothers of mine, you did for me" (Mt 25:40).

In this light, I invoke upon you the assistance of him, whom a meaningful saying of the Church Fathers describes as *Christus medicus*, and in entrusting your work to the protection of Mary, Consoler of the sick and Comforter of the dying, I lovingly bestow on all of you a special Apostolic Blessing.

Address on the Occasion of the International Charlemagne Prize of the City of Aachen, Germany

Wednesday, March 24, 2004

5. . . . I am thinking of a Europe that is united thanks to the work of the young. Young people understand one another with the greatest of ease, over and above geographical boundaries! How can a young generation be born, however, which is open to the true, the beautiful, the noble and to what is worthy of sacrifice, if in Europe the family no longer represents an institution open to life and disinterested love? A family of which the elderly are an integral part, with a view to what is most important: the active communication of values and of the sense of life.

Address to the Bishops of Australia on Their *Ad Limina* Visit

March 26, 2004

2. . . . Your own reports unequivocally describe some of the destructive consequences of this eclipse of the sense of God: the undermining of family life;

a drift away from the Church; a limited vision of life which fails to awaken in people the sublime call to "direct their steps toward a truth which transcends them" (*Fides et Ratio*, no. 5). . . .

7. Dear Brothers, I am pleased to acknowledge your steadfast efforts to *uphold the uniqueness of marriage as a life-long covenant based on generous mutual giving and unconditional love.* The Church's teaching on marriage and stable family life offers saving truth to individuals and a sure foundation upon which the aspirations of your nation can be anchored. Incisive and faithful explanation of Christian doctrine regarding marriage and the family is of utmost importance in order to counter the secular, pragmatic and individualistic outlook which has gained ground in the area of legislation and even a certain acceptance in the realm of public opinion (cf. *Ecclesia in Oceania*, 45). Of particular concern is the growing trend to equate marriage with other forms of cohabitation. This obfuscates the very nature of marriage and violates its sacred purpose in God's plan for humanity (cf. *Familiaris Consortio*, no. 3).

Raising families according to the splendor of Christ's truth is a sharing in God's work of creation. It lies at the heart of the call to promote a civilization of love. The deep-seated love of mothers and fathers for their children is also the Church's, as is the pain experienced by parents when their children fall victim to forces and trends which draw them away from the path of truth, leaving them disorientated and confused. *Bishops must continue to support parents* who, despite the often bewildering social difficulties of today's world, are in a position to exercise great influence and offer broader horizons of hope (cf. *Pastores Gregis*, no. 51). *It is the Bishop's particular task to ensure that within civil society—including the media and entertainment industry sectors—the values of marriage and family life are supported and defended* (cf. ibid., no. 52).

Address to Participants in the International UNIV Meeting

April 5, 2004

2. At your International Congress you are addressing a very timely theme: "Projecting culture: the language of advertising." There is a real need to know how to use suitable language in order to transmit positive messages and make their ideals and noble initiatives known and attractive. It is also necessary to be able to discern the limits and pitfalls of the language which the media propose to us. Sometimes, in fact, advertisements present a superficial and inadequate vision of life, of the individual person or the family, and of morality.

Address to the Members of the
Pontifical Academy of Social Sciences

April 30, 2004

Your Eminences,
Your Excellencies,
Dear Members of the Academy,

1. I greet you all with affection and esteem as we celebrate *the tenth anniversary of the Pontifical Academy of Social Sciences*. I thank your new President, Professor Mary Ann Glendon, and offer cordial good wishes as she begins her service. At the same time I express my deep gratitude to Professor Edmond Malinvaud for his commitment to the work of the Academy in studying such complex questions as labor and unemployment, forms of social inequality, and democracy and globalization. I am also grateful to Monsignor Marcelo Sánchez Sorondo for his efforts to make the work of the Academy accessible to a wider audience through the resources of modern communications.

2. The theme which you are presently studying—that of relations between generations—is closely connected to your research on globalization. In earlier times the care of grown children for their parents was taken for granted. The family was the primary place of an *inter-generational solidarity*. There was the solidarity of marriage itself, in which spouses took each other for better or worse and committed themselves to offer each other lifelong mutual assistance. This solidarity of the married couple soon extended to their children, whose education demanded a strong and lasting bond. This led in turn to solidarity between grown children and their aging parents.

At present relations between generations are undergoing significant changes as a result of various factors. In many areas there has been a weakening of the marriage bond, which is often perceived as a mere contract between two individuals. The pressures of a consumer society can cause families to divert attention from the home to the workplace or to a variety of social activities. Children are at times perceived, even before their birth, as an obstacle to the personal fulfillment of their parents, or are seen as one object to be chosen among others. Inter-generational relations are thus affected, since many grown children now leave to the state or society at large the care of their aged parents. The instability of the marriage bond in certain social settings likewise has led to a growing tendency for adult children to distance themselves from their parents and to delegate to third parties the natural obligation and divine command to honor one's father and mother.

3. Given the fundamental importance of solidarity in the building of healthy human societies (cf. *Sollicitudo Rei Socialis*, nos. 38-40), I encourage your study of these significant realities and express my hope that it will lead to a clearer appreciation of the need for *a solidarity which crosses generations and unites individuals and groups* in mutual assistance and enrichment. I am confident that your research in this area will make a valuable contribution to the development of the Church's social teaching.

Particular attention needs to be paid to the precarious situation of many elderly persons, which varies according to nations and regions (cf. *Evangelium Vitae*, no. 44; *Centesimus Annus*, no. 33). Many of them have insufficient resources or pensions, some suffer from physical maladies, while others no longer feel useful or are ashamed that they require special care, and all too many simply feel abandoned. These issues will certainly be more evident as the number of the elderly increases and the population itself ages as a result of the decline in the birthrate and the availability of better medical care.

4. In meeting these challenges, *every generation and social group has a role to play*. Special attention needs to be paid to the respective competencies of the State and the family in the building of an *effective solidarity between generations*. In full respect for the principle of subsidiarity (cf. *Centesimus Annus*, no. 48), public authorities must be concerned to acknowledge the effects of an individualism which—as your studies have already shown—can seriously affect relations between different generations. For its part, *the family*, as the origin and foundation of human society (cf. *Apostolicam Actuositatem*, no. 11; *Familiaris Consortio*, no. 42), also has an irreplaceable role in the building of inter-generational solidarity. There is no age when one ceases to be a father or mother, a son or daughter. We have a special responsibility not only toward those to whom we have given the gift of life, but also toward those from whom we have received that gift.

Dear Members of the Academy, as you carry forward your important work I offer you my prayerful good wishes and I cordially invoke upon you and your loved ones the abundant blessings of Almighty God.

Address to the Bishops of California, Nevada, and Hawaii on Their *Ad Limina* Visit

May 14, 2004

4. The lasting peace and harmony so longed for by individuals, families and society can only be won through that conversion which is a fruit of mercy

and constituent of genuine reconciliation. As Bishops you have the difficult yet satisfying duty of promoting the true Christian understanding of reconciliation. Perhaps no story better illustrates the profound drama of metanoia than the parable of the Prodigal Son, upon which I have elsewhere commented at length (cf. *Dives in Misericordia*, nos. 5-6). The prodigal son is in a certain sense all men and women. We all can be lured by the temptation to separate ourselves from the Father and thus suffer loss of dignity, humiliation and shame, but equally so we all can have the courage to turn back to the Father who embraces us with a love which, transcending even justice, manifests itself as mercy.

Address to Pilgrims Gathered in Rome for the Canonization of Five New Saints

May 17, 2004

3. I now greet with affection the Spanish-speaking pilgrims who have come to take part in the canonization of St. José Manyanet, a Spanish priest who was a chosen instrument in the nineteenth century to promote the good of the family together with the education of children and youth.

He placed his heart in the Holy Family. The "Gospel of the family," lived by Jesus of Nazareth together with Mary and Joseph, was the motor behind Fr. Manyanet's pastoral charity and the inspiration of his teaching. Furthermore, he worked so that the Holy Family would be known, venerated and imitated within families. This is his heritage and with his words, in his Catalonian language, I say to you today, the Religious founded by him, to the fathers and mothers of families and to the alumni and ex-alumni of his centers: "Make of your homes a Nazareth, of your families a Holy Family." May St. José Manyanet intercede for you!

Address to Participants in the Fifty-Third General Assembly of the Italian Bishops' Conference

May 20, 2004

3. Social communications has been another major topic of discussion at your Assembly, together with the presentation and examination of the Directory entitled: "Communication and Mission."

We are well aware of the penetrating influence that the media exercise today on mindsets and behavior, personal and collective, proposing a vision of life that unfortunately often tends to corrode basic ethical values, especially those that concern the family.

The media, however, also lend themselves to being used for and with very different purposes and results, making an important contribution to the affirmation of positive models of life and also to the spread of the Gospel. . . .

5. Dear Italian Bishops, I cordially share in the attention you devote to the life of this beloved Nation.

It is vital that the sincere search for the common good prevail over causes of disagreement and dissent so that Italy may function more smoothly and a new phase of development may begin, leading to the creation of a larger number of jobs, so necessary especially in certain southern regions.

A crucial theme for which we should redouble our efforts continues to be the family founded on marriage, the protection and acceptance of life and the primary responsibility of parents for their children's education. Today I repeat with you the words that were chosen as the theme for this year's Pro-Life Day: "There is no future without children!"

Truly necessary and urgent for the future of Italy are: an effort to combine social policies, the pastoral care of the Church and of all those who can influence public opinion, so that young couples may rediscover the joy of conceiving and raising children, taking part in a very special way in the Creator's work.

Address to the Bishops of San Antonio and Oklahoma City on Their *Ad Limina* Visit

May 22, 2004

Dear Brother Bishops,

1. It is with great joy that I welcome you, the Bishops from the ecclesiastical provinces of San Antonio and Oklahoma City, on the occasion of your visit *ad limina Apostolorum*. I am grateful that during the last few months I have had the pleasure of meeting so many Bishops from your country, which is home to a large and vibrant Catholic community. "We give thanks to God always for you all. . . remembering before our God and Father your work of faith and labor of love and steadfastness of hope in our Lord Jesus Christ" (1 Th 1:2-3). These visits not only strengthen the bond between us, but

they also offer a unique opportunity for us to look more closely at the good work already accomplished and the challenges still facing the Church in the United States.

In my last talks I discussed themes related to the *munus sanctificandi*. In particular I looked at the universal call to holiness and the importance of a loving communion with God and one another, as the key to personal and communal sanctification. "God created man in his own image and likeness: calling him to existence through love, he called him at the same time for love" (*Familiaris Consortio*, no. 11; cf. Gn 1:26-27). These essential relationships are based on God's love, and act as the point of reference for all human activity. *The vocation and responsibility of every person to love grants us not only the ability to cooperate with the Lord in his sanctifying mission but also gives us the desire to do so.* Accordingly, in this my final reflection on the sanctifying office, I wish to concentrate in a special way on one of the cornerstones of the Church itself, namely, the complex of interpersonal relationships known as the family (cf. *Familiaris Consortio*, no. 11).

2. Family life is sanctified in the joining of man and woman in the sacramental institution of holy matrimony. Consequently, it is fundamental that Christian marriage be comprehended in the fullest sense and be presented both as a natural institution and a sacramental reality. Many today have a clear understanding of the secular nature of marriage, which includes the rights and responsibilities modern societies hold as determining factors for a marital contract. There are nevertheless some who appear to lack a proper understanding of the intrinsically religious dimension of this covenant.

Modern society rarely pays heed to the permanent nature of marriage. In fact, the attitude toward marriage found in contemporary culture demands that the Church seek to offer better pre-marital instruction aimed at forming couples in this vocation and insist that her Catholic schools and religious education programs guarantee that young people, many of whom are from broken families themselves, are educated from a very early age in the Church's teaching on the sacrament of matrimony. In this regard, I thank the Bishops of the United States for their concern to provide a correct catechesis on marriage to the lay faithful of their dioceses. *I encourage you to continue to place a strong emphasis on marriage as a Christian vocation to which couples are called and to give them the means to live it fully* through marital preparation programs which are "serious in purpose, excellent in content, sufficient in length and obligatory in nature" (*Directory for the Pastoral Ministry of Bishops*, no. 202).

3. The Church teaches that the love of man and woman made holy in the sacrament of marriage is a mirror of God's everlasting love for his creation (cf. Preface of Marriage III). Similarly, *the communion of love present in family*

life serves as a model of the relationships which must exist in Christ's family, the Church. "Among the fundamental tasks of the Christian family is its ecclesial task: the family is placed at the service of the building up of the Kingdom of God in history by participating in the life and mission of the Church" (*Familiaris Consortio*, no. 49). In order to ensure that the family is capable of fulfilling this mission, the Church has a sacred responsibility to do all she can to assist married couples in making the family a "domestic church" and in fulfilling properly the "priestly role" to which every Christian family is called (cf. ibid., no. 55). A most effective way to accomplish this task is by assisting parents to become the first preachers of the Gospel and the main catechists in the family. This particular apostolate requires more than a mere academic instruction on family life; it requires the Church to share the hurts and struggles of parents and families, as well as their joys. Christian communities should thus make every effort to assist spouses in turning their families into schools of holiness by offering concrete support for family life ministry at the local level. Included in this responsibility is the satisfying task of leading back many Catholics who have drifted away from the Church but long to return now that they have a family.

4. The family as a community of love is reflected in the life of the Church. Indeed, the Church may be considered as a family God's Family gathered as sons and daughters of our heavenly Father. Like a family, the Church is a place where its members feel free to bring their sufferings, knowing that Christ's presence in the prayer of his people is the greatest source of healing. For this reason, the Church maintains an active involvement at all levels of family ministry and especially in those areas which reach out to youth and young adults. *Young people, faced with a secular culture which promotes instant gratification and selfishness over the virtues of self-control and generosity, need the Church's support and guidance.* I encourage you, along with your priests and lay collaborators, to have youth ministry as an essential part of your diocesan programs (cf. *Directory for the Pastoral Ministry of Bishops*, no. 203 and *Pastores Gregis*, no. 53). So many young people are seeking strong, committed and responsible role models who are not afraid to profess an unconditional love for Christ and his Church. In this regard, priests have always made and should continue to make a special and invaluable contribution to the lives of young Catholics.

As in any family, the Church's internal harmony can at times be challenged by a lack of charity and the presence of conflict among her members. This can lead to the formation of factions within the Church which often become so concerned with their special interests that they lose sight of the unity and solidarity which are the foundations of ecclesial life and the sources of communion in the family of God. To address this worrisome phenomenon

Bishops are charged to act with fatherly solicitude as men of communion to ensure that their particular Churches act as families, so "that there may be no discord in the body, but that the members may have the same care for one another" (1 Cor 12:25). This requires that the Bishop strive to remedy any division which can exist among his flock by attempting to rebuild a level of trust, reconciliation and mutual understanding in the ecclesial family.

5. My Brother Bishops, as I conclude these considerations on family life, I pray that you will continue your efforts *to promote personal and communal sanctification through devotions of popular piety*. For centuries the Holy Rosary, Stations of the Cross, prayer before and after meals and other devotional practices have helped to form a school of prayer in families and parishes, acting as rich and beautiful supplements to the sacramental life of Catholics. A renewal of these devotions will not only help the faithful in your country grow in personal holiness but will also act as a source of strength and sanctification for the Catholic Church in the United States.

As your nation marks in a special way the One-hundred and Fiftieth Anniversary of the proclamation of the dogma of the Immaculate Conception, I leave you with the words of my illustrious predecessor, Blessed Pope Pius IX: "We have, therefore, a very certain hope and complete confidence that the most Blessed Virgin will ensure by her most powerful patronage that all difficulties be removed and all errors dissipated, so that our Holy Mother the Catholic Church may flourish daily more and more throughout all the nations and countries, and may reign 'from sea to sea and from the river to the ends of the earth'" (*Ineffabilis Deus*). I invoke the intercession of Mary Immaculate, Patroness of the United States, who untainted by sin unceasingly prays for the sanctification of Christians, and I cordially impart my Apostolic Blessing as a pledge of strength and joy in Jesus Christ.

Regina Caeli

May 23, 2004

World Day of Social Communications

1. Today, in Italy and in other countries, is the liturgical Solemnity of the Ascension of the Lord, which shows how the humanity that Christ assumed and redeemed was raised by him to full communion with God.

On this same Sunday we are celebrating the *World Day of Social Communications*. The Church closely and fondly regards those who work in this vast sector and is eager to develop a frank and open dialogue with them, in order to foster their commitment to humanity's authentic progress.

2. This year the theme on which we are invited to reflect is: *The Media and the Family: a Risk and a Richness*. Thanks to the modern technologies, many nuclear families are able to have direct access to the *vast resources* of communications and information and make use of them for education, cultural enrichment and spiritual growth. Yet the media also have the capacity to *seriously damage* families when they present an inadequate or even distorted outlook on life, on the family, on religion and on morality.

It is therefore vital to learn how *to use them wisely and prudently*. This duty primarily concerns parents, who are responsible for giving their children a healthy and balanced education. It likewise involves the *public Authorities*, who are required to implement *suitable regulations* which ensure that the media always show respect for the truth and for the common good.

3. In these days prior to Pentecost, let us invoke with Mary the gift of the Holy Spirit, so that he may help all who work in the sector of social communications to carry out their work with authentic apostolic zeal.

Letter on the Fourth Centenary of the Death of St. Seraphino of Montegranaro, Patron of the Province

June 3, 2004

[St. Seraphino] was a great peacemaker in families, wisely alternating, according to the circumstances, forceful appeals, loving gestures of solidarity and words of encouraging consolation.

Address to the Bishops of Colorado, Wyoming, Utah, Arizona, New Mexico, and Western Texas on Their *Ad Limina* Visit

June 4, 2004

5. The rise of the prophetic mission of the laity is one of the great treasures unfolding in the Church of the third millennium. The Second Vatican Council rightly considered in detail the duty of the laity to "seek the kingdom

of God by engaging in temporal affairs and directing them according to God's will" *(Lumen Gentium, no. 31)*. It is also true however that over the last forty or so years, while political attention to human subjectivity has focused on individual rights, in the public domain there has been a growing reluctance to acknowledge that all men and women receive their essential and common dignity from God and with it the capacity to move toward truth and goodness (cf. *Centesimus Annus, no. 38)*. Detached from this vision of the fundamental unity and purpose of the whole human family, rights are at times reduced to self-centered demands: the growth of prostitution and pornography in the name of adult choice, the acceptance of abortion in the name of women's rights, the approval of same sex unions in the name of homosexual rights.

In the face of such erroneous yet pervasive thinking you must do everything possible to encourage the laity in their "special responsibility" for "evangelizing culture . . . and promoting Christian values in society and public life" (*Pastores Gregis*, no. 51). False secularistic forms of "humanism" which exalt the individual in such a manner that they become a veritable idolatry (cf. *Christifideles Laici*, no. 5) can be countered only by the rediscovery of the genuine inviolable dignity of every person. This sublime dignity is manifested in all its radiance when the person's origin and destiny are considered—created by God and redeemed by Christ, we are all called to be "children in the Son" (cf. ibid., no. 37). So, again I say to the people of the United States, it is the Paschal Mystery of Christ that is the only sure point of reference for all of humanity on its pilgrimage in search of authentic unity and true peace! (cf. *Ecclesia in America*, no. 70).

APOSTOLIC PILGRIMAGE TO BERN, SWITZERLAND

Meeting with the Catholic Youth of Switzerland

June 5, 2004

4. . . . . If you are able to open your hearts and minds with availability, you will discover "your vocation," in other words, the plan that God in his love has devised for you from eternity. . . .

5. You will be able to build a family founded on marriage, that pact of love between a man and a woman who commit themselves to a communion of stable and faithful life. Through your own witness, you will be able to confirm that even amid all the difficulties and obstacles, it is possible to live Christian marriage to the full as an experience filled with meaning and, as it were, "good news" for all families.

Or if this is your vocation, you will be a priest or a Religious, giving your life to Christ and to the Church with an undivided heart and thus becoming a sign of God's loving presence in today's world. Like so many who have gone before you, you will be able to be an undaunted and unflagging apostle, watchful in prayer, cheerful and welcoming in community service.

Angelus

June 6, 2004

2. Today I renew the entrustment of the Swiss People to the Blessed Virgin. May Mary watch over families, safeguarding conjugal love and supporting the mission of parents. May she comfort the elderly and help them to ensure that society does not lack their precious contribution. May she nourish in young people their sense of values and the commitment to abide by them. May she obtain for the entire national community the constant, unanimous desire to build together a prosperous and peaceful Country, which is both attentive and full of solidarity for people in difficulty.

Message to Bishop Egidio Caporello of Mantua for the Twelfth Centenary of the Diocese

June 19, 2004

4. Like the rest of Italy, Mantua has known rapid social changes in recent years and many financial difficulties, while it is confronting a growing number of different cultures and religions. A certain consumeristic and secularized mindset is undermining the unity and stability of families and, by attracting more and more Christians, causes them de facto to contribute to a progressive detachment from the values of the faith in social, civil and political milieus. It is vital to respond to these erosive forces and hence indispensable to rediscover the Christian roots of one's own culture.

All the faithful are called into question by this commitment. They will make an effective contribution to this urgent task if they know how to put Christ at the center of every personal, family and community project. It is by starting afresh from him that it becomes possible to build a more just and fraternal world.

Message for the Ninety-Fifth
Katholikentag in Germany

June 16, 2004

2. "Living by the power of God." The program of the *Katholikentag* is guided by this maxim, taken from the Second Letter to the Corinthians (13:4). It is an incentive to make all liturgical celebrations, conversations and prayers come alive through the power of God. I urge you to spend these days with open eyes and hearts so that you may once again be aware that the power of God is dynamically at work within you and, through your witness to faith, can also be lived in society.

During the events of this great Catholic meeting in which many other Christians are also taking part, may you feel the urge to raise your voices bravely as believing Christians whenever the foundations of the Christian faith and human coexistence are disputed, the lofty values of Christian marriage and of the family are overlooked and the uniqueness of life as a gift of God is at stake! Spur one another to be committed anew to the poor and the marginalized for peace and justice throughout the world! Bear witness to everyone to the hope that is in you (cf. 1 Pt 3:15).

Address to the First Group of Bishops of
Colombia on Their *Ad Limina* Visit

June 17, 2004

5. Another field of pastoral action that demands special attention is the promotion and defense of the family institution, attacked today on many fronts by multiple and subtle arguments. We are witnessing a trend, in some places most widespread, that tends to weaken its true nature.

I am aware of the commitment you devote to defending and promoting this institution that owes its origin to God and his plan of salvation (cf. *Familiaris Consortio*, no. 49). It is therefore necessary to continue to proclaim firmly the truth about marriage and the family established by God as an authentic service to society. Failing to do so would be a grave pastoral omission that would lead believers into error as well as those who have the serious responsibility of making decisions for the Nation's common good. This truth is not only valid for Catholics but for all men and women without distinction, since marriage and the family are an irreplaceable good for society, which cannot remain indifferent to its belittlement or the loss of its identity.

In this regard, family ministry, carried out above all by couples who belong to movements or associations for marriage spirituality and who set an example in the education of their children, must guide young couples and families in difficulty as well as those who are preparing for marriage in order to discover the values of Christian matrimony and to be faithful to the commitment they assume in receiving this sacrament. At the same time, it is important to teach them that in conceiving children, they must follow the criterion of responsible parenthood and must also see to their human and religious formation at home in an atmosphere of serene coexistence and tenderness, as an expression of God's love for each one of his children.

Address to the Ambassador of Spain to the Holy See

June 18, 2004

In this field some "social conquests" are misnamed, for in reality they only benefit some at the cost of the sacrifice of others, and public leaders, as the guarantors and not the source of the rights that are innate in all, must view them rather with concern and alarm.

Something similar sometimes happens with the family, the central and fundamental nucleus of every society, the unequalled hearth of solidarity and the natural school of peaceful coexistence, which deserves the greatest possible protection and help in carrying out its tasks. Its rights are a priority in comparison with those of larger social bodies. Among these, the right to be born and to grow up in a stable home in which the words "father" and "mother" can be said joyfully and without deception should not be forgotten. Thus, the smallest children are also prepared to open themselves confidently to life and to society, which will benefit as a whole if it does not listen to certain voices that seem to confuse marriage with other, quite different forms of union, if they are not actually opposed to it, or to consider children as mere objects for a person's own satisfaction.

Among other things, families have the right and duty to raise their children, doing so in accordance with their own moral and religious convictions; integral formation cannot escape the transcendent and spiritual dimension of human beings. The role of educational institutions bound to the Church fits into this context. They contribute to the common good like many others in various milieus which also render a service to citizens, and often to the least privileged. Nor should the teaching of the Catholic religion in State schools be undervalued, based precisely on the right of the families that ask for it, without discrimination or imposed conditions.

Address to the Bishops of the Provinces of Portland, Seattle, and Anchorage on Their *Ad Limina* Visit

June 24, 2004

2. Today creativity is especially needed in better shaping ecclesial institutions to fulfill their prophetic mission. This means *finding innovative ways to enable the light of Christ to shine brightly*, so that the gift of his grace may truly "make all things new" (Rev 21:5; cf. *Novo Millennio Ineunte*, no. 54). The Church's many institutions in the United States—schools, universities, hospitals and charitable agencies—must not only assist the faithful to think and act fully in accordance with the Gospel, overcoming every separation between faith and life (cf. *Christifideles Laici*, no. 34), but they must themselves embody *a clear corporate testimony* to its saving truth. This will demand constantly re-examining their priorities in the light of their mission and offering a convincing witness, within a pluralistic society, to the Church's teaching, particularly on respect for human life, marriage and family, and the right ordering of public life.

Address to the Participants in the European Symposium for University Teachers

June 25, 2004

Distinguished Ladies and Gentlemen,

1. I am pleased to meet you on the occasion of the *European Symposium for University Teachers* which is taking place in the context of the International Year of the Family. You have been engaged in reflecting and comparing *the foundations, experiences and prospects of families in Europe*. I extend my cordial greeting to each one of you. In particular, I greet Cardinal Camillo Ruini, to whom I am grateful for his courteous words on your behalf.

I express my deep appreciation for the theme you have chosen: *Europe's future is staked on the family*. It can be said that the family mirrors society, hence, also the Europe that is under construction. The development of families is and will be the most important indicator of cultural and institutional development on the Continent. It is therefore particularly appropriate that universities, and especially Christian teachers, follow attentively the dynamics of families, fostering a responsible and conscious outlook in young people.

2. In the first millennium *the encounter between Roman law and the Christian message* brought about what one might call the *European model of the family* that subsequently spread on a wide scale in the Americas and in Oceania. The vicissitudes of this model coincide with the events of the so-called "Western" civilization itself. In fact, in the middle of the past century, in the socially and economically better-developed communities, phenomena symptomatic of a deep crisis surfaced with disruptive consequences that are visible to everyone today (cf. Post-Synodal Apostolic Exhortation *Ecclesia in Europa*, no. 90). In the face of this crisis, the family has always been a *strong and cohesive element* and, despite being bitterly opposed, has remained the object of aspirations, desires, plans and yearning. The origin of this crisis is really cultural, to the point that the *younger generations* today seem to be strongly *attracted by the ideal of the traditional family* but *are almost incapable of assuming responsibility for it in the right way.*

3. Thus, it is possible to comprehend the importance of a congress such as yours, which looks at the family institution in the perspective of its foundations—philosophical, juridical and theological—for a full interpretation of current experiences that are often problematic and sometimes dramatic, and to grasp the many perspectives that are unfolding in the context of a renewed family model.

The main question, however, is precisely this: can we still speak of a family model today? The Church is convinced that in the context of our time it is more necessary than ever *to reassert the institutions of marriage and the family as realities that derive from the wisdom of God's will* and reveal their full significance and value in his creative and saving plan (cf. ibid.; cf. *Gaudium et Spes*, no. 48; *Familiaris Consortio*, nos. 11-16). To this end, side by side with the strictly pastoral initiatives is the role of all who work in the *context of culture and scientific investigation*, where the method of dialogue and comparison between the different disciplines concerned with family topics becomes highly significant.

4. In dealing with the European context, it is this method that is inspiring you in the course of this current Symposium. I hope that your timely initiative will contribute to ensuring that in Europe, today and tomorrow, families can carry out satisfactorily the *role inherent in their most eminent dignity.* To this

end, I assure you of my special remembrance in prayer and I invoke the intercession of the Holy Family of Nazareth, the model for every family.

I wish each one of you, dear friends, success in your work and a peaceful
stay in Rome. I accompany this wish with my Blessing, which I extend to all
your loved ones.

Address to the President of Malta

June 25, 2004

Mr. President,

I am pleased to welcome you to the Vatican so early in your term of office,
and through you I send heartfelt greetings to the people of Malta. Your visit
today occurs at an important moment in the history of your country. As
Malta takes its rightful place in the European Union, it has a vital role to
play in upholding the profoundly Christian identity of this Continent. In
this regard I would like to express the Holy See's sincere appreciation for
the support given by Your Excellency and the Government of Malta for the
inclusion of a reference to Europe's Christian heritage in the Preamble of the
Constitutional Treaty of the European Union.

Since the time of St. Paul, Malta has been renowned for its firm adherence
to the faith. I pray that it will persevere in this and I am confident that the
Maltese people, well known for their dedication to the Church and, in particular, their great respect for family life, will draw others to a deeper appreciation of the liberating message of the Gospel.

Upon you and all the beloved people of Malta I cordially invoke God's
abundant blessings of prosperity, joy and peace.

Address to Participants in the
Symposium on Catholic Education

July 3, 2004

3. Wherever students live, education must help them each day to grow into
more and more mature men and women, and "to be" better rather than "to
have" more. Scholastic formation is one aspect of education, but not the only
one. The essential connection between all the dimensions of education must

be constantly reinforced. A coordinated educational process will lead to ever greater unity in the personality and life of adolescents.

It is right to mobilize everyone and to join forces to work for young people: parents, teachers, educators, chaplaincy teams. They should all also remember that what they teach must be supported by their own witness and example. In fact, young people are sensitive to the witness of adults who are their models. The family continues to be the essential place for education.

Message to the Participants in the International Congress of Catholic Action

August 10, 2004

3. . . . Every Christian is bound to witness to the great changes in his life, worked by grace and motivated by charity. "This will be possible if the lay faithful are able to overcome in themselves the separation of the Gospel from life, to again take up in their daily activities in family, work and society, an integrated approach to life that is fully brought about by the inspiration and strength of the Gospel" (*Christifideles Laici*, no. 34). Catholic Action has always been and must still be today a nursery for the formation of the faithful who, enlightened by the social teaching of the Church, are employed on the front line to defend the sacred gift of life, the preservation of the dignity of the human person, the achievement of educational freedom, the promotion of the true meaning of marriage and the family, the practice of charity to the neediest, the quest for peace and justice and the application to the different interactive social realities of the principles of subsidiarity and solidarity.

PILGRIMAGE TO LOURDES ON THE OCCASION OF THE
150TH ANNIVERSARY OF THE PROMULGATION OF
THE DOGMA OF THE IMMACULATE CONCEPTION

Homily at Mass

August 15, 2004

7. . . . From this grotto I issue a special call to women. Appearing here, Mary entrusted her message to a young girl, as if to emphasize the special mission of women in our own time, tempted as it is by materialism and secularism: to be in today's society a witness of those essential values which are seen only

with the eyes of the heart. To you, women, falls the task of being sentinels of the Invisible! I appeal urgently to all of you, dear brothers and sisters, to do everything in your power to ensure that life, each and every life, will be respected from conception to its natural end. Life is a sacred gift, and no one can presume to be its master.

Address to the Ambassador of Guatemala to the Holy See

September 2, 2004

In the Messages I delivered on these Visits [to Guatemala], I wanted to express my affection for the beloved Guatemalan People, but also my concern at the human and social problems with which they have to deal. I am pleased to note that the protection of human life from conception to natural death is recognized in your Nation's Constitution, which does Guatemala honor. In this area as in others, when civil legislation embraces natural law peoples advance on the path to peace and progress.

VISIT TO LORETO

Homily at Mass for the Beatification of Pere Tarrés i Claret, Alberto Marvelli, and Pina Suro

September 5, 2004

8. *It is up to you lay people to witness to the faith through your own specific virtues*: fidelity and gentleness in the family.

General Audience

September 8, 2004, Nativity of the Blessed Virgin Mary

Mary as "blessed among women"

1. The liturgy today commemorates the Nativity of the Blessed Virgin Mary. This feast, very important to popular piety, leads us to admire in Mary the Child, the *purest dawn of the Redemption*. We are contemplating a little girl

like every other, yet at the same time the only one who was "blessed among women" (Lk 1:42). Mary was the immaculate "Daughter of Zion," destined to become the Mother of the Messiah.

2. Looking at the Child Mary, how can we fail to remember the many *defenseless children of Beslan, in Ossezia*, victims of a barbaric kidnapping and tragic massacre? They were *inside a school*, a place in which values are learned that give meaning to the history, culture and civilization of peoples: reciprocal respect, solidarity, justice and peace. Instead, between those walls they experienced outrage, hatred and death, the evil consequences of cruel fanaticism and an insane disregard for the human person.

At this moment our gaze broadens to take in *all innocent children* in every corner of the earth who are victims of the violence of adults. Children *forced to use weapons* and taught to hate and kill; children *induced to beg in the streets*, exploited for easy earnings; children *ill-treated and humiliated* by arrogant, abusive grown-ups; children *left to themselves*, deprived of the warmth of a family and prospects of a future; children who *die of hunger*, children *killed* in the many wars in various regions of the world.

3. It is a loud *cry of pain from children whose dignity is offended*. It cannot, it must not leave anyone indifferent. Dear brothers and sisters, before the cradle of the Infant Mary, let us respond with renewed awareness to the duty that behooves us all to *protect and defend* these frail creatures and *to build them a future of peace*. Let us pray together that the conditions for a serene and safe life may be created for them.

Prayer of the Holy Father for All the Innocent Children in the World

Brothers and Sisters, accepting the Holy Father's invitation, let us raise our prayer to God.
Let us say together: *Lord, hear us!*

1. For the children of Beslan who were torn from life with brutal violence while they were preparing to start the new school year, and for their parents and friends killed with them: that God in his mercy will throw open the doors of his house to them, let us pray:
Resp.: *Lord, hear us!*

2. For the injured, for the victims' families and for all the members of the Beslan community who are mourning with broken hearts the death of their loved ones: that, supported by the light of faith and comforted by the solidarity

of so many persons throughout the world, they may be able to forgive those who have harmed them, let us pray:

Resp.: *Lord, hear us!*

3. For all the children in so many parts of the world who are suffering and dying because of the violence and abuse of adults: that the Lord will enable them to feel the comfort of his love and melt the hardness of hearts that is the cause of their suffering, let us pray:

Resp.: *Lord, hear us!*

4. For the many people abducted in the tormented Land of Iraq, and in particular, for the two young Italian volunteer workers kidnapped yesterday in Baghdad: that they may all be treated with respect and quickly restored unharmed to the affection of their loved ones, let us pray:

Resp.: *Lord, hear us!*

5. For justice and peace in the world, that the Lord may illumine the minds of those who are subjected to the fatal suggestion of violence and open all hearts to dialogue and reconciliation, so as to build a future of hope and peace, let us pray:

Resp.: *Lord, hear us!*

The Holy Father:

God, our Father, you created men and women so that they might live together in communion. Make us understand that every child is a treasure of humanity and that violence to others is a dead end with no future. We ask you this through the intercession of the Virgin Mother of Jesus Christ Our Lord, who lives and reigns for ever and ever.

Message for Lent 2005

January 27, 2005

Dear Brothers and Sisters!

1. Each year, the Lenten Season is set before us as a good opportunity for the intensification of prayer and penance, opening hearts to the docile welcoming of the divine will. During Lent, a spiritual journey is outlined for us that prepares us to relive the Great Mystery of the Death and Resurrection of Christ. This is done primarily by listening to the Word of God more devoutly

and by practicing mortification more generously, thanks to which it is possible to render greater assistance to those in need.

This year, dear brothers and sisters, I wish to bring to your attention a theme which is rather current, well-illustrated by the following verse from Deuteronomy: *"Loving the Lord . . .means life to you, and length of days . . ."* (30:20). These are the words that Moses directs to the people, inviting them to embrace the Covenant with Yahweh in the country of Moab, *"that you and your descendants may live, loving the Lord, your God, obeying his voice, and cleaving to him."* (30:19-20). The fidelity to this divine Covenant is for Israel a guarantee of the future: *"that you may dwell in the land which the Lord swore to your fathers, to Abraham, to Isaac, and to Jacob, to give to them"* (30:20). According to the Biblical understanding, reaching old age is a sign of the Most High's gracious benevolence. Longevity appears, therefore, as a special divine gift.

It is upon this theme that I would like to ask you to reflect during this Lent, in order to deepen the awareness of the role that the elderly are called to play in society and in the Church, and thus to prepare your hearts for the loving welcome that should always be reserved for them. Thanks to the contribution of science and medicine, one sees in society today a lengthening of the human life span and a subsequent increase in the number of elderly. This demands a more specific attention to the world of so-called "old" age, in order to help its members to live their full potential by placing them at the service of the entire community. The care of the elderly, above all when they pass through difficult moments, must be of great concern to all the faithful, especially in the ecclesial communities of Western societies, where the problem is particularly present.

2. Human life is a precious gift to be loved and defended in each of its stages. The Commandment, "You shall not kill!" always requires respecting and promoting human life, from its beginning to its natural end. It is a command that applies even in the presence of illness and when physical weakness reduces the person's ability to be self-reliant. If growing old, with its inevitable conditions, is accepted serenely in the light of faith, it can become an invaluable opportunity for better comprehending the Mystery of the Cross, which gives full sense to human existence.

The elderly need to be understood and helped in this perspective. I wish, here, to express my appreciation to those who dedicate themselves to fulfilling these needs, and I also call upon other people of good will to take advantage of Lent for making their own personal contribution. This will allow many elderly not to think of themselves as a burden to the community, and sometimes even to their own families, living in a situation of loneliness that leads to the temptation of isolating themselves or becoming discouraged.

It is necessary to raise the awareness in public opinion that the elderly represent, in any case, a resource to be valued. For this reason, economic support and legislative initiatives, which allow them not to be excluded from social life, must be strengthened. In truth, during the last decade, society has become more attentive to their needs, and medicine has developed palliative cures that, along with an integral approach to the sick person, are particularly beneficial for long-term patients.

3. The greater amount of free time in this stage of life offers the elderly the opportunity to face the primary issues that perhaps had been previously set aside, due to concerns that were pressing or considered a priority nonetheless. Knowledge of the nearness of the final goal leads the elderly person to focus on that which is essential, giving importance to those things that the passing of years do not destroy.

Precisely because of this condition, the elderly person can carry out his or her role in society. If it is true that man lives upon the heritage of those who preceded him, and that his future depends definitively on how the cultural values of his own people are transmitted to him, then the wisdom and experience of the elderly can illuminate his path on the way of progress toward an ever more complete form of civilization.

How important it is to rediscover this mutual enrichment between different generations! The Lenten Season, with its strong call to conversion and solidarity, leads us this year to focus on these important themes which concern everyone. What would happen if the People of God yielded to a certain current mentality that considers these people, our brothers and sisters, as almost useless when they are reduced in their capacities due to the difficulties of age or sickness? Instead, how different the community would be, if, beginning with the family, it tries always to remain open and welcoming toward them.

4. Dear brothers and sisters, during Lent, aided by the Word of God, let us reflect upon how important it is that each community accompany with loving understanding those who grow old. Moreover, one must become accustomed to thinking confidently about the mystery of death, so that the definitive encounter with God occur in a climate of interior peace, in the awareness that He *"who knit me in my mother's womb"* (cf. Ps 139:13b) and who willed us *"in his image and likeness"* (cf. Gn 1:26) will receive us.

Mary, our guide on the Lenten journey, leads all believers, especially the elderly, to an ever more profound knowledge of Christ dead and risen, who is the ultimate reason for our existence. May she, the faithful servant of her divine Son, together with Saints Ann and Joachim, intercede for each one of us "now and at the hour of our death."

My Blessing to All!

SHRINE OF MARY, QUEEN OF THE APOSTLES,
YAOUNDÉ, CAMEROON

Message for the Thirteenth World Day of the Sick

February 11, 2005

Christ, hope for Africa

1. After ten years, in 2005, Africa will once again be hosting the principal celebrations for World Day of the Sick that will take place at the Shrine of Mary, Queen of the Apostles, in Yaoundé, Cameroon.

The choice of this venue will offer an opportunity to express real solidarity to the peoples of that Continent, tried by serious inadequacies in the health-care sector. A further step will thus be taken in implementing the commitment which the Christians of Africa made at the third World Day of the Sick ten years ago, that is, to be "Good Samaritans" to their brothers and sisters in difficulties.

Actually, in the Post-Synodal Apostolic Exhortation *Ecclesia in Africa*, complying with the observations of many Synod Fathers, I wrote that "contemporary Africa can be compared to the man who went down from Jerusalem to Jericho; he fell among robbers who stripped him, beat him and departed, leaving him half dead (cf. Lk 10:30-37)." And I added that "Africa is a Continent where countless human beings—men and women, children and young people—are lying, as it were, on the edge of the road, sick, injured, disabled, marginalized and abandoned. They are in dire need of Good Samaritans who will come to their aid" (no. 41).

2. World Day of the Sick aims to stimulate reflection on the subject of health, whose fullest meaning also alludes to the harmony of human beings with themselves and with the surrounding world. It is exactly this vision that Africa richly expresses in its cultural tradition, testified to by many art forms, both civil and religious, that are bursting with joy, rhythm and musicality.

Unfortunately, however, today this harmony is deeply disturbed. Numerous diseases wreak havoc on the Continent, including in particular the scourge of AIDS, "which is sowing suffering and death in many parts of Africa" (ibid., no. 116: loc. cit. no. 69). The conflicts and wars that afflict many regions of Africa stand in the way of interventions to prevent and treat these diseases. In the refugee camps people are languishing who are deprived even of the indispensable foodstuffs for survival.

I urge those who can to continue to do their utmost to put an end to these tragedies (cf. ibid., no. 117). I then remind people responsible for the sale of arms of what I said in that Document: "Those who foment wars in Africa by the arms trade are accomplices in abominable crimes against humanity" (ibid., no. 118).

3. As for the drama of AIDS, I have had the opportunity in other circumstances to stress that it is also symptomatic of a "pathology of the spirit." To fight it responsibly, it is necessary to increase its prevention by teaching respect for the sacred value of life and the correct approach to sexuality.

Indeed, if there are many contagious infections passed on through the blood especially during pregnancy—infections that must be combated with every possible means—those contracted through sexual intercourse are by far the most numerous and can only be avoided by responsible conduct and the observance of the virtue of chastity.

The Bishops participating in the above-mentioned Synod for Africa in 1994, referring to the effect of irresponsible sexual behavior on the spread of the disease, made a recommendation that I would like to propose anew here: "The companionship, joy, happiness and peace which Christian marriage and fidelity provide, and the safeguard which chastity gives, must be continuously presented to the faithful, particularly the young" (ibid., no. 116).

4. Everyone must feel involved in the battle against AIDS. In this area too, it is the task of government leaders and civil authorities to make available to citizens clear and correct information, and to earmark sufficient resources to provide education in health care for young people. I encourage international organizations to promote initiatives in this field that are inspired by wisdom and solidarity, and always to strive to defend human dignity and to protect the inviolable right to life.

Earnest applause goes to the pharmaceutical industries engaged in keeping low the costs of medicines helpful in the treatment of AIDS. Of course, financial resources are necessary for scientific research in the health-care sector and further resources are required to put the newly discovered drugs on the market, but in the face of emergencies such as AIDS, the preservation of human life must come before any other criterion.

I ask pastoral workers "to bring to their brothers and sisters affected by AIDS all possible material, moral and spiritual comfort. I urgently ask the world's scientists and political leaders, motivated by the love and respect due to every human person, to use every means available in order to put an end to this scourge" (ibid., no. 116).

I would like in particular to recall here with admiration the many health-care workers, chaplains and volunteers who, like Good Samaritans, assist persons with AIDS and care for their relatives. In this regard, the service of the thousands of Catholic health-care institutions that go to the help of people in

Africa afflicted by every kind of illness, and especially by AIDS, malaria and tuberculosis, is invaluable.

In recent years, I have noted that my appeals for persons with AIDS have not been in vain. I have seen with pleasure that various countries and institutions, with a coordinated effort, have supported practical campaigns for its prevention and for the care of the sick.

5. I am now addressing you in a special way, dear Brother Bishops of the Bishops' Conferences of other Continents, to ask you generously to join forces with the Pastors of Africa, to deal effectively with this and other emergencies. The Pontifical Council for Health Pastoral Care will continue, as in the past, to make its own contribution to coordinating and promoting this cooperation, asking every Bishops' Conference for its effective contribution.

The Church's attention to Africa's problems is not only motivated by philanthropic compassion for men and women in need but is also fostered by attachment to Christ the Redeemer, whose face she recognizes in the features of every suffering person. It is faith, therefore, that impels her to do her utmost in caring for the sick, as she has always done in the course of history. Hope enables her, despite the obstacles of every kind that she encounters, to persevere in this mission. Finally, charity suggests to her the right approach to the different situations, enabling her to perceive the particular features of each person and to respond to them.

With this attitude of deep sharing, the Church reaches out to life's injured in order to offer them Christ's love through the many forms of help that "creativity in charity" (Apostolic Letter *Novo Millennio Ineunte*, no. 50) suggests to her. She repeats to each one: courage, God has not forgotten you. Christ suffers with you. And by offering up your sufferings, you can collaborate with him in the redemption of the world.

6. The annual celebration of the World Day of the Sick offers everyone a possibility of understanding better the importance of pastoral health care. In our time, marked by a culture imbued with secularism, some have at times been tempted not to recognize the full value of this pastoral context.

They think that human destiny is played out in other fields. Instead, it is precisely in times of sickness that the need to find adequate responses to the ultimate questions about human life is the most pressing: questions on the meaning of pain, suffering and death itself, considered not only as an enigma that is hard to face, but a mystery in which Christ incorporates our lives in himself, opening them to a new and definitive birth for the life that will never end.

In Christ lies the hope of true, full health; the salvation that he brings is the true response to the ultimate questions about man. There is no contradiction between earthly health and eternal salvation, since the Lord died for the integral salvation of the human person and of all humanity (cf. 1 Pt 1:2-5; Liturgy of Holy Friday, *Adoration of the Cross*). Salvation consists of the final content of the New Covenant.

At the next World Day of the Sick, let us therefore proclaim the hope of total health for Africa and for all humanity, as we strive to work with greater determination at the service of this important cause.

7. In the Gospel passage of the Beatitudes, the Lord proclaims: *"Blessed are those who mourn, for they will be comforted"* (Mt 5:4). The contradiction that seems to exist between suffering and joy is overcome through the consoling action of the Holy Spirit. In conforming us to the mystery of the crucified and Risen Christ, the Holy Spirit opens us from this moment to the joy that will culminate in our beatific encounter with the Redeemer. In fact, the human being does not only aspire to physical or spiritual well-being, but to a "health" that is expressed in total harmony with God, with self and with humanity. This goal can only be reached through the mystery of the passion, death and Resurrection of Christ.

Mary Most Holy offers us an eloquent anticipation of this eschatological reality, especially through the mysteries of her Immaculate Conception and her Assumption into Heaven. In her, conceived without any shadow of sin, is found full acceptance of the divine will and service to human beings, and consequently, she is full of that deep harmony from which joy flows.

We therefore rightly turn to her, invoking her as *"Cause of our joy."* What the Virgin gives to us is a joy that endures even in trials. However, as I think of Africa, endowed with immense human, cultural and religious resources but afflicted also by unspeakable suffering, a heartfelt prayer rises to my lips:

O Mary, Immaculate Virgin,
Woman of suffering and hope,
be kind to every suffering person,
obtain fullness of life for each one.
Turn your maternal gaze
especially upon those in Africa
whose need is extreme,
struck down by AIDS
or other mortal illness.
Look upon the mothers who are mourning their children;
Look upon the grandparents who lack the resources
to support their orphaned grandchildren.
Embrace them all, keep them close to your Mother's heart.
Queen of Africa and of the whole world,
Virgin Most Holy, pray for us!

Letter to the Superior General of the Sisters of Divine Love

September 11, 2004

3. In the light of the great cultural and social changes that have occurred in our modern age, the foresight of Cardinal Marc' Antonio Barbarigo seems prophetic. Three centuries ago he engaged in the social advancement of women. Following in his footsteps, your Institute today is called to help women in difficulty rediscover their dignity in accordance with God's plan and their vocation of love. Recognizing the proper role of women in society helps to protect the values of the family, of life and of peace.

In this perspective, I would especially like to present to you for your consideration and commitment my Apostolic Letter *Mulieris Dignitatem*. The instructions it contains will help to bring you success in your mission at the service of the human and religious advancement of the world of women.

May Mary, Mother of the Church, guide you in this effort and obtain for your Religious Family the gift of numerous holy vocations. As I assure you of my special remembrance in prayer for this intention, I warmly impart my Blessing to you, Reverend Mother, and to the entire family of the Institute of Divine Love.

Address to the Bishops of New Zealand on Their *Ad Limina* Visit

September 13, 2004

2. New Zealand enjoys a proud heritage, steeped in rich cultural diversity, yet like many other countries is today suffering the effects of unrestrained secularism. This radical "split between the Gospel and culture" (*Evangelii Nuntiandi*, no. 20) is manifested as a "crisis of meaning" (cf. *Fides et Ratio*, no. 81): the distortion of reason by particular interest groups and exaggerated individualism are examples of this perspective of life which neglects the search for the ultimate goal and meaning of human existence. Your own reports indeed unequivocally indicate the pressing need for Christ's liberating message in a society experiencing the tragic consequences of the eclipse of the sense of God: the drift away from the Church; the undermining of family life; the facilitation of abortion and prostitution; a misguided vision of life which seeks pleasure and "success" rather than goodness and wisdom.

Address to the Members of the Episcopal Conference of the Pacific on Their *Ad Limina* Visit

September 18, 2004

3. Dear Brothers, the vibrant pastoral life of your dioceses, which your reports clearly describe, is an uplifting sign for all. The joyful liturgical celebrations, the keen participation of the young in the mission of the Church, the flowering of vocations, and the palpable presence of faith in the civic life of your nations, all attest to God's infinite goodness to his Church. Yet, with the prudence of a father's concern for his family, you have also expressed worries about the winds of change extending to your shores. The encroachment of secularism, particularly in the form of consumerism, and *the long reach of the most insidious aspects of the media*, which convey a deformed outlook on life, the family, religion and morality, *unsettle the very foundations of traditional cultural values.*

General Audience

October 6, 2004

"Listen, O daughter!" (Psalm 45[44])

1. The sweet feminine portrait that the liturgy has offered us forms the second scene of the diptych which makes up Psalm 45[44]. It is a serene and joyful nuptial song that we read in the Liturgy of Vespers. Thus, after meditating on the king who is celebrating his wedding (cf. vv. 2-10), our gaze now shifts to the figure of the queen, his bride (cf. vv. 11-18). This nuptial perspective enables us to dedicate the Psalm to all couples who live their marriage with inner intensity and freshness, a sign of a "great mystery," as St. Paul suggests: the mystery of the Father's love for humanity and Christ's love for his Church (cf. Eph 5:32). However, the Psalm unfolds a further horizon.

In fact, the Jewish king is in the limelight and in view of this the subsequent Judaic tradition saw in him the features of the Davidic Messiah, whereas Christianity transformed the hymn into a song in honor of Christ.

2. Now, however, our attention is held by the profile of the queen which the court poet, the author of the Psalm (cf. Ps 45[44]:2), paints with great delicacy and feeling. The reference to the Phoenician city of Tyre (cf. v. 13) leads us to suppose that she is a foreign princess. The appeal to forget her own

people and her father's house (cf. v. 11), which she has had to leave, thus acquires particular meaning.

The vocation to marriage is a turning point in life and changes a person's existence, as has already emerged in the Book of Genesis: "Therefore, a man leaves his father and his mother and cleaves to his wife, and they become one flesh" (Gn 2:24). The queen-bride, with her wedding procession that is bearing gifts, now advances toward the king who is entranced by her beauty (cf. Ps 45[44]:12-13).

3. The Psalmist's insistence in exalting the woman is important: she is "clothed with splendor" (v. 14), and this magnificence is illustrated by her wedding robes, woven of gold and richly embroidered (cf. vv. 14-15).

The Bible loves beauty as a reflection of God's splendor; even clothing can be raised to a sign of dazzling inner light and purity of soul.

The thought runs parallel, on the one hand, to the marvelous pages of the *Song of Songs* (cf. vv. 4 and 7), and on the other, to the echo in the Book of Revelation that portrays the "marriage of the Lamb," that is, of Christ, with the community of the redeemed, focusing on the symbolic value of the wedding robes: "The marriage of the Lamb has come, and his Bride has made herself ready; it was granted her to be clothed with fine linen, bright and pure, for the fine linen is the righteous deeds of the saints" (Rev 19.7-8).

4. Besides beauty, the joy is exalted that transpires from the festive procession of "maiden companions," the bridesmaids who accompany the bride "with joy and gladness" (Ps 45[44]:15-16). True joy, far deeper than mere merriment, is an expression of love that shares with a serene heart in the good of the beloved.

Now, according to the concluding hopes expressed, another reality radically inherent in marriage is also described: fertility. Indeed, "sons" are mentioned, and "peoples" (cf. vv. 17-18). The future, not only of the dynasty but of humanity, is brought about precisely because the couple offers new creatures to the world.

In our time, this is an important topic in the West, which is often unable to entrust its existence to the future by begetting and protecting new creatures who will continue the civilization of peoples and realize the history of salvation.

5. Many Fathers of the Church, as is well known, interpreted the portrait of the queen by applying it to Mary, from the very first words of the appeal: "Listen, O daughter, give ear . . ." (v. 11). This also happens, for example, in the *Homily on the Mother of God* by Chrysippus of Jerusalem. He was a Cappadocian who was part of the monks who founded the monastery of St.

Euthymius in Palestine. He became a priest and was the custodian of the Holy
Cross in the Basilica of Anastasius in Jerusalem.

"My discourse is addressed to you," he says, turning to Mary, "to you who
must go as bride to the great sovereign; to you I address my discourse, to you
who are about to conceive the Word of God in the way that he knows . . . .
'Listen, O daughter, give ear to my words'; indeed, the auspicious announcement of the world's redemption is coming true. Listen, and what you will hear
will gladden your heart . . . . 'Forget your own people and your father's house':
pay no attention to your earthly parents, for you will be transformed into a
heavenly queen. And 'listen,' he says, 'to how much the One who is Creator
and Lord of all things loves you.' Indeed, the 'king,' he says, 'will desire your
beauty;' the Father himself will take you as bride; the Holy Spirit will arrange all
the conditions that are necessary for these nuptials . . . . Do not believe you will
give birth to a human child, 'for he is your Lord and you will adore him.' Your
Creator has become your child; you will conceive and with all the others, you
will worship him as your Lord" (Marian texts of the first millennium, I, Rome,
1988, 605-606).

Psalm 44 is a nuptial song which we can dedicate to all married people who
wish to live out their matrimony with joy and interior freshness. In the scene
that introduces the bride-queen who occupies the place of honor, the psalmist
underscores the dignity of the woman as seen even in the magnificence of her
wedding dress. In beauty, Sacred Scripture sees a reflection of God's splendor. It
can be seen with precision in the biblical text of the Song of Songs and in the
Apocalypse of St. John, which, in the passage about the wedding of the Lamb,
reveals the symbol of Christ's bond with the community of the redeemed.*

Address to the Bishops of the Church in
New York on Their *Ad Limina* Visit

October 8, 2004

6. Brothers, I pray that at every opportunity you will be able to work together,
so that the Gospel may be more effectively proclaimed throughout your country. I wish to express my appreciation for all that you have already accomplished together, particularly in your statements on life issues, education and
peace. I invite you now to turn your attention to the many other pressing
issues that directly affect the Church's mission and her spiritual integrity, for
example the decline in Mass attendance and in recourse to the Sacrament of

---

*   This paragraph is an unofficial translation of the Italian.

Reconciliation, the threats to marriage and the religious needs of immigrants. Let your voice be clearly heard, announcing the message of salvation in season and out of season (cf. 2 Tim 4:1). Confidently preach the Good News so that all may be saved and come to the knowledge of the truth (cf. 1 Tim 2:4).

Address to the Ambassador of Brazil to the Holy See

October 11, 2004

I am pleased to consider the convergence of principles, of both the Holy See and your Government, concerning threats to world peace when it is affected by the absence of the Christian vision of respect for the human dignity of one's neighbor. I pray, therefore, that Brazilians will continue to promote and spread the values of faith, especially when it is a matter of explicitly recognizing the holiness of family life and safeguarding unborn infants from the moment of their conception.

Address to the Participants in the World Conference of Women Parliamentarians for the Protection of Children and Young Persons

October 18, 2004

1. I am pleased to address a cordial welcome to all of you, distinguished ladies and gentlemen, and I offer you a warm greeting. Through you, I would like my thoughts to reach the many nations of the world that belong to the Interparliamentary Union. I address a special greeting to the President of the Chamber of Deputies of Italy and the Latvian Parliamentarian who have interpreted your common sentiments.

2. Our meeting today fits into the context of the *World Conference of Women Parliamentarians for the Protection of Children and Young Persons,* sponsored by the Presidency of the Italian Parliament. The theme of your work that ends today concerns the hardship in which numerous children and adolescents live in various parts of the world. Your goal includes identifying together effective ways in which institutions can protect minors. In this regard, I express unqualified appreciation for this praiseworthy commitment to the youngest group of the population, while I encourage you to persevere in this direction with the awareness that children and youth are the hope and future of humanity.

They are the human family's most precious treasure, but at the same time, its frailest and most vulnerable members. Hence, it is always necessary to listen to them and pay constant attention to all their legitimate needs and aspirations. No one can be silent or indifferent, especially when innocent children suffer and are marginalized and their human dignity is wounded.

3. The immense cry of pain of abandoned and abused children from many regions of the earth must inspire in public institutions, private associations and all people of good will a new awareness of everyone's duty to protect, defend and educate these frail creatures with love and respect.

If it is to be effective, all action to safeguard children and adolescents should be accompanied by proper consideration of their fundamental rights. Juvenal has expressed this well in his well-known maxim: "The greatest reverence is due to a child" (cf. *The Satires*, XIV, 47). Furthermore, in the Gospel Jesus points to children as our "models" of life and firmly condemns those who do not respect them.

4. Distinguished ladies and gentlemen, I wish success to the study days of your Congress and I hope, thanks to the contribution of you all, that the dream of building a better future for the new generations may come true. Through the intercession of Mary, Mother of hope, may God grant that humanity see this prophecy of peace come true soon!

I accompany this wish with the assurance of my prayers, as I impart a heartfelt Blessing to you all.

General Audience

October 20, 2004

5. . . . Jesus asked those listening to him this disturbing question: "What shall a man give in return for his life?" (Mt 16:26). No exchange is possible, for life is a gift of God, and "in his hand is the life of every living thing and the breath of all mankind" (Jb 12:10).

Address to the Bishops of Angola, São Tomé, and Principe on Their *Ad Limina* Visit

October 22, 2004

4. . . . I am thinking at this time above all of those baptized persons in your communities whose irregular situation with regard to marriage prevents them

from being admitted to Eucharistic Communion (cf. *Ecclesia de Eucharistia*, no. 37). May the full power of God's grace be revealed in their lives, impelling them to conversion with the comforting prospect of taking part at last in God's banquet!

5. Next to this shadow, your quinquennial reports also recall the witness offered by countless families who live faithfulness to Christian marriage heroically, in a context of civil legislation or traditional customs that are not exactly conducive to monogamous marriage. This is evident in various phenomena such as concubinage (mentioned above) and polygamy, divorce and prostitution; some of this *immoral behavior leads to the spread of AIDS*. The very heavy toll of victims that this epidemic has taken and its serious threat to the social and economic stability make it impossible to ignore.

While doing everything in your power, dear Bishops, to *defend the holiness of the family and the priority place it occupies in society*, do not cease to proclaim, loud and clear, the liberating message of authentic Christian love. The many educational programs, both religious and secular, must stress the fact that *true love is chaste love* and, at the same time, that chastity offers a well-founded hope of getting the better of the forces that threaten the institution of the family and of freeing humanity from the devastating scourge of AIDS. Here I repeat the recommendation that I addressed to you in the Apostolic Exhortation *Ecclesia in Africa*: "The companionship, joy, happiness and peace which Christian marriage and fidelity provide, and the safeguard which chastity gives, must be continuously presented to the faithful, particularly the young" (no. 116).

Address to the Participants in the Ninth Meeting of the Post-Synodal Council of the General Secretariat for the Special Assembly for America of the Synod of Bishops

November 5, 2004

3. Among the present-day challenges, aside from the inauspicious activity of sects, there are other difficulties. For example, the negative consequences of globalization, especially when the economy is made an absolute value; growing urbanization with its inevitable cultural uprooting; drug trafficking and abuse; modern ideologies that hold the concept of family based on matrimony as "old-fashioned"; the progressive gap between the rich and the poor;

human-rights violations; migration and the complex problem of the foreign debt. And what can be said about the "culture of death," expressed in count-less ways, such as the arms race and the abominable phenomenon of violence unleashed by guerrilla warfare and international terrorism?

Address to the Bishops' Conference of the Indian Ocean (CEDOI) on Their *Ad Limina* Visit

November 9, 2004

7. Attention to families and to their harmonious development is one of your pastoral priorities. In your region, as in many regions of the world, social evolution is contributing to undermining the family structure. It is therefore necessary to remember the significance and value of marriage and the family in God's plan. Christian families must be authentic witnesses of the presence of Christ, who accompanies and sustains them in their daily lives. In fact, their mission is to "guard, reveal and communicate love, and this is a living reflection of a real sharing in God's love for humanity and the love of Christ the Lord for the Church his Bride" (*Familiaris Consortio*, no. 17). Likewise, families are the privileged place for the education of the young and the trans-mission of moral and spiritual values.

I therefore warmly encourage you to promote an effective family ministry, strongly proclaiming the teaching of the Gospel about family and marriage and offering young people the education they need to understand and accept their duties, taking care to instruct them before and after the celebration of matrimony. Special care must also be given to couples in difficulty, to broken families and to those who live in irregular marital situations.

8. Increasing watchfulness with regard to the education of young people is also more timely than ever. To respond to the challenges of Gospel witness today and in the future, their human and spiritual formation is an urgent need. I invite you to develop a pastoral ministry that awakens in young peo-ple enthusiasm for Christ and for serving their brethren. They will find solid reasons for founding their life on the hope that the Lord Jesus gives them and the ability to love as he loved. May all people generously engaged in cateche-sis take care to be first of all living examples of the teaching that it is their task to transmit in fidelity to the Church.

I hope that the young people in your region will allow themselves to be transformed by the encounter with Jesus, who comes to meet them to make them authentic witnesses of his Gospel and to lead them to true happiness.

May they always allow themselves to be led by him on the paths of faith and communicate to their brothers and sisters their own experience of the living God!

Letter to Cardinal Camillo Ruini for the Fiftieth Anniversary of the Foundation of the Italian Association of Radio Listeners and Television Viewers (AIART)

November 10, 2004

My Venerable Brother,
Cardinal Camillo Ruini,
President of the Italian Bishops' Conference,

1. I learned with pleasure that in these days the Italian Association of Radio Listeners and Television Viewers (AIART) is marking the fiftieth anniversary of its foundation, and I am pleased to address to you my cordial greeting, Your Eminence, and to those responsible for such a praiseworthy Association as well as to those taking part in the celebrations of this meaningful anniversary.

Promoted by Catholic Action when radio and television began to spread throughout Italy, AIART dedicates its attention to the protection and promotion of the values and the rights of the human person and of the family in the sphere of radio-television broadcasting. In the "Directory" on the pastoral service of social communications, approved by the Italian Bishops at their last General Assembly, it is affirmed that it has "the two-fold objective of critically forming the users and to make their voice heard, especially whenever a program offends the dignity of persons, above all minors" (no. 176).

2. The reasons that led to the Association's birth in 1954 are still valid today; indeed, in our media-oriented society, greater incisiveness and courage are needed to cultivate the taste for the beautiful with sensitivity for what is good and true. It is necessary to help consumers, especially families, to use television sensibly, to know how to choose with balance and wisdom the stations that are in harmony with the Christian perspective of the world and of the human person.

In this year's Message for the World Day of Social Communications I wanted to recall that communication, in each of its forms, must always set a standard of respect for the truth and dignity of the human person (cf. *Message* for *Thirty-Eighth World Day of Social Communications*, May 23: ORE, February 4, 6, no. 6). The legitimate demand for news and entertainment must be in keeping with the rights of each person and of families, never giving in to the enticements of those who want to confuse truth with opinions, and carefully preventing those most sacred and intimate aspects of family life from being exposed to sensationalism and banal vulgarity.

Address to Participants in the Nineteenth International Conference of the Pontifical Council for Health Pastoral Care

November 12, 2004

Your Eminence,
Venerable Brothers in the Episcopate,
Dear Brothers and Sisters,

1. I am pleased to welcome you on the occasion of the *International Conference of the Pontifical Council for Health Pastoral Care* which is taking place at this time. With your visit, you have wished to reaffirm your scientific and human commitment to those who are suffering.

I thank Cardinal Javier Lozano Barragán for his courteous words on behalf of you all. My grateful thoughts and appreciation go to everyone who has made a contribution to these sessions, as well as to the doctors and health-care workers throughout the world who dedicate their scientific and human skills and their spirituality to relieving pain and its consequences.

2. Medicine is always at the service of life. Even when medical treatment is unable to defeat a serious pathology, all its possibilities are directed to the alleviation of suffering. Working enthusiastically to help the patient in every situation means being aware of the inalienable dignity of every human being, even in the extreme conditions of terminal illness. Christians recognize this devotion as a fundamental dimension of their vocation: indeed, in carrying out this task they know that they are caring for Christ himself (cf. Mt 25:35-40).

"It is therefore through Christ, and in Christ, that light is thrown on the riddle of suffering and death which, apart from his Gospel, overwhelms us," the Council recalls (*Gaudium et Spes*, no. 22).

Those who open themselves to this light in faith find comfort in their own suffering and acquire the ability to alleviate that of others. Indeed, there is *a directly proportional relationship between the ability to suffer and the ability to help those who are suffering.* Daily experience teaches that the persons most sensitive to the suffering of others and who are the most dedicated to alleviating the suffering of others are also more disposed to accept, with God's help, their own suffering.

3. Love of neighbor, which Jesus vividly portrayed in the Parable of the Good Samaritan (cf. Lk 10:2ff.), enables us to *recognize the dignity of every person,* even when illness has become a burden. Suffering, old age, a comatose state or the imminence of death in no way diminish the intrinsic dignity of the person created in God's image.

Euthanasia is one of those tragedies caused by an ethic that claims to dictate who should live and who should die. Even if it is motivated by sentiments of a misconstrued compassion or of a misunderstood preservation of dignity, euthanasia actually eliminates the person instead of relieving the individual of suffering.

Unless compassion is combined with the desire to tackle suffering and support those who are afflicted, it leads to the cancellation of life in order to eliminate pain, thereby distorting the ethical status of medical science.

4. True compassion, on the contrary, encourages every reasonable effort for the patient's recovery. At the same time, it helps draw the line when it is clear that no further treatment will serve this purpose.

The refusal of *aggressive treatment* is neither a rejection of the patient nor of his or her life. Indeed, the object of the decision on whether to begin or to continue a treatment has nothing to do with the value of the patient's life, but rather with whether such medical intervention is beneficial for the patient.

The possible decision either not to start or to halt a treatment will be deemed ethically correct if the treatment is ineffective or obviously disproportionate to the aims of sustaining life or recovering health. Consequently, the decision to forego aggressive treatment is an expression of the respect that is due to the patient at every moment.

It is precisely this sense of loving respect that will help support patients to the very end. Every possible act and attention should be brought into play to lessen their suffering in the last part of their earthly existence and to encourage a life as peaceful as possible, which will dispose them to prepare their souls for the encounter with the heavenly Father.

5. Particularly in the stages of illness when proportionate and effective treatment is no longer possible, while it is necessary to avoid every kind of persistent or aggressive treatment, methods of "palliative care" are required. As the Encyclical *Evangelium Vitae* affirms, they must "seek to make suffering

more bearable in the final stages of illness and to ensure that the patient is supported and accompanied in his or her ordeal" (no. 65).

In fact, palliative care aims, especially in the case of patients with terminal diseases, at alleviating a vast gamut of symptoms of physical, psychological and mental suffering; hence, it requires the intervention of a team of specialists with medical, psychological and religious qualifications who will work together to support the patient in critical stages.

The Encyclical *Evangelium Vitae* in particular sums up the traditional teaching on the licit use of pain killers that are sometimes called for, with respect for the freedom of patients who should be able, as far as possible, "to satisfy their moral and family duties, and above all . . . to prepare in a fully conscious way for their definitive meeting with God" (no. 65).

Moreover, while patients in need of pain killers should not be made to forego the relief that they can bring, the dose should be effectively proportionate to the intensity of their pain and its treatment. All forms of euthanasia that would result from the administration of massive doses of a sedative for the purpose of causing death must be avoided.

To provide this help in its different forms, it is necessary to encourage the training of specialists in palliative care at special teaching institutes where psychologists and health-care workers can also be involved.

6. Science and technology, however, will never be able to provide a satisfactory response to the essential questions of the human heart; these are questions that faith alone can answer. The Church intends to continue making her own specific contribution, offering human and spiritual support to sick people who want to open themselves to the message of the love of God, who is ever attentive to the tears of those who turn to him (cf. Ps 39:13). Here, emphasis is placed on the importance of *health pastoral care* in which hospital chaplaincies have a special role and contribute so much to people's spiritual well-being during their hospital stay.

Then how can we forget the precious contribution of volunteers, who through their service give life to that *creativity in charity* which imbues hope, even in the unpleasant experience of suffering? Moreover, it is through them that Jesus can continue today to exist among men and women, doing good and healing them (cf. Acts 10:38).

7. Thus, the Church makes her own contribution to this moving mission for the benefit of the suffering. May the Lord deign to enlighten all who are close to the sick and encourage them to persevere in their different roles and various responsibilities.

May Mary, Mother of Christ, accompany everyone in the difficult moments of pain and illness, so that human suffering may be raised to the saving mystery of the Cross of Christ.

I accompany these hopes with my Blessing.

Address to the Members of the Pope John XXIII Communities' Associations

November 29, 2004

2. From the outset, that is, ever since Fr. Oreste Benzi opened his first family-house, your Community, which a few months ago acquired recognition as a private international Association of the Faithful of Pontifical Right, has distinguished itself by its special service to the lowliest and a style of true sharing that aspires to give new life and love to those who for various reasons have no family.

Address to the Italian Federation of Catholic Weeklies

December 3, 2004

2. Thanks be to God, Italy has a rich tradition of Catholic weeklies with outstanding priests and lay people who have marked their history. Among them I would like to recall Msgr. Andrea Spada, well-known to you, who died a few days ago. The contribution of Catholic journalists is also especially valuable today on the pastoral as well as the cultural and social levels.

Their service primarily offers information on the life of the Church, supported by the appropriate documentation and an analysis of ecclesial initiatives and their content. Then, in view of their wide local distribution, diocesan weeklies effectively help to spread in families, parishes and cities the Christian values that account for a large part of the spiritual heritage of the Italian People. I am thinking in particular of the protection of every dimension of human life, as well as of marriage and the family, which a misunderstood culture of "personal rights" is tending to distort, and lastly, of the values of truth, justice and solidarity.

Address to the Bishops of Louisville, Mobile, and New Orleans on Their *Ad Limina* Visit

December 4, 2004

5. Dear Brothers, in a spirit of gratitude and profound appreciation, let us commend to the Lord all the lay faithful of your particular Churches—the young people who are the hope of the future and even now are called to be a ferment of life and renewal in the Church and in American society, the married couples who strive to mirror in themselves and in their families the mystery of Christ's love for the Church, and the countless men and women who strive each day to bring the light of the Gospel to their homes, their workplaces and to the whole life of society. May they be ever more credible witnesses of the faith which has reconciled us to God (cf. Rom 5:1), the love which will transfigure the world, and the hope which looks forward to "new heavens and a new earth, where, according to his promise, the justice of God will reside" (2 Pt 3:13).

Address to Participants in the Congress of the Vatican Foundation "Centesimus Annus–Pro Pontifice"

December 4, 2004

3. It is therefore truly important to have a precise, motivated and complete approach to making the Church's social teaching known so as to avoid stressing any one aspect more than another, swayed by preconceived emotions or views, thus losing sight of its integral structure and using it instrumentally.

In addition, people must learn to use this doctrine as a valid reference in the context of family, professional and civil responsibilities. They must accept it as a shared criterion for personal and community decisions and actions, in continuity with the fine witness borne, especially since *Rerum Novarum*, by Christians, both lowly and great, who have lived the passion for the human cause in the light of the Gospel.

Address to the Ambassador of
Lithuania to the Holy See

December 6, 2004

I am eager to express anew my hope that the Representatives of the Lithuanian citizens, continuing to draw on the noble patrimony of human and Gospel ideals that marks the Nation's history, will work with sincere dedication to build a free society on sound ethical and moral foundations. In this perspective, I urge the Catholics who make up a large part of the population to collaborate with all people of good will to prevent Lithuanian society from being heavily influenced by the secularist and hedonistic model of life and its deceptive attractions. Knowing that they cannot be content with fighting the consequences of evil, believers are prepared to walk side by side with those who, through the appropriate legislation and balanced conduct, work to safeguard the family and life, from conception until natural death.

Address to the New Ambassador from
Peru to the Holy See

December 7, 2004

Peru has also undertaken to strengthen its national institutions as well as its projects for regional integration. It is to be hoped in this regard that the defense of human life and the institution of the family, today threatened from all sides by an erroneous concept of modernity or freedom, is not beyond the reach of Government measures, since the family, in accordance with the natural order established by the Creator, is the irreplaceable foundation of a nation's harmonious development.

Address to the Ambassador of
Thailand to the Holy See

December 16, 2004

In Your Excellency's remarks you mentioned King Bhumibol Adulyadej's recognition that the people of Thailand need to offer one another mutual support. His philosophy for economic reform makes that clear, as it seeks to help those at the lowest economic levels by providing access to local resources and technology. I urge your nation to continue to assist those who are most in need so that they may obtain the economic self-sufficiency to which they have a right. One of the most effective ways to ensure this is by safeguarding family life. In fact, family life shapes the social and ethical order of human work and is the true source of genuine economic progress (cf. Encyclical Letter *Laborem Exercens*, no. 10). In Asia the family has traditionally enjoyed a high level of esteem, regarded not only as the heart of interpersonal relationships but also as a place of economic security for its members. "The Family, therefore, must rightfully be seen as an essential agent of economic life, guided not by the market mentality but by the logic of sharing and solidarity among generations" (*Compendium of the Social Doctrine of the Church*, no. 248). It is my hope that your Government will foster an ever greater respect for the importance of the family, convincing young people that material wealth and quick economic gain are no replacement for the loving rapport found in "domestic society."

Address to the Ambassador of Norway to the Holy See

December 16, 2004

Your Excellency,

I am pleased to welcome you today and to accept the Letters of Credence by which you are appointed Ambassador Extraordinary and Plenipotentiary of the Kingdom of Norway to the Holy See. Though my visit to your country took place some years ago, I fondly recall the warmth and hospitality with which I was received. I thank you for the gracious greetings which you bring from His Majesty King Harald V and from Prime Minister Bondevik. I would ask you to convey to the Royal Family, the Government and all the people of Norway my good wishes and the assurance of my prayers for the well-being of the nation.

At the heart of the Holy See's diplomatic activity stands a steadfast commitment to defending the dignity of the human person. This promotion of human rights, social justice and solidarity, arises out of the recognition of the common origin of all life and points to the common destiny of all men and women. In this broad perspective, humanity's transcendent dimension is brought to light, countering the social fragmentation and secularism so sadly prevalent in many societies today and providing a sure foundation for solidarity and harmony in our world.

Within the international community Norway has long been esteemed for its generosity to developing nations. Tangible expressions of this are found, for example, in Norwegian participation in peace-keeping operations, assistance with aid projects, readiness to combat arms trafficking as well as championing of the causes of sustainable development and environmental protection. These acts of solidarity are an expression of a persevering desire to promote the common good and, at their most significant level, help to elicit a recognition of the essential nature of human life as a gift and of our world as a family of persons. In fact, genuine acts of solidarity are more than just unilateral gestures of good intent. They uphold God's universal plan for humanity and, in accord with this vision, address the complex challenges of justice, freedom of peoples and peace.

Mr. Ambassador, as you have correctly noted, Christianity has been of fundamental importance in Norway's history. It must be likewise in the present and in the future. In my pastoral visit to your country, I came as a pilgrim wishing to honor the lives of St. Olav and the other great Saints of the North, whose example still speaks today about the profound truths and values which have shaped Norwegian culture for over a thousand years. These guiding principles retain their significance for contemporary society, since they reveal "man's deepest sphere" and give "meaning to his life in the world" (cf. *Redemptor Hominis*, no. 10). Indeed, as seen in extraordinary ways through the witness of the Saints, the values at the heart of Christian Europe call all men and women "to direct their steps toward a truth which transcends them" (*Fides et Ratio*, no. 5) so that good may prevail and God may be honored. When individuals lose sight of this goal, which is their only guarantee of freedom and happiness, they become entrapped by impoverished ideologies and then fail to lift their gaze to the heights of life's purpose.

In this regard, one cannot but notice that an eclipse of the sense of God has cast its shadow not only over your own country but over other Nordic lands as well. In this disquieting process of secularization, as I have noted on many occasions, it is marriage and the family which come under greatest threat. For this reason I continue to urge both religious and civil leaders to uphold the sacred institution of marriage, willed by God in the very act of creation, with its concomitant of stable domestic life. The truth of human sexuality is illustrated in the beauty of married couples' love as a unique and exclusive gift of self to the other and the mutual acceptance of that wonderful gift by which they become cooperators with God in giving life to a new human person (cf. *Familiaris Consortio*, no. 14). Secular and pragmatic distortions of the reality of marriage can never be equated with the splendor of a life-long covenant based on generous self-giving and unconditional love and they will only damage the foundation upon which the legitimate aspirations of a nation are built.

From the beginning of my Pontificate I have made commitment to ecumenism a priority of my pastoral concern and action. Awareness of the common history shared by Christians has fostered brotherhood and dialogue, and united Christian witness for the advancement of the kingdom of God in our midst (cf. *Ut Unum Sint*, no. 41). To this end I encourage all the religious leaders of your nation to persevere along the path toward Christian unity. In this way they will help all Norwegians to draw on their rich heritage of over a thousand years of Christian faith: in Christ all people—nationals, migrants or foreigners—are brothers and sisters, and our gestures of solidarity toward them become acts of love and fidelity to Christ, who came that we might all have life and have it abundantly (cf. Jn 10:10).

With these words of encouragement I assure you that the Catholic Church will continue to work for the spiritual enrichment and social development of the Norwegian people. Through her witness of charity the Church reaches out to all men and women, irrespective of ethnicity or religion, facilitating the growth of a "culture of solidarity" and restoring life to the universal values of human coexistence (cf. *Ecclesia in Europa*, no. 85).

Mr. Ambassador, I am confident that the mission which you begin today will help to strengthen the cordial bonds of understanding and cooperation between Norway and the Holy See. As you take up your new responsibilities be assured that the various offices of the Roman Curia are ready to assist you in the fulfillment of your duties. Upon you, your family and your fellow citizens I invoke the abundant blessings of Almighty God.

Address to the Ambassador of Kenya to the Holy See

December 16, 2004

Your Excellency,

It is a pleasure for me to extend a cordial welcome to you today as I accept the Letters of Credence by which you are appointed Ambassador Extraordinary and Plenipotentiary of Kenya to the Holy See. Though my pastoral visits to your country took place some years ago now, they remain clearly etched in my mind as events of great joy. I thank you for the greetings which you bear from President Kibaki, the Government and all the citizens of Kenya. Please convey to them my sincere best wishes and assure them of my prayers for the well-being of the nation.

On arrival at Nairobi in 1995, I observed that your nation and indeed the whole continent of Africa was at a crossroads (cf. *Arrival Speech*, Nairobi, September 18, 1995). Its peoples and their leaders were being called to exercise all their wisdom in the difficult and urgent task of promoting democratic government and prudent economic development as essential elements to the building of a just society. The "winds of change" driving that common desire have not abated; indeed they have gathered strength with people demanding ever more insistently concrete action to ensure the development of a civic life marked by respect, fairness and integrity (cf. *Ecclesia in Africa*, no. 44).

Kenya, it can now be said, has set out along the road of truth and peace. Against the often disturbing backdrop of human tragedies which continue to afflict the continent of Africa and other regions, your nation has taken a leading role in promoting peace initiatives and social stability. In this regard, the recent United Nations Security Council's sitting in your capital has given Kenya much positive attention in the international media and rightly has brought praise for the nation's considerable contribution to peace-keeping missions and projects, especially in Sudan and Somalia. Such generous undertakings, as well as bringing immediate relief to the long-suffering peoples directly affected by conflict, will also elicit in your neighboring countries a deeper sense of shared responsibility for the defense and promotion of the fundamental human rights of the peoples of your region. When there is hesitation in the international community about the obligation to respect and implement human rights (cf. *Message for the 2003 World Day of Peace*, no. 5), misery ensues as is so evident today in Darfur.

In addition to a country's willing participation in the accords and agreements that promote international relations, authentic development also requires adherence to a sound plan of genuine national progress. In fact, the "unbreakable bond between the work of peace and respect for truth" (ibid., no. 8) suggests that the success of a government's participation in peace processes abroad will depend largely upon the degree of honesty and integrity with which it governs at home. In this regard, President Kibaki's determination to root out the scourge of corruption, which crushes the spirit of a nation, is to be applauded, and demands the active support of all politicians, civic leaders and bureaucrats in order that the common good may flourish. While much remains to be achieved, successes already attained in Kenya clearly give hope. Further strenuous efforts to guarantee an impartial judiciary and to ensure security through the rule of law and order are needed and will do much to favor a spirit of optimism among your people and to attract the kind of investment necessary to create the opportunities of employment which offer a brighter future to all and especially the young.

The family stands at the heart of the cultures of Africa. This is a treasure which must be preserved and never neglected, for the future of your people, and that of the world, passes through the family (cf. *Familiaris Consortio*, no. 86). It is only right therefore that civic and religious leaders should work together to ensure that the sacred institution of marriage, with its concomitant of stable home life, is affirmed and supported. Breakdown of domestic life is always a source of intractable problems which, in addition to causing incalculable distress to individuals, undermine the very fabric of society and its means of secure development.

The peoples of Kenya, though remaining confident about the future, are nevertheless suffering several acute social problems. Solutions cannot be restricted to the mere removal of hardships but instead require the courage to embrace a way of life faithful to God's plan for all men and women. In this regard, I note with grave concern the measures currently under debate in your country to facilitate abortion. In addition to violating life's essential dignity, abortion invariably causes untold emotional and psychological pain to the mother, who herself is frequently a victim of circumstances contrary to her deepest hopes and desires. Similarly, in regard to the tragedy of AIDS which the whole human family is currently facing, it must be recalled that at heart this is a question of behavior. Proposed remedies which either ignore or reject the only genuine foundation of health and happiness in this matter—sexual fidelity within marriage and abstinence without—are likely to increase rather than resolve the tragedy and indeed can be understood as new forms of colonialism. I therefore appeal to the Christian community of Kenya to bear steadfast witness to that intimate communion of life and love which defines the family, brings joy to communities, and provides the foundation upon which the aspirations of a nation can be built.

For her part the Catholic Church in Kenya will continue to support families in all possible ways, working as an ally in the pursuit of peace, stability and prosperity. Through her numerous schools, health-care facilities, and community development programs, she is already contributing much to securing a better future for the country. In this service the Church desires neither power nor privilege, but only the freedom to express her faith and love in works of goodness, justice and peace.

Your Excellency, as you enter the diplomatic community accredited to the Holy See, I assure you of the ready assistance of the various offices of the Roman Curia. May your mission serve to deepen the already strong bonds of understanding and cooperation between Kenya and the Holy See. Upon you, your family and your fellow citizens I cordially invoke the abundant blessings of Almighty God.

Address to the Ambassador of Malawi to the Holy See

December 16, 2004

The people of your Continent have much to offer the rest of the world concerning respect for the family. In this connection, I would encourage them to continue to promote stable family life as the proper environment in which to bring up children, thereby building firm foundations for the future of society. In particular, I would urge your Government to resist any attempts by outside agencies to impose programs of economic assistance tied to the promotion of sterilization and contraception. Not only are such campaigns "affronts to the dignity of the person and the family" (*Compendium of the Social Doctrine of the Church*, no. 234), but they also undermine the natural growth and progress of nations. However serious the social and health-care problems facing your country and your Continent, the good of your people demands the pursuit of authentic human development, responding not simply to their material needs but also to their cultural, moral and spiritual aspirations. "Development which is merely economic is incapable of setting man free; on the contrary, it will end by enslaving him further" (*Sollicitudo Rei Socialis*, no. 46).

Address to the Ambassador of Luxembourg to the Holy See

December 16, 2004

I am delighted to know that your Government is willing to help families by reinforcing the structures of assistance for children and has decided to continue the programs of religious instruction in secondary schools. Indeed, the young generations must benefit from a sound formation to prepare them to assume their responsibilities in the society of the future.

Above all, they need to be motivated by the strong ideals of freedom, respect and justice among individuals and peoples and the dignity of them all, which are also religious ideals. By having a clear awareness of the values that are at the root of their history and culture and finding fresh dynamism in them, young people will be able to turn more confidently to the future and work to build it with generosity and enthusiasm. Each will then discover that life has a truly altruistic meaning, far more fulfilling than the immediate satisfaction of material needs tied to the restrictive logic of a purely commercial and hedonistic vision of human destiny.

Likewise, to help them in their integral development, this kind of education would foster their inner life and form their conscience, with a view to their making decisions that correspond to the dignity of human persons.

It is also the mission of the Church, which seeks no advantages for herself, to remind our societies of the pressing invitation of the Gospel ideal. This is why she defends with such conviction the inalienable value of human life from conception to its natural end, as well as the greatness of marriage between a man and a woman as the basis of the family and of society. It is in this capacity that she permits herself to intervene in society's debates, to recall what serves the nobility of human dignity and what injures it, sometimes seriously, and to invite Governments to ponder on the importance of the economic, political and ethical decisions they make in order to build an ever more human society.

Speech to Delegates of the Forum of Family Associations

December 18, 2004

1. I greet with affection the Forum of Family Associations and thank the President, Prof. Luisa Santolini, for her words on behalf of you all. This meeting with you, the representatives of thousands of Italian families, is taking place close to Christmas. It is precisely by contemplating the mystery of God who became man and was welcomed into a human family that we can fully understand the value and beauty of the family.

Not only is the family at the heart of Christian life, but it is also the basis of social and civil life and thus constitutes a central chapter in Christian social teaching, as is clearly shown in the *Compendium of the Social Doctrine of the Church* (cf. nos. 209-245). It is vital to deepen continually the profound personal importance and the social, original and unrenounceable consequence of the union between a man and a woman, which is brought about in marriage and gives birth to the family community. Those who destroy this fundamental fabric of human coexistence injure society deeply and do damage that is often irreparable.

2. Attacks on marriage and the family are unfortunately growing stronger and more radical every day, both on the ideological and legislative fronts (cf. *Ecclesia in Europa*, no. 90). Attempts to reduce the family to a private emotional and socially unimportant experience; to confuse individuals' rights with those proper to the family nucleus constituted by the bond of marriage;

to equate *de facto* unions with marriage; to accept, and in certain cases to advocate, the suppression of innocent human lives by means of voluntary abortion; to distort the natural process of begetting children by introducing artificial forms of procreation, are but a few of the contexts in which the subversion taking place in society is blatantly obvious.

No civil progress can derive from the social devaluation of marriage and loss of respect for the inviolable dignity of human life. In many cases, what is presented as the progress of civilization or a scientific breakthrough is a defeat for human dignity and society.

3. The truth about human beings, their call to be welcomed with love and in love from conception cannot be sacrificed to the domination of technology and evil-doing over authentic rights. The legitimate longing for a child or for good health cannot be made an unconditional right to the point that it justifies the suppression of other human lives. Science and technology are truly at the service of humanity only if they safeguard and promote all the human beings involved in the process of procreation.

Catholic associations, together with all people of good will who believe in the values of the family and life, cannot yield to the pressures of a culture that is undermining the very foundations of respect for life and the promotion of families.

Hence, among the "manifold social service activities" already hoped for in *Familiaris Consortio*, whereby families should grow in awareness and assume the responsibility for transforming society (cf. no. 44), the prophetic voice of the Forum of Family Associations appears particularly relevant for Italy and for Europe.

4. In fact, the Forum, acting in a completely innovative and original way in Italian society, carries out the important and in many ways innovative task of being a voice for those who have no voice and a spokesman for the rights of the family, starting with those specified in the *Charter of the Rights of the Family* that is an integral part of the Agreement of your Association.

I thank you for all that you have done in the past ten years and for what you are. As I urge you to continue in your commitment to the service of life and of the family I impart my Apostolic Blessing with affection to you all.

Angelus

December 26, 2004

1. Today, the Feast of St. Stephen gives way to the Feast of the Holy Family. The Son of God prepared himself to carry out his redeeming mission, living a

hard-working and hidden life in the holy house of Nazareth. Thus, united by his Incarnation with every man and woman (cf. *Gaudium et Spes*, no. 22), he was able to sanctify human families.

2. May the Holy Family, which had to endure many painful trials, watch over *all the families of the world*, especially those in conditions of hardship. May it likewise help *the people of culture and political leaders to defend the family institution* founded on marriage and to support families as they face the serious challenges of our time.

3. In this "Year of the Eucharist," may Christian families rediscover the light and strength to journey on in unity and especially, through persevering participation in the *celebration of the Sunday Eucharist,* to develop as "domestic churches" (*Lumen Gentium*, no. 11). Mary, Queen of the Family, pray for us!

Address to the Diplomatic Corps
Accredited to the Holy See for the New Year

January 10, 2005

5. The first is the challenge of life. Life is the first gift which God has given us, it is the first resource which man can enjoy. The Church is called to proclaim "the Gospel of Life." And the State has as its primary task precisely the safeguarding and promotion of human life.

The challenge to life has grown in scale and urgency in recent years. It has involved particularly the *beginning of human life*, when human beings are at their weakest and most in need of protection. Conflicting views have been put forward regarding abortion, assisted procreation, the use of human embryonic stem cells for scientific research, and cloning. The Church's position, supported by reason and science, is clear: the human embryo is a subject identical to the human being which will be born at the term of its development. Consequently whatever violates the integrity and the dignity of the embryo is ethically inadmissible. Similarly, any form of scientific research which treats the embryo merely as a laboratory specimen is unworthy of man. Scientific research in the field of genetics needs to be encouraged and promoted, but, like every other human activity, it can never be exempt from moral imperatives; research using adult stem cells, moreover, offers the promise of considerable success.

The challenge to life has also emerged with regard to the very sanctuary of life: *the family.* Today the family is often threatened by social and cultural pressures which tend to undermine its stability; but in some countries the family is also threatened by legislation which—at times directly—challenges its natural structure, which is and must necessarily be that of a union between a man and a woman founded on marriage. The family, as a fruitful source of life and a fundamental and irreplaceable condition for the happiness of the individual spouses, for the raising of children and for the well-being of society, and indeed for the material prosperity of the nation, must never be undermined by laws based on a narrow and unnatural vision of man. There needs to prevail a just, pure and elevated understanding of human love, which finds in the family its primordial and exemplary expression. *Vince in bono malum.*

Address to Leaders of the Province of Rome

January 13, 2005

Distinguished Ladies and Gentlemen,

1. I am pleased to welcome you at the beginning of the New Year for the traditional exchange of greetings, and I offer each one of you my most cordial good wishes.

   I greet respectfully Hon. Mr. Francesco Storace, President of the Lazio Region, Hon. Mr. Walter Veltroni, Mayor of Rome, and Hon. Mr. Enrico Gasbarra, President of the Province of Rome. I thank them for expressing the common sentiments of those present. I also greet the Presidents and Members of the three Council Assemblies and their staff. My thoughts then go to all the inhabitants of the City, Province and Region; I affectionately wish them a year of serenity, spiritual and civil growth, and peace.

2. On this occasion, I would like first of all to tell you once again of my deep pleasure at the approval of the Statutes of the Lazio Region. Indeed, in addition to emphasizing Rome's role as a center of Catholicism, they explicitly recognize the primacy of the person and the fundamental value of life. They also recognize the rights of the family as a natural society founded on marriage, they propose to support families in the fulfillment of their social role, and they explicitly mention the regional permanent observer on families. The Statutes also provide for the Region to guarantee the right to study and freedom in the choice of education.

3. A further cause for satisfaction is the signing of the Protocol of Agreement between the Vicariate, the Municipality and the Region concerning the

construction of new parish complexes on the city outskirts. This Accord, rightly inspired by the principle of subsidiarity, will make it easier to build new parishes which, in addition to providing pastoral care, also upgrade the urban area and function as social centers where people can meet. Also on the agenda is collaboration between the Church and the Municipal, Provincial and Regional Institutions for the promotion of cultural events that will make the most of our great artistic, historical and spiritual heritage.

4. Among the problems that deserve special attention, I would like first to point out housing, especially for young families with a modest income. A joint effort by the institutions is indispensable in this regard, given the social implications that the lack of an adequate home entails for founding a new family and for having children.

The sad phenomena of drug addiction and more generally, hardship among youth, in turn require constant watchful attention and commitment, to provide young people with as good a future as possible.

Then what can be said of the urban traffic that becomes more congested and nerve-wracking from year to year? It causes considerable difficulties in the daily lives of many people and families. I very much hope that the bodies concerned can combine their contribution to improve the situation of urban traffic and transport. I eagerly hope that the matter of the condition of the roads and of city transport may be radically confronted with the contribution of all responsible bodies. With this in view, the opening of new communicating thoroughfares would certainly be helpful.

5. Honorable Representatives of the Regional, Provincial and Municipal Boards, I assure you of the support of my prayers for you and your daily work. With these sentiments, I cordially impart my Apostolic Blessing to you and gladly extend it to your families and to all who live and work in Rome, in its Province and throughout Lazio.

Address to the International Union of Schönstatt Families

January 20, 2005

Dear Brothers and Sisters of the International Union of Schönstatt Families,

1. On the occasion of the opening of your General Chapter you have come to Rome to reflect in prayer at the tombs of the Apostles and to renew your

fidelity to the Church before the Successor of Peter. I am delighted with your visit and warmly welcome you to the Pope's house. May these days spent in the "Eternal City" be a time of grace in which you all experience the closeness of God and of his saints!

2. "The future of humanity passes by way of the family" (Apostolic Exhortation *Familiaris Consortio*, no. 86). I encourage you to have a profound understanding of marriage and the family in the light of the faith. It is a positive sign that families actually represent the charism of your Federation. The family is a "school of love." May you transmit your enthusiasm for marriage and the family to others! More than ever, society needs healthy families in order to guarantee the common good. If we strengthen the sacred institution of marriage and the family according to God's plan, then love and solidarity among human beings will increase!

3. Dear brothers and dear sisters, the *Year of the Eucharist* is a pressing invitation to you all to find "in the supreme sacrament of love the wellspring of all communion" (*Message for the World Day of Peace 2005*, no. 12). Rediscover the great gift of the Eucharist! You will thus be able to "experience fully the beauty and the mission of the family" (Apostolic Letter *Mane Nobiscum Domine*, no. 30: ORE Special Insert, October 13, 2004).

Through the intercession of the *Mater Ter Admirabilis*, I impart to you with all my heart the Apostolic Blessing.

Message for the Thirty-Ninth World Communications Day

[May 8, 2009]

"The Communications Media: At the Service of Understanding Among Peoples"

January 24, 2005

Dear Brothers and Sisters,

1. We read in the Letter of St. James, "From the same mouth come blessing and cursing. My brothers and sisters, this ought not to be so" (Jas 3:10). The Sacred Scriptures remind us that words have an extraordinary power to bring people together or to divide them, to forge bonds of friendship or to provoke hostility.

Not only is this true of words spoken by one person to another: it applies equally to communication taking place at any level. Modern technology places at our disposal unprecedented possibilities for good, for spreading the truth of our salvation in Jesus Christ and for fostering harmony and reconciliation. Yet its misuse can do untold harm, giving rise to misunderstanding, prejudice and even conflict. The theme chosen for the 2005 World Communications Day—"The Communications Media: At the Service of Understanding Among Peoples"—addresses an urgent need: to promote the unity of the human family through the use made of these great resources.

2. One important way of achieving this end is through education. The media can teach billions of people about other parts of the world and other cultures. With good reason they have been called "the first Areopagus of the modern age . . . for many the chief means of information and education, of guidance and inspiration in their behavior as individuals, families, and within society at large" (*Redemptoris Missio*, no. 37). Accurate knowledge promotes understanding, dispels prejudice, and awakens the desire to learn more. Images especially have the power to convey lasting impressions and to shape attitudes. They teach people how to regard members of other groups and nations, subtly influencing whether they are considered as friends or enemies, allies or potential adversaries.

When others are portrayed in hostile terms, seeds of conflict are sown which can all too easily escalate into violence, war, or even genocide. Instead of building unity and understanding, the media can be used to demonize other social, ethnic and religious groups, fomenting fear and hatred. Those responsible for the style and content of what is communicated have a grave duty to ensure that this does not happen. Indeed, *the media have enormous potential for promoting peace and building bridges between peoples*, breaking the fatal cycle of violence, reprisal, and fresh violence that is so widespread today. In the words of St. Paul, which formed the basis of this year's Message for the World Day of Peace: "Do not be overcome by evil, but overcome evil with good" (Rom 12:21).

3. If such a contribution to peace-making is one of the significant ways the media can bring people together, its influence in favor of the swift mobilization of aid in response to natural disasters is another. It was heartening to see how quickly the international community responded to the recent tsunami that claimed countless victims. The speed with which news travels today naturally increases the possibility for timely practical measures designed to offer maximum assistance. In this way the media can achieve an immense amount of good.

4. The Second Vatican Council reminded us: "If the media are to be correctly employed, it is essential that all who use them know the principles of the moral order and apply them faithfully" (*Inter Mirifica*, no. 4).

The fundamental ethical principle is this: "The human person and the human community are the end and measure of the use of the media of social communication; communication should be by persons to persons for the integral development of persons" (*Ethics in Communications*, no. 21). In the first place, then, the communicators themselves need to put into practice in their own lives the values and attitudes they are called to instill in others. Above all, this must include a genuine commitment to the common good—a good that is not confined by the narrow interests of a particular group or nation but embraces the needs and interests of all, the good of the entire human family (cf. *Pacem in Terris*, no. 132). *Communicators have the opportunity to promote a true culture of life by distancing themselves from today's conspiracy against life* (cf. *Evangelium Vitae*, no. 17) and conveying the truth about the value and dignity of every human person.

5. The model and pattern of all communication is found in the Word of God himself. "In many and various ways God spoke of old to our fathers by the prophets; but in these last days he has spoken to us by a Son" (Heb 1:1). The Incarnate Word has established a new covenant between God and his people—a covenant which also joins us in community with one another. "For he is our peace, who has made us both one, and has broken down the dividing wall of hostility" (Eph 2:14).

My prayer on this year's World Communications Day is that the men and women of the media will play their part in *breaking down the dividing walls of hostility in our world*, walls that separate peoples and nations from one another, feeding misunderstanding and mistrust. May they use the resources at their disposal to strengthen the bonds of friendship and love that clearly signal the onset of the Kingdom of God here on earth.

Apostolic Letter *The Rapid Development* to Those Responsible for Communications

January 24, 2005

II. A Change of Mentality and Pastoral Renewal

7. In the communications media the Church finds a precious aid for spreading the Gospel and religious values, for promoting dialogue, ecumenical and inter-religious cooperation, and also for defending those solid principles which are indispensable for building a society which respects the dignity of

the human person and is attentive to the common good. The Church willingly employs these media to furnish information about itself and to expand the boundaries of evangelization, of catechesis and of formation, considering their use as a response to the command of the Lord: "Go into the whole world and proclaim the gospel to every creature" (Mk 16:15).

This is certainly not an easy mission in an age such as ours, in which there exists the conviction that the time of certainties is irretrievably past. Many people, in fact, believe that humanity must learn to live in a climate governed by an absence of meaning, by the provisional and by the fleeting (cf. *Fides et Ratio*, no. 91). In this context, the communications media can be used "to proclaim the Gospel or to reduce it to silence within men's hearts" (cf. Pontifical Council for Social Communications, Pastoral Instructive *Aetatis Novae*, no. 4). This poses a serious challenge for believers, especially for parents, families and all those responsible for the formation of children and young people. Those individuals in the Church community particularly gifted with talent to work in the media should be encouraged with pastoral prudence and wisdom, so that they may become professionals capable of dialoguing with the vast world of the mass media. . . .

IV. The Mass Media, the Crossroads of the Great Social Questions

10. . . . The positive development of the media at the service of the common good is a responsibility of each and every one (cf. CCC, no. 2494). Because of the close connections the media have with economics, politics and culture, there is required a management system capable of safeguarding the centrality and dignity of the person, the primacy of the family as the basic unit of society and the proper relationship among them.

Address to the Bishops of Spain on Their *Ad Limina* Visit

January 24, 2005

6. . . . At the same time, if [the Catholic faithful] are sustained by their Bishops, they will feel stronger in their faith in order to bear a public and credible witness to defending "effective respect for life in all its stages, the religious education of children, the protection of marriage and the family and the defense of the Name of God and of the human and social value of Christianity (Letter to the Archbishop of Santiago de Compostela, December 8, 2004). There

should then be an increase in pastoral activities that encourage the faithful to participate more regularly in Sunday Mass. Holy Mass must be experienced not as an obligation but rather as a requirement that is deeply rooted in every Christian's life.

Angelus

January 30, 2005

1. Today St. Peter's Square is gladdened by the presence of many children of Catholic Action who are concluding their "month of peace." I greet you with affection, dear boys and girls and children of the A.C.R.!

In today's Gospel, Jesus proclaims: *"Blessed are the peacemakers"* (Mt 5:9). These little ones can also be peacemakers! They too must train themselves in dialogue and must learn *"to defeat evil with good"* (cf. Rom 12:21), as I recalled for everyone in the recent *Message for the World Day of Peace*. It is necessary to defeat injustice with justice, falsehood with truth, vengeance with forgiveness, hate with love.

2. This lifestyle is not improvised but requires education, beginning in infancy. This education comes from wise teachings and above all from sound models in the family, in school and in every part of society. Parishes, oratories, associations, movements and ecclesial groups must more and more become *privileged places of this pedagogy of peace and love*, where growing together is learned.

3. Let us pray to Mary, Queen of Peace, so that she may *help youth*, who so much desire peace, to become its *courageous and tenacious builders*.

Address to the Congregation for Catholic Education

February 1, 2005

To my Venerable Brother Cardinal Zenon Grocholewski
Prefect of the Congregation for Catholic Education

1. I am pleased to offer my cordial greeting to you, to my venerable Brothers in the Episcopate and in the Priesthood, as well as to all the members of the Dicastery who are meeting on the occasion of the Plenary Assembly. I

wish you great success with your work in these days while you are examining certain questions that concern Seminaries, Ecclesiastical Faculties and
Catholic Universities.

2. You are paying special attention to the educational project at Seminaries,
which takes into account the fundamental complementarity of the four
dimensions of formation: human, intellectual, spiritual and pastoral (cf.
Pastores Dabo Vobis, nos. 43-59).

In light of current social and cultural changes, it can sometimes be useful for educators to avail themselves of the work of competent specialists to
help seminarians acquire a deeper understanding of the requirements of the
priesthood and to recognize celibacy as a gift of love for the Lord and for their
brethren. At the time of the young men's admission to the seminary, their
suitability for living a celibate life should be carefully assessed so that a moral
certainty regarding their emotional and sexual maturity may be reached
before they are ordained.

3. Your Plenary Meeting has also focused on the Ecclesiastical Faculties and
Catholic Universities that constitute a rich patrimony for the Church. In
the "great springtime for Christianity" that God is preparing (cf. Encyclical
Letter *Redemptoris Missio*, no. 86), they must be distinguished by the quality
of their teaching and research so as to take part officially in the dialogue with
the other faculties and universities.

Given the rapid developments in science and technology in our time,
these Institutions are called to a continuous renewal, to evaluate "the attain-
ments of science and technology in the perspective of the totality of the
human person" (*Ex Corde Ecclesiae*, no. 7). From this point of view, interdisciplinary dialogue is undoubtedly useful. The comparison with "a philosophy
of a *genuinely metaphysical* range" (*Fides et Ratio*, no. 83) and with theology
itself is proving fruitful.

4. Another interesting subject you are addressing at your meeting is Christian
education at scholastic institutions. Forty years ago, the conciliar Declaration
Gravissimum Educationis outlined in this regard certain principles that the
Congregation for Catholic Education was subsequently to develop further.

In the context of globalization and the changing mosaic of peoples and
cultures, the Church is aware of the urgent need for the mandate to preach
the Gospel and wishes to live it with renewed missionary dynamism. Catholic
education thus appears more and more as the fruit of a mission that must be
"shared" by priests, consecrated persons and lay faithful. The ecclesial service carried out by teachers of Catholic religion in schools fits into this horizon. Their teaching contributes to the students' integral development and to

knowledge of others in mutual respect. Hence, there is a lively hope that the teaching of religion will be recognized everywhere and will play an appropriate role in the educational plan of scholastic institutions.

5. Lastly, I would like to mention the efficient vocations promotion carried out by the Pontifical Society for Priestly Vocations, established by my Predecessor, Pius XII. It sustains first of all the "World Day of Prayer for Vocations," an annual occasion that is the center of vocational initiatives and events in all the Dioceses.

As I express deep gratitude to you for this praiseworthy institution, I willingly encourage those of you who dedicate time and energy to promoting a far-reaching vocations apostolate in the Ecclesial Communities. I think that the spiritual initiative it has embarked on in this year dedicated to the Eucharist is very timely. By arranging prayer shifts on each continent, it has created a chain of prayer that links Christian communities throughout the world.

6. In this regard, I would like to reaffirm that the Eucharist is the source and nourishment of every priestly and religious vocation. I would like, therefore, to express my appreciation of every initiative in this "network" of prayer for vocations, which I hope will encircle the whole world. May Mary, "Woman of the Eucharist," watch over all who are devoting their energies to the pastoral care of vocations.

I cordially impart my Apostolic Blessing to you and to all your loved ones.

Angelus

February 6, 2005

2. Pro-Life Day is being celebrated today here in Italy. In their Message for the occasion, the Italian Bishops emphasized the mystery of life as a relationship that demands trust. We must trust in life!

Unborn children are silently laying claim to trust in life. Many children, deprived of their family for various reasons and who can find a home that welcomes them through *adoption or a foster family,* also ask for trust.

Letter to the Bishops of France

February 11, 2005

7. . . . It is the duty of the State, for its part, out of respect for the established rules, also to guarantee to the families who so desire the opportunity to give

their children the catechesis they need, especially by planning convenient times for it. Moreover, without a moral dimension, young people can only be tempted by violence and by forms of conduct that do not do them justice, as is regularly seen. . . .

8. . . . My thoughts go in particular to the persons and families affected by financial and social difficulties. May ever greater solidarity be built up so that no one is left out! May greater attention be paid in this period to the people who are homeless and hungry!

Message to the Ambassador of Austria to the Holy See

March 7, 2005

6. . . . The Church wishes to collaborate with the State for the good of men and women, wherever she can make her own specific contribution. The Holy See notes with pleasure that a fertile and well-tested collaboration exists in Austria between the State and the Church for the good of, and in the interests of, all the cities and all the citizens, independently of their religious denomination or confession. I would like here expressly to emphasize the collaboration between the Church and the State in the sectors of education, health care and social services. This collaboration benefits people of all social classes and all ages. In this context, it is necessary to remember that the Austrian Government is taking positive and encouraging steps with a series of family policies. It is to be hoped that the fundamental "yes to life" is expressed ever better and more frequently politically in a "yes to children." No one can ever be denied the right to life, which is the presupposition of all the other rights. A society can truly be described as "human" if human life in all its phases, that is, from conception until natural death, enjoys the full and effective protection of this right. The Church never tires of recalling it. The Church is also aware that her demand for the unconditional protection of human life and the dignity of the person can always count on the understanding and support of people of good will. She also notes with pleasure that young people are ready to commit themselves to this.

Message to the Bishops of
Tanzania on Their *Ad Limina* Visit

March 11, 2005

Dear Brother Bishops,

1. While I regret that I cannot receive you in the Vatican at this time, nevertheless I gladly welcome you, *the Pastors of the Church in Tanzania*, on your visit *ad limina Apostolorum*. I greet you all from Gemelli Hospital, where I offer my prayers and my sufferings for you: in these days I feel especially close to you. As I address you for the first time in this new millennium, in consideration of your Quinquennial Reports, I wish to speak with you about three integral parts of your pastoral ministry: care of the family, care of the clergy, and care for the common good of society in your region.

2. The world can learn much from the high value that is placed upon *the family as a building block of African society*. Today the Church is called to give special priority to the pastoral care of the family, because of the great cultural changes taking place in the modern world. The new ideas and ways of life that are being proposed must be carefully assessed in the light of the Gospel, so that those values essential for the health and well-being of society may be preserved (cf. *Ecclesia in Africa*, no. 80). For example, the unjust practice of linking programs of economic assistance to the promotion of sterilization and contraception must be strenuously resisted. Such programs are "affronts to the dignity of the person and the family" (*Compendium of the Social Doctrine of the Church*, no. 234) and they threaten to undermine the authentic Christian understanding of the nature and purpose of marriage.

According to the design of the Creator, the sacred bond of matrimony symbolizes the new and eternal Covenant sanctioned in the Blood of Christ (cf. *Familiaris Consortio*, no. 13). One and indissoluble by nature, it has to remain open to the generation of new life, by which the spouses cooperate in God's creative work. As authentic teachers of the faith, continue to proclaim these principles and to *build up the Church in your country as the Family of God* (cf. *Ecclesia in Africa*, no. 92). Only in this way can healthy foundations be laid for the future of African society and indeed the future of the local Church.

The promotion of genuine family values is all the more urgent on account of the terrible scourge of AIDS afflicting your country and so much of the African Continent. Fidelity within marriage and abstinence outside it are the only sure ways to limit the further spread of infection. Communicating this message must be a key element in the Church's response to the epidemic. It especially grieves me to consider the many thousands of children left as orphans in the wake of the merciless virus. The Church plays a vital part in providing the care and compassion that is needed for these innocent victims, tragically deprived of the love of their parents.

3. The principal co-workers of the Bishop in carrying out his mission are the priests of the diocese, to whom the Bishop is called to be *a father, a brother and a friend* (cf. *Directory for the Pastoral Ministry of Bishops*, no. 76). As you help them to grow in holiness and in single-hearted commitment to discipleship, see that you enkindle within them a genuine longing for the Kingdom of God. Continue to encourage them in their gifts, sustain them in their difficulties and form them to meet the demands of priestly life today. I know that you appreciate the importance of seminary formation and the need to assign your best priests to this task. Without neglecting the intellectual and pastoral aspects of the training, I ask you always to exercise particular vigilance over the spiritual formation. Only a commitment to prayer, rooted in a mature understanding of the priest's personal configuration to Christ, will enable him to practice the generous self-giving in pastoral charity to which he is called (cf. *Pastores Dabo Vobis*, no. 23). Likewise, by ensuring that all the clergy receive suitable ongoing formation, you help them to "rekindle the gift of God that is within . . . through the laying on of hands" (2 Tim 1:6).

4. As an Episcopal Conference, you have already taken important steps to combat the material deprivation afflicting so many of your people. The success of your initiative in organizing the International Forum of 2002 is clearly seen in the government's stated intention to make use of its conclusions in formulating public policy. Such cooperation between Church and State on matters of great social concern deserves to be commended, and it is to be hoped that others will follow the lead you have given in this area. I am confident that you will continue to press for concrete measures designed to alleviate poverty and to increase educational provision, so that the poor may be enabled to help themselves and one another.

Your country has already contributed in significant ways to building peace and stability in East Africa. I have spoken in the past of the generosity with which you provided a home for thousands of refugees fleeing persecution in their own countries (cf. *Address to the Ambassador of Tanzania to the Holy See*, January 11, 1997), and I urge you to continue to extend this Christ-like welcome to your suffering brothers and sisters. In this way, you prove yourselves true neighbors to them. One of the true challenges for the future will be to maintain and strengthen respectful relations with the Muslim community, especially in the Zanzibar archipelago. A serious commitment to inter-religious dialogue and a firm resolve to work together in addressing your country's social and economic problems will give a shining example to other nations of the harmony that should always exist between diverse ethnic and religious groups.

5. Dear brother Bishops, as you look to the future with confidence, pray for the guidance of the Holy Spirit in the preparations that will be made for the Second Special Assembly for Africa of the Synod of Bishops, so that the joys and sorrows, the griefs and the hopes of the people of your Continent may find an echo in the hearts of all who follow Christ (cf. *Gaudium et Spes*, no. 1). Seek always to evangelize the culture of your people in such a way that *Christ speaks from the heart of your local churches with a truly African voice.*

I pray that this Year of the Eucharist may be for you "a precious opportunity to grow in awareness of the incomparable treasure which Christ has entrusted to his Church" (*Mane Nobiscum Domine*, no. 29). Commending you and your priests, deacons, religious and lay faithful to the intercession of Mary, Star of Evangelization, I cordially impart my Apostolic Blessing as a pledge of grace and strength in her Son, our Lord and Savior Jesus Christ.

PART II

Papal Documents and
Teachings of
Pope Benedict XVI

CHAPTER I

To the World Meetings of Families

Letter to the Participants in the Fifth World Meeting of Families

May 17, 2005

To Cardinal Alfonso López Trujillo,
President of the Pontifical Council for the Family,

On February 22 this year, the venerable Holy Father John Paul II convoked the *Fifth World Meeting of Families* to take place in Valencia, Spain, selecting as its theme: "The transmission of faith in the family," and fixing the date for the first week in July 2006.

I am pleased to confirm the convocation of this important World Meeting of Families. In this regard, I am determined, as was John Paul II, to encourage the "marvelous news" (*Familiaris Consortio*, no. 51), the "Gospel of the Family," whose value is central to the Church and to society.

I myself had the opportunity to be the General Relator at the Special Assembly of the Synod of Bishops on the Family, celebrated in Rome in 1980. The Apostolic Exhortation *Familiaris Consortio* that resulted from this Assembly makes a deep analysis of the identity and mission of the family, which it describes as the "domestic Church" and sanctuary of life.

Today, if they are to give a truly human face to society, no people can ignore the precious good of the family, founded on marriage. "The matrimonial covenant, by which a man and a woman establish between themselves a *partnership* of the whole of life, is by its nature ordered toward the good of the spouses and the procreation and education of offspring" (c. 1055): this is the foundation of the family and the patrimony and common good of humanity.

Thus, the Church cannot cease to proclaim that in accordance with God's plans (cf. Mt 19:3-9), marriage and the family are irreplaceable and permit no other alternatives.

Today more than ever, the Christian family has a very noble mission that it cannot shirk: the transmission of the faith, which involves the gift of self to Jesus Christ who died and rose, and insertion into the Ecclesial Community.

Parents are the first evangelizers of children, a precious gift from the Creator (cf. *Gaudium et Spes*, no. 50), and begin by teaching them to say their first prayers. In this way a moral universe is built up, rooted in the will of God, where the child grows in the human and Christian values that give life its full meaning.

On this occasion, I would like to send my cordial greeting to Archbishop Agustín García-Gasco Vicente, Archbishop of Valencia, the particular Church which is preparing for this Ecclesial Meeting and will welcome families from the rest of Spain and from other countries.

Already from this moment, I commend to the Lord and bless the families who will be taking part in this Meeting or joining it in spirit. May the Virgin Mary, our Mother, who was with her Son at the Wedding of Cana, intercede for all the families of the world.

APOSTOLIC JOURNEY TO SPAIN FOR
THE FIFTH WORLD MEETING OF FAMILIES

Address at the Welcome Ceremony, Airport of Manises

July 8, 2006

3. My reason for this long-awaited visit is to take part in the Fifth World Meeting of Families, whose theme is "The Transmission of Faith in the Family." I wish to set forth the central role, for the Church and for society, proper to the family based on marriage. The family is a unique institution in God's plan, and the Church cannot fail to proclaim and promote its fundamental importance, so that it can live out its vocation with a constant sense of responsibility and joy.

Address at the Prayer Vigil in Valencia, Spain

July 8, 2006

Dear Brothers and Sisters,

I am most happy to take part in this prayer meeting which is meant to cele-brate with great joy God's gift of the family. I feel very close in prayer to all those who have recently experienced this city's mourning and in our hope in the Risen Christ, which provides light and strength even at times of immense human tragedy.

United by the same faith in Christ, we have gathered here from so many parts of the world as a community which with gratitude and joy bears wit-ness that human beings were created in the image and likeness of God for love, and that complete human fulfillment only comes about when we make a sincere gift of ourselves to others. The family is the privileged setting where every person learns to give and receive love. That is why the Church con-stantly wishes to demonstrate her pastoral concern for this reality, so basic for the human person. This is what she teaches in her Magisterium: "God, who is love and who created man and woman for love, has called them to love. By creating man and woman he called them to an intimate communion of life and love in Marriage. 'So they are no longer two but one flesh' (Mt 19:6)" (*Compendium of the Catechism of the Catholic Church*, no. 337).

This is the truth that the Church tirelessly proclaims to the world. My beloved predecessor Pope John Paul II said that "man has been made 'in the image and likeness' of God not only by his being human, but also by the com-munion of the persons that man and woman have formed since the begin-ning. They become the image of God, not so much in their aloneness as in their communion" (*Catechesis*, November 14, 1979). That is why I confirmed the calling of this Fifth World Meeting of Families in Spain, and specifically here in Valencia, a city rich in tradition and proud of the Christian faith lived and nurtured in so many of its families.

The family is an intermediate institution between individuals and society, and nothing can completely take its place. The family is itself based primarily on a deep interpersonal relationship between husband and wife, sustained by affection and mutual understanding. To enable this, it receives abundant help from God in the sacrament of Matrimony, which brings with it a true vocation to holiness. Would that our children might experience more the harmony and affection between their parents, rather than disagreements and discord, since the love between father and mother is a source of great security for children and it teaches them the beauty of a faithful and lasting love.

The family is a necessary good for peoples, an indispensable foundation for society and a great and lifelong treasure for couples. It is a unique good for children, who are meant to be the fruit of the love, of the total and generous self-giving of their parents. To proclaim the whole truth about the family, based on marriage as *a domestic Church and a sanctuary of life*, is a great respon-sibility incumbent upon all.

Father and mother have said a complete "yes" in the sight of God, which constitutes the basis of the sacrament which joins them together. Likewise, for the inner relationship of the family to be complete, they also need to say a "yes" of acceptance to the children whom they have given birth to or adopted, and each of which has his or her own personality and character. In this way, children will grow up in a climate of acceptance and love, and upon reaching sufficient maturity, will then want to say "yes" in turn to those who gave them life.

The challenges of present-day society, marked by the centrifugal forces generated especially in urban settings, make it necessary to ensure that families do not feel alone. A small family can encounter difficult obstacles when it is isolated from relatives and friends. The ecclesial community therefore has the responsibility of offering support, encouragement and spiritual nourishment which can strengthen the cohesiveness of the family, especially in times of trial or difficulty. Here parishes have an important role to play, as do the various ecclesial associations, called to cooperate as networks of support and a helping hand for the growth of families in faith.

Christ has shown us what is always to be the supreme source of our life and thus of the lives of families: "This is my commandment, that you love one another as I have loved you. No one had greater love than this, to lay down one's life for one's friends" (Jn 15:12-13). The love of God himself has been poured out upon us in Baptism. Consequently, families are called to experience this same kind of love, for the Lord makes it possible for us, through our human love, to be sensitive, loving and merciful like Christ.

Together with passing on the faith and the love of God, one of the greatest responsibilities of families is that of training free and responsible persons. For this reason the parents need gradually to give their children greater freedom, while remaining for some time the guardians of that freedom. If children see that their parents—and, more generally, all the adults around them—live life with joy and enthusiasm, despite all difficulties, they will themselves develop that profound "joy of life" which can help them to overcome wisely the inevitable obstacles and problems which are part of life. Furthermore, when families are not closed in on themselves, children come to learn that every person is worthy of love, and that there is a basic, universal brotherhood which embraces every human being.

This Fifth World Meeting invites us to reflect on a theme of particular importance, one fraught with great responsibility: *the transmission of faith in the family*. This theme is nicely expressed in the *Catechism of the Catholic Church*: "As a mother who teaches her children to speak and so to understand and communicate, the Church our Mother teaches us the language of faith in order to introduce us to the understanding and the life of faith" (no. 171).

This is symbolically in the liturgy of Baptism: with the handing over of the lighted candle, the parents are made part of the mystery of new life as children of God given to their sons and daughters in the waters of baptism. To hand down the faith to children, with the help of individuals and institutions like the parish, the school or Catholic associations, is a responsibility which parents cannot overlook, neglect or completely delegate to others. "The Christian family is called the domestic church because the family manifests and lives out the communal and familiar nature of the Church as the family of God. Each family member, in accord with his or her own role, exercises the baptismal priesthood and contributes toward making the family a community of grace and of prayer, a school of human and Christian virtues, and the place where the faith is first proclaimed to children" (*Compendium of the Catechism of the Catholic Church*, no. 350). And what is more: "Parents, in virtue of their participation in the fatherhood of God, have the first responsibility for the education of their children and they are the first heralds of the faith for them. They have the duty to love and respect their children as *persons* and as *children of God* . . . in particular, they have the mission of educating their children in the Christian faith" (ibid., no. 460).

The language of faith is learned in homes where this faith grows and is strengthened through prayer and Christian practice. In the reading from *Deuteronomy* we have heard the prayer constantly repeated by the Chosen People, the "Shema Israel," which Jesus himself would have heard and recited in his home in Nazareth. He himself would refer to it during his public life, as we see in the Gospel of Mark (12:29). This is the faith of the Church, which is born of God's love which comes through your families. To live the fullness of this faith, in all its wondrous newness, is a great gift. All the same, at those times when God's face seems to be hidden, believing can be difficult and takes great effort.

This meeting provides a new impetus for proclaiming the Gospel of the family, reaffirming the strength and identity of the family founded upon marriage and open to the generous gift of life, where children are accompanied in their bodily and spiritual growth. This is the best way to counter a widespread hedonism which reduces human relations to banality and empties them of their authentic value and beauty. To promote the values of marriage does not stand in the way of fully experiencing the happiness that man and women encounter in their mutual love. Christian faith and ethics are not meant to stifle love, but to make it healthier, stronger and more truly free. Human love needs to be purified and to mature if it is to be fully human and the principle of a true and lasting joy (cf. *Address at St. John Lateran*, June 5, 2006).

And so I invite government leaders and legislators to reflect on the evident benefits which homes in peace and harmony assure to individuals and the family, the neuralgic center of society, as the Holy See has stated in the *Charter of the Rights of the Family.* The purpose of laws is the integral good of man, in response to his needs and aspirations. This good is a significant help to society, of which it cannot be deprived, and for peoples a safeguard and a purification. The family is also a school which enables men and women to grow to the full measure of their humanity. The experience of being loved by their parents helps children to become aware of their dignity as children.

Children need to be brought up in the faith, to be loved and protected. Along with their basic right to be born and to be raised in the faith, children also have the right to a home which takes as its model the home of Nazareth, and to be shielded from all dangers and threats. I am the grandfather of the world, we have heard.

I would now like to say a word to grandparents, who are so important for every family. They can be—and so often are—the guarantors of the affection and tenderness which every human being needs to give and receive. They offer little ones the perspective of time, they are memory and richness of families. In no way should they ever be excluded from the family circle. They are a treasure which the younger generation should not be denied, especially when they bear witness to their faith at the approach of death.

I now wish to recite a part of the prayer which you have prayed in asking for the success of this World Meeting of Families.

O God, who in the Holy Family
left us a perfect model of family life
lived in faith and obedience to your will.
Help us to be examples of faith and love for your commandments.
Help us in our mission of transmitting the faith that we received from
    our parents.
Open the hearts of our children
so that the seed of faith, which they received in Baptism, will grow
    in them.
Strengthen the faith of our young people,
that they may grow in knowledge of Jesus.
Increase love and faithfulness in all marriages,
especially those going through times of suffering or difficulty.

(. . .)

United to Joseph and Mary,
we ask this through Jesus Christ your Son, our Lord. Amen.

Homily at Mass in Valencia, Spain

July 9, 2006

Dear Brothers and Sisters,

In this Holy Mass which it is my great joy to celebrate, together with many of my Brothers in the Episcopate and a great number of priests, I give thanks to the Lord for all of you, the joyful throng of beloved families gathered in this place, and the many others who in distant lands are following this celebration by radio and television. I greet all of you with an affectionate embrace.

Both Esther and Paul, as we have just heard in today's readings, testify that the family is called to work for the handing on of the faith. Esther admits: "Ever since I was born, I have heard in the tribe of my family that you, O Lord, took Israel out of all the nations" (14:5). Paul follows the tradition of his Jewish ancestors by worshiping God with a pure conscience. He praises the sincere faith of Timothy and speaks to him about "a faith that lived first in your grandmother Lois and your mother Eunice, and now, I am sure, lives in you" (2 Tim 1:15). In these biblical testimonies, the family includes not only parents and children, but also grandparents and ancestors. The family thus appears to us as a community of generations and the guarantee of a patrimony of traditions.

None of us gave ourselves life or singlehandedly learned how to live. All of us received from others both life itself and its basic truths, and we have been called to attain perfection in relationship and loving communion with others. The family, founded on indissoluble marriage between a man and a woman, is the expression of this relational, filial and communal aspect of life. It is the setting where men and women are enabled to be born with dignity, and to grow and develop in an integral manner.

Once children are born, through their relationship with their parents they begin to share in a family tradition with even older roots. Together with the gift of life, they receive a whole patrimony of experience. Parents have the right and the inalienable duty to transmit this heritage to their children: to help them find their own identity, to initiate them to the life of society, to foster the responsible exercise of their moral freedom and their ability to love on the basis of their having been loved and, above all, to enable them to encounter God. Children experience human growth and maturity to the extent that they trustingly accept this heritage and training which they gradually make their own. They are thus enabled to make a personal synthesis between what has been passed on and what is new, a synthesis that every individual and generation is called to make.

At the origin of every man and woman, and thus in all human fatherhood and motherhood, we find God the Creator. For this reason, married couples must accept the child born to them, not simply as theirs alone, but also as a child of God, loved for his or her own sake and called to be a son or daughter of God. What is more: each generation, all parenthood and every family has its origin in God, who is Father, Son and Holy Spirit.

Esther's father had passed on to her, along with the memory of her forebears and her people, the memory of a God who is the origin of all and to whom all are called to answer. The memory of God the Father, who chose a people for himself and who acts in history for our salvation. The memory of this Father sheds light on our deepest human identity: where we come from, who we are, and how great is our dignity. Certainly we come from our parents and we are their children, but we also come from God who has created us in his image and called us to be his children. Consequently, at the origin of every human being there is not something haphazard or chance, but a loving plan of God. This was revealed to us by Jesus Christ, the true Son of God and a perfect man. He knew whence he came and whence all of us have come: from the love of his Father and our Father.

Faith, then, is not merely a cultural heritage, but the constant working of the grace of God who calls and our human freedom, which can respond or not to his call. Even if no one can answer for another person, Christian parents are still called to give a credible witness of their Christian faith and hope. The need to ensure that God's call and the good news of Christ will reach their children with the utmost clarity and authenticity.

As the years pass, this gift of God which the parents have helped set before the eyes of the little ones will also need to be cultivated with wisdom and gentleness, in order to instill in them a capacity for discernment. Thus, with the constant witness of their parents' conjugal love, permeated with a living faith, and with the loving accompaniment of the Christian community, children will be helped better to appropriate the gift of their faith, to discover the deepest meaning of their own lives and to respond with joy and gratitude.

The Christian family passes on the faith when parents teach their children to pray and when they pray with them (cf. *Familiaris Consortio*, no. 60); when they lead them to the sacraments and gradually introduce them to the life of the Church; when all join in reading the Bible, letting the light of faith shine on their family life and praising God as our Father.

In contemporary culture, we often see an excessive exaltation of the freedom of the individual as an autonomous subject, as if we were self-created and self-sufficient, apart from our relationship with others and our responsibilities in their regard. Attempts are being made to organize the life of society on the basis of subjective and ephemeral desires alone, with no reference to objective, prior truths such as the dignity of each human being and his inalienable rights and duties, which every social group is called to serve.

The Church does not cease to remind us that true human freedom derives from our having been created in God's image and likeness. Christian education is consequently an education in freedom and for freedom. "We do not do good as slaves, who are not free to act otherwise, but we do it because we are personally responsible for the world; because we love truth and goodness, because we love God himself and therefore his creatures as well. This is the true freedom to which the Holy Spirit wants to lead us" (*Homily for the Vigil of Pentecost*, June 9, 2006).

Jesus Christ is the perfect human being, an example of filial freedom, who teaches us to share with others his own love: "As the Father has loved me, so I have loved you; abide in my love" (Jn 15:9). And so the Second Vatican Council teaches that "Christian married couples and parents, following their own way, should support one another in grace all through life with faithful love, and should train their children, lovingly received from God, in Christian doctrine and evangelical virtues. Because in this way they present to all an example of unfailing and generous love, they build up the brotherhood of charity, and they stand as witnesses and cooperators of the fruitfulness of Mother Church, as a sign of and a share in that love with which Christ loved his Bride and gave himself for her" (*Lumen Gentium*, no. 41).

The joyful love with which our parents welcomed us and accompanied our first steps in this world is like a sacramental sign and prolongation of the benevolent love of God from which we have come. The experience of being welcomed and loved by God and by our parents is always the firm foundation for authentic human growth and authentic development, helping us to mature on the way toward truth and love, and to move beyond ourselves in order to enter into communion with others and with God.

To help us advance along the path of human maturity, the Church teaches us to respect and foster the marvelous reality of the indissoluble marriage between man and woman which is also the origin of the family. To recognize and assist this institution is one of the greatest services which can be rendered nowadays to the common good and to the authentic development of individuals and societies, as well as the best means of ensuring the dignity, equality and true freedom of the human person.

This being the case, I want to stress the importance and the positive role which the Church's various family associations are playing in support of marriage and the family. Consequently, "I wish to call on all Christians to collaborate cordially and courageously with all people of good will who are serving the family in accordance with their responsibility" (*Familiaris Consortio*, no. 86), so that by joining forces in a legitimate plurality of initiatives they

will contribute to the promotion of the authentic good of the family in contemporary society.

Let us return for a moment to the first reading of this Mass, drawn from
the Book of Esther. The Church at prayer has seen in this humble queen
interceding with all her heart for her suffering people, a prefigurement of
Mary, whom her Son has given to us all as our Mother; a prefigurement of the
Mother who protects by her love God's family on its earthly pilgrimage. Mary
is the image and model of all mothers, of their great mission to be guardians of
life, of their mission to be teachers of the art of living and of the art of loving.

The Christian family—father, mother and children—is called, then, to do
all these things not as a task imposed from without, but rather as a gift of the
sacramental grace of marriage poured out upon the spouses. If they remain
open to the Spirit and implore his help, he will not fail to bestow on them the
love of God the Father made manifest and incarnate in Christ. The presence
of the Spirit will help spouses not to lose sight of the source and criterion of
their love and self-giving, and to cooperate with him to make it visible and
incarnate in every aspect of their lives. The Spirit will also awaken in them
a yearning for the definitive encounter with Christ in the house of his Father
and our Father. And this is the message of hope that, from Valencia, I wish to
share with all the families of the world. Amen.

Angelus

July 9, 2006

Before concluding this celebration, we turn to the Virgin Mary, like the many
families which invoke her in the privacy of their homes, so that she will be
present to them with maternal concern. Through the intercession of Mary,
open your homes and your hearts to Christ, so that he will be your strength
and your joy, and help you to live in harmony and to proclaim before the
world the invincible power of true love.

At this time, I wish to thank all those who contributed to the successful outcome of this Meeting. Above all I express my profound gratitude to
Cardinal Alfonso López Trujillo, President of the Pontifical Council for the
Family, and to Archbishop Agustín García-Gasco of Valencia, who brought
to a happy end this great World Meeting of Families. In a particular way, I
wish to acknowledge the generous and efficient work of the many volunteers
from so many nations, and I thank them for their selfless cooperation in all
the events. I offer a special word of thanks to the many consecrated persons

and religious communities, especially the cloistered communities, who have accompanied all the celebrations with persevering prayer.

I now have the joy of announcing that the next World Meeting of Families will be held in 2009 in Mexico City. To the beloved pilgrim Church in the noble nation of Mexico and, in a personal way, to Cardinal Norberto Rivera Carrera, the Archbishop of Mexico City, I express even now my gratitude for his generous offer.

In English:*

I greet all the English-speaking participants who have gathered from various parts of the world. I trust that your experiences here will have strengthened your commitment to promoting the integrity of family life. May God abundantly bless you and all those you represent, and through the intercession of Mary, Mother of the Church, may you and your families be filled with the wisdom of her Son.

Dear French-speaking families, I greet you with joy with the announcement that the next World Meeting of Families will take place in 2009, in Mexico City. I invite you to root your life and your conjugal love in the sacrament you received on the day of your matrimony, which makes you icons and witnesses of God's love. Such a love must always be able to achieve forgiveness in the heart of the couple; this is the way that opens up a future for conjugal and family relationships. Thus you will be witnesses of true love to your children, giving them self-confidence and helping them discover for themselves the Christ who wants to help them to build an integrated personality of their own and to entrust them with the responsibility for their own existence. May you be able to announce to all who surround you that, as Christ has shown us, there is no greater love than to give and to give oneself to God and to one's brothers and sisters.

I cordially greet the pilgrims, especially the families from German-speaking countries. As a community of life and of love founded on God, the family remains the privileged place for handing on the faith. Let us accompany families with our prayer. Let us not grow tired in our commitment to promoting marriage and the family, which is always necessary in today's social context. Dear friends, I am happy to invite you, already today, to the next World Meeting of Families in Mexico City in 2009. May God grant His blessing to families and to all of us!

---

*   Four paragraphs in this section, the greetings to French-, German-, Portugese-, and Polish-speaking families, are an unofficial translation of the Italian.

I greet with great affection the Portuguese-speaking families present here or in communion with us, calling down upon all the maternal care of the Virgin Mary so that in every Christian heart there may be kept burning the flame of faith, of love and of harmony as the supreme and precious inheritance to be passed on to the children during the life of their parents. Dear families, may you be blessed in your efforts for the good of humanity and of the Church. God willing, the next World Meeting of Families will be in 2009, in Mexico City.

I cordially greet the Polish families, those participating here in Valencia at the Fifth World Meeting of Families and those who are doing so spiritually in their homes. My wish is that every family should be a community of prayer, of handing on the faith, and the place where the spirit is formed. May Mary, Queen of Families, support your efforts and constantly guide you. Already today I invite you to the next World Meeting of Families which, God willing, will be held in Mexico in the year 2009. May God bless you all.

I warmly embrace all the families here present, as well as those who have taken part in this celebration through radio, television and the other communications media. I commend all families to the protection of the Holy Family of Nazareth. Following its quiet example, may families help their children to grow in wisdom, age and grace before God and men (cf. Lk 2:52).

Letter to Cardinal Alfonso López Trujillo for the Next World Meeting of Families

October 1, 2007

To His Eminence Cardinal Alfonso López Trujillo,
President of the Pontifical Council for the Family,

On July 9, 2006, at the end of the Fifth World Meeting of Families in Valencia, Spain, I had the opportunity to announce that the Sixth Meeting of Families would be held in Mexico. It will be taking place from January 16 to 18, 2009 on the theme: *"The family, teacher of human and Christian values,"* in continuity with last year's unforgettable event.

As the first school of life and faith and the "domestic Church," the family is called to educate the new generations in the human and Christian values so that in modeling its life on the example of Christ, it may shape within them a harmonious personality.

In this task, so crucial for the human person who cannot be reduced merely to knowing how to use realities within his reach but strives above all to seek and to commit himself to the ideals and models of behavior which make him "superior to bodily things" (*Gaudium et Spes*, no. 14), it is also necessary to rely on schools, parishes and the various ecclesial groups that encourage the human being's integral education.

At a time when there is frequently a gap between what people say they are doing and the actual way they live and behave, this upcoming World Meeting of Families is resolved to encourage Christian homes to form an upright moral conscience, which will help them, strengthened by God's grace, to follow faithfully his will which he revealed to us through Jesus Christ and has inscribed in the depths of every person's heart (ibid., no. 16).

I would like on this occasion to offer a cordial greeting to my Brother Bishops of this beloved Nation, especially Cardinal Norberto Rivera Carrera, Archbishop of Mexico City, the Ecclesial Community which will give hospitality to the families from many different parts of the world who will be taking part in this important Gathering.

I ask the Lord to illuminate with his grace the preparatory process and celebration of this event and to grant that it may be a special opportunity for families to rejoice in their own vocation and mission, both those present and those united in spirit.

With these sentiments, as I recommend you to the Holy Family of Nazareth, I bless you with all my affection.

Letter to Cardinal Tarcisio Bertone, Papal Legate for the Sixth World Meeting of Families*

December 28, 2008

To our Venerable Brother,
His Eminence, Tarcisio Cardinal Bertone, SDB,
Secretary of State,

Seeking to improve the condition of society for the future, many pastors and lay faithful from around the whole world will soon gather in Mexico City for the Sixth World Meeting of Families, at whose heart is the family as teacher of human Christian values. This theme is considered to be of utmost importance because "The family is called to carry out its task of education in the Church thus sharing in her life and mission. The Church wishes to carry out

---

*   This text is an unofficial translation of the Latin in the Italian compendium.

her educational mission above all through families who are capable of undertaking this task by the Sacrament of Matrimony, through the state of grace which follows from it" (John Paul II, *Gratissimam Sane*, no. 16). In fact, parents are the primary teachers of human values for their own children when, supported by divine grace, they try to pass on to them the virtues of faith in Christ, active charity and great hope "and they also possess a fundamental competence in this area: they are educators because they are parents" (ibid.).

It is helpful to recall and to offer to call Christian families the shining examples of those faithful who, in times both ancient and more recent, left behind in their own lives an example of fortitude and a memory of virtue not only for their children but also for many other people (cf. 2 Mc 6:31). Thus, among many others, Saints Basil and Aemilia stand out in the East for having four saints among nine children while, in the West, Saints Gordianus and Silvia were the parents of the Supreme Pontiff St. Gregory the Great. At the beginning of the new millennium, Holy Mother Church added to the ranks of the beatified Maria Teresa Ferragud Roig, who, along with her four virgin daughters consecrated to Christ, achieved the palm of martyrdom and heavenly glory; the married couple Luigi Beltrame Quattrocchi and Maria Corsini in Italy and, in France, Louis Martin and Zelia Maria Guérin, from whom was born the patroness of missions and the flower of Carmel, St. Therese of Lisieux.

I am quite convinced that an event of this kind can be of great benefit to society as a whole and to every individual. Therefore I gladly accepted the invitation of my Venerable Brother, His Eminence, Norbert Cardinal Rivera Carrera, Archbishop of Mexico City. Since I am unable to be present there myself, I am confidently sending you, Venerable Brother, my first and most diligent assistant in carrying out the tasks of every day, so that you may fittingly represent me personally there and may bring my fatherly encouragement and kind greeting to those who gather. Therefore by this letter I name you MY LEGATE to the Sixth World Meeting of Families, which will be celebrated in Mexico from the thirteenth to the eighteenth of January.

I fervently commend your legation and the whole Meeting of Families to the powerful intercession of the Blessed Virgin Mary of Guadalupe and of St. Joseph and of all those blessed parents, that they may entreat the Son of the God for all the assistance, rights and guidance needed by the rulers of nations and by families themselves so that the dignity of all men may be truly acknowledged and reverently honored. I ask you to bestow in my name and with love to all the participants in this memorable event the Apostolic Blessing and the assurance of my communion.

Message to Participants in the Recitation of the Rosary on the Occasion of the Sixth World Day of Families

January 17, 2009

Dear Brothers and Sisters,
Dear Families,

I wish all of you who have gathered to celebrate the Sixth World Meeting of Families under the motherly gaze of Our Lady of Guadalupe "Grace . . . and peace from God the Father and the Lord Jesus Christ" (2 Thes 1:2).

You have just finished praying the Holy Rosary, contemplating the Joyful Mysteries of the Son of God made man who was born into the family of Mary and Joseph and grew up in Nazareth in the intimacy of the home, amid his daily occupations, prayer and relations with neighbors. His family welcomed him and protected him lovingly, initiated him into the observance of the religious traditions and laws of his people and accompanied him to human maturity and the mission for which he had been destined. "And Jesus," says the Gospel according to St. Luke, "increased in wisdom and in stature, and in favor with God and man" (Lk 2:52).

The Joyful Mysteries have alternated with the accounts of several Christian families from the five continents that are, as it were, an echo and a reflection in our time of the history of Jesus and his family. These accounts have shown us how the seed of the Gospel continues to germinate and bear fruit in various situations in today's world.

The theme of this Sixth World Meeting of Families, *"The Family, Teacher of Human and Christian Values,"* reminds us that the home environment is a school of humanity and Christian life for all its members, with beneficial consequences for people, the Church and society. In fact, the home is called to live and to foster reciprocal love and truth, respect and justice, loyalty and collaboration, service and availability to others, especially the weakest. The Christian home, which must "show forth to all men Christ's living pres-ence in the world and the authentic nature of the Church" (*Gaudium et Spes*, no. 48), must be imbued with God's presence, placing in his hands everyday events and asking his help in carrying out its indispensable mission.

For this reason prayer in the family at the most suitable and significant moments is of supreme importance since, as the Lord himself assured us: "Where two or three are gathered in my name, there am I in the midst of them" (Mt 18:20). And the Teacher is certainly with the family that listens

and meditates on the Word of God, that learns from him what is most important in life (cf. Lk 10:41-42) and puts his teachings into practice (cf. Lk 11:28).
In this way, personal and family life is transformed, gradually improved and
enriched with dialogue, faith is transmitted to the children, the pleasure of
being together grows and the home is further united and consolidated, like
the house built upon rock (cf. Mt 7:24-25). May Pastors not cease to help
families to benefit fully from the Word of God in Sacred Scripture.

With the strength that stems from prayer the family is transformed into a
community of disciples and missionaries of Christ. In the family the Gospel
is welcomed, passed on and it radiates. As my venerable Predecessor Pope
Paul VI said: "The parents not only communicate the Gospel to their children, but from their children they can themselves receive the same Gospel as
deeply lived by them" (*Evangelii Nuntiandi*, no. 71).

By living filial trust and obedience to God, fidelity and the generous
acceptance of children, care for the weakest and promptness in forgiving, the
Christian family becomes a living Gospel legible to all (cf. 2 Cor 3:2), as a
sign of credibility that is perhaps more persuasive and better able to challenge
the world today. The family should also bring its witness of life and explicit
profession of faith to the various contexts of its surroundings, such as the
school and various other associations. It should also be committed to the
catechetical formation of the children and the pastoral activities of its parish
community, especially those related to preparation for marriage or specifically
addressed to family life.

Coexistence in the home is a gift for people and a source of inspiration for
social coexistence, showing that freedom and solidarity are complementary,
that the good of each one must take into account the good of the others
and that strict justice demands openness to understanding and forgiveness
for the sake of the common good. Indeed, social relations can take as a reference point the values that constitute authentic family life in order to become
increasingly humanized every day and directed toward building "the civilization of love."

Furthermore, the family is also a vital cell of society, the first and decisive
resource for its development. It is also, frequently, the last resort for people
whose needs the established structures cannot meet satisfactorily.

Because of its essential role in society, the family has a right to have its
proper identity recognized that is not to be confused with other forms of
coexistence. It is likewise entitled to expect proper cultural, legal, financial,
social, and health-care protection and, most particularly, to receive support
that, taking into account the number of children, provides sufficient financial
resources to allow it to choose the type of education and school freely.

It is therefore necessary to promote a family culture and policy that the
families themselves can develop in an organized manner. For this reason I

encourage them to join associations that promote the identity and rights of the family, in accordance with an anthropological vision consistent with the Gospel, while I invite the said organizations to cooperate with one another to ensure that their coordinated activity may be more effective.

To conclude, I urge all of you to have great trust, for the family is in the Heart of God, Creator and Savior. Working for families is working for the worthy and luminous future of humanity and for the construction of the Kingdom of God. Let us humbly invoke divine grace so that it may help us to collaborate with enthusiasm and joy in the noble cause of the family, called to be evangelized and evangelizing, human and humanizing. this beautiful task, may we be accompanied by the maternal intercession and heavenly protection of the Most Holy Virgin Mary, whom I invoke today with the glorious title of Our Lady of Guadalupe, and to whom, as Mother, I entrust the families of the whole world.

Videoconference after Closing Mass for the Sixth World Day of Families

January 18, 2009

Dear Brothers and Sisters,

I warmly greet you all at the end of this solemn Eucharistic celebration with which the *Sixth World Meeting of Families* in Mexico City is ending. I thank God for the many families who, sparing no effort, have gathered together around the altar of the Lord.

I particularly greet Cardinal Tarcisio Bertone, Secretary of State, who has presided at this celebration as my Legate. I would like to express my affection and gratitude to Cardinal Ennio Antonelli, and likewise to the members of the Pontifical Council for the Family of which he is President, to Cardinal Norberto Rivera Carrera, Archbishop and Primate of Mexico, and the Central Commission that has overseen the organization of this Sixth World Meeting. I extend my gratitude to all who with their self-sacrificing dedication and devotion made the Meeting possible. I also greet the Cardinals and Bishops present at the celebration, especially the members of the Mexican Bishops' Conference, and to the Authorities of this beloved nation, who have generously hosted this important event and made it possible.

You Mexicans know well that you are very close to the Pope's heart. I think of you and offer to God the Father your joys and your hopes, your plans and your anxieties. In Mexico the Gospel has put down deep roots, forging its traditions, its culture and the identity of its noble people. It is necessary to guard this rich patrimony so that it may continue to be a source of the moral and spiritual energy needed to face today's challenges with courage and creativity, and may be handed on as a precious gift to the new generations.

With joy and interest I have participated in this World Meeting, above all with my prayers, giving specific guidance and attentively following its preparation and development. Today, through the means of communication, I have come on a spiritual pilgrimage to this Marian Shrine, the heart of Mexico and of all America, to entrust all the world's families to Our Lady of Guadalupe.

This World Meeting of Families has aimed to encourage Christian homes so that their members may be people who are free and rich in human and Gospel values, on their way toward holiness; that is the best service that we Christians can offer contemporary society. The Christian response to the challenges that confront the family and human life in general must face consists in reinforcing trust in the Lord and the vigor that derives from faith itself, which is nourished in attentive listening to the Word of God.

How beautiful it is to gather as a family to let God speak to the hearts of its members through his living and effective Word. In prayer, especially in the recitation of the Rosary, as it was recited yesterday, the family contemplates the mysteries of the life of Jesus, interiorizes the values on which it meditates and feels called to embody them in its life.

The family is an indispensable foundation for society and for peoples, just as it is an irreplaceable good for children, whose coming into the world as the fruit of love, of the total and generous gift of their parents, deserve to be born. As Jesus demonstrated by honoring the Virgin Mary and St. Joseph, the family occupies a fundamental role in a person's upbringing. It is a true school of humanity and perennial values. No one has given life to himself.

From others we received life, which develops and matures with the truths and values that we learn in our relationship and communion with others. In this regard, the family founded on the indissoluble matrimony of a man and a woman is the expression of the relational, filial and communal dimensions. It is the setting in which men and women can be born with dignity, and can grow and develop in an integral manner (cf. *Homily at Holy Mass for the Fifth World Meeting of Families*, Valencia, July 9, 2006).

However, this educational task is complicated by a deceptive concept of freedom, in which caprice and the subjective impulses of the individual are exalted to the point of leaving each person locked within the prison of his own self. The true freedom of the human being derives from his creation in the image and likeness of God. For this reason freedom must be exercised responsibly, always opting for the authentic good so that it may become love, a gift of self. For this reason, more than theories, the intimacy and love that are characteristic of the family community are needed. It is at home that people truly learn to live, to value life and health, freedom and peace, justice and truth, work, harmony and respect.

Today more than ever the witness and public commitment of all the baptized is necessary to reaffirm the dignity and the unique, irreplaceable value of the family founded on the marriage of a man and a woman open to life, and also of human life in all of its stages.

Legal and administrative measures must be promoted that support families with their inalienable rights, necessary if they are to continue to carry out their extraordinary mission. The witnesses given at yesterday's celebration show that today too the family can stand firm in the love of God and renew humanity in the new millennium.

I wish to express my closeness and to assure my prayers for all the families that bear witness to fidelity in especially difficult circumstances. I encourage the many families who, at times living in the midst of setbacks and misunderstandings, set an example of generosity and trust in God, in the hope that they will not lack the assistance they need. I am also thinking of the families who are suffering because of poverty, sickness, marginalization or emigration and, most especially, of Christian families that are being persecuted for their faith. The Pope is very close to all of you and accompanies you in your daily efforts.

Before concluding this meeting, I am pleased to announce that the *Seventh World Meeting of Families* will take place, God willing, in Italy, in the city of Milan in the year 2012, on the theme: "The family, work and celebration." I am deeply grateful to Cardinal Dionigi Tettamanzi, Archbishop of Milan, for his kindness in accepting this important commitment.

I entrust all the families of the world to the protection of the Most Holy Virgin, so widely venerated in the noble land of Mexico under the title of Guadalupe. To her, the one who always reminds us that our happiness lies in doing Christ's will (cf. Jn 2:5), I now say:

Most Holy Mother of Guadalupe,
who have shown your love
and your tenderness to the peoples of the American continent,
fill with joy and hope all the peoples and families of the world.

We entrust to you,
who go before us and guide us on our journey of faith
toward the eternal Homeland,
the joys, the plans, the anxieties and
the desires of all families.

O Mary,
to you we turn, trusting in your tenderness as Mother.
Do not ignore the prayers we address to you
for the whole world's families
in this crucial period in history;
instead, welcome us all in your heart as Mother
and guide us on our way toward the heavenly Homeland.

Amen.

Homily at Mass with Organizers of the Sixth World Meeting of Families

April 23, 2009

Dear Friends,

A short while ago we said in the Responsorial Psalm "I will bless the Lord at all times; his praise shall continually be in my mouth" (Ps 34[33]:1). Let us praise him today for the Sixth World Meeting of Families, celebrated successfully in Mexico City last January, in whose organization and program you took part in various ways. I am deeply grateful to you. I also offer a cordial greeting to Cardinals Ennio Antonelli, President of the Pontifical Council for the Family, and Norberto Rivera Carrera, Archbishop Primate of Mexico, the leader of this pilgrimage to Rome.

In reading the Acts of the Apostles we heard from St. Peter's lips, "We must obey God rather than men" (Acts 5:29). This fully agrees with what John's Gospel tells us: "He who believes in the Son has eternal life; he who does not obey the Son shall not see life" (Jn 3:36). Thus the word of God speaks to us of an obedience that is not mere subjection nor a mere fulfillment of mandates but is born from intimate communion with God and consists in an insight that can discern what "comes from above" and "is above all." It is a fruit of the Holy Spirit which God grants "without measure."

Dear friends, our contemporaries need to discover this obedience which is not theoretical but vital, which means opting for a practical form of behavior based on obedience to God's will which renders us completely free. Christian families with their domestic life, simple and happy, sharing day after day their joys, hopes and anxieties, lived in the light of faith, are schools of obedience and an environment of true freedom. Those who have lived their marriage in accordance with God's plan for many years, like some of those present, testify to the goodness of the Lord who helps and encourages us.

Christ is truly present in the Eucharist; he is the Bread which comes down from Heaven to replenish our energy and enable us to face the effort and exertion of the journey. He is beside us. May he also be the best friend of those who are receiving First Communion today, transforming them within so that they may be his enthusiastic witnesses to others.

Let us now continue our Eucharistic celebration, invoking the loving intercession of our Heavenly Mother, Our Lady of Guadalupe, so that we may receive Jesus and have life and, strengthened with the Eucharistic Bread, may be servants of true joy for the world.

Letter to Cardinal Ennio Antonelli, President of the Pontifical Council for the Family, on the Occasion of the Seventh World Meeting of Families

August 23, 2010

Venerable Brother,
Cardinal Ennio Antonelli,
President of the Pontifical Council for the Family,

At the end of the Sixth World Meeting of Families in Mexico City in January 2009, I announced that the next Meeting of Catholic families from all over the world would take place with the Successor of Peter in Milan in 2012 on the theme "The Family: Work and Celebration." Now wishing to begin the preparations for this important event, I am glad to announce that, God willing, it will take place from May 30 to June 3. At the same time I will provide further details concerning the theme and the arrangements.

Work and celebration are closely connected with the lives of families: they condition decisions, influence relations between spouses and between parents and children and affect the relationship of the family with society and with the Church. Sacred Scripture (cf. Gn 1-2) tells us that the family, work and holidays are gifts and blessings to help us to live a fully human life. Daily experience shows that the authentic development of the person includes both the individual, family and community dimensions and functional activities and relations, as well as openness to hope and to unlimited Good.

In our day, unfortunately, the organization of work, conceived of and implemented in terms of market competition and the greatest profit, and the conception of a holiday as an opportunity to escape and to consume commodities, contribute to dispersing the family and the community and spreading an individualistic lifestyle. It is therefore necessary to promote reflection and commitment which aim at reconciling the needs and schedule of work with those of the family. They must also aim at recovering the true meaning of celebration, especially on Sunday, the weekly Easter, the day of the Lord and the day of man, the day of the family, of the community and of solidarity.

The upcoming World Meeting of Families affords a privileged opportunity to rethink work and celebration in the perspective of a family that is united and open to life, thoroughly integrated in society and in the Church, attentive to the quality of relationship in addition to the economy of the family nucleus itself. The event, to be truly fruitful, must not, therefore, remain isolated, but must fit into an adequate process of ecclesial and cultural preparation. I therefore hope that during 2011, the thirtieth anniversary of the Apostolic Exhortation *Familiaris Consortio*, the "magna carta" of the pastoral care of families, a worthwhile journey may be undertaken, promoting initiatives at parish, diocesan and national levels, which aims to shed light on experiences of work and of celebration in their truest and most positive aspects, with particular concern for their effect on the practical life of families. May Christian families and ecclesial communities of the whole world therefore feel challenged and involved, and set out promptly on their way toward "Milan 2012."

The Seventh World Meeting, like the previous ones will last for five days and will culminate with the "Feast of Testimonies" on Saturday evening and with solemn Mass on Sunday morning. These two celebrations, at both of which I shall preside, will be a gathering of the "family of families." The overall event will be especially arranged to ensure that the various dimensions complement each other: community prayer, theological and pastoral reflection, moments of brotherhood and exchanges between guest families and those that live in the area, as well as media coverage.

From this moment may the Lord reward St. Ambrose's Archdiocese of Milan with heavenly favors for its generous availability and commitment to organization, at the service of the universal Church and of families from so many nations.

As I invoke the intercession of the Holy Family of Nazareth, dedicated to daily work and assiduous in celebrating the feasts of its people, I warmly impart the Apostolic Blessing to you Venerable Brother and to your collaborators and with special affection willingly extend it to all the families involved in the preparation of the important Meeting in Milan.

CHAPTER II

To the Participants at the Plenary Assemblies of the Pontifical Council for the Family

Address to the Participants in the Plenary Assembly of the Pontifical Council for the Family

May 13, 2006

Your Eminences,
Reverend Brothers in the Episcopate and in the Priesthood,
Dear Brothers and Sisters,

It gives me great pleasure to meet you at the end of the Plenary Session of the Pontifical Council for the Family, created by my Venerable Predecessor, John Paul II, on May 9, 1981, which is celebrating its twenty-fifth anniversary in these days. I address my cordial greeting to each one of you with a special thought for Cardinal Alfonso López Trujillo, whom I thank for having interpreted your common sentiments.

This meeting has given you an opportunity to examine the challenges and pastoral projects concerning the family, rightly considered a domestic church and a sanctuary of life. It is a vast, complex and delicate field of apostolate to which you devote energy and enthusiasm, with the intention of promoting the "Gospel of the family and of life." In this regard, how can we forget the broad and far-sighted vision of my Predecessors and especially of John Paul II, who have courageously promoted the cause of the family, considering it a decisive and irreplaceable value for the common good of the peoples?

The family, founded on marriage, is the "patrimony of humanity," a fundamental social institution; it is the vital cell and pillar of society and this concerns believers and non-believers alike. It is a reality that all States must hold in the highest regard because, as John Paul II liked to repeat, "the future of humanity passes by way of the family" (*Familiaris Consortio*, no. 86).

In the Christian vision, moreover, marriage, which Christ raised to the most exalted dignity of a sacrament, confers greater splendor and depth on the conjugal bond and more powerfully binds the spouses who, blessed by the Lord of the Covenant, promise each other faithfulness until death in love that is open to life.

For them, the Lord is the center and heart of the family. He accompanies them in their union and sustains them in their mission to raise children to maturity. In this way the Christian family not only cooperates with God in generating natural life, but also in cultivating the seeds of divine life given in Baptism. These are the well-known principles of the Christian view of marriage and the family. I recalled them once again last Thursday, when I spoke to the members of the John Paul II Institute for Studies on Marriage and the Family.

In today's world, where certain erroneous concepts concerning the human being, freedom and love are spreading, we must never tire of presenting anew the truth about the family institution, as God has desired it since creation. Unfortunately, the number of separations and divorces is increasing.

They destroy family unity and create numerous problems for children, the innocent victims of these situations. In our day it is especially the stability of the family that is at risk; to safeguard it one often has to swim against the tide of the prevalent culture, and this demands patience, effort, sacrifice and the ceaseless quest for mutual understanding. Today, however, it is possible for husbands and wives to overcome their difficulties and remain faithful to their vocation with recourse to God's support, with prayer and participating devotedly in the sacraments, especially the Eucharist. The unity and strength of families helps society to breathe the genuine human values and to be open to the Gospel. The apostolate of many of the Movements called to work in this context in harmonious understanding with the dioceses and parishes contributes to this.

Furthermore, a particularly sensitive topic today is the respect due to the human embryo, which ought always to be born from an act of love and should already be treated as a person (cf. *Evangelium Vitae*, no. 60). The progress of science and technology in the area of bioethics is transformed into a threat when human beings lose the sense of their own limitations and, in practice, claim to replace God the Creator. The Encyclical *Humanae Vitae* reasserts clearly that human procreation must always be the fruit of the conjugal act with its twofold unitive and procreative meaning (cf. no. 12).

The greatness of conjugal love in accordance with the divine plan demands it, as I recalled in the Encyclical *Deus Caritas Est*: "*Eros*, reduced to pure 'sex,' has become a commodity, a mere 'thing' to be bought and sold, or rather, man himself becomes a commodity. . . . Here we are actually dealing with a debasement of the human body" (no. 5).

Thanks to God, many, especially young people, are rediscovering the value of chastity, which appears more and more as a reliable guarantee of authentic love. The historical period in which we live asks Christian families to witness with courageous coherence to the fact that procreation is the fruit of love. Such a witness will not fail to encourage politicians and legislators to safeguard the rights of the family. Indeed, it is well known that juridical solutions for the so-called "de facto" unions are gaining credibility; although they reject the obligations of marriage, they claim enjoyment of the same rights.

Furthermore, at times there are even attempts to give marriage a new definition in order to legalize homosexual unions, attributing to them the right to adopt children. Vast areas of the world are suffering from the so-called "demographic winter," with the consequent gradual ageing of the population. Families sometimes seem ensnared by the fear of life and of parenthood. It is necessary to restore their trust, so that they can continue to carry out their noble mission of procreation in love.

I am grateful to your Pontifical Council because at various continental and national meetings, it seeks to enter into dialogue with those who have political and legislative responsibility in this regard, as it also strives to set up a vast network of conversations with Bishops, offering the local Churches the opportunity of courses for those with pastoral responsibilities.

Next, I take this opportunity to repeat my invitation to all the diocesan communities to take part with their delegations in the Fifth World Meeting of Families that will take place next July in Valencia, Spain, and in which, please God, I will have the joy of participating.

Thank you again for your work; may the Lord continue to make it fruitful! For this I assure you of my remembrance in prayer while, invoking Mary's motherly protection, I impart to all of you my Blessing, which I willingly extend to families so that they will continue to build their homes on the model of the Holy Family of Nazareth.

Address to the Participants in the Plenary
Assembly of the Pontifical Council for the Family

April 5, 2008

Your Eminences,
Venerable Brothers in the Episcopate and in the Priesthood,
Dear Brothers and Sisters,

I am pleased to meet you at the end of the Eighteenth Plenary Assembly
of the Pontifical Council for the Family on the theme: *"Grandparents: their
witness and presence in the family."* I thank you for accepting my suggestion at
the Meeting in Valencia when I said: "In no way should [grandparents] ever
be excluded from the family circle. They are a treasure which the younger
generation should not be denied, especially when they bear witness to their
faith" (*Address at the Fifth World Meeting of Families*, Valencia, July 8, 2006). I
greet in particular Cardinal Ricardo Vidal, Archbishop of Cebu and a member of the Committee of the Presidency, who has expressed your common
sentiments, and I address an affectionate thought to dear Cardinal Alfonso
López Trujillo who has guided this Dicastery with passion and competence
for eighteen years. We miss him and offer him our best wishes for a prompt
recovery, together with our prayers.

The theme you have discussed is very familiar to all. Who does not remember their grandparents? Who can forget their presence and their witness by
the domestic hearth? How many of us bear their names as a sign of continuity
and gratitude! It is a custom in families, after their departure, to remember
their birthdays with the celebration of Mass for the repose of their souls and
if possible, a visit to the cemetery. These and other gestures of love and faith
are a manifestation of our gratitude to them. They gave themselves, they sacrificed themselves for us, and in certain cases also gave their lives.

The Church has always paid special attention to grandparents, recognizing them as a great treasure from both the human and social, as well as
religious and spiritual viewpoints. My venerable Predecessors Paul VI and
John Paul II—we have just celebrated the third anniversary of the latter's
death—emphasized on various occasions the Ecclesial Community's respect
for the elderly, for their dedication and their spirituality. In particular, during
the Jubilee of the Year 2000, John Paul II summoned the world's elderly to
St. Peter's Square in September and said on that occasion: "Despite the limitations brought on by age, I continue to enjoy life. For this I thank the Lord.
It is wonderful to be able to give oneself to the very end for the sake of the
Kingdom of God!" These words were contained in the Letter that about a

year earlier, in October 1999, he had addressed to the elderly and which have preserved intact their human, social and cultural timeliness.

Your Plenary Assembly has discussed the theme of grandparents' presence in the family, the Church and society with a look that can include the past, present and future. Let us briefly analyze these three moments. In the past, grandparents had an important role in the life and growth of the family. Even with their advancing age they continued to be present with their children, their grandchildren and even their great-grandchildren, giving a living witness of caring, sacrifice and a daily gift of themselves without reserve. They were witnesses of a personal and community history that continued to live on in their memories and in their wisdom. Today, the economic and social evolution has brought profound transformations to the life of families. The elderly, including many grandparents, find themselves in a sort of "parking area": some realize they are a burden to their family and prefer to live alone or in retirement homes with all the consequences that such decisions entail.

Unfortunately, it seems that the "culture of death" is advancing on many fronts and is also threatening the season of old-age. With growing insistence, people are even proposing euthanasia as a solution for resolving certain difficult situations. Old age, with its problems that are also linked to the new family and social contexts because of modern development, should be evaluated carefully and always in the light of the truth about man, the family and the community. It is always necessary to react strongly to what dehumanizes society. Parish and diocesan communities are forcefully challenged by these problems and are seeking today to meet the needs of the elderly. Ecclesial movements and associations exist which have embraced this important and urgent cause. It is necessary to join forces to defeat together all forms of marginalization, for it is not only they—grandfathers, grandmothers, senior citizens—who are being injured by the individualistic mindset, but everyone. If grandparents, as is said often and on many sides, are a precious resource, it is necessary to put into practice coherent choices that allow them to be better valued.

May grandparents return to being a living presence in the family, in the Church and in society. With regard to the family, may grandparents continue to be witnesses of unity, of values founded on fidelity and of a unique love that gives rise to faith and the joy of living. The so-called new models of the family and a spreading relativism have weakened these fundamental values of the family nucleus. The evils of our society—as you justly observed during your work—are in need of urgent remedies. In the face of the crisis of the family, might it not be possible to set out anew precisely from the presence and witness of these people—grandparents—whose values and projects are more resilient? Indeed, it is impossible to plan the future without referring to a past full of significant experiences and spiritual and moral reference points. Thinking of grandparents, of their testimony of love and fidelity to life, reminds us of the Biblical figures of Abraham and Sarah, of Elizabeth and Zechariah, of Joachim and Anne, as well as of the elderly Simeon and Anna and even Nicodemus: they all remind us that at every age the Lord asks each one for the contribution of his or her own talents.

Let us now turn our gaze toward the sixth World Meeting of Families which will be celebrated in Mexico in January 2009. I greet and thank Cardinal Norberto Rivera Carrera, Archbishop of Mexico, present here, for all he has already done in these months of preparation together with his collaborators. All Christian families of the world look to this Nation, "ever faithful" to the Church, which will open the doors to all the families of the world. I invite the Ecclesial Communities, especially family groups, movements and associations of families, to prepare themselves spiritually for this event of grace. Venerable and dear Brothers, I thank you once again for your visit and for the work you have done during these days; I assure you of my remembrance in prayer and cordially impart the Apostolic Blessing to you and to your loved ones.

Address to the Participants in the Plenary Assembly of the Pontifical Council for the Family

February 8, 2010

Your Eminences,
Venerable Brothers in the Episcopate,
Dear Brothers and Sisters,

At the beginning of the Nineteenth Plenary Assembly of the Pontifical Council for the Family I am glad to greet you with my cordial welcome! This year the institutional event sees your Dicastery particularly renewed. Not only does it have a new Cardinal President and Bishop Secretary but also several Cardinals and Bishops on the Administrative Committee and some new Officials and married couple Members, as well as numerous new consultors. As I warmly thank those who have finished their service at the Pontifical Council and those who are still contributing their invaluable work to it, I invoke upon everyone abundant gifts from the Lord. My grateful thoughts go in particular to the late Cardinal Alfonso López Trujillo who led your Dicastery for eighteen years with passionate dedication to the cause of the family and of life in today's world. Lastly, I would like to express to Cardinal

Ennio Antonelli my warmest gratitude for his cordial words on behalf of you all and for having wished to illustrate the topics of this important Assembly.

The activities of the Dicastery today fit between the Sixth World Meeting of Families celebrated in Mexico City in 2009, and the Seventh, scheduled to take place in Milan in 2012. While I renew my gratitude to Cardinal Norberto Rivera Carrera for the generous work of his Archdiocese for the preparation and realization of the Meeting in 2009, I express from this moment my affectionate gratitude to the Ambrosian Church and to her Pastor, Cardinal Dionigi Tettamanzi, for his willingness to host the Seventh World Meeting of Families. In addition to arranging these extraordinary events, in order to increase knowledge of the fundamental value of the family for the life of the Church and of society, the Pontifical Council is carrying ahead various initiatives. They include the project "The Family, a Subject of Evangelization," with which it intends to prepare a collection from across the world of valid experiences in the different contexts of the pastoral care of the family, so that they may serve as inspiration and encouragement for new initiatives. They also include "The Family, a Resource for Society," with which the Council aims to introduce into public opinion the benefits that the family brings to society, to its coherence and to its development.

Another of the Dicastery's important tasks is the compilation of a *Vademecum* for preparation for Marriage. My beloved Predecessor, Venerable John Paul II, said in his Apostolic Exhortation *Familiaris Consortio* that this preparation is "more than ever necessary in our times," and that it must be "seen and put into practice as a gradual and continuous process. It includes three main stages: remote, proximate and immediate" (no. 66). With reference to these instructions, the Dicastery proposes to outline properly the features of the three states of this formation process and the response to the vocation to married life. Remote preparation concerns children, adolescents and young people. It involves the family, the parish and school, places in which they are taught to understand life as a vocation to love, which is subsequently specified in the form of marriage or of virginity for the Kingdom of Heaven, but is always a vocation to love. In this stage, furthermore, the meaning of sexuality must gradually emerge as a relational capacity and a positive energy to be integrated into authentic love. The proximate preparation concerns engaged couples and must become a journey of faith and Christian life which leads to deeper knowledge of the mystery of Christ, of the Church and of the meaning of grace and responsibility in marriage (cf. ibid.). Its duration and the way in which it is undertaken will necessarily differ according to situations, possibilities and needs. However, it is to be hoped that it will offer a course of catecheses, as well as accounts of experiences in the Christian community. All this should provide for the interventions of the priest and of various experts, as well as the presence of animators, the guidance of a few exemplary couples of Christian spouses, dialogue with the future spouses individually and as a group, and an atmosphere of friendship and prayer. In addition, it is necessary to take pains to ensure that on this occasion the engaged couple revive their personal relationship with the Lord Jesus, especially by listening to the word of God, by receiving the Sacraments and above all by taking part in the Eucharist. It is only by making Christ the center of their personal life and their life as a couple that authentic love and self-giving to others is possible: "He who abides in me, and I in him, he it is that bears much fruit, for apart from me you can do nothing," Jesus reminds us (Jn 15:5). The immediate preparation takes place just before the marriage. In addition to the examination of those to be married as prescribed by Canon Law, preparation may include catechesis on the Rite of Marriage and its meaning, spiritual retreats and guidance. These aim to guarantee that the celebration of marriage is perceived by the faithful and particularly by those who are preparing for it as a gift to the entire Church that contributes to her spiritual development. It is also right that Bishops promote the sharing of significant experiences and offer incentives for serious pastoral commitment in this important area. They should pay special attention to ensuring that the vocation of the spouses becomes an enrichment for the whole Christian community and especially in today's context a missionary and prophetic witness.

Your Plenary Assembly has "The Rights of the Child" as its theme. This was chosen with reference to the twentieth anniversary of the Convention approved by the United Nations General Assembly in 1989. Following Christ's example, the Church down the centuries has encouraged the protection of the dignity and rights of minors and has taken care of them in many ways. Unfortunately in various cases some of her members, acting in opposition to this commitment, have violated these rights: conduct which she does not and will not fail to deplore and condemn. The tenderness and teaching of Jesus, who saw children as a model to imitate in order to enter the Kingdom of God (cf. Mt 18:1-6; 19:13-14), have always constituted a pressing appeal to foster deep respect and care for them. Jesus' harsh words against those who cause one of these little ones to sin (cf. Mk 9:42), engage everyone always to adhere to this degree of respect and love. Thus the Convention on the Rights of the Child was accepted favorably by the Holy See since it contains positive statements on adoption, health care, education, the protection of the disabled and the defense of little ones against violence, neglect and sexual or labor exploitation.

In its Preamble the Convention describes the family "as a natural environment for the growth and wellbeing of all its members and of children in particular." Indeed, it is precisely the family founded on the marriage between a man and a woman that can give children the greatest help. They want to be loved by a mother and a father who love each other, and they need to live and grow together with both their parents, because the maternal and paternal figures are complementary in the raising of children and the development of their personality and identity. It is therefore important that everything possible be done to enable them to grow up in a united and stable family. To this end, it is necessary to urge spouses never to lose sight of the profound reasons and sacramentality of the conjugal covenant and to strengthen it by listening to the word of God and by prayer, constant dialogue, reciprocal acceptance and mutual forgiveness. A family environment that is not serene, the separation of the parental couple, particularly with divorce, is not without consequences on the children. On the other hand, supporting the family and promoting its true good, its rights, its unity and its stability is the best way to protect the rights and authentic needs of minors.

Venerable and dear Brothers and Sisters, thank you for your visit! I am spiritually close to you and to the work you carry out in favor of families and I cordially impart the Apostolic Blessing to each one of you and to all who share in this precious service to the Church.

Address to the Participants in the Plenary Assembly of the Pontifical Council for the Family

December 1, 2011

Your Eminences,
Venerable Brothers in the Episcopate and in the Priesthood,
Dear Brothers and Sisters,

I am pleased to welcome you on the occasion of the Plenary Assembly of the Pontifical Council for the Family, on a double thirtieth anniversary: that of the Apostolic Exhortation *Familiaris Consortio*, published on November 22, 1981 by Bl. John Paul II and of the Dicastery itself, which he established on March 9 with the Motu Proprio *Familia a Deo instituta*, as a sign of the importance to be attributed to the family apostolate in the world and at the same time, as an effective tool to help promote it at every level (cf. John Paul II, *Familiaris Consortio*, no. 73). I cordially greet Cardinal Ennio Antonelli, thanking him for his words introducing our meeting, as well as the Bishop Secretary, the staff and all of you gathered here.

The new evangelization depends largely on the Domestic Church (cf. ibid., no. 65). In our time, as in times past, the eclipse of God, the spread of ideologies contrary to the family and the degradation of sexual ethics are connected. And just as the eclipse of God and the crisis of the family are linked, so the new evangelization is inseparable from the Christian family. The family is indeed the *way* of the Church because it is the "human space" of our encounter with Christ. Spouses, "not only receive the love of Christ and become a saved community, but they are also called upon to communicate Christ's love to their brethren, thus becoming a saving community" (ibid., no. 49). The family founded on the Sacrament of Marriage is a particular realization of the Church, saved and saving, evangelized and evangelizing community. Just like the Church, it is called to welcome, radiate and show the world the love and presence of Christ. The reception and transmission of divine love are realized in the mutual commitment of the spouses, in generous and responsible procreation, in the care and education of children, work and social relationships, with attention to the needy, in participation in church activities, in commitment to civil society. The Christian Family to the extent it succeeds in living love as communion and service as a reciprocal gift open to all, as a journey of permanent conversion supported by the grace of God, reflects the splendor of Christ in the world and the beauty of the divine Trinity. St. Augustine has a famous phrase: *"immo vero vides Trinitatem, si caritatem vides"*—"Well, if you see charity, yes indeed you see the Trinity" (*De Trinitate*, VIII, 8). And the family is one of the fundamental places where you live and are educated in love and charity.

In the wake of my Predecessors, I too have repeatedly urged Christian spouses to evangelize both with their witness of life and their involvement in pastoral activities. I did so recently in Ancona, at the end of the Italian National Eucharistic Congress. There I wanted to meet with couples and priests. In fact, the two sacraments called "at the service of communion" (CCC, no. 1534), Holy Orders and Matrimony, are traced to the sole source of the Eucharist "both these states of life share the same root in the love of Christ who gives himself for humanity's salvation. They are called to a common mission: to witness to, and make present, this love at the service of the community in order to build up the People of God. . . . This perspective makes it possible to overcome a reductive vision of the family, which sees it merely as the object of pastoral action. . . . The family is a source of wealth for married couples, an irreplaceable good for children, an indispensable foundation of society and a vital community for the journey of the Church" (*Homily in Ancona*, September 11, 2011). By virtue of this the "family is the privileged place of human and Christian education and remains, for this end, as the closest ally of the priestly ministry. . . . No vocation is a private matter, and even less so is the vocation to marriage because its horizon is the entire Church" (ibid.).

There are some areas where the role of Christian families, in collaboration with priests and under the guidance of Bishops, is particularly urgent: the education of children, adolescents and young people in loving, understood as gift of self and communion; the preparation of engaged couples for married life with a journey of faith; the formation of married couples, especially young couples; the experiences of associations with charitable and educational purposes, and civic commitment; and the pastoral care of families for families, a life-long commitment, giving due value to the time dedicated to work and to rest.

Dear friends, we are preparing for the Seventh World Meeting of Families to be held in Milan from May 30 to June 3, 2012. It will be a great joy for me and for us all to come together, to pray and to celebrate with the families who will come from around the world, accompanied by their Pastors. I thank the Ambrosian Church for her great effort made so far and for that in the coming months. I invite the families of Milan and Lombardy to open the doors of their houses to accommodate the pilgrims who will come from all over the world. In hospitality we experience joy and enthusiasm: it is nice to make acquaintances and friendships, recounting the experience of family life and the faith experience associated with it. In my Letter convoking the Meeting in Milan I asked for "an adequate process of ecclesial and cultural preparation," so that the event will be a success and actively involve the Christian communities around the world. I thank those who have already taken steps in that direction and call on those who have not yet done so to make the most of the next few months. Your Dicastery has already provided valuable help in drawing up a catechism with the theme "The Family: Work and Rest"; it has also proposed a "family week" for the parishes, associations and movements, and other praiseworthy initiatives.

Thank you again for coming and for the work you do to promote the family at the service of the Gospel. While I assure you of my remembrance in prayer. I impart a special heartfelt Apostolic Blessing to each one of you and your loved ones.

CHAPTER III

To the Meetings and the National Days of the Family

Message to Bishops Who Lead Episcopal Commissions for the Family and Life in Latin America and the Caribbean

March 28, 2011

To my Venerable Brother,
Cardinal Ennio Antonelli,
President of the Pontifical Council for the Family,

I am pleased to greet you cordially, Your Eminence, and the other cardinals, bishops and priests who are participating in the meeting of the leaders of the Episcopal Commissions for the Family and Life of Latin America and the Caribbean, which is taking place in Bogotá.

As I reiterated in the Fifth General Conference of the Episcopate of Latin America and the Caribbean, the family is the value dearest to the peoples of those noble lands. For this reason, family ministry has an important part to play in the evangelizing activity of each of the different particular Churches, promoting a culture of life and working to ensure that the rights of families are recognized and respected.

One notes, however, with sadness, that homes are coming under increasingly adverse conditions caused by rapid cultural changes, by social instability, by the flows of migrants, by poverty, by educational programs that trivialize sexuality and by false ideologies. We cannot remain indifferent to these challenges. In the Gospel we find the light needed to respond to them without losing heart. Christ with his grace urges us to work with diligence and enthusiasm to accompany each one of the family members in discovering God's plan of love for the human person. No effort is therefore wasted in promoting anything that can help to ensure that each family, founded on the indissoluble union between a man and a woman, accomplishes its mission of being a living cell of society, a nursery of virtues, a school of constructive and peaceful coexistence, an instrument of harmony and a privileged environment in which human life is welcomed and protected, joyfully and responsibly, from its beginning until its natural end.

It is also worthwhile to continue to encourage parents in their fundamental right and obligation to educate the new generations in faith and in the values that ennoble human existence.

I have no doubt that the continental mission launched in Aparecida, and which is awakening so many hopes everywhere, will serve to revive the pastoral care of marriage and the family in the beloved countries of Latin America and the Caribbean. The Church can count on Christian families, calling them to be true instruments of evangelization and of the apostolate and inviting them to become aware of their invaluable mission in the world.

I therefore encourage all the participants in this important meeting to develop in their reflections the broad pastoral themes outlined by the bishops gathered in Aparecida. Thus they will enable the family to experience a profound encounter with Christ through listening to His Word, prayer, sacramental life and the practice of charity.

In this way, one will help put into practice a solid spiritual life that encourages in all its members a strong aspiration to holiness, without fear of displaying the beauty of the high ideals and ethical and moral demands of life in Christ. To promote this, it is necessary to develop further the training of all those who, in one way or another, are dedicated to the evangelization of families. It is likewise important to plot ways for collaboration with all men and women of good will in order to continue to safeguard intensely all human life, marriage and the family, throughout the region.

I conclude by expressing my affection and solidarity to all the families of Latin America and the Caribbean, particularly those who find themselves in difficult situations. As I entrust to the powerful protection of the Most Holy Virgin Mary the fruits of this laudable initiative, I impart to you a heartfelt Apostolic Blessing, which I extend with great pleasure to those engaged in the evangelization and the promotion of the well-being of families.

Homily at Mass for the National Day of Croatian Catholic Families

June 5, 2011

Dear Brothers and Sisters!

In this Mass at which it is my joy to preside, concelebrating with numerous brothers in the Episcopate and with a great number of priests, I give thanks to the Lord for all the beloved families gathered here, and for all the others who are linked with us through radio and television. I offer particular thanks to Cardinal Josip Bozanić, Archbishop of Zagreb, for his kind words at the beginning of this Mass. I address my greetings to all and express my great affection with an embrace of peace!

We have recently celebrated the Ascension of the Lord and we prepare ourselves to receive the great gift of the Holy Spirit. In the first reading, we saw how the apostolic community was united in prayer in the Upper Room with Mary, the mother of Jesus (cf. Acts 1:12-14). This is a picture of the Church with deep roots in the paschal event: indeed, the Upper Room is the place where Jesus instituted the Eucharist and the priesthood during the Last Supper, and where, having risen from the dead, he poured out the Holy Spirit upon the Apostles on the evening of Easter Sunday (cf. Jn 20:19-23). The Lord directed his disciples "not to depart from Jerusalem, but to wait for the promise of the Father" (Acts 1:4); he asked that *they might remain together* to prepare themselves to receive the gift of the Holy Spirit. And they gathered together in prayer with Mary in the Upper Room, waiting for the promised event (cf. Acts 1:14). Remaining together was the condition given by Jesus for them to experience the coming of the Paraclete, and prolonged prayer served to maintain them in harmony with one another. We find here a formidable lesson for every Christian community. Sometimes it is thought that missionary efficacy depends primarily upon careful planning and its intelligent implementation by means of specific action. Certainly, the Lord asks for our cooperation, but his initiative has to come first, before any response from us: his Spirit is the true protagonist of the Church, to be invoked and welcomed.

In the Gospel, we heard the first part of the so-called "high-priestly prayer" of Jesus (cf. Jn 17:1-11a)—at the conclusion of his farewell discourses—full of trust, sweetness and love. It is called "the high-priestly prayer" because in it Jesus is presented as a priest interceding for his people as he prepares to leave this world. The passage is dominated by the double theme of the *hour* and the *glory*. It deals with the hour of death (cf. Jn 2:4; 7:30; 8:20), the hour in which the Christ must pass from this world to the Father (13:1). But at the same time it is also the hour of his glorification which is accomplished by means of the Cross, called by John the Evangelist "exaltation," namely the raising up, the elevation to glory: the hour of the death of Jesus, the hour of supreme love, is the hour of his highest glory. For the Church too, for every Christian, the highest glory is the Cross, which means living in charity, in total gift to God and to others.

Dear brothers and sisters! I very willingly accepted the invitation given to me by the Bishops of Croatia to visit this country on the occasion of the first National Gathering of Croatian Catholic Families. I express my sincere appreciation for this attention and commitment to the family, not only because today this basic human reality, in your nation as elsewhere, has to face difficulties and threats, and thus has special need of evangelization and support, but also because Christian families are a decisive resource for education in the faith, for the up-building of the Church as a communion and for her missionary presence in the most diverse situations in life. I know the generosity and the dedication with which you, dear Pastors, serve the Lord and the Church. Your daily labor for the faith formation of future generations, as well as for marriage preparation and for the accompaniment of families, is the fundamental path for regenerating the Church anew and for giving life to the social fabric of the nation. May you remain dedicated to this important pastoral commitment!

Everyone knows that the Christian family is a special sign of the presence and love of Christ and that it is called to give a specific and irreplaceable contribution to evangelization. Blessed John Paul II, who visited this noble country three times, said that "the Christian family is called upon to take part actively and responsibly in the mission of the Church in a way that is original and specific, by placing itself, in what it is and what it does as an "'intimate community of life and love,' at the service of the Church and of society" (*Familiaris Consortio*, no. 50). The Christian family has always been the first way of transmitting the faith and still today retains great possibilities for evangelization in many areas.

Dear parents, commit yourselves always to teach your children to pray, and pray with them; draw them close to the Sacraments, especially to the Eucharist, as we celebrate the 600th anniversary of the Eucharistic miracle of Ludbreg; and introduce them to the life of the Church; in the intimacy of the home do not be afraid to read the sacred Scriptures, illuminating family life with the light of faith and praising God as Father. Be like a little Upper Room, like that of Mary and the disciples, in which to live unity, communion and prayer!

By the grace of God, many Christian families today are acquiring an ever deeper awareness of their missionary vocation, and are devoting themselves seriously to bearing witness to Christ the Lord. Blessed John Paul II once said: "An authentic family, founded on marriage, is in itself 'good news' for the world." And he added: "In our time the families that collaborate actively in evangelization are ever more numerous [. . .] the hour of the family has arrived in the Church, which is also the hour of the missionary family" (*Angelus*, October 21, 2001). In today's society the presence of exemplary Christian families is more necessary and urgent than ever. Unfortunately, we are forced to acknowledge the spread of a secularization which leads to the exclusion of God from life and the increasing disintegration of the family, especially in Europe. Freedom without commitment to the truth is made into an absolute, and individual well-being through the consumption of material goods and transient experiences is cultivated as an ideal, obscuring the quality of inter-personal relations and deeper human values; love is reduced to sentimental emotion and to the gratification of instinctive impulses, without a commit-ment to build lasting bonds of reciprocal belonging and without openness to life. We are called to oppose such a mentality! Alongside what the Church says, the testimony and commitment of the Christian family—your concrete testimony—is very important, especially when you affirm the inviolability of human life from conception until natural death, the singular and irreplace-able value of the family founded upon matrimony and the need for legislation which supports families in the task of giving birth to children and educating them. Dear families, be courageous! Do not give in to that secularized men-tality which proposes living together as a preparation, or even a substitute for marriage! Show by the witness of your lives that it is possible, like Christ, to love without reserve, and do not be afraid to make a commitment to another person! Dear families, rejoice in fatherhood and motherhood! Openness to life is a sign of openness to the future, confidence in the future, just as respect for the natural moral law frees people, rather than demeaning them! The good of the family is also the good of the Church. I would like to repeat some-thing I have said in the past: "the edification of each individual Christian family fits into the context of the larger family of the Church which supports it and carries it with her . . . And the Church is reciprocally built up by the family, a 'small domestic church'" (Address of His Holiness Benedict XVI to the Participants in the Ecclesial Diocesan Convention of Rome, June 6, 2005). Let us pray to the Lord, that families may come more and more to be small churches and that ecclesial communities may take on more and more the quality of a family!

Dear Croatian families, living the communion of faith and charity, be ever more transparent witnesses to the promise that the Lord, ascending into heaven, makes to each one of us: "I am with you always, to the close of the age" (Mt 28:20). Dear Croatian Christians, hear yourselves called to evangelize with the whole of your life; hear the powerful word of the Lord: "Go therefore and make disciples of all nations" (Mt 28:19). May the Virgin Mary, Queen of Croatia, accompany you always on your way. Amen! Praised be Jesus and Mary!

Regina Caeli

June 5, 2011

Dear Brothers and Sisters!

Before concluding this solemn celebration, I wish to thank you for your fervent and devout participation, through which you express your love and your commitment to the family, as Bishop Župan—to whom I also express my warm gratitude—has just reminded us.

I have come here today to confirm you in your faith. This is the gift I bring you: the faith of Peter, the faith of the Church! But at the same time you give me this same faith, enriched with your experience, your joys and sufferings. In a special way you give me your faith lived in the family, so that I may keep it in the patrimony of the whole Church.

I know that you find great strength in Mary, the Mother of Christ and our Mother. So we now turn to her, spiritually oriented toward her Shrine at Marija Bistrica, and we entrust to her all Croatian families: parents, children, grandparents; the journey of husband and wife, the task of education, professional activities and home-making. We invoke her intercession that public institutions may always sustain the family, the basic cell of the social fabric.

Dear Brothers and Sisters, within a year we will celebrate the Seventh World Meeting of Families in Milan. We entrust to our Lady the preparation of this important church event.

Message for the Second National Congress for the Family in Ecuador

November 1, 2011

To my Venerable Brother,
Metropolitan Archbishop Antonio Arregui Yarza of Guayaquil,
President of the Bishops' Conference of Ecuador,

On the occasion of the Second National Congress for the Family I greet with affection the pastors and faithful of the Church in Ecuador, which—in the context of the Continental Mission, proposed by the Latin American and Caribbean Bishops' Conferences at Aparecida, and in preparation for the Seventh World Meeting for Families that will take place in Milan—will seek to begin a process of reflection on the Gospel that will enable married Christians and their homes to respond to their identity, vocation and mission.

The theme of the Congress, "The Ecuadorian Family on Mission: Work and Rest at the Service of the Individual and of the Common Good," recognizes that the family, born from the covenant of love and of the total and sincere reciprocal gift of a man and a woman in marriage, is not a private affair, closed in on itself. By its vocation it carries out a marvelous service, crucial to the good of society and to the Church's mission. In fact, society is not the mere sum of individuals but rather the fruit of relationships between people: between husband and wife, parents and children, and between siblings, relationships which are founded on family life and the bonds of love that stem from it. Through children each family gives society the human riches it has experienced. It can rightly be said that the health and quality of social relations depend on the health and quality of family relationships.

In this regard, work and rest especially concern and are deeply bound to family life: they condition its decisions, influence relationships between the spouses and between parents and children and affect the family's ties with society and with the Church.

Through work, human beings experience themselves as subjects who share in God's plan of creation. Hence the lack of work and its precariousness threaten human dignity. Not only do they create situations of injustice and poverty that degenerate all too often into despair, crime and violence but they even cause people to have an identity crisis. It is, therefore, urgent to find effective measures, serious and appropriate projects, as well as the necessary determination to find ways to enable all to have access to a dignified, permanent and well paid job. This will enable them to be sanctified and to play an active role in the development of society, combining hard and responsible work with sufficient time for a rich, fruitful and harmonious family life. A serene and constructive home atmosphere, with its domestic duties and affections, is the first school of work and the best place for people to discover their potential, increase their eagerness to improve themselves and to achieve their noblest aspirations. Furthermore, family life teaches people to overcome selfishness, to foster solidarity, not to scorn sacrifice for the happiness of others, to value what is good and upright and to apply themselves with conviction and generosity for the benefit of the commonweal and for each other's good, inasmuch as they are responsible for themselves, for others and for the surrounding context.

Rest, for its part, humanizes time by opening it to the encounter with God, with others and with nature. It follows that families need to recover the genuine feeling of rest, especially on Sunday, the Day of the Lord and of man. In the celebration of Sunday Mass the family experiences here and now the Real Presence of the Risen Lord, receives new life, welcomes the gift of the Spirit, increases its love for the Church, listens to God's word, shares the Eucharistic Bread and opens to brotherly love.

With these sentiments, while I renew the expression of my closeness and cordiality to the most beloved sons and daughters of this nation, I entrust the results of this Congress to the powerful intercession of *Nuestra Señora de la Presentación del Quinché*, the heavenly Patroness of Ecuador. As a pledge of abundant divine favors, I gladly impart to everyone present the implored Apostolic Blessing.

CHAPTER IV

To the Pontifical Academy for Life

Address to Participants in the Twelfth General Assembly of the Pontifical Academy for Life and Congress on "The Human Embryo in the Pre-Implantation Phase"

February 27, 2006

Venerable Brothers in the Episcopate and in the Priesthood,
Distinguished Ladies and Gentlemen,

I address a respectful and cordial greeting to everyone on the occasion of the General Assembly of the Pontifical Academy for Life and the International Congress on: *"The human embryo in the pre-implantation phase,"* which has just begun.

I greet in particular Cardinal Javier Lozano Barragàn, President of the Pontifical Council for Health Pastoral Care, as well as Bishop Elio Sgreccia, President of the Pontifical Academy for Life, whom I thank for the kind words with which he has presented clearly the special interest of the themes treated on this occasion, and I greet Cardinal-elect Carlo Caffarra, a long-standing friend.

Indeed, the study topic chosen for your Assembly, *"The human embryo in the pre-implantation phase,"* that is, in the very first days subsequent to conception, is an extremely important issue today, both because of the obvious repercussions on philosophical-anthropological and ethical thought, and also because of the prospects applicable in the context of the biomedical and juridical sciences.

It is certainly a fascinating topic, however difficult and demanding it may be, given the delicate nature of the subject under examination and the complexity of the epistemological problems that concern the relationship between the revelation of facts at the level of the experimental sciences and the consequent, necessary anthropological reflection on values.

As it is easy to see, neither Sacred Scripture nor the oldest Christian Tradition can contain any explicit treatment of your theme. St. Luke, nevertheless, testifies to the active, though hidden, presence of the two infants.

He recounts the meeting of the Mother of Jesus, who had conceived him in her virginal womb only a few days earlier, with the mother of John the Baptist, who was already in the sixth month of her pregnancy: "When Elizabeth heard Mary's greeting, the baby leapt in her womb" (Lk 1:41).

St Ambrose comments: Elizabeth "perceived the arrival of Mary, he (John) perceived the arrival of the Lord the woman, the arrival of the Woman, the child, the arrival of the Child" (*Comm. in Luc.* 2:19, 22-26).

Even in the absence of explicit teaching on the very first days of life of the unborn child, it is possible to find valuable information in Sacred Scripture that elicits sentiments of admiration and respect for the newly conceived human being, especially in those who, like you, are proposing to study the mystery of human procreation.

The sacred books, in fact, set out to show God's love for every human being even before he has been formed in his mother's womb.

"Before I formed you in the womb I knew you, and before you were born I consecrated you" (Jer 1:5), God said to the Prophet Jeremiah. And the Psalmist recognizes with gratitude: "You did form my inward parts, you did knit me together in my mother's womb. I praise you, for you are fearful and wonderful. Wonderful are your works! You know me right well" (Ps 139[138]:13-14). These words acquire their full, rich meaning when one thinks that God intervenes directly in the creation of the soul of every new human being.

God's love does not differentiate between the newly conceived infant still in his or her mother's womb and the child or young person, or the adult and the elderly person. God does not distinguish between them because he sees an impression of his own image and likeness (Gn 1:26) in each one. He makes no distinctions because he perceives in all of them a reflection of the face of his Only-begotten Son, whom "he chose . . . before the foundation of the world . . . . He destined us in love to be his sons . . . according to the purpose of his will" (Eph 1:4-6).

This boundless and almost incomprehensible love of God for the human being reveals the degree to which the human person deserves to be loved in himself, independently of any other consideration—intelligence, beauty, health, youth, integrity, and so forth. In short, human life is always a good, for it "is a manifestation of God in the world, a sign of his presence, a trace of his glory" (*Evangelium Vitae*, no. 34).

Indeed, the human person has been endowed with a very exalted dignity, which is rooted in the intimate bond that unites him with his Creator: a reflection of God's own reality shines out in the human person, in every person, whatever the stage or condition of his life.

Therefore, the Magisterium of the Church has constantly proclaimed the sacred and inviolable character of every human life from its conception until its natural end (cf. ibid., no. 57). This moral judgment also applies to the origins of the life of an embryo even before it is implanted in the mother's womb, which will protect and nourish it for nine months until the moment of birth: "Human life is sacred and inviolable at every moment of existence, including the initial phase which precedes birth" (ibid., no. 61).

I know well, dear scholars, with what sentiments of wonder and profound respect for the human being you carry out your demanding and fruitful work of research precisely on the origin of human life itself it is a mystery on whose significance science will be increasingly able to shed light, even if it will be difficult to decipher it completely.

Indeed, as soon as reason succeeds in overcoming a limit deemed insurmountable, it will be challenged by other limits as yet unknown. Man will always remain a deep and impenetrable enigma.

In the fourth century, St. Cyril of Jerusalem already offered the following reflection to the catechumens who were preparing to receive Baptism: "Who prepared the cavity of the womb for the procreation of children? Who breathed life into the inanimate fetus within it? Who knit us together with bones and sinews and clothed us with skin and flesh (cf. Jb 10:11), and as soon as the child is born, causes the breast to produce an abundance of milk? How is it that the child, in growing, becomes an adolescent, and from an adolescent is transformed into a young man, then an adult and finally an old man, without anyone being able to identify the precise day on which the change occurred?"

And he concluded: "O Man, you are seeing the Craftsman you are seeing the wise Creator" (*Catechesi Battesimale*, 9, 15-16).

At the beginning of the third millennium these considerations still apply. They are addressed not so much to the physical or physiological phenomenon as rather to its anthropological and metaphysical significance. We have made enormous headway in our knowledge and have defined more clearly the limits of our ignorance but it always seems too arduous for human intelligence to realize that in looking at creation, we encounter the impression of the Creator.

In fact, those who love the truth, like you, dear scholars, should perceive that research on such profound topics places us in the condition of seeing and, as it were, touching the hand of God. Beyond the limits of experimental methods, beyond the boundaries of the sphere which some call meta-analysis, wherever the perception of the senses no longer suffices or where neither the perception of the senses alone nor scientific verification is possible, begins the adventure of transcendence, the commitment to "go beyond" them.

Dear researchers and experts, I hope you will be more and more successful, not only in examining the reality that is the subject of your endeavor, but also in contemplating it in such a way that, together with your discoveries, questions will arise that lead to discovering in the beauty of creatures a reflection of the Creator.

In this context, I am eager to express my appreciation and gratitude to the Pontifical Academy for Life for its valuable work of "study, formation and information" which benefits the Dicasteries of the Holy See, the local Churches and scholars attentive to what the Church proposes on their terrain of scientific research and on human life in its relations with ethics and law.

Because of the urgency and importance of these problems, I consider the foundation of this Institution by my venerable Predecessor, John Paul II, providential. I therefore desire to express with sincere cordiality to all of you, the personnel and the members of the Pontifical Academy for Life, my closeness and support.

With these sentiments, as I entrust your work to Mary's protection, I impart the Apostolic Blessing to you all.

Address to Participants in the Symposium on the Theme "Stem Cells: What Future for Therapy?"

September 16, 2006

Venerable Brothers in the Episcopate and in the Priesthood,
Distinguished Ladies and Gentlemen,

I address a cordial greeting to you all. This meeting with you, scientists and scholars dedicated to specialized research in the treatment of diseases that are a serious affliction to humanity, is a special comfort to me.

I am grateful to the organizers who have promoted this Congress on a topic that has become more and more important in recent years. The specific theme of the Symposium is appropriately formulated with a question open to hope: *"Stem cells: what future for therapy?"*

I thank Bishop Elio Sgreccia, President of the Pontifical Academy for Life, for his kind words, also on behalf of the International Federation of Catholic

Medical Associations (FIAMC), an association that has cooperated in organizing the Congress and is represented here by Prof. Gianluigi Gigli, outgoing President, and Prof. Simon de Castellvi, President-elect.

When science is applied to the alleviation of suffering and when it discovers on its way new resources, it shows two faces rich in humanity: through the sustained ingenuity invested in research, and through the benefit announced to all who are afflicted by sickness.

Those who provide financial means and encourage the necessary structures for study share in the merit of this progress on the path of civilization.

On this occasion, I would like to repeat what I said at a recent Audience: "Progress becomes true progress only if it serves the human person and if the human person grows: not only in terms of his or her technical power, but also in his or her moral awareness" (cf. General Audience, August 16, 2006).

In this light, somatic stem-cell research also deserves approval and encouragement when it felicitously combines scientific knowledge, the most advanced technology in the biological field and ethics that postulate respect for the human being at every stage of his or her existence.

The prospects opened by this new chapter in research are fascinating in themselves, for they give a glimpse of the possible cure of degenerative tissue diseases that subsequently threaten those affected with disability and death.

How is it possible not to feel the duty to praise all those who apply themselves to this research and all who support the organization and cover its expenses?

I would like in particular to urge scientific structures that draw their inspiration and organization from the Catholic Church to increase this type of research and to establish the closest possible contact with one another and with those who seek to relieve human suffering in the proper ways.

May I also point out, in the face of the frequently unjust accusations of insensitivity addressed to the Church, her constant support for research dedicated to the cure of diseases and to the good of humanity throughout her 2,000-year-old history.

If there has been resistance—and if there still is—it was and is to those forms of research that provide for the planned suppression of human beings who already exist, even if they have not yet been born. Research, in such cases, irrespective of efficacious therapeutic results is not truly at the service of humanity.

In fact, this research advances through the suppression of human lives that are equal in dignity to the lives of other human individuals and the lives of the researchers themselves.

History itself has condemned such a science in the past and will condemn it in the future, not only because it lacks the light of God but also because it lacks humanity.

I would like to repeat here what I already wrote some time ago: Here there is a problem that we cannot get around; no one can dispose of human life. An insurmountable limit to our possibilities of doing and of experimenting must be established. The human being is not a disposable object, but every single individual represents God's presence in the world (cf. J. Ratzinger, *God and the World*, Ignatius Press, 2002).

In the face of the actual suppression of the human being there can be no compromises or prevarications. One cannot think that a society can effectively combat crime when society itself legalizes crime in the area of conceived life.

On the occasion of recent Congresses of the Pontifical Academy for Life, I have had the opportunity to reassert the teaching of the Church, addressed to all people of good will, on the human value of the newly conceived child, also when considered prior to implantation in the uterus.

The fact that you at this Congress have expressed your commitment and hope to achieve new therapeutic results from the use of cells of the adult body without recourse to the suppression of newly conceived human beings, and the fact that your work is being rewarded by results, are confirmation of the validity of the Church's constant invitation to full respect for the human being from conception. The good of human beings should not only be sought in universally valid goals, but also in the methods used to achieve them.

A good result can never justify intrinsically unlawful means. It is not only a matter of a healthy criterion for the use of limited financial resources, but also, and above all, of respect for the fundamental human rights in the area of scientific research itself.

I hope that God will grant your efforts—which are certainly sustained by God who acts in every person of good will and for the good of all—the joy of discovering the truth, wisdom in consideration and respect for every human being, and success in the search for effective remedies to human suffering.

To seal this hope, I cordially impart an affectionate Blessing to all of you, to your collaborators and to your relatives, as well as to the patients who will benefit from your ingenuity and resourcefulness and the results of your work, with the assurance of my special remembrance in prayer.

Address to Participants in the General Assembly of the Pontifical Academy for Life

February 24, 2007

Dear Brothers and Sisters,

It is a true joy for me to receive the Members of the Pontifical Academy for Life in this Audience, held on the occasion of the Thirteenth General

Assembly, and those who are participating at this Congress on the theme: *"The Christian conscience in support of the right to life."*

I greet Cardinal Javier Lozano Barragán, the Archbishops and Bishops present, brother priests, the Congress speakers and all of you, gathered from various countries. I greet in particular, Archbishop Elio Sgreccia, President of the Pontifical Academy for Life, whom I thank for the kind words addressed to me and for the work he does together with the Vice-President, the Chancellor and the Board of Directors who carry out the delicate and vast tasks of the Pontifical Academy.

The theme to which you have called the participants' attention, and therefore also that of the Ecclesial Community and of public opinion, is very significant: the Christian conscience, in fact, has an internal need to nourish and strengthen itself with the multiple and profound motivations that work in favor of the right to life.

It is a right that must be sustained by all, because it is the first fundamental right of all human rights. The Encyclical *Evangelium Vitae* strongly affirms this: "Even in the midst of difficulties and uncertainties, every person sincerely open to truth and goodness can, by the light of reason and the hidden action of grace, come to recognize in the natural law written in the heart (cf. Rom 2:14-15) the sacred value of human life from its very beginning until its end, and can affirm the right of every human being to have this primary good respected to the highest degree. Upon the recognition of this right, every human community and the political community itself are founded" (no. 2).

The same Encyclical recalls that "believers in Christ must defend and promote this right, aware as they are of the wonderful truth recalled by the Second Vatican Council: 'By his Incarnation the Son of God has united himself in some fashion with every human being' (*Gaudium et Spes*, no. 22). This saving event reveals to humanity not only the boundless love of God who 'so loved the world that he gave his only Son' (Jn 3:16), but also the incomparable value of every human person" (ibid.).

Therefore, the Christian is continually called to be ever alert in order to face the multiple attacks to which the right to life is exposed. In this he knows that he can count on motives that are deeply rooted in the natural law and that can therefore be shared by every person of upright conscience.

In this perspective, above all after the publication of the Encyclical *Evangelium Vitae,* much has been done to make the subject matter of these motivations better known in the Christian community and in civil society, but it must be admitted that the attacks on the right to life throughout the world have broadened and multiplied, also assuming new forms.

The pressures to legalize abortion are increasing in Latin American countries and in developing countries, also with recourse to the liberalization of new forms of chemical abortion under the pretext of safeguarding reproductive health: policies for demographic control are on the rise, notwithstanding that they are already recognized as dangerous also on the economic and social plane.

At the same time, the interest in more refined biotechnological research is growing in the more developed countries in order to establish subtle and extensive eugenic methods, even to obsessive research for the "perfect child," with the spread of artificial procreation and various forms of diagnosis tending to ensure good selection.

A new wave of discriminatory eugenics finds consensus in the name of the presumed well-being of the individual, and laws are promoted especially in the economically progressive world for the legalization of euthanasia.

All of this comes about while, on another front, efforts are multiplying to legalize cohabitation as an alternative to matrimony and closed to natural procreation.

In these situations the conscience, sometimes overwhelmed by the powerful collective media, is insufficiently vigilant concerning the gravity of the problems at play, and the power of the strongest weakens and seems to paralyze even people of good will.

For this reason it is necessary to appeal to the conscience, and in particular, to the Christian conscience. The *Catechism of the Catholic Church* tells us, "Conscience is a judgment of reason whereby the human person recognizes the moral quality of a concrete act that he is going to perform, is in the process of performing or has already completed. In all he says and does, man is obliged to follow faithfully what he knows to be just and right" (no. 1778).

From this definition it emerges that the moral conscience, to be able to judge human conduct rightly, above all must be based on the solid foundation of truth, that is, it must be enlightened to know the true value of actions and the solid criteria for evaluation. Therefore, it must be able to distinguish good from evil, even where the social environment, pluralistic culture and superimposed interests do not help it do so.

The formation of a *true* conscience, because it is founded on the truth, and *upright*, because it is determined to follow its dictates without contradictions, without betrayal and without compromises, is a difficult and delicate undertaking today, but indispensable.

Unfortunately, many factors hinder this undertaking. In the first place, in the current phase of secularization, called post-modern and marked by disputable forms of tolerance, not only is the rejection of Christian tradition growing, but distrust for the capacity of reason to perceive the truth also distances us from the taste for reflection.

According to some, for individual conscience to be unbiased it must free itself both from references to tradition and those based on human reason.

Hence, the conscience, which as an act of reason aims at the truth of things, ceases to be light and becomes a simple screen upon which the society of the media projects the most contradictory images and impulses.

One must be re-educated to the desire to know authentic truth, to defend one's own freedom of choice in regard to mass behavior and the lures of propaganda, to nourish passion for moral beauty and a clear conscience. This is the delicate duty of parents and educators who assist them; and it is the duty of the Christian community with regard to its faithful.

Concerning the Christian conscience, its growth and nourishment, one cannot be content with fleeting contact with the principal truths of faith in infancy, but a program of accompaniment is necessary along the various stages of life, opening the mind and the heart to welcome the fundamental duties upon which the existence of the individual and the community rest.

Only in this way will it be possible to prepare youth to comprehend the values of life, love, marriage and the family. Only in this way can they be brought to appreciate the beauty and the sanctity of the love, joy and responsibility of being parents and collaborators of God in giving life.

In the absence of a continuous and qualified formation, the capacity for judgment of the problems posed by biomedicine in the areas of sexuality, new-born life, procreation, and also in the way to treat and care for patients and the weaker sectors of society, becomes even more problematic.

It is certainly necessary to speak about the moral criteria that regard these themes with professionals, doctors and lawyers, to engage them to elaborate a competent judgment of conscience, and if need be, also a courageous objection of conscience, but an equal need rises from the basic level for families and parish communities in the process of the formation of youth and adults.

Under this aspect, next to Christian formation, whose aim is the knowledge of the Person of Christ, of his Word and Sacraments in the itinerary of faith of children and adolescents, one must consistently fuse the discourse on moral values that regard the body, sexuality, human love, procreation, respect for life at every moment, at the same time with valid and precise motives, reporting behavior contrary to these primary values.

In this specific field the work of priests must be opportunely flanked by the commitment of lay educators, also specialists, dedicated to the duty to guide the ecclesial reality with their knowledge enlightened by faith.

Therefore, I ask the Lord to send among you, dear brothers and sisters, and among those dedicated to science, medicine, law and politics, witnesses endowed with true and upright consciences in order to defend and promote the "splendor of the truth" and to sustain the gift and mystery of life.

I trust in your help dearest professionals, philosophers, theologians, scientists and doctors. In a society at times chaotic and violent, with your cultural qualifications, by teaching and by example, you can contribute to awakening in many hearts the eloquent and clear voice of conscience.

The Second Vatican Council teaches us that "man has in his heart a law inscribed by God. His dignity lies in observing this law, and by it he will be judged" (*Gaudium et Spes*, no. 16). The Council has offered wise directives so that "the faithful should learn to distinguish carefully between the rights and the duties which they have as belonging to the Church and those which fall to them as members of the human society," and "they will strive to unite the two harmoniously, remembering that in every temporal affair they are to be guided by a Christian conscience, since not even in temporal business may any human activity be withdrawn from God's dominion" (*Lumen Gentium*, no. 36).

For this very reason the Council exhorts lay believers to welcome "what is decided by the Pastors as teachers and rulers of the Church," and then recommends that "Pastors . . . should recognize and promote the dignity and responsibility of the laity in the Church. They should willingly use their prudent advice" and concludes that "[m]any benefits for the Church are to be expected from this familiar relationship between the laity and the Pastors" (cf. *Lumen Gentium*, no. 37).

When the value of human life is at stake, this harmony between the magisterial function and the committed laity becomes singularly important: life is the first good received from God and is fundamental to all others; to guarantee the right to life for all and in an equal manner for all is the duty upon which the future of humanity depends. The importance of your study meeting emerges also from this perspective.

I entrust the work and the results to the intercession of the Virgin Mary, whom the Christian tradition hails as the true "Mother of all the living." May she assist and guide you! To seal this wish I willingly impart to all of you, to your families and collaborators, the Apostolic Blessing.

Address to Participants in the Congress on the Theme "Close by the Incurable Sick Person and the Dying: Scientific and Ethical Aspects"

February 25, 2008

Dear Brothers and Sisters,

With deep joy I offer my greeting to all of you who are taking part in the Congress of the Pontifical Academy for Life on the theme: *"Close by the Incurable Sick Person and the Dying: Scientific and Ethical Aspects."* The

Congress is taking place in conjunction with the Fourteenth General Assembly of the Academy, whose members are also present at this Audience. I first of all thank the President, Bishop Sgreccia, for his courteous words of greeting; with him, I thank the entire Presidency, the Board of Directors of the Pontifical Academy, all the collaborators and ordinary members, the honorary and the corresponding members. I would then like to address a cordial and grateful greeting to the relators of this important Congress, as well as to all the participants who come from various countries of the world. Dear friends, your generous commitment and witness are truly praiseworthy.

A mere glance at the titles of the Congress reports suffices to perceive the vast panorama of your reflections and the interest they hold for the present time, especially in today's secularized world. You seek to give answers to the many problems posed every day by the constant progress of the medical sciences, whose activities are increasingly sustained by high-level technological tools.

In view of all this, the urgent challenge emerges for everyone, and in a special way for the Church enlivened by the Risen Lord, to bring into the vast horizon of human life the splendor of the revealed truth and the support of hope.

When a life is extinguished by unforeseen causes at an advanced age, on the threshold of earthly life or in its prime, we should not only see this as a biological factor which is exhausted or a biography which is ending, but indeed as a new birth and a renewed existence offered by the Risen One to those who did not deliberately oppose his Love. The earthly experience concludes with death, but through death full and definitive life beyond time unfolds for each one of us. The Lord of life is present beside the sick person as the One who lives and gives life, the One who said: "I came that they may have life, and have it abundantly" (Jn 10:10). "I am the Resurrection and the life; he who believes in me, though he die, yet shall he live (Jn 11:25), and "I will raise him up on the last day" (Jn 6:54). At that solemn and sacred moment, all efforts made in Christian hope to improve ourselves and the world entrusted to us, purified by grace, find their meaning and are made precious through the love of God the Creator and Father. When, at the moment of death, the relationship with God is fully realized in the encounter with "him who does not die, who is Life itself and Love itself, then we are in life; then we 'live'" (Spe Salvi, no. 27). For the community of believers, this encounter of the dying person with the Source of Life and Love is a gift that has value for all, that enriches the communion of all the faithful. As such, it deserves the attention and participation of the community, not only of the family of close relatives but, within the limits and forms possible, of the whole community that was bound to the dying person. No believer should die in loneliness and neglect. Mother Teresa of Calcutta took special care to gather the poor and the forsaken so that they might experience the Father's warmth in the embrace of sisters and brothers, at least at the moment of death.

But it is not only the Christian community which, due to its particular bonds of supernatural communion, is committed to accompanying and celebrating in its members the mystery of suffering and death and the dawn of new life. The whole of society, in fact, is required through its health-care and civil institutions to respect the life and dignity of the seriously sick and the dying. Even while knowing that "it is not science that redeems man" (*Spe Salvi*, no. 26), our entire society and in particular the sectors linked to medical science are bound to express the solidarity of love and the safeguard and respect of human life at every moment of its earthly development, especially when it is suffering a condition of sickness or is in its terminal stage. In practice, it is a question of guaranteeing to every person who needs it the necessary support, through appropriate treatment and medical interventions, diagnosed and treated in accordance with the criteria of medical proportionality, always taking into account the moral duty of administering (on the part of the doctor) and of accepting (on the part of the patient) those means for the preservation of life that are "ordinary" in the specific situation. On the other hand, recourse to treatment with a high risk factor or which it would be prudent to judge as "extraordinary," is to be considered morally licit but optional. Furthermore, it will always be necessary to assure the necessary and due care for each person as well as the support of families most harshly tried by the illness of one of their members, especially if it is serious and prolonged. Also with regard to employment procedures, it is usual to recognize the specific rights of relatives at the moment of a birth; likewise, and especially in certain circumstances, close relatives must be recognized as having similar rights at the moment of the terminal illness of one of their family members. A supportive and humanitarian society cannot fail to take into account the difficult conditions of families who, sometimes for long periods, must bear the burden of caring at home for seriously-ill people who are not self-sufficient. Greater respect for individual human life passes inevitably through the concrete solidarity of each and every one, constituting one of the most urgent challenges of our time.

As I recalled in the Encyclical *Spe Salvi*: "The true measure of humanity is essentially determined in relationship to suffering and to the sufferer. This holds true both for the individual and for society. A society unable to accept its suffering members and incapable of helping to share their suffering and to bear it inwardly through 'com-passion' is a cruel and inhuman society" (no. 38). In a complex society, strongly influenced by the dynamics of productivity and the needs of the economy, frail people and the poorest families risk being overwhelmed in times of financial difficulty and/or illness. More and more lonely elderly people exist in big cities, even in situations of serious illness and close to death. In such situations, the pressure of euthanasia is felt, especially when a utilitarian vision of the person creeps in. In this regard, I take this opportunity to reaffirm once again the firm and constant ethical condemnation of every form of direct euthanasia, in accordance with the Church's centuries-old teaching.

The synergetic effort of civil society and the community of believers must aim not only to ensure that all live a dignified and responsible life, but also, experience the moment of trial and death in terms of brotherhood and solidarity, even when death occurs within a poor family or in a hospital bed. The Church, with her already functioning institutions and new initiatives, is called to bear a witness of active charity, especially in the critical situations of non-self-sufficient people deprived of family support, and for the seriously ill in need of palliative treatment and the appropriate religious assistance. On the one hand, the spiritual mobilization of parish and diocesan communities, and on the other, the creation or improvement of structures dependent on the Church, will be able to animate and sensitize the whole social environment, so that solidarity and charity are offered and witnessed to each suffering person and particularly to those who are close to death. For its part, society cannot fail to guarantee assistance to families that intend to commit themselves to nursing at home, sometimes for long periods, sick people afflicted with degenerative pathologies (tumors, neuro-degenerative diseases, etc.), or in need of particularly demanding nursing care. The help of all active and responsible members of society is especially required for those institutions of specific assistance that require numerous specialized personnel and particularly expensive equipment. It is above all in these sectors that the synergy between the Church and the institutions can prove uniquely precious for ensuring the necessary help to human life in the time of frailty.

While I hope that at this International Congress, celebrated in connection with the Jubilee of the Lourdes Apparitions, it will be possible to identify new proposals to alleviate the situation of those caught up in terminal forms of illness, I exhort you to persevere in your praiseworthy commitment to the service of life in all its phases. With these sentiments, I assure you of my prayers in support of your work and accompany you with a special Apostolic Blessing.

Address to the Members of the
Pontifical Academy for Life

February 21, 2009

Your Excellencies,
Venerable Brothers in the Episcopate and in the Priesthood,
Distinguished Academicians,
Ladies and Gentlemen,

I am particularly pleased to be able to receive you on the occasion of the Fifteenth General Assembly of the Pontifical Academy for Life. In 1994, my venerable Predecessor Pope John Paul II instituted it under the presidency of Prof. Jerôme Lejeune, a scientist, interpreting with farsightedness the delicate task it would carry out in the course of the years. I thank the President, Archbishop Rino Fisichella, for his words introducing this meeting which confirm the Academy's important commitment to the promotion and defense of human life.

Ever since the mid-nineteenth century when the Augustinian Abbot, Gregor Mendel, discovered the laws of the heredity of characteristics, for which he is considered the founder of genetics, this science has truly taken giant steps in the understanding of that language which is at the foundation of biological information and determines the development of a living being. It is for this reason that modern genetics has a particularly important place in the biological disciplines that have contributed to the wonderful development of the knowledge of the invisible architecture of the human body and the cellular and molecular processes that dictate its multiple activities. Science today has succeeded in revealing both the different hidden mechanisms of human physiology and the processes linked to the appearance of certain defects inherited from the parents. It has also revealed processes that make some people more exposed to the risk of contracting a disease. This knowledge, the result of intelligence and the efforts of countless experts, has made possible not only a more effective and early diagnosis of genetic diseases but also treatment destined to relieve the sufferings of the sick and, in some cases even to restore the hope of recovering their health. Since the sequencing of the entire human genome became available, the difference between one person and another and between the different human populations has also become the object of genetic research. This has permitted us to glimpse the possibility of new achievements.

The context of research still remains very open today and every day new horizons, still largely unexplored, are disclosed. The efforts of the researcher in these most enigmatic and precious areas demand special support; for this reason, collaboration among the different sciences is a support that can never be lacking in order to achieve results that are effective and at the same time achieve authentic progress for all humanity. This complementarity allows one to avoid the risk of a widespread genetic reductionism which tends to identify the person exclusively in terms of genetic information and interactions with the environment. It must be stressed that man will always be greater than all the elements that form his body; indeed, he carries within him the power of thought which always aspires to the truth about himself and about the world. The words of Blaise Pascal a great thinker who was also a gifted scientist charged with significance spring to mind: "Man is only a reed, the most feeble thing in nature, but he is a thinking reed. The entire universe need not arm itself to crush him. A vapor, a drop of water suffices to kill him. But, if the universe were to crush him, man would still be more noble than that which killed him, because he knows that he dies and he knows the advantage that the universe has over him; the universe, instead, knows nothing" (*Pensées*, 347).

Every human being, therefore, is far more than a unique combination of genetic information that is transmitted by his or her parents. Human generation can never be reduced to the mere reproduction of a new individual of the human species, as happens with any animal. The arrival of each person in the world is always a new creation. The words of a Psalm recall this with profound wisdom: "For it was you who created my being; knit me together in my mother's womb . . . my body held no secret from you when I was being fashioned in secret" (Ps 139[138]:13, 15). Consequently, if one wishes to enter into the mystery of human life, no branch of science must isolate itself, claiming to have the last word. Rather, it must participate in the common vocation to reach the truth, though with the different methodologies and subject matter proper to each science. Your Congress, however, analyzed not only the great challenges that genetics must tackle but also extended its Constitution to the risks of eugenics, certainly not a new practice and which in the past has been employed in unprecedented forms of authentic discrimination and violence. The disapproval of eugenics used with violence by a state regime or as the result of hatred for a race or a people is so deeply rooted in consciences that it was formally expressed in the *Universal Declaration of Human Rights*. Despite this, still today disturbing manifestations of this odious practice that presents itself with various features are appearing. Of course, the eugenic and racial ideologies that humiliated man in the past and caused tremendous suffering are not being proposed again, but a new mentality is being introduced that tends to justify a different view of life and personal dignity founded on personal desires and individual rights. Hence there is a tendency to give priority to functional ability, efficiency, perfection and physical beauty to the detriment of life's other dimensions which are deemed unworthy. The respect that is due to every human being, even bearing a developmental defect or a genetic disease that might manifest itself during life, is thus weakened while children whose life is considered not worth living are penalized from the moment of conception.

It is necessary to reiterate that every form of discrimination practiced by any authority with regard to persons, peoples or races on the basis of differences traceable to real or presumed genetic factors is an attack on the whole of humanity. What must be strongly reaffirmed is the equal dignity of every human being by the very fact that he has been born. A person's biological, mental and cultural development or state of health must never become a discriminatory factor. On the contrary, it is necessary to consolidate the culture of acceptance and love showing real solidarity toward those who suffer. It must break down the barriers that society often builds by discriminating against those who are disabled or affected by pathologies, or, worse, even reaching the selection and rejection of life in the name of an abstract ideal of health and physical perfection. If the human being is reduced to an object of experimental manipulation from the very earliest stages of his development this means that biotechnological medicine has surrendered to the will of the stronger. Trust in science must not make one forget the primacy of ethics when human life is at stake.

I am confident, dear friends, that your research in this sector may continue with the due scientific commitment and attention that the ethical factor demands on such important and crucial matters for the coherent development of personal existence. This is the hope with which I desire to conclude this meeting. As I invoke upon your work an abundance of heavenly light, I impart with affection a special Apostolic Blessing to you all.

Address to the Members of the Pontifical Academy for Life

February 13, 2010

Dear Brothers in the Episcopate and in the Priesthood,
Distinguished Members of the Pontificia Academia Pro Vita,
Distinguished Ladies and Gentlemen,

I am pleased to welcome you and to offer you a cordial greeting on the occasion of the General Assembly of the Pontifical Academy for Life. It is called to reflect on themes pertaining to the relationship between bioethics and the natural moral law which, because of the constant developments in this branch of science, appear ever more important in the context of our day. I address a special greeting to Archbishop Rino Fisichella, President of this Academy, and I thank him for his courteous words on behalf of those present. I likewise wish to extend my personal thanks to each one of you for the invaluable and irreplaceable commitment you devote to life in your various fields.

The problems that gravitate around the theme of bioethics demonstrate the priority given to the *anthropological issue* in the questions put to you. As I said in my latest Encyclical Letter *Caritas in Veritate*: "A particularly crucial battleground in today's struggle between the supremacy of technology and human moral responsibility is the field of *bioethics*, where the very possibility of integral human development is radically called into question. In this most delicate and critical area, the fundamental question asserts itself forcefully: is man the product of his own labors or does he depend on God? Scientific discoveries in this field and the possibilities of technological intervention seem so advanced as to force a choice between two types of reasoning: reason open to transcendence or reason closed within immanence" (no. 74). In the face of such questions that touch so decisively on human life in its perennial tension between immanence and transcendence and that have immense importance for the culture of the future generations, it is necessary to set up an integral pedagogical project that allows these topics to be treated in a positive, balanced and constructive perspective, especially regarding the relationship between faith and reason.

Bioethical issues often bring to the fore the reference to the dignity of the person. This is a fundamental principle which faith in the Crucified and Risen Jesus Christ has always defended, especially when, in respect of the simplest and most defenseless people, it is disregarded. God loves each human being uniquely and profoundly. Bioethics moreover, like every discipline, needs a reference that can guarantee a consistent reading of ethical issues that inevitably emerge in the face of the disputes that may arise from their interpretation. In this sphere the normative reference to the natural moral law comes into its own. Indeed, the recognition of human dignity as an inalienable right is founded primarily on this law, which is not written by a human hand but is engraved in human hearts by God the Creator. Every juridical order is required to recognize this law as inviolable and every individual is called to respect and promote it (cf. *Catechism of the Catholic Church*, nos. 1954-1960). Without the founding principle of human dignity the search for a source for the rights of the person would be arduous, and it would be impossible to reach an ethical judgment on the scientific breakthroughs that intervene directly in human life. It is necessary, therefore, to repeat firmly that there can be no understanding of human dignity as linked merely to external elements, such as scientific progress, graduality in the formation of human life or facile pietism in the face of limited situations. When respect for the dignity of the person is invoked, it is fundamental that it should be full, total and without restrictions other than those entailed in the recognition that it is always human life that is involved. Human life, of course, experiences its own development and the horizon of scientific and bioethical research is open; yet it is necessary to reassert that when it is a matter of contexts that concern the human being, scientists can never think that they are merely dealing with inanimate and manipulable matter. In fact, from the very first instant of the human being's life is characterized by the fact that it is *human life* and for this reason possesses its own dignity everywhere and in spite of all (cf. Congregation for the Doctrine of the Faith, *Dignitas Personae* on Certain Bioethical Questions, no. 5). Otherwise, we should always be threatened by the risk of an exploitative use of science, with the inevitable consequence of slipping into arbitrary decisions, discrimination and the financial interest of the strongest.

Combining bioethics and the natural moral law makes it possible to ensure as best we can the necessary and unavoidable reference to that dignity which human life intrinsically possesses from its first moment until its natural end. On the contrary, in today's context, despite the increasing reference to the rights that guarantee the person's dignity, it is clear that recognition of these rights is not always applied to human life in its natural development or in its weakest stages. A similar contradiction demands that a commitment be assumed in the various social and cultural contexts to see that human life is recognized everywhere as an inalienable subject of law, and never as an object subjected to the arbitrary will of the strongest. History has shown how dangerous and harmful a State can be that proceeds to legislate on issues which affect the person and society, even claiming to be the source and principle of ethics. Without the universal principles that permit the verification of a common denominator for all humanity, the risk of drifting into relativism in the area of legislation should not be underestimated (cf. CCC, no. 1959). The natural moral law, strong in its universal character, makes it possible to ward off this danger and, above all, offers the legislator a guarantee for the authentic respect of both the person and the entire order of creatures. It is, as it were, a catalyzing source of consensus between people of different cultures and religions and permits them to overcome differences. This is because it asserts the existence of an order impressed within nature by the Creator and recognized as an instance of true rational ethical judgment in order to pursue good and avoid evil. Natural moral law "belongs to the great heritage of human wisdom. Revelation, with its light, has contributed to further purifying and developing it" (Pope John Paul II, *Address to Participants in the Bi-Annual Plenary Assembly of the Congregation for the Doctrine of the Faith*, February 6, 2004).

Distinguished Members of the Pontifical Academy for Life, in the contemporary context your commitment appears to be ever more delicate and difficult, but the increasing sensitivity to human life is an encouragement to continue with ever greater dynamism and courage in this important service to life and to teaching the future generations the Gospel values. I hope you will all persevere in your study and research, so that the work of promoting and defending life may be more and more effective and fruitful. I accompany you with the Apostolic Blessing, which I gladly extend to all who share with you in this daily commitment.

Address to the Participants in the General Assembly of the Pontifical Academy for Life

February 26, 2011

Your Eminences,
Venerable Brothers in the Episcopate and in the Priesthood,
Brothers and Sisters,

I welcome you with joy on the occasion of the annual Assembly of the Pontifical Academy for Life. I greet in particular the President, Bishop Ignacio de Paula, and thank him for his courteous words. I address my cordial welcome to each one of you! During these days of work you have treated topics of important timeliness, which profoundly call into question contemporary society and challenge us to find ever more adequate responses for the good of the human person.

The topic of post-abortion syndrome—that is, the grave psychological distress experienced by women who have had recourse to voluntary abortion—reveals the irrepressible voice of the moral conscience and the most serious wound it suffers every time that human action betrays the innate vocation to the good of the human being, to which it bears witness.

In this reflection it would be useful also to focus attention on the at times obscured conscience of the fathers of children who often leave pregnant women on their own. The *Catechism of the Catholic Church* teaches that the moral conscience is that "judgment of reason whereby the human person recognizes the moral quality of a concrete act that he is going to perform, is in the process of performing, or has already completed" (no. 1778).

Indeed it is a duty of the moral conscience to discern good from evil in the different situations of life, so that, on the basis of this judgment, the human being may freely turn toward goodness. To those who would like to deny the existence of the human moral conscience, reducing its voice to the result of external conditioning or to a purely emotional phenomenon, it is important to reaffirm that the moral quality of human action is neither an extrinsic or optional value, nor is it a prerogative of Christians or believers; rather it brings together every human being.

It is through the moral conscience that God speaks to every person and invites him to defend human life at every moment. The profound dignity of the moral conscience and the reason for its inviolability is inherent in this personal bond with the Creator.

The human being in his wholeness—mind, emotions, will—fulfills his vocation to the good in his conscience, so that the choice of good or evil in the concrete situations of life ends by profoundly marking the human person in every expression of his being. The whole person, in fact, is injured when his action is contrary to the dictates of his conscience. Yet, even when man rejects the truth and goodness that the Creator proposes to him, God does not abandon him but, precisely through the voice of his conscience, continues to see him and to speak to him so that he will recognize his error and open himself to divine Mercy which can heal any wound.

Doctors in particular cannot fail in the grave duty to defend from deception the conscience of many women who believe abortion is the solution to family, financial and social problems or those that relate to their baby's health. Especially in the latter situation the woman is all too often convinced, at times by doctors themselves, that abortion is not only a morally licit choice, but is even a "therapeutic" action that is only right, in order to prevent the child and his family from suffering and from being an "unjust" burden on society.

Against a cultural background characterized by the eclipse of the sense of life, in which the common perception of the moral gravity of abortion and of other kinds of attacks on human life, special fortitude is demanded of doctors so that they may continue to assert that abortion resolves nothing but kills the child, destroys the woman and blinds the conscience of the child's father, all too often ruining family life. This duty, however, does not only concern the medical profession and health-care workers. The whole of society must defend the right to life of the child conceived and the true good of the woman who will never, in any circumstance, be able to find fulfillment in the decision of abortion.

It will likewise be necessary, as your work has shown, to provide women who having unfortunately already had an abortion are now experiencing the full moral and existential tragedy of it. Many dioceses and volunteer organizations offer psychological and spiritual support for full human recovery. The solidarity of the Christian community cannot dispense with this type of co-responsibility.

In this regard I would like to recall the invitation addressed by Venerable John Paul II to women who have had an abortion: "The Church is aware of the many factors which may have influenced your decision, and she does not doubt that in many cases it was a painful and even shattering decision. The wound in your heart may not yet have healed. Certainly what happened was and remains terribly wrong. But do not give in to discouragement and do not lose hope. Try rather to understand what happened and face it honestly. If you have not already done so, give yourselves over with humility and trust to repentance. The Father of mercies is ready to give you his forgiveness and his peace in the Sacrament of Reconciliation. To the same Father and his mercy you can with sure hope entrust your child. With the friendly and expert help and advice of other people, and as a result of your own painful experience, you can be among the most eloquent defenders of everyone's right to life" (*Evangelium Vitae*, no. 99).

The moral conscience of researchers and of the entire civil society is also closely involved in the second topic, which is the subject of your work today; the use of umbilical cord banks, for clinical and research purposes. Medical and scientific research is a value, hence a commitment, not only for researchers but for the whole civil community. From it stems the duty to promote ethically effective research by institutions and the value of solidarity of individuals in taking part in research that aims to further the common good. This value and the need for solidarity are very clearly highlighted in the case of the use of umbilical cord stem cells. These are important clinical applications and promising research at the scientific level, but their implementation relies heavily on generosity in donating umbilical cord blood at the moment of birth, and on updating structures to enable women giving birth to donate this blood if they so wish.

I therefore invite you all to become champions of a true and conscious human and Christian solidarity. In this regard, many medical researchers rightly view with perplexity the ever increasing number of private banks for the preservation of umbilical cord blood for the exclusive use of individuals

In addition to lacking true scientific superiority with regard to cord donation this option—as your Assembly's work shows—undermines the genuine spirit of solidarity that must constantly motivate the search for the common good to which science and medical research ultimately aspire.

Dear brothers and sisters, I renew the expression of my gratitude to the President and to all the Members of the Pontifical Academy for Life for the scientific and ethical value with which you carry out your commitment to serving the good of the human person. I hope that you will keep ever alive the spirit of authentic service that makes minds and hearts sensitive to recognizing the needs of our contemporaries. I cordially impart the Apostolic Blessing to each one of you and to your loved ones.

CHAPTER V

To the Pontifical John Paul II Institute for Studies on Marriage and the Family

Address to Members of the Pontifical John Paul II Institute for Studies on Marriage and the Family on the Twenty-Fifth Anniversary of Its Foundation

May 11, 2006

Your Eminences,
Venerable Brothers in the Episcopate and in the Priesthood,
Dear Brothers and Sisters,

I meet you today with great joy on this twenty-fifth anniversary of the foundation of the *Pontifical John Paul II Institute for Studies on Marriage and Family* at the Pontifical Lateran University. I greet you all with affection and I thank you for the great affection that I have encountered. I warmly thank Msgr. Livio Melina for his kind words and also for his briefness. We will be able to read what he wished to say, while more time will be left for friendly exchanges.

The beginning of your Institute is connected with a singular event: on that day, May 13, 1981, my beloved Predecessor John Paul II suffered the well-known serious attack on his life during the Audience at which he was to have announced the creation of your Institute.

This event has special importance at this commemoration, which we are celebrating a little more than a year after his death. You have wished to emphasize it with the fitting initiative of a Congress on *The legacy of John Paul II on marriage and family: loving human love*.

You rightly feel that this legacy of yours is very special, since the vision that is one of the structural centers of his mission and reflections was addressed to you and you are its perpetuators: God's plan for marriage and the family.

This bequest is not merely a collection of doctrines or ideas but first and foremost a teaching endowed with enlightening unity on the meaning of human love and life. The presence of numerous families at this Audience—therefore not only the students of the present and the past but above all the students of the future—is a particularly eloquent testimony of how the teaching of this truth has been received and has borne fruit.

As a young priest, Karol Wojtyla already had the idea of "teaching how to love." It was later to fill him with enthusiasm when, as a young Bishop, he confronted the difficult times that followed the publication of my Predecessor Paul VI's prophetic and ever timely Encyclical *Humanae Vitae*.

It was then that he realized the need for a systematic study of this topic. It was the basis of this teaching which he later offered to the entire Church in his unforgettable *Catechesis on human love*.

Thus, *two* fundamental *elements* were highlighted that in recent years you have sought to examine more deeply and that give novelty to your Institute as an academic reality with a specific mission in the Church.

The *first element* concerns the fact that marriage and the family are rooted in the inmost nucleus of the truth about man and his destiny. Sacred Scripture reveals that the vocation to love is part of the authentic image of God which the Creator has desired to impress upon his creature, calling them to resemble him precisely to the extent in which they are open to love.

Consequently, the sexual difference that distinguishes the male from the female body is not a mere biological factor but has a far deeper significance. It expresses that form of love with which man and woman, by becoming one flesh, as Sacred Scripture says, can achieve an authentic communion of people open to the transmission of life and who thus cooperate with God in the procreation of new human beings.

A *second element* marks the newness of John Paul II's teaching on human love: his original way of interpreting God's plan precisely in the convergence of divine revelation with the human experience. Indeed, in Christ, fullness of the revelation of the Father's love, is also expressed the full truth of the human vocation to love that can only be found completely in the sincere gift of self.

In my recent Encyclical, *Deus Caritas Est*, I wanted to emphasize that it is precisely through love that "the Christian image of God and the resulting image of mankind and its destiny" (no. 1) shines forth.

In other words, God used the way of love to reveal the intimate mystery of his Trinitarian life. Furthermore, the close relationship that exists between the image of God-Love and human love enables us to understand that: "Corresponding to the image of a monotheistic God is monogamous marriage. Marriage based on exclusive and definitive love becomes the icon of the relationship between God and his people and vice versa. God's way of loving becomes the measure of human love" (no. 11).

It is here that the duty incumbent on the Institute for Studies on Marriage and Family in academic structures overall stands out: to illumine the truth of love as a path to fullness in every form of human life. The great challenge of the new evangelization that John Paul II proposed with such enthusiasm needs to be sustained with a truly profound reflection on human love, since precisely this love is the privileged path that God chose to reveal himself to man and in this love he calls human beings to communion in the Trinitarian life.

This approach enables us also to overcome a private conception of love that is so widespread today. Authentic love is transformed into a light that guides the whole of life toward its fullness, generating a society in which human beings can live. The communion of life and love which is marriage thus emerges as an authentic good for society.

Today, the need to avoid confusing marriage with other types of unions based on weak love is especially urgent. It is only the rock of total, irrevocable love between a man and a woman that can serve as the foundation on which to build a society that will become a home for all mankind.

The importance of the Institute's work in the Church's mission explains its structure: in fact, John Paul II approved a single Institute but with different headquarters located on the five continents, for the purpose of offering a reflection that would display the riches of the one truth in the plurality of cultures.

This unity of vision in research and teaching, embracing the diversity of places and sensibilities, constitutes a value which you must safeguard, developing the riches embedded in each culture. This feature of the Institute has proven to be particularly suited to the study of a reality such as that of the marriage and family. Your work can express how the gift of creation lived in the different cultures was raised to a redeeming grace by Christ's redemption.

To be successful in your mission as the faithful heirs of the Institute's Founder, beloved John Paul II, I ask you to look to Mary Most Holy, Mother of Fair Love. The redeeming love of the Incarnate Word must be transformed into "fountains of living water in the midst of a thirsting world" (*Deus Caritas Est*, no. 42), for every marriage and in every family.

I offer you all, dear teachers, students of today and yesterday and the staff in charge, as well as all the families who look up to your Institute, my most cordial good wishes, which I accompany with a special Apostolic Blessing.

Address to Participants in an International Congress Organized by the John Paul II Institute for Studies on Marriage and the Family

April 5, 2008

Your Eminences,
Venerable Brothers in the Episcopate and in the Priesthood,
Dear Brothers and Sisters,

I meet you with great joy on the occasion of the International Congress on "*"Oil on the wounds": A response to the ills of abortion and divorce,*" promoted by the John Paul II Pontifical Institute for Studies on Marriage and Family in collaboration with the *Knights of Columbus*. I congratulate you on the topical and complex theme that has been the subject of your reflections in these days and in particular for the reference to the Good Samaritan (Lk 10:25-37), which you chose as a key to approach the evils of abortion and divorce that bring so much suffering to the lives of individuals, families and society. Yes, the men and women of our day sometimes truly find themselves stripped and wounded on the wayside of the routes we take, often without anyone listening to their cry for help or attending to them to alleviate and heal their suffering. In the often purely ideological debate a sort of conspiracy of silence is created in their regard. Only by assuming an attitude of merciful love is it possible to approach in order to bring help and enable victims to pick themselves up and resume their journey through life.

In a cultural context marked by increasing individualism, hedonism and all too often also by a lack of solidarity and adequate social support, human freedom, as it faces life's difficulties, is prompted in its weakness to make decisions that conflict with the indissolubility of the matrimonial bond or with the respect due to human life from the moment of conception, while it is still protected in its mother's womb. Of course, divorce and abortion are decisions of a different kind, which are sometimes made in difficult and dramatic circumstances that are often traumatic and a source of deep suffering for those who make them. They also affect innocent victims: the infant just conceived and not yet born, children involved in the break-up of family ties. These decisions indelibly mark the lives of all those involved. The Church's ethical opinion with regard to divorce and procured abortion is unambivalent and known to all: these are grave sins which, to a different extent and taking into account the evaluation of subjective responsibility, harm the dignity of the human person, involve a profound injustice in human and social relations and offend God himself, Guarantor of the conjugal covenant and the Author of life. Yet the Church, after the example of her Divine Teacher, always has the people themselves before her, especially the weakest and most innocent who are victims of injustice and sin, and also those other men and women who, having perpetrated these acts, stained by sin and wounded within, are seeking peace and the chance to begin anew.

The Church's first duty is to approach these people with love and consideration, with caring and motherly attention, to proclaim the merciful closeness of God in Jesus Christ. Indeed, as the Fathers teach, it is he who is the true Good Samaritan, who has made himself close to us, who pours oil and wine on our wounds and takes us into the inn, the Church, where he has us treated, entrusting us to her ministers and personally paying in advance for our recovery. Yes, the Gospel of love and life is also always the *Gospel of mercy*, which is addressed to the actual person and sinner that we are, to help us up after any fall and to recover from any injury. My beloved Predecessor, the Servant of God John Paul II, the third anniversary of whose death we celebrated recently, said in inaugurating the new Shrine of Divine Mercy in Krakow: "Apart from the mercy of God there is no other source of hope for mankind" (August 17, 2002). On the basis of this mercy the Church cultivates an indomitable trust in human beings and in their capacity for recovery. She knows that with the help of grace human freedom is capable of the definitive and faithful gift of self which makes possible the marriage of a man and woman as an indissoluble bond; she knows that even in the most difficult circumstances human freedom is capable of extraordinary acts of sacrifice and solidarity to welcome the life of a new human being. Thus, one can see that the "No" which the Church pronounces in her moral directives on which public opinion sometimes unilaterally focuses, is in fact a great "Yes" to the dignity of the human person, to human life and to the person's capacity to love. It is an expression of the constant trust with which, despite their frailty, people are able to respond to the loftiest vocation for which they are created: the vocation to love.

On that same occasion, John Paul II continued: "This fire of mercy needs to be passed on to the world. In the mercy of God the world will find peace" (ibid., 8). The great task of disciples of the Lord Jesus who find themselves the travelling companions of so many brothers, men and women of good will, is hinged on this. Their program, the program of the Good Samaritan, is a "'heart which sees.' This heart sees where love is needed and acts accordingly" (*Deus Caritas Est*, no. 31). In these days of reflection and dialogue you have stooped down to victims suffering from the wounds of divorce and abortion. You have noted first of all the sometimes traumatic suffering that afflicts the so-called "children of divorce," marking their lives to the point of making their way far more difficult. It is in fact inevitable that when the conjugal covenant is broken, those who suffer most are the children who are the living sign of its indissolubility. Supportive pastoral attention must therefore aim to ensure that the children are not the innocent victims of conflicts between parents who divorce. It must also endeavor to ensure that the continuity of the link with their parents is guaranteed as far as possible, as well as the links with their own family and social origins, which are indispensable for a balanced psychological and human growth.

You also focused on the tragedy of procured abortion that leaves profound and sometimes indelible marks in the women who undergo it and in the people around them, as well as devastating consequences on the family and society, partly because of the materialistic mentality of contempt for life that it encourages. What selfish complicity often lies at the root of an agonizing decision which so many women have had to face on their own, who still carry in their heart an open wound! Although what has been done remains a grave injustice and is not in itself remediable, I make my own the exhortation in *Evangelium Vitae* addressed to women who have had an abortion: "Do not give in to discouragement and do not lose hope. Try rather to understand what happened and face it honestly. If you have not already done so, give yourselves over with humility and trust to repentance. The Father of mercies is ready to give you his forgiveness and his peace in the Sacrament of Reconciliation. To the same Father and his mercy you can with sure hope entrust your child" (no. 99).

I express deep appreciation for all those social and pastoral initiatives being taken for the reconciliation and treatment of people injured by the drama of abortion and divorce. Together with numerous other forms of commitment, they constitute essential elements for building that civilization of love that humanity needs today more than ever.

As I implore the Merciful Lord God that he will increasingly liken you to Jesus the Good Samaritan, that his spirit will teach you to look with new eyes at the reality of the suffering brethren, that he will help you to think with new criteria and spur you to act with generous dynamism with a view to an authentic civilization of love and life, I impart a special Apostolic Blessing to you all.

Message for the Fortieth Anniversary of the Encyclical *Humanae Vitae*

October 2, 2008

To Msgr. Livio Melina,
President of the John Paul II Pontifical Institute,
for Studies on Marriage and Family,

I learned with joy that the Pontifical Institute of which you are President and the Catholic University of the Sacred Heart have opportunely organized an International Congress on the occasion of the fortieth anniversary of the publication of the Encyclical *Humanae Vitae*, an important Document that treats one of the essential aspects of the vocation to marriage and the specific journey of holiness that results from it. Indeed, having received the gift of love, husband and wife are called in turn to give themselves to each other without reserve. Only in this way are the acts proper and exclusive to spouses truly acts of love which, while they unite them in one flesh, build a genuine personal communion. Therefore, the logic of the totality of the gift intrinsically configures conjugal love and, thanks to the sacramental outpouring of the Holy Spirit, becomes the means to achieve authentic conjugal charity in their own life.

The possibility of procreating a new human life is included in a married couple's integral gift of themselves. Since, in fact, every form of love endeavors to spread the fullness on which it lives, conjugal love has its own special way of communicating itself: the generation of children. Thus it not only resembles but also shares in the love of God who wants to communicate himself by calling the human person to life. Excluding this dimension of communication through an action that aims to prevent procreation means denying the intimate truth of spousal love, with which the divine gift is communicated: "If the mission of generating life is not to be exposed to the arbitrary will of men, one must necessarily recognize insurmountable limits to the possibility of man's domination over his own body and its functions; limits which no man, whether a private individual or one invested with authority, may licitly surpass" (*Humanae Vitae*, no. 17). This is the essential nucleus of the teaching that my Venerable Predecessor Paul VI addressed to married couples and which the Servant of God John Paul II, in turn, reasserted on many occasions, illuminating its anthropological and moral basis.

Forty years after the Encyclical's publication we can understand better how decisive this light was for understanding the great "yes" that conjugal love involves. In this light, children are no longer the objective of a human project but are recognized as an authentic gift, to be accepted with an attitude of responsible generosity toward God, the first source of human life. This great "yes" to the beauty of love certainly entails gratitude, both of the parents in receiving the gift of a child, and of the child himself, in knowing that his life originates in such a great and welcoming love.

It is true, moreover, that serious circumstances may develop in the couple's growth which make it prudent to space out births or even to suspend them. And it is here that knowledge of the natural rhythms of the woman's fertility becomes important for the couple's life. The methods of observation which enable the couple to determine the periods of fertility permit them to administer what the Creator has wisely inscribed in human nature without interfering with the integral significance of sexual giving. In this way spouses, respecting the full truth of their love, will be able to modulate its expression in conformity with these rhythms without taking anything from the totality of the gift of self that union in the flesh expresses. Obviously, this requires maturity in love which is not instantly acquired but involves dialogue and reciprocal listening, as well as a special mastery of the sexual impulse in a journey of growth in virtue.

In this perspective, knowing that the Congress is also taking place through an initiative of the Catholic University of the Sacred Heart, I am likewise eager to express in particular my appreciation for all that this university institution does to support the *International Paul VI Institute for Research in Human Fertility and Infertility for Responsible Procreation* (ISI), which it gave to my unforgettable Predecessor, Pope John Paul II, thereby desiring to make, so to speak, an institutionalized response to the appeal launched by Pope Paul VI in paragraph number 24 of the Encyclical, to "men of science." A task of the ISI, in fact, is to improve the knowledge of the *natural* methods for controlling human fertility and of *natural* methods for overcoming possible infertility. Today, "thanks to the progress of the biological and medical sciences, man has at his disposal ever more effective therapeutic resources; but he can also acquire new powers, with unforeseeable consequences, over human life at its very beginning and in its first stages" (*Instruction On Respect for Human Life in Its Origin and on the Dignity of Procreation*, [*Donum Vitae*], no. 1). In this perspective, "many researchers are engaged in the fight against sterility. While fully safeguarding the dignity of human procreation, some have achieved results which previously seemed unattainable.

"Scientists therefore are to be encouraged to continue their research with the aim of preventing the causes of sterility and of being able to remedy them so that sterile couples will be able to procreate in full respect for their own personal dignity and that of the child to be born" (ibid., no. 8). It is precisely this goal that is proposed by the ISI Paul VI and by other similar centers, with the encouragement of the ecclesiastical authority.

We may ask ourselves: how is it possible that the world today, and also many of the faithful, find it so difficult to understand the Church's message which illustrates and defends the beauty of conjugal love in its natural expression? Of course, in important human issues the technical solution often appears the easiest. Yet it actually conceals the basic question that concerns the meaning of human sexuality and the need for a responsible mastery of it so that its practice may become an expression of personal love. When love is at stake, technology cannot replace the maturation of freedom. Indeed, as we well know, not even reason suffices: it must be the heart that sees. Only the eyes of the heart succeed in understanding the proper needs of a great love, capable of embracing the totality of the human being. For this, the service that the Church offers in her pastoral care of marriages and families must be able to guide couples to understand with their hearts the marvelous plan that God has written into the human body, helping them to accept all that an authentic process of maturation involves.

The Congress that you are celebrating therefore represents an important moment of reflection and care for couples and families, offering them the results of years of research in both the anthropological and ethical dimensions, as well as that which is strictly scientific, with regard to truly responsible procreation. In this light I can only congratulate you and express the hope that this work will bear abundant fruit and contribute to supporting couples on their way with ever greater wisdom and clarity, encouraging them in their mission to be credible witnesses of the beauty of love in the world. With these hopes, as I invoke the Lord's help on the work of the congress, I impart a special Apostolic Blessing to all.

Address to Participants in a Meeting Promoted by the John Paul II Institute for Studies on Marriage and the Family

May 13, 2011

Your Eminences,
Dear Brothers in the Episcopate and in the Priesthood,
Dear Brothers and Sisters,

With joy I welcome you today, a few days after the Beatification of Pope John Paul II who, thirty years ago, as we heard, chose to found at the same time the Pontifical Council for the Family and your Pontifical Institute, two entities that show how firmly convinced he was of the family's importance for the Church and for society.

I greet the representatives of your great community that now reaches across all the continents, as well as the praiseworthy Foundation for Marriage and Family which I created to support your mission. I thank your President, Msgr. Melina, for his words on behalf of you all.

The new Blessed John Paul II, who, as was mentioned, was the victim of that terrible attack in St. Peter's Square thirty years ago, entrusted to you, in particular, the study, research and dissemination of his "Catecheses on human love" that contain a profound reflection on the human body. Joining the theology of the body with that of love in order to find unity in the human journey: this is the theme I would like to point out to you as a horizon for your work.

Shortly after the death of Michelangelo, Paolo Veronese was summoned by the Inquisition, accused of having depicted inappropriate figures in his "Last Supper." The artist replied that even in the Sistine Chapel bodies were depicted nude, with little reverence. It was the Inquisitor himself who took Michelangelo's defense, with a reply that has become famous: "But in these figures what is there that is not inspired by the Holy Spirit?" As people of the modern age, we struggle to understand these words because the body appears to us as inert matter, heavy, opposed to knowledge and to the freedom proper to the spirit. However the bodies Michelangelo depicted are robed in love, life, splendor. He wanted in this way to show that our bodies hide a mystery. In them the spirit is manifest and active. They are called to be spiritual bodies, as St. Paul says (cf. 1 Cor 15:44).

Consequently we can ask ourselves: can this destiny of the body enlighten the stages of its journey? If our body is called to be spiritual, should not its history be that of the covenant between body and spirit? Indeed, far from being opposed to the spirit, the body is the place where the spirit can dwell. In this light it is possible to understand that our bodies are not inert, heavy matter but, if we know how to listen, they speak the language of true love.

The first word of this language is found in the creation of the human person. The body speaks to us of an origin that we have not conferred upon ourselves. "You knit me in my mother's womb," the Psalmist says to the Lord (Ps 139:13). We can affirm that the body, in revealing our origin to us, bears within itself a filial significance because it reminds us that we are generated, and leads us back, through our parents who passed on life to us, to God the Creator. Only when he recognizes the originating love which has given this life can the human person accept himself, be reconciled with nature and with the world.

The creation of Adam is followed by the creation of Eve. The flesh received from God is required to make possible the union of love between man and woman and transmit life. Before the Fall the bodies of Adam and Eve appear in perfect harmony. There is a language in them that they did not create, an *eros* rooted in their nature which invites them to receive one another reciprocally from the Creator, so as to be able to give themselves.

Thus we understand that in love the human person is "re-created." *Incipit vita nuova* [a new life begins], as Dante said, (*Vita Nuova* I, 1), the life of the new unity of the two in one flesh. The true appeal of sexuality is born of the vastness of this horizon that opens up: integral beauty, the universe of the other person and of the "we" that is born of the union, the promise of communion that is hidden therein, the new fruitfulness, the path toward God, the source of love, which love opens up.

The union in one flesh then becomes a union for the whole of life, until the man and woman become one spirit as well. Thus a journey begins in which the body teaches us the value of time, of that slow maturation in love. In this light the virtue of chastity takes on new meaning. It is not a "no" to the pleasures and joys of life, but a great "yes" to love as a profound communication between persons, a communication that requires time and respect as they journey together toward fullness and as a love that becomes capable of generating life and of generously welcoming the new life that is born.

It is true that the body also has a negative language: one hears talk of oppression of the other, of the desire to possess and exploit. However, we know that this language is not part of God's original plan but, rather, is the result of sin. When it is separated from its filial meaning, from its connection with the Creator, the body rebels against the person, loses its capacity to let communion shine through and becomes a place for the appropriation of the other. Is this not perhaps the drama of that sexuality which today remains enclosed in the narrow circle of one's own body and emotions, but which in reality can only find fulfillment in that call to something greater?

In this regard John Paul II spoke of the humility of the body. One of Claudel's characters says to his beloved: "I am not able to keep the promise that my body made to you," which prompts the reply: "You can break the body, but not the promise" (*Le soulier de satin* [*The Satin Slipper*], Day 3, Scene XIII).

The power of this promise explains how the Fall is not the last word about the body in salvation history. God also offers the human person a process of the redemption of the body, the language of which is preserved in the family. If after the Fall Eve is given the name "Mother of the Living," this testifies to the fact that the power of sin is not capable of obliterating the original language of the body, the blessing of life that God continues to offer when a man and woman are joined in one flesh. The family: this is the place where the theology of the body and the theology of love are interwoven. Here we learn the goodness of the body, its witness to a good origin, in the experience of the love we receive from our parents. Here lives the self-giving in a single flesh, in the conjugal charity that unites the spouses. Here we experience that the fruitfulness of love and life is interwoven with that of other generations. It is in the family that the human person discovers that he or she is not in a relationship as an autonomous person, but as a child, spouse or parent, whose identity is founded in being called to love, to receive from others and to give him or herself to others.

This journey of creation finds its fullness in the Incarnation, in the coming of Christ. God took a body, revealed himself in it. The upward movement of the body is hence integrated in another, more original movement, the humble movement of God who lowers himself toward the body, in order to raise it to him. As Son, he received a filial body in gratitude and in listening to the Father, and he gave this body for us, by so doing to generate the new body of the Church. The liturgy of the Feast of the Ascension sings the story of the flesh, sinner in Adam, assumed and redeemed by Christ. It is a flesh that becomes ever filled increasingly with light and the Spirit, filled with God.

Thus we see the depth of the theology of the body. When it is interpreted in the whole of tradition, it does not run the risk of superficiality and allows us to understand the greatness of the vocation to love, which is a call to a communion of persons in the twofold form of life of virginity and marriage.

Dear friends, your Institute has been placed under the protection of Our Lady. Concerning Mary Dante said some words that are enlightening for a theology of the body: "For in thy womb rekindling shone the love" (*Paradiso*, Canto XXXIII, 7). The Love which generates the Church was incarnate in her female body. May the Mother of the Lord continue to protect you on your journey and make fruitful your studies and your teaching in service to the Church's mission for the family and society. May you be accompanied by the Apostolic Blessing which I cordially impart to you all. Thank you.

To the Pontifical Council for Culture

Address to Participants in the International Conference Promoted by the Pontifical Council for Culture

November 12, 2011

Dear Brother Bishops,
Your Excellencies, Distinguished Guests,
Dear Friends,

I wish to thank Cardinal Gianfranco Ravasi, President of the Pontifical Council for Culture, for his kind words and for promoting this International Conference on *Adult Stem Cells: Science and the Future of Man and Culture*. I would also like to thank Archbishop Zygmunt Zimowski, President of the Pontifical Council for Pastoral Care of Health Workers, and Bishop Ignacio Carrasco de Paula, President of the Pontifical Academy for Life for their contribution to this particular endeavor. A special word of gratitude goes to the many benefactors whose support has made this event possible. In this regard, I would like to express the Holy See's appreciation of all the work that is done, by various institutions, to promote cultural and formative initiatives aimed at supporting top-level scientific research on adult stem cells and exploring the cultural, ethical and anthropological implications of their use.

Scientific research provides a unique opportunity to explore the wonder of the universe, the complexity of nature and the distinctive beauty of life, including human life. But since human beings are endowed with immortal souls and are created in the image and likeness of God, there are dimensions of human existence that lie beyond the limits of what the natural sciences are competent to determine. If these limits are transgressed, there is a serious risk that the unique dignity and inviolability of human life could be subordinated to purely utilitarian considerations. But if instead these limits are duly respected, science can make a truly remarkable contribution to promoting and safeguarding the dignity of man: indeed herein lies its true utility. Man, the agent of scientific research, will sometimes, in his biological nature, form the object of that research. Nevertheless, his transcendent dignity entitles him always to remain the ultimate beneficiary of scientific research and never to be reduced to its instrument.

In this sense, the potential benefits of adult stem cell research are very considerable, since it opens up possibilities for healing chronic degenerative illnesses by repairing damaged tissue and restoring its capacity for regeneration. The improvement that such therapies promise would constitute a significant step forward in medical science, bringing fresh hope to sufferers and their families alike. For this reason, the Church naturally offers her encouragement to those who are engaged in conducting and supporting research of this kind, always with the proviso that it be carried out with due regard for the integral good of the human person and the common good of society.

This proviso is most important. The pragmatic mentality that so often influences decision-making in the world today is all too ready to sanction whatever means are available in order to attain the desired end, despite ample evidence of the disastrous consequences of such thinking. When the end in view is one so eminently desirable as the discovery of a cure for degenerative illnesses, it is tempting for scientists and policy-makers to brush aside ethical objections and to press ahead with whatever research seems to offer the prospect of a breakthrough. Those who advocate research on embryonic stem cells in the hope of achieving such a result make the grave mistake of denying the inalienable right to life of all human beings from the moment of conception to natural death. The destruction of even one human life can never be justified in terms of the benefit that it might conceivably bring to another. Yet, in general, no such ethical problems arise when stem cells are taken from the tissues of an adult organism, from the blood of the umbilical cord at the moment of birth, or from fetuses who have died of natural causes (cf. Congregation for the Doctrine of the Faith, Instruction *Dignitas Personae*, no. 32).

It follows that dialogue between science and ethics is of the greatest importance in order to ensure that medical advances are never made at unacceptable human cost. The Church contributes to this dialogue by helping to form consciences in accordance with right reason and in the light of revealed truth. In so doing she seeks, not to impede scientific progress, but on the contrary to guide it in a direction that is truly fruitful and beneficial to humanity. Indeed, it is her conviction that everything human, including scientific research, "is not only received and respected by faith, but is also purified, elevated and perfected" (ibid., no. 7). In this way science can be helped to serve the common good of all mankind, with a particular regard for the weakest and most vulnerable.

In drawing attention to the needs of the defenseless, the Church thinks not only of the unborn but also of those without easy access to expensive medical treatment. Illness is no respecter of persons, and justice demands that every effort be made to place the fruits of scientific research at the disposal of all who stand to benefit from them, irrespective of their means. In addition to purely ethical considerations, then, there are issues of a social, economic and political nature that need to be addressed in order to ensure that advances in medical science go hand in hand with just and equitable provision of health-care services. Here the Church is able to offer concrete assistance through her extensive health-care apostolate, active in so many countries across the globe and directed with particular solicitude to the needs of the world's poor.

Dear friends, as I conclude my remarks, I want to assure you of a special remembrance in prayer and I commend to the intercession of Mary, *Salus Infirmorum*, all of you who work so hard to bring healing and hope to those who suffer. I pray that your commitment to adult stem cell research will bring great blessings for the future of man and genuine enrichment to his culture. To you, your families and your collaborators, as well as to all the patients who stand to benefit from your generous expertise and the results of your work, I gladly impart my Apostolic Blessing. Thank you very much!

CHAPTER VII

To the Tribunal of the Roman Rota

Address to the Members of the
Tribunal of the Roman Rota

January 28, 2006

Distinguished Prelate Auditors,
Officials and Collaborators of the Apostolic Tribunal of the Roman Rota,

Almost a year has passed since your Tribunal's last meeting with my beloved Predecessor, John Paul II. It was the last in a long series of meetings. Of the great legacy of canon law that he has also bequeathed to us, I would like in particular to focus on the Instruction *Dignitas Connubii, On the Procedures to Follow in Handling Causes of the Nullity of Marriage*. It was intended to set out a sort of *vademecum* which not only contains the respective norms in force on this subject but enriches them with further, relevant measures necessary for their correct application.

The greatest contribution of this Instruction, which I hope will be applied in its entirety by those who work in the ecclesiastical tribunals, consists in pointing out, in the causes of matrimonial nullity, the extent and manner in which to apply the norms contained in the canons concerning ordinary contentious judgment, as well as the observance of the special norms dictated for causes on the state of persons and for the public good.

As you well know, the attention dedicated to trials of the nullity of marriage increasingly transcends the context of experts. In fact, for many of the faithful, ecclesiastical sentences in this sector bear upon whether or not they may receive Eucharistic Communion.

199

It is this very aspect, so crucial from the viewpoint of Christian life, which explains why the subject of the nullity of marriage arose again and again at the recent Synod on the Eucharist. It might seem at first glance that there is a great divergence between the pastoral concern shown during the Synod's work and the spirit of the collection of juridical norms in *Dignitas Connubii*, almost to the point of their being in opposition.

On the one hand, it would appear that the Synod Fathers were asking the ecclesiastical tribunals to strive to ensure that members of the faithful who are not canonically married regularize their marital situation as soon as possible and return to the Eucharistic Banquet.

On the other, canonical legislation and the recent Instruction would seem instead to limit this pastoral thrust, as though the main concern were rather to proceed with the foreseen juridical formalities at the risk of forgetting the pastoral aim of the process.

This approach conceals a false opposition between law and pastoral ministry in general. Here, I do not intend to go deeply into this issue which John Paul II already treated on several occasions, especially in his Address to the Roman Rota in 1990 (January 18, 1990; cf. ORE, January 29, 1990, 6).

At this first meeting with you, I prefer to concentrate on love for the truth, which is the fundamental meeting point between canon law and pastoral ministry. With this affirmation, moreover, I associate myself in spirit with precisely what my venerable Predecessor said to you in his Address last year (January 29, 2005; ORE, February 2, 3).

The canonical proceedings for the nullity of marriage are essentially a means of ascertaining the truth about the conjugal bond. Thus, their constitutive aim is not to complicate the life of the faithful uselessly, nor far less to exacerbate their litigation, but rather to render a service to the truth.

Moreover, the institution of a trial in general is not in itself a means of satisfying any kind of interest but rather a qualified instrument to comply with the duty of justice to give each person what he or she deserves.

Precisely in its essential structure, the trial is instituted in the name of justice and peace. In fact, the purpose of the proceedings is the declaration of the truth by an impartial third party, after the parties have been given equal opportunities to support their arguments and proof with adequate room for discussion. This exchange of opinions is normally necessary if the judge is to discover the truth, and consequently, to give the case a just verdict. Every system of trial must therefore endeavor to guarantee the objectivity, speed and efficacy of the judges' decisions.

In this area too, the relationship between faith and reason is of fundamental importance. If the case corresponds with right reason, the fact that the Church has recourse to legal proceedings to resolve interecclesial matters of a juridical kind cannot come as a surprise. A tradition has thus taken shape which is now centuries old and has been preserved in our day in ecclesiastical tribunals throughout the world.

It is well to keep in mind, moreover, that in the age of classical medieval law, canon law made an important contribution to perfecting the institutional structure of the trial itself.

Its application in the Church concerns first and foremost cases in which, since the matter remains to be resolved, the parties could reach an agreement that would settle their litigation but for various reasons this does not happen.

In seeking to determine what is right, not only does recourse to proceedings not aim to exacerbate conflicts, but it seeks to make them more humane by finding objectively adequate solutions to the requirements of justice.

Of course, this solution on its own does not suffice, for people need love, but when it is inevitable, it is an important step in the right direction.

Indeed, trials may also revolve around matters whose settlement is beyond the competence of the parties involved since they concern the rights of the entire Ecclesial Community. The process of declaring the nullity of a marriage fits precisely into this context: in fact, in its twofold natural and sacramental dimension, marriage is not a good that spouses can dispose of nor, given its social and public nature, can any kind of self-declaration be conjectured.

At this point the second observation spontaneously arises: no trial is against the other party, as though it were a question of inflicting unjust damage. The purpose is not to take a good away from anyone but rather to establish and protect the possession of goods by people and institutions.

In addition to this point, valid in every trial, there is another, more specific point in the hypothesis of matrimonial nullity. Here, the parties are not contending for some possession that must be attributed to one or the other. The trial's aim is rather to declare the truth about the validity or invalidity of an actual marriage, in other words, about a reality that establishes the institution of the family and deeply concerns the Church and civil society.

Consequently, it can be said that in this type of trial the Church herself is the one to whom the request for the declaration is addressed. Given the natural presumption of the validity of a marriage that has been formally contracted, my Predecessor, Benedict XIV, an outstanding canon lawyer, conceived of and made obligatory in such proceedings the participation of the defender of the bond at the said trial (cf. Apostolic Constitution *Dei Miseratione*, November 3, 1741). Thus, the dialectic of the proceedings whose aim was to ascertain the truth was better guaranteed.

Just as the dialectic of the proceedings leads us to understand the criterion of the search for the truth, so it can help us grasp the other aspect of the question: its pastoral value, which cannot be separated from love for the truth.

Indeed, pastoral love can sometimes be contaminated by complacent attitudes toward the parties. Such attitudes can seem pastoral, but in fact they do not correspond with the good of the parties and of the Ecclesial Community itself; by avoiding confrontation with the truth that saves, they can even turn out to be counterproductive with regard to each person's saving encounter with Christ.

The principle of the indissolubility of marriage forcefully reaffirmed here by John Paul II (cf. Addresses of January 21, 2000, and January 28, 2002) pertains to the integrity of the Christian mystery.

Today, unfortunately, we may observe that this truth is sometimes obscured in the consciences of Christians and of people of good will. For this very reason, the service that can be offered to the faithful and to non-Christian spouses in difficulty is deceptive: it reinforces in them, if only implicitly, the tendency to forget the indissolubility of their union.

Thus, the possible intervention of the ecclesiastical institution in causes of nullity risks merely registering a failure.

However, the truth sought in processes of the nullity of marriage is not an abstract truth, cut off from the good of the people involved. It is a truth integrated in the human and Christian journey of every member of the faithful. It is very important, therefore, that the declaration of the truth is reached in reasonable time.

Divine Providence certainly knows how to draw good from evil, even when the ecclesiastical institutions neglect their duty or commit errors.

It is nonetheless a grave obligation to bring the Church's institutional action in her tribunals ever closer to the faithful. Besides, pastoral sensitivity must be directed to avoiding matrimonial nullity when the couple seeks to marry and to striving to help the spouses solve their possible problems and find the path to reconciliation. That same pastoral sensitivity to the real situations of individuals must nonetheless lead to safeguarding the truth and applying the norms prescribed to protect it during the trial.

I hope that these reflections will serve to help people understand better that love of the truth links the institution of canonical causes of the nullity of marriage with the authentic pastoral sense that must motivate these processes. With this key to interpretation, the Instruction *Dignitas Connubii* and the concerns expressed during the last Synod can be seen to converge.

Dear friends, the Ecclesial Community is deeply grateful to you for your discreet approach to the arduous and fascinating task of bringing about this harmony. With the sincere hope that your judicial activity will contribute to the good of all who turn to you and will encourage them in their personal encounter with the Truth that is Christ, I bless you with gratitude and affection.

Address to the Members of the
Tribunal of the Roman Rota

January 27, 2007

Dear Prelate Auditors,
Officials and Collaborators of the Tribunal of the Roman Rota,

I am particularly pleased to meet you once again on the occasion of the inauguration of the judicial year.

I cordially greet the College of Prelate Auditors, starting with the Dean, Bishop Antoni Stankiewicz, whom I thank for his words introducing our meeting. I then greet the Officials, the Advocates and the other Collaborators of this Tribunal, as well as the Members of the *Studio Rotale* and all those present. I willingly take this opportunity to renew to you the expression of my esteem and, at the same time, to reaffirm the importance of your ecclesial ministry in as vital a sector as judicial activity. I am very mindful of the valuable work you are required to carry out diligently and scrupulously on behalf of this Apostolic See and with its mandate. Your sensitive task of service to the truth in justice is supported by the illustrious traditions of this Tribunal, which each one of you must feel bound to respect.

Last year, at my first meeting with you, I sought to explore ways to overcome the apparent antithesis between the institution of causes of the nullity of marriage and genuine pastoral concern. In this perspective, the love of truth emerges as a point of convergence between processual research and the pastoral service of the person. We must not forget, however, that in causes of the nullity of marriage, the legal truth presupposes the "truth of the marriage" itself. Yet the expression "truth of the marriage" loses its existential importance in a cultural context that is marked by relativism and juridical positivism, which regard marriage as a mere social formalization of emotional ties.

Consequently, not only is it becoming incidental, as human sentiments can be, but it is also presented as a legal superstructure of the human will that can be arbitrarily manipulated and even deprived of its heterosexual character.

This crisis of the meaning of marriage is also influencing the attitude of many of the faithful. The practical effects of what I have called "the hermeneutic of discontinuity and rupture" with regard to the teaching of the Second Vatican Council, (cf. *Address to the Roman Curia*, December 22, 2005), is felt especially acutely in the sphere of marriage and the family.

Indeed, it seems to some that the conciliar teaching on marriage, and in particular, the description of this institution as *"intima communitas vitae et amoris"* [*the intimate partnership of life and love*] (*Gaudium et Spes*, no. 48), must lead to a denial of the existence of an indissoluble conjugal bond because this would be a question of an "ideal" to which "normal Christians" cannot be "constrained."

In fact, the conviction that the pastoral good of the person in an irregular marital situation requires a sort of canonical regularization, independently of the validity or nullity of his/her marriage, independently, that is, of the "truth" of his/her personal status, has also spread in certain ecclesiastical milieus. The process of the declaration of matrimonial nullity is actually considered as a legal means for achieving this objective, according to a logic in which the law becomes the formalization of subjective claims. In this regard, it should first be pointed out that the Council certainly described marriage as *intima communitas vitae et amoris*, but this partnership is determined, in accordance with the tradition of the Church, by a whole set of principles of the divine law which establish its true and permanent anthropological meaning (cf. ibid.).

Furthermore, the Magisteriums of Paul VI and John Paul II, as well as the legislative action of both the Latin and Eastern Codes, have followed up the Council in faithful hermeneutical continuity with regard to both the doctrine and the discipline of marriage and indeed, persevered in its effort for "reform" or "renewal in continuity" (cf. *Address to the Roman Curia*). This development was based on the indisputable presupposition that marriage has a truth of its own—that is, the human knowledge, illumined by the Word of God, of the sexually different reality of the man and of the woman with their profound needs for complementarity, definitive self-giving and exclusivity—to whose discovery and deepening reason and faith harmoniously contribute.

The *anthropological and saving truth of marriage*—also in its juridical dimension—is already presented in Sacred Scripture. Jesus' response to those Pharisees who asked his opinion about the lawfulness of repudiation is well known: "Have you not read that he who made them from the beginning *made them male and female*, and said, 'For this reason *a man shall leave his father and mother and be joined to his wife, and the two shall become one*'? So they are no longer two but one. What therefore God has joined together, let no man put asunder" (Mt 19:4-6).

The citations of Genesis (1:27; 2:24) propose the matrimonial truth of the "principle," that truth whose fullness is found in connection with Christ's union with the Church (cf. Eph 5:30-31) and was the object of such broad and deep reflections on the part of Pope John Paul II in his cycles of catecheses on human love in the divine design.

On the basis of this dual unity of the human couple, it is possible to work out an authentic *juridical anthropology of marriage*. In this sense, Jesus' conclusive words are especially enlightening: "What therefore God has joined together, let no man put asunder." Every marriage is of course the result of the free consent of the man and the woman, but in practice their freedom expresses the natural capacity inherent in their masculinity and femininity.

The union takes place by virtue of the very plan of God who created them male and female and gives them the power to unite forever those natural and complementary dimensions of their persons.

The indissolubility of marriage does not derive from the definitive commitment of those who contract it but is intrinsic in the nature of the "powerful bond established by the Creator" (John Paul II, *Catechesis*, General Audience, November 21, 1979, no. 2: ORE, November 26, 1979, 1).

People who contract marriage must be definitively committed to it because marriage is such in the plan of creation and of redemption. And the essential juridical character of marriage is inherent precisely in this bond which represents for the man and for the woman a requirement of justice and love from which, for their good and for the good of all, they may not withdraw without contradicting what God himself has wrought within them.

It is necessary to study this aspect further, not only in consideration of your role as canon lawyers, but also because the overall understanding of the institution of marriage must also include clarity with regard to its juridical dimension. However, conceptions of the nature of this relationship can be radically divergent. For positivism, the legality of the conjugal bond would be solely the result of the application of a formally valid and effective human norm. In this way, the human reality of life and conjugal love remains extrinsic to the "juridical" institution of marriage. A hiatus is created between law and human existence which radically denies the possibility of an anthropological foundation of the law.

The traditional role of the Church is quite different in the understanding of the juridical dimension of the conjugal union following the teachings of Jesus, of the Apostles and of the Holy Fathers. St. Augustine, for instance, in citing St. Paul, forcefully affirms: "*Cui fidei [coniugali] tantum iuris tribuit Apostolus, ut eam potestatem appellaret, dicens: Mulier non habet potestatem corporis sui, sed vir; similiter autem et vir non habet potestatem corporis sui, sed mulier* (1 Cor 7:4)" (*De Bono Coniugali*, 4, 4).

St. Paul who so profoundly explains in his Letter to the Ephesians the "mysterion mega" of conjugal love in relation to Christ's union with the Church (5:22-31), did not hesitate to apply to marriage the strongest legal terms to designate the juridical bond by which spouses are united in their sexual dimension. So too, for St. Augustine, lawfulness is essential in each one of the three goods (*proles, fides, sacramentum*) that form the backbone of his doctrinal exposition on marriage.

With regard to the subjective and libertarian relativization of the sexual experience, the Church's tradition clearly affirms the natural juridical character of marriage, that is, the fact that it belongs by nature to the context of justice in interpersonal relations.

In this perspective, the law is truly interwoven with life and love as one of the intrinsic obligations of its existence. Therefore, as I wrote in my first Encyclical, "From the standpoint of creation, *eros* directs man toward marriage, to a bond which is unique and definitive; thus, and only thus, does it fulfill its deepest purpose" (*Deus Caritas Est*, no. 11).

Thus, love and law can be united to the point of ensuring that husband and wife *mutually owe to one another* the love *with which they spontaneously love one another*: the love in them is the fruit of their free desire for the good of one another and of their children; which, moreover, is also a requirement of love for one's own true good.

All the activity of the Church and of the faithful in the context of the family, must be based on this *truth about marriage and its intrinsic juridical dimension*. In spite of this, as I recalled earlier, the relativistic mindset, in more or less open or subtle ways, can also insinuate itself into the ecclesial community.

You are well aware that this is a risk of our time which is sometimes expressed in a distorted interpretation of the canonical norms in force. One must react to this tendency with courage and faith, constantly applying the *hermeneutic of renewal in continuity* and not allowing oneself to be seduced by forms of interpretation that involve a break with the Church's tradition.

These paths lead away from the true essence of marriage, as well as from its intrinsic juridical dimension and, under various more or less attractive names, seek to conceal a false conjugal reality.

So it is that the point is sometimes reached of maintaining that nothing is right or wrong in a couple's relationship, provided it corresponds with the achievement of the subjective aspirations of each party. In this perspective, the idea of marriage "*in facto esse*" oscillates between merely factual relations and the juridical-positivistic aspect, overlooking its essence as an intrinsic bond of justice between the persons of the man and of the woman.

The contribution of ecclesiastical tribunals to overcoming the crisis of the meaning of marriage, in the Church and in civil society, could seem to some people of somewhat secondary or minor importance.

However, precisely because marriage has an intrinsically juridical dimension, being wise and convinced servants of justice in this sensitive and most important sector has the significant value of witness and is of deep reassurance to all. Dear Prelate Auditors, you are committed on a front in which responsibility for the truth makes itself felt in a special way in our times.

In being faithful to your task, make sure that your action fits harmoniously into an overall rediscovery of the beauty of that "truth about marriage," the truth of the "principle," which Jesus fully taught us and of which the Holy Spirit continually reminds us in the Church today.

Dear Prelate Auditors, Officials and collaborators, these are the considerations to which I felt impelled to call your attention, in the certainty that I would find in you judges and magistrates ready to share and make your own so important and serious a doctrine.

To each and every one I express in particular my pleasure and my total confidence that the Apostolic Tribunal of the Roman Rota, an effective and authoritative manifestation of the juridical wisdom of the Church, will continue to carry out consistently its own, far from easy *munus*, at the service of the divine plan followed by the Creator and the Redeemer in the institution of marriage.

As I invoke divine help upon your work, I cordially impart a special Apostolic Blessing to you all.

Address to the Members of the
Tribunal of the Roman Rota

January 26, 2008

Dear Prelate Auditors,
Officials and Collaborators of the Tribunal of the Roman Rota,

The occurrence of the first centenary of the restoration of the Apostolic Tribunal of the Roman Rota, ratified by St. Pius X in 1908 with his Apostolic Constitution Sapienti Consilio, has just been recalled in the cordial words of your Dean, Bishop Antoni Stankiewicz. This circumstance enhances the sense of appreciation and gratitude with which I am meeting you, already for the third time. I offer my cordial greeting to each and every one of you. I see personified in you, esteemed Prelate Auditors, and in all those who take part in various capacities in the work of this Tribunal, an institution of the Apostolic See whose roots, embedded in canonical tradition, have proven an inexhaustible source of vitality. It is your task to keep this tradition alive, in the conviction that you are thereby rendering an ever timely service to the overall administration of justice in the Church.

This centenary is a favorable opportunity for reflecting on a fundamental aspect of the Rota's activity: the value of rotal jurisprudence in the ensemble of the administration of justice in the Church. It is a dimension highlighted in the very description of the Rota given by the Apostolic Constitution *Pastor Bonus*: "The Roman Rota is a court of higher instance at the Apostolic

See, usually at the appellate stage, with the purpose of safeguarding rights within the Church; it fosters unity of jurisprudence, and, by virtue of its own decisions, provides assistance to lower tribunals" (no. 126). In their annual Discourses, my beloved Predecessors frequently spoke with appreciation and trust of the Roman Rota's jurisprudence, both in general and with reference to practical matters and especially matrimonial topics.

If it is only right and proper to remember the ministry of justice exercised by the Rota during its centuries-old existence—and especially in the last one hundred years—it is also appropriate on this occasion to endeavor to examine the meaning of this service, the annual volume of whose decisions demonstrate that it is a practical instrument. We might wonder in particular why rotal sentences possess a juridical importance that exceeds the immediate context of the causes in which they are issued. Regardless of the formal value that every ordinary juridical process can attribute to previous proceedings, there is no doubt that in a certain way, its individual decisions concern the whole of society. Indeed, they continue to determine what all can expect from the tribunals, which undoubtedly influences the tenor of social life. Any legal system must seek to offer solutions in which, as well as the prudential evaluation of individual cases, the same principles and general norms of justice are applied. Only in this way is a trusting atmosphere created in the tribunals' activity and the arbitrary nature of subjective criteria avoided. Furthermore, within each judicial organization the hierarchy that exists between the various tribunals is such that possible recourse to higher tribunals in itself provides for the unity of jurisprudence.

The above-mentioned considerations are also perfectly applicable to ecclesiastical tribunals. Indeed, since canonical processes concern the juridical aspects of salvific goods or of other temporal goods which serve the Church's mission, the requirement of unity in the essential criteria of justice and the need to be able to reasonably foresee the direction that judicial decisions will take becomes a public ecclesial good of particular importance for the People of God's internal life and its institutional witness in the world. In addition to the intrinsic value of reasonableness inherent in the work of a Tribunal that usually decides cases in the last instance, it is clear that the value of the Roman Rota's jurisprudence is dependent upon its nature as a higher instance which can appeal to the Apostolic See. The legal measures which recognize this value (cf. c. 19, *Code of Canon Law*; Apostolic Constitution *Pastor Bonus*, no. 126) do not create, but rather, declare this value. It derives ultimately from the need to administer justice in accordance with equal parameters in all that is precisely in itself essentially equal.

As a result, the value of rotal jurisprudence is not a factual sociological issue since it has a properly juridical character, placed at the service of substantial justice. It would therefore be improper to admit to any opposition between rotal jurisprudence and the decisions of local tribunals that are called to play an indispensable role in rendering the administration of justice immediately accessible, and in being able to investigate and resolve practical cases at times linked to peoples' culture and mentality. In any case, all rulings must always be based on the principles and common norms of justice. This requirement, common to any juridical order, has specific significance in the Church to the extent that the requirements of communion are at stake. This involves the protection of what is common to the universal Church, entrusted in a particular way to the Supreme Authority and to the bodies that participate *ad normam iuris* in its sacred authority.

In the matrimonial context, rotal jurisprudence has carried out very conspicuous work in the past one hundred years. In particular, it has made significant contributions that are expressed in the codification in force. In this light, one cannot think that the importance of the jurisprudential interpretation of law by the Rota has diminished. Indeed, the application of current canon law requires precisely that it reflect the true sense of justice, linked first of all to marriage's very essence. The Roman Rota is constantly called to carry out an arduous task which has a strong influence on the work of all tribunals: that of understanding the existence or non-existence of the matrimonial reality, which is intrinsically anthropological, theological and juridical. For a better understanding of the role of jurisprudence, I would like to insist on what I said to you last year concerning the "intrinsic juridical dimension of marriage" (cf. Address to Roman Rota, January 27, 2007). Law cannot be reduced to a mere collection of positive rules that tribunals are required to apply. The only way to give a solid foundation to the jurisprudential task is to conceive of it as a true exercise of *prudentia iuris*. This prudence is quite the opposite of arbitrariness or relativism, for it permits events to reveal the presence or absence of the specific relationship of justice which marriage is, with its real human and saving meaning. Only in this way do jurisprudential maxims acquire their true value without becoming a compilation of abstract and repetitive rules, exposed to the risk of subjective or arbitrary interpretations.

The objective assessment of the facts in the light of the Magisterium and the law of the Church thus constitutes a very important aspect of the Roman Rota's activity and exercises great influence on ministers of justice of the tribunals of local Churches. Rotal jurisprudence should be seen as exemplary juridical wisdom carried out with the authority of the Tribunal permanently constituted by the Successor of Peter for the good of the whole Church. Thanks to this work, the concrete reality in causes of matrimonial nullity is objectively judged in light of criteria that constantly reaffirm the reality of matrimonial indissolubility, open to every man and woman in accordance with the plan of God, Creator and Savior. Constant effort is needed to attain that unity of the criteria of justice which essentially characterizes the notion of jurisprudence itself and is a fundamental presupposition for its activity. In the Church, precisely because of her universality and the diversity of the juridical cultures in which she is called to operate, there is always a risk that "local forms of jurisprudence" develop, *sensim sine sensu,* ever more distant from the common interpretation of positive law and also from the Church's teaching on matrimony. I hope that appropriate means may be studied to make rotal jurisprudence more and more manifestly unitive as well as effectively accessible to all who exercise justice, in order to ensure its uniform application in all Church tribunals.

The value of interventions of the Ecclesiastical Magisterium on matrimonial and juridical issues, including the Roman Pontiff's Discourses to the Roman Rota, should also be seen in this realistic perspective. They are a ready guide for the work of all Church tribunals, since they authoritatively teach the essential aspects of the reality of marriage. In his last Address to the Rota, my venerable Predecessor John Paul II put people on guard against the positivistic mentality in the understanding of law, which tends to make a distinction between laws and jurisprudential approaches and the Church's doctrine. He affirmed: "In fact, the authentic interpretation of God's Word, exercised by the Magisterium of the Church, has juridical value to the extent that it concerns the context of law, without requiring any further formal procedure to become juridically and morally binding. For a healthy juridical interpretation, it is indispensable to understand the whole body of the Church's teachings and to place every affirmation systematically in the flow of tradition. It will thus be possible to avoid selective and distorted interpretations and useless criticisms at every step" (John Paul II, Address to Roman Rota, January 29, 2005).

This centenary is destined to go beyond the formal commemoration. It will become an opportunity for a reflection that must temper your commitment, enlivening it with an ever deeper ecclesial sense of justice which is a true service to saving communion. I encourage you to pray daily for the Roman Rota and for all who work in the sector of the administration of justice in the Church, with recourse to the motherly intercession of Mary Most Holy, *Speculum iustitiae.* This invitation might seem merely devotional and somewhat extrinsic to your ministry; but we must not forget that everything in the Church is brought about through the force of prayer, which transforms our entire existence and fills us with the hope that Jesus brings to us. This prayer, inseparable from daily commitment that is serious and competent, will bring light and strength, faithfulness and authentic renewal to the life of this venerable Institution through which, *ad normam iuris,* the Bishop of Rome exercises his primatial solicitude for the administration of justice throughout the People of God. Therefore, may my Blessing today, full of affection and gratitude, embrace both you who are present here and all those worldwide who serve the Church and all the faithful in this field.

Address to the Members of the Tribunal of the Roman Rota

January 29, 2009

Distinguished Judges,
Officials and Collaborators of the Tribunal of the Roman Rota,

The solemn inauguration of the judiciary activity of your Tribunal offers me once again this year the joy of receiving its distinguished members: Monsignor Dean, whom I thank for his gracious words of greeting, the College of Prelate Auditors, the Officials of the Tribunal and the Advocates of the *Studium Rotale.* I offer all of you my own cordial greetings, together with the expression of my appreciation for the important responsibilities which you carry out as faithful collaborators of the Pope and of the Holy See.

You are expecting from the Pope, at the beginning of your working year, a word of light and guidance in the fulfillment of your demanding work. There are any number of topics which we might discuss on this occasion, but now, some twenty years after the Addresses of Pope John Paul II regarding psychic incapacity in the causes of matrimonial nullity (February 5, 1987: ORE, February 23, 1987, 6; and January 25, 1988: ORE, February 15, 1988, 7), it seems fitting to question the extent to which these interventions have had an adequate reception in ecclesiastical tribunals.

This is not the moment to draw up a balance sheet, but no one can fail to see that there continues to be a concrete and pressing problem in this regard. In some cases, unfortunately, one can still perceive the urgent need to which my venerable Predecessor pointed: that of preserving the ecclesial community "from the scandal of seeing the value of Christian marriage being destroyed in practice by the exaggerated and almost automatic multiplication of declarations of nullity, in cases of the failure of marriage, on the pretext of some immaturity or psychic weakness on the part of the contracting parties" (Address to the Roman Rota, February 5, 1987, no. 9).

In our meeting today, I wish to draw the attention of those engaged in the practice of law to the need to handle cases with the depth and seriousness required by the ministry of truth and charity proper to the Roman Rota.

Indeed, responding to the need for procedural precision, the aforementioned Addresses provide, on the basis of the principles of Christian anthropology, fundamental criteria not only for the weighing of expert psychiatric and psychological reports, but also for the judicial settlement of causes. In this regard it is helpful to recall several clear-cut distinctions. First of all, the distinction between "the psychic maturity which is seen as the goal of human development" and, on the other hand, "the canonical maturity which is the basic minimum required for establishing the validity of marriage" (Address to the Roman Rota, February 5, 1987, no. 6). Second, the distinction between incapacity and difficulty, inasmuch as "incapacity alone, and not difficulty in giving consent and in realizing a true community of life and love, invalidates a marriage" (ibid., no. 7). Third, the distinction between the canonical approach to normality, which, based on an integral vision of the human person, "also includes moderate forms of psychological difficulty," and the clinical approach, which excludes from the concept of normality every limitation of maturity and "every form of psychic illness" (Address to the Roman Rota, January 25, 1988, no. 5). And finally, the distinction between the "minimum capacity sufficient for valid consent" and the ideal capacity "of full maturity in relation to happy married life" (ibid.).

Furthermore, based on the engagement of the faculties of the intellect and the will in the formation of matrimonial consent, Pope John Paul II, in the aforementioned Address of February 5, 1987, reaffirmed the principle that true incapacity "is to be considered only when an anomaly of a serious nature is present which, however it may be defined, must substantially vitiate the capacity to understand and/or to will" (Address to the Roman Rota, February 5, 1987, no. 7).

In this regard it seems fitting to recall that the norm of the Code of Canon Law regarding mental incapacity, so far as its application is concerned, was amplified and completed by the recent Instruction *Dignitas Connubii* of January 25, 2005. The Instruction requires that, for such incapacity to be established, at the time of the celebration of marriage there must already have been present a specific mental anomaly (art. 209 § 1) which seriously impairs the use of reason (art. 209 § 2, no. 1; c. 1095, no. 1) or the critical and elective faculty with regard to making serious decisions, particularly concerning the free choice of a state of life (art. 209 § 2, no. 2; c. 1095, no. 2), or which produces in the contracting party not only a serious difficulty but also the impossibility of fulfilling the duties inherent in the obligations of marriage (art. 209 § 2, no. 3; c. 1095, no. 3).

On this occasion, however, I would like to reconsider the theme of the incapacity to contract marriage, as treated in Canon 1095, also in the light of the relationship between the human person and marriage, and to recall several fundamental principles which must guide those engaged in the practice of law.

First of all, there is a need for a new and positive appreciation of the capacity to marry belonging in principle to every human person by virtue of his or her very nature as a man or a woman. We tend in fact to risk falling into a kind of anthropological pessimism which, in the light of today's cultural context, would consider marriage as practically impossible. Apart from the fact that this context is not uniform in the various parts of the world, genuine incapacity to consent cannot be confused with the real difficulties facing many people, especially the young, which lead them to conclude that marital union is, as a rule, inconceivable and impracticable. Rather, a reaffirmation of the innate human capacity for marriage is itself the starting point for enabling couples to discover the natural reality of marriage and its importance for salvation. Ultimately, what is at stake is the truth about marriage itself and its intrinsic juridical nature (cf. Benedict XVI, Address to the Roman Rota, January 27, 2007), which is an indispensable premise for the ability to understand and evaluate the capacity required to marry.

Capacity in this sense has to be seen in relation to the essential nature of marriage as "the intimate partnership of life and conjugal love established by the Creator and endowed with its proper laws" (*Gaudium et Spes*, no. 48), and, in a particular way, with essential and inherent obligations which are to be accepted by the couple (c. 1095, no. 3). This capacity is not calculated in relation to a specific degree of existential or actual realization of the conjugal union by the fulfillment of the essential obligations, but rather in relation to the effective will of each of the partners, which makes that realization possible and operative from the very moment that the marriage is contracted. To speak of capacity or incapacity, therefore, is meaningful to the extent that it concerns the act itself of contracting marriage, since the bond which comes into being by the will of the spouses constitutes the juridical reality of the biblical "one flesh" (Gn 2:24; Mk 10:8; Eph 5:31; cf. c. 1061 §1), and its continuing validity does not depend on the subsequent conduct of the couple during their married life. In a very different way, a reductionist approach which disregards the truth about marriage sees the effective establishment of a genuine communion of life and love, idealized at the level of a purely human well-being, as essentially dependent on purely accidental factors, rather than on the exercise of human freedom sustained by grace. It is true that this freedom of human nature, "wounded in the natural powers proper to it," and "inclined to sin" (*Catechism of the Catholic Church*, no. 405), is limited and imperfect, but it is not thereby unauthentic and insufficient for carrying out that act of self-determination by the parties which is the conjugal covenant, which gives rise to marriage and to the family founded on it.

Obviously certain anthropological and "humanistic" currents of thought, aimed at self-realization and egocentric self-transcendence, so idealize the human person and marriage that they end up denying the psychic capacity of a great number of people, basing this on elements which do not correspond to the essential requirements of the conjugal bond. Faced with such conceptions, those engaged in the practice of ecclesial law cannot prescind from the healthy realism spoken of by my venerable Predecessor (cf. John Paul II, Address to the Roman Rota, January 27, 1997, no. 4), since capacity refers to the minimum needed for those marrying to give their being as a male person and a female person in order to establish that bond to which the vast majority of human beings are called. It follows that, as a matter of principle, causes of nullity due to psychic incapacity require the judge to employ the service of experts to ascertain the existence of a genuine incapacity (c. 1680; art. 203 1), which is always an exception to the natural principle of the capacity needed to understand, decide for and carry out the mutual self-giving from which the conjugal bond arises.

This then, distinguished members of the Tribunal of the Roman Rota, is what I wished to present to you on this solemn occasion, which is always a pleasant one for me. I exhort you to persevere with deep Christian conscientiousness in the exercise of your office, whose great importance for the life of the Church is evident from all that I have said. May the Lord always assist you in your demanding work by the light of his grace, in pledge of which I impart to all of you, with deep affection, my Apostolic Blessing.

Address to the Members of the
Tribunal of the Roman Rota

January 29, 2010

Dear Members of the Tribunal of the Roman Rota,

I am pleased to meet you once again for the inauguration of the Judicial Year. I cordially greet the College of Prelate Auditors, beginning with the Dean, Bishop Antoni Stankiewicz, whom I thank for the words he has addressed to me on behalf of all present. I extend my greeting to the Promoters of Justice, the Defenders of the Bond, the other Officials, the Advocates, and all of this Apostolic Tribunal's Collaborators, as well as the Members of the *Studium Rotale*. I gladly take this opportunity to renew the expression of my profound esteem and sincere gratitude for your ecclesial ministry, and at the same time I underline the necessity of your judicial activity. The valuable work that the

Prelate Auditors are called to carry out diligently, in the name and under the mandate of the Apostolic See, is supported by the authoritative and well-established traditions of this Tribunal, which each one of you is bound to respect.

Today I wish to reflect on the essential nucleus of your ministry, seeking to analyze its relationship with justice, charity and truth. I will refer especially to some of the observations made in the Encyclical *Caritas in Veritate*, which, although considered within the context of the social doctrine of the Church, can also illuminate other ecclesial areas. It is necessary to take note of the widespread and deeply-rooted, though not always evident, tendency to place justice and charity in opposition to one another, as if the two were mutually exclusive. In this regard, with reference more specifically to the life of the Church, some maintain that pastoral charity could justify every step toward declaring the nullity of the marriage bond in order to assist people who find themselves in irregular matrimonial situations. Truth itself, even if lip service be paid to it, tends thus to be viewed through a manipulative lens that would seek to adapt it, case by case, to the different requirements that emerge.

Setting out from the expression "administration of justice," I wish to point out first of all that your ministry is essentially a work of justice: a virtue "that consists in the constant and firm will to give their due to God and neighbor" (CCC, no. 1807)—the human and Christian value of which it is more important than ever to rediscover, even within the Church. Canon Law is at times undervalued, as if it were a mere technical instrument at the service of any given subjective interest, even one that is not founded on truth. Instead, Canon Law must always be considered in its essential relationship with justice, in the recognition that, in the Church, the goal of juridical activity is the salvation of souls and that it "constitutes a special participation in the mission of Christ the Shepherd . . . . in realizing the order that Christ himself desired" (John Paul II, cf. Address to the Rota Romana, January 18, 1990: ORE, January 29, 1990, 6, no. 5). In this perspective, one must also bear in mind, in any situation, that the process and the sentence are linked fundamentally to justice and must be placed at its service. The process and the sentence have a great relevance both for the parties to a dispute, and for the entire ecclesial body, and this acquires a most singular value when it entails a pronouncement on the nullity of a marriage which directly concerns the human and supernatural good of the spouses, as well as the public good of the Church. Over and above this dimension of justice that may be termed "objective," there is another inseparable dimension which concerns those who "implement the law," namely, those who make justice possible. I wish to underscore that they must be characterized by the high practice of human and Christian virtues, particularly prudence and justice, but also fortitude.

This last virtue becomes more relevant the more injustice appears to be the easiest approach to take, insofar as it implies accommodating the desires and expectations of the parties or even the conditioning of the social context. Against this background, the Judge who seeks to be just and wishes to live up to the classic paradigm of "animate justice" (cf. Aristotle, *Nicomachean Ethics*, V, 1132a), has the grave responsibility before God and men of his function, which includes due timeliness in every phase of the process: *"quam primum, salva iustitia"* [as soon as possible, while safeguarding justice] (Pontifical Council for Legislative Texts, Instruction *Dignitas Connubii*, no. 72). All those who work in the field of law, each according to his proper function, must be guided by justice. I am thinking particularly of the advocates, who must not only pay full attention to respecting the truth of the evidence, but also carefully avoid assuming, as lawyers *di fiducia*, patronage of causes which, according to their conscience, cannot be objectively supported.

The action, therefore, of those who administer justice cannot prescind from charity. Love for God and for neighbor should inform every activity, even if it appears to be the most technical and bureaucratic. The perspective and the measure of charity will help focus attention on the fact that the judge is always dealing with people, beset by problems and difficulties. The principle that *"charity goes beyond justice"* (Encyclical *Caritas in Veritate*, no. 6) applies equally to the specific sphere of those engaged in the administration of justice. Consequently, the approach toward people, while admittedly observing a specific modality linked to the process, must seek, with sensitivity and concern for the individuals involved, to facilitate contact with the competent tribunal by the parties to the case. At the same time, it is important to take definite steps, every time one glimpses hope for a favorable outcome, to induce the spouses if possible to convalidate their marriage and restore conjugal living (cf. CIC, c. 1676). Moreover, one should try to establish between the parties a climate of human and Christian openness that is based on the search for the truth (cf. *Dignitas Connubii*, art. 65 §§ 2-3).

It must be reiterated that every work of authentic charity includes an indispensable reference to justice, all the more so in our case. "Love—*caritas*—is an extraordinary force which leads people to opt for courageous and generous engagement in the field of justice and peace" (*Caritas in Veritate*, no. 1). "If we love others with charity, then first of all we are just toward them. Not only is justice not extraneous to charity, not only is it not an alternative or parallel path to charity: justice is 'inseparable from charity,' and intrinsic to it" (*Caritas in Veritate*, no. 6). Charity without justice is not charity, but a counterfeit, because charity itself requires that objectivity which is typical of justice and which must not be confused with inhuman coldness. In this regard, as my Predecessor, Venerable Pope John Paul II, said in his Address on the relationship between pastoral care and the law: "The judge . . . must always guard against the risk of misplaced compassion, which could degenerate into sentimentality, itself pastoral only in appearance" (Address to the Rota Romana, January 18, 1990).

One must avoid pseudo-pastoral claims that would situate questions on a purely horizontal plane, in which what matters is to satisfy subjective requests to arrive at a declaration of nullity at any cost, so that the parties may be able to overcome, among other things, obstacles to receiving the Sacraments of Penance and the Eucharist. The supreme good of readmission to Eucharistic Communion after sacramental Reconciliation demands, instead, that due consideration be given to the authentic good of the individuals, inseparable from the truth of their canonical situation. It would be a false "good" and a grave lack of justice and love to pave the way for them to receive the sacraments nevertheless, and would risk causing them to live in objective contradiction to the truth of their own personal condition.

Regarding truth, in my Addresses to this Apostolic Tribunal in 2006 and 2007 (January 28, 2006, and January 27, 2007), I stressed that it is possible to arrive at the truth on the essence of marriage and the reality of every personal situation that is submitted to the judgment of the tribunal, and also the truth of matrimonial processes (cf. *Dignitas Connubii*, nos. 65 §§ 1-2, 95 § 1, 167, 177, 178). Today I wish to emphasize that both justice and charity postulate love for truth and essentially entail searching for truth. In particular, charity makes the reference to truth even more exacting. "To defend the truth, to articulate it with humility and conviction, and to bear witness to it in life are therefore exacting and indispensable forms of charity. Charity, in fact, 'rejoices in the truth' (1 Cor 13:6)" (*Caritas in Veritate*, no. 1). "Only in truth does charity shine forth, only in truth can charity be authentically lived . . . Without truth, charity degenerates into sentimentality. Love becomes an empty shell, to be filled in an arbitrary way. In a culture without truth, this is the fatal risk facing love. It falls prey to contingent subjective emotions and opinions, the word 'love' is abused and distorted, to the point where it comes to mean the opposite" (ibid., no. 3).

One must keep in mind that an emptying of this kind can take place not only in the act of judging but also in the theoretical concepts that greatly influence concrete judgments. The problem arises when the very essence of marriage, rooted in the nature of man and woman, is more or less obscured, as it is the essence of marriage that makes it possible to express objective judgments on a specific marriage. In this sense, existential, person-centered and relational consideration of the conjugal union can never be at the expense of indissolubility, an essential property which, in Christian marriage, obtains, with unity, a special firmness by reason of the sacrament (cf. CIC, c. 1056).

Moreover, it must not be forgotten that matrimony is favored by the law. Consequently, in case of doubt, it must be considered valid until the contrary has been proven (cf. CIC, c. 1060). Otherwise, there is a grave risk of losing any objective reference point for pronouncements on nullity, by transforming every conjugal difficulty into a symptom of failure to establish a union whose essential nucleus of justice—the indissoluble bond—is effectively denied.

Distinguished Prelate Auditors, Officials and Advocates, I entrust these reflections to you, knowing well the spirit of faithfulness that inspires you and the commitment that you strengthen as you implement fully the Church's norms, in the search for the true good of the People of God. As comfort for your valuable work, upon each of you and upon your daily work I invoke the maternal protection of Mary Most Holy, *Speculum Iustitiae* (Mirror of Justice), and I affectionately impart my Apostolic Blessing.

Address to the Members of the
Tribunal of the Roman Rota

January 22, 2011

Dear Members of the Tribunal of the Roman Rota,

I am glad to meet you at this annual event on the occasion of the inauguration of the Judicial Year. I address a cordial greeting to the College of Prelate Auditors, starting with the Bishop Antoni Stankiewicz, the Dean, whom I thank for his courteous words. I greet the Officials, the Advocates and the other collaborators of this Tribunal, as well as all those present. This moment offers me an opportunity to express once again my appreciation of the work you are carrying out in the service of the Church and to encourage you to an ever greater commitment in such a delicate and important sector for pastoral care and for the *salus animarum*.

The post-conciliar discussion on canon law was centered on the relationship between law and pastoral care. The well-known assertion of the Venerable Servant of God, John Paul II, whose opinion was that "it is not true that, to be more pastoral, the law should be less juridical" (cf. Address to the Roman Rota, January 18, 1990, no. 4), expresses the radical surmounting of an apparent antithesis.

"The juridical and the pastoral dimensions," John Paul II, said, "are united inseparably in the Church, a pilgrim on this earth. Above all, one aspect of their harmony emerges from their common goal: the salvation of souls" (ibid.). At my first meeting with you in 2006 I tried to highlight the authentic pastoral meaning of causes of the nullity of marriage founded on love for the truth (cf. Address to the Roman Rota, January 28, 2006). Today I would like to pause to consider the juridical dimension that is inherent in the pastoral activity of preparation and admission to marriage, to seek to shed light on the connection between this work and the judicial matrimonial process.

The canonical dimension of preparation for marriage may not be an element that is immediately apparent. In fact, on the one hand one observes that in courses for the preparation of marriage canonical issues have a rather modest—if not insignificant—place since there is a tendency to think that the future spouses have little interest in problems reserved for experts.

On the other hand, although the need for the juridical work that precedes marriage and that aim to ascertain that "nothing stands in the way of its valid and licit celebration" (*Code of Canon Law*, c. 1066), escapes no one, there is a widespread view which holds that the examination of the parties engaged to be married and the publication of marriage banns or other appropriate means for carrying out the necessary inquiries which are to precede marriage (cf. ibid., c. 1067)—including courses for the preparation of marriage—are exclusively formal requirements. In fact it is often maintained that in admitting couples to marriage pastors must have a broad-minded approach, since people's natural right to marry is at stake.

It is right in this regard to reflect on the juridical dimension of marriage itself. It is a subject that I mentioned in the context of a reflection on the truth about marriage, in which I said, among other things: "With regard to the subjective and libertarian relativization of the sexual experience, the Church's tradition clearly affirms the natural juridical character of marriage, that is, the fact that it belongs by nature to the context of justice in interpersonal relations. In this perspective, the law is truly interwoven with life and love as one of the intrinsic obligations of its existence" (Address to the Roman Rota, January 27, 2007). Thus, there is no such thing as one marriage according to life and another according to law: marriage is one thing alone, it constitutes a real legal bond between the man and the woman, a bond which sustains the authentic conjugal dynamic of life and love.

The marriage celebrated by the spouses, with which pastoral care is concerned and which is the focus of canonical doctrine, is a single, natural and salvific reality whose richness certainly gives rise to a variety of approaches yet without losing its essential identity. The juridical aspect is intrinsically linked to the essence of marriage. This is understood in the light of a non-positivistic notion of law, but considered in the perspective of relationality in accordance with justice.

The right to marry, *ius connubii*, must be seen in this perspective. In other words it is not a subjective claim that pastors must fulfill through a merely formal recognition independent of the effective content of the union. The right to contract marriage presupposes that the person can and intends to celebrate it truly, that is, in the truth of its essence as the Church teaches it. No one can claim the right to a nuptial ceremony. Indeed the *ius connubii* refers to the right to celebrate an authentic marriage.

The *ius connubii* would not, therefore, be denied where it was evident that the fundamental requirements for its exercise were lacking, namely, if the required capacity for marriage were patently lacking or the person intended to choose something which was incompatible with the natural reality of marriage.

I would like to reaffirm in this regard what I wrote after the Synod of Bishops on the Eucharist: "Given the complex cultural context which the Church today encounters in many countries, the Synod also recommended devoting maximum pastoral attention to training couples preparing for marriage and to ascertaining beforehand their convictions regarding the obligations required for the validity of the sacrament of Matrimony. Serious discernment in this matter will help to avoid situations where impulsive decisions or superficial reasons lead two young people to take on responsibilities that they are then incapable of honoring (cf. *Propositio* 40). The good that the Church and society as a whole expect from marriage and from the family founded upon marriage is so great as to call for full pastoral commitment to this particular area. Marriage and the family are institutions that must be promoted and defended from every possible misrepresentation of their true nature, since whatever is injurious to them is injurious to society itself" (*Sacramentum Caritatis*, no. 29).

Preparation for marriage, in its various phases described by Pope John Paul II in the Apostolic Exhortation *Familiaris Consortio* (November 22, 1981), certainly has aims that transcend the juridical dimension because its horizon is constituted by the integral, human and Christian, good of the married couple and of their future children (cf. no. 66), aimed definitively at the holiness of their life (cf. CIC, c. 1063, 2°).

It should never be forgotten, however, that the immediate objective of this preparation is to promote the free celebration of a true marriage, that is, the constitution of a bond of justice and love between the spouses, characterized by unity and indissolubility, ordained for the good of the spouses and for the procreation and upbringing of their offspring, and which among baptized people constitutes one of the sacraments of the New Covenant. This preparation does not address an extrinsic ideological message to the couple, nor, still less, does it impose a cultural model; rather, the engaged couple are put in a position to discover the truth of a natural inclination and a capacity for committing themselves which they bear inscribed in their relational entity as man-woman. From this derives the law, as an essential component of the marital relationship, rooted in a natural potential of the spouses that the consensual gift of self actualizes.

Reason and faith compete to illumine this truth of life, however, although it must remain clear that, as Venerable John Paul II taught further, "the Church does not refuse to celebrate a marriage for the person who is *bene dispositus*, even if he is imperfectly prepared from the supernatural point of view, provided the person has the right intention to marry according to the natural reality of marriage" (Address to the Roman Rota, January 30, 2003, no. 8).

In this perspective particular care must be given to following through the preparation for marriage, whether it is remote preparation, proximate preparation or immediate preparation (cf. John Paul II, *Familiaris Consortio*, no. 66).

Among the means for ascertaining whether the project of the engaged couple is truly conjugal the prematrimonial examination stands out. This examination has a mainly juridical purpose: to ascertain that nothing impedes the valid and licit celebration of the wedding. However juridical does not mean formal, as though it were a bureaucratic step, like filling up a form based on set questions. Instead it is a unique pastoral opportunity—one to be made the most of with the full seriousness and attention that it requires—in which, through a dialogue full of respect and cordiality, the pastor seeks to help the person to face seriously the truth about himself or herself and about his or her own human and Christian vocation for marriage.

In this sense the dialogue, always conducted separately with each of the engaged pair without lessening the possibility of further conversations with the couple—requires an atmosphere of full sincerity in which stress should be put on the fact that the contracting parties themselves are those first concerned and first obliged in conscience to celebrate a valid marriage.

In this way, with the various means available for a careful preparation and verification, an effective pastoral action can be developed which seeks to prevent the nullity of marriage. It is necessary to make every effort to interrupt, as far as possible, the vicious circle that often exists between a predictable admission to marriage, without an adequate preparation and a serious examination of the prerequisites for its celebration, and a legal declaration sometimes equally facile but of a contrary nature, in which the marriage itself is considered null solely on the basis of the observation of its failure.

It is true that not all the causes of an eventual declaration of nullity can be identified or expressed in the preparation for marriage; yet likewise it would not be right to hinder admission to marriage on the basis of unfounded presumptions, such as that of considering that, in this day and age, people would generally be incapable of marriage or would only appear to have a desire for it. In this perspective it seems important that there should be an even more incisive awareness concerning the responsibility in this matter of those entrusted with the care of souls. Canon Law in general, and especially matrimonial and procedural law, certainly require a special preparation but the knowledge of the basic aspects and of the immediately practical aspects of canon law, relative to its functions, constitute a formative requirement of primary importance for all pastoral workers, particularly those who are active in the pastoral care of families.

In addition, all this requires that the work of ecclesiastical tribunals transmit a univocal message on what is essential in marriage, in harmony with the Magisterium and with canon law and speaking unanimously. Given the need for the unity of jurisprudence, entrusted to the care of this Tribunal, the other ecclesiastical tribunals must conform to the rotal jurisprudence (cf. John Paul II, Address to the Roman Rota, January 17, 1998, no. 4). I recently insisted on the need to judge correctly causes relative to consensual incapacity (cf. Address to the Roman Rota, January 29, 2009).

This question continues to be very timely. Unfortunately incorrect positions still endure, such as that of identifying the discretion of judgment required for the marriage (cf. CIC, c. 1095, no. 2) with the hoped for prudence in the decision to get married, thus confusing an issue of capacity with another which does not undermine the validity since it concerns the level of practical wisdom with which a decision is taken which is, in any case, truly matrimonial. The misunderstanding would be yet more serious were there a wish to assign an invalidating effect to rash decisions made in married life.

In the context of nullity because of the exclusion of an essential property of marriage (cf. CIC, c. 1101 § 2), a serious commitment is likewise necessary so that the judiciary pronouncements reflect the truth about marriage, the same truth that must illumine the moment of admission to marriage. I am thinking in particular of the question of the exclusion of the *bonum coniugum*. In relation to this exclusion the same danger that threatens the correct application of the norms on incapacity seems to be repeated, and that is, the search for causes of nullity in behavior that do not concern the constitution of the conjugal bond but rather its realization in life. It is necessary to resist the temptation to transform the simple shortcomings of the spouses in their conjugal existence into defects of consent.

Real exclusion can occur in fact only when the ordination toward the good of the spouses is harmed (cf. CIC, c. 1055 § 1), excluded by a positive act of will. Cases in which there is failure to recognize the other as spouse or in which the essential ordering of the community of conjugal life to the good of the other is excluded are quite exceptional. The clarification of these hypotheses of exclusion of the *bonum coniugum* must be attentively assessed by the jurisprudence of the Roman Rota.

In concluding my reflections, I return to considering the relationship between the law and pastoral ministry. It is often the object of misunderstandings, to the detriment of law, but also of pastoral care.

Instead, it is necessary to encourage in all sectors, and in a particular way in the field of marriage and of the family, a positive dynamic, sign of profound harmony between the pastoral and the juridical which will certainly prove fruitful in the service rendered to those who are approaching marriage.

Dear Members of the Tribunal of the Roman Rota, I entrust you all to the powerful intercession of the Blessed Virgin Mary, so that you may never lack divine help in carrying out your daily work with faithfulness, in a spirit of fruitful service and I very willingly impart to you all a special Apostolic Blessing.

Motu Proprio *Quaerit Semper*

August 30, 2011

Motu Proprio *Quaerit Semper* with which the Apostolic Constitution *Pastor Bonus* is amended and certain competences transferred from the Congregation for Divine Worship and the Discipline of the Sacraments to the new Office set up at the Tribunal of the Roman Rota for processes of dispensation from ratified and non-consummated marriage and for cases concerning the nullity of sacred ordination.

The Holy See has always sought to adapt its structures of governance to the pastoral needs that arise in the life of the Church in every period of history, thereby modifying the structure and competence of the Dicasteries of the Roman Curia.

The Second Vatican Council moreover confirmed this criterion, reaffirming the need to adapt the Dicasteries to the needs of our time and of different regions and rites, especially with regard to their number, their titles, their competence, their procedures and how they coordinate their activities (cf. Decree *Christus Dominus*, no. 9).

Following these principles, my Predecessor, Blessed John Paul II, proceeded to an overall reorganization of the Roman Curia through the Apostolic Constitution *Pastor Bonus*, promulgated on June 28, 1988 (*AAS* 80 [1988] 841-930), defining the competence of the different Dicasteries, taking into account the *Code of Canon Law*, promulgated five years earlier, and the norms that were then being drawn up for the Eastern Churches. Later, both my Predecessor and I intervened with further measures, modifying the structure and competence of certain Dicasteries, the better to respond to changed needs.

In present circumstances it has seemed appropriate for the Congregation for Divine Worship and the Discipline of the Sacraments to focus mainly on giving a fresh impetus to promoting the Sacred Liturgy in the Church, in accordance with the renewal that the Second Vatican Council desired, on the basis of the Constitution *Sacrosanctum Concilium*.

I have therefore deemed it opportune to transfer to a new Office, set up at the Tribunal of the Roman Rota, the competence for processes of dispensation from ratified and non-consummated marriage and cases concerning the nullity of sacred ordination.

Consequently, on the advice of the Cardinal Prefect of the Congregation for Divine Worship and the Discipline of the Sacraments and with the favorable opinion of the Dean of the Tribunal of the Roman Rota, having heard the opinion of the Supreme Tribunal of the Apostolic Signatura and of the Pontifical Council for Legislative Texts, I decree the following:

Art. 1

Articles 67 and 68 of the above-mentioned Apostolic Constitution *Pastor Bonus* are abrogated.

Art. 2

Article 126 of the Apostolic Constitution *Pastor Bonus* is amended as follows:

> "Article 126 § 1. The Roman Rota is a court of higher instance at the Apostolic See, usually at the appellate stage, with the purpose of safeguarding rights within the Church; it fosters unity of jurisprudence and, by virtue of its own decisions, provides assistance to lower tribunals.
>
> § 2. An Office has been set up at this Tribunal to examine the fact of non-consummation in a marriage and the existence of a just cause for granting a dispensation. It therefore receives all the acts, together with the *votum* of the Bishop and the remarks of the Defender of the Bond, weighs them according to its own special procedure and, if the case warrants it, submits a petition to the Supreme Pontiff requesting the dispensation.
>
> § 3. This Office is also competent to examine cases concerning the nullity of sacred ordination, in accordance with both universal and proper law, *congrua congruis referendo*."

Art. 3

The Office for processes of dispensation from ratified and non-consummated marriage and for cases concerning the nullity of sacred ordination is presided over by the Dean of the Roman Rota, assisted by Officials, Delegated Commissioners and Consultors.

Art. 4

On the day of the entry into force of these regulations, any processes of dispensation from ratified and non-consummated marriage and cases concerning the nullity of sacred ordination still pending at the Congregation for Divine Worship and the Discipline of the Sacraments will be transferred to the new Office at the Tribunal of the Roman Rota and will be decided by the latter.

I order that everything established by this Apostolic Letter *Motu Proprio data* be fully observed in all its parts, notwithstanding anything to the contrary, even if worthy of particular mention, and I establish that it be promulgated through publication in the daily newspaper *L'Osservatore Romano* and that it come into force on October 1, 2011.

CHAPTER VIII

Addresses and Messages

Homily at Mass Before the
Basilica of St. John Lateran

May 26, 2005

Dear Brothers in the Episcopate and in the Priesthood,
Dear Brothers and Sisters,

On the feast of *Corpus Domini*, the Church relives the mystery of Holy Thursday in the light of the Resurrection. There is also a Eucharistic procession on Holy Thursday, when the Church repeats the exodus of Jesus from the Upper Room to the Mount of Olives.

In Israel, the night of the Passover was celebrated in the home, within the intimacy of the family; this is how the first Passover in Egypt was commemorated, the night in which the blood of the paschal lamb, sprinkled on the crossbeam and doorposts of the houses, served as protection against the destroyer.

On that night, Jesus goes out and hands himself over to the betrayer, the destroyer, and in so doing, overcomes the night, overcomes the darkness of evil. Only in this way is the gift of the Eucharist, instituted in the Upper Room, fulfilled: Jesus truly gives his Body and his Blood. Crossing over the threshold of death, he becomes living Bread, true manna, endless nourishment for eternity. The flesh becomes the Bread of Life. . . .

The Holy Thursday procession accompanies Jesus in his solitude toward the *via crucis*. The *Corpus Domini* procession responds instead in a symbolic way to the mandate of the Risen One: I go before you to Galilee. Go to the extreme ends of the world, take the Gospel to the world. . . . In the *Corpus*

Domini procession, we walk with the Risen One on his journey to meet the entire world, as we said. By doing precisely this, we too answer his mandate: "Take, eat . . . Drink of it, all of you" (Mt 26:26ff.).

Address to Participants in the Fifty-Fourth Assembly of the Italian Bishops' Conference

May 30, 2005

One crucial issue that demands of us the maximum pastoral attention is the family. In Italy, even more than in other countries, the family truly is the fundamental cell of society. It is deeply rooted in the hearts of the young generations and bears the brunt of many problems, providing support and remedies to situations that would otherwise be desperate.

Yet also in Italy, families in today's cultural atmosphere are exposed to the many risks and threats with which we are all familiar. The inner frailty and instability of many conjugal unions is combined with the widespread social and cultural tendency to dispute the unique character and special mission of the family founded on marriage.

Then, Italy itself is one of the nations where the low birth rate is the most serious and constant, with consequences that are already felt by the whole body of society. This is why for some time you Italian Bishops have been joining your voice to that of John Paul II, primarily in defending the sacredness of human life and the value of the institution of marriage, but also in promoting the role of the family in the Church and in society, requesting financial and legislative measures that support young families in having children and raising them.

In the same spirit, you are currently involved in enlightening and motivating the decisions of Catholics and of all citizens concerning the upcoming referendums on the law on assisted procreation. Your clear and concrete commitment is a sign of your concern as Pastors for every human being, who can never be reduced to a means but is always an end, as our Lord Jesus Christ teaches us in his Gospel and as human reason itself tells us. In this commitment and in all the many different kinds of work that are part of a Pastor's mission and duty, I am close to you with my words and my prayers, trusting in the light and grace of the Holy Spirit who acts in the conscience and heart.

The same concern for the true good of human beings that impels us to take care of the future of families and of respect for human life, is expressed in attention to the poor we have among us, to the sick, to immigrants, to peoples decimated by disease, war and famine.

Dear Italian Brother Bishops, I want to thank you and your faithful for your generous charity, making the Church that new people in which no one is a stranger. Let us always remember the Lord's words: what you have done "for one of my least brothers, you did it for me" (Mt 25:40). . . .

I assure you of my daily prayers for you and for your Churches, for the whole of the beloved Italian Nation, for its present and its Christian future, for the task it is called to carry out in Europe and in the world, and I impart with affection a special Apostolic Blessing to you, to your priests and to every Italian family.

Address to Pilgrims from the Diocese of Verona, Italy

June 4, 2005

Dear Brothers and Sisters of the Diocese of Verona,

I am delighted to welcome you on your pilgrimage to the Tombs of the Apostles. I cordially greet you all, starting with your Bishop, whom I thank for expressing your common sentiments. I greet the priests, the men and women religious, the leaders of the ecclesial associations and movements, as well as the civil Authorities who wished to be present at this meeting.

At the end of the diocesan Synod, with today's pilgrimage to the Apostolic See, you desire to express the bonds of communion that bind the diocesan Community of Verona to the Church of Rome and to reaffirm your full adherence to the magisterium of the Successor of Peter, constituted by Christ, "Pastor of all the faithful," who is "to promote the common good of the universal Church and the particular good of all the Churches" (*Christus Dominus*, no. 2).

You have come here to be strengthened in the faith and I, only recently called to this weighty task, am glad to greet, through you, such an ancient and illustrious Ecclesial Community as that of St. Zeno, very venerated in my Country as well, and to encourage you to persevere in your commitment to Christian witness in the contemporary world.

Your Synod, which began three years ago, has reached its culmination in the Year of the Eucharist. This happy coincidence helps us to understand better that the Eucharist is the heart of the Church and of Christian life. *"Ecclesia de Eucharistia"*—*"the Church draws her life from the Eucharist"*—this is what the Servant of God John Paul II has left written for us in his last Encyclical. All the contexts of your Diocese must live on the Eucharist: from the families, small domestic churches, to every social and pastoral section of the parishes and of the territory.

At Bari last Sunday, at the end of the [Italian] National Eucharistic Congress, I wanted to recall that "Christ is truly present among us in the Eucharist. His presence is not static. It is a dynamic presence that grasps us, to make us his own, to make us assimilate him. Christ draws us to him, he makes us come out of ourselves to make us all one with him. In this way he also integrates us in the communities of brothers and sisters, and communion with the Lord is always also communion with our brothers and sisters" (Homily, Solemnity of *Corpus Domini*, Bari, May 29, 2005).

It is true: our spiritual life essentially depends upon the Eucharist. Without it, faith and hope are extinguished and charity cools.

This is why, dear friends, I urge you to take better and better care of the quality of the Eucharistic celebrations, especially those on Sunday, so that Sunday may truly be the Lord's Day and confer fullness of meaning on every-day events and activities, demonstrating the joy and beauty of the faith.

The family was rightly one of the main themes of your Synod, as it has been in the pastoral guidelines of the Church in Italy and throughout the world. Indeed, in your Diocese, moreover, as elsewhere, divorce and de facto unions are on the increase, and this constitutes for Christians an urgent appeal to proclaim and bear witness to the Gospel of Life and of the Family in its integrity.

The family is called to be an "intimate partnership of life and love" (*Gaudium et Spes*, no. 48), because it is founded on indissoluble marriage. Despite the difficulties and the social and cultural conditioning of this period of history, Christian spouses must not cease to be in their lives a sign of God's faithful love: may they collaborate actively with priests in the pastoral guid-ance of engaged couples, young married couples and families, and in bringing up the new generations.

Dear brothers and sisters, yesterday we celebrated the Solemnity of the Sacred Heart of Jesus: only in this inexhaustible source of love will you be able to find the necessary energy for your mission.

The Church was born from the Heart of the Redeemer, from his pierced side, and she is ceaselessly renewed in the sacraments.

May it be your concern to draw spiritual nourishment from prayer and an intense sacramental life; deepen your personal knowledge of Christ and strive with all your might for the "high standard of ordinary Christian living" which is what holiness is, as our beloved John Paul II used to say.

May Mary Most Holy, whose Immaculate Heart we are commemorating today, obtain as a gift for all the members of your Diocese total fidelity to Christ and to his Church. I entrust the post-synodal journey that awaits you to the intercession of the heavenly Mother of the Redeemer and to the support of the saints and blesseds of your region.

For my part, I assure you of my remembrance in prayer, as I affectionately impart a special Apostolic Blessing to your Bishop, to you and to your entire diocesan Community.

Address to Participants in the Ecclesial Diocesan Convention of Rome

June 6, 2005

Dear Brothers and Sisters,

I very willingly accepted the invitation to introduce our Diocesan Convention with a Reflection, first of all because it gives me the chance to meet you, of having direct contact with you, and then too, because I can help you acquire a deeper understanding of the sense and purpose of the pastoral journey the Church of Rome is making.

I greet with affection each one of you, Bishops, priests, deacons, men and women religious, and in particular you lay people and families who consciously take on those duties of responsibility and Christian witness that have their root in the sacrament of Baptism and, for those who are married, in the sacrament of Marriage. I cordially thank the Cardinal Vicar and the couple, Luca and Adriana Pasquale, for their words on behalf of you all.

This Convention and the guidelines it will provide for the pastoral year are a new stage on the journey begun by the Church of Rome, based on the Diocesan Synod, with the "City Mission," desired by our deeply loved Pope John Paul II in preparation for the Great Jubilee of 2000.

In that Mission all the components of our Diocese—parishes, religious communities, associations and movements—were mobilized, not only for a mission to the people of Rome, but to be themselves "a people of God in mission," putting into practice John Paul II's felicitous expression: "The parish must seek itself outside itself" and find itself, that is, in the places where the people live. So it was that during the City Mission thousands of Christians of Rome, mainly lay people, became missionaries and took the word of faith first to the families in the various districts of the city, and then to the different workplaces, hospitals, schools and universities, and the environments of culture and leisure time.

After the Holy Year, my beloved Predecessor asked you not to stop on this journey and not to lose the apostolic energies kindled or the fruits of grace gathered. Therefore, since 2001, the fundamental pastoral policy of the Diocese has been to give the mission a permanent form, and to impress a more decidedly missionary approach on the life and activities of the parishes and of every other ecclesial situation.

I want to tell you first of all that I fully intend to confirm this decision: indeed, it is proving to be more and more necessary. There are no alternatives to it in a social and cultural context in which many forces are working to distance us from the faith and from Christian life.

For two years now the missionary commitment of the Church of Rome has focused above all on the family. This is not only because today this fundamental human reality is subjected to a multitude of problems and threats and is therefore especially in need of evangelization and practical support, but also because Christian families constitute a crucial resource for education in the faith, for the edification of the Church as communion and for her ability to be a missionary presence in the most varied situations of life, as well as to act as a Christian leaven in the widespread culture and social structures.

We will also continue along these lines in the coming pastoral year, and so the theme of our Convention is "Family and Christian community: formation of the person and transmission of the faith."

The assumption from which it is necessary to set out, if we are to understand the family mission in the Christian community and its tasks of forming the person and transmitting the faith, is always that of the meaning of marriage and the family in the plan of God, Creator and Savior. This will therefore be the focus of my Reflection this evening and I will refer to the teaching of the Apostolic Exhortation *Familiaris Consortio* (Part II, nos. 12-16).

Marriage and the family are not in fact a chance sociological construction, the product of particular historical and financial situations. On the other hand, the question of the right relationship between the man and the woman is rooted in the essential core of the human being and it is only by starting from here that its response can be found.

In other words, it cannot be separated from the ancient but ever new human question: Who am I? What is a human being? And this question, in turn, cannot be separated from the question about God: Does God exist? Who is God? What is his face truly like?

The Bible gives one consequential answer to these two queries: the human being is created in the image of God, and God himself is love. It is therefore the vocation to love that makes the human person an authentic image of God: man and woman come to resemble God to the extent that they become loving people.

This fundamental connection between God and the person gives rise to another: the indissoluble connection between spirit and body: in fact, the human being is a soul that finds expression in a body and a body that is enlivened by an immortal spirit.

The body, therefore, both male and female, also has, as it were, a theological character: it is not merely a body; and what is biological in the human being is not merely biological but is the expression and the fulfillment of our humanity.

Likewise, human sexuality is not juxtaposed to our being as person but part of it. Only when sexuality is integrated within the person does it successfully acquire meaning.

Thus, these two links, between the human being with God and in the human being, of the body with the spirit, give rise to a third: the connection between the person and the institution.

Indeed, the totality of the person includes the dimension of time, and the person's "yes" is a step beyond the present moment: in its wholeness, the "yes" means "always," it creates the space for faithfulness. Only in this space can faith develop, which provides a future and enables children, the fruit of love, to believe in human beings and in their future in difficult times.

The freedom of the "yes," therefore, reveals itself to be freedom capable of assuming what is definitive: the greatest expression of freedom is not the search for pleasure without ever coming to a real decision; this apparent, permanent openness seems to be the realization of freedom, but it is not true. The true expression of freedom is the capacity to choose a definitive gift in which freedom, in being given, is fully rediscovered.

In practice, the personal and reciprocal "yes" of the man and the woman makes room for the future, for the authentic humanity of each of them. At the same time, it is an assent to the gift of a new life.

Therefore, this personal "yes" must also be a publicly responsible "yes," with which the spouses take on the public responsibility of fidelity, also guaranteeing the future of the community. None of us, in fact, belongs exclusively to himself or herself: one and all are therefore called to take on in their inmost depths their own public responsibility.

Marriage as an institution is thus not an undue interference of society or of authority. The external imposition of form on the most private reality of life is instead an intrinsic requirement of the covenant of conjugal love and of the depths of the human person.

Today, the various forms of the erosion of marriage, such as free unions and "trial marriage," and even pseudo-marriages between people of the same sex, are instead an expression of anarchic freedom that are wrongly made to pass as true human liberation. This pseudo-freedom is based on a trivialization of the body, which inevitably entails the trivialization of the person. Its premise is that the human being can do to himself or herself whatever he or she likes:

thus, the body becomes a secondary thing that can be manipulated, from the human point of view, and used as one likes. Licentiousness, which passes for the discovery of the body and its value, is actually a dualism that makes the body despicable, placing it, so to speak, outside the person's authentic being and dignity.

The truth about marriage and the family, deeply rooted in the truth about the human being, has been actuated in the history of salvation, at whose heart lie the words: "God loves his people." The biblical revelation, in fact, is first and foremost the expression of a history of love, the history of God's Covenant with humankind.

Consequently, God could take the history of love and of the union of a man and a woman in the covenant of marriage as a symbol of salvation history. The inexpressible fact, the mystery of God's love for men and women, receives its linguistic form from the vocabulary of marriage and the family, both positive and negative: indeed, God's drawing close to his people is presented in the language of spousal love, whereas Israel's infidelity, its idolatry, is designated as adultery and prostitution.

In the New Testament God radicalizes his love to the point that he himself becomes, in his Son, flesh of our flesh, a true man. In this way, God's union with humankind acquired its supreme, irreversible form.

Thus, the blue-print of human love is also definitely set out, that recip rocal "yes" which cannot be revoked· it does not alienate men and women but sets them free from the different forms of alienation in history in order to restore them to the truth of creation.

The sacramental quality that marriage assumes in Christ, therefore, means that the gift of creation has been raised to the grace of redemption. Christ's grace is not an external addition to human nature, it does not do violence to men and women but sets them free and restores them, precisely by raising them above their own limitations. And just as the Incarnation of the Son of God reveals its true meaning in the Cross, so genuine human love is self-giving and cannot exist if it seeks to detach itself from the Cross.

Dear brothers and sisters, this profound link between God and the human being, between God's love and human love, is also confirmed in certain tendencies and negative developments that have weighed heavily on us all. In fact, the debasement of human love, the suppression of the authentic capacity for loving, is turning out in our time to be the most suitable and effective weapon to drive God away from men and women, to distance God from the human gaze and heart.

Similarly, the desire to "liberate" nature from God leads to losing sight of the reality of nature itself, including the nature of the human being, reducing it to a conglomeration of functions so as to have them available at will to build what is presumed to be a better world and presumed to be a happier humanity. Instead, the Creator's design is destroyed, and so is the truth of our nature.

Even in the begetting of children marriage reflects its divine model, God's love for man. In man and woman, fatherhood and motherhood, like the body and like love, cannot be limited to the biological: life is entirely given only when, by birth, love and meaning are also given, which make it possible to say yes to this life.

From this point it becomes clear how contrary to human love, to the profound vocation of the man and the woman, are the systematic closure of a union to the gift of life and even more, the suppression or manipulation of newborn life.

No man and no woman, however, alone and single-handed, can adequately transmit to children love and the meaning of life. Indeed, to be able to say to someone "your life is good, even though I may not know your future," requires an authority and credibility superior to what individuals can assume on their own.

Christians know that this authority is conferred upon that larger family which God, through his Son Jesus Christ and the gift of the Holy Spirit, created in the story of humanity, that is, upon the Church. Here they recognize the work of that eternal, indestructible love which guarantees permanent meaning to the life of each one of us, even if the future remains unknown.

For this reason, the edification of each individual Christian family fits into the context of the larger family of the Church, which supports it and carries it with her and guarantees that it has, and will also have in the future, the meaningful "yes" of the Creator. And the Church is reciprocally built up by the family, a "small domestic church," as the Second Vatican Council called it (*Lumen Gentium*, no. 11; *Apostolicam Actuositatem*, no. 11), rediscovering an ancient Patristic expression (cf. St. John Chrysostom, *In Genesim Serm.* VI, 2; VII, 1).

In the same sense, *Familiaris Consortio* affirms that "Christian marriage . . . constitutes the natural setting in which the human person is introduced into the great family of the Church" (no. 15).

There is an obvious consequence to all this: the family and the Church— in practice, parishes and other forms of Ecclesial Community—are called to collaborate more closely in the fundamental task that consists, inseparably, in the formation of the person and the transmission of the faith.

We know well that for an authentic educational endeavor, communicating a correct theory or doctrine does not suffice. Something far greater and more human is needed: the daily experienced closeness that is proper to love, whose most propitious place is above all the family community, but also in a parish, movement or ecclesial association, in which there are people who care for their brothers and sisters because they love them in Christ, particularly children and young people, but also adults, the elderly, the sick and families themselves. The great Patron of educators, St. John Bosco, reminded his spiritual sons that "education is something of the heart and that God alone is its master" (*Epistolario*, 4, 209).

The central figure in the work of educating, and especially in education in the faith, which is the summit of the person's formation and is his or her most appropriate horizon, is specifically the form of witness. This witness becomes a proper reference point to the extent that the person can account for the hope that nourishes his life (cf. 1 Pt 3:15) and is personally involved in the truth that he proposes.

On the other hand, the witness never refers to himself but to something, or rather, to Someone greater than he, whom he has encountered and whose dependable goodness he has sampled. Thus, every educator and witness finds an unequalled model in Jesus Christ, the Father's great witness, who said nothing about himself but spoke as the Father had taught him (cf. Jn 8:28).

This is the reason why prayer, which is personal friendship with Christ and contemplation in him of the face of the Father, is indispensably at the root of the formation of the Christian and of the transmission of the faith. The same is, of course, also true for all our missionary commitment, and particularly for the pastoral care of families: therefore, may the Family of Nazareth be for our families and our communities the object of constant and confident prayer as well as their life model.

Dear brothers and sisters, and especially you, dear priests, I am aware of the generosity and dedication with which you serve the Lord and the Church. Your daily work forming the new generations in the faith, in close connection with the sacraments of Christian initiation, as well as marriage preparation and offering guidance to families in their often difficult progress, particularly in the important task of raising children, is the fundamental way to regenerating the Church ever anew, and also to reviving the social fabric of our beloved city of Rome.

Continue, therefore, without letting yourselves be discouraged by the difficulties you encounter. The educational relationship is delicate by nature: in fact, it calls into question the freedom of the other who, however gently, is always led to make a decision. Neither parents nor priests nor catechists, nor any other educators can substitute for the freedom of the child, adolescent or young person whom they are addressing. The proposal of Christianity in particular challenges the very essence of freedom and calls it to faith and conversion.

Today, a particularly insidious obstacle to the task of educating is the massive presence in our society and culture of that relativism which, recognizing nothing as definitive, leaves as the ultimate criterion only the self with its desires. And under the semblance of freedom it becomes a prison for each one, for it separates people from one another, locking each person into his or her own "ego."

With such a relativistic horizon, therefore, real education is not possible without the light of the truth; sooner or later, every person is in fact condemned to doubting in the goodness of his or her own life and the relationships of which it consists, the validity of his or her commitment to build with others something in common.

Consequently, it is clear that not only must we seek to get the better of relativism in our work of forming people, but we are also called to counter its destructive predominance in society and culture. Hence, as well as the words of the Church, the witness and public commitment of Christian families is very important, especially in order to reassert the inviolability of human life from conception until its natural end, the unique and irreplaceable value of the family founded on marriage and the need for legislative and administrative measures that support families in the task of bringing children into the world and raising them, an essential duty for our common future. I also offer you my heartfelt thanks for this commitment.

I would like to entrust to you a last message concerning the care of vocations to the priesthood and to the consecrated life: we all know the Church's great need of them!

First of all, prayer is crucial in order that these vocations be born and reach maturity, and that those called will always continue to be worthy of their vocation; prayer should never be lacking in any family or Christian community.

However, the life witness of priests and men and women religious and their joy in having been called by the Lord is also fundamental.

Equally so is the essential example that children receive in their own family and the conviction of families themselves that for them too, the vocation of a child of theirs is a great gift from the Lord. Indeed, the choice of virginity for the love of God and the brethren, which is required for priesthood and for consecrated life, goes hand in hand with the estimation of Christian marriage: both, in two different and complementary ways, make visible in a certain way the mystery of God's Covenant with his people.

Dear brothers and sisters, I consign these thoughts to you as a contribution to your work in the evening sessions of the Convention, and later, during the coming pastoral year. I ask the Lord to give you courage and enthusiasm, so that our Church of Rome, each parish, religious community, association or movement, may participate more intensely in the joy and labors of the mission; thus, each family and the entire Christian community will rediscover in the Lord's love the key that opens the door of hearts and makes possible a true education in the faith and people's formation.

My affection and my Blessing go with you today and in the future.

Angelus

June 12, 2005

Dear Brothers and Sisters,

The Year of the Eucharist continues. It was desired by our beloved Pope John Paul II to reawaken ever greater wonder toward this Sacrament in the consciences of believers.

One of the recurring themes in this special Eucharistic period is that of Sunday, the Lord's Day, a topic that was also at the heart of the recent Italian Eucharistic Congress held in Bari.

At the closing celebration, I too emphasized how participation in Sunday Mass must not be felt as an imposition or burden by Christians, but rather as a necessity and joy. Gathering together with our brothers and sisters to listen to the Word of God and to be nourished by Christ, sacrificed for us, is a beautiful experience that gives life meaning and imbues our hearts with peace. We Christians cannot live without Sunday.

Parents, therefore, are called to help their children to discover the value and importance of responding to the invitation of Christ, who summons the whole Christian family to Sunday Mass. An especially significant stage in this educational journey is First Communion, a true celebration for the parish community which welcomes its smallest children to the Lord's Table for the first time.

To highlight the importance of this event for families and parishes, next October 15, God willing, I will be holding a special catechetical meeting in the Vatican for children who have received their First Communion this year, especially those from Rome and Lazio. This festive gathering will be taking place toward the end of the Year of the Eucharist and during the Ordinary Assembly of the Synod of Bishops, focused on the Eucharistic mystery. It will be a suitable and beautiful opportunity to reaffirm the essential role of the Eucharist in the formation and spiritual growth of young children.

From this moment I entrust this meeting to the Virgin Mary, so that she may teach us to love Jesus more and more, in constant meditation on his Word and in adoration of his presence in the Eucharist; I also ask her to help us enable the young generations to discover the "precious pearl" of the Eucharist, which gives life true and full meaning. With this intention, we now turn to the Holy Virgin.

Address to the Ambassador of Switzerland to the Holy See

June 16, 2005

Mr. Ambassador,

I am pleased to welcome you on the occasion of the presentation of the Letters accrediting you as Ambassador Extraordinary and Plenipotentiary of the Swiss Confederation to the Holy See, and I thank you for your kind words. I would be most grateful if you would kindly convey to the President of the Swiss Confederation and to the Federal Council my gratitude for their courteous greetings, and reciprocate by expressing to them my cordial good wishes for all the inhabitants of Switzerland.

How could I fail to mention, at the beginning of our meeting, the Visit of my Predecessor Pope John Paul II to your Country and his memorable meeting with the young people, a sign of hope for all Swiss Catholics?

At the same time, I am delighted with the cordial diplomatic relations that exist between your Country and the Holy See. I am equally pleased with the open dialogue between the representatives of the Swiss Confederation and the Country's Bishops, in an attempt to find satisfactory solutions, for both the Confederation and the Cantons, to any difficulties in their mutual relations that might still exist.

After the example of most Western European countries, Swiss society has experienced a considerable evolution in its customs and, under the combined pressures of technological progress and the wishes of a part of public opinion, new laws have been proposed in various sectors that affect respect for life and for the family. This concerns the delicate questions of the transmission of life, of sickness and of the end of life, but also the place of the family and respect for marriage.

On all these issues that are related to the fundamental values, the Catholic Church has clearly expressed herself through the voices of her Pastors and will continue to do so as long as necessary, to recall ceaselessly the inalienable greatness of human dignity that demands respect for human rights and, first and foremost, of the right to life.

I would like to encourage Swiss society to remain open to the surrounding world, to retain its place in the world and in Europe, and to put its talents at the service of the human community, especially in the poorest countries that will not be able to develop without this assistance.

Likewise, I hope that your Country will continue to be open to those who arrive in search of work or protection, convinced that its wealth also lies in the welcome it offers to others.

In a world where many conflicts are still in progress, it is important that the dialogue between cultures does not only involve the national leaders, but that it involve one and all, in families, in the places of education, in the world of work and in social relations, in order to build a true culture of peace.

Your Excellency, may I greet through you the Pastors and faithful of the Catholic Church who live in Switzerland. I know that they are concerned with preserving the vital link of communion with the Successor of Peter and harmoniously living with their Christian brothers of other traditions.

As you observed, Your Excellency, your young compatriots of the Pontifical Swiss Guard exemplify this connection between Switzerland and the Holy See, witnessing to a great sense of service.

At the time when you are inaugurating your mission, Mr. Ambassador, please accept my very best wishes, and the assurance that you will always find welcome and understanding among my collaborators. Upon you, Your Excellency, upon your family, upon your collaborators and upon the entire Swiss People, I invoke an abundance of God's Blessings.

Address to the Ambassador of Malta to the Holy See

June 16, 2005

To give life to a united and supportive Europe is a commitment of all its peoples. Indeed, Europe must be able to combine the legitimate interests of each nation with the requirements of the common good of the whole Continent.

I am grateful to you, Mr. Ambassador, for expressing the renewed desire of your Country to play the lead in this new phase of the Continent's history, by helping to reinforce its capacity for dialogue, for the defense and promotion of the family founded on marriage, for the Christian traditions and for openness to and an encounter with the different cultures and religions.

Address to the President of the Italian Republic

June 24, 2005

Mr. President,

I have the joy today of reciprocating the most cordial visit that you were pleased to pay me as Head of the Italian State last May 3 on the occasion of the new pastoral service to which the Lord has called me. First of all, therefore, I would like to thank you and through you, to thank the Italian People for the warm welcome they have accorded me from the very first day of my pastoral service as Bishop of Rome and Pastor of the universal Church.

For my part, I assure the citizens of Rome and then the whole Italian Nation of my commitment to do my utmost for the religious and civil good of those whom the Lord has entrusted to my pastoral care.

The proclamation of the Gospel which, in communion with the Italian Bishops, I am called to make to Rome and to Italy, is not only at the service of the Italian people's growth in faith and in the Christian life but also of its progress on the paths of concord and peace. Christ is the Savior of the whole person, spirit and body, his spiritual and eternal destiny and his temporal and earthly life. Thus, when his message is heard, the civil community also becomes more responsible and attentive to the needs of the common good and shows greater solidarity with the poor, the abandoned and the marginalized.

Reviewing Italian history, one is struck by the innumerable works of charity that the Church, with great sacrifices, set up for the relief of all kinds of suffering. Today the Church intends to journey on along this same path, without any ambition for power and without requesting social or financial privileges. The example of Jesus Christ, who "went about doing good works and healing all" (Acts 10:38), remains the Church's supreme norm of conduct among the peoples.

Relations between the Church and the Italian State are founded on the principle spelled out by the Second Vatican Council, which says: "The political community and the Church are autonomous and independent of each other in their own fields. Nevertheless, both are devoted to the personal vocation of man, though under different titles" (*Gaudium et Spes*, no. 76).

This principle was already present in the Lateran Pacts and was subsequently confirmed in the Agreements that modified the Concordat. Therefore, a healthy secularism of the State, by virtue of which temporal realities are governed according to their own norms but which does not exclude those ethical references that are ultimately founded in religion, is legitimate. The autonomy of the temporal sphere does not exclude close harmony with the superior and complex requirements that derive from an integral vision of man and his eternal destiny.

I am eager to assure you, Mr. President, and all the Italian People, that the Church desires to maintain and to foster a cordial spirit of collaboration and understanding at the service of the spiritual and moral growth of the Country; it would be seriously harmful, not only for her but also for Italy, to attempt to weaken or to break these very special ties that bind her to the Country. The Italian culture is deeply imbued with Christian values, as can be seen in the splendid masterpieces that the Nation has produced in all fields of thought and art.

My hope is that the Italian People will not only not deny the Christian heritage that is part of their history but will guard it jealously and make it produce new fruits worthy of the past. I am confident that Italy, under the wise and exemplary guidance of those who are called to govern it, will continue to carry out in the world its civilizing mission in which it has so distinguished itself down the centuries. By virtue of its history and its culture, Italy can make a very worthwhile contribution, particularly to Europe, helping it to rediscover the Christian roots that enabled it to achieve greatness in the past and can still serve to deepen the profound unity of the Continent.

Mr. President, as you can easily understand, I have many concerns at the beginning of my pastoral service on the Chair of Peter. I would like to point out some of them which, because of their universally human character, cannot but also concern those who are responsible for government. I am alluding to the problem of the protection of the family founded on marriage, as it is recognized also in the Italian Constitution (no. 29), the problem of the defense of human life from conception to its natural end and lastly, the problem of education and consequently of school, an indispensable training ground for the formation of the new generations.

The Church, accustomed as she is to scrutinizing God's will engraved in the very nature of the human creature, sees in the family a most important value that must be defended from any attack that aims to undermine its solidity and call its very existence into question.

The Church recognizes human life as a primary good, the premise for all other goods. She therefore asks that it be respected both at its initial and its final stages and stresses the duty to provide adequate palliative treatment that makes death more human.

As for schools, her role is connected with the family as a natural expansion of its task of formation. In this regard, save the competence of the State to dictate the general norms of instruction, I cannot but express the hope that the right of parents to choose education freely will be respected, and that in so doing they will not have to bear the additional burden of further expenses. I trust that Italian legislators, in their wisdom, will be able to find "human" solutions to the problems mentioned here, in other words, solutions that respect the inviolable values implicit in them.

Lastly, expressing my hope that the Nation will continue to advance on the path of spiritual and material well-being, I join you, Mr. President, in urging all the citizens and all the members of society always to live and work in a spirit of genuine harmony, in a context of open dialogue and mutual trust, in the commitment to serve and promote the common good and the dignity of every person. I would like to conclude, Mr. President, by recalling the esteem and affection that the Italian People feels for you, as well as its full confidence in fulfilling the duties inherent in your exalted office.

I have the joy of joining in this affectionate esteem and trust, as I entrust you and your Consort, Mrs. Franca Ciampi, the leaders of the life of the Nation and the entire Italian People to the protection of the Virgin Mary, so intensely venerated in the countless shrines dedicated to her. With these sentiments, I invoke upon you all the Blessing of God, a pledge of every desired good.

Address to Members of the "Little Work of Divine Providence" Lay Movement

June 28, 2005

Dear Brothers and Sisters,

"Blessed are the peacemakers, for they shall be called sons of God" (Mt 5:9). How timely and necessary this Beatitude is!

Persevere, dear friends, each one in your own province and in accordance with your own possibilities, in offering your collaboration for the safeguard of the dignity of every person, for the defense of human life in the service of a determined action of authentic peace in every social milieu. I address this invitation especially to you, dear young people, whom I see are very numerous.

Thank you for your commitment. My beloved Predecessor John Paul II, whose process of Beatification begins this very day, used to like to repeat that you young people are the hope and future of the Church and of humanity. In the heart of each one, therefore, may the desire to give life to a world of true and stable peace never cease to grow.

Address to Participants in the Archdiocesan Pilgrimage from Madrid

July 4, 2005

The Church in Madrid desires to be present in all the fields of daily life and also in the means of social communications. This is an important aspect, for the Spirit impels us to take to every man and woman the love that God the Father revealed in Jesus Christ.

This love is caring, generous and unconditional, and is not only offered to those who listen to his message but also to those who do not know it or reject it.

Each one of the faithful must feel called, as if sent by Christ, to seek out those who have drifted away from the community, like the disciples of Emmaus who succumbed to disappointment (cf. Lk 24:13-35). It is necessary to go to the very fringes of society to take to everyone the light of Christ's message about the meaning of life, the family and society, reaching out to those who live in the desert of neglect and poverty and loving them with the love of the Risen Christ.

In every apostolate and in Gospel proclamation, as St. Paul says, "If I . . . have not love, I am nothing" (1 Cor 13:2).

General Audience*

November 2, 2005

My affectionate greetings go out also to you representatives of the National Association of Large Families. Your welcome presence provides me with an opportunity to recall the centrality of the family, the foundational cell of society and the primary place where life is welcomed and served.

In today's social context, nuclear families with many children stand as a testimony of faith, of courage and of optimism because without children there is no future! I hope for further social and legislative actions to protect and support larger families who enrich the whole country and offer it hope.

Address to the Bishops of the Czech Republic on Their *Ad Limina* Visit**

November 18, 2005

Your Eminence and venerable brothers!

The visit *ad limina Apostolorum* is one of the most intense moments of ecclesial communion and fraternal sharing of the episcopal ministry. On this

---

*   This excerpt is an unofficial translation of the Italian.

**   This address is an unofficial translation of the Italian.

occasion, each bishop can pause before the Lord together with his con-
freres to reflect on the life of his own community from the perspective of
the intimate relationship that links the particular Churches to the Universal
Church. Together with the Successor of Peter you wish to give evidence of
full adhesion to Christ and generous availability for the faithful of the flock
entrusted to you. You are welcome, dear brothers, in this See of Rome, which
is also the spiritual focal point for Catholics in every part of the world.

In my meetings with each of you I had the opportunity to come to know
a very lively Church which feels itself called to be the leaven in a secularized
society and is, at the same time, interested, often with nostalgia in the liberating but also demanding message of the Gospel. You have highlighted the
growing number of your fellow citizens who identify themselves as members
of no Church but you have also noted the interest with which civil society
follows the activity of the Catholic Church and its programs. I think that the
material and spiritual devastation of the previous regime has left in your fellow citizens, who have now regained full freedom, the anxiety to make up for
lost time, to rush on headlong without perhaps paying enough attention to
the importance of spiritual values that provide civic and material gains with
resilience and consistency. That, however, opens up a vast field of mission
for the Christian community. Just as the tiny mustard seed, once it develops,
becomes a large bush that offers hospitality to the birds of the air, so your
Churches can welcome those who seek valid reasons for their own lives and
their own existential choices. Your communities, so united, fervent and sensitive to the theme of universal charity, already give solid witness that attracts
more than a few people even in the realm of culture. It is a sign of hope for
the formation of a mature laity that knows how to assume its proper share of
the Church's responsibilities.

I know, dear brothers, that you are engaged in following your priests and
consecrated communities with fatherly affection. These are the gifts that
Christ the Good Shepherd gives to the Czech people through your ministry.
You have given a favorable description of the clergy and religious, presenting them as people who are active and hardworking, disciplined and united.
Along with you I express lively thanksgiving to the Lord for this presence that
is so meaningful for the Church. This picture that gives cause for consolation
should not, however, let us forget other aspects that cause understandable
concern. First of all, the scarcity of priests: this is a fact that rightly leads you
to give special urgency to pastoral work for vocations. From this same point
of view, the commitment to forming solid Christian families shows itself to
be particularly important for the life of the Church because the possibility of
counting on healthy and generous new generations depends on the family as
the chance to show them the beauty of a life entirely consecrated to Christ
and their brothers and sisters. It is right, then, that you made a priority of

your commitment to care for families, both those in formation and those already formed and perhaps in difficulty. The family, which is the cell of society on the natural level, is the fundamental school for Christian formation on the spiritual level. The Second Vatican Council rightly presented it as the "domestic church," noting that in it, "parents should, by their word and example, be the first preachers of the faith to their children; they should encourage them in the vocation which is proper to each of them, fostering with special care vocation to a sacred state" (LG, no. 11).

Along with this programmatic point of your pastoral work, you have turned your attention to the "extended family" which is the parish, well aware that it is in this sphere that the believer experiences the Church as the Mystical Body of Christ and learns how to live out the social dimension of the faith. From this point of view, the involvement of the laity in the activity of the parish and their introduction to a healthy and rich liturgical life are very important. The Christian community is a reality of persons with its own rules, a living body that, in Jesus, exists in the world to bear witness to the power of the Gospel. Thus, it brings together brothers and sisters who have no desire for power or selfish interests but who live in the joy of the charity of God who is Love.

In such a context, the state should have no problem in recognizing in the Church a partner that does not come with any prejudice in its activities of service to the citizens. In fact, the Church carries out its activity in the religious context to allow believers to express their faith without, however, invading civil authority's area of competence. With its apostolic commitment and its contributions to charity, health and education, the Church can promote the progress of society in a climate of great religious freedom. As has been noted, the Church does not seek privileges but only the ability to carry out its mission. When this right of the Church is recognized it is, in fact, the whole society that benefits.

Venerable brothers, there you have a few reflections that I wanted to share with you in this first meeting. I am spiritually close to you in the exercise of your pastoral ministry and I particularly exhort you to continue ecumenical dialogue faithfully. I know that this is intense, just as the dialogue with your fellow citizens in the cultural realm about the basic values that hold every civil society together is also intense. May the Lord support your pastoral efforts with His grace, through the intercession of His Immaculate Mother. I accompany you with a cordial Apostolic Blessing that I bestow on you, on your priests, on consecrated persons and on all the lay faithful who form part of the flock entrusted to you by Divine Providence.

Address to Participants in the Conference on the Human Genome Organized by the Pontifical Council for Health Pastoral Care

November 19, 2005

Your Eminence,
Venerable Brothers in the Episcopate and in the Priesthood,
Distinguished Ladies and Gentlemen,

I address my cordial greeting to you all, with a special thought of gratitude to Cardinal Javier Lozano Barragán for the kind greeting he has expressed on behalf of those present.

I offer a special greeting to the Bishops and priests who are taking part in this Conference as well as the speakers, who have certainly made a highly qualified contribution to the problems addressed in these days: their reflections and suggestions will be the subject of an attentive evaluation by the competent ecclesial bodies.

Placing myself in the pastoral perspective proper to the Pontifical Council that has sponsored this Conference, I would like to point out that today, especially in the area of breakthroughs in medical science, the Church is being given a further possibility of carrying out the precious task of enlightening consciences, in order to ensure that every new scientific discovery will serve the integral good of the person, with constant respect for his or her dignity.

In underlining the importance of this pastoral task, I would like first of all to say a word of encouragement to those in charge of promoting it.

The contemporary world is marked by the process of secularization. Through complex cultural and social events, it has not only claimed a just autonomy for science and the organization of society, but has all too often also obliterated the link between temporal realities and their Creator, even to the point of neglecting to safeguard the transcendent dignity of human beings and respect for human life itself.

Today, however, secularization in the form of radical secularism no longer satisfies the more aware and alert minds. This means that possible and perhaps new spaces are opening up for a profitable dialogue with society and not only with the faithful, especially on important themes such as those relating to life.

This is possible because, in peoples with a long Christian tradition, there are still seeds of humanism which the disputes of nihilistic philosophy have not yet reached. Indeed, these seeds tend to germinate more vigorously, the more serious the challenges become.

Believers, moreover, know well that the Gospel is in an intrinsic harmony with the values engraved in human nature. Thus, God's image is deeply impressed in the soul of the human being, the voice of whose conscience it is far from easy to silence.

With the Parable of the Sower, Jesus in the Gospel reminds us that there is always good ground on which the seed may fall, spring up and bear fruit. Even people who no longer claim to be members of the Church or even those who have lost the light of faith, nonetheless remain attentive to the human values and positive contributions that the Gospel can make to the good of the individual and of society.

It is particularly easy to become aware of this by reflecting on the topic of your Conference: the people of our time, whose sensitivity, moreover, has been heightened by the terrible events that have clouded the twentieth century and the beginning of the twenty-first, easily understand that human dignity cannot be identified with the genes of the human being's DNA and is not diminished by the possible presence of physical differences or genetic defects.

The principle of "non-discrimination" on the basis of physical or genetic factors has deeply penetrated consciences and is formally spelled out in the charters of human rights. The truest foundation of this principle lies in the dignity inherent in every human person because he or she is created in the image and likeness of God (cf. Gn 1:26).

What is more, a serene analysis of scientific data leads to a recognition of the presence of this dignity in every phase of human life, starting from the very moment of conception. The Church proclaims and proposes this truth not only with the authority of the Gospel, but also with the power that derives from reason. This is precisely why she feels duty bound to appeal to every person of good will in the certainty that the acceptance of these truths cannot but benefit individuals and society.

Indeed, it is necessary to preserve ourselves from the risks of a science and technology that claim total autonomy from the moral norms inscribed in the nature of the human being.

There are many professional bodies and academies in the Church that are qualified to evaluate innovations in the scientific environment, particularly in the world of biomedicine; then there are doctrinal bodies specifically designated to define the moral values to be safeguarded and to formulate norms required for their effective protection; lastly, there are pastoral Dicasteries, such as the Pontifical Council for Health Pastoral Care, whose task is to ensure that the Church's pastoral presence is effective.

This third task is not only invaluable with regard to an ever more adequate humanization of medicine, but also in order to guarantee a prompt response to the expectations by each individual of effective spiritual assistance.

Consequently, it is necessary to give pastoral health care a new impetus. This implies renewal and the deepening of the pastoral proposal itself. It should take into account the growing mass of knowledge spread by the media and the higher standard of education of those they target.

We cannot ignore the fact that more and more frequently, not only leg-islators but citizens too are called to express their thoughts on problems that can be described as scientific and difficult. If they lack an adequate education, indeed, if their consciences are inadequately formed, false values or deviant information can easily prevail in the guidance of public opinion.

Updating the training of pastors and educators to enable them to take on their own responsibilities in conformity with their faith, and at the same time in a respectful and loyal dialogue with non-believers, is the indispensable task of any up-to-date pastoral health care. Today, especially in the field of the applications of genetics, families can lack adequate information and have difficulty in pre-serving the moral autonomy they need to stay faithful to their own life choices.

In this sector, therefore, a deeper and more enlightened formation of con-sciences is necessary. Today's scientific discoveries affect family life, involving families in unexpected and sensitive decisions that require responsible treat-ment. Pastoral work in the field of health care thus needs properly trained and competent advisers.

This gives some idea of the complex and demanding management needed in this area today.

In the face of these growing needs in pastoral care, as the Church con-tinues to trust in the light of the Gospel and the power of Grace, she urges those responsible to study a proper methodology in order to help individuals, families and society, combining faithfulness and dialogue, theological study and the ability for mediation.

In this, she sets great store especially by the contribution of all, such as you who are gathered here to take part in this International Conference and who have at heart the fundamental values that support human coexistence. I gladly take this opportunity to express to you all my grateful appreciation for your contribution in a sector so important for the future of humanity.

With these sentiments, I invoke from the Lord an abundance of enlight-enment on your work, and as a testimony of my esteem and affection, I impart a special Blessing to you all.

Address at a Meeting on Family and Life Issues in Latin America

December 3, 2005

Dear Brothers in the Episcopate,

1. I am pleased to receive you on the occasion of the Third Meeting of the Presidents of the Episcopal Commissions for the Family and Life of Latin

America. I should like to express my gratitude for the words addressed to me by Cardinal Alfonso López Trujillo, President of the Pontifical Council for the Family.

Together with the whole Church, I witnessed Pope John Paul II's concern for this most important topic. For my part, I make my own this same concern, which will have a far-reaching effect on the future of the Church and the peoples since, as my Predecessor said in his Apostolic Exhortation *Familiaris Consortio*, *"The future of humanity passes by way of the family!"*

"It is therefore indispensable and urgent that every person of good will should endeavor to save and foster the values and requirements of the family." And he added: "Christians also have the mission of *proclaiming with joy and conviction the 'Good News' about the family*, for the family absolutely needs to hear ever anew and to understand ever more deeply the authentic words that reveal its identity, its inner resources and the importance of its mission in the City of God and in that of man" (Conclusion, no. 86).

The Apostolic Exhortation cited together with the Letter to Families *Gratissimam Sane* and the Encyclical *Evangelium Vitae* constitute, as it were, a luminous triptych that must inspire your task as Pastors.

2. I wish to thank you in particular for your pastoral concern which seeks to safeguard the fundamental values of marriage and the family. They are threatened by the current phenomenon of secularization that prevents the social conscience from discovering adequately the identity and mission of the family institution and recently, by the pressure of unjust laws that fail to recognize its fundamental rights.

In light of this situation, I am pleased to note the increase in and consolidation of the particular Churches' work for this human institution, which is rooted in God's loving plan and represents the irreplaceable *model* for the common good of humanity. Homes that give a generous response to the Lord abound and there is also a wealth of pastoral experiences, a sign of new vitality, in which family identity is reinforced by means of better marriage preparation.

3. Your duty as Pastors consists in presenting in its full richness the extraordinary value of marriage, which as a natural institution is a "patrimony of humanity." Moreover, its elevation to the loftiest dignity of a sacrament must be seen with gratitude and wonder, as I recently said, affirming:

"The sacramental quality that marriage assumes in Christ therefore means that the gift of creation has been raised to the grace of redemption. Christ's grace is not an external addition to human nature, it does not do violence to men and women but sets them free and restores them, precisely by raising them above their own limitations" (Address to the Ecclesial Diocesan Convention of Rome, June 6, 2005; ORE, June 15, 6).

4. The spouses' love and total gift of self, with their special connotations of exclusivity, fidelity, permanence in time and openness to life, are at the root of this communion of life and love that constitutes the married state (cf. *Gaudium et Spes*, no. 48).

Today, it is necessary to proclaim with renewed enthusiasm that the Gospel of the family is a process of human and spiritual fulfillment in the certainty that the Lord is always present with his grace. This proclamation is often distorted by false concepts of marriage and the family that do not respect God's original plan. In this regard, people have actually reached the point of suggesting new forms of marriage, some unknown to popular cultures in that its specific nature is altered.

Also in the life context, new models are being proposed that dispute this fundamental right. As a result, the elimination of embryos or their arbitrary use in the name of scientific progress, which fails to recognize its own limits and to accept all the moral principles that make it possible to safeguard the dignity of the person, becomes a threat to the human being who is reduced to an object or a mere instrument. When such levels are reached, society itself is affected and every kind of risk shakes its foundations.

5. In Latin America, as in all other places, children have the right to be born and to be raised in a family founded on marriage, where parents are the first educators of the faith for their children in order for them to reach full human and spiritual maturity.

Children truly are the family's greatest treasure and most precious good. Consequently, everyone must be helped to become aware of the intrinsic evil of the crime of abortion. In attacking human life in its very first stages, it is also an aggression against society itself. Politicians and legislators, therefore, as servants of the common good, are duty bound to defend the fundamental right to life, the fruit of God's love.

6. It is certain that for pastoral action in so delicate and complex an area, in which various disciplines are involved and fundamental issues faced, a *careful training* of pastoral workers in the Dioceses is essential.

Priests, therefore, as the immediate collaborators of the Bishops, must receive a sound training in this field that will enable them to face competently and with conviction the problems that arise in their pastoral activity.

As for lay people, especially those who devote their energy to this service of families, they in turn need a proper and sound formation that will help them witness to the greatness and lasting value of marriage in today's society.

7. Dear brothers and sisters, as you know well, the Fifth World Meeting of Families is not far off. It will be held in Valencia, Spain, on the theme: *The transmission of faith in the family*.

In this regard, I would like to offer my cordial greeting to Archbishop Agustín García-Gasco of that city, who is taking part in this Meeting and who, with the Pontifical Council for the Family, is sharing the challenging task of its preparation. I encourage you all so that numerous delegations of the Bishops' Conferences, Dioceses and movements of Latin America will be able to take part in this important ecclesial event.

For my part, I firmly support the holding of this Meeting and place it under the loving protection of the Holy Family.

Dear Pastors, I cordially impart my Apostolic Blessing to you and to all the families in Latin America.

Encyclical Letter *Deus Caritas Est,*
On Christian Love

December 25, 2005

Part I: The Unity of Love in Creation and in Salvation History

A problem of language

2. God's love for us is fundamental for our lives, and it raises important questions about who God is and who we are. In considering this, we immediately find ourselves hampered by a problem of language. Today, the term "love" has become one of the most frequently used and misused of words, a word to which we attach quite different meanings. Even though this Encyclical will deal primarily with the understanding and practice of love in sacred Scripture and in the Church's Tradition, we cannot simply prescind from the meaning of the word in the different cultures and in present-day usage.

Let us first of all bring to mind the vast semantic range of the word "love": we speak of love of country, love of one's profession, love between friends, love of work, love between parents and children, love between family members, love of neighbor and love of God. Amid this multiplicity of meanings, however, one in particular stands out: love between man and woman, where body and soul are inseparably joined and human beings glimpse an apparently irresistible promise of happiness. This would seem to be the very epitome of love; all other kinds of love immediately seem to fade in comparison. So we need to ask: are all these forms of love basically one, so that love, in its many and varied manifestations, is ultimately a single reality, or are we merely using the same word to designate totally different realities?

"Eros" and "Agape"—difference and unity

3. That love between man and woman which is neither planned nor willed, but somehow imposes itself upon human beings, was called *eros* by the ancient Greeks. Let us note straight away that the Greek Old Testament uses the word *eros* only twice, while the New Testament does not use it at all: of the three Greek words for love, *eros*, *philia* (the love of friendship) and *agape*, New Testament writers prefer the last, which occurs rather infrequently in Greek usage. As for the term *philia*, the love of friendship, it is used with added depth of meaning in St. John's Gospel in order to express the relationship between Jesus and his disciples. The tendency to avoid the word *eros*, together with the new vision of love expressed through the word *agape*, clearly point to something new and distinct about the Christian understanding of love. In the critique of Christianity which began with the Enlightenment and grew progressively more radical, this new element was seen as something thoroughly negative. According to Friedrich Nietzsche, Christianity had poisoned *eros*, which for its part, while not completely succumbing, gradually degenerated into vice (cf. *Jenseits von Gut und Böse*, IV, 168). Here the German philosopher was expressing a widely-held perception: doesn't the Church, with all her commandments and prohibitions, turn to bitterness the most precious thing in life? Doesn't she blow the whistle just when the joy which is the Creator's gift offers us a happiness which is itself a certain foretaste of the Divine? . . .

9. . . . . The Prophets, particularly Hosea and Ezekiel, described God's passion for his people using boldly erotic images. God's relationship with Israel is described using the metaphors of betrothal and marriage; idolatry is thus adultery and prostitution. Here we find a specific reference—as we have seen—to the fertility cults and their abuse of *eros*, but also a description of the relationship of fidelity between Israel and her God. The history of the love-relationship between God and Israel consists, at the deepest level, in the fact that he gives her the *Torah*, thereby opening Israel's eyes to man's true nature and showing her the path leading to true humanism. It consists in the fact that man, through a life of fidelity to the one God, comes to experience himself as loved by God, and discovers joy in truth and in righteousness—a joy in God which becomes his essential happiness: "Whom do I have in heaven but you? And there is nothing upon earth that I desire besides you . . . for me it is good to be near God" (Ps 73 [72]:25, 28). . . .

11. The first novelty of biblical faith consists, as we have seen, in its image of God. The second, essentially connected to this, is found in the image of man. The biblical account of creation speaks of the solitude of Adam, the

first man, and God's decision to give him a helper. Of all other creatures, not one is capable of being the helper that man needs, even though he has assigned a name to àll the wild beasts and birds and thus made them fully a part of his life. So God forms woman from the rib of man. Now Adam finds the helper that he needed: "This at last is bone of my bones and flesh of my flesh" (Gn 2:23). Here one might detect hints of ideas that are also found, for example, in the myth mentioned by Plato, according to which man was originally spherical, because he was complete in himself and self-sufficient. But as a punishment for pride, he was split in two by Zeus, so that now he longs for his other half, striving with all his being to possess it and thus regain his integrity (Plato, *Symposium*, XIV-XV, 189c-192d). While the biblical narrative does not speak of punishment, the idea is certainly present that man is somehow incomplete, driven by nature to seek in another the part that can make him whole, the idea that only in communion with the opposite sex can he become "complete." The biblical account thus concludes with a prophecy about Adam: "Therefore a man leaves his father and his mother and cleaves to his wife and they become one flesh" (Gn 2:24).

Two aspects of this are important. First, *eros* is somehow rooted in man's very nature; Adam is a seeker, who "abandons his mother and father" in order to find woman; only together do the two represent complete humanity and become "one flesh." The second aspect is equally important. From the standpoint of creation, *eros* directs man toward marriage, to a bond which is unique and definitive; thus, and only thus, does it fulfill its deepest purpose. Corresponding to the image of a monotheistic God is monogamous marriage. Marriage based on exclusive and definitive love becomes the icon of the relationship between God and his people and vice versa. God's way of loving becomes the measure of human love. This close connection between *eros* and marriage in the Bible has practically no equivalent in extra-biblical literature. . . .

Jesus Christ—the incarnate love of God

13. Jesus gave this act of oblation an enduring presence through his institution of the Eucharist at the Last Supper. He anticipated his death and resurrection by giving his disciples, in the bread and wine, his very self, his body and blood as the new manna (cf. Jn 6:31-33). The ancient world had dimly perceived that man's real food—what truly nourishes him as man—is ultimately the *Logos*, eternal wisdom: this same *Logos* now truly becomes food for us—as love. The Eucharist draws us into Jesus' act of self-oblation. More than just statically receiving the incarnate *Logos*, we enter into the very dynamic of his self-giving. The imagery of marriage between God and Israel is now realized in a way previously inconceivable: it had meant standing in God's

presence, but now it becomes union with God through sharing in Jesus' self-gift, sharing in his body and blood. The sacramental "mysticism," grounded in God's condescension toward us, operates at a radically different level and lifts us to far greater heights than anything that any human mystical elevation could ever accomplish.

Address at St. Martha's Dispensary in Vatican City on the Feast of the Holy Family

December 30, 2005

Dear Friends,

I greet with deep affection all of you who work in this Center named after St. Martha, the sister of Mary and Lazarus and an example of great availability to the divine Teacher. I thank you for your warm family welcome, as well as for the courteous words your representative addressed to me on behalf of you all.

I greet Sr. Chiara and the other Sisters, the doctors, the volunteers and each one of the families who find invaluable help here.

The service you carry out is inspired by the example of St. Martha who took care of Jesus, who as a man had human needs: he was thirsty and hungry, he was weary after his journey, he needed a moment of rest, to be away from the crowds for a while and from the city of Jerusalem. Like Martha, you too strive to serve Jesus in the people you meet.

My Visit acquires special significance because it is taking place in the Christmas season: in these days our gaze comes to rest on the Infant Jesus. In coming here, I find Jesus himself in the children for whom you lovingly care. They are the subject of your attention, just as the newborn Messiah in the Crib is the focus of Mary and Joseph's care.

In each one of them, as in the Bethlehem Grotto, Jesus knocks at the door of our hearts, asking us to make room in our lives for him. God is like that: he does not impose himself, he never uses force to enter, but asks, as a child does, to be welcomed. In a certain sense, God too presents himself in need of attention: he waits for us to open our hearts to him, to take care of him. And every time we turn lovingly to "one of these least brothers of mine," as the Lord said, it is he whom we are serving (cf. Mt 25:40).

Today, we are celebrating the Feast of the Holy Family of Nazareth. Finding myself among you and noting your dedication to children and their parents, I would like to stress the fundamental vocation of the family to be the first and principal place where life is welcomed. The modern concept of family, partly in reaction to the past, gives great importance to conjugal love, emphasizing its subjective aspects of freedom of choice and feelings.

On the other hand, people are finding it harder to perceive and understand the value of the call to collaborate with God in procreating human life. Besides, contemporary societies, despite being equipped with so many means, do not always succeed in facilitating the mission of parents, either on the level of spiritual and moral motivations or on that of practical living conditions.

There is a great need, both from the cultural and the political and legislative viewpoints, to support the family, and initiatives such as your dispensary are more useful than ever in this regard. These realities are small but important, and, thanks be to God, the Church is rich in them and does not cease to put them at the service of all.

Dear brothers and sisters, before leaving you, I invite you to pray with me for all the families of Rome and the world, and especially for those in difficult conditions, particularly because they are obliged to live far from their country of origin.

Let us pray for the parents who do not succeed in guaranteeing their children what they need for their health, education and a dignified and serene life. Let us invoke the motherly protection of Mary for everyone: *Ave Maria . . .*

I now impart my heartfelt Apostolic Blessing to you and to your dear ones, as I wish you all a peaceful, prosperous New Year.

Homily for the *Te Deum* and First Vespers of the Solemnity of Mary, Mother of God

December 31, 2005

Dear Brothers and Sisters,

At the end of a year which has been particularly eventful for the Church and for the world, mindful of the Apostle's order, "walk . . . established in the faith . . . abounding in thanksgiving" (cf. Col 2:6-7), we are gathered together this evening to raise a hymn of thanksgiving to God, Lord of time and of history.

I am thinking with a profound and spiritual sentiment of twelve months ago, when for the last time beloved Pope John Paul II made himself the voice of the People of God to give thanks to the Lord, like this evening, for the numerous benefits granted to the Church and to humanity. In the same evocative setting of the Vatican Basilica, it is now my turn to ideally gather from every corner of the earth the praise and thanksgiving raised to God at the end of 2005 and on the eve of 2006. Yes, it is our duty, as well as a need of our hearts, to praise and thank the eternal One who accompanies us through time, never abandoning us, and who always watches over humanity with the fidelity of his merciful love.

We may well say that the Church lives to praise and thank God. She herself has been an "action of grace" down the ages, a faithful witness of a love that does not die, of a love that embraces people of every race and culture, fruitfully disseminating principles of true life.

As the Second Vatican Council recalls, "the Church prays and likewise labors so that into the People of God, the Body of the Lord and the Temple of the Holy Spirit, may pass the fullness of the whole world, and that in Christ, the head of all things, all honor and glory may be rendered to the Creator, the Father of the universe" (*Lumen Gentium*, no. 17).

Sustained by the Holy Spirit, she "presses forward amid the persecutions of the world and the consolations of God" (St. Augustine, *De Civitate Dei*, XVIII, 51, 2), drawing strength from the Lord's help. Thus, in patience and in love, she overcomes "her sorrows and her difficulties, both those that are from within and those that are from without," and reveals "in the world, faithfully, however darkly, the mystery of her Lord until, in the consummation, it shall be manifested in full light" (*Lumen Gentium*, no. 8). The Church lives from Christ and with Christ. He offers her his spousal love, guiding her through the centuries; and she, with the abundance of her gifts, accompanies men and women on their journey so that those who accept Christ may have life and have it abundantly.

This evening I make myself first of all the voice of the Church of Rome to raise to Heaven our common hymn of praise and thanksgiving. In the past twelve months, our Church of Rome has been visited by many other Churches and Ecclesial Communities, to deepen the dialogue of truth in charity that unites all the baptized, and together to experience more keenly the desire for full communion. Many believers of other religions, however, also wanted to testify to their cordial and brotherly esteem for this Church and her Bishop, aware that the serene and respectful encounter conceals the heart of a harmonious action in favor of all humanity.

And what can be said of the many people of good will who have turned their gaze to this See in order to build up a fruitful dialogue on the great values concerning the truth about man and life to be defended and promoted? The Church always desires to be welcoming, in truth and in charity.

As regards the journey of the Diocese of Rome, I wish to reflect briefly on the diocesan pastoral program, which this year has focused attention on the family, choosing as a theme: *"Family and Christian community: formation of the person and transmission of the faith."*

My venerable Predecessors always made the family the center of their attention, especially John Paul II, who dedicated numerous Interventions to it. He was convinced, and said so on many occasions, that the crisis of the family is a serious threat to our civilization itself.

Precisely to underline the importance of the family based on marriage in the life of the Church and of society, I also wished to make my contribution by speaking at the Diocesan Congress in St. John Lateran last June 6. I am delighted because the diocesan program is going smoothly with a far-reaching apostolic action which is carried out in the parishes, at the prefectures and in the various ecclesial associations.

May the Lord grant that the common effort lead to an authentic renewal of Christian families.

I take this opportunity to greet the representatives of the religious and civil Communities of Rome present at this end-of-year celebration. I greet in the first place the Cardinal Vicar, the Auxiliary Bishops, priests, Religious and lay faithful from various parishes who have gathered here; I also greet the City Mayor and the other Authorities. I extend my thoughts to the entire Roman community whose Pastor the Lord called me to be, and I renew to everyone the expression of my spiritual closeness.

At the beginning of this celebration, enlightened by the Word of God, we sang the "Te Deum" with faith. There are so many reasons that render our thanksgiving intense, making it a unanimous prayer. While we consider the many events that have marked the succession of months in this year that is coming to its end, I would like to remember especially those who are in difficulty: the poorest and the most abandoned people, those who have lost hope in a well-grounded sense of their own existence, or who involuntarily become the victims of selfish interests without being asked for their support or their opinion.

Making their sufferings our own, let us entrust them all to God, who knows how to bring everything to a good end; to him let us entrust our aspiration that every person's dignity as a child of God be respected.

Let us ask the Lord of life to soothe with his grace the sufferings caused by evil, and to continue to fortify our earthy existence by giving us the Bread and Wine of salvation to sustain us on our way toward the Heavenly Homeland.

While we take our leave of the year that is drawing to a close and set out for the new one, the liturgy of this First Vespers ushers us into the Feast of Mary, Mother of God, *Theotokos*. Eight days after the birth of Jesus, we will be celebrating the one whom God chose in advance to be the Mother of the Savior "when the fullness of time had come" (Gal 4:4).

The mother is the one who gives life but also who helps and teaches how to live. Mary is a Mother, the Mother of Jesus, to whom she gave her blood and her body. And it is she who presents to us the eternal Word of the Father, who came to dwell among us. Let us ask Mary to intercede for us.

May her motherly protection accompany us today and forever, so that Christ will one day welcome us into his glory, into the assembly of the Saints: *Aeterna fac cum sanctis tuis in gloria numerari.*

Amen!

Homily at Mass and Celebration of Baptism in the Sistine Chapel

January 8, 2006
Dear Parents and Godparents,
Dear Brothers and Sisters,

What happens in Baptism? What do we hope for from Baptism? You have given a response on the threshold of this Chapel: We hope for eternal life for our children. This is the purpose of Baptism. But how can it be obtained? How can Baptism offer eternal life? What is eternal life?

In simpler words, we might say: we hope for a good life, the true life, for these children of ours; and also for happiness in a future that is still unknown. We are unable to guarantee this gift for the entire span of the unknown future, so we turn to the Lord to obtain this gift from him.

We can give two replies to the question, "How will this happen?" This is the first one: through Baptism each child is inserted into a gathering of friends who never abandon him in life or in death because these companions are God's family, which in itself bears the promise of eternity.

This group of friends, this family of God, into which the child is now admitted, will always accompany him, even on days of suffering and in life's dark nights; it will give him consolation, comfort and light.

This companionship, this family, will give him words of eternal life, words of light in response to the great challenges of life, and will point out to him the right path to take. This group will also offer the child consolation and comfort, and God's love when death is at hand, in the dark valley of death. It will give him friendship, it will give him life. And these totally trustworthy companions will never disappear.

No one of us knows what will happen on our planet, on our European Continent, in the next fifty, sixty, or seventy years. But we can be sure of one thing: God's family will always be present and those who belong to this family will never be alone. They will always be able to fall back on the steadfast friendship of the One who is life.

And, thus, we have arrived at the second answer. This family of God, this gathering of friends is eternal, because it is communion with the One who conquered death and holds in his hand the keys of life. Belonging to this circle, to God's family, means being in communion with Christ, who is life and gives eternal love beyond death.

And if we can say that love and truth are sources of life, are life itself—and a life without love is not life—we can say that this companionship with the One who is truly life, with the One who is the Sacrament of life, will respond to your expectation, to your hope.

Yes, Baptism inserts us into communion with Christ and therefore gives life, life itself. We have thus interpreted the first dialogue we had with him here at the entrance to the Sistine Chapel.

Now, after the blessing of the water, a second dialogue of great importance will follow. This is its content: Baptism, as we have seen, is a gift; the gift of life. But a gift must be accepted, it must be lived.

A gift of friendship implies a "yes" to the friend and a "no" to all that is incompatible with this friendship, to all that is incompatible with the life of God's family, with true life in Christ.

Consequently, in this second dialogue, three "nos" and three "yeses" are spoken. We say "no" and renounce temptation, sin and the devil. We know these things well but perhaps, precisely because we have heard them too often, the words may not mean much to us.

If this is the case, we must think a little more deeply about the content of these "nos." What are we saying "no" to? This is the only way to understand what we want to say "yes" to.

In the ancient Church these "nos" were summed up in a phrase that was easy to understand for the people of that time: they renounced, they said, the "pompa diabuli," that is, the promise of life in abundance, of that apparent life that seemed to come from the pagan world, from its permissiveness, from its way of living as one pleased.

It was therefore "no" to a culture of what seemed to be an abundance of life, to what in fact was an "anticulture" of death. It was "no" to those spectacles in which death, cruelty and violence had become an entertainment.

Let us remember what was organized at the Colosseum or here, in Nero's gardens, where people were set on fire like living torches. Cruelty and violence had become a form of amusement, a true perversion of joy, of the true meaning of life.

This "pompa diabuli," this "anticulture" of death was a corruption of joy, it was love of deceit and fraud and the abuse of the body as a commodity and a trade.

And if we think about it now, we can say that also in our time we need to say "no" to the widely prevalent culture of death.

It is an "anticulture" manifested, for example, in drugs, in the flight from reality to what is illusory, to a false happiness expressed in deceit, fraud, injustice and contempt for others, for solidarity, and for responsibility for the poor and the suffering; it is expressed in a sexuality that becomes sheer irresponsible enjoyment, that makes the human person into a "thing," so to speak, no longer considered a person who deserves personal love which requires fidelity, but who becomes a commodity, a mere object.

Let us say "no" to this promise of apparent happiness, to this *"pompa"* of what may seem to be life but is in fact merely an instrument of death, and to this "anticulture," in order to cultivate instead the culture of life. For this reason, the Christian "yes," from ancient times to our day, is a great "yes" to life. It is our "yes" to Christ, our "yes" to the Conqueror of death and the "yes" to life in time and in eternity.

Just as in this baptismal dialogue the "no" is expressed in three renunciations, so too the "yes" is expressed in three expressions of loyalty: "yes" to the living God, that is, a God Creator and a creating reason who gives meaning to the cosmos and to our lives; "yes" to Christ, that is, to a God who did not stay hidden but has a name, words, a body and blood; to a concrete God who gives us life and shows us the path of life; "yes" to the communion of the Church, in which Christ is the living God who enters our time, enters our profession, enters daily life.

We might also say that the Face of God, the content of this culture of life, the content of our great "yes," is expressed in the Ten Commandments, which are not a pack of prohibitions, of "noes," but actually present a great vision of life.

They are a "yes" to a God who gives meaning to life (the first three Commandments); a "yes" to the family (Fourth Commandment); a "yes" to life (Fifth Commandment); a "yes" to responsible love (Sixth Commandment); a "yes" to solidarity, to social responsibility, to justice (Seventh Commandment); a "yes" to the truth (Eighth Commandment); a "yes" to respect for others and for their belongings (Ninth and Tenth Commandments).

This is the philosophy of life, the culture of life that becomes concrete and practical and beautiful in communion with Christ, the living God, who walks with us in the companionship of his friends, in the great family of the Church. Baptism is a gift of life.

It is a "yes" to the challenge of really living life, of saying "no" to the attack of death that presents itself under the guise of life; and it is a "yes" to the great gift of true life that became present on the Face of Christ, who gives himself to us in Baptism and subsequently in the Eucharist.

I said this as a brief comment on the words in the baptismal dialogue that interpret what happens in this Sacrament. In addition to the words, we have gestures and symbols, but I will just point them out very briefly.

We have already made the first gesture: it is the Sign of the Cross, which is given to us as a shield that must protect this child in his life; and as an "indicator" that points out the way of life, for the Cross sums up Jesus' life.

Then, there are the elements: water, the anointing with oil, the white garment and the flame of the candle.

Water is the symbol of life: Baptism is new life in Christ. The oil is the symbol of strength, health and beauty, for it truly is beautiful to live in communion with Christ. Then, there is the white garment, as an expression of the culture of beauty, of the culture of life. And lastly, the flame of the candle is an expression of the truth that shines out in the darkness of history and points out to us who we are, where we come from and where we must go.

Dear Godparents, dear parents, dear brothers and sisters, let us thank the Lord today, for God does not hide behind clouds of impenetrable mystery but, as today's Gospel said, has opened the heavens, he has shown himself, he talks to us and is with us; he lives with us and guides us in our lives.

Let us thank the Lord for this gift and pray for our children, so that they may truly have life: authentic, eternal life. Amen.

Address to Members of the Regional Board of Lazio and to the Civil Authorities of Rome

January 12, 2006

During those days [at the end of John Paul II's life], Rome and Lazio, like the rest of Italy and all humanity, truly lived a profound spiritual experience of faith and prayer, of brotherhood and the rediscovery of the goods that make our life dignified and rich in meaning. Nor can such an experience remain barren in the context of the civil community, its tasks and its multiple responsibilities and relations.

I am thinking in particular of that highly sensitive area that is as crucial to the formation and happiness of people as to the future of society: the family.

For the past three years the Diocese of Rome has made the family the focus of its pastoral commitment, in order to help the family face the new causes of crises and challenges widespread in our cultural context by a clearer and more convinced awareness of its real nature and consequent duties.

Indeed, as I said last June 6, speaking to the Convention the Diocese organized on these topics: "Marriage and the family are not in fact a chance sociological construction, the product of particular historical and financial situations. On the contrary, the question of the right relationship between man and woman is rooted in the essential core of the human being and it is only by starting from here that its response can be found" (Address to Ecclesial Diocesan Convention, St. John Lateran, June 6, 2005: ORE, June 15, 6).

I therefore added: "Marriage as an institution is thus not an undue interference of society or of authority. The external imposition of form on the most private reality of life is instead an intrinsic requirement of the covenant of conjugal love" (ibid., 6).

Here, it is not a question of specific norms of Catholic morals but of elementary truths that concern our common humanity: respecting them is essential for the good of the person and of society. Consequently, they also call into question your responsibilities as public Administrators and your legal competences in two directions.

On the one hand, all measures that can sustain young couples in forming a family, and the family itself, in the procreation and education of children, are as expedient as ever: in this regard, problems such as the cost of housing, nurseries and kindergarten schools for the tiniest children immediately spring to mind.

On the other, it is a serious error to obscure the value and roles of the legitimate family founded on marriage by attributing legal recognition to other improper forms of union for which there is really no effective social need.

The protection of unborn human life likewise requires attention: care must be taken that pregnant women in difficult conditions do not lack material help, and that drugs which in some way conceal the gravity of abortion are not introduced as an anti-life choice.

Then, in a society that is ageing, assistance to the elderly and the whole range of problems that concern the health care of citizens is becoming increasingly important. I would like to encourage you in the efforts you are making in these areas and to stress that in the health sector, the continuing scientific and technological developments as well as the commitment to containing costs must be promoted, keeping firmly to the superior principle of the centrality of the patient.

The many cases of suffering and of mental illness deserve special attention. This is partly in order not to leave without adequate help those families which often find they have to cope with very difficult situations.

I am pleased at the development in recent years of various forms of collaboration among the public Administrative Boards of Rome, the Province and the Region, and the ecclesial volunteer organizations, in the work aimed at alleviating both old and new forms of poverty, which unfortunately afflict a large part of the population and many immigrants in particular.

General Audience

January 25, 2006

"Sing a new song!" (Psalm 144[143])

3. It is above all the family (cf. v. 12) that is founded on generations of young people. Sons, the hope of the future, are compared to strong saplings; daughters are like sturdy columns supporting the house, similar to those of a temple.

From the family we pass on to agriculture and farming, to the fields with its crops stored in the barns, with large flocks of grazing sheep and the working animals that till the fertile fields (cf. vv. 13-14).

Angelus

February 5, 2006

Dear Brothers and Sisters,

Pro-Life Day is being celebrated today throughout Italy and is a precious opportunity for prayer and reflection on the themes of the defense and promotion of human life, especially when it is found to be in difficult conditions.

Many of the lay faithful who work in this area are present in St. Peter's Square, some of whom are involved in the Pro-Life Movement. I address my cordial greeting to them, with a special thought for Cardinal Camillo Ruini who has accompanied them, and I once again express my appreciation for the work they do to ensure that life is always received as a gift and accompanied with love.

As I invite you to meditate on the Message of the Italian Bishops, which has as its theme *"Respecting life,"* I think back to beloved Pope John Paul II, who paid constant attention to these problems. I would like in particular to recall the Encyclical *Evangelium Vitae*, which he published in 1995 and which represents an authentic milestone in the Church's Magisterium on a most timely and crucial issue.

Inserting the moral aspects in a vast spiritual and cultural framework, my venerable Predecessor frequently reasserted that human life has a value of paramount importance which demands recognition, and the Gospel asks that it always be respected.

In the light of my recent Encyclical Letter on Christian love, I would like to underline the importance of the *service of love* for the support and promotion of human life. In this regard, even before active initiatives, it is fundamental to foster a correct *attitude toward the other:* the culture of life is in fact based on attention to others without any forms of exclusion or discrimination. *Every* human life, as such, deserves and demands always to be defended and promoted.

We are well aware that all too often this truth risks being opposed by the hedonism widespread in the so-called society of well-being: life is exalted as long as it is pleasurable, but there is a tendency to no longer respect it as soon as it is sick or handicapped. Based on deep love for every person it is possible instead to put into practice effective forms of service to life: to newborn life and to life marked by marginalization or suffering, especially in its terminal phase.

The Virgin Mary received with perfect love the Word of life, Jesus Christ, who came into the world so that human beings might "have life . . . abundantly" (Jn 10:10). Let us entrust to her expectant mothers, families, health-care workers and volunteers who are committed in so many ways to the service of life. Let us pray in particular for people in the most difficult situations.

Address to the Clergy of Rome

March 2, 2006

The next intervention dedicated to the family was made by the parish priest of St. Sylvia. Here, I cannot but fully agree. Furthermore, during the ad limina visits I always speak to Bishops about the family, threatened throughout the world in various ways.

The family is threatened in Africa because it is difficult to find the way from "traditional marriage" to "religious marriage," because there is a fear of finality.

Whereas in the West the fear of the child is caused by the fear of losing some part of life, in Africa it is the opposite. Until it is certain that the wife will also bear children, no one dares to enter marriage definitively. Therefore, the number of religious marriages remains relatively small, and even many "good" Christians with an excellent desire to be Christians do not take this final step.

Marriage is also threatened in Latin America, for other reasons, and is badly threatened, as we know, in the West. So it is all the more necessary for us as Church to help families, which are the fundamental cell of every healthy society.

Only in families, therefore, is it possible to create a communion of generations in which the memory of the past lives on in the present and is open to the future. Thus, life truly continues and progresses. Real progress is impossible without this continuity of life, and once again, it is impossible without the religious element. Without trust in God, without trust in Christ who in addition gives us the ability to believe and to live, the family cannot survive.

We see this today. Only faith in Christ and only sharing the faith of the Church saves the family; and on the other hand, only if the family is saved can the Church also survive. For the time being, I do not have an effective recipe for this, but it seems to me that we should always bear it in mind.

We must therefore do all that favors the family: family circles, family catechesis, and we must teach prayer in the family. This seems to me to be very important: wherever people pray together the Lord makes himself present with that power which can also dissolve "sclerosis" of the heart, that hardness of heart which, according to the Lord, is the real reason for divorce.

Nothing else, only the Lord's presence, helps us to truly relive what the Creator wanted at the outset and which the Redeemer renewed. Teach family prayer and thus invite people to pray with the Church and then seek all the other ways. . . .

We can tangibly feel today all that you said about the problem of adolescents, their loneliness and their being misunderstood by adults. It is interesting that these young people who seek closeness in discotheques are actually suffering from great loneliness and, of course, also from misunderstanding.

This seems to me, in a certain sense, an expression of the fact that parents, as has been said, are largely absent from the formation of the family. And mothers too are obliged to work outside the home. Communion between them is very fragile.

Each family member lives in a world of his or her own: they are isolated in their thoughts and feelings, which are not united. The great problem of this time—in which each person, desiring to have life for himself, loses it because he is isolated and isolates the other from him—is to rediscover the deep communion which in the end can only stem from a foundation that is common to all souls, from the divine presence that unites all of us.

I think that the condition for this is to overcome loneliness and misunderstanding, because the latter also results from the fact that thought today is fragmented. Each one seeks his own way of thinking and living and there is no communication in a profound vision of life. Young people feel exposed to new horizons which previous generations do not share; therefore, continuity in the vision of the world is absent, caught up as it is in an ever more rapid succession of new inventions.

Address to the Members of the European People's Party

March 30, 2006

Your support for the Christian heritage, moreover, can contribute significantly to the defeat of a culture that is now fairly widespread in Europe, which relegates to the private and subjective sphere the manifestation of one's own religious convictions. Policies built on this foundation not only entail the repudiation of Christianity's public role; more generally, they exclude engagement with Europe's religious tradition, which is so clear, despite its denominational variations, thereby threatening democracy itself, whose strength depends on the values that it promotes (cf. *Evangelium Vitae*, no. 70). Given that this tradition, precisely in what might be called its polyphonic unity, conveys values that are fundamental for the good of society, the European Union can only be enriched by engaging with it. It would be a sign of immaturity, if not indeed weakness, to choose to oppose or ignore it, rather than to dialogue with it. In this context one has to recognize that a certain secular intransigence shows itself to be the enemy of tolerance and of a sound secular vision of state and society. I am pleased, therefore, that the European Union's constitutional treaty envisages a structured and ongoing relationship with religious communities, recognizing their identity and their specific contribution. Above all, I trust that the effective and correct implementation of this relationship will start now, with the cooperation of all political movements irrespective of party alignments. It must not be forgotten that, when Churches or ecclesial communities intervene in public debate, expressing reservations or recalling various principles, this does not constitute a form of intolerance or an interference, since such interventions are aimed solely at enlightening consciences, enabling them to act freely and responsibly, according to the true demands of justice, even when this should conflict with situations of power and personal interest.

As far as the Catholic Church is concerned, the principal focus of her interventions in the public arena is the protection and promotion of the dignity of the person, and she is thereby consciously drawing particular attention to principles which are not negotiable. Among these the following emerge clearly today:

- protection of life in all its stages, from the first moment of conception until natural death;
- recognition and promotion of the natural structure of the family—as a union between a man and a woman based on marriage—and its defense from attempts to make it juridically equivalent to radically different forms of union which in reality harm it and contribute to its destabilization, obscuring its particular character and its irreplaceable social role;
- the protection of the right of parents to educate their children.

These principles are not truths of faith, even though they receive further light and confirmation from faith; they are inscribed in human nature itself and therefore they are common to all humanity. The Church's action in promoting them is therefore not confessional in character, but is addressed to all people, prescinding from any religious affiliation they may have. On the contrary, such action is all the more necessary the more these principles are denied or misunderstood, because this constitutes an offence against the truth of the human person, a grave wound inflicted onto justice itself.

Dear friends, in exhorting you to be credible and consistent witnesses of these basic truths through your political activity, and more fundamentally through your commitment to live authentic and consistent lives, I invoke upon you and your work the continued assistance of God, in pledge of which I cordially impart my Blessing to you and to those accompanying you.

Address to the Bishops of Ghana on Their *Ad Limina* Visit

April 24, 2006

Dear Brother Bishops,

In these days of joyful celebration of the Resurrection of our Lord and Savior, I welcome you, the Bishops of Ghana, on the occasion of your pilgrimage to Rome for your visit *ad limina apostolorum*. Through you I offer my warm affection to the priests, Religious and lay faithful of your Dioceses. In a special way, I thank Bishop Lucas Abadamloora for the kind words of greeting he offered me on your behalf. I wish to recognize in particular Ghana's native son, Cardinal Peter Poreku Dery, who recently joined the ranks of the College of Cardinals, and I also take this opportunity to greet Cardinal Peter Turkson, Archbishop of Cape Coast. You have all come to Rome, this city where the Apostles Peter and Paul gave of themselves completely in imitation of Christ: Peter just a short distance from where we are today and Paul along the Ostian way. As good and faithful servants of the Gospel, it is my constant prayer that, like the Princes of the Apostles, "God may make you worthy of his call, and may fulfill every good resolve and work of faith by his power, so that the name of our Lord Jesus Christ may be glorified in you, and you in him" (2 Thes 1:11-12).

Your country has made great strides in recent years to deal with the scourge of poverty and to strengthen the economy. Notwithstanding this laudable progress, much still remains to be done to overcome this condition which impedes a large portion of the population. Extreme and widespread poverty often results in a general moral decline leading to crime, corruption, attacks on the sanctity of human life or even a return to the superstitious practices of the past. In this situation, people can easily lose trust in the future. The Church, however, shines forth as a beacon of hope in the life of the Christian. One of the most effective ways in which she does this is by helping the faithful gain a better understanding of the promises of Jesus Christ. Accordingly, there is a particular and pressing need for the Church, as a beacon of hope, to intensify her efforts to provide Catholics with comprehensive programs of formation which will help them to deepen their Christian faith and thus enable them to take their rightful place both in the Church of Christ and in society.

An essential part of any adequate formation process is the role of the lay catechist. It is appropriate, therefore, that I offer a word of gratitude to the many committed men and women who selflessly serve your local Church in this way. As Pope John Paul II noted in his Post-Synodal Apostolic Exhortation *Ecclesia in Africa*: "in the midst of the Christian community the catechists' responsibility is to be acknowledged and held in respect" (cf. no. 91). I know that these faithful men and women are often impeded in their task by a lack of resources or hostile environments, and yet they remain undaunted messengers of Christ's joy. Mindful of how grateful local Churches are for the assistance offered by catechists, I encourage you and your priests to continue to do all you can to ensure that these evangelists receive the spiritual, doctrinal, moral and material support they require to carry out their mission properly.

In many countries, including your own, young people constitute almost half of the population. The Church in Ghana is young. In order to reach out to today's youth it is necessary that the Church address their problems in a frank and loving way. A solid catechetical foundation will strengthen them in their Catholic identity and give them the necessary tools to confront the challenges of changing economic realities, globalization and disease. It will also assist them in responding to the arguments often put forward by religious sects. Consequently, it is important that future pastoral planning at both national and local levels carefully takes into account the needs of the young and tailors youth programs to address these needs appropriately (cf. *Christifideles Laici*, no. 46).

It is also the Church's task to assist Christian families to live faithfully and generously as true "domestic churches" (cf. *Lumen Gentium*, no. 11). In fact, sound catechesis relies on the support of strong Christian families which are never selfish in character, constantly directed toward the other and founded upon the Sacrament of Matrimony. In reviewing your Quinquennial Reports, I noted that many of you are concerned about the proper celebration of Christian marriage in Ghana. I share your concern and therefore invite the faithful to place the Sacrament of Matrimony at the center of their family life. While Christianity always seeks to respect the venerable traditions of cultures and peoples, it also seeks to purify those practices which are contrary to the Gospel. For this reason it is essential that the entire Catholic community continue to stress the importance of the monogamous and indissoluble union of man and woman, consecrated in holy matrimony. For the Christian, traditional forms of marriage can never be a substitute for sacramental marriage.

The gift of self to the other is also at the heart of the Sacrament of Holy Orders. Those who receive this sacrament are configured in a particular way to Christ the Head of the Church. They are therefore called to give of themselves completely for the sake of their brothers and sisters. This can only happen when God's will is no longer seen as something imposed from without, but becomes "my own will based on the realization that God is in fact more deeply present to me than I am to myself" (cf. *Deus Caritas Est*, no. 17). The priesthood must never be seen as a way of improving one's social standing or standard of living. If it is, then priestly gift of self and docility to God's designs will give way to personal desires, rendering the priest ineffective and unfulfilled. I therefore encourage you in your continuous endeavors to ensure the suitability of candidates for the priesthood and to guarantee proper priestly formation for those who are studying for the sacred ministry. We must strive to help them discern Christ's will and nurture this gift so that they may become effective and fulfilled ministers of his joy.

My dear Brothers, I am aware that this year is a special Jubilee for the Church in Ghana. In fact, just yesterday, April 23rd, was the Hundredth Anniversary of the arrival of missionaries in the northern part of your Country. It is my special prayer that missionary zeal will continue to fill you and your beloved people, strengthening you in your efforts to spread the Gospel. As you return to your homes, I ask that you take consolation from the words the Apostle Peter offered to the early Christians: "Blessed be the God and Father of our Lord Jesus Christ!

By his great mercy we have been born anew to a living hope through the resurrection of Jesus Christ from the dead" (1 Pt 1:3). Commending your ministry to Mary, Queen of the Apostles, I cordially impart my Apostolic Blessing to you and to all those entrusted to your pastoral care.

Address to the Ambassador of Spain to the Holy See

May 20, 2006

Mr. Ambassador,

I am pleased to receive the Letters accrediting you as Ambassador Extraordinary and Plenipotentiary of the Kingdom of Spain to the Holy See. I cordially thank you for your words, and likewise for the appreciated greetings from His Majesty King Juan Carlos I, from the Royal Family, from your Government and from the Spanish Nation. Please convey to them my best wishes for prosperity and spiritual well-being for themselves and for all Spaniards, whom I keep very present in my prayers.

On various occasions I have had the opportunity to visit your Country, of which I treasure very pleasant memories both for the friendliness of the people I met and the abundance and great value of the many works of art and cultural expressions scattered throughout the Land.

It is an enviable patrimony that denotes a brilliant history, deeply imbued with Christian values and enriched by the lives of outstanding Gospel witnesses, both inside and outside its frontiers.

This patrimony includes works whose creators expressed in them their own ideals and faith. If this is ignored or glossed over, it will lose a large part of its attraction and meaning, but the works will continue to be, as it were, "speaking stones."

As you said, Your Excellency, the centuries-old diplomatic relations between Spain and the Holy See reflect the constant ties of the Spanish People with the Catholic faith. The great vitality that the Church in your Country has had and still has is, as it were, a special invitation to reinforce these relations and to foster a close collaboration between the Church and public institutions, which is both loyal and respectful of each other's province and autonomy to achieve the integral good of the people who, as citizens of their Homeland, are also to a large extent beloved children of the Church.

An important path for this cooperation was marked out by the Agreements signed by the Spanish State and the Holy See to guarantee the Catholic Church: "the free and public exercise of her own activities, especially those of worship, jurisdiction and teaching" (Art. I of the First Agreement, January 3, 1979).

Indeed, Mr. Ambassador, the Church, as you know, impels believers to love justice and to take an honest part in public or professional life with a sense of respect and solidarity, so as "to promote organically and institutionally the common good" (*Deus Caritas Est*, no. 29).

She is also involved in the promotion and defense of human rights because of the high esteem in which she holds the integral dignity of the person, in whatever place or situation he or she may be. Using her own means, she devotes all her commitment to ensuring that none of these rights are violated or suppressed, either by individuals or institutions.

For this reason the Church proclaims wholeheartedly the fundamental right to life from conception to its natural end, the right to be born, to form and to live in a family, and not to let the family be supplanted by other institutions or different forms.

In this regard, the upcoming World Meeting of Families in Valencia, Spain, to which I am very much looking forward, will give me the opportunity to celebrate the beauty and fruitfulness of the family founded on marriage, its exalted vocation and indispensable social value.

The Church also insists on the inalienable right of individuals to profess their own religious faith without hindrance, both publicly and privately, as well as the right of parents to have their children receive an education that complies with their values and beliefs without either explicit or implicit discrimination.

In this regard, it pleases me to note the great demand for the teaching of Catholic religion in Spanish State schools. This means that people recognize the importance of this subject for the personal and cultural growth and training of the young. Its importance to the development of the student's personality is the basic principle of the Agreement between the Spanish State and the Holy See on teaching and on cultural subjects, which establishes that the Catholic religion will be taught "in similar conditions to those of the other basic disciplines" (Art. II).

In her evangelizing mission, charitable activity is also a special task of the Church as well as attention to any needy person who is hoping for a friendly, fraternal and impartial hand to alleviate his or her situation. In present-day Spain, as in its long history, the Church's numerous institutions for social assistance prove that this dimension of her activity has been particularly fruitful, in all areas and with extensive goals.

Furthermore, since she is not inspired by either political or ideological strategies (cf. *Deus Caritas Est*, nos. 31b; 33), the Church encounters on her path people and institutions of any origin who are also responsive to the duty of helping the destitute, whoever they may be.

Founded on this "duty of humanity," collaboration in the area of social assistance and humanitarian aid has reached many places and it is to be hoped that it will be ever further encouraged.

Mr. Ambassador, at the end of this Meeting, I repeat to you my best wishes for the success of the lofty mission that has been entrusted to you, so that relations between Spain and the Holy See will be strengthened and progress will be made that reflects the respect and deep affection for the Pope of so many Spaniards.

I also hope that your stay in Rome will bring you fruitful human, cultural and Christian experiences, and that you and your distinguished family will feel at home here but will not forget the beautiful lands in the extreme west of Europe where you come from and where the Gospel very soon took root and spread under the patronage of the Apostle James, contributing to nourish and keep alive Europe's Christian roots.

I ask you to convey my respects to Their Majesties the King and Queen of Spain, and to the Authorities of this noble Nation, and I invoke abundant Blessings from the Most High upon you, your loved ones and the collaborators of this diplomatic Representation.

Address to the Media of the Italian Bishops' Conference

June 2, 2006

With the advent of Illuminism, Western culture began to drift more and more swiftly away from its Christian foundations. Especially in the most recent period, the break-up of the family and of marriage, attacks on human life and its dignity, the reduction of faith to a subjective experience and the consequent secularization of public awareness are seen as the stark and dramatic consequences of this distancing.

Yet, in various parts of Europe experiences and forms of Christian culture exist that are growing stronger or re-emerging with increased vitality. In particular, the Catholic faith is still substantially present in the life of the Italian People, and the signs of its renewed vitality are visible to all.

Homily at the Prayer Vigil with Ecclesial Movements and New Communities

June 3, 2006

Pentecost is this: Jesus, and through him God himself, actually comes to us and draws us to himself. "He sends forth the Holy Spirit"—this is what Scripture says. What effect does this have?

I would like first of all to pick out two aspects: the Holy Spirit, through whom God comes to us, brings us life and freedom. Let us look at both these things a little more closely.

"I came that they might have life, and have it abundantly," Jesus says in the Gospel of John (10:10). Life and freedom: these are the things for which we all yearn. But what is this—where and how do we find "life"?

I think that the vast majority of human beings spontaneously have the same concept of life as the Prodigal Son of the Gospel. He had his share of the patrimony given to him and then felt free; in the end, what he wanted was to live no longer burdened by the duties of home, but just to live. He wanted everything that life can offer. He wanted to enjoy it to the full—living, only living, immersed in life's abundance, missing none of all the valuable things it can offer.

In the end he found himself caring for pigs and even envying those animals—his life had become so empty and so useless. And his freedom was also proving useless.

When all that people want from life is to take possession of it, it becomes ever emptier and poorer; it is easy to end up seeking refuge in drugs, in the great deception. And doubts surface as to whether, in the end, life is truly a good.

No, we do not find life in this way. Jesus' words about life in abundance are found in the Good Shepherd discourse. His words are set in a double context.

Concerning the shepherd, Jesus tells us that he lays down his life. "No one takes [my life] from me, but I lay it down of my own accord" (cf. Jn 10:18). It is only in giving life that it is found; life is not found by seeking to possess it. This is what we must learn from Christ; and the Holy Spirit teaches us that it is a pure gift, that it is God's gift of himself. The more one gives one's life for others, for goodness itself, the more abundantly the river of life flows.

Secondly, the Lord tells us that life unfolds in walking with the Shepherd who is familiar with the pasture—the places where the sources of life flow.

We find life in communion with the One who is life in person—in communion with the living God, a communion into which we are introduced by the Holy Spirit, who is called in the hymn of Vespers *"fons vivus,"* a living source.

The pasture where the sources of life flow is the Word of God as we find it in Scripture, in the faith of the Church. The pasture is God himself who we learn to recognize in the communion of faith through the power of the Holy Spirit.

Dear friends, the Movements were born precisely of the thirst for true life; they are Movements for life in every sense.

Where the true source of life no longer flows, where people only appropriate life instead of giving it, wherever people are ready to dispose of unborn life because it seems to take up room in their own lives, it is there that the life of others is most at risk.

If we want to protect life, then we must above all rediscover the source of life; then life itself must re-emerge in its full beauty and sublimeness; then we must let ourselves be enlivened by the Holy Spirit, the creative source of life. . . .

The Holy Spirit, in giving life and freedom, also gives unity. These are three gifts that are inseparable from one another. I have already gone on too long; but let me say a brief word about unity.

To understand it, we might find a sentence useful which at first seems rather to distance us from it. Jesus said to Nicodemus, who came to him with his questions by night: "The wind blows where it wills" (Jn 3:8). But the Spirit's will is not arbitrary. It is the will of truth and goodness.

Therefore, he does not blow from anywhere, now from one place and then from another; his breath is not wasted but brings us together because the truth unites and love unites.

The Holy Spirit is the Spirit of Jesus Christ, the Spirit who unites the Father with the Son in Love, which in the one God he gives and receives. He unites us so closely that St. Paul once said: "You are all one in Jesus Christ" (Gal 3:28).

With his breath, the Holy Spirit impels us toward Christ. The Holy Spirit acts corporeally; he does not only act subjectively or "spiritually."

The Risen Christ said to his disciples, who supposed that they were seeing only a "spirit": "It is I myself; touch me, and see; for a spirit has not flesh and bones as you see that I have" (cf. Lk 24:39).

This applies for the Risen Christ in every period of history. The Risen Christ is not a ghost, he is not merely a spirit, a thought, only an idea.

He has remained incarnate—it is the Risen One who took on our flesh—and always continues to build his Body, making us his Body. The Spirit breathes where he wills, and his will is unity embodied, a unity that encounters the world and transforms it.

Address to Participants in the Ecclesial Convention of the Diocese of Rome

June 5, 2006

With this Convention and with the pastoral year that will be inspired by its content, the Diocese of Rome is journeying on through the long period that began ten years ago now with the City Mission desired by John Paul II, my beloved Predecessor.

Actually, its goal is still the same: to revive the faith in our communities and seek to reawaken or inspire it in all the individuals and families of this great city, where the faith was preached and the Church already established by the first generation of Christians, and the Apostles Peter and Paul in particular.

In the past three years you have focused your attention especially on the family in order to consolidate this fundamental human reality with the Gospel truth—today, unfortunately, seriously undermined and threatened—and to help it carry out its indispensable mission in the Church and in society.

The priority we are now giving to the education in the faith of the new generations does not mean that we are abandoning our commitment to the family, which is primarily responsible for education.

Rather, we are responding to the widespread concern of many believing families, who fear, in today's social and cultural context, that they might not succeed in passing on to their children the precious heritage of the faith.

Angelus

June 11, 2006

Dear Brothers and Sisters,

On this Sunday that follows Pentecost, we are celebrating the Solemnity of the Most Holy Trinity. Thanks to the Holy Spirit, who helps us understand Jesus' words and guides us to the whole truth (cf. Jn 14:26; 16:13), believers can experience, so to speak, the intimacy of God himself, discovering that he is not infinite solitude but communion of light and love, life given and received in an eternal dialogue between the Father and the Son in the Holy Spirit—Lover, Loved and Love, to echo St. Augustine.

In this world no one can see God, but he has made himself known so that, with the Apostle John, we can affirm: "God is love" (1 Jn 4:8, 16), and "we have come to know and to believe in the love God has for us" (Encyclical *Deus Caritas Est*, no. 1; cf. 1 Jn 4:16).

Those who encounter Christ and enter into a friendly relationship with him welcome into their hearts Trinitarian Communion itself, in accordance with Jesus' promise to his disciples: "If a man loves me, he will keep my word, and my Father will love him, and we will come to him and make our home with him" (Jn 14:23).

For those who have faith, the entire universe speaks of the Triune God. From the spaces between the stars to microscopic particles, all that exists refers to a Being who communicates himself in the multiplicity and variety of elements, as in an immense symphony.

All beings are ordered to a dynamic harmony that we can similarly call "love." But only in the human person, who is free and can reason, does this dynamism become spiritual, does it become responsible love, in response to God and to one's neighbor through a sincere gift of self. It is in this love that human beings find their truth and happiness.

Among the different analogies of the ineffable mystery of the Triune God that believers are able to discern, I would like to cite that of the family. It is called to be a community of love and life where differences must contribute to forming a "parable of communion."

The Virgin Mary, among all creatures, is a masterpiece of the Most Holy Trinity. In her humble heart full of faith, God prepared a worthy dwelling place for himself in order to bring to completion the mystery of salvation. Divine Love found perfect correspondence in her, and in her womb the Only-begotten Son was made man.

Let us turn to Mary with filial trust, so that with her help we may progress in love and make our life a hymn of praise to the Father through the Son in the Holy Spirit.

Address to the Bishops of Lithuania, Estonia, and Latvia on Their *Ad Limina* Visit

June 23, 2006

Your Eminences,
Venerable Brothers in the Episcopate,

Thank you for your pleasant visit. You have come from the peaceful lands of the Baltic *ad limina Apostolorum*, to strengthen your communion with the Successor of Peter and to bring him the cordial greeting of those entrusted to your pastoral care. I extend my grateful thoughts to each one of you, addressed first of all to Cardinal Jānis Pujats, Archbishop of Riga, and to Archbishop Sigitas Tamkevicius, Metropolitan Archbishop of Kaunas.

They have expressed sentiments of convinced attachment to the ministry of the Bishop of Rome on your behalf and on behalf of your diocesan Communities, to which I assure my remembrance in prayer. In the past few days I have listened to and shared with attention what each one of you personally wished to point out to me concerning the functioning of his own Diocese, the generous commitment of the priests, the hope of the lay people and the direction in which civil society is moving.

As I thank you for your spontaneous trust, in a spirit of collegial co-responsibility for the People of God, I encourage you to discern the seeds of good that God has sown in your Communities in order to carry out an increasingly convinced, courageous and tireless missionary action.

Among the many topics I would like to discuss with you, I will reflect today on one of great importance even in your countries: the family. Side by side with exemplary families, there are often others that are unfortunately marked by the frailty of conjugal bonds, the scourge of abortion and the demographic crisis, little attention to teaching authentic values to the children, the precariousness of employment, social mobility that weakens relations between the generations and a growing sense of inner bewilderment among the young people.

A modernity that is not rooted in authentic human values is destined to be dominated by the tyranny of instability and confusion. For this reason, every Ecclesial Community, rich in its faith and supported by God's grace, is called to be a reference point and to enter into dialogue with the Community of which it is an integral part.

The Church, teacher of life, draws from natural law and the Word of God those principles which indicate the indispensable foundations on which to build the family according to the Creator's plan. Dear and venerable Brothers, never tire of always being courageous defenders of life and of the family; persevere in the efforts you have undertaken for the human and religious formation of engaged couples and young families. This is a highly deserving task which I hope will also be appreciated and supported by the institutions of civil society.

The duty of guiding the People of God, of protecting it, defending it and training it in truth and love, is entrusted to you as Pastors. Christ, the Supreme High Priest, is its true Head and, as the Second Vatican Council teaches, he is present among believers in the person of the Bishops, assisted by the priests (cf. *Lumen Gentium*, no. 21).

"Just as . . . St. Peter and the rest of the Apostles constitute a unique apostolic college, so in like fashion the Roman Pontiff, Peter's Successor, and the Bishops, the successors of the Apostles, are related with and united to one another" (ibid., no. 22). The Bishops placed in charge of the particular Churches "exercise their pastoral office over the portion of the People of God assigned to them, not over other Churches nor the Church universal" (ibid., no. 23).

It is important, therefore, that an affective and effective collegiality between the Successor of Peter and all the Pastors be reinforced with full respect for the ministry of each one. Thus, as a well-structured, harmonious body, the People of God can grow in holiness and in missionary vitality, thanks to the contribution of each one of its members.

Venerable Brothers, tirelessly foster communion among yourselves and within each one of your Dioceses, making the most of the contribution of all. Love the priests, your first collaborators who are co-responsible for pastoral care, and give them spiritual and if necessary also material support.

The better able they are to have at their disposal the indispensable guarantees for a dignified living standard, the more serenely they will be able to dedicate themselves to the pastoral ministry entrusted to them. See to their constant formation, also with renewal courses that help them to deepen their knowledge of the teachings of the Second Vatican Council and to appreciate the rich content of the liturgical texts and documents of the Church translated into your respective languages.

Nurture missionary zeal in them so that they will proclaim and witness with joy and enthusiasm to the Good News. May every priest be like the "apple of the Bishop's eye," always followed with fatherly affection and esteem. If priests are enlivened by trust and an authentic Gospel spirit, they will be able to accompany effectively the promising reawakening of lay people, already active in your ecclesiastical district area.

Venerable Brothers, I know that you appropriately combine with concern for your priests another important preoccupation: vocations and the formation of seminarians and aspirants to the consecrated life. The secularized mindset that has also burst into your Communities is increasingly discouraging young men from responding positively to Christ's invitation to follow him more closely, and for this reason you should promote an attentive youth and vocations ministry. Do not hesitate to propose explicitly to youth the Gospel ideal, the beauty of the *sequela Christi sine glossa* without compromises; help all who set out on the path of the priesthood and the consecrated life to respond generously to the Lord Jesus, who never ceases to look lovingly upon his Church and upon humanity.

As for seminarians, ensure that they have formation teachers endowed with a solid humanity and deep piety and who are open to dialogue and collaboration, teachers faithful to the teaching of the Magisterium and credible Gospel witnesses.

Venerable Brothers, the Lord has chosen you to work in his vineyard in a society that only recently emerged from the sad winter of persecution. While the wounds that Communism inflicted on your peoples have not yet completely healed, the influence of a secularism that exalts the mirages of consumerism and makes man the measure of himself is growing. All this makes your pastoral action even more difficult, but without losing confidence, persevere tirelessly in proclaiming the Gospel of Christ, the word of salvation for the people of every epoch and every culture.

The Gospel does not humiliate human freedom and authentic social progress; on the contrary, it helps human beings to fulfill themselves completely and renews society through the gentle and exacting law of love.

May the powerful intercession of Mary, our heavenly Mother, sustain you in your mission and may the example of the martyrs who remained faithful to Christ during the terrible persecutions of past times be an encouragement to you. I assure you of my fraternal and prayerful closeness, as I warmly bless you, the priests, the men and women religious and all the lay faithful entrusted to your pastoral care.

Address to the Ambassador of Uruguay to the Holy See

June 30, 2006

Mr. Ambassador,

I am pleased to offer you a cordial welcome, Your Excellency, at this ceremony for the presentation of the Letters accrediting you as Ambassador Extraordinary and Plenipotentiary of the Oriental Republic of Uruguay to the Holy See.

I thank you for the kind words you have addressed to me, as well as for the thoughtful greeting you have been so good as to convey from H.E. Mr. Tabaré Vázquez Rosas, President of the Republic. I ask you to express to him my very best wishes for his personal well-being and that of his family, as well as for the prosperity and peaceful coexistence in solidarity of this noble Nation.

On its path through history, Uruguay has continued to make its own the Christian ideals of justice and peace. Various concepts of the human being and human destiny coexist in its heart peacefully and with mutual respect, but without diminishing the sincere and real appreciation of the religious dimension and, in particular, of the Church's mission.

A demonstration of affection for the Holy See by so many Uruguayans, as Your Excellency has said, constitutes the undying memory of the two Visits to your Country made by my Predecessor, John Paul II, which lives on, commemorated by a monument in the place where he celebrated his first Mass in Montevideo.

In this perspective, it is to be hoped that the Christian vision of man, created in the image and likeness of God and called to a supernatural destiny, can be openly expressed in the education of the new generations.

In fact, the educational task must not be limited to the merely technical and professional dimension but must include every aspect of the person: his social side and his desire for transcendence, which is expressed in love, one of his noblest dimensions.

The loftiest values rooted in peoples' hearts and in the social fabric are as it were the soul of peoples, which make them strong in adversity, generous in loyal collaboration and eager to build a better future full of life where all, without exception, have the opportunity to develop the full dignity of the human being.

Therefore, certain tendencies that attempt to limit the inviolable value of human life itself, from conception to its natural end, or separate it from its natural context, such as human love in marriage and the family, are viewed with concern.

The Church certainly encourages a generous "culture of life" which creates hope and not only for strictly denominational reasons. As you well know, Mr. Ambassador, there are many eminent people also in your Country who for ethical and rational reasons are similarly preoccupied.

Related to this by their very nature are the issues of the family, the essential structure of society, and that of the union in marriage of a man and a woman, in accordance with a plan imprinted in human nature by the Creator.

There are numerous people in the mass media who denigrate or deride the important value of marriage and the family, thereby encouraging selfishness and confusion rather than the generosity and sacrifice necessary to protect the health of this authentic "primary cell" of the human community.

Promoting the family, helping it to carry out its indispensable tasks, means at the same time gaining social cohesion and above all, respecting its rights which cannot be eroded by other forms of union that claim to usurp them.

Today, the vast problem of poverty and marginalization is a pressing challenge to governors and those in charge of public institutions. On the other hand, the so-called "globalization process" has created new possibilities but also new risks that must be faced in the larger concert of nations.

It is an opportunity to go on weaving, as it were, a network of understanding and solidarity between peoples—without reducing everything to merely commercial or pragmatic exchanges—where there is also room for the human problems of every location, especially the problems of emigrants who are forced to leave their country in search of a better standard of life, which sometimes has serious consequences on their personal, family and social contexts.

The Church, considering the practice of charity as an essential dimension of her being and mission, pays careful attention by means of self-denial to the needy of any condition or provenance, and collaborates in this task with the various public bodies and institutions so that no one in search of support is left without a friendly hand to help in overcoming difficulties.

To do this, she offers her personal and material resources, but above all human closeness in the endeavor to relieve the most grievous poverty, loneliness and neglect, knowing that "a pure and generous love is the best witness to the God in whom we believe and by whom we are driven to love" (Encyclical *Deus Caritas Est*, no. 31c).

Mr. Ambassador, before ending this Meeting, I would like to express to you my best wishes that the mission you are beginning will be fruitful and will contribute to reinforcing the diplomatic relations of your Country with the Holy See, at the same time making them easier and more cordial.

I ask you once again to convey my sentiments and hopes to His Excellency the President of the Republic and to the other Authorities of your Country, while I invoke the maternal protection of Our Lady of the Thirty-Three upon you, Your Excellency, your distinguished family, your collaborators and the beloved sons and daughters of Uruguay.

Angelus

July 2, 2006

Dear Brothers and Sisters,

Next Saturday and Sunday, the Fifth World Meeting of Families will be held in Spain, in the city of Valencia. The first of these meetings was held in Rome in 1994, on the occasion of the International Year of Families promoted by the United Nations. On that occasion, our beloved John Paul II wrote a long and passionate meditation on the family that he addressed in the form of a "Letter" to the families of the whole world. This great gathering of families was followed by others: in Rio de Janeiro in 1997, in Rome in 2000 for the Jubilee of Families, and in Manila in 2003 where, however, he was unable to go in person but sent an audiovisual Message. It is important that families today also receive the memorable appeal that John Paul II addressed to them twenty-five years ago in his Apostolic Exhortation *Familiaris Consortio:* "Family, become what you are!" (cf. no. 17).

The theme of the upcoming Meeting in Valencia is the transmission of the faith in the family. This commitment has inspired the motto of my Apostolic Visit to this city: *"Family: live and transmit the faith!"* In so many secularized communities, the first urgent need for believers in Christ is indeed the renewal of the faith of adults so that they can communicate it to the new generations.

Moreover, the process of the Christian initiation of children and young people can become a useful opportunity for parents to renew their ties with the Church and learn even more about the beauty and truth of the Gospel.

In short, the family is a living organism in which there is a reciprocal exchange of gifts. The important thing is that the Word of God, which keeps the flame of faith alive, never be lacking.

In a most significant gesture, during the rite of Baptism the father or god-father lights a candle from the great Paschal Candle, the symbol of the Risen Christ, and turning to the relatives of the child, the celebrant says: "[this child] of yours has been enlightened by Christ. [He/she is] to walk always as [a child] of the light." If it is to be authentic, this gesture, in which there is all the meaning of the transmission of faith in the family, must be preceded and accompanied by the commitment of the parents to deepen their knowledge of their own faith, reviving its flame through prayer and the assiduous reception of the Sacraments of Confession and the Eucharist.

Let us pray to the Virgin Mary for the success of the upcoming great Meeting in Valencia and for all the families in the world so that they may be genuine communities of love and life, in which the flame of the faith is passed on from generation to generation.

Greetings:*

I greet you, dear French-speaking pilgrims. May your vacation be for you a time of rest and of more intense family life that strengthens relationships among the generations and allows young people in particular to enter into dialogue with adults about the essential questions of faith and of the meaning of existence. I impart to you my Apostolic Blessing.

I welcome all the English-speaking visitors gathered for this *Angelus* prayer. As I prepare to visit Spain for the conclusion of the Fifth World Meeting of Families, I ask your prayers for all families, that they will live in accordance with their God-given vocation and benefit from just governmental policies which safeguard their fundamental role in society. May the Lord bless our families with his joy and peace!

I extend a happy greeting to all the German-speaking pilgrims and visitors. Today's Sunday scriptural readings describe how God created man for immortality. Suffering and death do not get the last word over creation. This

---

*   The four paragraphs greeting French-, German-, and Spanish-speaking pilgrims are an unofficial translation of the Italian.

becomes clear through the works performed by Jesus Christ. He heals the sick and raises the dead. Christ, who vanquished death through His suffering and death, gives new life to us as well. Remain in communion with the Lord; with Him we have the fullness of life. I wish you all a blessed Sunday and a good summer holiday.

I cordially greet the Spanish-speaking pilgrims present here and all those who are joining this Marian prayer through radio and television. I earnestly invite you to pray for the spiritual fruits of the Fifth World Meeting of Families, which will take place next weekend in Valencia, Spain. May the Virgin Mary, who formed the Home of Nazareth together with Joseph and Jesus, be the model of the evangelizing family that passes on the faith to today's world. A blessed Sunday to you!

The Fifth World Meeting of Families began yesterday in Spain. Its theme is "Transmitting the faith in the family." I will travel to Valencia myself for the conclusion of this event. I urge you to participate spiritually in this important meeting and I ask you to support it by your prayers. May this meeting renew the spirit of piety in your families and strengthen them as communities of life and of love. I heartily greet all Polish families.

Letter to Cardinal Fiorenzo Angelini on the Fiftieth Anniversary of His Episcopal Ordination

July 6, 2006

To my Venerable Brother,
Cardinal Fiorenzo Angelini,

On July 29 this year, Your Eminence, you will be celebrating the fiftieth anniversary of your episcopal Ordination, which took place in the Church of Sant'Ignazio in the city of Rome, where you were born on August 1, 1916. This means that three days later, you will also be celebrating your nineti-eth birthday.

On this happy occasion I am very pleased to express my most cordial con-gratulations to you and to offer you my best wishes, with the assurance of a special remembrance in prayer, as I join in your thanksgiving to the Lord for the many gifts with which he has been pleased to enrich your life and ministry for the edification of the Church in Rome, in Italy and throughout the world.

In this context of grateful praise, I would like to recall, at least briefly, what Divine Providence has granted you to achieve in these fifty years.

When the Holy Father Pius XII of venerable memory appointed you titular Bishop of Messene, you had already been serving for more than ten years as General Chaplain of the Men's Branch of Catholic Action, and for just a few months, as Delegate for hospitals and medical centers in the Diocese of Rome.

The episcopal dignity further invigorated the zeal that already distinguished you, attested in particular by the construction of the Church of San Leone Magno al Prenestino and the Pius XII "Centro per un Mondo Migliore" on the Via dei Laghi.

Subsequent to your episcopal ordination, you dedicated yourself without respite to health pastoral care, enabling it to be organized and furthering its organization at the diocesan level, with positive results in Italy and abroad.

Bl. John XXIII appointed you National Chaplain to the Italian Catholic Doctors' Association, which you had founded and which became such a flourishing association that it was able to promote the International Federation of the Catholic Doctors' Association.

In addition to this formative action in the medical sphere was your action in support of the pastoral care of hospital chaplains, and then, your commitment to encouraging scientific research in the field of medicine, whose constant aim was to promote and safeguard the human person.

Your intentions were always perfectly in tune with those of beloved Pope John Paul II, and you were involved in a collaboration that gave birth to the Pontifical Council for the Pastoral Assistance to Health-Care Workers [today known as the "Pontifical Council for Health Pastoral Care"], whose presidency the Holy Father entrusted to you.

Under your guidance, this Dicastery was able to foster in the particular Churches scattered throughout the world that privileged attention to the sick in which, in the light of the Gospel teachings, Christians cannot but share.

In this context, you also promoted a series of annual International Conferences at the Vatican on topics of great importance in the health-care sector; and you saw to the publication of the first census of Catholic Health Care Institutions in the World, as well as compiling and publishing the first "Charter of Health-Care Workers."

It was while you were President that the World Day of the Sick was established and plans were made for the Pontifical Academy for Life.

The firm conviction that the defense of life and pastoral attention to human suffering overcome ideological barriers likewise prompted you, Venerable Brother, to pay visits to and to participate in conventions in various nations, in the most varied and difficult political situations, in order to take everywhere the proclamation of the fundamental human and Christian values and to invite everyone to join forces in service to the suffering.

Recognizing this most generous commitment in a sector of fundamental importance, Pope John Paul II created you Cardinal at the Consistory of June 28, 1991.

In more recent years, comforted by this new sign of papal benevolence and in spiritual continuity with a life spent serving human beings, especially those who are suffering, you founded the International Institute for Research on the Face of Christ in collaboration with the Benedictine Congregation of the Sisters Reparatrix of the Holy Face of Our Lord Jesus Christ, thereby promoting the annual celebration of International Congresses, the tenth of which was celebrated this year.

Thanks to the above-mentioned Religious Congregation, in accordance with the desire formally expressed by its founder, Servant of God Abbot Ildebrando Gregori, your pastoral concern is still expressed through new initiatives, rewarded by precious vocations to the consecrated life and by health-care and educational institutions in Poland, Romania, India and the Democratic Republic of the Congo.

Recounting God's works means praising him. That is why, Your Eminence, I have wished to recall the intense work you have done and are still doing in the Lord's vineyard in order to give thanks to the Lord and at the same time to recognize the merit of a man who has been able to make himself a docile, wise and zealous instrument of the Lord's divine plan.

I know that I am faithfully interpreting your most heartfelt intentions, Venerable Brother, in addressing every expression of gratitude to the Virgin Most Holy, whom you have always recognized as the inspiration and support of your ministry since your Roman Seminary years, when you learned to call on her with the beautiful invocation, "*Mater mea, fiducia mea*."

May the Virgin's intercession continue to obtain an abundance of heavenly gifts for you, as a pledge of which I impart to you with affection a special Apostolic Blessing that I willingly extend to the Sisters Reparatrix of the Holy Face of Our Lord Jesus Christ, and to all your loved ones.

Interview Before His Apostolic Journey to Bavaria

August 5, 2006

VR [Vatican Radio]: The issue of the family. A month ago you were in Valencia for the World Meeting of Families. Anyone who was listening carefully, as we tried to do at Vatican Radio, noticed how you never mentioned the words "homosexual marriage," you never spoke about abortion or about contraception. Careful observers thought that was very interesting. Clearly your idea is to go around the world preaching the faith rather than as an "apostle of morality." What are your comments?

Benedict XVI: Obviously, yes. Actually, I should say I had only two opportunities to speak for twenty minutes. And when you have so little time you cannot immediately begin with "no." Firstly, you have to know what we really want, right? Christianity, Catholicism, is not a collection of prohibitions: it is a positive option. It is very important that we look at it again because this idea has almost completely disappeared today. We have heard so much about what is not allowed that now it is time to say: we have a positive idea to offer, that man and woman are made for each other, that the scale of sexuality, *eros, agape,* indicates the level of love and it is in this way that marriage develops, first of all as a joyful and blessing-filled encounter between a man and a woman, and then, the family, which guarantees continuity among generations and through which generations are reconciled to each other and even cultures can meet. So, firstly, it is important to stress what we want. Secondly, we can also see why we do not want some things. I believe we need to see and reflect on the fact that it is not a Catholic invention that man and woman are made for each other so that humanity can go on living: all cultures know this. As far as abortion is concerned, it is part of the fifth, not the sixth, commandment: "You shall not kill!" We have to presume this is obvious and always stress that the human person begins in the mother's womb and remains a human person until his or her last breath. The human person must always be respected as a human person. But all this is clearer if you say it first in a positive way.

Meeting with Priests of the Diocese of Albano

August 31, 2006

The Family

Fr. Angelo Pennazza, parish priest in Pavona:
Your Holiness, in the "Catechism of the Catholic Church" we read that "Holy Orders and Matrimony are directed toward the salvation of others. . . . They confer a particular mission in the Church and serve to build up the People of God" (no. 1534). This seems to us truly fundamental, not only for our pastoral action but also for our way of being priests. What can we priests do to express this proposal in pastoral praxis and, according to what you yourself have just reaffirmed, to communicate positively the beauty of Marriage which can still make the men and women of our time fall in love? What can the sacramental grace of spouses contribute to our lives as priests?

Benedict XVI:

Two tremendous questions! The first one is: how is it possible to communicate the beauty of marriage to the people of today? We see how many young people are reluctant to marry in church because they are afraid of finality; indeed, they are even reluctant to have a civil wedding. Today, too many young people and even to some who are not so young, definitiveness appears as a constriction, a limitation of freedom. And what they want first of all is freedom. They are afraid that in the end they might not succeed. They see so many failed marriages. They fear that this juridical form, as they understand it, will be an external weight that will extinguish love.

It is essential to understand that it is not a question of a juridical bond, a burden imposed with marriage. On the contrary, depth and beauty lie precisely in finality. Only in this way can love mature to its full beauty. But how is it possible to communicate this? I think this problem is common to us all.

For me, in Valencia—and Your Eminence, you can confirm this—it was an important moment not only when I talked about this, but when various families presented themselves to me with one or more children; one family was virtually a "parish," it had so many children! The presence and witness of these families really was far stronger than any words.

They presented first of all the riches of their family experience: how such a large family truly becomes a cultural treasure, an opportunity for the education of one and all, a possibility for making the various cultural expressions of today coexist, the gift of self, mutual help also in suffering, etc.

But their testimony of the crises they had suffered was also significant. One of these couples had almost reached the point of divorcing. They explained that they then learned to live through this crisis, this suffering of the otherness of the other, and to accept each other anew. Precisely in overcoming the moment of crisis, the desire to separate, a new dimension of love developed and opened the door to a new dimension of life, which nothing but tolerating the suffering of the crisis could reopen.

This seems to me very important. Today, a crisis point is reached the moment the diversity of temperament is perceived, the difficulty of putting up with each other every day for an entire life. In the end, then, they decided: let us separate. From these testimonies we understood precisely that in crises, in bearing the moment in which it seems that no more can be borne, new doors and a new beauty of love truly open.

A beauty consisting of harmony alone is not true beauty. Something is missing, it becomes insufficient. True beauty also needs contrast. Darkness and light complement each other. Even a grape, in order to ripen, does not only need the sun but also the rain, not only the day but also the night.

We priests ourselves, both young and old, must learn the need for suffering and for crises. We must put up with and transcend this suffering. Only in this way is life enriched. I believe that the fact the Lord bears the stigmata for eternity has a symbolic value. As an expression of the atrocity of suffering and death, today the stigmata are seals of Christ's victory, of the full beauty of his victory and his love for us. We must accept, both as priests and as married persons, the need to put up with the crises of otherness, of the other, the crisis in which it seems that it is no longer possible to stay together.

Husbands and wives must learn to move ahead together, also for love of the children, and thus be newly acquainted with one another, love one another anew with a love far deeper and far truer. So it is that on a long journey, with its suffering, love truly matures.

It seems to me that we priests can also learn from married people precisely because of their suffering and sacrifices. We often think that celibacy on its own is a sacrifice. However, knowing the sacrifices married people make—let us think of their children, of the problems that arise, of the fears, suffering, illnesses, rebellion, and also of the problems of the early years when nights are almost always spent sleeplessly because of the crying of small children—we must learn our sacrifice from them, from their sacrifices. And at the same time we must learn that it is beautiful to mature through sacrifices and thus to work for the salvation of others.

Fr. Pennazza, you correctly mentioned the Council which says that Marriage is a Sacrament for the salvation of others: first of all for the salvation of the other, of the husband and of the wife, but also of the children, the sons and daughters, and lastly of the entire community. And thus, priesthood too matures in the encounter.

I then think that we ought to involve families. Family celebrations seem to me to be very important. On the occasion of celebrations it is right that the family, the beauty of families, appear. Even testimonies—although they are perhaps somewhat too fashionable—can in some instances truly be a proclamation, a help for us all.

To conclude, I consider it very significant that in St. Paul's Letter to the Ephesians, God's marriage with humanity through the Incarnation of the Lord is achieved on the Cross, on which is born the new humanity: the Church.

Precisely from these divine nuptials Christian marriage is born. As St. Paul says, it is the sacramental concretization of what happens in this great mystery. Thus, we must learn ever anew this bond between the Cross and the Resurrection, between the Cross and the beauty of the Redemption, and insert ourselves into this sacrament. Let us pray to the Lord to help us proclaim this mystery well, to live this mystery, to learn from married couples how they live it in order to help us live the Cross, so that we may also attain moments of joy and of the Resurrection.

Youth

Fr. Gualtiero Isacchi, Director of Diocesan Service for the Pastoral Care of Youth:
Young people are the focus of a more decisive attention on the part of our dioceses and of the entire Church in Italy. The World Days have led them to this discovery: there are a great many young people and they are enthusiastic. Yet, our parishes in general are not adequately equipped to welcome them; parish communities and pastoral workers are not sufficiently trained to talk to them; the priests involved in the various tasks do not have the time required to listen to them. They are remembered when they become a problem or when we need them to enliven some celebration or festivity . . . . How can a priest today express a preferential option for young people in view of his busy pastoral agenda? How can we serve young people based on their own scale of values instead of involving them in "our own things"?

Benedict XVI:

I would like first of all to stress what you have said. On the occasion of the World Youth Days and at other events—as recently, on the Eve of Pentecost—it appears that young people are also in search of God. The young want to see if God exists and what God tells us. Consequently, there is a certain willingness, in spite of all the difficulties of our time. An enthusiasm also exists. Therefore, we must do all we can to try to keep alive this flame that shows itself on occasions such as the World Youth Days.

What shall we do? This is our common question. I think that precisely here, an "integrated pastoral care" should be put into practice, for in fact not every parish priest can cope adequately with youth. He therefore needs a pastoral apostolate that transcends the limits of the parish and that also transcends the limits of the priest's work; a pastoral apostolate that involves numerous pastoral workers.

It seems to me that under the Bishop's coordination, a way should be found, on the one hand, to integrate young people into the parish so that they may be the leaven of parish life; and on the other, also to obtain for these youth the help of extra-parochial personnel. These two things must go hand-in-hand. It is necessary to suggest to young people that not only in the parish but also in various contexts they must integrate themselves into the life of the dioceses so as to meet subsequently in the parish; so it is necessary to encourage all initiatives along these lines.

I think that volunteer experience is very important nowadays. It is vital not to leave young people to the mercy of discos but to have useful tasks for them to do in which they see they are necessary, realize that they can do something good. By feeling this impulse to do something useful for humanity, for someone, for a group, young people also become aware of this incentive to strive to find the "track" of a positive commitment, of a Christian ethic.

It seems to me very important that young people truly find tasks that demonstrate that they are needed, that guide them on the way of a positive service of assistance inspired by Christ's love for men and women, so that they themselves seek the sources from which to draw strength and commitment.

Another experience is offered by the prayer groups where, in their own youthful context, the young learn to listen to the Word of God, to learn the Word of God and to enter into contact with God. This also means learning the common form of prayer, the Liturgy, which at first sight might perhaps seem rather inaccessible to them. They learn that the Word of God exists and seeks us out, despite all the distance of the times, and speaks to us today. We offer to the Lord the fruit of the earth and of the work of our hands and we find it transformed into a gift of God. We speak as children to the Father and we then receive the gift of the Lord himself. We receive the mission to go out into the world with the gift of his Presence.

It would also be useful to have liturgy schools that young people could attend. Moreover, opportunities for young people to present and introduce themselves are vital. I heard that here in Albano a play on the life of St. Francis was performed. Committing oneself in this sense means desiring to penetrate the personality of St. Francis, of his time, and thereby widening one's own personality. It is only an example, something apparently fairly unusual. It can be a lesson to broaden the personality, to enter into a context of Christian tradition, to reawaken the thirst for a better knowledge of the sources from which this saint drew. He was not only an environmentalist or a pacifist. He was above all a convert.

I read with great pleasure that Bishop Sorrentino of Assisi, precisely to obviate this "abuse" of the figure of St. Francis, on the occasion of the eighth centenary of his conversion wished to establish a "Year of Conversion" to see what the true "challenge" is. Perhaps we can all animate youth a little to make the meaning of conversion understood by also finding a link with the figure of St. Francis and seeking a route that broadens life. Francis was first a kind of "playboy." He then felt that this was not enough. He heard the Lord's voice: "Rebuild my House." Little by little, he came to understand what "building the House of the Lord" means.

I do not, therefore, have very practical answers, because I find myself facing a mission where I already find young people gathered, thanks be to God. But it seems to me that one ought to make use of all the possibilities offered today by the Movements, Associations and Volunteer Groups and in other activities for youth. It is also necessary to present young people to the parish so that it sees who the young people are. Vocations' promotion is necessary. The whole thing must be coordinated by the Bishop. It seems to me that pastoral workers are found through the same authentic cooperation of young people who are training. And thus, it is possible to open the way to conversion, to the joy that God exists and is concerned about us, that we have access to God and can help others "rebuild his House."

It seems to me that this, finally, is our mission, sometimes difficult, but in the end very beautiful: to "build God's House" in the contemporary world.

Thank you for your attention and I ask you to forgive me for my disconnected answers. Let us collaborate so that "God's House" in our time will grow and many young people will find the path of service to the Lord.

Address to Participants in the Plenary Assembly of the Pontifical Council for the Laity

September 22, 2006

Dear Brothers and Sisters, while I express my deep appreciation to you for the activity of animation and service that you carry out, I cordially hope that the Plenary Assembly will help to make the lay faithful ever more aware of their mission in the Church, especially within the parish community, which is a "family" of Christian families.

I assure you of my constant remembrance of this in prayer, and as I invoke upon each one Mary's motherly protection, I willingly impart my Blessing to all of you, to your relatives and to the communities to which you belong.

Angelus

October 8, 2006

Dear Brothers and Sisters,

This Sunday, the Gospel presents to us Jesus' words on marriage. He answered those who asked him whether it was lawful for a man to divorce his wife, as provided by a decree in Mosaic law (cf. Dt 24:1), that this was a concession made to Moses because of man's "hardness of heart," whereas the truth about marriage dated back to "the beginning of creation" when, as is written of God in the Book of Genesis, "male and female he created them; for this reason a man shall leave his father and mother and be joined to his wife, and the two shall become one" (Mk 10:6-7; cf. Gn 1:27; 2:24).

And Jesus added: "So they are no longer two but one. What therefore God has joined together, let not man put asunder" (Mk 10:8-9). This is God's original plan, as the Second Vatican Council also recalled in the Constitution

Gaudium et Spes: "The intimate partnership of life and love which constitutes the married state has been established by the Creator and endowed by him with its own proper laws: it is rooted in the contract of its partners . . . God himself is the author of marriage" (no. 48).

My thoughts now go to all Christian spouses: I thank the Lord with them for the gift of the Sacrament of Marriage, and I urge them to remain faithful to their vocation in every season of life, "in good times and in bad, in sickness and in health," as they promised in the sacramental rite.

Conscious of the grace they have received, may Christian husbands and wives build a family open to life and capable of facing united the many complex challenges of our time.

Today, there is a special need for their witness. There is a need for families that do not let themselves be swept away by modern cultural currents inspired by hedonism and relativism, and which are ready instead to carry out their mission in the Church and in society with generous dedication.

In the Apostolic Exhortation *Familiaris Consortio,* the Servant of God John Paul II wrote that "the sacrament of marriage makes Christian couples and parents witnesses of Christ 'to the end of the earth,' missionaries, in the true and proper sense, of love and life" (cf. no. 54). Their mission is directed both to inside the family—especially in reciprocal service and the education of the children—and to outside it. Indeed, the domestic community is called to be a sign of God's love for all.

The Christian family can only fulfill this mission if it is supported by divine grace. It is therefore necessary for Christian couples to pray tirelessly and to persevere in their daily efforts to maintain the commitments they assumed on their wedding day.

I invoke upon all families, especially those in difficulty, the motherly protection of Our Lady and of her husband Joseph. Mary, Queen of the family, pray for us!

Message for the Ninety-Third
World Day of Migrants and Refugees (2007)

The Migrant Family

October 18, 2006

Dear Brothers and Sisters!

On the occasion of the coming World Day of Migrants and Refugees, and looking at the Holy Family of Nazareth, icon of all families, I would like to invite you to reflect on the condition of the migrant family. The evangelist Matthew narrates that shortly after the birth of Jesus, Joseph was forced to leave for Egypt by night, taking the child and his mother with him, in order to flee the persecution of king Herod (cf. Mt 2:13-15). Making a comment on this page of the Gospel, my venerable Predecessor, the Servant of God Pope Pius XII, wrote in 1952: "The family of Nazareth in exile, Jesus, Mary and Joseph, emigrants and taking refuge in Egypt to escape the fury of an evil king, are the model, the example and the support of all emigrants and pilgrims of every age and every country, of all refugees of any condition who, compelled by persecution and need, are forced to abandon their homeland, their beloved relatives, their neighbors, their dear friends, and move to a foreign land" (*Exsul Familia*, AAS 44, 1952, 649). In this misfortune experienced by the Family of Nazareth, obliged to take refuge in Egypt, we can catch a glimpse of the painful condition in which all migrants live, especially, refugees, exiles, evacuees, internally displaced persons, those who are persecuted. We can take a quick look at the difficulties that every migrant family lives through, the hardships and humiliations, the deprivation and fragility of millions and millions of migrants, refugees and internally displaced people. The Family of Nazareth reflects the image of God safeguarded in the heart of every human family, even if disfigured and weakened by emigration.

The theme of the next World Day of Migrants and Refugees—*The migrant family*—is in continuity with those of 1980, 1986 and 1993. It intends to underline further the commitment of the Church not only in favor of the individual migrant, but also of his family, which is a place and resource of the culture of life and a factor for the integration of values. The migrant's family meets many difficulties. The distance of its members from one another and unsuccessful reunification often result in breaking the original ties. New relationships are formed and new affections arise. Some migrants forget the past and their duties, as they are subjected to the hard trial of distance and solitude. If the immigrant family is not ensured of a real possibility of inclusion and participation, it is difficult to expect its harmonious development. The International Convention for the protection of the rights of all migrant workers and members of their families, which was enforced on July 1st, 2003, intends to defend men and women migrant workers and the members of their respective families. This means that the value of the family is recognized, also in the sphere of emigration, which is now a structural phenomenon of our societies. The Church encourages the ratification of the international legal instruments that aim to defend the rights of migrants, refugees and their families and, through its various Institutions and Associations, offers its advocacy that is becoming more and more necessary. To this end, it has opened Centers where migrants are listened to, Houses where they are welcomed, Offices for services offered to persons and families, with other initiatives set up to respond to the growing needs in this field.

Much is already being done for the integration of the families of immigrants, although much still remains to be done. There are real difficulties connected with some "defense mechanisms" on the part of the first generation immigrants, which run the risk of becoming an obstacle to the greater maturity of the young people of the second generation. This is why it is necessary to provide for legislative, juridical and social intervention to facilitate such an integration. In recent times, there is an increase in the number of women who leave their countries of origin in search of better conditions of life, in view of more promising professional prospects. However, women who end up as victims of trafficking of human beings and of prostitution are not few in number. In family reunification, social workers, especially religious women, can render an appreciated service of mediation that merits our gratitude more and more.

Regarding the integration of the families of immigrants, I feel it my duty to call your attention to the families of refugees, whose conditions seem to have gone worse in comparison with the past, also specifically regarding the reunification of family nuclei. In the camps assigned to them, in addition to logistic difficulties, and those of a personal character linked to the trauma and emotional stress caused by the tragic experiences they went through, sometimes there is also the risk of women and children being involved in sexual exploitation, as a survival mechanism. In these cases an attentive pastoral presence is necessary. Aside from giving assistance capable of healing the wounds of the heart, pastoral care should also offer the support of the Christian community, able to restore the culture of respect and have the true value of love found again. It is necessary to encourage those who are interiorly-wrecked to recover trust in themselves. Everything must also be done to guarantee the rights and dignity of the families and to assure them housing facilities according to their needs. Refugees are asked to cultivate an open and positive attitude toward their receiving society and maintain an active willingness to accept offers to participate in building together an integrated community that would be a "common household" for all.

Among migrants, there is a category that needs to be considered in a special way: the students from other countries, who are far from home, without an adequate knowledge of the language, at times without friends and often with a scholarship that is insufficient for their needs. Their condition is even worse if they are married. Through its Institutions, the Church exerts every effort to render the absence of family support for these young students less painful. It helps them integrate in the cities that receive them, by putting them in contact with families that are willing to offer them hospitality and facilitate knowing one another. As I had the opportunity to say on another occasion, helping foreign students is "an important field of pastoral action . . . Indeed, young people who leave their own country in order to study encounter many problems and especially the risk of an identity crisis" (*L'Osservatore Romano*, December 15, 2005).

Dear Brothers and Sisters, may the World Day of Migrants and Refugees become a useful occasion to build awareness, in the ecclesial community and public opinion, regarding the needs and problems, as well as the positive potentialities of migrant families. My thoughts go in a special way to those who are directly involved in the vast phenomenon of migration, and to those who expend their pastoral energy in the service of human mobility. The words of the apostle Paul, *"caritas Christi urget nos"* (2 Cor 5:14), urge us to give ourselves preferentially to our brothers and sisters who are most in need. With these sentiments, I invoke divine assistance on each one and I affectionately impart to all a special Apostolic Blessing.

PASTORAL VISIT TO VERONA FOR THE
FOURTH NATIONAL ECCLESIAL CONVENTION

Homily at Mass in Bentegodi Stadium*

October 19, 2006

But, as I noted earlier, Italy is also very fertile terrain for Christian witness. The Church here is, in fact, very much alive—and we see that—and it maintains a broad presence among people of every age and state. Christian traditions are still often rooted and continue to bear fruit. Meanwhile, a great effort of evangelization and catechesis is underway, addressed in particular to the younger generations but more and more also to families. The inadequacy of a closed-minded rationalism and an excessively individualistic ethics is being more clearly felt; specifically, the great risk involved in cutting ourselves off from the Christian roots of our civilization is being noticed. This feeling, which is widespread among the Italian people, is frequently and forcefully expressed by many important exponents of culture, even among those who do not share or at least do not practice our faith. The Church and Italian Catholics are therefore called to seize this great opportunity and, first of all, to be aware of it. Our attitude should never one of renunciation and turning in on ourselves: rather, we need to keep our dynamism alive and if possible increase it; we need to open up new relationships with confidence and not spare any effort that can contribute to Italy's the cultural and moral growth. In fact, it is up to us—not with our meager resources but with the power that comes from the Holy Spirit—to offer positive and convincing answers to the expectations and questions of our people. If we succeed in this, the Church in Italy will render a great service not only to this nation but also to Europe and to the world, because the trap of

---

*   This text is an unofficial translation of the Italian.

secularism is everywhere and equally universal is the need for a faith lived out in relation to the challenges of our time . . .

Education

In practical terms, in order for the experience of Christian faith and love to be accepted and experienced and handed on from one generation to the next, the education of the person is a fundamental and decisive question. Concern for intellectual formation must not overlook formation of a person's freedom and ability to love. That is why recourse to the assistance of Grace is also necessary. Only in this way can a person effectively resist that risk for the sorts of human family that are characterized by an imbalance between a very swift growth in our technical ability and a much slower growth of our moral resources. A real education needs to reawaken the courage to make firm decisions which nowadays are considered a shackle that kills our freedom but are really indispensable for growing and achieving something great in our lives, particularly for allowing love to mature into its full beauty and, thus, to give depth and meaning to our own freedom. It is out of this concern for the human person and his formation that we say "no" to weak and deviant forms of love and other counterfeit versions of freedom, such as the reduction of reason only to what can be calculated and manipulated. Indeed, such a "no" is actually a "yes" to authentic love, to the reality of the human person as created by God. I want to express here all my appreciation for the great work of formation and education that the individual Churches never tire of carrying out in Italy, for their pastoral attention to the younger generations and to families: thank you for this attentiveness! Among the many forms of this involvement I would be remiss not to recall in particular the Catholic schools, because to some degree age-old prejudices against it endure which are no longer justifiable, causing harmful delays in accrediting them and permitting them to operate.

. . . Special attention and extraordinary commitment are required today for those great challenges that put vast segments of the human family in serious danger: wars and terrorism, hunger and thirst, and some terrible epidemics. But the risk of political and legislative choices also needs to be confronted with equal determination and clarity of purpose when they contradict fundamental values, anthropological principles and ethics rooted in the nature of human being, particularly regarding the protection of human life at every phase from conception to natural death and to the promotion of the family based on marriage, avoiding the introduction into the public order of other forms of unions that would contribute to destabilization by obscuring marriage's unique and irreplaceable role in society. The open and courageous witness that the Church and Italian Catholics have given and continue to give on this subject are a precious service to Italy and also helpful and stimulating for many other nations.

This commitment and this witness are certainly part of that great "yes" that we as believers in Christ say to the humanity that God loves.

Address to the President of the Republic of Italy

November 20, 2006

This specific contribution [to the political sphere] is mainly made by the lay faithful, who, acting with full responsibility and making use of the right to participate in public life, work with other members of society "to build a just order in society" (ibid.).

In their action, moreover, they rely on the "fundamental values and anthropological principles and ethics rooted in the nature of the human being" (ibid.), which are also recognizable through the proper use of reason.

Thus, when they undertake to confront with their words and actions today's great challenges, such as war and terrorism, hunger and thirst, the extreme poverty of so many human beings, several terrible epidemics, but also the safeguard of human life in all its stages from conception until natural death and the promotion of the family founded on marriage and primarily responsible for education, they are not acting in their own special interests or on behalf of principles that can only be perceived by those who profess a specific religious creed: they do so, instead, in the context of, and abiding by, the rules of democratic coexistence for the good of the whole of society and on behalf of values that every upright person can share.

Proof of this is the fact that the majority of the values that I mentioned are proclaimed by the Italian Constitution, which was drafted almost sixty years ago by people holding different ideals.

Message for the World Day of Peace

[January 1, 2007]

The Human Person, the Heart of Peace

December 8, 2006

The right to life and to religious freedom

4. The duty to respect the dignity of each human being, in whose nature the image of the Creator is reflected, means in consequence that *the person cannot*

be disposed of at will. Those with greater political, technical, or economic power may not use that power to violate the rights of others who are less fortunate. Peace is based on respect for the rights of all. Conscious of this, the Church champions the fundamental rights of each person. In particular she promotes and defends respect for the *life* and the *religious freedom* of everyone. Respect for the right to life at every stage firmly establishes a principle of decisive importance: *life is a gift which is not completely at the disposal of the subject.* Similarly, the affirmation of the right to religious freedom places the human being *in a relationship with a transcendent principle which withdraws him from human caprice.* The right to life and to the free expression of personal faith in God is not subject to the power of man. Peace requires the establishment of *a clear boundary between what is at man's disposal and what is not*: in this way unacceptable intrusions into the patrimony of specifically human values will be avoided.

5. As far as *the right to life* is concerned, we must denounce its widespread violation in our society: alongside the victims of armed conflicts, terrorism and the different forms of violence, there are the silent deaths caused by hunger, abortion, experimentation on human embryos and euthanasia. How can we fail to see in all this an attack on peace? Abortion and embryonic experimentation constitute a direct denial of that attitude of acceptance of others which is indispensable for establishing lasting relationships of peace. As far as *the free expression of personal faith* is concerned, another disturbing symptom of lack of peace in the world is represented by the difficulties that both Christians and the followers of other religions frequently encounter in publicly and freely professing their religious convictions. Speaking of Christians in particular, I must point out with pain that not only are they at times prevented from doing so; in some States they are actually persecuted, and even recently tragic cases of ferocious violence have been recorded. There are regimes that impose a single religion upon everyone, while secular regimes often lead not so much to violent persecution as to systematic cultural denigration of religious beliefs. In both instances, a fundamental human right is not being respected, with serious repercussions for peaceful coexistence. This can only promote *a mentality and culture that is not conducive to peace.*

Address to the Ambassador of the Kyrgyz Republic to the Holy See

December 14, 2006

The extraordinary natural beauty of Kyrgyzstan is a blessing for your nation. Such dramatic evidence of the hand of the Creator gladdens the hearts of your people and helps them lift their thoughts toward the Almighty. Indeed, the people of Kyrgyzstan know well the importance of religious freedom and understand that if the spiritual dimension of persons is repressed or even denied, the soul of a nation is crushed. During the tragic epoch of intimidation in Central Asian history, while the supremacy of force endured, religious believers in your country nurtured a hope for freedom and justice, a future in which the supremacy of truth about the human person and the purpose of society would prevail. Today, that hope is experienced in a variety of ways including the tolerance demonstrated between religious and ethnic communities, the respect for the role of the family at the heart of your society, and the flourishing of your nation's fine arts. Such traits and values, which have in fact long adorned your history, assume a heightened importance of regional significance when we consider Kyrgyzstan's unique geographical position as a cultural crossroads.

As the Kyrgyz Republic continues to forge its national identity, it must be borne in mind that the important component of economic development contains a moral aspect, of crucial importance to the well-being and peaceful progress of a nation. It is here that the demand for justice is satisfied (cf. *Sollicitudo Rei Socialis*, no. 10). The right to meaningful work and an acceptable standard of living, the assurance of a fair distribution of goods and wealth, and the responsible use of natural resources all depend upon a concept of growth which is not limited to merely satisfying material necessities. Instead, such a notion must also highlight the dignity of every human person—the proper subject of all progress—and thereby enhance the common good of all humanity.

Address and Christmas Greetings to the Members of the Roman Curia

December 22, 2006

The *Visit to Valencia, Spain,* was under the banner of the theme of marriage and the family. It was beautiful to listen, before the people assembled from all continents, to the testimonies of couples—blessed by a numerous throng of children—who introduced themselves to us and spoke of their respective journeys in the Sacrament of Marriage and in their large families.

They did not hide the fact that they have also had difficult days, that they have had to pass through periods of crisis. Yet, precisely through the effort of supporting one another day by day, precisely through accepting one another ever anew in the crucible of daily trials, living and suffering to the full their initial "yes," precisely on this Gospel path of "losing oneself," they had matured, rediscovered themselves and become happy.

Their "yes" to one another in the patience of the journey and in the strength of the Sacrament with which Christ had bound them together, had become a great "yes" to themselves, their children, to God the Creator and to the Redeemer, Jesus Christ. Thus, from the witness of these families a wave of joy reached us, not a superficial and scant gaiety that is all too soon dispelled, but a joy that developed also in suffering, a joy that reaches down to the depths and truly redeems man.

Before these families with their children, before these families in which the generations hold hands and the future is present, the problem of Europe, which it seems no longer wants to have children, penetrated my soul. To foreigners this Europe seems to be tired, indeed, it seems to be wishing to take its leave of history.

Why are things like this? This is the great question. The answers are undoubtedly very complex. Before seeking these answers, it is only right to thank the many married couples in our Europe who still say "yes" to children today and accept the trials that this entails: social and financial problems, as well as worries and struggles, day after day; the dedication required to give children access to the path toward the future.

In mentioning these difficulties, perhaps the reasons also become clearer why for many the risk of having children appears too great.

A child needs loving attention. This means that we must give children some of our time, the time of our life. But precisely this "raw material" of life—time—seems to be ever scarcer. The time we have available barely suffices for our own lives; how could we surrender it, give it to someone else?

To have time and to give time—this is for us a very concrete way to learn to give oneself, to lose oneself in order to find oneself.

In addition to this problem comes the difficult calculation: what rules should we apply to ensure that the child follows the right path and in so doing, how should we respect his or her freedom? The problem has also become very difficult because we are no longer sure of the norms to transmit; because we no longer know what the correct use of freedom is, what is the correct way to live, what is morally correct and what instead is inadmissible.

The modern spirit has lost its bearings, and this lack of bearings prevents us from being indicators of the right way to others. Indeed, the problem goes even deeper. Contemporary man is insecure about the future. Is it permissible to send someone into this uncertain future? In short, is it a good thing to be a person?

This deep lack of self-assurance—plus the wish to have one's whole life for oneself—is perhaps the deepest reason why the risk of having children appears to many to be almost unsustainable.

In fact, we can transmit life in a responsible way only if we are able to pass on something more than mere biological life, and that is, a meaning that prevails even in the crises of history to come and a certainty in the hope that is stronger than the clouds that obscure the future.

Unless we learn anew the foundations of life—unless we discover in a new way the certainty of faith—it will be less and less possible for us to entrust to others the gift of life and the task of an unknown future.

Connected with that, finally, is also the problem of definitive decisions: can man bind himself forever? Can he say a "yes" for his whole life? Yes, he can. He was created for this. In this very way human freedom is brought about and thus the sacred context of marriage is also created and enlarged, becoming a family and building the future.

At this point, I cannot be silent about my concern about the legislation for *de facto* couples. Many of these couples have chosen this way because—at least for the time being—they do not feel able to accept the legally ordered and binding coexistence of marriage. Thus, they prefer to remain in the simple *de facto* state. When new forms of legislation are created which relativize marriage, the renouncement of the definitive bond obtains, as it were, also a juridical seal.

In this case, deciding for those who are already finding it far from easy becomes even more difficult.

Then there is in addition, for the other type of couple, the relativization of the difference between the sexes.

The union of a man and a woman is being put on a par with the pairing of two people of the same sex, and tacitly confirms those fallacious theories that remove from the human person all the importance of masculinity and femininity, as though it were a question of the purely biological factor.

Such theories hold that man—that is, his intellect and his desire—would decide autonomously what he is or what he is not. In this, corporeity is scorned, with the consequence that the human being, in seeking to be emancipated from his body—from the "biological sphere"—ends by destroying himself.

If we tell ourselves that the Church ought not to interfere in such matters, we cannot but answer: are we not concerned with the human being? Do not believers, by virtue of the great culture of their faith, have the right to make a pronouncement on all this? Is it not their—our—duty to raise our voices to defend the human being, that creature who, precisely in the inseparable unity of body and spirit, is the image of God? The Visit to Valencia became for me a quest for the meaning of the human being.

Angelus

December 31, 2006

Dear Brothers and Sisters,

On this last Sunday of the year we are celebrating the *Feast of the Holy Family of Nazareth*. I address with joy all the families of the world, wishing them the peace and love that Jesus brought us in coming among us at Christmas.

In the Gospel we do not find discourses on the family but an *event* which is worth more than any words: God *wanted to be born and to grow up in a human family*. In this way he consecrated the family as the first and ordinary means of his encounter with humanity.

In his life spent at Nazareth, Jesus honored the Virgin Mary and the righteous Joseph, remaining under their authority throughout the period of his childhood and his adolescence (cf. Lk 2:41-52). In this way he shed light on the primary value of the family in the education of the person.

Jesus was introduced by Mary and Joseph into the religious community and frequented the synagogue of Nazareth. With them, he learned to make the pilgrimage to Jerusalem, as the Gospel passage offered for our meditation by today's liturgy tells us.

When he was twelve years old, he stayed behind in the Temple and it took his parents all of three days to find him. With this act he made them understand that he "had to see to his Father's affairs," in other words, to the mission that God had entrusted to him (cf. Lk 2:41-52).

This Gospel episode reveals the most authentic and profound vocation of the family: that is, to accompany each of its members on the path of the discovery of God and of the plan that he has prepared for him or her.

Mary and Joseph taught Jesus primarily by their example: in his parents he came to know the full beauty of faith, of love for God and for his Law, as well as the demands of justice, which is totally fulfilled in love (cf. Rom 13:10).

From them he learned that it is necessary first of all to do God's will, and that the spiritual bond is worth more than the bond of kinship.

The Holy Family of Nazareth is truly the "prototype" of every Christian family which, united in the Sacrament of Marriage and nourished by the Word and the Eucharist, is called to carry out the wonderful vocation and mission of being the living cell not only of society but also of the Church, a sign and instrument of unity for the entire human race.

Let us now invoke for every family, especially families in difficulty, the protection of Mary Most Holy and of St. Joseph. May they sustain such families so that they can resist the disintegrating forces of a certain contemporary culture which undermines the very foundations of the family institution.

May they help Christian families to be, in every part of the world, living images of God's love.

After the Angelus:*

On this joyful Feast of the Holy Family I am happy to welcome all the English-speaking pilgrims present for today's *Angelus*. In the Holy Family of Nazareth we are given the true model of a Christian home. Let us resolve to make our own homes radiate with Christ's loving harmony and peace.

Our hearts also turn today to all those for whom family life is marred by sadness, tragedy or violence. May they be uplifted by the hope which Jesus brings to each one of us.

Upon all of you and your loved ones I invoke God's abundant Blessings of joy and peace!

Looking back with gratitude on God's goodness, I greet you, dear German-speaking pilgrims and visitors on this last day of the year 2006. Today the Church also celebrates the feast of the Holy Family. May Jesus, Mary and Joseph, so beautifully represented here in the manger in St. Peter's Square, be for you a pledge of God's care and encourage you to encounter each other with good will, affection and Christian love. I wish you all a peaceful Sunday and a good transition from the old year to the new with God's blessing.

I welcome the Spanish-speaking pilgrims participating in the *Angelus* prayer on this Sunday when we celebrate the Holy Family. Let us pray for all the families of the world, that they may live the faith and pass it on in their homes and so be witnesses of love in the world. Happy Lord's Day!

I greet all the Poles. Let us give thanks to God for the past year and for all the good things we have received and particularly for the pilgrimage to Poland. I recall my journey in the footsteps of the Servant of God John Paul II and your witness of faith. Today, on the Sunday of the Holy Family, I pray that your families may be a worthy place for educating children and young people. May God bless you!

Finally, I greet all the Italian-speaking pilgrims. I wish you a good Sunday and a calm end of the year.

---

*   The four paragraphs greeting German-, Spanish-, Polish-, and Italian-speaking pilgrims are an unofficial translation of the Italian.

Homily at Mass and Baptism of Children

January 7, 2007

Dear Brothers and Sisters,

This year too, we are meeting for a real family celebration, the Baptism of thirteen children in this wonderful Sistine Chapel, where with their creativity, Michelangelo and other outstanding artists achieved masterpieces that illustrate the wonders of the history of salvation.

I would like immediately to greet all of you present here: the parents, the godparents, the relatives and friends who accompany these newborn babies at such an important moment for their lives and for the Church. Every child who is born brings us God's smile and invites us to recognize that life is his gift, a gift to be welcomed with love and preserved with care, always and at every moment.

The Christmas Season, which ends precisely today, has made us contemplate the Child Jesus in the poor grotto of Bethlehem, lovingly tended by Mary and Joseph. God entrusts every child who is born to his parents: so how important is the family founded on marriage, the cradle of life and love!

The House of Nazareth where the Holy Family lived is the model and school of simplicity, patience and harmony for all Christian families. I pray the Lord that your families too may be welcoming places where these little ones can not only grow in good health but also in faith and love for God, who today, with Baptism, makes them his children.

The Rite of Baptism of these children is taking place on the day in which we celebrate the Feast of the Baptism of the Lord, an event which, as I said, brings the Christmas Season to a close.

So far, we have heard the account of the Evangelist Luke, who presents Jesus who remained hidden in the crowd while he went to John the Baptist to be baptized. Jesus had also been baptized, and, St. Luke tells us, "was praying" (3:21). Jesus speaks with his Father. And we may be certain that he did not only speak for himself but also of us and for us; he also spoke of me, of each one of us and for each one of us.

And then the Evangelist tells us that above the Lord in prayer, Heaven was opened.

Jesus entered into contact with the Father, Heaven opened above him. At this moment we can think that Heaven has also opened here, above these children of ours who, through the Sacrament of Baptism, come into contact with Jesus. Heaven opens above us in the Sacrament. The more we live in contact with Jesus in the reality of our Baptism, the more Heaven will open above us. And from Heaven—let us return to the Gospel—that day a voice came which said to Jesus: "You are my beloved Son" (Lk 3:22).

In Baptism, the Heavenly Father also repeats these words for each one of these infants. He says: "You are my child." Baptism is adoption and admission into God's family, into communion with the Most Holy Trinity, into communion with the Father, the Son and the Holy Spirit. For this very reason, Baptism should be administered in the Name of the Most Holy Trinity. These words are not merely a formula; they are reality. They mark the moment when your children are reborn as children of God. From being the children of human parents, they also become the children of God in the Son of the living God.

However, we must now meditate on the words in the Second Reading of this liturgy where St. Paul tells us: "He saved us, not because of deeds done by us in righteousness, but in virtue of his own mercy, by the washing of regeneration and renewal in the Holy Spirit" (Ti 3:5).

A washing of regeneration: Baptism is not only a word, it is not only something spiritual but also implies matter. All the realities of the earth are involved. Baptism does not only concern the soul. Human spirituality invests the totality of the person, body and soul. God's action in Jesus Christ is an action of universal efficacy. Christ took flesh and this continues in the sacraments in which matter is taken on and becomes part of the divine action.

We can now ask precisely why water should be the sign of this totality. Water is the element of fertility. Without water there is no life. Thus, in all the great religions water is seen as the symbol of motherhood, of fruitfulness. For the Church Fathers, water became the symbol of the maternal womb of the Church.

Tertullian, a Church writer of the second and third centuries, said something surprising. He said: "Never is Christ without water." By these words, Tertullian meant that Christ is never without the Church. In Baptism we are adopted by the Heavenly Father, but in this family that he establishes there is also a mother, Mother Church. Man cannot have God as Father, the ancient Christian writers were already saying, unless he has the Church as mother.

We perceive in a new way that Christianity is not merely an individual, spiritual reality, a simple subjective decision that I take, but something real and concrete, we could also say something material. Adoption as children of God, of the Trinitarian God, is at the same time being accepted into the family of the Church, it is admission as brothers and sisters into the great family of Christians. And only if, as children of God, we are integrated as brothers and sisters into the reality of the Church can we say "Our Father," to our Heavenly Father. This prayer always implies the "we" of God's family.

Now, however, let us return to the Gospel in which John the Baptist says: "I baptize you with water; but he who is mightier than I is coming . . . he will baptize you with the Holy Spirit and with fire" (Lk 3:16).

We have seen water; but now the question is unavoidable: of what does the fire that St. John the Baptist referred to consist? To see this reality of the fire, present in Baptism with water, we must note that John's baptism was a human gesture, an act of penance, a human impulse for God, to ask the forgiveness of sins and the chance to begin a new life. It was only a human desire, a step toward God with their own effort.

Now this is not enough. The distance would be too great. In Jesus Christ we see that God comes to meet us. In Christian Baptism, instituted by Christ, we do not only act with the desire to be cleansed through the prayer to obtain forgiveness.

In Baptism God himself acts, Jesus acts through the Holy Spirit. In Christian Baptism the fire of the Holy Spirit is present. God acts, not only us. God is present here today. He takes on your children and makes them his own.

But naturally, God does not act in a magical way. He acts only with our freedom. We cannot renounce our freedom. God challenges our freedom, invites us to cooperate with the fire of the Holy Spirit. These two things must go together. Baptism will remain throughout life a gift of God, who has set his seal on our souls. But it will then be our cooperation, the availability of our freedom to say that "yes" which makes divine action effective.

These children of yours, whom we will now baptize, are not yet able to collaborate, to manifest their faith. For this reason, your presence, dear fathers and mothers, and yours, dear godfathers and godmothers, acquires a special value and significance. Always watch over your little ones, so that they may learn to know God as they grow up, love him with all their strength and serve him faithfully. May you be their first educators in faith, offering together with your teaching also the examples of a coherent Christian life. Teach them to pray and to feel as living members of the concrete family of God, of the Ecclesial Community.

The attentive study of the Catechism of the Catholic Church or of the Compendium of this Catechism can offer you important help. It contains the essential elements of our faith and can be a particularly useful and immediate means, for you yourselves, to grow in the knowledge of the Catholic faith and to transmit it integrally and faithfully to your children. Above all, do not forget that it is your witness, it is your example, that has the greatest effect on the human and spiritual maturation of your children's freedom. Even caught up in the sometimes frenetic daily activities, do not neglect to foster prayer, personally and in the family, which is the secret of Christian perseverance.

Let us entrust these children and their families to the Virgin Mother of Jesus, Our Savior, presented in today's liturgy as the beloved Son of God: may Mary watch over them and accompany them always, so that they can fully carry out the project of salvation which God has for each one. Amen.

Address to Members of the Regional Board of Lazio and the Civil Authorities of Rome

January 11, 2007

This same concern for the human being that impels us to be close to the poor and the sick makes us attentive to that fundamental human good of the family based on marriage. Today, the intrinsic value and authentic motivations of marriage and the family need to be understood better. To this end, the Church's pastoral commitment has been considerable and must increase further.

But a twofold policy of and for the family, which calls into question the responsibility of its members, is also necessary. In other words, it is a matter of increasing initiatives that can make the forming of a family and subsequently having and raising children easier and less burdensome for young couples; that encourage the employment of youth, contain housing costs as much as possible and increase the number of kindergartens and nursery schools.

Indeed, those projects that aim to attribute to other forms of union inappropriate legal recognition, inevitably lead to weakening and destabilizing the legitimate family founded on marriage and appear to be dangerous and counterproductive.

Educating the new generations is the pastoral priority on which the Diocese of Rome is currently focusing attention. The social and civil importance of this problem certainly escapes none of you.

Therefore, while I am grateful for the support you already offer to certain forms of the Church's educational commitment, including the after-school recreation facilities, I am confident that in this area too it will be possible to develop a fruitful collaboration with respect for the temperament and tasks proper to each one of those concerned.

Angelus

January 14, 2007

Dear Brothers and Sisters,

The annual *World Day of Migrants and Refugees* is being celebrated this Sunday. For the occasion, I have addressed to all people of good will and to Christian communities in particular a special Message on *The migrant family*.

We can look to the Holy Family of Nazareth, icon of all families, because it reflects the image of God cherished in the heart of every human family, even when it is weakened and at times disfigured by life's trials.

The Evangelist Matthew recounts that shortly after Jesus' birth, St. Joseph was forced to flee to Egypt, taking the Child and his Mother with him, in order to escape King Herod's persecution (cf. Mt 2:13-15).

In the drama of the Family of Nazareth we perceive the sorrowful plight of so many migrants, especially refugees, exiles, displaced people, evacuees and the persecuted. We recognize in particular the difficulties of the migrant family: hardship, humiliation, poverty and fragility.

The phenomenon of human mobility is actually vast and diversified. According to recent calculations by the United Nations, migrants, due to financial reasons, amount today to almost 200 million, approximately 9 million are refugees and about 2 million, international students.

We must add to this large number of brothers and sisters the internally displaced and those whose situation is illegal, bearing in mind that in one way or another each one of them depends on a family.

It is therefore important to protect migrants and their families with the help of specific legislative, juridical and administrative protection, and also by means of a network of services, consultation centers and structures that provide social and pastoral assistance.

I hope that a balanced management of migratory flows and of human mobility in general will soon be achieved so as to benefit the entire human family, starting with practical measures that encourage legal emigration and the reunion of families, and paying special attention to women and minors.

Indeed, the human person must always be the focal point in the vast field of international migration. Only respect for the human dignity of all migrants, on the one hand, and recognition by the migrants themselves of the values of the society that has taken them in, on the other, enable families to be properly integrated into the social, economic and political systems of the host nation.

Dear friends, the reality of migration should never be viewed solely as a problem, but also and above all as a great resource for humanity's development.

Moreover, the migrant family is in a special way a resource as long as it is respected as such; it must not suffer irreparable damage but must be able to stay united or to be reunited and carry out its mission as the cradle of life and the primary context where the human person is welcomed and educated.

Let us ask the Lord for this together, through the intercession of the Blessed Virgin Mary and St. Frances Xavier Cabrini, Patroness of migrants.

Message for the Forty-First
World Communications Day

[May 20, 2007]

"Children and the Media: A Challenge for Education"

January 24, 2007

Dear Brothers and Sisters,

1. The theme of the Forty-first World Communications Day, "Children and the Media: A Challenge for Education," invites us to reflect on two related topics of immense importance. The formation of children is one. The other, perhaps less obvious but no less important, is the formation of the media.

The complex challenges facing education today are often linked to the pervasive influence of the media in our world. As an aspect of the phenomenon of globalization, and facilitated by the rapid development of technology, the media profoundly shape the cultural environment (cf. Pope John Paul II, Apostolic Letter *The Rapid Development*, no. 3). Indeed, some claim that the formative influence of the media rivals that of the school, the Church, and maybe even the home. "Reality, for many, is what the media recognize as real" (Pontifical Council for Social Communications, *Aetatis Novae*, no. 4).

2. The relationship of children, media, and education can be considered from two perspectives: the formation of children by the media; and the formation of children to respond appropriately to the media. A kind of reciprocity emerges which points to the responsibilities of the media as an industry and to the need for active and critical participation of readers, viewers and listeners. Within this framework, training in the proper use of the media is essential for the cultural, moral and spiritual development of children.

How is this common good to be protected and promoted? Educating children to be discriminating in their use of the media is a responsibility of parents, Church, and school. The role of parents is of primary importance. They have a right and duty to ensure the prudent use of the media by training the conscience of their children to express sound and objective judgments which will then guide them in choosing or rejecting programs available (cf. Pope John Paul II, Apostolic Exhortation *Familiaris Consortio*, no. 76). In doing so, parents should have the encouragement and assistance of schools and parishes in ensuring that this difficult, though satisfying, aspect of parenting is supported by the wider community.

Media education should be positive. Children exposed to what is aesthetically and morally excellent are helped to develop appreciation, prudence and the skills of discernment. Here it is important to recognize the fundamental value of parents' example and the benefits of introducing young people to children's classics in literature, to the fine arts and to uplifting music. While popular literature will always have its place in culture, the temptation to sensationalize should not be passively accepted in places of learning. Beauty, a kind of mirror of the divine, inspires and vivifies young hearts and minds, while ugliness and coarseness have a depressing impact on attitudes and behavior.

Like education in general, media education requires formation in the exercise of freedom. This is a demanding task. So often freedom is presented as a relentless search for pleasure or new experiences. Yet this is a condemnation not a liberation! True freedom could never condemn the individual—especially a child—to an insatiable quest for novelty. In the light of truth, authentic freedom is experienced as a definitive response to God's "yes" to humanity, calling us to choose, not indiscriminately but deliberately, all that is good, true and beautiful. Parents, then, as the guardians of that freedom, while gradually giving their children greater freedom, introduce them to the profound joy of life (cf. *Address to the Fifth World Meeting of Families*, Valencia, July 8, 2006).

3. This heartfelt wish of parents and teachers to educate children in the ways of beauty, truth and goodness can be supported by the media industry only to the extent that it promotes fundamental human dignity, the true value of marriage and family life, and the positive achievements and goals of humanity. Thus, the need for the media to be committed to effective formation and ethical standards is viewed with particular interest and even urgency not only by parents and teachers but by all who have a sense of civic responsibility.

While affirming the belief that many people involved in social communications want to do what is right (cf. Pontifical Council for Social Communications, *Ethics in Communications*, 4), we must also recognize that those who work in this field confront "special psychological pressures and ethical dilemmas" (*Aetatis Novae*, no. 19) which at times see commercial competitiveness compelling communicators to lower standards. Any trend to produce programs and products—including animated films and video games—which in the name of entertainment exalt violence and portray anti-social behavior or the trivialization of human sexuality is a perversion, all the more repulsive when these programs are directed at children and adolescents. How could one explain this "entertainment" to the countless innocent young people who actually suffer violence, exploitation and abuse? In this regard, all would do well to reflect on the contrast between Christ who "put his arms around [the

children] laid his hands on them and gave them his blessing" (Mk 10:16) and
the one who "leads astray . . . these little ones" for whom "it would be better
. . . if a millstone were hung round his neck" (Lk 17:2). Again I appeal to the
leaders of the media industry to educate and encourage producers to safeguard
the common good, to uphold the truth, to protect individual human dignity
and promote respect for the needs of the family.

4. The Church herself, in the light of the message of salvation entrusted to
her, is also a teacher of humanity and welcomes the opportunity to offer assistance to parents, educators, communicators, and young people. Her own parish and school programs should be in the forefront of media education today.
Above all, the Church desires to share a vision of human dignity that is central to all worthy human communication. "Seeing with the eyes of Christ, I
can give to others much more than their outward necessities; I can give them
the look of love which they crave" (*Deus Caritas Est*, no. 18).

Angelus

February 4, 2007

Dear Brothers and Sisters,

Today, *Pro-Life Day*, organized by the Bishops' Conference on the theme:
"Love and desire life," is being celebrated in Italy. I cordially greet all those
who are gathered in St. Peter's Square to witness their commitment in support of life, from its conception to its natural end. I join the Italian Bishops in
renewing the appeal made several times by my venerable Predecessors to all
men and women of good will to welcome the great and mysterious gift of life.

Life, which is a work of God, should not be denied to anyone, even the
tiniest and most defenseless unborn child, and far less to a child with serious
disabilities. At the same time, echoing the Pastors of the Church in Italy, I
advise you not to fall into the deceptive trap of thinking that life can be disposed of, to the point of "legitimizing its interruption with euthanasia, even
if it is masked by a veil of human compassion."

The "Week of life and of the family" begins in our Diocese of Rome today.
It is an important opportunity to pray and reflect on the family, which is
the "cradle" of life and of every vocation. We are well aware that the family
founded on marriage is the natural environment in which to bear and raise
children and thereby guarantee the future of all of humanity.

However, we also know that marriage is going through a deep crisis and
today must face numerous challenges. It is consequently necessary to defend,
help, safeguard and value it in its unrepeatable uniqueness.

If this commitment is in the first place the duty of spouses, it is also a priority duty of the Church and of every public institution to support the family by means of pastoral and political initiatives that take into account the real needs of married couples, of the elderly and of the new generations.

A peaceful family atmosphere, illumined by faith and the holy fear of God also nurtures the budding and blossoming of vocations to the service of the Gospel. I am referring in particular not only to those who are called to follow Christ on the path of the priesthood but also to all men and women religious, the consecrated people we remembered last Friday on the "World Day of Consecrated Life."

Dear brothers and sisters, let us pray that through a constant effort to promote life and the family institution, our communities may be places of communion and hope in which, despite the many difficulties, the great "yes" to authentic love and to the reality of the human being and the family is renewed in accordance with God's original plan. Let us ask the Lord, through the intercession of Mary Most Holy, to grant that respect for the sacredness of life will grow so that people will be ever more aware of the real needs of families and that the number of those who help to build the civilization of love in the world will increase.

General Audience

February 7, 2007

One thing is sure: together with the gratitude of the early Church, of which St. Paul speaks, we must also add our own, since thanks to the faith and apostolic commitment of the lay faithful, of families, of spouses like Priscilla and Aquila, Christianity has reached our generation.

It could grow not only thanks to the Apostles who announced it. In order to take root in people's land and develop actively, the commitment of these families, these spouses, these Christian communities, of these lay faithful was necessary in order to offer the "humus" for the growth of the faith. As always, it is only in this way that the Church grows.

This couple in particular demonstrates how important the action of Christian spouses is. When they are supported by the faith and by a strong spirituality, their courageous commitment for the Church and in the Church becomes natural. The daily sharing of their life prolongs and in some way is sublimated in the assuming of a common responsibility in favor of the Mystical Body of Christ, even if just a little part of it. Thus it was in the first generation and thus it will often be.

A further lesson we cannot neglect to draw from their example: every home can transform itself in a little church. Not only in the sense that in them must reign the typical Christian love made of altruism and of reciprocal care, but still more in the sense that the whole of family life, based on faith, is called to revolve around the singular lordship of Jesus Christ.

Not by chance does Paul compare, in the *Letter to the Ephesians*, the matrimonial relationship to the spousal communion that happens between Christ and the Church (cf. Eph 5:25-33). Even more, we can maintain that the Apostle indirectly models the life of the entire Church on that of the family. And the Church, in reality, is the family of God.

Therefore, we honor Aquila and Priscilla as models of conjugal life responsibly committed to the service of the entire Christian community. And we find in them the model of the Church, God's family for all times.

Address to the Ambassador of Colombia to the Holy See

February 9, 2007

As Pastor of the universal Church, I cannot refrain from expressing to Your Excellency my anxiety for the laws that concern those very sensitive issues such as the transmission and defense of life, sickness, the identity of the family and respect for marriage. On these topics and in the light of natural reason and the moral and spiritual principles that derive from the Gospel, the Catholic Church will continue ceaselessly to proclaim the inalienable greatness of human dignity.

It is also necessary to appeal to the responsibility of the lay people present in legislative bodies, in the Government and in the administration of justice to ensure that laws always express principles and values that are in conformity with natural law and that foster the authentic common good.

Address to the Ambassador of Costa Rica to the Holy See

February 10, 2007

On the other hand, Your Excellency, as you pointed out, this dialogue [about promoting justice] must exclude all the different forms of violence and help in building a more human future with the collaboration of all.

In this regard, it is appropriate to recall that social improvements are not only achieved by applying the necessary technical means but also by promoting reforms that take into account an ethical consideration of the person, the family and society.

It is consequently necessary to cultivate moral values such as honesty, discipline and responsibility for the common good. In this way it will be possible to avoid personal and collective selfishness in every context, as well as corruption which hinders every form of progress.

It is well known that the future of a nation must be based on peace, the harvest of righteousness (cf. Jas 3:18), building the kind of society which, starting with those in charge of politics, parliament, administration and the law, encourages concord, harmony and respect for individuals as well as the defense of their fundamental rights.

In this regard, the policies that the Government of Costa Rica has implemented in the international arena to promote peace and human rights in the world, and its traditional closeness to the positions maintained by the Holy See in various international forums on matters as important as the defense of human life and the promotion of marriage and the family, deserve praise.

Address to Participants in the International Congress on Natural Moral Law

February 12, 2007

Venerable Brothers in the Episcopate and in the Priesthood,
Esteemed Professors,
Ladies and Gentlemen,

It is with particular pleasure that I welcome you at the beginning of the Congress' work in which you will be engaged in the following days on a theme of considerable importance for the present historical moment, namely, the natural moral law.

I thank Bishop Rino Fisichella, Rector Magnificent of the Pontifical Lateran University, for the sentiments expressed in the address with which he has introduced this meeting.

There is no doubt that we are living in a moment of extraordinary development in the human capacity to decipher the rules and structures of matter, and in the consequent dominion of man over nature.

We all see the great advantages of this progress and we see more and more clearly the threat of destruction of nature by what we do.

There is another less visible danger, but no less disturbing: the method that permits us to know ever more deeply the rational structures of matter makes us ever less capable of perceiving the source of this rationality, creative Reason. The capacity to see the laws of material being makes us incapable of seeing the ethical message contained in being, a message that tradition calls *lex naturalis*, natural moral law.

This word for many today is almost incomprehensible due to a concept of nature that is no longer metaphysical, but only empirical. The fact that nature, being itself, is no longer a transparent moral message creates a sense of disorientation that renders the choices of daily life precarious and uncertain.

Naturally, the disorientation strikes the younger generations in a particular way, who must in this context find the fundamental choices for their life.

It is precisely in the light of this contestation that all the urgency of the necessity to reflect upon the theme of natural law and to rediscover its truth common to all men appears. The said law, to which the Apostle Paul refers (cf. Rom 2:14-15), is written on the heart of man and is consequently, even today, accessible.

This law has as its first and general principle, "to do good and to avoid evil." This is a truth which by its very evidence immediately imposes itself on everyone. From it flows the other more particular principles that regulate ethical justice on the rights and duties of everyone.

So does the principle of respect for *human life* from its conception to its natural end, because this good of life is not man's property but the free gift of God. Besides this is the duty to seek the truth as the necessary presupposition of every authentic personal maturation.

Another fundamental application of the subject is *freedom*. Yet taking into account the fact that human freedom is always a freedom shared with others, it is clear that the harmony of freedom can be found only in what is common to all: the truth of the human being, the fundamental message of being itself, exactly the *lex naturalis*.

And how can we not mention, on one hand, the demand of *justice* that manifests itself in giving *unicuique suum* and, on the other, the expectation of *solidarity* that nourishes in everyone, especially if they are poor, the hope of the help of the more fortunate?

In these values are expressed unbreakable and contingent norms that do not depend on the will of the legislator and not even on the consensus that the State can and must give. They are, in fact, norms that precede any human law: as such, they are not subject to modification by anyone.

The natural law, together with fundamental rights, is the source from which ethical imperatives also flow, which it is only right to honor.

In today's ethics and philosophy of Law, petitions of juridical positivism are widespread. As a result, legislation often becomes only a compromise between different interests: seeking to transform private interests or wishes into law that conflict with the duties deriving from social responsibility.

In this situation it is opportune to recall that every juridical methodology, be it on the local or international level, ultimately draws its legitimacy from its rooting in the natural law, in the ethical message inscribed in the actual human being.

Natural law is, definitively, the only valid bulwark against the arbitrary power or the deception of ideological manipulation. The knowledge of this law inscribed on the heart of man increases with the progress of the moral conscience.

The first duty for all, and particularly for those with public responsibility, must therefore be to promote the maturation of the moral conscience. This is the fundamental progress without which all other progress proves non-authentic.

The law inscribed in our nature is the true guarantee offered to everyone in order to be able to live in freedom and to be respected in their own dignity.

What has been said up to this point has very concrete applications if one refers to the family, that is, to "the intimate partnership of life and the love which constitutes the married state . . . established by the Creator and endowed by him with its own proper laws" (Gaudium et Spes, no. 48).

Concerning this, the Second Vatican Council has opportunely recalled that the institution of marriage has been "confirmed by the divine law," and therefore "this sacred bond . . . for the good of the partner, of the children and of society no longer depends on human decision alone" (ibid.).

Therefore, no law made by man can override the norm written by the Creator without society becoming dramatically wounded in what constitutes its basic foundation. To forget this would mean to weaken the family, penalizing the children and rendering the future of society precarious.

Lastly, I feel the duty to affirm yet again that not all that is scientifically possible is also ethically licit. Technology, when it reduces the human being to an object of experimentation, results in abandoning the weak subject to the arbitration of the stronger. To blindly entrust oneself to technology as the only guarantee of progress, without offering at the same time an ethical code that penetrates its roots in that same reality under study and development, would be equal to doing violence to human nature with devastating consequences for all.

The contribution of scientists is of primary importance. Together with the progress of our capacity to dominate nature, scientists must also contribute to help understand the depth of our responsibility for man and for nature entrusted to him.

On this basis it is possible to develop a fruitful dialogue between believers and non-believers; between theologians, philosophers, jurists and scientists, which can offer to legislation as well precious material for personal and social life.

Therefore, I hope these days of study will bring not only a greater sensitivity of the learned with regard to the natural moral law, but will also serve to create conditions so that this theme may reach an ever fuller awareness of the inalienable value that the *lex naturalis* possesses for a real and coherent progress of private life and the social order.

With this wish, I assure you of my remembrance in prayer for you and for your academic commitment to research and reflection, while I impart to all with affection the Apostolic Blessing.

Letter to the President of the Republic of Korea

February 15, 2007

For over fifty years, the Korean people have suffered the consequences of division. Families have been split, close relatives have been separated from one another. Please let them know that I am spiritually close to them in their suffering. On compassionate grounds, I pray for a speedy solution to the problem which impedes so many from communicating with one another.

Sadly, the modern world is marked by an increasing number of threats to the dignity of human life. I wish therefore to commend all those in your country who work to uphold and defend the sanctity of life, marriage and the family, areas in which, as you know, the Catholic Church in Korea is particularly active. The risk of a nuclear arms race in the region is a further source of concern, fully shared by the Holy See. I urge all interested parties to make every effort to resolve the present tensions through peaceful means and to refrain from any gesture or initiative that might endanger the negotiations, while ensuring that the most vulnerable part of the North Korean population has access to humanitarian aid.

Address to Papal Representatives in Latin American Countries in Preparation for the Fifth General Conference of the Latin American Episcopal Council (CELAM)

February 17, 2007

An immense missionary and evangelizing potential is offered by the young who account for more than two thirds of the population, whereas family "feeling [is] a primordial trait of your Latin American culture," as my venerable Predecessor John Paul II said at the meeting in Puebla, Mexico, in January 1979 (Homily, Palafoxiano Seminary, Puebla, January 28, 1979, in Puebla and Beyond [Maryknoll: Orbis Books, 1979], 78).

The family institution deserves priority attention; it is showing signs of breaking up under the pressure of lobbies that can have a negative effect on legislative processes. Divorce and de facto unions are on the rise, while adultery is viewed with unjustifiable tolerance.

It is necessary to reassert that marriage and the family are based on the deepest nucleus of the truth about man and his destiny; only on the rock of faithful and permanent conjugal love between a man and woman is it possible to build a community worthy of the human being.

Post-Synodal Apostolic Exhortation *Sacramentum Caritatis*, On the Eucharist as the Source and Summit of the Church's Life and Mission

February 22, 2007

The Eucharist and the Sacraments

Initiation, the ecclesial community and the family

19. It should be kept in mind that the whole of Christian initiation is a process of conversion undertaken with God's help and with constant reference to the ecclesial community, both when an adult is seeking entry into the Church, as happens in places of first evangelization and in many secularized regions, and when parents request the sacraments for their children. In this regard, I would like to call particular attention to the relationship between Christian initiation and the family. In pastoral work it is always important to make Christian families part of the process of initiation. Receiving Baptism, Confirmation and First Holy Communion are key moments not only for the individual receiving them but also for the entire family, which should be supported in its educational role by the various elements of the ecclesial community (cf. *Propositio* 15). Here I would emphasize the importance of First Holy Communion. For many of the faithful, this day continues to be memorable as the moment when, even if in a rudimentary way, they first came to

understand the importance of a personal encounter with Jesus. Parish pastoral programs should make the most of this highly significant moment. . . .

V. The Eucharist and Matrimony

The Eucharist, a nuptial sacrament

27. The Eucharist, as the sacrament of charity, has a particular relationship with the love of man and woman united in marriage. A deeper understanding of this relationship is needed at the present time (cf. John Paul II, *Familiaris Consortio*, no. 57). Pope John Paul II frequently spoke of the nuptial character of the Eucharist and its special relationship with the sacrament of Matrimony: "The Eucharist is the sacrament of our redemption. It is the sacrament of the Bridegroom and of the Bride" (*Mulieris Dignitatem*, no. 26). Moreover, "the entire Christian life bears the mark of the spousal love of Christ and the Church. Already Baptism, the entry into the People of God, is a nuptial mystery; it is so to speak the nuptial bath which precedes the wedding feast, the Eucharist" (CCC, no. 1617). The Eucharist inexhaustibly strengthens the indissoluble unity and love of every Christian marriage. By the power of the sacrament, the marriage bond is intrinsically linked to the Eucharistic unity of Christ the Bridegroom and his Bride, the Church (cf Eph 5:31-32). The mutual consent that husband and wife exchange in Christ, which establishes them as a community of life and love, also has a Eucharistic dimension. Indeed, in the theology of St. Paul, conjugal love is a sacramental sign of Christ's love for his Church, a love culminating in the Cross, the expression of his "marriage" with humanity and at the same time the origin and heart of the Eucharist. For this reason the Church manifests her particular spiritual closeness to all those who have built their family on the sacrament of Matrimony (cf. *Propositio* 8). The family—the domestic Church (cf. *Lumen Gentium*, no. 11)—is a primary sphere of the Church's life, especially because of its decisive role in the Christian education of children (cf. *Propositio* 8). In this context, the Synod also called for an acknowledgment of the unique mission of women in the family and in society, a mission that needs to be defended, protected and promoted (cf. *Mulieris Dignitatem*; cf. Congregation for the Doctrine of the Faith, *Letter to the Bishops of the Catholic Church on the Collaboration of Men and Women in the Church and in the World* [May 31, 2004]). Marriage and motherhood represent essential realities which must never be denigrated.

The Eucharist and the unicity of marriage

28. In the light of this intrinsic relationship between marriage, the family and the Eucharist, we can turn to several pastoral problems. The indissoluble, exclusive and faithful bond uniting Christ and the Church, which finds sacramental expression in the Eucharist, corresponds to the basic anthropological fact that man is meant to be definitively united to one woman and vice versa (cf. Gn 2:24, Mt 19:5). With this in mind, the Synod of Bishops addressed the question of pastoral practice regarding people who come to the Gospel from cultures in which polygamy is practiced. Those living in this situation who open themselves to Christian faith need to be helped to integrate their life-plan into the radical newness of Christ. During the catechumenate, Christ encounters them in their specific circumstances and calls them to embrace the full truth of love, making whatever sacrifices are necessary in order to arrive at perfect ecclesial communion. The Church accompanies them with a pastoral care that is gentle yet firm (cf. *Propositio* 9), above all by showing them the light shed by the Christian mysteries on nature and on human affections.

The Eucharist and the indissolubility of marriage

29. If the Eucharist expresses the irrevocable nature of God's love in Christ for his Church, we can then understand why it implies, with regard to the sacrament of Matrimony, that indissolubility to which all true love necessarily aspires (cf. *Catechism of the Catholic Church*, no. 1640). There was good reason for the pastoral attention that the Synod gave to the painful situations experienced by some of the faithful who, having celebrated the sacrament of Matrimony, then divorced and remarried. This represents a complex and troubling pastoral problem, a real scourge for contemporary society, and one which increasingly affects the Catholic community as well. The Church's pastors, out of love for the truth, are obliged to discern different situations carefully, in order to be able to offer appropriate spiritual guidance to the faithful involved (cf. *Familiaris Consortio*, no. 84; cf. Congregation for the Doctrine of the Faith, Letter to the Bishops of the Catholic Church Concerning the Reception of Holy Communion by Divorced and Remarried Members of the Faithful *Annus Internationalis Familiae* [September 14, 1994]). The Synod of Bishops confirmed the Church's practice, based on Sacred Scripture (cf. Mk 10:2- 12), of not admitting the divorced and remarried to the sacraments, since their state and their condition of life objectively contradict the loving union of Christ and the Church signified and made present in the Eucharist. Yet the divorced and remarried continue to belong to the Church, which accompanies them with special concern and encourages them to live as fully as possible the Christian life through regular participation at Mass, albeit

without receiving communion, listening to the word of God, Eucharistic adoration, prayer, participation in the life of the community, honest dialogue with a priest or spiritual director, dedication to the life of charity, works of penance, and commitment to the education of their children.

When legitimate doubts exist about the validity of the prior sacramental marriage, the necessary investigation must be carried out to establish if these are well-founded. Consequently there is a need to ensure, in full respect for canon law (cf. Pontifical Council for Legislative Texts, Instruction on the Norms to be Observed at Ecclesiastical Tribunals in Matrimonial Proceedings *Dignitas Connubii* [January 25, 2005]), the presence of local ecclesiastical tribunals, their pastoral character, and their correct and prompt functioning (cf. *Propositio* 40). Each Diocese should have a sufficient number of persons with the necessary preparation, so that the ecclesiastical tribunals can operate in an expeditious manner. I repeat that "it is a grave obligation to bring the Church's institutional activity in her tribunals ever closer to the faithful" (Benedict XVI, Address to the Tribunal of the Roman Rota for the Inauguration of the Judicial Year [January 28, 2006]). At the same time, pastoral care must not be understood as if it were somehow in conflict with the law. Rather, one should begin by assuming that the fundamental point of encounter between the law and pastoral care is *love for the truth*: truth is never something purely abstract, but "a real part of the human and Christian journey of every member of the faithful" (cf. *Propositio* 40). Finally, where the nullity of the marriage bond is not declared and objective circumstances make it impossible to cease cohabitation, the Church encourages these members of the faithful to commit themselves to living their relationship in fidelity to the demands of God's law, as friends, as brother and sister; in this way they will be able to return to the table of the Eucharist, taking care to observe the Church's established and approved practice in this regard. This path, if it is to be possible and fruitful, must be supported by pastors and by adequate ecclesial initiatives, nor can it ever involve the blessing of these relations, lest confusion arise among the faithful concerning the value of marriage (cf. *Propositio* 40).

Given the complex cultural context which the Church today encounters in many countries, the Synod also recommended devoting maximum pastoral attention to training couples preparing for marriage and to ascertaining beforehand their convictions regarding the obligations required for the validity of the sacrament of Matrimony. Serious discernment in this matter will help to avoid situations where impulsive decisions or superficial reasons lead two young people to take on responsibilities that they are then incapable of honoring (cf. *Propositio* 40). The good that the Church and society as a whole expect from marriage and from the family founded upon marriage is so great as to call for full pastoral commitment to this particular area. Marriage and the family are institutions that must be promoted and defended from every possible misrepresentation of their true nature, since whatever is injurious to them is injurious to society itself.

Address to Participants in the Plenary Assembly of the Pontifical Council for Social Communications

March 9, 2007

Your Eminences,
Dear Brother Bishops,
Dear Brothers and Sisters in Christ,

I am glad to welcome you to the Vatican today on the occasion of the annual Plenary Assembly of the Pontifical Council for Social Communications. My thanks go firstly to Archbishop Foley, President of the Council, for his kind introductory comments. To all of you, I wish to express my gratitude for your commitment to the apostolate of social communications, the importance of which cannot be underestimated in our increasingly technological world.

The field of social communications is fast-changing. While the print media struggles to maintain circulation, other forms of media such as radio, television and the internet are developing at an extraordinary rate. Against the backdrop of globalization, this ascendancy of the electronic media coincides with its increasing concentration in the hands of a few multinational conglomerates whose influence crosses all social and cultural boundaries.

What have been the outcomes and effects of this rise in the media and entertainment industries? I know this question is one that commands your close attention. Indeed, given the media's pervasive role in shaping culture, it concerns all people who take seriously the well-being of civic society.

Undoubtedly much of great benefit to civilization is contributed by the various components of the mass media. One need only think of quality documentaries and news services, wholesome entertainment, and thought-provoking debates and interviews. Furthermore, in regard to the internet it must be duly recognized that it has opened up a world of knowledge and learning that previously for many could only be accessed with difficulty, if at all. Such contributions to the common good are to be applauded and encouraged.

On the other hand, it is also readily apparent that much of what is transmitted in various forms to the homes of millions of families around the world is destructive. By directing the light of Christ's truth upon such shadows the

Church engenders hope. Let us strengthen our efforts to encourage all to place the lit lamp on the lamp-stand where it shines for everyone in the home, the school, and society (cf. Mt 5:14-16)!

In this regard, my message for this year's World Communications Day draws attention to the relationship between the media and young people. My concerns are no different from those of any mother or father, or teacher, or responsible citizen. We all recognize that "beauty, a kind of mirror of the divine, inspires and vivifies young hearts and minds, while ugliness and coarseness have a depressing impact on attitudes and behavior" (no. 2). The responsibility to introduce and educate children and young people into the ways of beauty, truth and goodness is therefore a grave one. It can be supported by media conglomerates only to the extent that they promote fundamental human dignity, the true value of marriage and family life, and the positive achievements and goals of humanity.

I appeal again to the leaders of the media industry to advise producers to safeguard the common good, to uphold the truth, to protect individual human dignity and promote respect for the needs of the family. And in encouraging all of you gathered here today, I am confident that care will be taken to ensure that the fruits of your reflections and study are effectively shared with particular Churches through parish, school and diocesan structures.

To all of you, your colleagues and the members of your families at home I impart my Apostolic Blessing.

Homily at Mass for the Pope's Eightieth Birthday

April 15, 2007

I have always considered it a great gift of Divine Mercy to have been granted birth and rebirth, so to speak, on the same day, in the sign of the beginning of Easter. Thus, I was born as a member of my own family and of the great family of God on the same day.

Yes, I thank God because I have been able to experience what "family" means; I have been able to experience what "fatherhood" means, so that the words about God as Father were made understandable to me from within; on the basis of human experience, access was opened to me to the great and benevolent Father who is in Heaven. . . .

Birth and rebirth, an earthly family and the great family of God: this is the great gift of God's multiple mercies, the foundation which supports us.

Homily at Mass in Piazza Ducale, Vigevano

April 21, 2007

And lastly, what can be said of the family? It is the structural element of social life, which is why the fabric of the Ecclesial Community [after warm applause]—and I see that we agree—and civil society itself can only be renewed by working on behalf of families.

Address to Directors, Medical Staff, Patients, and Relatives During His Visit to the "San Matteo" Polyclinic, Pavia

April 22, 2007

A hospital is a place which in a certain way we might call "holy," where one experiences not only the frailty of human nature but also the enormous potential and resources of human ingenuity and technology at the service of life.

Human life! However often it is explored, this gift always remains a mystery.

I am aware that this hospital structure, your "San Matteo" Polyclinic, is well known in this City and in the rest of Italy, in particular for its pioneering surgery on several occasions. Here, you seek to alleviate suffering in the attempt to restore the person to complete health and this often happens, partly thanks to modern scientific discoveries; and here, truly comforting results are obtained.

I strongly hope that the necessary scientific and technological progress will constantly go hand in hand with the awareness that together with the good of the sick person, one is promoting those fundamental values, such as the respect for and defense of life in all its stages, on which the authentically human quality of coexistence depends.

Being here with you, it comes naturally to me to think of Jesus, who in the course of his earthly existence always showed special attention to the suffering, healing them and giving them the possibility of returning to a life of family and social relations which illness had compromised.

I am also thinking of the first Christian community, where, as we read in these days in the Acts of the Apostles, many cases of healing and miracles accompanied the Apostles' preaching.

The Church, following the example of her Lord, always expresses special preference for the suffering and, as the President said, sees Christ himself in the suffering and does not cease to offer to the sick the necessary technical assistance and human love, knowing that she is called to express Christ's love and concern for them and for those who care for them.

Technical progress, technology and human love should always go together!

Moreover, Jesus' words, "As you did it to one of the least of these my brethren, you did it to me" (Mt 25:40; 45), resonate with special timeliness in this place. In every person stricken with illness it is Jesus himself who waits for our love.

Suffering is of course repugnant to the human spirit; yet, it is true that when it is accepted with love and compassion and illumined by faith, it becomes a precious opportunity that mysteriously unites one to Christ the Redeemer, the Man of sorrows who on the Cross took upon himself human suffering and death.

With the sacrifice of his life, he redeemed human suffering and made it the fundamental means of salvation.

Dear sick people, entrust to the Lord the hardships and sorrows that you have to face and in his plan they will become a means of purification and redemption for the whole world.

Dear friends, I assure each and every one of you of my remembrance in prayer and, as I invoke Mary Most Holy, *Salus infirmorum—Health of the Sick*—so that she may protect you and your families, the directors, the doctors and the whole community of the Polyclinic, I impart to you all with affection a special Apostolic Blessing.

APOSTOLIC JOURNEY TO BRAZIL FOR THE
FIFTH GENERAL CONFERENCE OF THE BISHOPS OF
LATIN AMERICA AND THE CARIBBEAN

Regina Caeli

May 13, 2007

I warmly greet all the English-speaking groups present today. Families stand at the heart of the Church's mission of evangelization, for it is in the home that our life of faith is first expressed and nurtured. Parents, you are the primary witnesses to your children of the truths and values of our faith: pray with and for your children; teach them by your example of fidelity and joy! Indeed, every disciple, spurred on by word and strengthened by sacrament, is called to mission. It is a duty from which no one should shy away, for nothing is more beautiful than to know Christ and to make him known to others! May Our Lady of Guadalupe be your model and guide. God bless you all!

APOSTOLIC JOURNEY TO BRAZIL FOR THE FIFTH
GENERAL CONFERENCE OF THE BISHOPS OF
LATIN AMERICA AND THE CARIBBEAN

Address at the Opening of the Fifth General Conference of the Bishops of Latin America and the Caribbean

May 13, 2007

5. Other priority areas

In order to bring about this renewal of the Church that has been entrusted to your care in these lands, let me draw your attention to some areas that I consider priorities for this new phase.

The family

The family, the "patrimony of humanity," constitutes one of the most important treasures of Latin American countries. The family was and is the school of faith, the training-ground for human and civil values, the hearth in which human life is born and is generously and responsibly welcomed. Undoubtedly, it is currently suffering a degree of adversity caused by secularism and by ethical relativism, by movements of population internally and externally, by poverty, by social instability and by civil legislation opposed to marriage which, by supporting contraception and abortion, is threatening the future of peoples.

In some families in Latin America there still unfortunately persists a chauvinist mentality that ignores the "newness" of Christianity, in which the equal dignity and responsibility of women relative to men is acknowledged and affirmed.

The family is irreplaceable for the personal serenity it provides and for the upbringing of children. Mothers who wish to dedicate themselves fully to bringing up their children and to the service of their family must enjoy conditions that make this possible, and for this they have the right to count on the support of the State. In effect, the role of the mother is fundamental for the future of society.

The father, for his part, has the duty to be a true father, fulfilling his indispensable responsibility and cooperating in bringing up the children. The children, for their integral growth, have a right to be able to count on their father and mother, who take care of them and accompany them on their way toward the fullness of life. Consequently there has to be intense and vigorous pastoral care of families. Moreover, it is indispensable to promote authentic family policies corresponding to the rights of the family as an essential subject in society. The family constitutes part of the good of peoples and of the whole of humanity.

Regina Caeli

May 20, 2007

A further motive for reflection and prayer that the annual occasion of the World Communications Day offers today is the theme: "Children and the Media: A Challenge for Education." The educational challenges of today's world are often compared to the influence of the mass media, which compete with school, Church and even the family.

In this context, an adequate formation in the correct use of the media is essential: parents, teachers and the Ecclesial Community are called to collaborate to educate children and youth to be selective and to develop a critical attitude, cultivating a taste for what is aesthetically and morally valid.

But the media must also bring their contribution to this educational commitment, promoting the dignity of the human person, marriage and family, and the achievements and aims of civilization.

Programs that instill violence and anti-social behavior or vulgarize human sexuality are unacceptable, all the more so if they are proposed to minors.

I therefore renew the appeal to those responsible in the media industry and to social communications workers to safeguard the common good, respect the truth and protect the dignity of the person and the family.

Address to the Members of the
Italian Episcopal Conference for their
Fifty-Seventh General Assembly

May 24, 2007

You have given a clear witness of this attention to the common good through the *Note* approved by the Permanent Episcopal Council regarding the family founded on matrimony and the legislative initiatives in matters of *de facto* unions, moving in full consonance with the constant teaching of the Apostolic See.

In this context, the recent manifestation in favor of the family, which took place through the initiative of the Catholic laity but shared also by many non-Catholics, was a great and extraordinary festival of the people, which confirmed how the family itself is profoundly rooted in the heart and life of Italians.

This event has certainly contributed to making visible to all the family's meaning and role in society, which particularly needs to be understood and recognized today in the face of a culture that deludes itself in promoting the happiness of individuals by unilaterally insisting on the freedom of the individual person. However, each State initiative in favor of the family as such cannot fail to be valued and encouraged. . . .

Lastly, I would like to recall the meeting that will bring us together again at Loreto, at the beginning of September, for the pilgrimage and encounter under the name, *"Agorà of the Italian youth,"* and that wishes to insert youth more profoundly into the Church's journey following the Convention of Verona and to prepare them for the World Youth Day next year in Sydney.

We know well that Christian formation of the new generations is perhaps the most difficult but also the extremely important duty that the Church faces.

We will therefore go to Loreto together with our young people, so that the Virgin Mary may help them and that they be ever more in love with Jesus Christ and thus remain within the Church, recognized as a trustworthy companion, and communicate to their brethren the joyful certainty of being loved by God.

Address to the Bishops of Mozambique on Their *Ad Limina* Visit

May 26, 2007

The evangelization of Christian life and the budding of vocations depend on the formation of authentically Christian families that accept the model, demands and grace of Christian marriage. I know that there are no lack of difficulties due to the limitations of some ancient customs and also to the instability of domestic life, sorely tried by a so-called "modern" society permeated with sensualism and individualism.

The crisis will not abate unless there is a dynamic and solidly founded pastoral care of the family, with the support of family associations coordinated at the diocesan and national level.

Address to Participants in a Meeting Sponsored by the Young Entrepreneurs of the Italian Manufacturers' Association

May 26, 2007

Besides the centrality of man in the economy, your reflection in the course of these years has faced other highly topical issues, for example, that of the family in Italian business. Several times I have been able to repeat the importance of the family founded on marriage as the supporting element of a society's life and development.

To work in favor of the family means to contribute to renewing the social fabric and also to ensuring the foundations of an authentic economic development.

Letter to the Bishops, Priests, Consecrated Persons, and Lay Faithful of the Catholic Church in the People's Republic of China

May 27, 2007

The Lay Faithful and the Family

15. In the most difficult periods of the recent history of the Catholic Church in China, the lay faithful, both as individuals and families and as members of spiritual and apostolic movements, have shown total fidelity to the Gospel, even paying a personal price for their faithfulness to Christ. My dear lay people, you are called, today too, to incarnate the Gospel in your lives and to bear witness to it by means of generous and effective service for the good of the people and for the development of the country: and you will accomplish this mission by living as honest citizens and by operating as active and responsible co-workers in spreading the word of God to those around you, in the country or in the city. You who in recent times have been courageous witnesses of the faith, must remain the hope of the Church for the future! This demands from you an ever more engaged participation in all areas of Church life, in communion with your respective Pastors.

Since the future of humanity passes by way of the family, I consider it indispensable and urgent that lay people should promote family values and safeguard the needs of the family. Lay people, whose faith enables them to know God's marvelous design for the family, have an added reason to assume this concrete and demanding task: the family in fact "is the normal place where the young grow to personal and social maturity. It is also the bearer of the heritage of humanity itself, because through the family, life is passed on from generation to generation. The family occupies a very important place in Asian cultures; and, as the Synod Fathers noted, family values like filial respect, love and care for the aged and the sick, love of children and harmony are held in high esteem in all Asian cultures and religious traditions." (John Paul II, Post-Synodal Apostolic Exhortation *Ecclesia in Asia*, no. 46; Cf. Benedict XVI, Address at Fifth World Meeting of Families in Spain [Valencia, July 8, 2006]: "The family is a necessary good for peoples, an indispensable foundation for society and a great and lifelong treasure for couples. It is a unique good for children, who are meant to be the fruit of the love, of the total and generous self-giving of their parents. To proclaim the whole truth about the family based on marriage as *a domestic Church and a sanctuary of life*, is a great responsibility incumbent upon all . . . Christ has shown us what is always the supreme source of our life and thus of the lives of families: 'This is my commandment, that you love one another as I have loved you. No one has greater love than this, to lay down one's life for one's friends' (Jn 15:12-13). The love of God himself has been poured out upon us in Baptism. Consequently, families are called to experience this same kind of love, for the Lord makes it possible for us, through our human love, to be sensitive, loving and merciful like Christ.")

The above-mentioned values form part of the relevant Chinese cultural context, but also in your land there is no lack of forces that influence the family negatively in various ways. Therefore the Church which is in China, aware that the good of society and her own good are profoundly linked to the good of the family (cf. *Gaudium et Spes*, no. 47), must have a keener and more urgent sense of her mission to proclaim to all people God's plan for marriage and the family, ensuring the full vitality of each (cf. *Familiaris Consortio*, no. 3).

Christian initiation of adults

16. The recent history of the Catholic Church in China has seen a large number of adults coming to the faith, thanks partly to the witness of the local Christian community. You, Pastors, are called to devote particular care to their Christian initiation via an appropriate and serious period of catechumenate aimed at helping them and preparing them to lead the life of Jesus' disciples.

In this regard, I would mention that evangelization is never purely intellectual communication, but rather includes experience of life, purification and transformation of the whole of existence, and a journey in communion. Only in this way is a proper relationship established between thought and life.

Looking then to the past, it is unfortunately the case that many adults have not always been sufficiently initiated into the complete truth of Christian life and have not even known the richness of the renewal brought by the Second Vatican Council. It therefore seems necessary and urgent to offer them a solid and thorough Christian formation, in the shape of a post-baptismal catechumenate. (As the Synod Fathers of the Seventh Ordinary Assembly of the Synod of Bishops observed [October 1-30, 1987], in the formation of Christians "a post-baptismal catechesis in the form of a catechumenate can also be helpful by presenting again some elements from the Rite of Christian Initiation of Adults with the purpose of allowing a person to grasp and live the immense, extraordinary richness and responsibility received at Baptism": *Christifideles Laici*, no. 61; cf. *Catechism of the Catholic Church*, 1230-1231).

Address to Superiors and Employees of the Governorate of Vatican City State and the Patrons of the Vatican Museums

May 31, 2007

A little while ago, in the Governorate Chapel, I blessed a beautiful image of the Blessed Mother, whom you venerate as "Mother of the Family." I also blessed the new organ expressly desired to accompany the song of the liturgical assembly that unites you for the daily Holy Mass.

The Church's presence amid your offices and workplaces reminds you each day that the paternal glance of God, in his providence, follows you and takes care of each one of you.

May prayer, which is confident dialogue with the Lord, and also midweek participation in the celebration of the Divine Sacrifice that unites us to Christ the Savior, be the secret and strength of your days and sustain you always, especially in difficult moments.

I have also been informed that the projects of the Governorate include a fountain dedicated to St. Joseph, subsidized by generous donors. The Spouse of the Virgin Mary, head of the Holy Family and Patron of the Church, can quite rightly be considered the example and model for those committed in the numerous services of the Governorate, who for the most part carry out services that are humble and silent, but which are an indispensable support for the activity of the Holy See.

I hope, therefore, that the project will be successfully completed. And I ask St. Joseph to protect you and your families always.

Besides the protection of St. Joseph I invoke upon you the maternal assistance of the Virgin Mary, Mother of the Church, who watches us from above this building. I entrust all of you to her: may her maternal smile accompany you and may her intercession obtain for you God's choicest Blessings.

While I wholeheartedly bless you, once again I thank you for your work.

Address to the Members of the Bishops' Conference of the Central African Republic on Their *Ad Limina* Visit

June 1, 2007

Furthermore, a change in mindset must be brought about to allow society to have access to genuine human and spiritual development. This long-term task concerns in the first place the family and marriage. By resolutely engaging to live in conjugal fidelity and in the unity of the couple, Christians show everyone the greatness and truth of marriage.

It is by a freely consenting "yes," forever, that a man and a woman express their genuine humanity and openness to giving new life. Thus, the serious preparation for marriage of young people must help them overcome their reluctance to found a permanent family open to the future. I also ask you to develop support for families, especially by encouraging their Christian education. They will then be able to account more vigorously for the faith that enlivens them, both to their children and to society.

Address to the New Ambassador of the Republic of Estonia to the Holy See

June 1, 2007

In a special way, the Church is committed to the promotion of the sanctity of marriage, the basic role and mission of the family, the education of children and respect for God's gift of life from conception to natural death. Since the health of any society depends in no small measure on the health of its families (cf. *Sacramentum Caritatis*, no. 29), I trust that this witness will contribute to the consolidation of family and community life and, together with wise and far-sighted social policies, will help to revitalize Estonia's long history of strong and united families. For it is in the family, above all, that the young are trained in goodness, generosity, forgiveness and fraternal concern for others, and given a sense of personal responsibility for building a world of freedom, solidarity and hope.

Address to Participants in the Convention of the Diocese of Rome

June 11, 2007

Dear Brothers and Sisters,

For the third consecutive year our diocesan Convention gives me the possibility of meeting and speaking to you all, addressing the theme on which the Church of Rome will be focusing in the coming pastoral year, in close continuity with the work carried out in the year now drawing to a close.

I greet with affection each one of you, Bishops, priests, deacons, men and women religious, lay people who generously take part in the Church's mission. I thank the Cardinal Vicar in particular for the words he has addressed to me on behalf of you all.

The theme of the Convention is *"Jesus is Lord: educating in the faith, in the 'sequela' in witnessing"*: a theme that concerns us all because every disciple professes that Jesus is Lord and is called to grow in adherence to him, giving and receiving help from the great company of brothers and sisters in the faith.

Nevertheless, the verb "to educate," as part of the title of the Convention, suggests special attention to children, boys and girls and young people, and highlights the duty proper first of all to the family: thus, we are continuing the program that has been a feature of the pastoral work of our Diocese in recent years.

It is important to start by reflecting on the first affirmation, which gives our Convention its tone and meaning: "Jesus is Lord." We find it in the solemn declaration that concludes Peter's discourse at Pentecost, in which the head of the Apostles said: "Let all the house of Israel therefore know assuredly that God has made him both Lord and Christ, this Jesus whom you crucified" (Acts 2:36). The conclusion of the great hymn to Christ contained in Paul's Letter to the Philippians is similar: "every tongue [should] confess that Jesus Christ is Lord, to the glory of God the Father" (2:11).

Again, in the final salutation of his First Letter to the Corinthians, St. Paul exclaimed: "If anyone has no love for the Lord, let him be accursed. *Maranà tha*: Our Lord, come!" (1 Cor 16:22), thereby handing on to us the very ancient Aramaic invocation of Jesus as Lord.

Various other citations could be added: I am thinking of the twelfth chapter of the same Letter to the Corinthians in which St. Paul says: "No one can say 'Jesus is Lord' except by the Holy Spirit" (1 Cor 12:3).

Thus, the Apostle declares that this is the fundamental confession of the Church, guided by the Holy Spirit. We might think also of the tenth chapter of the Letter to the Romans where the Apostle says, "if you confess with your lips that Jesus is Lord" (Rom 10:9), thus reminding the Christians of Rome that these words, "Jesus is Lord," form the common confession of the Church, the sure foundation of the Church's entire life.

The whole confession of the Apostolic Creed, of the Nicene Creed, developed from these words. St. Paul also says in another passage of his First Letter to the Corinthians: "Although there may be so-called gods in heaven or on earth . . . "—and we know that today too there are many so-called "gods" on earth—for us there is only "one God, the Father, from whom are all things and for whom we exist, and one Lord, Jesus Christ, through whom are all things and through whom we exist" (1 Cor 8:5-6).

Thus, from the outset the disciples recognized the Risen Jesus as the One who is our brother in humanity but is also one with God; the One who, with his coming into the world and throughout his life, in his death and in his Resurrection, brought us God and in a new and unique way made God present in the world: the One, therefore, who gives meaning and hope to our life; in fact, it is in him that we encounter the true Face of God that we find what we really need in order to live.

Educating in the faith, in the *sequela*, and in witnessing means helping our brothers and sisters, or rather, helping one another to enter into a living relationship with Christ and with the Father. This has been from the start the fundamental task of the Church as the community of believers, disciples and friends of Jesus. The Church, the Body of Christ and Temple of the Holy Spirit, is that dependable company within which we have been brought forth and educated to become, in Christ, sons and heirs of God.

In the Church, we receive the Spirit through whom "we cry, 'Abba! Father!'" (cf. Rom 8:14-17). We have just heard in St. Augustine's homily that God is not remote, that he has become the "Way" and the "Way" himself has come to us. He said: "Stand up, you idler, and start walking!" Starting to walk means moving along the path that is Christ himself, in the company of believers; it means while walking, helping one another to become truly friends of Jesus Christ and children of God.

Daily experience tells us—as we all know—that precisely in our day educating in the faith is no easy undertaking. Today, in fact, every educational task seems more and more arduous and precarious. Consequently, there is talk of a great "educational emergency," of the increasing difficulty encountered in transmitting the basic values of life and correct behavior to the new generations, a difficulty that involves both schools and families and, one might say, any other body with educational aims.

We may add that this is an inevitable emergency: in a society, in a culture, which all too often make relativism its creed—relativism has become a sort of dogma—in such a society the light of truth is missing; indeed, it is considered dangerous and "authoritarian" to speak of truth, and the end result is doubt about the goodness of life—is it good to be a person? is it good to be alive?—and in the validity of the relationships and commitments in which it consists.

So how would it be possible to suggest to children and to pass on from generation to generation something sound and dependable, rules of life, an authentic meaning and convincing objectives for human existence both as an individual and as a community?

For this reason, education tends to be broadly reduced to the transmission of specific abilities or capacities for doing, while people endeavor to satisfy the desire for happiness of the new generations by showering them with consumer goods and transitory gratification. Thus, both parents and teachers are easily tempted to abdicate their educational duties and even no longer to understand what their role, or rather, the mission entrusted to them, is.

Yet, in this way we are not offering to young people, to the young generations, what it is our duty to pass on to them. Moreover, we owe them the true values which give life a foundation.

However, this situation obviously fails to satisfy; it cannot satisfy because it ignores the essential aim of education which is the formation of a person to enable him or her to live to the full and to make his or her own contribution to the common good. However, on many sides the demand for authentic education and the rediscovery of the need for educators who are truly such is increasing.

Parents, concerned and often worried about their children's future, are asking for it, many teachers who are going through the sad experience of the deterioration of their schools are asking for it, society overall is asking for it, in Italy as in many other nations, because it sees the educational crisis cast doubt on the very foundations of coexistence.

In a similar context, the Church's commitment to providing education in the faith, in discipleship and in witnessing to the Lord Jesus is more than ever acquiring the value of a contribution to extracting the society in which we live from the educational crisis that afflicts it, clamping down on distrust and on that strange "self-hatred" that seems to have become a hallmark of our civilization.

However, none of this diminishes the difficulties we encounter in leading children, adolescents and young people to meet Jesus Christ and to establish a lasting and profound relationship with him. Yet precisely this is the crucial challenge for the future of the faith, of the Church and of Christianity, and it is therefore an essential priority of our pastoral work: to bring close to Christ and to the Father the new generation that lives in a world largely distant from God.

Dear brothers and sisters, we must always be aware that we cannot carry out such a task with our own strength but only with the power of the Spirit. We need enlightenment and grace that come from God and act within hearts and consciences. For education and Christian formation, therefore, it is above all prayer and our personal friendship with Jesus that are crucial: only those who know and love Jesus Christ can introduce their brothers and sisters into a living relationship with him. Indeed, moved by this need, I thought: it would be helpful to write a book on Jesus to make him known.

Let us never forget the words of Jesus: "I have called you friends, for all that I have heard from my Father I have made known to you. You did not choose me, but I chose you and appointed you that you should go and bear fruit and that your fruit should abide" (Jn 15:15-16).

Our communities will thus be able to work fruitfully and to teach the faith and discipleship of Christ while being in themselves authentic "schools" of prayer (cf. Apostolic Letter *Novo Millennio Ineunte*, no. 33), where the primacy of God is lived.

Furthermore, it is education and especially Christian education which shapes life based on God who is love (cf. 1 Jn 4:8, 16), and has need of that closeness which is proper to love. Especially today, when isolation and loneliness are a widespread condition to which noise and group conformity is no real remedy, personal guidance becomes essential, giving those who are growing up the assurance that they are loved, understood and listened to.

In practice, this guidance must make tangible the fact that our faith is not something of the past, that it can be lived today and that in living it we really find our good. Thus, boys and girls and young people may be helped to free themselves from common prejudices and will realize that the Christian way of life is possible and reasonable, indeed, is by far the most reasonable.

The entire Christian community, with all its many branches and components, is challenged by the important task of leading the new generations to the encounter with Christ: on this terrain, therefore, we must express and manifest particularly clearly our communion with the Lord and with one another, as well as our willingness and readiness to work together to "build a network," to achieve with an open and sincere mind every useful form of synergy, starting with the precious contribution of those women and men who have consecrated their lives to adoring God and interceding for their brethren.

However, it is very obvious that in educating and forming people in the faith the family has its own fundamental role and primary responsibility. Parents, in fact, are those through whom the child at the start of life has the first and crucial experience of love, of a love which is actually not only human but also a reflection of God's love for him.

Therefore, the Christian family, the small "domestic Church," and the larger family of the Church must take care to develop the closest collaboration, especially with regard to the education of children (cf. *Lumen Gentium*, no. 11).

Everything that has matured in the three years in which our diocesan pastoral ministry has devoted special attention to the family should not only be implemented but also further increased.

For example, the attempts to involve parents and even godparents more closely, before and after Baptism, in order to help them understand and put into practice their mission as educators in the faith have already produced appreciable results and deserve to be continued and to become the common heritage of each parish. The same applies for the participation of families in catechesis and in the entire process of the Christian initiation of children and adolescents.

Of course, many families are unprepared for this task and there is no lack of families which—if they are not actually opposed to it—do not seem to be interested in the Christian education of their own children: the consequences of the crisis in so many marriages are making themselves felt here.

Yet, it is rare to meet parents who are wholly indifferent to the human and moral formation of their children and consequently unwilling to be assisted in an educational task which they perceive as ever more difficult.

Therefore, an area of commitment and service opens up for our parishes, oratories, youth communities and above all for Christian families themselves, called to be near other families to encourage and assist them in raising their children, thereby helping them to find the meaning and purpose of life as a married couple.

Let us now move on to other subjects concerning education in the faith.

As children gradually grow up, their inner desire for personal autonomy naturally increases. Especially in adolescence, this can easily lead to them taking a critical distance from their family. Here, the closeness which can be guaranteed by the priest, Religious, catechist or other educators capable of making the friendly Face of the Church and love of Christ concrete for the young person, becomes particularly important.

If it is to produce positive effects that endure in time, our closeness must take into account that the education offered is a free encounter and that Christian education itself is formation in true freedom. Indeed, there is no real educational proposal, however respectful and loving it may be, which is not an incentive to making a decision, and the proposal of Christianity itself calls freedom profoundly into question, calling it to faith and conversion.

As I said at the Ecclesial Convention in Verona: "A true education must awaken the courage to make definitive decisions, which today are considered a mortifying bind to our freedom. In reality, they are indispensable for growth and in order to achieve something great in life, in particular, to cause love to mature in all its beauty: therefore, to give consistency and meaning to freedom itself" (Address, October 19, 2006: ORE, October 25, 2006, 9).

When they feel that their freedom is respected and taken seriously, adolescents and young people, despite their changeability and frailty, are not in fact unwilling to let themselves be challenged by demanding proposals: indeed, they often feel attracted and fascinated by them.

They also wish to show their generosity in adhering to the great, perennial values that constitute life's foundations. The authentic educator likewise takes seriously the intellectual curiosity which already exists in children and, as the years pass, is more consciously cultivated. Constantly exposed to, and often confused by, the multiplicity of information, and by the contrasting ideas and interpretations presented to them, young people today nevertheless still have a great inner need for truth. They are consequently open to Jesus Christ who, as Tertullian reminds us, "called himself truth, not custom" (*De Virginibus Velandis*, I, 1).

It is up to us to seek to respond to the question of truth, fearlessly juxtaposing the proposal of faith with the reason of our time. In this way we will help young people to broaden the horizons of their intelligence, to open themselves to the mystery of God, in whom is found life's meaning and direction, and to overcome the conditioning of a rationality which trusts only what can be the object of experiment and calculation. Thus, it is very important to develop what last year we called "the pastoral care of intelligence."

The task of education passes through freedom but also requires authority. Therefore, especially when it is a matter of educating in faith, the figure of the witness and the role of witnessing is central. A witness of Christ does not merely transmit information but is personally involved with the truth Christ proposes and, through the coherency of his own life, becomes a dependable reference point.

However, he does not refer to himself, but to Someone who is infinitely greater than he is, in whom he has trusted and whose trustworthy goodness he has experienced. The authentic Christian educator is therefore a witness who finds his model in Jesus Christ, the witness of the Father who said nothing about himself but spoke as the Father had taught him (cf. Jn 8:28). This relationship with Christ and with the Father is for each one of us, dear brothers and sisters, the fundamental condition for being effective educators in the faith.

Our Convention very rightly speaks of education not only in faith and discipleship but also in witnessing to the Lord Jesus. Bearing an active witness to Christ does not, therefore, concern only priests, women religious and lay people who as formation teachers have tasks in our communities, but children and young people themselves, and all who are educated in the faith.

Therefore, the awareness of being called to become witnesses of Christ is not a corollary, a consequence somehow external to Christian formation, such as, unfortunately, has often been thought and today too people continue to think. On the contrary, it is an intrinsic and essential dimension of education in the faith and discipleship, just as the Church is missionary by her very nature (cf. *Ad Gentes*, no. 2).

If children, through a gradual process from the beginning of their formation, are to achieve permanent formation as Christian adults, the desire to be and the conviction of being sharers in the Church's missionary vocation in all the situations and circumstances of life must take root in the believers' soul. Indeed, we cannot keep to ourselves the joy of the faith. We must spread it and pass it on, and thereby also strengthen it in our own hearts.

If faith is truly the joy of having discovered truth and love, we inevitably feel the desire to transmit it, to communicate it to others. The new evangelization to which our beloved Pope John Paul II called us passes mainly through this process.

A concrete experience that will increase in the youth of the parishes and of the various ecclesial groups the desire to witness to their own faith is the "Young People's Mission" which you are planning, after the success of the great "City Mission."

By educating in the faith, a very important task is entrusted to Catholic schools. Indeed, they must carry out their mission on the basis of an educational project which places the Gospel at the center and keeps it as a decisive reference point for the person's formation and for the entire cultural program.

In convinced synergy with families and with the Ecclesial Community, Catholic schools should therefore seek to foster that unity between faith, culture and life which is the fundamental goal of Christian education. State schools too can be sustained in their educational task in various ways by the presence of teachers who are believers—in the first place, but not exclusively, teachers of Catholic religion—and of students with a Christian formation, as well as by the collaboration of many families and of the Christian community itself.

The healthy secularism of schools, like that of the other State institutions, does not in fact imply closure to Transcendence or a false neutrality with regard to those moral values which form the basis of an authentic formation of the person. A similar discourse naturally applies for universities and it is truly a good omen that university ministry in Rome has been able to develop in all the Athenaeums, among teachers as much as students, and that a fruitful collaboration has developed between the civil and Pontifical academic institutions.

Today, more than in the past, the education and formation of the person are influenced by the messages and general climate spread by the great means of communication and which are inspired by a mindset and culture marked by relativism, consumerism and a false and destructive exaltation, or rather, profanation, of the body and of sexuality.

Therefore, precisely because of the great "yes" that as believers in Christ we say to the man loved by God, we certainly cannot fail to take interest in the overall orientation of the society to which we belong, in the trends that motivate it and in the positive or negative influence that it exercises on the formation of the new generations.

The very presence of the community of believers, its educational and cultural commitment, the message of faith, trust and love it bears are in fact an invaluable service to the common good and especially to the children and youth who are being trained and prepared for life.

Dear brothers and sisters, there is one last point to which I would like to draw your attention: it is supremely important for the Church's mission and requires our commitment and first of all our prayer. I am referring to vocations to follow the Lord Jesus more closely in the ministerial priesthood and in the consecrated life.

In recent decades, the Diocese of Rome has been gladdened by the gift of many priestly ordinations which have made it possible to bridge the gap in the previous period, and also to meet the requests of many Sister Churches in need of clergy; but the most recent indications seem less favorable and prompt the whole of our diocesan community to renew to the Lord, with humility and trust, its request for laborers for his harvest (cf. Mt 9:37-38; Lk 10:2).

With delicacy and respect we must address a special but clear and courageous invitation to follow Jesus to those young men and women who appear to be the most attracted and fascinated by friendship with him. In this perspective, the Diocese will designate several new priests specifically to the care of vocations, but we know well that prayer and the overall quality of our Christian witness, the example of life set by priests and consecrated souls, the generosity of the people called and of the families they come from, are crucial in this area.

Dear brothers and sisters, I entrust to you these reflections as a contribution to the dialogue of these evenings, and to the work of the next pastoral year. May the Lord always give us the joy of believing in him, of growing in his friendship, of following him in the journey of life and of bearing witness to him in every situation, so that we may be able to pass on to those who will come after us the immense riches and beauty of faith in Jesus Christ. May my affection and my blessing accompany you in your work. Thank you for your attention!

Address to the Bishops of Slovakia on Their *Ad Limina* Visit

June 15, 2007

With regard to the reality of families, I have learned that Slovakia too is beginning to be affected by the crisis of marriage and the birth rate. This is first and foremost due to financial considerations which induce young engaged couples to postpone their marriage.

In addition, the dwindling social esteem of the value of marriage is being recorded, combined with a weakness in the new generations who are often afraid to make permanent decisions and lifelong commitments.

Another destabilizing factor is undoubtedly the systematic attack on marriage and the family conducted by certain areas of culture and by the mass media. In this framework, what should the Church do other than intensify prayer and continue to be strongly committed to supporting families as they face the challenges of the present time?

Thanks be to God, the pastoral care in your Country of the sacraments connected with the family, is well structured: Marriage, the Baptism of children, First Communion and Confirmation have obligatory preparation periods, and it is a constant commitment for you as Pastors and for the priests who assist you to help families start out on an authentic journey of faith and of Christian life as a community.

The groups, movements and lay ecclesial associations involved on the front line in the promotion of conjugal and family life and in the dissemination of the Church's teaching on matrimony, the family, sexual morals and bioethical themes, can be an effective source of help in your pastoral action.

At the crossroads between the pastoral care of the family and that of young people is the *pastoral care of vocations*.

Slovakia is a Nation which subsequent to 1990 experienced a vigorous flourishing of vocations to the priesthood and the consecrated life.

In addition to the only seminary that stayed open under the dictatorship, five others have come into being in these years, and today almost all parishes are provided with their own pastor.

We thank the Lord for this wealth of priests, and especially of young priests. However, as was foreseeable, this springtime could not last long, so today every Christian community is encouraged to give priority to a careful pastoral vocations promotion.

The formation of altar servers is a good step in this direction. Many parishes are taking it, in collaboration with the seminaries.

Of course, the increase in the number and quality of vocations also depends on the spiritual life of families: working for and with families is therefore a particularly appropriate way to encourage the birth and consolidation of vocations to the priesthood and consecrated life.

Nor should it be forgotten that this must all be nourished by constant and intense prayer.

Visit of His Beatitude Chrysostomos II, Archbishop of Nea Justiniana and All Cyprus, to His Holiness Benedict XVI

June 16, 2007

Common Declaration

> "Blessed be God and Father of Our Lord Jesus Christ, who has blessed us in Christ with every spiritual blessing in the heavenly places" (Eph 1:3).

1. We, Benedict XVI, Pope and Bishop of Rome, and Chrysostomos II, Archbishop of Nea Justiniana and All Cyprus, full of hope for the future of our Churches' relations, thank God with joy for this fraternal meeting in our common faith in the Risen Christ. This visit has enabled us to observe how these relations have increased, both at a local level and in the context of the theological dialogue between the Catholic Church and the Orthodox Church as a whole. The Delegation of the Church of Cyprus has always made a positive contribution to this dialogue; among other things, for instance, in 1983 it hosted the Coordination Committee of the International Joint Commission for Theological Dialogue, so that in addition to doing the demanding preparatory

work, the Catholic and Orthodox Members were able to visit and admire the great spiritual riches and wealth of art works of the Church of Cyprus.

2. On the happy occasion of our fraternal encounter at the tombs of Sts. Peter and Paul, the *"coryphaei* of the Apostles," as liturgical tradition says, we would like to declare of common accord our sincere and firm willingness, in obedience to the desire of Our Lord Jesus Christ, to intensify our search for full unity among all Christians, making every possible effort deemed useful to the life of our Communities. We desire that the Catholic and Orthodox faithful of Cyprus live a fraternal life in full solidarity, based on our common faith in the Risen Christ. We also wish to sustain and encourage the theological dialogue which is preparing through the competent International Commission to address the most demanding issues that marked the historical event of the division.

For full communion in the faith, the sacramental life and the exercise of the pastoral ministry, it is necessary to reach substantial agreement. To this end, we assure our faithful of our fervent prayers as Pastors in the Church and ask them to join us in a unanimous invocation *"that they may all be one . . . so that the world may believe"* (Jn 17:21).

3. At our meeting, we reviewed the historical situations in which our Churches are living. In particular, we examined the situation of division and tensions that have marked the Island of Cyprus for more than thirty years, with its tragic daily problems which impair the daily life of our communities and of individual families. More generally, we considered the situation in the Middle East, where the war and conflicts between peoples risk spreading with disastrous consequences. We prayed for the peace that "comes from the heavenly places." It is the intention of our Churches to play a role of peacemaking in justice and solidarity and, to achieve all this, it is our constant wish to foster fraternal relations among all Christians and loyal dialogue between the different religions present and active in the Region. May faith in the one God help the people of these ancient and celebrated regions to rediscover friendly coexistence, in reciprocal respect and constructive collaboration.

4. We therefore address this appeal to all those who, everywhere in the world, raise their hand against their own brethren, exhorting them firmly to lay down their weapons and to take steps to heal the injuries caused by war. We also ask them to spare no effort to ensure that human rights are always defended in every nation: respect for the human person, an image of God, is in fact a fundamental duty for all. Thus, among the human rights to be safeguarded, freedom of religion should be at the top of the list. Failure to respect this right constitutes a very serious offence to the dignity of the human being,

who is struck deep within his heart where God dwells. Consequently, to profane, destroy or sack the places of worship of any religion is an act against humanity and the civilization of the peoples.

5. We did not omit to reflect on a new opportunity that is opening for more intense contact and more concrete collaboration between our Churches. In fact, the building of the European Union is progressing, and Catholics and Orthodox are called to contribute to creating a climate of friendship and cooperation. At a time when secularization and relativism are growing, Catholics and Orthodox in Europe are called to offer a renewed common witness to the ethical values, ever ready to account for their faith in Jesus Christ, Lord and Savior. The European Union, which will not be able to restrict itself to merely economic cooperation, needs sound cultural foundations, shared ethical references and openness to the religious dimension. It is essential to revive the Christian roots of Europe which made its civilization great down the centuries and to recognize that in this regard the Western and Eastern Christian traditions have a common task to achieve.

6. At our encounter, therefore, we considered our Churches' long journey through history and the great tradition which has come down to our day, starting with the proclamation of the first disciples, who came to Cyprus from Jerusalem after the persecution of Stephen, and reviewing Paul's voyage from the coasts of Cyprus to Rome as it is recounted in the Acts of the Apostles (Acts 11:19; 27:4ff.). The rich patrimony of faith and the solid Christian tradition of our lands should spur Catholics and Orthodox to a renewed impetus in proclaiming the Gospel in our age, in being faithful to our Christian vocation and in responding to the demands of the contemporary world.

7. The treatment of bioethical issues gives rise to serious concern. Indeed, there is a risk that certain techniques, applied to genetics, intentionally conceived to meet legitimate needs, actually go so far as to undermine the dignity of the human being created in the image of God. The exploitation of human beings, abusive experimentation and genetic experiments which fail to respect ethical values are an offence against life and attack the safety and dignity of every human person, in whose existence they can never be either justified or permitted.

8. At the same time, these ethical considerations and a shared concern for human life prompt us to invite those nations which, with God's grace, have made significant progress in the areas of the economy and technology, not to forget their brothers and sisters who live in countries afflicted by poverty, hunger and disease. We therefore ask the leaders of nations to encourage and promote an equitable distribution of the goods of the earth in a spirit of solidarity with the poor and with all those who are destitute in the world.

9. We also concurred in our anxiety about the risk of destroying the creation. Man received it so that he might implement God's plan. However, by setting himself up at the center of the universe, forgetting the Creator's mandate and shutting himself in a selfish search for his own well-being, the human being has managed the environment in which he lives by putting into practice decisions that threaten his own existence, whereas the environment requires the respect and protection of all who dwell in it.

10. Let us address together this prayer to the Lord of history, so that he will strengthen our Churches' witness in order that the Gospel proclamation of salvation may reach the new generations and be a light for all men and women. To this end, we entrust our desires and commitments to the *Theotokos*, the Mother of God *Hodegetria*, who points out the way to Our Lord Jesus Christ.

Address to the Bishops of Togo on Their *Ad Limina* Visit

June 22, 2007

Dear Brothers in the Episcopate, you have the opportunity to carry out your pastoral ministry by participating in your own capacity in the life of the people entrusted to your care.

In fact, "as a body organized within the community and the nation, the Church has both the right and the duty to participate fully in building a just and peaceful society with all the means at her disposal" (*Ecclesia in Africa*, no. 107).

I praise in particular your commitment to the protection of and respect for life which you have had the opportunity to express on numerous occasions, and quite recently demonstrating it once again in detail by your opposition to abortion.

Moreover, the promotion of the truth and dignity of marriage as well as the preservation of essential family values must feature among your principal priorities.

Pastoral care of the family is an essential element for evangelization and enables young people to discover what a commitment that is unique and faithful entails. I therefore urge you to pay special attention to the formation of couples and families.

Through her work of social assistance and her action in the health-care sector in which numerous competent men and women religious and lay people are involved, the Church also expresses God's loving presence to people suffering or in distress and contributes to the progress of justice and respect for human dignity.

In this same perspective, I encourage you to continue your efforts to promote Catholic schools, which provide an integral education at the service of families and of the transmission of faith. Their role, despite the great difficulties they can encounter, is essential to enabling young people to acquire a sound human, cultural and religious formation.

May educators and teachers themselves be models of Christian life for the young!

Address to Members of the Bishops' Conference of Puerto Rico on Their *Ad Limina* Visit

June 30, 2007

The family is also a permanent challenge for you. It is threatened on all sides by the snares of the modern world such as the prevalent materialism, the search for instant pleasure and the lack of steadfast fidelity by couples who are constantly influenced by the media.

When marriage is not built on the rock of true love and mutual self-giving, it is easily swept away by the current of divorce and also looks askance at the value of life, especially that of unborn children.

This panorama reveals the need to intensify, as you are already doing, an effective family apostolate which helps Christian spouses to assume the fundamental values of the Sacrament they have received.

In this regard, faithful to Christ's teaching, through your magisterium you proclaim the truth about the family as a domestic Church and sanctuary of life in the face of certain trends in contemporary society that seek to eclipse or to confuse the one, irreplaceable value of marriage between a man and a woman.

Address to Bishops from the Dominican Republic on Their *Ad Limina* Visit

July 5, 2007

Dear Brothers in the Episcopate,

At this collective meeting during your visit *ad limina Apostolorum*, I rejoice to share the same faith in Jesus Christ which accompanies our journey and is alive and present in the communities entrusted to your pastoral care. I address my affectionate greeting to you as well as to the diocesan Churches over which you preside with such great dedication and generosity.

I am grateful to Archbishop Ramón Benito de la Rosa y Carpio of Santiago de los Caballeros, President of the Dominican Bishops' Conference, for his kind words on behalf of all. At the same time, I feel I closely share in your anxieties and aspirations. I ask God to grant that this visit to Rome may be a source of blessings for all the priests, religious communities and pastoral workers who collaborate with you amid the beloved Dominican People, aware of the challenges of the globalized world which are to be reckoned with today.

In your quinquennial reports, I noted that your Church is a community that is alive, dynamic, participatory and missionary; it feels challenged by Jesus' mandate to proclaim the Gospel to the whole creation (cf. Mk 16:15) and strives to ensure that this proclamation reaches everyone.

To achieve this goal, the message must be clear and precise so that the words of life proclaimed may be converted into personal attachment to Jesus, our Savior.

Thus, "it is urgent to rediscover and to set forth once more the authentic reality of the Christian faith, which is not simply a set of propositions to be accepted with an intellectual assent. Rather, faith is a lived knowledge of Christ, a living remembrance of his commandments and a truth to be lived out" (*Veritatis Splendor*, no. 88).

The priority of your pastoral ministry must be to ensure that the truth about Christ and the truth about man penetrate more deeply the different strata of Dominican society, since "[t]here is no true evangelization if the name, the teaching, the life, the promises, the kingdom and the mystery of Jesus of Nazareth, the Son of God, are not proclaimed" (*Evangelii Nuntiandi*, no. 22).

This work, which is not exempt from difficulties, develops among a people whose spirit is open and sensitive to the Good News.

There is no doubt that the symptoms of a process of secularization are also making themselves felt in your Country in which for many people God does not represent the origin and destination of life nor its ultimate meaning. Yet, basically, as you well know, this people has a profoundly Christian soul, demonstrated by the lively and active Ecclesial Communities in which so many people, families and groups are doing their best to live and witness to their faith.

The family is also a priority objective of the new evangelization. It is the true "domestic Church," especially when it is the fruit of lively Christian communities which produce young people who have a true vocation to the Sacrament of Marriage.

Families are not alone in having to face great challenges; the Ecclesial Community supports them, enlivens their faith and ensures their perseverance in a Christian project of life that is all too often subject to so many ups and downs and dangers.

The Church desires that the family truly be the place where the person is born, matures and is educated for life, and where parents, by loving their children tenderly, prepare them for healthy interpersonal relationships which embody moral and human values in the midst of a society so heavily marked by hedonism and religious indifference.

At the same time, in collaboration with the public institutions, Ecclesial Communities will be on the alert to safeguard the stability of families and to encourage their spiritual and material progress. This will lead to an improvement in the upbringing of children.

For this reason, it is to be hoped that the Authorities of your beloved Country collaborate increasingly in this indispensable task of working for families.

In this regard, my Predecessor stressed in his *Message for the World Day of Peace* in 1994: "The family has a right to the full support of the State in order to carry out fully its particular mission" (no. 5).

I am not unaware of the problems which the family institution encounters in your Nation, especially with the drama of divorce and the pressures to legalize abortion, in addition to the spread of unions that do not comply with the Creator's plan for marriage.

I know that you take special care of priestly vocations in order to meet all the needs of your Dioceses. Indeed, the promotion of priestly and religious vocations must be a priority for the Bishops and a commitment of all the faithful.

I therefore fervently implore the Lord of the harvest that he will continue to give to your seminaries—which must be seen as the very heart of the Diocese (cf. *Optatam Totius*, no. 5)—numerous candidates to the priesthood who will one day serve their brethren as "servants of Christ and stewards of the mysteries of God" (1 Cor 4:1).

In addition to an integral formation, a profound discernment is necessary on the human and Christian suitability of seminarians in order to ensure as well as possible that their future ministry will be exercised with dignity.

Taking into account that "the presbyterate thus appears as a true family" (*Pastores Dabo Vobis*, no. 74), it is desirable that the bonds of charity between the Bishop and his priests be very strong and cordial. If young men see that priests live a true spirituality of communion around their Bishop, witnessing to union and charity among themselves, to Gospel charity and missionary availability, they themselves will feel more attracted to the priestly vocation.

It is of paramount importance that Bishops pay special attention to their principal collaborators, the priests (cf. *Presbyterorum Ordinis*, no. 8), that they be impartial in their dealings with them, closely acquainted with their personal and pastoral needs, fatherly to them in their difficulties and that they give constant encouragement to their priests' work and endeavors and, in the context of the new evangelization, that they reach out to those who have distanced themselves.

The theme this year of the Third Pastoral Plan: "Disciple of the Lord, welcome those who are close and seek out those who are distant," has a vast application in the complex context of migration which involves so many families.

Devote much effort to reach groups of your compatriots who are abroad, but I also warmly ask you to accompany with great love the Haitian immigrants who have left their Country in search of better living conditions for themselves and their families, as you are already doing.

I am pleased to observe that you have already been in contact with your brother Bishops of Haiti in the endeavor to alleviate the situation of poverty and wretchedness which is an offence to the dignity of so many people in this Sister Nation.

In your episcopal ministry many pastoral challenges are closely related to the evangelization of culture which must promote human and evangelical values in their full integrity.

The field of culture is one of "the modern equivalents of the Areopagus," in which the Gospel must be made present with its full impact (cf. *Redemptoris Missio*, no. 37). It is impossible to do this task without the social communications media: radio, television broadcasts, videos and computer networks can be most useful for spreading the Gospel far and wide.

This task particularly involves lay people, since it is part of their distinctive task to "take on themselves this renewal of the temporal order. Guided by the light of the Gospel and the mind of the Church, prompted by Christian love, they should act in this domain in a direct way and in their own specific manner" (*Apostolicam Actuositatem*, no. 7).

It is therefore necessary to give them an appropriate religious formation which makes them capable of facing the numerous challenges of contemporary society. It is up to them to promote the human and Christian values which illumine the political, economic and cultural reality of the Country, in order to establish a fair and more equitable social order in accordance with the Church's social doctrine.

At the same time, consistent with ethical and moral norms, they must set an example of honesty and transparency in the management of public activities, in the face of the sly and widespread blight of corruption which at times also creeps into the areas of political and economic power, as well as into other public and social milieus.

Lay people must be the leaven in society, acting in public life to illumine with Gospel values the various areas in which a people's identity is forged. With their daily activities, they must "testify how the Christian faith constitutes the only fully valid response . . . to the problems and hopes that life poses to every person and society" (*Christifideles Laici*, no. 34).

Their condition as citizens and followers of Christ must not induce them to lead "two parallel lives in their existence: on the one hand, the so-called 'spiritual' life with its values and demands; and on the other, the so-called 'secular' life, that is, life in a family, at work, in social relationships, in the responsibilities of public life and in culture" (ibid., no. 59).

On the contrary, there must be an effort to make consistency in life and in faith an eloquent testimony of the truth of the Christian message.

Together with you, I would like to entrust all these suggestions and desires to the Virgin of Altagracia, the title with which you honor your Mother and Patroness of the Nation, so that she will continue to accompany your pastoral work.

I entrust you to her with full hope as I impart to you my Apostolic Blessing, which I cordially extend to your particular Churches, your priests, religious communities and consecrated persons as well as to the Catholic faithful of the Dominican Republic.

Meeting with Clergy of the Dioceses of Belluno-Feltre and Treviso

July 24, 2007

Your Holiness, I am Fr. Claudio. The question I wanted to ask you is about the formation of conscience, especially in young people, because today it seems more and more difficult to form a consistent conscience, an upright conscience. Good and evil are often confused with having good and bad feelings, the more emotive aspect. So I would like to hear your advice. Thank you.

Benedict XVI: Your Excellency, dear Brothers, I would like first of all to express my joy and gratitude for this beautiful meeting. I thank the two Pastors, Bishop Andrich and Bishop Mazzocato, for their invitation. I offer my heartfelt thanks to all of you who have come here in such large numbers during the holiday season. To see a church full of priests is encouraging because it shows us that there are priests. The Church is alive, despite the increasing problems in our day and especially in the Western hemisphere. The Church is still alive and has priests who truly desire to proclaim the Kingdom of God; she is growing and standing up to these complications that we perceive in our cultural situation today. Now, to a certain extent, this first question reflects a problem of Western culture, since in the last two centuries the concept of "conscience" has undergone a profound transformation. Today, the idea prevails that only what is quantifiable can be rational, which stems from reason. Other things, such as the subjects of religion and morals, should not enter into common reason because they cannot be proven or, rather, put to the "acid test," so to speak. In this situation, where morals and religion are as it were almost expelled from reason, the subject is the only ultimate criterion of morality and also of religion, the subjective conscience which knows no other authority. In the end, the subject alone decides, with his feelings and experience, on the possible criteria he has discovered. Yet, in this way the subject becomes an isolated reality and, as you said, the parameters change from one day to the next. In the Christian tradition, "conscience," "con-scientia," means "with knowledge": that is, ourselves, our being is open and can listen to the voice of being itself, the voice of God. Thus, the voice of the great values is engraved in our being and the greatness of the human being is precisely that he is not closed in on himself, he is not reduced to the material, something quantifiable, but possesses an inner openness to the essentials and has the possibility of listening. In the depths of our being, not only can we listen to the needs of the moment, to material needs, but we can also hear the voice of the Creator himself and thus discern what is good and what is bad. Of course, this capacity for listening must be taught and encouraged. The commitment to the preaching that we do in church consists of precisely this: developing this very lofty capacity with which God has endowed human beings for listening to the voice of truth and also the voice of values. I would say, therefore, that a first step would be to make people aware that our very nature carries in itself a moral message, a divine message that must be deciphered. We can become increasingly better acquainted with it and listen to it if our inner hearing is open and developed. The actual question now is how to carry out in practice this education in listening, how to make human beings capable of it despite all the forms of modern deafness, how to ensure that this listening, the *Ephphatha* of Baptism, the opening of the inner senses, truly takes place. In taking stock of the current situation, I would propose the combination of a secular approach and a religious approach, the approach of faith. Today, we all see that man can destroy the foundations of his existence, his earth, hence, that we can no longer simply do what we like or what seems useful and promising at the time with this earth of ours, with the reality entrusted to us. On the contrary, we must respect the inner laws of creation, of this earth, we must learn these laws and obey these laws if we wish to survive. Consequently, this obedience to the voice of the earth, of being, is more important for our future happiness than the voices of the moment, the desires of the moment. In short, this is a first criterion to learn: that being itself, our earth, speaks to us and we must listen if we want to survive and to decipher this message of the earth. And if we must be obedient to the voice of the earth, this is even truer for the voice of human life. Not only must we care for the earth, we must respect the other, others: both the other as an individual person, as my neighbor, and others as communities who live in the world and have to live together. And we see that it is only with full respect for this creature of God, this image of God which man is, and with respect for our coexistence on this earth, that we can develop. And here we reach the point when we need the great moral experiences of humanity. These experiences are born from the encounter with the other, with the community. We need the experience that human freedom is always a shared freedom and can only function if we share our freedom with respect for the values that are common to us all. It seems to me that with these steps it will be possible to make people see the need to obey the voice of being, to respect the dignity of the other, to accept the need to live our respective freedom together as *one* freedom, and through all this to recognize the intrinsic value that can make a dignified communion of life possible among human beings. Thus, as has been said, we come to the great experiences of humanity in which the voice of being is expressed. We especially come to the experiences of this great historical pilgrimage of the People of God that began with Abraham. In him, not only do we find the fundamental human experiences but also, we can hear through these experiences the voice of the Creator himself, who loves us and has spoken to us. Here, in this context, respecting the human experiences that point out the way to us today and in the future, I believe that the Ten Commandments always have a priority value in which we see the important signposts on our way. The Ten Commandments reinterpreted, relived in the light of Christ, in the light of the life of the Church and of her experiences, point to certain fundamental and essential values. Together, the Fourth and Sixth Commandments suggest the importance of our body, of respecting the laws of the body and of sexuality and love, the value of faithful love, of the family; the Fifth Commandment points to the value of life and also the value of community life; the Seventh Commandment regards the value of sharing the earth's goods and of a fair distribution of these goods and of the stewardship of God's creation; the Eighth Commandment points to the great value of truth. If, therefore, in the Fourth, Fifth and Sixth Commandments we have love of neighbor, in the Seventh we have the truth. None of this works without communion with God, without respect for God and God's presence in the world. In any case, a world without God becomes an arbitrary and egoistic world. There is light and hope only if God appears. Our life has a meaning which we must not produce ourselves but which precedes us and guides us. In this sense, therefore, I would say that together, we should take the obvious routes which today even the lay conscience can easily discern. We should therefore seek to guide people to the deepest voices, to the true voice of the conscience that is communicated through the great tradition of prayer, of the moral life of the Church. Thus, in a process of patient education, I think we can all learn to live and to find true life.

I am Fr. Mauro. Your Holiness, in exercising our pastoral ministry we are increasingly burdened by many duties. Our tasks in the management and administration of parishes, pastoral organization and assistance to people in difficulty are piling up. I ask you, what are the priorities we should aim for in our ministry as priests and parish priests to avoid fragmentation on the one hand and on the other, dispersion? Thank you.

Benedict XVI: That is a very realistic question, is it not? I am also somewhat familiar with this problem, with all the daily procedures, with all the necessary audiences, with all that there is to do. Yet, it is necessary to determine the right priorities and not to forget the essential: the proclamation of the Kingdom of God. On hearing your question, I remembered the Gospel of two weeks ago on the mission of the seventy disciples. For this first important mission which Jesus had them undertake, the Lord gave them three orders which on the whole I think express the great priorities in the work of a disciple of Christ, a priest, in our day too. The three imperatives are: to pray, to provide care, to preach. I think we should find the balance between these three basic imperatives and keep them ever present as the heart of our work. Prayer: which is to say, without a personal relationship with God nothing else can function, for we cannot truly bring God, the divine reality or true human life to people unless we ourselves live them in a deep, true relationship of friendship with God in Jesus Christ. Hence, the daily celebration of the Holy Eucharist is a fundamental encounter where the Lord speaks to me and I speak to the Lord who gives himself through my hands. Without the prayer of the Hours, in which we join in the great prayer of the entire People of God beginning with the Psalms of the ancient people who are renewed in the faith of the Church, and without personal prayer, we cannot be good priests for we would lose the essence of our ministry. The first imperative is to be a man of God, in the sense of a man in friendship with Christ and with his Saints. Then comes the second command. Jesus said: tend the sick, seek those who have strayed, those who are in need. This is the Church's love for the marginalized and the suffering. Rich people can also be inwardly marginalized and suffering. "To take care of" refers to all human needs, which are always profoundly oriented to God. Thus, as has been said, it is necessary for us to know our sheep, to be on good terms with the people entrusted to us, to have human contact and not to lose our humanity, because God was made man and consequently strengthened all dimensions of our being as humans. However, as I said, the human and the divine always go hand in hand. To my mind, the sacramental ministry is also part of this "tending" in its multiple forms. The ministry of Reconciliation is an act of extraordinary caring which the person needs in order to be perfectly healthy. Thus, this sacramental care begins with Baptism, which is the fundamental renewal of our life, and extends to the Sacrament of Reconciliation and the Anointing of the Sick. Of course, all the other sacraments and also the Eucharist involve great care for souls. We have to care for people but above all—this is our mandate—for their souls. We must think of the many illnesses and moral and spiritual needs that exist today and that we must face, guiding people to the encounter with Christ in the sacrament, helping them to discover prayer and meditation, being silently recollected in church with this presence of God. And then, preaching. What do we preach? We proclaim the Kingdom of God. But the Kingdom of God is not a distant utopia in a better world which may be achieved in fifty years' time, or who knows when. The Kingdom of God is God himself, God close to us who became very close in Christ. This is the Kingdom of God: God himself is near to us and we must draw close to this God who is close for he was made man, remains man and is always with us in his Word, in the Most Holy Eucharist and in all believers. Therefore, proclaiming the Kingdom of God means speaking of God today, making present God's words, the Gospel which is God's presence and, of course, making present the God who made himself present in the Holy Eucharist. By interweaving these three priorities and, naturally, taking into account all the human aspects, including our own limitations that we must recognize, we can properly fulfill our priesthood. This humility that recognizes the limitations of our own strength is important as well. All that we cannot do, the Lord must do. And there is also the ability to delegate and to collaborate. All this must always go with the fundamental imperatives of praying, tending and preaching. . . .

I am Fr. Samuele. We have accepted your invitation to pray, care for people and preach. We are taking you seriously by caring for you yourself; so, to express our affection, we have brought you several bottles of wholesome wine from our region, which we will make sure that you receive through our Bishop. So now for my question. We are seeing an enormous increase in situations of divorced people who remarry, live together and ask priests to help them with their spiritual life. These people often come to us with a heartfelt plea for access to the sacraments. These realities need to be faced and the sufferings they cause must be shared. Holy Father, may I ask you

what are the human, spiritual and pastoral approaches with which one can combine compassion and truth? Thank you.

Benedict XVI: Yes, this is indeed a painful problem and there is certainly no simple solution to resolve it. This problem makes us all suffer because we all have people close to us who are in this situation. We know it causes them sorrow and pain because they long to be in full communion with the Church. The previous bond of matrimony reduces their participation in the life of the Church. What can be done? I would say: as far as possible, we would naturally put prevention first. Hence, preparation for marriage becomes ever more fundamental and necessary. Canon Law presupposes that man as such, even without much education, intends to contract a marriage in harmony with human nature, as mentioned in the first chapters of Genesis. He is a human being, his nature is human and consequently he knows what marriage is. He intends to behave as human nature dictates to him. Canon Law starts from this presupposition. It is something compulsory: man is man, nature is what it is and tells him this. Today, however, this axiom, which holds that man prompted by his nature will make one faithful marriage, has been transformed into a somewhat different axiom. *"Volunt contrahere matrimonium sicut ceteri homines."* It is no longer nature alone that speaks, but the *"ceteri homines"*: what everyone does. And what everyone does today is not simply to enter into natural marriage, in accordance with the Creator, in accordance with creation. What the *"ceteri homines"* do is to marry with the idea that one day their marriage might fail and that they will then be able to move on to another one, to a third or even a fourth marriage. This model of what "everyone does" thus becomes one that is contrary to what nature says. In this way, it becomes normal to marry, divorce and remarry, and no one thinks this is something contrary to human nature, or in any case those who do are few and far between. Therefore, to help people achieve a real marriage, not only in the sense of the Church but also of the Creator, we must revive their capacity for listening to nature. Let us return to the first query, the first question: rediscovering within what everyone does, what nature itself tells us, which is so different from what this modern custom dictates. Indeed, it invites us to marry for life, with lifelong fidelity including the suffering that comes from growing together in love. Thus, these preparatory courses for marriage must be a rectification of the voice of nature, of the Creator, within us, a rediscovery, beyond what all the *"ceteri homines"* do, of what our own being intimately tells us. In this situation, therefore, distinguishing between what everyone else does and what our being tells us, these preparatory courses for marriage must be a journey of rediscovery. They must help us learn anew what our being tells us. They must help couples reach the true decision of marriage in accordance with the Creator and the Redeemer. Hence, these preparatory courses are of great importance in order to "learn oneself," to learn the true intention for marriage. But preparation is not enough; the great crises come later. Consequently, ongoing guidance, at least in the first ten years, is of the utmost importance. In the parish, therefore, it is not only necessary to provide preparatory courses but also communion in the journey that follows, guidance and mutual help. May priests, but not on their own, and families, which have already undergone such experiences and are familiar with such suffering and temptations, be available in moments of crisis. The presence of a network of families that help one another is important and different movements can make a considerable contribution. The first part of my answer provides for prevention, not only in the sense of preparation but also of guidance and for the presence of a network of families to assist in this contemporary situation where everything goes against faithfulness for life. It is necessary to help people find this faithfulness and learn it, even in the midst of suffering. However, in the case of failure, in other words, when the spouses are incapable of adhering to their original intention, there is always the question of whether it was a real decision in the sense of the sacrament. As a result, one possibility is the process for the declaration of nullity. If their marriage were authentic, which would prevent them from remarrying, the Church's permanent presence would help these people to bear the additional suffering. In the first case, we have the suffering that goes with overcoming this crisis and learning a hard-fought for and mature fidelity. In the second case, we have the suffering of being in a new bond which is not sacramental, hence, does not permit full communion in the sacraments of the Church. Here it would be necessary to teach and to learn how to live with this suffering. We return to this point, to the first question of the other diocese. In our generation, in our culture, we have to rediscover the value of suffering in general, and we have to learn that suffering can be a very positive reality which helps us to mature, to become more ourselves, and to be closer to the Lord who suffered for us and suffers with us. Even in the latter situation, therefore, the presence of the priest, families, movements, personal and communitarian communion in these situations, the helpful love of one's neighbor, a very specific love, is of the greatest importance. And I think that only this love, felt by the Church and expressed in the solidarity of many, can help these people recognize that they are loved by Christ and are members of the Church despite their difficult situation. Thus, it can help them to live the faith. . . .

Fr. Alberto: Holy Father, young people are our future and our hope: but they sometimes see life as a difficulty rather than an opportunity; not as a gift for themselves and for others but as something to be consumed on the spot; not as a future to be built but as aimless wandering. The contemporary mindset demands that young people be happy and perfect all of

the time. The result is that every tiny failure and the least difficulty are no longer seen as causes for growth but as a defeat. All this often leads to irreversible acts such as suicide, which wound the hearts of those who love them and of society as a whole. What can you tell us educators who feel all too often that our hands are tied and that we have no answers? Thank you.

Benedict XVI: I think you have just given us a precise description of a life in which God does not figure. At first sight, it seems as if we do not need God or indeed, that without God we would be freer and the world would be grander. But after a certain time, we see in our young people what happens when God disappears. As Nietzsche said: "The great light has been extinguished, the sun has been put out." Life is then a chance event. It becomes a thing that I must seek to do the best I can with and use life as though it were a thing that serves my own immediate, tangible and achievable happiness. But the big problem is that were God not to exist and were he not also the Creator of my life, life would actually be a mere cog in evolution, nothing more; it would have no meaning in itself. Instead, I must seek to give meaning to this component of being. Currently, I see in Germany, but also in the United States, a somewhat fierce debate raging between so-called "creationism" and evolutionism, presented as though they were mutually exclusive alternatives: those who believe in the Creator would not be able to conceive of evolution, and those who instead support evolution would have to exclude God. This antithesis is absurd because, on the one hand, there are so many scientific proofs in favor of evolution which appears to be a reality we can see and which enriches our knowledge of life and being as such. But on the other, the doctrine of evolution does not answer every query, especially the great philosophical question: where does everything come from? And how did everything start which ultimately led to man? I believe this is of the utmost importance. This is what I wanted to say in my lecture at Regensburg: that reason should be more open, that it should indeed perceive these facts but also realize that they are not enough to explain all of reality. They are insufficient. Our reason is broader and can also see that our reason is not basically something irrational, a product of irrationality, but that reason, creative reason, precedes everything and we are truly the reflection of creative reason. We were thought of and desired; thus, there is an idea that preceded me, a feeling that preceded me, that I must discover, that I must follow, because it will at last give meaning to my life. This seems to me to be the first point: to discover that my being is truly reasonable, it was thought of, it has meaning. And my important mission is to discover this meaning, to live it and thereby contribute a new element to the great cosmic harmony conceived of by the Creator. If this is true, then difficulties also become moments of growth, of the process and progress of my very being, which has meaning from conception until the very last moment of life. We can get to know this reality of meaning that precedes all of us, we can also rediscover the meaning of pain and suffering; there is of course one form of suffering that we must avoid and must distance from the world: all the pointless suffering caused by dictatorships and erroneous systems, by hatred and by violence. However, in suffering there is also a profound meaning, and only if we can give meaning to pain and suffering can our life mature. I would say, above all, that there can be no love without suffering, because love always implies renouncement of myself, letting myself go and accepting the other in his otherness; it implies a gift of myself and therefore, emerging from myself. All this is pain and suffering, but precisely in this suffering caused by the losing of myself for the sake of the other, for the loved one and hence, for God, I become great and my life finds love, and in love finds its meaning. The inseparability of love and suffering, of love and God, are elements that must enter into the modern conscience to help us live. In this regard, I would say that it is important to help the young discover God, to help them discover the true love that precisely in renunciation becomes great and so also enables them to discover the inner benefit of suffering, which makes me freer and greater. Of course, to help young people find these elements, companionship and guidance are always essential, whether through the parish, Catholic Action or a Movement. It is only in the company of others that we can also reveal this great dimension of our being to the new generations.

PASTORAL VISIT TO LORETO ON THE OCCASION OF THE
AGORÀ OF ITALIAN YOUTH

Prayer Vigil with Young People

September 1, 2007

Responses of the Holy Father to Questions Posed by Young People

Question posed by Piero Tisti and Giovanna Di Mucci:

"Many of us young people in the suburbs do not have a center, a place or people with whom we can identify. Often we are without a history, a perspective or even a future. It seems that what we really wait for never happens. From this come the experience of solitude and at times, an improper dependence on others. Your Holiness, is there someone or something by means of which we can become important? How is it possible to hope when reality negates every dream of happiness, every project of life?"

Response of the Holy Father:

Thank you for this question and for your very realistic presentation of the situation. It is not always easy to respond concerning the peripheries of this world with great problems and we do not want to live an easy optimism; but on the other hand, we must have the courage to go forwards.

I will therefore anticipate the essence of my answer: Yes, there is hope today too; each one of you is important because each is known and desired by God and God has his plan for each one. It is our task to discover and respond to it, so that despite these precarious and marginalized situations, we will be able to put into practice God's plan for us.

However, to go into detail, you have realistically presented to us the situation of a society: in the outskirts it seems hard to move ahead, to change the world for the better. Everything seems concentrated in the great centers of economic and political power, the great bureaucracies dominate, and those in the outskirts truly seem excluded from this life.

Then, one aspect of this situation of marginalization that affects so many people is that the important cells of social life that can also build centers on the fringes are fragmented: the family, which should be the place where generations meet—from great grandfather to grandchild—, should not only be a place where generations meet but also where they learn to live, learn the essential virtues, and this is in danger.

Thus, all the more should we do our utmost to ensure that the family survives, that today too, it is the vital cell, the center in the periphery.

Therefore, the parish, the living cell of the Church, must also really be a place of inspiration, life and solidarity which helps people build together centers in the periphery. And I must say here, there is often talk about the Church in the suburbs and in the center, which would be Rome, but in fact in the Church there are no suburbs because where Christ is, the whole center is there.

Wherever the Eucharist is celebrated, wherever the Tabernacle stands, there is Christ; hence, there is the center and we must do all we can to ensure that these living centers are effective, present and truly a force that counters this marginalization.

The living Church, the Church of the little communities, the parish Church, the movements, must form as many centers in the outskirts and thus help to overcome the difficulties that the leading politics obviously cannot manage to resolve, and at the same time, we must also think that despite the great focuses of power, contemporary society itself is in need of solidarity, of a sense of lawfulness, of the initiative and creativity of all.

I know that this is easier said than done, but I see here people who are working to increase the number of centers in the peripheries, to increase hope, and thus it seems to me that we should take up the initiative. The Church must be present precisely in the suburbs; Christ must be present, the center of the world must be present.

We have seen and we see today in the Gospel that for God there are no peripheries. In the vast context of the Roman Empire, the Holy Land was situated on the fringe; Nazareth was on the margins, an unknown town. Yet that very situation was, de facto, to become the center that changed the world!

And thus, we must form centers of faith, hope, love and solidarity, centers of a sense of justice and lawfulness and of cooperation. Only in this way will modern society be able to survive. It needs this courage, it needs to create centers even if, obviously, hope does not seem to exist. We must counter this desperation, we must collaborate with great solidarity in doing our best to increase hope, so that men and women may collaborate and live.

The world—we see it—must be changed, but it is precisely the mission of young people to change it! We cannot change it with our own strength alone but in communion of faith and in journeying on together. In communion with Mary, with all the Saints, in communion with Christ, we can do something essential, and I encourage you and invite you to trust in Christ, to trust in God.

Being in the great company of the Saints and moving forward with them can change the world, creating centers in the outskirts, so that the company of Saints may truly become visible and thus the hope of all may become realistic, and every one may say: "I am important in the totality of history. The Lord will help us." Thank you.

Question posed by Sara Simonetta:

"I believe in the God who has touched my heart, but I have many insecurities, questions and fears that I carry within. It is not easy to speak about God with my friends; many of them see the Church as a reality that judges youth, that opposes their desire for happiness and love. Faced with this refusal, I feel all of my solitude as human and I want to feel near God. Your Holiness, in this silence, where is God?"

Response of the Holy Father:

Yes, even though we are believers, we all know God's silence. In the Psalm we have just recited, there is this almost despairing cry: "Make haste to answer me, O Lord . . . Do not hide your face!" and a little while ago a book of the spiritual experiences of Mother Teresa was published and what we already all knew was a little more clearly shown: with all her charity and the power of her faith, Mother Teresa suffered from God's silence.

On the one hand, we must also bear God's silence in order to understand our brothers who do not know God.

On the other, with the Psalm we can always cry to God once again: "Answer us, show your face!"

And without a doubt, in our life, if our hearts are open, we can find the important moments when God's presence really becomes tangible even for us.

I now remember a little story that John Paul II told at the Spiritual Exercises he preached in the Vatican when he was not yet Pope. He recounted that after the war he was visited by a Russian official who was a scientist and who said to him as a scientist: "I am certain that God does not exist. Yet, if I am in the mountains, surrounded by his majestic beauty, by his grandeur, I am equally sure that the Creator does exist and that God exists."

The beauty of creation is one of the sources where we can truly touch God's beauty, we can see that the Creator exists and is good, which is true as Sacred Scripture says in the Creation Narrative, that is, that God conceived of this world and made it with his heart, his will and his reason, and he found it good.

We too must be good in order to have an open heart and to perceive God's true presence. Then, hearing the Word of God in the solemn liturgical celebrations, in celebrations of faith, in the great music of faith, we feel this presence. I remember at this moment another little story which a Bishop on his *ad limina* visit told me a little while ago.

There was a very intelligent woman who was not a Christian. She began to listen to the great music of Bach, Handel and Mozart. She was fascinated and said one day: "I must find the source of this beauty," and the woman converted to Christianity, to the Catholic faith, because she had discovered that this beauty has a source, and the source is the presence of Christ in hearts, it is the revelation of Christ in this world.

Hence, great feasts of faith, of liturgical celebration, but also personal dialogue with Christ: he does not always respond, but there are times when he really responds. Then there is the friendship, the company of faith.

Now, gathered here in Loreto, we see that faith unites, friendship creates a company of travelling companions. And we sense that all this does not derive from nothing but truly has a source, that the silent God is also a God who speaks, that he reveals himself and above all, that we ourselves can be witnesses of his presence, and from our faith a light truly shines also for others.

Thus, I would say on the one hand, we must accept that God is silent in this world, but we must not be deaf to his words or blind to his appearance on so many occasions. We see the Lord's presence, especially in creation, in the beautiful liturgy, in friendship within the Church, and full of his presence, we can also give light to others.

Thus, I come to the second part, or rather, the first part of your question: it is difficult to speak to friends today about God and perhaps even more difficult to talk about the Church, because they see in God only the limit of our freedom, a God of commandments, of prohibitions, and the Church as an institution that limits our freedom, that imposes prohibitions upon us.

Nonetheless, we must try to make the living Church visible to them, not this idea of a center of power in the Church with these labels, but the community of companions where, in spite of all life's problems that exist for everyone, is born our joy of living.

Here, a third memory springs to mind. I was in Brazil, in Fazenda da Esperança, this great community where drug addicts are treated and rediscover hope, the joy of living in this world; and they witnessed what the actual discovery that God exists meant for their recovery from despair.

They thus understood that their life has meaning and they rediscovered the joy of being in this world, the joy of facing the problems of human life.

Therefore, in every human heart, despite all the problems that exist, is a thirst for God, and when God disappears, the sun that gives light and joy also disappears.

This thirst for the infinite that is in our hearts is also demonstrated even in the reality of drugs: the human being wants to extend the quality of life, to have more than life, to have the infinite, but drugs are a lie, they are a fraud, because they do not extend life but destroy it.

The great thirst that speaks to us of God and sets us on the path that leads to him is true, but we must help one another. Christ came to create a network of communion in the world, where all together we might carry one another, and thus help one another together to find the ways that lead to life and to understand that the Commandments of God are not limits to our freedom but the paths that guide us to the other, toward the fullness of life.

Let us pray to the Lord to help us understand his presence, to be full of his Revelation, his joy, to help one another to go forward in the company of faith and with Christ to increasingly find the true Face of God, and hence, true life.

Address of His Holiness Benedict XVI

Dear young people who are the hope of the Church in Italy! I am happy to meet you in this remarkable place, on this special evening, rich in prayer, song, periods of silence, full of hope and profound emotion. This valley, where in the past also my beloved Predecessor John Paul II met many of you, has henceforth become your *agora*, your square without walls and barriers, where a thousand streets converge and from which they branch out.

I listened with attention to those who have spoken on behalf of you all. You have come to this peaceful, authentic and joyful place of encounter for thousands of different reasons: some of you because you belong to a group or were invited by some friend, some by deep conviction, some with several doubts in your heart and some merely out of curiosity. . . . Whatever the reason that drew you here, I can tell you, although it requires courage to say it, that it was the Holy Spirit who has brought us together. Yes, that is exactly the case; the Spirit has led you here; you have come here with your doubts and certainties, with your joys and your anxieties. It is now up to all of us, to all of you, to open your hearts and offer everything to Jesus.

Say to him: here I am; of course, I am not yet as you would like me to be, I cannot even manage to understand myself fully but with your help I am ready to follow you. Lord Jesus, this evening I would like to speak to you, making my own the inner attitude and trusting abandonment of that young woman who, 2,000 years ago, said her "yes" to the Father who chose her to be your Mother. The Father chose her because she was docile and obedient to his will. Like her, like little Mary, each one of you, dear young friends, should say to God with faith: "Here I am; let it be done to me according to your word."

What an amazing spectacle of young and stirring faith we are experiencing this evening! And this evening, thanks to you, Loreto has become the spiritual capital of youth; the center toward which multitudes of the young people who populate the five Continents converge in spirit.

At this moment, we feel as though we were surrounded by the expectations and hopes of millions of young people across the world: at this very minute there are some who are watching, others who are asleep, yet others who are studying or working; some are hoping and some despairing, some believe and others are not able to believe, some love life and others, instead, are throwing it away.

I would like my words to reach them all: the Pope is close to you, he shares your joys and your pain, and he especially shares in the most intimate hopes that are in your soul. For each one of you he asks the Lord for the gift of a full and happy life, a life filled with meaning, a true life.

Today, unfortunately, all too often a full and happy existence is seen by many young people as a difficult dream—we heard so many testimonies— sometimes almost impossible to accomplish. So many of your peers are looking to the future with apprehension and ask many questions. Worried, they ask: How is it possible to be integrated in a society marked by a multitude of grave injustices and suffering? How should I react to the selfishness and violence that sometimes seem to prevail? How can I give life full meaning?

With love and conviction, I repeat to you young people present here, and through you to your peers throughout the world: Do not be afraid, Christ can fill your heart's deepest aspirations! Are there dreams that cannot come true when it is God's Spirit who inspires and nourishes them in your heart? Can anything block our enthusiasm when we are united with Christ? Nothing and no one, the Apostle Paul would say, will ever separate us from God's love, in Christ Jesus Our Lord (cf. Rom 8:35-39).

Let me tell you again this evening: if you stay united with Christ, each one of you will be able to do great things. This is why, dear friends, you must not be afraid to dream with your eyes open of important projects of good and you must not let yourselves be discouraged by difficulties. Christ has confidence in you and wants you to be able to realize all your most noble and lofty dreams of genuine happiness. Nothing is impossible for those who trust in God and entrust themselves to him.

Look at the young Mary; the Angel proposed something truly inconceivable to her: participation, in the most involving way possible, in the greatest of God's plans, the salvation of humanity. Facing this proposal, Mary, as we heard in the Gospel, was distressed for she realized the smallness of her being before the omnipotence of God; and she asked herself: "How is it possible? Why should it be me?" Yet, ready to do the divine will, she promptly said her "yes" which changed her life and the history of all humanity. It is also thanks to her "yes" that we are meeting here this evening.

I ask myself and I ask you: can God's requests to us, however demanding they may seem, ever compare with what God asked the young Mary? Dear young men and women, since Mary truly knows what it means to respond generously to the Lord's requests, let us learn from her to say our own "yes."

Mary, dear young people, knows your noblest and deepest aspirations. Above all, she well knows your great desire for love, with your need to love and to be loved. By looking at her, by following her docilely, you will discover the beauty of love; not a "disposable" love that is transient and deceptive, imprisoned in a selfish and materialistic mindset, but true, deep love.

In the very depths of their hearts, every young man, every young woman who are looking out on life, cherish the dream of a love that will give full meaning to their futures. For many, this is fulfilled in the choice of marriage and in the formation of a family in which the love between a man and a woman is lived as a definitive gift, sealed by the "yes" spoken before God on their wedding day, a "yes" for their whole life.

I know well that today this dream is always less easy to realize. How many failures of love surround us! How many couples bow their heads, give up and separate! How many families fall to pieces! How many young people, even among you, have witnessed the separation and divorce of their parents!

I would like to say to those in such sensitive and complex situations: the Mother of God, the Community of believers and the Pope are beside you and are praying that the crisis that marks today's families may not become an irreversible failure. May Christian families, with the support of divine Grace, stay faithful to that solemn commitment of love joyfully assumed before the priest and the Christian community on the solemn day of their marriage.

In the face of so many failures these questions are often asked: Am I any better than my friends and my parents who have tried and failed? Why should I myself succeed where so many have given up? This human fear can be daunting to even the more courageous spirits but in this night that awaits us, in front of her Holy House, Mary will repeat to each one of you, dear young friends, the words that she herself heard the Angel say to her: Do not be afraid, do not fear!

The Holy Spirit is with you and will never leave you. Nothing is impossible to those who trust in God. This applies for those who are destined to married life and still more for those to whom God proposes a life of total detachment from earthly goods, to be dedicated full time to his Kingdom. Some of you have set out toward the priesthood, toward the consecrated life; some of you aspire to be missionaries, knowing how many and what risks this entails.

I am thinking of the missionaries, priests, women religious and lay people, who have fallen in the trenches of love at the service of the Gospel. Fr. Giancarlo Bossi, for whom we prayed when he was kidnapped in the Philippines, will have much to tell us about this and today we rejoice to have him with us. Through him, I would like to greet and thank all those who spend their lives for Christ on the frontiers of evangelization.

Dear young people, if the Lord calls you to live more intimately at his service, respond generously. You may be certain: life dedicated to God is never spent in vain.

Dear young people, I shall end my talk here, not without first having embraced you with a father's heart. I embrace you one by one and greet you warmly. I greet the Bishops present, starting with Archbishop Angelo Bagnasco, President of the Italian Bishops' Conference, and Archbishop Gianni Danzi who has welcomed us into his Ecclesial Community. I greet the priests, the Religious and the animators who have accompanied you. I greet the Civil Authorities and all who organized this Meeting. We will be "virtually" united later and we will see one another again tomorrow morning, at the end of this night of Vigil, for the crowning point of our Meeting when Jesus makes himself truly present in his Word and in the mystery of the Eucharist.

From this moment, I would like to make an appointment with you young people in Sydney where, in a year's time, the next World Youth Day will be held. I know Australia is far away and for young Italians it is literally at the other end of the world. . . . Let us pray that the Lord who works every miracle will grant that many of you may be there. May he grant it to me, may he grant it to you. This is one of our many dreams which tonight, as we pray together, we entrust to Mary. Amen.

APOSTOLIC JOURNEY TO AUSTRIA FOR THE
850TH ANNIVERSARY OF THE FOUNDATION OF
THE SHRINE OF MARIAZELL

Address at the Meeting with
Authorities and Diplomatic Corps

September 7, 2007

Life

It was in Europe that the notion of human rights was first formulated. The fundamental human right, the presupposition of every other right, is the right to life itself. This is true of life from the moment of conception until its natural end. Abortion, consequently, cannot be a human right—it is the very opposite. It is "a deep wound in society," as the late Cardinal Franz König never tired of repeating.

In stating this, I am not expressing a specifically ecclesial concern. Rather, I wish to act as an advocate for a profoundly human need, speaking out on behalf of those unborn children who have no voice. In doing so, I do not close my eyes to the difficulties and the conflicts which many women are experiencing, and I realize that the credibility of what we say also depends on what the Church herself is doing to help women in trouble.

In this context, then, I appeal to political leaders not to allow children to be considered as a form of illness, nor to abolish in practice your legal system's acknowledgment that abortion is wrong. I say this out of a concern for humanity. But that is only one side of this disturbing problem. The other is the need to do everything possible to make European countries once again open to welcoming children. Encourage young married couple to establish new families and to become mothers and fathers! You will not only assist them, but you will benefit society as a whole. I also decisively support you in your political efforts to favor conditions enabling young couples to raise children. Yet all this will be pointless, unless we can succeed in creating once again in our countries a climate of joy and confidence in life, a climate in which children are not seen as a burden, but rather as a gift for all.

Another great concern of mine is the debate on what has been termed "actively assisted death." It is to be feared that at some point the gravely ill or elderly will be subjected to tacit or even explicit pressure to request death or to administer it to themselves. The proper response to end-of-life suffering is loving care and accompaniment on the journey toward death—especially with the help of palliative care—and not "actively assisted death." But if humane accompaniment on the journey toward death is to prevail, structural reforms would be needed in every area of the social and healthcare system, as well as organized structures of palliative care. Concrete steps would also have to be taken: in the psychological and pastoral accompaniment of the seriously ill and dying, their family members, and physicians and healthcare personnel. In this field the hospice movement has done wonders. The totality of these tasks, however, cannot be delegated to it alone. Many other people need to be prepared or encouraged in their willingness to spare neither time nor expense in loving care for the gravely ill and dying.

Address to the New Ambassador of the Slovak Republic to the Holy See

September 13, 2007

The combined efforts of Church and civil society to instruct young people in the ways of goodness are all the more crucial at a time when they are tempted to disparage the values of marriage and family so vital to their future happiness and to a nation's social stability. The family is the nucleus in which a person first learns human love and cultivates the virtues of responsibility, generosity and fraternal concern. Strong families are built on the foundation of strong marriages. Strong societies are built on the foundation of strong families. Indeed, all civic communities should do what they can to promote economic and social policies that aid young married couples and facilitate their desire to raise a family. Far from remaining indifferent to marriage, the State must acknowledge, respect and support this venerable institution as the stable union between a man and a woman who willingly embrace a life-long commitment of love and fidelity (cf. *Familiaris Consortio*, no. 40). The members of your National Council are engaged in serious discussions on how to promote marriage and foster family life. The Catholic Bishops, too, in your country are worried about increases in the rate of divorce and the number of children conceived out of wedlock. Thanks to the efforts of the Council for Family and Youth, the Conference of Bishops has expanded educational initiatives that raise awareness of the noble vocation to marriage, thus preparing young people to assume its responsibilities. Such programs open the door to further collaboration between Church and State and help to ensure a healthy future for your country.

General Audience

September 19, 2007

John Chrysostom was anxious to accompany his writings with the person's integral development in his physical, intellectual and religious dimensions. The various phases of his growth are compared to as many seas in an immense ocean: "The first of these seas is childhood" (*Homily*, 81, 5 *On Matthew's Gospel*).

Indeed, "it is precisely at this early age that inclinations to vice or virtue are manifest." Thus, God's law must be impressed upon the soul from the outset "as on a wax tablet" (*Homily* 3, 1 *On John's Gospel*): This is indeed the most important age. We must bear in mind how fundamentally important it is that the great orientations which give man a proper outlook on life truly enter him in this first phase of life.

Chrysostom therefore recommended: "From the tenderest age, arm children with spiritual weapons and teach them to make the Sign of the Cross on their forehead with their hand" (*Homily*, 12, 7 *On First Corinthians*).

Then come adolescence and youth: "Following childhood is the sea of adolescence, where violent winds blow . . . , for concupiscence . . . grows within us" (*Homily* 81, 5 *On Matthew's Gospel*).

Lastly comes engagement and marriage: "Youth is succeeded by the age of the mature person who assumes family commitments: this is the time to seek a wife" (ibid.).

He recalls the aims of marriage, enriching them—referring to virtue and temperance—with a rich fabric of personal relationships. Properly prepared spouses therefore bar the way to divorce: everything takes place with joy and children can be educated in virtue. Then when the first child is born, he is "like a bridge; the three become one flesh, because the child joins the two parts" (*Homily* 12, 5 *On the Letter to the Colossians*), and the three constitute "a family, a Church in miniature" (*Homily* 20, 6 *On the Letter to the Ephesians*).

Address to Participants in the Conference of the Executive Committee of Centrist Democratic International

September 21, 2007

There are some who believe that it is legitimate to destroy human life in its earliest or final stages. Equally troubling is the growing crisis of the family, which is the fundamental nucleus of society based on the indissoluble bond of marriage between a man and a woman. Experience has shown that when the truth about man is subverted or the foundation of the family undermined, peace itself is threatened and the rule of law is compromised, leading inevitably to forms of injustice and violence.

Address to Members of the International Theological Commission

October 5, 2007

When the fundamental requirements of human dignity, of human life, of the family institution, of a fair social order, in other words, basic human rights, are at stake, no law devised by human beings can subvert the law that the Creator has engraved on the human heart without the indispensable foundations of society itself being dramatically affected. Natural law thus becomes the true guarantee offered to each one in order that he may live in freedom, have his dignity respected and be protected from all ideological manipulation and every kind of arbitrary use or abuse by the stronger. No one can ignore this appeal. If, by tragically blotting out the collective conscience, skepticism and ethical relativism were to succeed in deleting the fundamental principles of the natural moral law, the foundations of the democratic order itself would be radically damaged. To prevent this obscuring, which is a crisis of human civilization even before it is a Christian one, all consciences of people of good will, of lay persons and also of the members of the different Christian denominations, must be mobilized so that they may engage, together and effectively, in order to create the necessary conditions for the inalienable value of the natural moral law in culture and in civil and political society to be fully understood. Indeed, on respect for this natural moral law depends the advance of individuals and society on the path of authentic progress in conformity with right reason, which is participation in the eternal Reason of God.

Letter to the President of the Italian Bishops' Conference on the Occasion of the Centenary of the Italian Catholic Social Week

October 12, 2007

The daily news demonstrates that contemporary society is facing many ethical and social emergencies that could undermine its stability and seriously jeopardize its future. Particularly relevant is the current anthropological question which embraces respect for human life and the attention to be paid to the needs of the family founded on the marriage of a man and a woman. As has been affirmed several times, it is not a matter of solely "Catholic" values and principles but of defending and protecting common human values, such as justice, peace and the safeguarding of creation.

What can then be said of the problems concerning work in relation to the family and young people? When lack of steady work does not permit young people to have a family of their own, society's authentic and full development is seriously jeopardized.

Message for the Ninety-Fourth World Day of Migrants and Refugees

October 18, 2007

Precisely from this perspective the question is raised of how to respond to the expectations of the young migrants? What can be done to help them? Of course, it is necessary to aim first of all at support for the family and schools. But how complex the situations are, and how numerous the difficulties these young people encounter in their family and school contexts! In families, the traditional roles that existed in the countries of origin have broken down, and a clash is often seen between parents still tied to their culture and children quickly acculturated in the new social contexts. Likewise, the difficulty should not be underestimated which the young people find in getting inserted into the educational course of study in force in the country where they are hosted. Therefore, the scholastic system itself should take their conditions into consideration and provide specific formative paths of integration for the immigrant boys and girls that are suited to their needs. The commitment will also be important to create a climate of mutual respect and dialogue among all the students in the classrooms based on the universal principles and values that are common to all cultures. Everyone's commitment—teachers, families and students—will surely contribute to helping the young migrants to face in the best way possible the challenge of integration and offer them the possibility to acquire what can aid their human, cultural and professional formation. This holds even more for the young refugees for whom adequate programs will have to be prepared, both in the scholastic and the work contexts, in order to guarantee their preparation and provide the necessary bases for a correct insertion into the new social, cultural and professional world.

Address to Members of the International Congress of Catholic Pharmacists

October 29, 2007

Mr. President,
Dear Friends,

I am happy to welcome you, members of the International Congress of Catholic Pharmacists, on the occasion of your twenty-fifth Congress, whose theme is: "The new boundaries of the pharmaceutical act."

The current development of an arsenal of medicines and the resulting possibilities for treatment oblige pharmacists to reflect on the ever broader functions they are called to fulfill, particularly as intermediaries between doctor and patient; they have an educational role with patients to teach them the proper dosage of their medication and especially to acquaint them with the ethical implications of the use of certain drugs. In this context, it is not possible to anaesthetize consciences, for example, concerning the effects of particles whose purpose is to prevent an embryo's implantation or to shorten a person's life. The pharmacist must invite each person to advance humanity, so that every being may be protected from the moment of conception until natural death, and that medicines may fulfill properly their therapeutic role. No person, moreover, may be used thoughtlessly as an object for the purpose of therapeutic experimentation; therapeutic experimentation must take place in accordance with protocols that respect fundamental ethical norms. Every treatment or process of experimentation must be with a view to possible improvement of the person's physical condition and not merely seeking scientific advances. The pursuit of good for humanity cannot be to the detriment of people undergoing treatment. In the moral domain, your Federation is invited to address the issue of conscientious objection, which is a right your profession must recognize, permitting you not to collaborate either directly or indirectly by supplying products for the purpose of decisions that are clearly immoral such as, for example, abortion or euthanasia.

It would also be advisable that the different pharmaceutical structures, laboratories at hospital centers and surgeries, as well as our contemporaries all together, be concerned with showing solidarity in the therapeutic context, to make access to treatment and urgently needed medicines available at all levels of society and in all countries, particularly to the poorest people.

Prompted by the Holy Spirit, may you as Catholic pharmacists find in the life of faith and in the Church's teaching elements that will guide you in your professional approach to the sick, who are in need of human and moral support if they are to live with hope and find the inner resources that will help them throughout their lives. It is also your duty to help young people who enter the different pharmaceutical professions to reflect on the increasingly delicate ethical implications of their activities and decisions. To this end, it is important that all Catholic health-care professionals and people of good will join forces to deepen their formation, not only at a technical level but also with regard to bioethical issues, as well as to propose this formation to the profession as a whole. The human being, because he or she is the image of God, must always be the center of research and choices in the biomedical context. At the same time, the natural principle of the duty to provide care for the sick person is fundamental. The biomedical sciences are at the service of the human being; if this were not the case, they would have a cold and inhuman character. All scientific knowledge in the health sector and every therapeutic procedure is at the service of the sick person, viewed in his integral being, who must be an active partner in his treatment and whose autonomy must be respected.

As I entrust you as well as the sick people you are called to treat to the intercession of Our Lady and of St. Albert the Great, I impart my Apostolic Blessing to you and to all the members of your Federation and your families.

Address to Members of the "New Families Movement"

November 3, 2007

Dear Brothers and Sisters,

Welcome and thank you for coming to visit me. You come from the five continents and belong to *The New Families Movement* which came into being forty years ago in the context of the *Focolare Movement*. You are thus a branch of *Focolare* and today form a network of at least 800,000 families working in 182 nations, all committed to making their home a "focolare" [hearth] which radiates in the world the witness of a Gospel-style family life. I offer each one of you my most cordial greeting, which I extend also to those who have wished to accompany you at our meeting. I greet in a special way your leaders who have conveyed your common sentiments and described to me your Movement's working methods as well as its goals. I thank you for the greetings you have brought me from Chiara Lubich, to whom I send my warm good wishes, thanking her because she continues to guide the large family of the *Focolare* with wisdom and unswerving attachment to the Church.

As has just been recalled, it is precisely in the context of this vast and praiseworthy institution that you, dear married couples, place yourselves at the service of the world of families with an important and ever timely pastoral action that has four orientations: spirituality, education, sociability and solidarity. Your task is effectively a silent and deep commitment to evangelization with the goal of testifying that only family unity, a gift of God-Love, can make the family a true nest of love, a home that welcomes life and a school of virtue and Christian values for children. As you confront the many social and economic, cultural and religious issues that challenge contemporary society in every part of the world, your work, truly providential, is a sign of hope and an encouragement for Christian families to be a privileged "space" where the beauty of making Jesus Christ the focus and of faithfully following his Gospel is proclaimed in everyday life, sometimes despite many difficulties. Indeed, your meeting's theme: *"A house built on the rock—the Gospel lived, a response to the problems of families today,"* emphasizes the importance of this ascetical and pastoral itinerary. The secret is precisely to live the Gospel!

Rightly, therefore, in the work of the assembly during these days, in addition to contributions that illustrate the situation of today's families in the different cultural contexts, you have planned to deepen your knowledge of the Word of God and to hear the testimonies that show how the Holy Spirit acts in hearts and in family life, even in complex and difficult situations. Only think of the uncertainties of engaged couples as they face definitive decisions for the future, of the crisis of couples, of separations and divorces as well as irregular unions, of the condition of widows, of families in difficulty and of welcoming abandoned minors. I warmly hope that also thanks to your commitment, pastoral strategies may be identified to cope with the increasing needs of families today and the multiple challenges that face them, so that they will not fail in their special mission in the Church and in society.

In this regard, in the Post-Synodal Apostolic Exhortation *Christifideles Laici*, my venerable and beloved Predecessor John Paul II noted that the Church maintains that for the faithful, "the first and basic expression of the social dimension . . . is the married couple and the family" (no. 40). To bring this vocation to fruition, the family, aware that it is the primary cell of society, must not forget that it can find strength in a Sacrament desired by Christ to reinforce the love between man and woman: a love understood as a gift of self, reciprocal and profound. As John Paul II likewise observed: "The family has the mission to guard, reveal and communicate love, and this is a living reflection of and a real sharing in God's love for humanity and the love of Christ the Lord for the Church, his Bride" (*Familiaris Consortio*, no. 17). Thus, according to the divine plan, the family is a sacred and sanctifying place and the Church, which has always been close to the family, supports it in this mission, especially today when the internal and external threats to it are so numerous. In order not to succumb to discouragement, divine help is essential; thus, every Christian family must look with trust to the Holy Family, the original "domestic Church" in which "through God's mysterious design, it was in that family that the Son of God spent long years of a hidden life. It is therefore the prototype and example for all Christian families" (ibid., no. 86).

Dear brothers and sisters, the humble and holy Family of Nazareth, the icon and model of every human family, will not let you go without its heavenly support. Nonetheless, your ceaseless recourse to prayer, to listening to the Word of God and to an intense sacramental life is indispensable, together with a constant effort to live Christ's commandment of love and forgiveness. Love does not seek its own interests, it does not harbor rancor for evil received but rejoices in truth. Love "bears all things, believes all things, hopes all things, endures all things" (1 Cor 13:5-7). Dear brothers and sisters, continue your journey and be witnesses of this Love which will make you increasingly the "heart" and "leaven" of the entire *New Families Movement*. I assure you of my remembrance in prayer for each one of you, for your activities and all those you meet in your apostolate, and with affection I now impart to you all the Apostolic Blessing.

Address to Participants in the Twenty-Second International Congress of the Pontifical Council for Health Pastoral Care

November 17, 2007

Your Eminence,
Venerable Brothers in the Episcopate and in the Priesthood,
Dear Brothers and Sisters,

I am pleased to meet you on the occasion of this International Conference organized by the Pontifical Council for Health Pastoral Care. I address my cordial greeting to each of you, which goes in the first place to Cardinal Javier Lozano Barragán, with sentiments of gratitude for the kind expressions he addressed to me in the name of all. With him I greet the Secretary and the other members of the Pontifical Council, the distinguished persons present and all those who are taking part in this meeting to reflect together on the theme of the pastoral care of the aged sick. This is a central aspect of pastoral health care today, which, thanks to the increase in life span, concerns an ever greater population who have multiple needs, but at the same time indubitable human and spiritual resources.

If it is true that human life in every phase is worthy of the maximum respect, in some sense it is even more so when it is marked by age and sickness. Old age constitutes the last step of our earthly pilgrimage, which has distinct phases, each with its own lights and shadows. One may ask: does a human being who moves toward a rather precarious condition due to age and sickness still have a reason to exist? Why continue to defend life when the challenge of illness becomes dramatic, and why not instead accept euthanasia as a liberation? Is it possible to live illness as a human experience to accept with patience and courage?

The person called to accompany the aged sick must confront these questions, especially when there seems to be no possibility of healing. Today's efficiency mentality often tends to marginalize our suffering brothers and sisters, as if they were only a "weight" and "a problem" for society. The person with a sense of human dignity knows that they are to respect and sustain them while they face serious difficulties linked to their condition. Indeed, recourse to the use of palliative care when necessary is correct, which, even though it cannot heal, can relieve the pain caused by illness.

Alongside the indispensable clinical treatment, however, it is always necessary to show a concrete capacity to love, because the sick need understanding, comfort and constant encouragement and accompaniment. The elderly in particular must be helped to travel in a mindful and human way on the last stretch of earthly existence in order to prepare serenely for death, which—we Christians know—is a passage toward the embrace of the Heavenly Father, full of tenderness and mercy.

I would like to add that this necessary pastoral solicitude for the aged sick cannot fail to involve families, too. Generally, it is best to do what is possible so that the families themselves accept them and assume the duty with thankful affection, so that the aged sick can pass the final period of their life in their home and prepare for death in a warm family environment. Even when it would become necessary to be admitted to a health-care structure, it is important that the patient's bonds with his loved ones and with his own environment are not broken. In the most difficult moments of sickness, sustained by pastoral care, the patient is to be encouraged to find the strength to face his hard trial in prayer and with the comfort of the sacraments. He is to be surrounded by brethren in the faith who are ready to listen and to share his sentiments. Truly, this is the true objective of "pastoral" care for the aged, especially when they are sick, and more so if gravely sick.

On many occasions, my Venerable Predecessor John Paul II, who especially during his sickness offered an exemplary testimony of faith and courage, exhorted scientists and doctors to undertake research to prevent and treat illnesses linked to old age without ever ceding to the temptation to have recourse to practices that shorten the life of the aged and sick, practices that would turn out to be, in fact, forms of euthanasia. May scientists, research-ers, doctors, nurses, as well as politicians, administrative and pastoral workers never forget that the temptation of euthanasia appears as "one of the more alarming symptoms of the 'culture of death,' which is advancing above all in prosperous societies" (*Evangelium Vitae*, no. 64). Man's life is a gift of God that we are all called to guard always. This duty also belongs to health-care workers, whose specific mission is to be "ministers of life" in all its phases, particularly in those marked by fragility connected with infirmity. A general commitment is needed so that human life is respected, not only in Catholic hospitals, but in every treatment facility.

It is faith in Christ that enlightens Christians regarding sickness and the condition of the aged person, as in every other event and phase of existence. Jesus, dying on the Cross, gave human suffering a transcendent value and meaning. Faced with suffering and sickness, believers are invited to remain calm because nothing, not even death, can separate us from the love of Christ. In him and with him it is possible to face and overcome every physical and spiritual trial and to experience, exactly in the moment of greatest weakness, the fruits of Redemption. The Risen Lord manifests himself to those who believe in him as the *Living One* who transforms human existence, giving even sickness and death a salvific sense.

Dear brothers and sisters, while I invoke upon each one of you and your daily work the maternal protection of Mary, *Salus infirmorum*, and of the Saints who have spent their lives at the service of the sick, I exhort you to always work to spread the "Gospel of life." With these sentiments, I warmly impart the Apostolic Blessing, willingly extending it to your loved ones, co-workers and particularly to the aged patients.

Address to the Bishops of
Kenya on Their *Ad Limina* Visit

November 19, 2007

My dear Brother Bishops,

It is with great joy that I welcome you, the Bishops of Kenya, on your quin-quennial visit to the tombs of the Apostles Peter and Paul, a visit which serves to strengthen the bonds of fraternal love and communion between us. I thank Archbishop Njue for his kind words addressed to me on your behalf. Your solicitude for one another and for the people entrusted to your care, your love of the Lord and your devotion to the Successor of Peter are for me a source of profound joy and thanksgiving.

Every Bishop has a particular responsibility to build up the unity of his flock, mindful of our Lord's prayer "that they may be one, even as you, Father, are in me and I in you" (Jn 17:21). United in one faith, sharing one Baptism and believing in the one Lord, (cf. Eph 4:5), the Church is one throughout the world, yet at the same time she is marked by a rich diversity of traditions and cultural expressions. In Africa, the color and vibrancy with which the faithful manifest their religious sentiments has added a new dimension to the rich tapestry of Christian culture worldwide, while at the same time your people's strong attachment to the traditional values associated with family life can help to express the shared faith which is at the heart of the mystery of the Church's unity (cf. *Ecclesia in Africa*, no. 63). Christ himself is the source and guarantee of our unity since he has overcome all forms of division through his death on the Cross and has reconciled us to God in the one body (cf. Eph 2:14). I thank you, dear Brothers, for preaching the love of Christ and exhorting your people to tolerance, respect and love of their brothers and sisters and of all persons. In this way you exercise the prophetic ministry that the Lord has entrusted to the Church, and in particular to the Successors of the Apostles (cf. *Pastores Gregis*, no. 26).

Indeed it is the Bishops who, as ministers and signs of communion in Christ, are pre-eminently called to make manifest the unity of his Church. The collegial nature of the episcopal ministry traces its origins to the Twelve Apostles, called together by Christ and given the task of proclaiming the Gospel and making disciples of all nations. Their pastoral mission is continued by the members of the episcopal College in such a way that "whoever listens to them is listening to Christ" (*Lumen Gentium*, no. 20). I urge you to continue your fraternal cooperation with one another in the spirit of the community of Christ's disciples, united in your love for him and in the Gospel that you proclaim. While each of you has an individual contribution to make to the common collegial voice of the Church in your country, it is important to ensure that this variety of perspectives always serves to enrich the unity of the Body of Christ, just as the unity of the Twelve was deepened and strengthened by the different gifts of the Apostles themselves. Your dedication to working together on issues of ecclesial and social concern will bring great fruit for the life of the Church in Kenya and for the effectiveness of your episcopal ministry.

Within each diocese, the vibrancy and harmony of the presbyterate offers a clear sign of the vitality of the local Church. Structures of consultation and participation are necessary, but can be ineffective if the proper spirit is missing. As Bishops, we must constantly strive to build up the sense of community among our priests, united in the love of Christ and in their sacramental ministry. Life can be difficult for priests today. They can feel isolated or alone and overwhelmed by their pastoral responsibilities. We must be close to them and encourage them, in the first place, to remain firmly rooted in prayer, because only those who are themselves nourished are able to nourish others in turn. Let them drink deeply from the wells of Sacred Scripture and from the daily and reverent celebration of the most holy Eucharist. Let them give themselves generously to praying the Liturgy of the Hours, a prayer that is made "in communion with all who pray throughout history, a prayer in communion with Jesus Christ" (Address to the Priests and Permanent Deacons of Bavaria, September 14, 2006). By praying in this way they include and represent others who may lack the time or energy or capacity to pray, and thus the power of prayer, the presence of Jesus Christ, renews their priesthood and flows out into the world (cf. ibid.). Help your priests in this way to grow in solidarity with one another, with their people, and with you, as your consecrated co-workers. Respectful dialogue and closeness between Bishop and priests not only builds up the local Church but also edifies the entire community. Indeed, visible unity among the spiritual leaders can be a powerful antidote against division within the wider family of God's people.

A key focus of unity in a community is the institution of marriage and family life, which the people of Africa hold in particular esteem. The devoted love of Christian married couples is a blessing for your country, expressing sacramentally the indissoluble covenant between Christ and his Church. This precious treasure must be guarded at all costs. All too often, the ills besetting some parts of African society, such as promiscuity, polygamy and the spread of sexually transmitted diseases, can be directly related to disordered notions of marriage and family life. For this reason it is important to assist parents in teaching their children how to live out a Christian vision of marriage, conceived as an indissoluble union between one man and one woman, essentially equal in their humanity (cf. *Ecclesia in Africa*, no. 82) and open to the generation of new life.

While this understanding of Christian family life finds a deep resonance in Africa, it is a matter of great concern that the globalized secular culture is exerting an increasing influence on local communities as a result of campaigns by agencies promoting abortion. This direct destruction of an innocent human life can never be justified, however difficult the circumstances that may lead some to consider taking such a grave step. When you preach the Gospel of Life, remind your people that the right to life of every innocent human being, born or unborn, is absolute and applies equally to all people with no exception whatsoever. This equality "is the basis of all authentic social relationships which, to be truly such, can only be founded on truth and justice" (*Evangelium Vitae*, no. 57). The Catholic community must offer support to those women who may find it difficult to accept a child, above all when they are isolated from their family and friends. Likewise, the community should be open to welcome back all who repent of having participated in the grave sin of abortion, and should guide them with pastoral charity to accept the grace of forgiveness, the need for penance, and the joy of entering once more into the new life of Christ.

The Church in Kenya is well known for the fine contribution made by its educational institutions in forming generations of young people in sound ethical principles and in opening their minds to engage in peaceful and respectful dialogue with members of other social or religious groups. At a time when a secularist and relativist mentality is increasingly asserting itself through global means of social communication, it is all the more essential that you continue to promote the quality and the Catholic identity of your schools, universities and seminaries. Take the steps necessary in order to affirm and clarify their proper institutional status. Society greatly benefits from educated Catholics who know and practice the Church's social doctrine. Today there is a particular need for highly trained professionals and persons of integrity in the area of medicine, where advances in technology continue to raise serious moral questions. Ecumenical and inter-religious dialogue likewise present major challenges that can only be addressed adequately on the basis of sound catechesis in the principles of Catholic doctrine, as expounded in the *Catechism of the Catholic Church*. I know that you will continue to be vigilant over the quality and content of teaching that is offered to young people through the Church's educational institutions, so that the light of Christ's truth may shine ever more brightly over the land and the people of Kenya.

My dear Brother Bishops, as you guide your people into the unity for which Christ prayed, do so with ardent charity and firm authority, unfailing in patience and in teaching (cf. 2 Tim 4:2). Please convey my affectionate greetings and my prayerful encouragement to your beloved people, and to all those who are active in the service of the Church, through prayer or in parishes and mission stations, in education, humanitarian activity and health care. To each of you and to those entrusted to your pastoral care, I cordially impart my Apostolic Blessing.

PASTORAL VISIT TO ST. JOHN THE BAPTIST HOSPITAL IN ROME

Homily at Mass

December 2, 2007

Dear Brothers and Sisters,

"Let us go to the house of the Lord!" These words that we repeated in the response of the Responsorial Psalm clearly express the feelings that fill our hearts today, the First Sunday of Advent. The reason why we can go ahead

joyfully, as the Apostle Paul has exhorted us, lies in the fact that our salvation is now at hand. The Lord is coming! With this knowledge we set out on the journey of Advent, preparing ourselves to celebrate with faith the extraordinary event of the Lord's birth. In the coming weeks, day after day the liturgy will offer for our reflection Old Testament texts that recall the lively, constant desire that kept alive in the Jewish people the expectation of the Messiah's coming. Watchful in prayer, let us too seek to prepare our hearts to receive the Lord, who will come to show us his mercy and give us his salvation.

Precisely during this time of waiting, Advent is a season of hope, and it is to Christian hope that I wished to dedicate my second Encyclical, officially presented the day before yesterday; it begins with the words St. Paul addressed to the Christians of Rome: "*Spe salvi facti sumus*—in hope we were saved" (Rom 8:24). In the Encyclical, I write among other things that "we need the greater and lesser hopes that keep us going day by day. But these are not enough without the great hope, which must surpass everything else. This great hope can only be God, who encompasses the whole of reality and who can bestow upon us what we, by ourselves, cannot attain" (no. 31). May the certainty that God alone can be our steadfast hope enliven us all, gathered here this morning in this house where illness is combated with the support of solidarity. And I would like to make the most of my Visit to your hospital, managed by the Association of the Italian Knights of the Sovereign Military Order of Malta, to present the Encyclical in spirit to the Christian community of Rome, and especially to those who, like you, are in direct contact with suffering and illness, for precisely through suffering like the sick do we have need of hope, the certainty that God exists and does not abandon us, that he lovingly takes us by the hand and accompanies us. It is a text I invite you to examine deeply, to find in it the reasons for this "trustworthy hope, by virtue of which we can face our present: the present, even if it is arduous" (no. 1).

Dear brothers and sisters, "May the God of hope who fills us with all joy and peace in faith through the power of the Holy Spirit be with you all!" With this wish which the priest addresses to the assembly at the beginning of Holy Mass, I offer you my cordial greeting. I greet first of all the Cardinal Vicar, Camillo Ruini, and Cardinal Pio Laghi, Patron of the Sovereign Military Order of Malta, the Prelates and priests present and the chaplains and Sisters who serve here. I greet with respect His Most Eminent Highness Fra Andrew Bertie, Prince and Grand Master of the Sovereign Military Order of Malta, whom I thank for the sentiments he has expressed on behalf of the management, the administrative, health-care and nursing staffs and all those who in their various capacities work in this hospital. I extend my greeting to the distinguished Authorities, with a special thought for the Health-care

Director as well as the Patients' Representative, whom I thank for the words they addressed to me at the beginning of the Celebration.

But my most affectionate greeting is for you, dear sick people, and for your relatives who share your anxieties and hopes. The Pope is spiritually close to you and assures you of his daily prayers; he invites you to find support and comfort in Jesus and never to lose trust. The Advent liturgy will repeat to us throughout the coming weeks not to tire of calling on him; it will exhort us to go forth to meet him, knowing that he himself comes constantly to visit us. In trial and in sickness, God mysteriously visits us, and if we abandon ourselves to his will, we can experience the power of his love. Precisely because they are inhabited by people troubled by suffering, hospitals and clinics can become privileged places to witness to Christian love, which nourishes hope and inspires resolutions of fraternal solidarity. In the Collect we prayed: "O God, inspire in us the determination to meet with good works your Christ who comes." Yes! Let us open our hearts to every person, especially if he or she is in difficulty, because by doing good to those in need we prepare to welcome Jesus, who, in them, comes to visit us.

Dear brothers and sisters, this is what you seek to do in this hospital, where everyone's concern focuses on the professional and loving acceptance of the patients, the preservation of their dignity and the commitment to improve the quality of their life. Down the centuries the Church has made herself particularly "close" to the suffering. Your praiseworthy Sovereign Military Order of Malta has chosen to share in this spirit: from the very outset it was dedicated to the assistance of pilgrims in the Holy Land with a Hospice-Infirmary. While it pursued its aim of the defense of Christianity, the Sovereign Military Order of Malta spared no effort in treating the sick, especially the poor and the outcast. This hospital is also a testimony of this fraternal love. Having come into existence in the 1970s, it has today become a stronghold with a high standard of technology and a home of solidarity, where side by side with the health-care staff numerous volunteers work with generous dedication.

Dear Knights of the Sovereign Military Order of Malta, dear doctors, nurses and all who work here, you are all called to carry out an important service to the sick and to society, a service that demands self-denial and a spirit of sacrifice. In every sick person, whoever he or she may be, may you be able to recognize and serve Christ himself; make them perceive with your acts and words the signs of his merciful love. To carry out this "mission" well, endeavor, as St. Paul instructs us in the Second Reading, to "put on the armor of light" (Rom 13:12), which consists in the Word of God, the gifts of the Spirit, the grace of the Sacraments, the theological and cardinal virtues; fight evil and abandon sin that darkens our life. At the beginning of a new liturgical year, let us renew our good resolutions of evangelical life. "It is full time now for you to wake from sleep" (Rom 13:11), the Apostle urges; it is time to convert, to throw off the lethargy of sin, to prepare ourselves confidently to welcome "the Lord who comes." It is for this reason that Advent is a season of prayer and watchful waiting.

The Gospel passage that has just been proclaimed exhorts us to be "watchful," which is among other things the key word of the whole of this liturgical period: "Watch, therefore, for you do not know on what day your Lord is coming" (Mt 24:42). Jesus, who came among us at Christmas and will return in glory at the end of time, does not tire of visiting us continuously in everyday events. He asks us to be alert to perceive his presence, his advent, and recommends that we watch and wait for him since his coming is not programmed or foretold but will be sudden and unexpected. Only those who are alert are not taken by surprise. He warns: may it not happen to you as in Noah's day, when men ate and drank heedlessly and were swept away unprepared by the flood (cf. Mt 24:37-38). What does the Lord want to make us understand with this warning, other than we must not let ourselves be absorbed by material realities and concerns to the point of being ensnared by them? We must live in the eyes of the Lord with the conviction that he can make himself present. If we live in this way, the world will become better.

"Watch, therefore." Let us listen to Jesus' Gospel invitation and prepare ourselves to relive with faith the mystery of the Redeemer's birth, which filled all the world with joy; let us prepare ourselves to welcome the Lord in his constant coming to us in the events of life, in joy and in pain, in health and in sickness; let us prepare ourselves to meet him at his definitive coming. His nearness is always a source of peace, and if suffering, a legacy of human nature, sometimes becomes unbearable, with the Savior's advent "suffering—without ceasing to be suffering—becomes, despite everything, a hymn of praise" (*Spe Salvi*, no. 37). Comforted by these words, let us continue the Eucharistic Celebration, invoking upon the sick, their relatives and all who work in this hospital and in the entire Order of the Knights of Malta the motherly protection of Mary, the Virgin of waiting and hope, as also of the joy which already exists in this world, because when we feel the closeness of the living Christ, there the remedy to suffering and his joy is already present. Amen.

Letter to the President of the Brazilian Episcopal Conference on the Occasion of the Fraternity Campaign of 2008*

December 8, 2007

To my Venerable Brother in the Episcopate,
The Most Reverend Gerald Lyrio Rocł ı,
President of the National Conference (Brazilian Bishops,
Archbishop of Mariana (MG),

At the start of the spiritual journey of Lent, the road to the Pasch of the Lord's Resurrection, I wish once again to join in the Fraternity Campaign for 2008, which has as its theme *"Fraternity and Defense of Life"* and as its motto, *"Therefore choose life."* It is a time of conversion for all Christians in the sense of seeking to regain an even greater fidelity to God the creator and giver of life.

In his Encyclical *Evangelium Vitae*, my venerable predecessor, Pope John Paul II, revealed the mentality of individualism and hedonism that, with a distorted concept of science, has been the cause of new violations of life, particularly abortion and euthanasia. We must certainly combat all threats against life; the Second Vatican Council, in its condemnation of everything that is opposed to life or violates the integrity of the human person and its dignity, reminded us that these attitudes "do more harm to those who practice them than those who suffer from the injury" since they greatly offend the honor due to the Creator (cfr. GS, no. 27).

For this reason, in my *Inaugural Discourse at the Fifth General Conference of the Episcopate of Latin America and the Caribbean*, I wanted to recall that the paths traced by a culture without God and without His commandments, or even opposed to God, end up being "a culture opposed to the human being and opposed to the good of the people of Latin America" (no. 4).

The final document from Aparecida shows us that the encounter with Christ is the starting point for negating these paths of death and for choosing life; but it is also the point where we begin to recognize fully the sacramentality of life and of the dignity of the human person (no. 356). In inaugurating the Fraternity Campaign for this year, I express anew the wish that the various bodies of the civil society will desire to support the will of the people,

---

*   This text is an unofficial translation of the Italian.

the majority of whom reject all forms contrary to the ethical requirements of justice and respect for human life from its beginning to its natural end.

With these good wishes, I invoke the Lord's protection, that his loving hand be extended over all of Brazil, and that the new life in Christ may fully engage humanity in its personal, familial, social and cultural dimensions, spreading His gifts of peace and prosperity, and reawakening in every heart the sentiments of fraternity and lively cooperation.

With a special Apostolic Blessing.

Message for the World Day of Peace

[January 1, 2008]

The Human Family, a Community of Peace

December 8, 2007

1. At the beginning of a New Year, I wish to send my fervent good wishes for peace, together with a heartfelt message of hope to men and women throughout the world. I do so by offering for our common reflection the theme which I have placed at the beginning of this message. It is one which I consider particularly important: *the human family, a community of peace*. The first form of communion between persons is that born of the love of a man and a woman who decide to enter a stable union in order to build together *a new family*. But the peoples of the earth, too, are called to build relationships of solidarity and cooperation among themselves, as befits members of the one *human family*: "All peoples"—as the Second Vatican Council declared—"are one community and have one origin, because God caused the whole human race to dwell on the face of the earth (cf. Acts 17:26); they also have one final end, God" (*Nostra Aetate*, no. 1).

The family, society and peace

2. The natural family, as an intimate communion of life and love, based on marriage between a man and a woman (cf. *Gaudium et Spes*, no. 48), constitutes "the *primary place of 'humanization'* for the person and society" (*Christifideles Laici*, no. 40), and a "*cradle of life and love*" (*Christifideles Laici*, no. 40). The family is therefore rightly defined as the first natural society, "*a divine institution that stands at the foundation of life of the human person as the prototype of every social order*" (Pontifical Council for Justice and Peace, *Compendium of the Social Doctrine of the Church*, no. 211).

3. Indeed, in a healthy family life we experience some of the fundamental elements of peace: justice and love between brothers and sisters, the role of authority expressed by parents, loving concern for the members who are weaker because of youth, sickness or old age, mutual help in the necessities of life, readiness to accept others and, if necessary, to forgive them. For this reason, the family is *the first and indispensable teacher of peace*. It is no wonder, therefore, that violence, if perpetrated in the family, is seen as particularly intolerable. Consequently, when it is said that the family is "the primary living cell of society" (*Apostolicam Actuositatem*, no. 11), something essential is being stated. The family is the foundation of society for this reason too: *because it enables its members in decisive ways to experience peace*. It follows that the human community cannot do without the service provided by the family. Where can young people gradually learn to savor the genuine "taste" of peace better than in the original "nest" which nature prepares for them? *The language of the family is a language of peace*; we must always draw from it, lest we lose the "vocabulary" of peace. In the inflation of its speech, society cannot cease to refer to that "grammar" which all children learn from the looks and the actions of their mothers and fathers, even before they learn from their words.

4. The family, since it has the duty of educating its members, *is the subject of specific rights*. The *Universal Declaration of Human Rights*, which represents a landmark of *juridic civilization of truly universal value*, states that "the family is the natural and fundamental group unit of society and is entitled to protection by society and the State" (Art. 16/3). For its part, the Holy See sought to acknowledge a special *juridic dignity* proper to the family by publishing the *Charter of the Rights of the Family*. In its Preamble we read: "the rights of the person, even if they are expressed as rights of the individual, have a fundamental social dimension which finds an innate and vital expression in the family" (Holy See, *Charter of the Rights of the Family*, November 24, 1983, Preamble, A). The rights set forth in the *Charter* are an expression and explicitation of the natural law written on the heart of the human being and made known to him by reason. The denial or even the restriction of the rights of the family, by obscuring the truth about man, *threatens the very foundations of peace*.

5. Consequently, whoever, even unknowingly, circumvents the institution of the family undermines peace in the entire community, national and international, since he weakens what is in effect *the primary agency of peace*. This point merits special reflection: everything that serves to weaken the family based on the marriage of a man and a woman, everything that directly or indirectly stands in the way of its openness to the responsible acceptance of

a new life, everything that obstructs its right to be primarily responsible for the education of its children, constitutes an objective obstacle on the road to peace. The family needs to have a home, employment and a just recognition of the domestic activity of parents, the possibility of schooling for children, and basic health care for all. When society and public policy are not committed to assisting the family in these areas, they deprive themselves of an essential resource in the service of peace. The social communications media, in particular, because of their educational potential, have a special responsibility for promoting respect for the family, making clear its expectations and rights, and presenting all its beauty.

Humanity is one great family

6. The social community, if it is to live in peace, is also called to draw inspiration from the values on which the family community is based. This is as true for local communities as it is for national communities; it is also true for the international community itself, for the human family which dwells *in that common house which is the earth*. Here, however, we cannot forget that the family comes into being from the responsible and definitive "yes" of a man and a women, and it continues to live from the conscious "yes" of the children who gradually join it. The family community, in order to prosper, needs the generous consent of all its members. This realization also needs to become a shared conviction on the part of all those called to form the *common human family*. We need to say our own "yes" to this vocation which God has inscribed in our very nature. We do not live alongside one another purely by chance; all of us are progressing along *a common path as men and women, and thus as brothers and sisters*. Consequently, it is essential that we should all be committed to living our lives in an attitude of responsibility before God, acknowledging him as the deepest source of our own existence and that of others. By going back to this supreme principle we are able to perceive the unconditional worth of each human being, and thus to lay the premises for building a humanity at peace. Without this transcendent foundation society is a mere aggregation of neighbors, not a community of brothers and sisters called to form one great family.

The family, the human community and the environment

7. The family needs a home, a fit environment in which to develop its proper relationships. *For the human family, this home is the earth*, the environment that God the Creator has given us to inhabit with creativity and responsibility. We need to care for the environment: it has been entrusted to men and women to be protected and cultivated with responsible freedom, with the good of all as a constant guiding criterion. Human beings, obviously, are

of supreme worth vis-à-vis creation as a whole. Respecting the environment does not mean considering material or animal nature more important than man. Rather, it means not selfishly considering nature to be at the complete disposal of our own interests, for future generations also have the right to reap its benefits and to exhibit toward nature the same responsible freedom that we claim for ourselves. Nor must we overlook the poor, who are excluded in many cases from the goods of creation destined for all. Humanity today is rightly concerned about the ecological balance of tomorrow. It is important for assessments in this regard to be carried out prudently, in dialogue with experts and people of wisdom, uninhibited by ideological pressure to draw hasty conclusions, and above all with the aim of reaching agreement on a model of sustainable development capable of ensuring the well-being of all while respecting environmental balances. If the protection of the environment involves costs, they should be justly distributed, taking due account of the different levels of development of various countries and the need for solidarity with future generations. Prudence does not mean failing to accept responsibilities and postponing decisions; it means being committed to making joint decisions after pondering responsibly the road to be taken, decisions aimed at strengthening that covenant between human beings and the environment, which should mirror the creative love of God, from whom we come and toward whom we are journeying.

8. In this regard, it is essential to "sense" that the earth is "our common home" and, in our stewardship and service to all, to choose the path of dialogue rather than the path of unilateral decisions. Further international agencies may need to be established in order to confront together the stewardship of this "home" of ours; more important, however, is the need for ever greater conviction about the need for responsible cooperation. The problems looming on the horizon are complex and time is short. In order to face this situation effectively, there is a need to act in harmony. One area where there is a particular need to intensify dialogue between nations is that of the *stewardship of the earth's energy resources*. The technologically advanced countries are facing two pressing needs in this regard: on the one hand, to reassess the high levels of consumption due to the present model of development, and on the other hand to invest sufficient resources in the search for alternative sources of energy and for greater energy efficiency. The emerging counties are hungry for energy, but at times this hunger is met in a way harmful to poor countries which, due to their insufficient infrastructures, including their technological infrastructures, are forced to undersell the energy resources they do possess. At times, their very political freedom is compromised by forms of protectorate or, in any case, by forms of conditioning which appear clearly humiliating.

Family, human community and economy

9. An essential condition for peace within individual families is that they should be built upon the solid foundation of shared spiritual and ethical values. Yet it must be added that the family experiences authentic peace when no one lacks what is needed, and when the family patrimony—the fruit of the labor of some, the savings of others, and the active cooperation of all—is well-managed in a spirit of solidarity, without extravagance and without waste. The peace of the family, then, requires an *openness to a transcendent patrimony of values*, and at the same time a concern for the prudent management of both material goods and inter-personal relationships. The failure of the latter results in the breakdown of reciprocal trust in the face of the uncertainty threatening the future of the nuclear family.

10. Something similar must be said for that other family which is humanity as a whole. The human family, which today is increasingly unified as a result of globalization, also needs, in addition to a foundation of shared values, an economy capable of responding effectively to the requirements of a common good which is now planetary in scope. Here too, a comparison with the natural family proves helpful. Honest and straightforward relationships need to be promoted between individual persons and between peoples, thus enabling everyone to cooperate on a just and equal footing. Efforts must also be made to ensure a *prudent use of resources* and an *equitable distribution of wealth*. In particular, the aid given to poor countries must be guided by sound economic principles, avoiding forms of waste associated principally with the maintenance of expensive bureaucracies. Due account must also be taken of the moral obligation to ensure that the economy is not governed solely by the ruthless laws of instant profit, which can prove inhumane.

The family, the human community and the moral law

11. A family lives in peace if all its members *submit to a common standard*: this is what prevents selfish individualism and brings individuals together, fostering their harmonious coexistence and giving direction to their work. This principle, obvious as it is, *also holds true for wider communities*: from local and national communities to the international community itself. For the sake of peace, a common law is needed, one which would foster true freedom rather than blind caprice, and protect the weak from oppression by the strong. The family of peoples experiences many cases of arbitrary conduct, both within individual States and in the relations of States among themselves. In many situations the weak must bow not to the demands of justice, but to the naked power of those stronger than themselves. It bears repeating: power must always be disciplined by law, and this applies also to relations between sovereign States.

12. The Church has often spoken on the subject of the nature and function of law: the *juridic norm*, which regulates relationships between individuals, disciplines external conduct and establishes penalties for offenders, has as its criterion the *moral norm* grounded in nature itself. Human reason is capable of discerning this moral norm, at least in its fundamental requirements, and thus ascending to the creative reason of God which is at the origin of all things. The moral norm must be the rule for decisions of conscience and the guide for all human behavior. Do juridic norms exist for relationships between the nations which make up the human family? And if they exist, are they operative? The answer is: yes, such norms exist, but to ensure that they are truly operative *it is necessary to go back to the natural moral norm as the basis of the juridic norm*; otherwise the latter constantly remains at the mercy of a fragile and provisional consensus.

13. Knowledge of the natural moral norm is not inaccessible to those who, in reflecting on themselves and their destiny, strive to understand the inner logic of the deepest inclinations present in their being. Albeit not without hesitation and doubt, they are capable of discovering, at least in its essential lines, *this common moral law* which, over and above cultural differences, enables human beings to come to a common understanding regarding the most important aspects of good and evil, justice and injustice. It is essential to go back to this fundamental law, committing our finest intellectual energies to this quest, and not letting ourselves be discouraged by mistakes and misunderstandings. Values grounded in the natural law are indeed present, albeit in a fragmentary and not always consistent way, in international accords, in universally recognized forms of authority, in the principles of humanitarian law incorporated in the legislation of individual States or the statutes of international bodies. *Mankind is not "lawless."* All the same, there is an urgent need to persevere in dialogue about these issues and to encourage the legislation of individual States to converge toward a recognition of fundamental human rights. The growth of a global juridic culture depends, for that matter, on a constant commitment to strengthen the profound human content of international norms, lest they be reduced to mere procedures, easily subject to manipulation for selfish or ideological reasons.

Overcoming conflicts and disarmament

14. Humanity today is unfortunately experiencing great division and sharp conflicts which *cast dark shadows on its future*. Vast areas of the world are caught up in situations of increasing tension, while the danger of an increase in the number of countries possessing nuclear weapons causes well-founded apprehension in every responsible person. Many civil wars are still being

fought in Africa, even though a number of countries there have made progress on the road to freedom and democracy. The Middle East is still a theatre of conflict and violence, which also affects neighboring nations and regions and risks drawing them into the spiral of violence. On a broader scale, one must acknowledge with regret the growing number of *States engaged in the arms race*: even some developing nations allot a significant portion of their scant domestic product to the purchase of weapons. The responsibility for this baneful commerce is not limited: the countries of the industrially developed world profit immensely from the sale of arms, while the ruling oligarchies in many poor countries wish to reinforce their stronghold by acquiring ever more sophisticated weaponry. In difficult times such as these, it is truly necessary for all persons of good will to come together to reach concrete agreements aimed at *an effective demilitarization*, especially in the area of nuclear arms. At a time when the process of nuclear non-proliferation is at a stand-still, I feel bound to entreat those in authority to resume with greater determination negotiations for a *progressive and mutually agreed dismantling of existing nuclear weapons*. In renewing this appeal, I know that I am echoing the desire of all those concerned for the future of humanity.

15. Sixty years ago the United Nations Organization solemnly issued the *Universal Declaration of Human Rights* (1948-2008). With that document the human family reacted against the horrors of the Second World War by acknowledging its own unity, based on the equal dignity of all men and women, and by putting respect for the fundamental rights of individuals and peoples at the center of human coexistence. This was a decisive step forward along the difficult and demanding path toward harmony and peace. This year also marks the *twenty-fifth anniversary* of the Holy See's adoption of the *Charter of the Rights of the Family* (1983-2008) and the *fortieth anniversary* of the celebration of the first *World Day of Peace* (1968-2008). Born of a providential intuition of Pope Paul VI and carried forward with great conviction by my beloved and venerable predecessor Pope John Paul II, the celebration of this Day of Peace has made it possible for the Church, over the course of the years, to present in these Messages an instructive body of teaching regarding this fundamental human good. In the light of these significant anniversaries, I invite every man and woman to have a more lively sense of belonging to the one human family, and to strive to make human coexistence increasingly reflect this conviction, which is essential for the establishment of true and lasting peace. I likewise invite believers to implore tirelessly from God the great gift of peace. Christians, for their part, know that they can trust in the intercession of Mary, who, as the Mother of the Son of God made flesh for the salvation of all humanity, is our common Mother.

To all my best wishes for a joyful New Year!

Address to the New Ambassador of the Republic of Seychelles to the Holy See

December 13, 2007

Your Excellency,

I am pleased to accept the Letters by which you are accredited Ambassador Extraordinary and Plenipotentiary of the Republic of Seychelles to the Holy See. I recall with pleasure your visit last year in the company of President James Alix Michel and I am most grateful for the greetings which you have brought from him. For my part, I gladly reciprocate with the assurance of my heartfelt prayers for your beloved country and all its people.

Seychelles has been blessed by Providence not only with great natural beauty and a sound economic life, but also with the social harmony and cohesiveness born of shared values and a strong commitment to solidarity in the pursuit of the common good. Your nation can indeed be grateful for its high standard of living, the fruit of the vision and sacrifice of many generations of citizens. Within the broader context of the African continent, Seychelles is well known for the quality and extent of its educational system and the breadth of its network of health services, available to all citizens. This impressive infrastructure offers great promise for the future of the nation, since it provides a firm foundation for continued economic growth and also, even more importantly, for the realization of the deepest hopes and aspirations of the younger generation.

In this regard, I am grateful for Your Excellency's reference to the importance of acknowledging and fostering those spiritual values, born of your nation's Christian roots, which have been decisive in shaping the present of Seychelles and which offer a sure foundation for its future. The Church in Seychelles is rightly proud of its contribution to the life of the nation, particularly through its historic commitment to the education of the young and to the training of the faithful in the virtues essential for integral human development and the building of a free, just and prosperous society. The Catholic community wishes to persevere in this commitment, and, in a spirit of sincerity and respectful cooperation, to work for the promotion of the common good through the preaching of the Gospel, the work of forming consciences in sound religious and moral principles, and the provision of charitable assistance to all, without regard to race or religion.

On this occasion I cannot fail to express my appreciation for the cordial relations existing between the Republic of Seychelles and the Holy See, marked as they are by reciprocal trust and ready collaboration. I likewise express my gratitude for the Government's efforts to support religious education at the primary level and to contribute to the building of new churches and educational structures. This commitment is a concrete sign of the relationship of trust and responsible cooperation which has long existed between the civil authorities and the Catholic community in the service of the young, who represent the hope of society. The nation has, in fact, made the needs of the young and their sound formation a notable priority, and this will surely bear rich fruit as the young men and women of today gradually take their place as the responsible citizens and leaders of tomorrow. I have great confidence in the youth of Seychelles, and through you I send all of them my affectionate greetings and my hearty encouragement to persevere in cultivating the virtues of honesty, fidelity and generous service to others which not only bring personal happiness and deep fulfillment, but also create a society of ever greater fraternity, freedom, justice and peace.

Among the greatest resources of Seychelles is its strong family life, grounded in the mutual love of husband and wife and strengthened by the gift of children. As the first cell of society, the family rightly looks to society for the encouragement it needs in its irreplaceable mission. I can only encourage the efforts being made by all people of good will, in every sphere of national life and policy, to "guarantee and foster the genuine identity of family life" (cf. *Compendium of the Social Doctrine of the Church*, no. 252), by promoting and defending this fundamental institution, acknowledging and meeting the challenges faced by young families, and supporting parents in their responsibilities as the first educators of their children. The future of the state depends in large part on families that are strong in their communion and stable in their commitment (cf. ibid., no. 213).

Your Excellency, as you now begin your mission on behalf of the Republic of Seychelles, please accept my personal good wishes for your demanding work. Know that the various offices of the Holy See are ready to assist and support you in the fulfillment of your duties. With these sentiments I cordially invoke upon you, your family, and all the beloved people of Seychelles God's richest blessings of joy and peace.

General Audience

December 19, 2007

Christ's birth

Dear Brothers and Sisters,

In these days, as we come gradually closer to the great Feast of Christmas, the liturgy impels us to intensify our preparation, placing at our disposal many biblical texts of the Old and New Testaments that encourage us to focus clearly on the meaning and value of this annual feast day. If, on the one hand, Christmas makes us commemorate the incredible miracle of the birth of the Only-Begotten Son of God from the Virgin Mary in the Bethlehem Grotto, on the other, it also urges us to wait, watching and praying, for our Redeemer himself, who on the last day "will come to judge the living and the dead." Perhaps we today, even we believers, really await the Judge, but we all expect justice. We see so much injustice in the world, in our little world, at home, in the neighborhood, but also in the great world of States and societies. And we expect justice to be done. Justice is an abstract concept: one does justice. We are waiting for one to come in concrete terms who can do justice. And in this sense we pray: Come, Lord Jesus Christ, as Judge, come in your own way. The Lord knows how to enter the world and create justice. Let us pray that the Lord, the Judge, will respond to us, that he will truly create justice in the world. We are waiting for justice but it cannot be merely the expression of a certain requirement with regard to others. Waiting for justice in the Christian sense means above all that we ourselves begin to live under the eyes of the Judge, in accordance with the criteria of the Judge; that we begin to live in his presence, doing justice in our own lives. Thus, by doing justice, putting ourselves in the Judge's presence, we wait for justice in reality. And this is the meaning of Advent, of vigilance. The watchfulness of Advent means living under the eyes of the Judge and thus preparing ourselves and the world for justice. In this way, therefore, living under the eyes of the God-Judge, we can open the world to the coming of his Son and predispose hearts to welcome "the Lord who comes." The Child whom the shepherds adored in a grotto on the night of Bethlehem about 2,000 years ago, never tires of visiting us in our daily lives while we journey on as pilgrims toward the Kingdom. In his expectation, therefore, the believer becomes an interpreter of the hopes of all humanity; humanity yearns for justice and thus, although often unconsciously, is waiting for God, waiting for salvation which God alone can give to us. For us Christians, this expectation is marked by assiduous prayer, as appears clearly in the particularly evocative series of prayers proposed to us during these days of the Christmas Novena, in Mass, in the Gospel acclamation and in the celebration of Vespers before the Canticle of the *Magnificat*.

Each one of the invocations that implores the coming of Wisdom, of the Sun of justice, of the God-with-us, contains a prayer addressed by the people to the One awaited so that he will hasten his coming. However, invoking the gift of the birth of the promised Savior also means committing ourselves to preparing his way, to having a worthy dwelling-place ready for him, not only in the area that surrounds us but especially within our souls. Letting ourselves be guided by the Evangelist John, let us seek in these days, therefore, to turn our minds and hearts to the eternal Word, to the *Logos*, to the Word that was made flesh, from whose fullness we have received grace upon grace (cf. Jn 1:14, 16). This faith in the *Logos* Creator, in the Word who created the world, in the One who came as a Child, this faith and its great hope unfortunately appear today far from the reality of life lived every day, publicly or privately. This truth seems too great. As for us, we fend for ourselves according to the possibilities we find, or at least this is how it seems. Yet, in this way the world becomes ever more chaotic and even violent; we see it every day. And the light of God, the light of Truth, is extinguished. Life becomes dark and lacks a compass.

Thus, how important it is that we really are believers and that as believers we strongly reaffirm, with our lives, the mystery of salvation that brings with it the celebration of Christ's Birth! In Bethlehem, the Light which brightens our lives was manifested to the world; the way that leads us to the fullness of our humanity was revealed to us. If people do not recognize that God was made man, what is the point of celebrating Christmas? The celebration becomes empty. We Christians must first reaffirm the truth about the Birth of Christ with deep and heartfelt conviction, in order to witness to all the awareness of an unprecedented gift which is not only a treasure for us but for everyone. From this stems the duty of evangelization which is, precisely, the communication of this *"eu-angelion,"* this "Good News." This was recently recalled in the Document of the Congregation for the Doctrine of the Faith entitled *Doctrinal Note on Some Aspects of Evangelization,* which I would like to submit to your reflection and your personal and community study (December 3, 2007).

Dear friends, in this preparation for Christmas, now at hand, the Church's prayer for the fulfillment of the hopes of peace, salvation and justice which the world today urgently needs becomes more intense. Let us ask God to grant that violence be overcome by the power of love, that opposition give way to reconciliation and that the desire to oppress be transformed into the desire for forgiveness, justice and peace. May the kind and loving good wishes that we exchange in these days reach all the contexts of our daily lives. May peace be in our hearts so that they are open to the action of God's grace. May peace dwell in families and may they spend Christmas united in front of the crib and the tree decorated with lights. May the message of solidarity and good will that comes from Christmas contribute to creating a deeper sensitivity to the old and new forms of poverty, to the common good, in which we are all called to participate. May all members of the family community, especially children, the elderly, the weakest, feel the warmth of this feast and may it extend subsequently to all the days in the year.

May Christmas be a feast of peace and joy for everyone: joy in the Birth of the Savior, the Prince of Peace. Like the shepherds, let us hasten toward

Bethlehem from this very moment. In the heart of the Holy Night, we too will be able to contemplate the Babe wrapped in swaddling clothes, lying in a manger, together with Mary and Joseph (cf. Lk 2:12, 16). Let us ask the Lord to open our hearts, so that we may enter into the mystery of his Birth. May Mary, who gave her virginal womb to the Word of God, whom as Mother she contemplated as a baby in her motherly arms and whom she continues to offer to everyone as the Redeemer of the world, help us make this Christmas an opportunity for growth in the knowledge and love of Christ. This is the wish that I express with affection to all of you who are present here, to your families and to all your loved ones.

Happy Christmas to you all!

Angelus

December 30, 2007

Dear Brothers and Sisters,

Today, we are celebrating the Feast of the Holy Family. As we follow the Gospels of Matthew and Luke, let us fix our gaze on Jesus, Mary and Joseph and adore the mystery of a God who chose to be born of a woman, the Blessed Virgin, and to enter this world in the way common to all humankind. By so doing he sanctified the reality of the family, filling it with divine grace and fully revealing its vocation and mission. The Second Vatican Council dedicated much attention to the family. Married partners, it said, must be witnesses of faith to each other and to their children (cf. *Lumen Gentium*, no. 35). The Christian family thus shares in the Church's prophetic vocation: with its way of living it "proclaims aloud both the present power of the Kingdom of God and the hope of the blessed life" (ibid.). Then, as my venerable Predecessor John Paul II tirelessly repeated, the good of the person and of society is closely connected to the "healthy state" of the family (cf. *Gaudium et Spes*, no. 47). The Church, therefore, is committed to defending and to fostering "the dignity and supremely sacred value of the married state" (ibid.). To this end, an important event is being held in Madrid this very day, whose participants I now address in Spanish.

I greet the participants in the Meeting for Families that is taking place in Madrid this Sunday, together with the Cardinals, Bishops and priests who have accompanied them. In contemplating the mystery of the Son of God who came into the world surrounded by the love of Mary and Joseph, I ask Christian families to experience the loving presence of the Lord in their lives. I likewise encourage them, drawing inspiration from Christ's love for humanity, to bear witness to the world of the beauty of human love, marriage and the family. Founded on the indissoluble union between a man and a woman, the family constitutes the privileged context in which human life is welcomed and protected from its beginning to its natural end. Thus, parents have the right and the fundamental obligation to raise their children in the faith and values which give dignity to human life. It is worthwhile working for the family and marriage because it is worthwhile working for the human being, God's most precious creature. I have a special word for children, so that they may love and pray for their fathers and mothers and their siblings; to young people, so that encouraged by their parents' love, they may follow generously their own vocation to marriage, priestly or religious life; to the elderly and the sick, so that they may find needed help and understanding. And you, dear spouses, may you always count on God's grace so that your love may be increasingly fruitful and faithful every day. I entrust the outcome of this celebration to the hands of Mary, who *"with her 'yes' she opened the door of our world to God"* (*Spe Salvi*, no. 49). Many thanks and happy holidays!

Let us now turn to the Blessed Virgin, praying for the good of the family and for all the families in the world.

After the Angelus:*

I greet you, dear French-speaking pilgrims who have come for the *Angelus*. On this Sunday when we celebrate the Holy Family, we pray most especially for the families of the world, asking the Lord to grant them the grace to live out their mission in the service of life, that they may be centers of sanctity for all their members. Happy holidays to you all! With my Apostolic Blessing.

I offer a warm welcome to the English-speaking visitors gathered for this *Angelus* prayer. Today, in the heart of the Christmas Season, the Church celebrates the Holy Family of Jesus, Mary and Joseph. May the mystery of God's love, made incarnate in the Child Jesus and reflected in the home of Mary and Joseph in Nazareth, dwell in your hearts and in your families throughout the coming year. Upon all of you I invoke an abundance of Christmas joy and peace!

I greet most heartily the German-speaking pilgrims and visitors on this Sunday within the Octave of Christmas on which the Church celebrates the Feast of the Holy Family. Let us ask Jesus Christ, the Son of God, who was born into a human family, that he watch over all parents and their children

---

*   The five paragraphs greeting French-, German-, Spanish-, Polish-, and Italian-speaking pilgrims are an unofficial translation of the Italian.

and strengthen the bonds of love and mutual care among them. I wish all of you a happy and peaceful Christmas season and a good passage from the old year to the new.

I warmly greet the Spanish-speaking pilgrims who have joined us in the Marian prayer of the *Angelus*. On this Feast of the Holy Family, I invite all of you to imitate the endearing shared life—full of love and respect—that characterizes the home of Nazareth where Jesus grew up, and that is a source of joy, hope and peace for all of humankind. Happy Sunday.

I greet the Poles. Today is the Sunday of the Holy Family. I ask God to strengthen Polish families strong in faith, hope and charity. May the conjugal love between men and women be the cradle of life and the foundation for the spiritual growth of future generations. May God bless you.

Finally, I greet with affection the Italian-speaking pilgrims, in particular the faithful of the Church of the Annunciation in Montesarchio, the altar servers from Breno along with their parents, the friends and volunteers of *Fraterna Domus*, the young people from Vertemate and the Little Choir of Angels from Moniego. I wish you all a peaceful Sunday and every good thing for the new year.

Homily at Mass on the Forty-First World Day of Peace

January 1, 2008

Dear Brothers and Sisters,

Today, we are beginning a new year and Christian hope takes us by the hand; let us begin it by invoking divine Blessings upon it and imploring, through the intercession of Mary, Mother of God, the gift of peace: for our families, for our cities, for the whole world. With this hope, I greet all of you present here, starting with the distinguished Ambassadors of the Diplomatic Corps accredited to the Holy See who have gathered at this celebration on the occasion of the World Day of Peace. I greet Cardinal Tarcisio Bertone, my Secretary of State, and Cardinal Renato Raffaele Martino and all members of the Pontifical Council for Justice and Peace. I am particularly grateful to them for their commitment to spread the Message for the World Day of Peace whose theme this year is: "The human family, a community of peace."

Peace. In the First Reading from the Book of Numbers we heard the invocation: "The Lord . . . give you peace" (6:26); may the Lord grant peace to each one of you, to your families and to the whole world. We all aspire to live in peace but true peace, the peace proclaimed by the Angels on Christmas night, is not merely a human triumph or the fruit of political agreements; it is first and foremost a divine gift to be ceaselessly implored, and at the same time a commitment to be carried forward patiently, always remaining docile to the Lord's commands. This year, in my Message for today's World Day of Peace, I wanted to highlight the close relationship that exists between the family and building peace in the world. The natural family, founded on the marriage of a man and a woman, is "a 'cradle of life and love'" and "the first and indispensable teacher of peace." For this very reason the family is "the primary 'agency' of peace," and "the denial or even the restriction of the rights of the family, by obscuring the truth about man, threatens the very foundations of peace" (cf. nos. 1-5). Since humanity is a "great family," if it wants to live in peace it cannot fail to draw inspiration from those values on which the family community is based and stands. The providential coincidence of various recurrences spur us this year to make an even greater effort to achieve peace in the world. Sixty years ago, in 1948, the General Assembly of the United Nations published the "Universal Declaration of Human Rights"; forty years ago my venerable Predecessor Paul VI celebrated the first World Day of Peace; this year, in addition, we will be commemorating the twenty-fifth anniversary of the Holy See's adoption of the "Charter of the Rights of the Family." "In the light of these significant anniversaries"—I am repeating here what I wrote precisely at the end of the Message—"I invite every man and woman to have a more lively sense of belonging to the one human family, and to strive to make human coexistence increasingly reflect this conviction, which is essential for the establishment of true and lasting peace" (no. 15).

Our thoughts now turn spontaneously to Our Lady, whom we invoke today as the Mother of God. It was Pope Paul VI who moved to January 1 the Feast of the Divine Motherhood of Mary, which was formerly celebrated on October 11. Indeed, even before the liturgical reform that followed the Second Vatican Council, the memorial of the circumcision of Jesus on the eighth day after his birth—as a sign of submission to the law, his official insertion in the Chosen People—used to be celebrated on the first day of the year and the Feast of the Name of Jesus was celebrated the following Sunday. We perceive a few traces of these celebrations in the Gospel passage that has just been proclaimed, in which St. Luke says that eight days after his birth the Child was circumcised and was given the name "Jesus," "the name given by the Angel before he was conceived in [his Mother's] . . . womb" (Lk 2:21). Today's feast, therefore, as well as being a particularly significant Marian feast, also preserves a strongly Christological content because, we might say, before the Mother, it concerns the Son, Jesus, true God and true Man.

The Apostle Paul refers to the mystery of the divine motherhood of Mary, the *Theotokos*, in his Letter to the Galatians. "When the time had fully come," he writes, "God sent forth his Son, born of woman, born under the law" (4:4). We find the mystery of the Incarnation of the Divine Word and the Divine Motherhood of Mary summed up in a few words: the Virgin's great privilege is precisely to be Mother of the Son who is God. The most logical and proper place for this Marian feast is therefore eight days after Christmas. Indeed, in the night of Bethlehem, when "she gave birth to her first-born son" (Lk 2:7), the prophecies concerning the Messiah were fulfilled. "The virgin shall be with child and bear a son," Isaiah had foretold (7:14); "Behold, you will conceive in your womb and bear a son," the Angel Gabriel said to Mary (Lk 1:31); and again, an Angel of the Lord, the Evangelist Matthew recounts, appeared to Joseph in a dream to reassure him and said: "Do not fear to take Mary for your wife, for that which is conceived in her is of the Holy Spirit; she will bear a son" (Mt 1:20-21).

The title "Mother of God," together with the title "Blessed Virgin," is the oldest on which all the other titles with which Our Lady was venerated are based, and it continues to be invoked from generation to generation in the East and in the West. A multitude of hymns and a wealth of prayers of the Christian tradition refer to the mystery of her divine motherhood, such as, for example, a Marian antiphon of the Christmas season, *Alma Redemptoris mater*, with which we pray in these words: "*Tu quae genuisti, natura mirante, tuum sanctum Genitorem, Virgo prius ac posterius*—You, in the wonder of all creation, have brought forth your Creator, Mother ever virgin." Dear brothers and sisters, let us today contemplate Mary, ever-virgin Mother of the Only-Begotten Son of the Father; let us learn from her to welcome the Child who was born for us in Bethlehem. If we recognize in the Child born of her the Eternal Son of God and accept him as our one Savior, we can be called and we really are children of God: sons in the Son. The Apostle writes: "God sent forth his Son, born of woman, born under the law, to redeem those who were under the law, so that we might receive adoption as sons" (Gal 4:4).

The Evangelist Luke repeats several times that Our Lady meditated silently on these extraordinary events in which God had involved her. We also heard this in the short Gospel passage that the Liturgy presents to us today. "Mary kept all these things, pondering them in her heart" (Lk 2:19). The Greek verb used, *sumbállousa*, literally means "piecing together" and makes us think of a great mystery to be discovered little by little. Although the Child lying in a manger looks like all children in the world, at the same time he is totally different: he is the Son of God, he is God, true God and true man. This mystery—the Incarnation of the Word and the divine Motherhood of Mary—is great and certainly far from easy to understand with the human mind alone.

Yet, by learning from Mary, we can understand with our hearts what our eyes and minds do not manage to perceive or contain on their own. Indeed, this is such a great gift that only through faith are we granted to accept it, while not entirely understanding it. And it is precisely on this journey of faith that Mary comes to meet us as our support and guide. She is mother because she brought forth Jesus in the flesh; she is mother because she adhered totally to the Father's will. St. Augustine wrote: "The divine motherhood would have been of no value to her had Christ not borne her in his heart, with a destiny more fortunate than the moment when she conceived him in the flesh" (*De Sancta Virginitate*, 3, 3). And in her heart Mary continued to treasure, to "piece together" the subsequent events of which she was to be a witness and protagonist, even to the death on the Cross and the Resurrection of her Son Jesus.

Dear brothers and sisters, it is only by pondering in the heart, in other words, by piecing together and finding unity in all we experience, that, following Mary, we can penetrate the mystery of a God who was made man out of love and who calls us to follow him on the path of love; a love to be expressed daily by generous service to the brethren. May the new year which we are confidently beginning today be a time in which to advance in that knowledge of the heart, which is the wisdom of saints. Let us pray, as we heard in the First Reading, that the Lord may "make his face to shine" upon us, "and be gracious" to us (cf. Nm 6:24-7) and bless us. We may be certain of it: if we never tire of seeking his Face, if we never give in to the temptation of discouragement and doubt, if also among the many difficulties we encounter we always remain anchored to him, we will experience the power of his love and his mercy. May the fragile Child who today the Virgin shows to the world make us peacemakers, witnesses of him, the Prince of Peace. Amen!

Angelus

January 1, 2008

Dear Brothers and Sisters,

We have begun a new year and I hope that it may be serene and profitable for all. I entrust it to the heavenly protection of Mary, whom we invoke in today's liturgy with her most ancient and important title, that of Mother of God. With her "yes" to the Angel on the day of the Annunciation, the Virgin conceived in her womb, through the work of the Holy Spirit, the Eternal Word, and on Christmas Night gave birth to him. At Bethlehem, in the fullness of time, Jesus was born of Mary; the Son of God was made man for our salvation, and the Virgin became the true Mother of God. This immense gift that Mary has received is not reserved to her alone, but is for us all. In her fruitful virginity, in fact, God has given "to men the goods of eternal salvation . . . , because by means of her we have received the Author of Life" (cf. Collect Prayer). Mary, therefore, after having given flesh to the Only-Begotten Son of God, became the mother of believers and of all humanity.

And it is precisely in the name of Mary, Mother of God and of humanity, that we have been celebrating for forty years on the first day of the year the World Day of Peace. The theme I selected for this year's celebration is: *"The human family, a community of peace."* The same love that builds and unites the family, the vital cell of society, supports the construction between the peoples of the earth of those relationships of solidarity and collaboration that are suitable to members of the one human family. Vatican Council II recalls this when it affirms that "all people comprise a single community, and have a single origin . . . . One also is their final goal: God" (cf. *Nostra Aetate*, no. 1). A strict bond therefore exists between families, society and peace. "Consequently, whoever, even unknowingly, circumvents the institution of the family," I note in the Message for this year's World Day of Peace, "undermines peace in the entire community, national and international, since he weakens what is in effect *the primary 'agency' of peace"* (no. 5). And then, "We do not live alongside one another purely by chance; all of us are progressing along a common path as men and women, and thus as brothers and sisters" (no. 6). It is thus truly important that each one assumes the appropriate responsibilities before God and recognizes in him the original source of his own existence and that of others. From this knowledge flows a duty to make humanity into a true community of peace, based on a "common law . . . , one which would foster true freedom . . . and protect the weak from oppression by the strong" (no. 11).

May Mary, Mother of the Prince of Peace, sustain the Church in her tireless work at the service of peace, and help the community of peoples, which celebrates in 2008 the sixtieth anniversary of the Universal Declaration of Human Rights, to travel a road of authentic solidarity and stable peace.

Address to the Members of the Regional Board of Lazio and the Civil Authorities of Rome

January 10, 2008

If we look at the reality of our situation, we cannot deny that we are facing a true and large-scale "educational emergency," as I emphasized last June 11, speaking to the Convention of the Diocese of Rome (ORE, June 20, 2007, 3). Indeed, it seems ever more difficult to convincingly propose solid certainties and criteria on which the new generations can build their lives. This is well known to both parents and teachers, who for this reason are all too often tempted to abdicate their own educational duties. Moreover, in the contemporary social context permeated by relativism as well as nihilism, they themselves have trouble in finding reliable reference points to sustain and guide them in their role as educators and in the way they lead their life as a whole.

Such an emergency, distinguished Representatives of the Boards of Rome and Lazio, cannot leave either the Church or your Boards indifferent. Clearly at stake, in fact, with the formation of individuals, are the actual foundations of coexistence and of society's future. The Diocese of Rome, for its part, is paying truly special attention to this difficult task being carried out in the different educational contexts, from the family and school to the parishes, associations and movements, oratories, cultural initiatives, sports and free time. In this context, I express deep gratitude to the Lazio Region for its support of oratories and other centers for children organized by parishes and Ecclesial Communities, as well as for its contribution to building new parish complexes in the areas of Lazio that are still without them. However, I wish above all to encourage a converging, widescale commitment in order to enable civil institutions, each in its own capacity, to redouble their efforts to face the various dimensions of the current educational emergency, constantly inspired by the guiding criterion of the centrality of the human person.

It is clear here that respect and support for the family founded on marriage are imperative. As I wrote in the recent Message for the World Day of Peace, "The natural family, as an intimate communion of life and love, based on marriage between a man and a woman, constitutes 'the *primary place of "humanization"* for the person and society,' and a '*cradle of life and love*'" (ORE, December 19/26, 2007, 8, no. 2). Unfortunately, we see every day how insistent and threatening are the attacks on marriage and the misunderstandings of this fundamental human and social reality. Thus, it is especially necessary that public administrations do not support these negative trends but, on the contrary, offer families convinced and concrete support, in the certainty that they are thereby acting for the common good.

Address to the Vatican's General Inspectorate for Public Security

January 11, 2008

This year, when I was drafting my Message for the World Day of Peace celebrated on January 1, I was thinking precisely of families. In this text, whose theme is *The human family, a community of peace,* I recalled that "the natural family, as an intimate communion of life and love, based on marriage between a man and a woman, constitutes the primary place for the 'humanization' of the person and society, the 'cradle of life and love.'" The family, therefore, is rightly defined as the first natural society, "a divine institution that stands at the foundation of life of the human person as the prototype of every social order" (no. 2).

Homily at Mass and Baptism of Children

January 13, 2008

Dear Brothers and Sisters,

Today's celebration is always a cause of special joy for me. Indeed, the administration of the Sacrament of Baptism on the Feast of the Baptism of the Lord is one of the most expressive moments of our faith, in which we can almost see the mystery of life through the signs of the liturgy. In the first place, there is human life. It is represented here in particular by these thirteen children who are the fruit of your love, dear parents, to whom I address my cordial greeting, which I extend to the godparents and the other relatives and friends present. Then comes the mystery of divine life which God gives to these little ones today through rebirth in water and the Holy Spirit. God is life, as some of the pictures that embellish this Sistine Chapel marvelously evoke.

Yet it does not seem out of place if we immediately juxtapose the experience of life with the opposite experience, that is, the reality of death. Sooner or later everything that begins on earth comes to its end, like the meadow grass that springs up in the morning and by evening has wilted. In Baptism, however, the tiny human being receives a new life, the life of grace, which enables him or her to enter into a personal relationship with the Creator forever, for the whole of eternity. Unfortunately, human beings are capable of extinguishing this new life with their sin, reducing themselves to being in a situation which Sacred Scripture describes as "second death." Whereas for other creatures who are not called to eternity, death means solely the end of existence on earth, in us sin creates an abyss in which we risk being engulfed forever unless the Father who is in Heaven stretches out his hand to us. This, dear brothers and sisters, is the mystery of Baptism: God desired to save us by going to the bottom of this abyss himself so that every person, even those who have fallen so low that they can no longer perceive Heaven, may find God's hand to cling to and rise from the darkness to see once again the light for which he or she was made. We all feel, we all inwardly comprehend that our existence is a desire for life which invokes fullness and salvation. This fullness is given to us in Baptism.

We have just heard the account of the Baptism of Jesus in the Jordan. It was a different Baptism from that which these babies are about to receive but is deeply connected with it. Basically, the whole mystery of Christ in the world can be summed up in this term: "baptism," which in Greek means "immersion." The Son of God, who from eternity shares the fullness of life with the Father and the Holy Spirit, was "immersed" in our reality as sinners to make us share in his own life: he was incarnate, he was born like us, he grew up like us and, on reaching adulthood, manifested his mission which began precisely with the "baptism of conversion" administered by John the Baptist. Jesus' first public act, as we have just heard, was to go down into the Jordan, mingling among repentant sinners, in order to receive this baptism. John was naturally reluctant to baptize him, but because this was the Father's will, Jesus insisted (cf. Mt 3:13-15).

Why, therefore, did the Father desire this? Was it because he had sent his Only-Begotten Son into the world as the Lamb to take upon himself the sins of the world (cf. Jn 1:29)? The Evangelist recounts that when Jesus emerged from the waters, the Holy Spirit descended upon him in the form of a dove, while the Father's voice from Heaven proclaimed him "my beloved Son in whom I am well pleased" (Mt 3:17). From that very moment, therefore, Jesus was revealed as the One who came to baptize humanity in the Holy Spirit: he came to give men and women life in abundance (cf. Jn 10:10), eternal life, which brings the human being back to life and heals him entirely, in body and in spirit, restoring him to the original plan for which he was created. The purpose of Christ's existence was precisely to give humanity God's life and his Spirit of love so that every person might be able to draw from this inexhaustible source of salvation. This is why St. Paul wrote to the Romans that we were baptized into the death of Christ in order to have his same life as the Risen One (cf. Rom 6:3-4). For this reason Christian parents, such as you today, bring their children to the baptismal font as soon as possible, knowing that life which they have communicated calls for a fullness, a salvation that God alone can give. And parents thus become collaborators of God, transmitting to their children not only physical but also spiritual life.

Dear parents, I thank the Lord with you for the gift of these children and I invoke his assistance so that he may help you to raise them and incorporate them into the spiritual Body of the Church. As you offer them what they need for their growth and salvation may you always be committed, helped by their godparents, to developing in them faith, hope and charity, the theological virtues proper to the new life given to them in the Sacrament of Baptism.

You will guarantee this by your presence and your affection; you will guarantee it first of all and above all by prayer, presenting them daily to God and entrusting them to him in every season of their life. If they are to grow healthy and strong, these babies will of course need both material care and many other kinds of attention; yet, what will be most necessary to them, indeed indispensable, will be to know, love and serve God faithfully in order to have eternal life. Dear parents, may you be for them the first witnesses of an authentic faith in God!

In the Rite of Baptism there is an eloquent sign that expresses precisely the transmission of faith. It is the presentation to each of those being baptized of a candle lit from the flame of the Easter candle: it is the light of the Risen Christ, which you will endeavor to pass on to your children. Thus, from one generation to the next we Christians transmit Christ's light to one another in such a way that when he returns he may find us with this flame burning in our hands. During the Rite I shall say to you: "Parents and godparents, this light is entrusted to you to be kept burning brightly." Dear brothers and sisters, always feed the flame of the faith by listening to and meditating on the Word of God and assiduous communion with Jesus in the Eucharist. May you be assisted in this marvelous if far from easy role by the holy Protectors after whom these thirteen children will be named. Above all, may these Saints help those being baptized to reciprocate your loving care as Christian parents. May the Virgin Mary in particular accompany both them and you, dear parents, now and forever. Amen!

Angelus

January 13, 2008

After the Angelus

Today, the World Day of Migrants and Refugees is celebrated, which this year places young migrants at the center of attention. There are, in fact, many youth who are driven for various reasons to live far from their families and their countries. Young girls and minors are particularly at risk. Some children and adolescents are born and raised in "refugee camps": they also have a right to a future! I express my appreciation for those committed to assisting migrant youth, their families and for their employment and scholastic integration. I invite Ecclesial Communities to kindly welcome the youth and the very young with their parents, trying to understand their histories and support their integration. Dear young migrants, commit yourselves together with your peers to build a more just and fraternal society, fulfilling your duties, respecting the laws and never allowing yourselves to be affected by violence. I entrust all of you to Mary, Mother of all humanity.

Letter to the Faithful of the Diocese and City of Rome on the Urgent Task of Educating Young People

January 21, 2008

Dear Faithful of Rome,

I thought of addressing this Letter to you in order to speak to you about a problem of which you yourselves are aware and to which the various members of our Church are applying themselves: the problem of education. We all have at heart the good of the people we love, especially our children, adolescents and young people. Indeed, we know that it is on them that the future of our City depends. Therefore, it is impossible not to be concerned about the formation of the new generations, about their ability to give their lives a direction and to discern good from evil, and about their health, not only physical but also moral.

Educating, however, has never been an easy task and today seems to be becoming ever more difficult. Parents, teachers, priests and everyone who has direct educational responsibilities are well aware of this. Hence, there is talk of a great "educational emergency," confirmed by the failures we encounter all too often in our efforts to form sound people who can cooperate with others and give their own lives meaning. Thus, it is natural to think of laying the blame on the new generations, as though children born today were different from those born in the past. There is also talk of a "generation gap" which certainly exists and is making itself felt, but is the effect rather than the cause of the failure to transmit certainties and values.

Must we therefore blame today's adults for no longer being able to educate? There is certainly a strong temptation among both parents and teachers as well as educators in general to give up, since they run the risk of not even understanding what their role or rather the mission entrusted to them is.

In fact, it is not only the personal responsibilities of adults or young people, which nonetheless exist and must not be concealed, that are called into question but also a widespread atmosphere, a mindset and form of culture which induce one to have doubt about the value of the human person, about the very meaning of truth and good, and ultimately about the goodness of life. It then becomes difficult to pass on from one generation to the next something that is valid and certain, rules of conduct, credible objectives around which to build life itself.

Dear brothers and sisters of Rome, at this point I would like to say some very simple words to you: Do not be afraid! In fact, none of these difficulties is insurmountable. They are, as it were, the other side of the coin of that great and precious gift which is our freedom, with the responsibility that rightly goes with it. As opposed to what happens in the technical or financial fields, where today's advances can be added to those of the past, no similar accumulation is possible in the area of people's formation and moral growth, because the person's freedom is ever new. As a result, each person and each generation must make his own decision anew, alone. Not even the greatest values of the past can be simply inherited; they must be claimed by us and renewed through an often anguishing personal option.

When the foundations are shaken, however, and essential certainties are lacking, the impelling need for those values once again makes itself felt: thus today, the request for an education which is truly such is in fact increasing. Parents, anxious and often anguished about the future of their children, are asking for it; a great many teachers going through the sorrowful experience of their schools' deterioration are asking for it; society overall, seeing doubts cast on the very foundations of coexistence, is asking for it; children and young people themselves who do not want to be left to face life's challenges on their own are also asking for it in their inmost being. Those who believe in Jesus Christ, moreover, have a further and stronger reason for not being afraid: they know in fact that God does not abandon us, that his love reaches us wherever we are and just as we are, in our wretchedness and weakness, in order to offer us a new possibility of good.

Dear brothers and sisters, to make my considerations more meaningful, it might be useful to identify several common requirements of an authentic education. It needs first of all that closeness and trust which are born from love: I am thinking of the first and fundamental experience of love which children have, or at least should have, from their parents. Yet every true teacher knows that if he is to educate he must give a part of himself, and that it is only in this way that he can help his pupils overcome selfishness and become in their turn capable of authentic love.

In a small child there is already a strong desire to know and to understand, which is expressed in his stream of questions and constant demands for explanations. Therefore, an education would be most impoverished if it were limited to providing notions and information and neglected the important question about the truth, especially that truth which can be a guide in life.

Suffering is also part of the truth of our life. So, by seeking to shield the youngest from every difficulty and experience of suffering, we risk raising brittle and ungenerous people, despite our good intentions: indeed, the capacity for loving corresponds to the capacity for suffering and for suffering together.

We thus arrive, dear friends of Rome, at what is perhaps the most delicate point in the task of education: finding the right balance between freedom and discipline. If no standard of behavior and rule of life is applied even in small daily matters, the character is not formed and the person will not be ready to face the trials that will come in the future. The educational relationship, however, is first of all the encounter of two kinds of freedom, and successful education means teaching the correct use of freedom. As the child gradually grows up, he becomes an adolescent and then a young person; we must therefore accept the risk of freedom and be constantly attentive in order to help him to correct wrong ideas and choices. However, what we must never do is to support him when he errs, to pretend we do not see the errors or worse, that we share them as if they were the new boundaries of human progress.

Education cannot, therefore, dispense with that authoritativeness which makes the exercise of authority possible. It is the fruit of experience and competence, but is acquired above all with the coherence of one's own life and personal involvement, an expression of true love. The educator is thus a witness of truth and goodness. He too, of course, is fragile and can be mistaken, but he will constantly endeavor to be in tune with his mission.

Dear faithful of Rome, from these simple observations it becomes clear that in education a sense of responsibility is crucial: the responsibility of the educator, of course, but also, as he grows up, the responsibility of the child, the student, the young person who enters the world of work. Those who can measure up to themselves and to others are responsible. Those who believe seek further; indeed, they seek to respond to God who loved them first.

Responsibility is in the first place personal, but there is also a responsibility which we share as citizens in the same city and of one nation, as members of the human family and, if we are believers, as children of the one God and members of the Church. Indeed, ideas, lifestyles, laws, the orientations in general of the society in which we live and the image it has of itself through the mass media exercise a great influence on the formation of the new generations, for good but often also for evil. However, society is not an abstraction; in the end we are ourselves all together, with the orientations, rules and representatives we give one another, although the roles and responsibilities of each person are different. Thus, the contribution of each one of us, of each person, family or social group, is necessary if society, starting with our City of Rome, is to become a more favorable context for education.

Lastly, I would like to offer you a thought which I developed in my recent Encyclical Letter *Spe Salvi* on Christian hope: the soul of education, as of the whole of life, can only be a dependable hope. Today, our hope is threatened on many sides and we even risk becoming, like the ancient pagans, people "having no hope and without God in the world," as the Apostle Paul wrote to the Christians of Ephesus (Eph 2:12). What may be the deepest difficulty for a true educational endeavor consists precisely in this: the fact that at the root of the crisis of education lies a crisis of trust in life.

I cannot finish this Letter, therefore, without a warm invitation to place our hope in God. He alone is the hope that withstands every disappointment; his love alone cannot be destroyed by death; his justice and mercy alone can heal injustices and recompense the suffering experienced. Hope that is addressed to God is never hope for oneself alone, it is always also hope for others; it does not isolate us but renders us supportive in goodness and encourages us to educate one another in truth and in love.

I express my affection for you and assure you of my special remembrance in prayer, as I impart my Blessing to you all.

Message for the Forty-Second World Communications Day

[May 4, 2008]

"The Media: At the Crossroads Between Self-Promotion and Service. Searching for the Truth in Order to Share it with Others."

January 24, 2008

Dear Brothers and Sisters!

1. The theme of this year's World Communications Day—*"The Media: At the Crossroads between Self-Promotion and Service. Searching for the Truth in order to Share it with Others"*—sheds light on the important role of the media in the life of individuals and society. Truly, there is no area of human experience, especially given the vast phenomenon of globalization, in which the media have not become an integral part of interpersonal relations and of social, economic, political and religious development. As I said in my Message for this year's World Day of Peace (January 1, 2008): "The social communications media, in particular, because of their educational potential, have a special responsibility for promoting respect for the family, making clear its expectations and rights, and presenting all its beauty" (no. 5).

2. In view of their meteoric technological evolution, the media have acquired extraordinary potential, while raising new and hitherto unimaginable

questions and problems. There is no denying the contribution they can make to the diffusion of news, to knowledge of facts and to the dissemination of information: they have played a decisive part, for example, in the spread of literacy and in socialization, as well as the development of democracy and dialogue among peoples. Without their contribution it would truly be difficult to foster and strengthen understanding between nations, to breathe life into peace dialogues around the globe, to guarantee the primary good of access to information, while at the same time ensuring the free circulation of ideas, especially those promoting the ideals of solidarity and social justice. Indeed, the media, taken overall, are not only vehicles for spreading ideas: they can and should also be instruments at the service of a world of greater justice and solidarity. Unfortunately, though, they risk being transformed into systems aimed at subjecting humanity to agendas dictated by the dominant interests of the day. This is what happens when communication is used for ideological purposes or for the aggressive advertising of consumer products. While claiming to represent reality, it can tend to legitimize or impose distorted models of personal, family or social life. Moreover, in order to attract listeners and increase the size of audiences, it does not hesitate at times to have recourse to vulgarity and violence, and to overstep the mark. The media can also present and support models of development which serve to increase rather than reduce the technological divide between rich and poor countries. . . .

4. The role that the means of social communication have acquired in society must now be considered an integral part of the "anthropological" question that is emerging as the key challenge of the third millennium. Just as we see happening in areas such as human life, marriage and the family, and in the great contemporary issues of peace, justice and protection of creation, so too in the sector of social communications there are essential dimensions of the human person and the truth concerning the human person coming into play. When communication loses its ethical underpinning and eludes society's control, it ends up no longer taking into account the centrality and inviolable dignity of the human person. As a result it risks exercising a negative influence on people's consciences and choices and definitively conditioning their freedom and their very lives. For this reason it is essential that social communications should assiduously defend the person and fully respect human dignity. Many people now think there is a need, in this sphere, for "info-ethics," just as we have bioethics in the field of medicine and in scientific research linked to life.

Angelus

February 3, 2008

Another prayer intention is offered to us by the Pro-Life Day, being celebrated in Italy today, whose theme is *"Serving Life."* I greet and thank all who are gathered here in St. Peter's Square in order to witness to their commitment to defend and promote life and to reassert that "a people's civilization is measured by its capacity to serve life" (*Message of the Italian Bishops' Conference for the Thirtieth National Pro-Life Day*). May each one, according to his own possibilities, professionalism and competence, always feel impelled to love and serve life from its beginning to its natural end. In fact, welcoming human life as a gift to be respected, protected and promoted is a commitment of everyone, all the more so when it is weak and needs care and attention, both before birth and in its terminal phase. I join the Italian Bishops in encouraging all those who, with an effort but also with joy, discreetly and with great dedication, assist elderly or disabled relatives and those who regularly give part of their time to help those people of every age whose lives are tried by so many different forms of poverty.

Address to the Bishops of
Costa Rica on Their *Ad Limina* Visit

February 8, 2008

You are justifiably concerned about the constant deterioration of the family institution with grave repercussions both on the social structure and on ecclesial life. In this regard it is necessary to promote the good of the family, to defend its rights in the appropriate institutions and to develop a pastoral viewpoint that protects it and provides direct help in difficulty. Thus, adequate pre-matrimonial catechesis is of paramount importance, as well as daily closeness that brings encouragement to each home and makes Jesus' greeting ring out in it: "Today, salvation has come to this house" (Lk 19:9). Do not forget the groups of married couples and families who must help one another to achieve their lofty and indispensable vocation, or the specific services that alleviate the painful situations created by the separation of husband and wife, by a precarious financial situation or by domestic violence whose victims are above all women.

Address to Participants in the International Convention on the Theme "Woman and Man, the *Humanum* in Its Entirety"

February 9, 2008

God entrusts to women and men, according to their respective capacities, a specific vocation and mission in the Church and in the world. Here I am thinking of the family, a community of love open to life, the fundamental cell of society. In it the woman and the man, thanks to the gift of maternity and paternity, together carry out an irreplaceable role in regard to life. Children from their conception have the right to be able to count on their father and mother to take care of them and to accompany their growth. The State, for its part, must uphold with appropriate social policies everything that promotes the stability and unity of matrimony, the dignity and responsibility of couples, their rights and irreplaceable duty as educators of their children. Besides, it is necessary to enable the woman to collaborate in the building of society, appreciating her typical "feminine genius."

Address to the Fathers of the General Congregation of the Society of Jesus

February 21, 2008

This [force of secularization] is the reason why I asked you for a renewed commitment to promoting and defending Catholic doctrine, "especially . . . its key points, under severe attack today by the secular culture" (*Letter to Fr. Kolvenbach*, January 10, 2008), of which I gave some examples in my Letter. The themes, continuously discussed and called into question today, of the salvation of all humanity in Christ, of sexual morality, of marriage and the family, must be explored and illumined in the context of contemporary reality but preserving that harmony with the Magisterium which avoids causing confusion and dismay among the People of God.

Address to the Bishops of
El Salvador on Their *Ad Limina* Visit

February 28, 2008

Dear Brothers in the Episcopate,

I receive you with great joy today when your *ad limina* visit has brought you to the tombs of the Apostles to strengthen the bonds of communion with the Apostolic See of your respective particular Churches. My joy is even greater because this is my first opportunity to meet you as the Successor of Peter. I thank Archbishop Fernando Sáenz Lacalle of San Salvador, President of your Bishops' Conference, for his thoughtful words on your behalf. Through you, I send a special greeting to your priests, Religious and lay faithful, who with generosity and tireless effort live and proclaim the Good News of redemption, the one, true hope for all people which Christ has brought to us.

The majority of the Salvadoran People is distinguished by lively faith and a strong religious sentiment. The Gospel, brought there by the first missionaries and preached fervently by Pastors full of love for God such as Archbishop Óscar Arnulfo Romero, has put down deep roots in this beautiful Land and has yielded abundant fruits of Christian life and holiness. Dear Brother Bishops, the transforming capacity of the message of salvation has once again become reality: the Church is required to proclaim it because "the Word of God is not fettered" (2 Tm 2:9) and is living and active (cf. Heb 4:12).

As Pastors of the Church, your hearts are moved to consider the serious needs of the people entrusted to your care, whom you wish to serve with love and dedication. Their plight of poverty obliges many of them to emigrate in search of a better standard of living. Emigration often has negative consequences for the stability of marriage and the family. I also know of the efforts you are making to foster reconciliation and peace in your Country and thus to overcome painful past events.

At the same time, you addressed a Pastoral Letter in 2005 to the issue of violence, considered the most serious problem in your Nation. In analyzing its causes, you recognize that increased violence is an immediate consequence of other, deeper social scourges such as poverty, lack of education, the gradual erosion of those values that have always tempered the Salvadoran soul, and the break-up of families. Indeed, the family is an indispensable good for the Church and society as well as a fundamental element for building peace (cf. *Message for the World Day of Peace 2008*, no. 3). For this reason, you feel the need to revitalize and strengthen in all your dioceses adequate and effective pastoral care, which offers young people a solid spiritual and emotional formation that will help them discover the beauty of God's plan for human love and enable them to live consistently the authentic values of marriage and the family, such as mutual tenderness and respect, self-control, the total gift of self and constant fidelity.

In the face of widespread poverty, people are feeling the critical need to improve the structures and financial conditions that will enable everyone to lead a dignified life. It should not be forgotten, however, that man is not a mere product of the material or social conditions in which he lives. He needs something more; he aspires to more than science or any human initiative can possibly give him. There is within him an immense thirst for God. Yes, dear Brother Bishops, men and women are yearning for God in the depths of their hearts and he is the only One who can satisfy their thirst for fullness and life, because he alone can give us the certainty of unconditional love, of a love stronger than death (cf. *Spe Salvi*, no. 26). "Man needs God, otherwise he remains without hope" (ibid., no. 23).

It is therefore necessary to encourage in your diocesan communities an ambitious and daring evangelization effort directed to facilitating this intimate encounter with the living Christ, which is at the origin and heart of Christian existence (cf. *Deus Caritas Est*, no. 1). Pastoral care must thus be centered on "Christ himself, who is to be known, loved and imitated, so that in him we may live the life of the Trinity, and with him transform history until its fulfillment in the heavenly Jerusalem" (*Novo Millennio Ineunte*, no. 29). It is necessary to help the faithful to increasingly discover the spiritual riches of their Baptism, through which they are "called to the fullness of Christian life and to the perfection of love" (*Lumen Gentium*, no. 40). These spiritual riches will also illuminate their commitment to bear witness to Christ at the heart of human society (cf. *Gaudium et Spes*, no. 43). To fulfill this most exalted vocation they must be firmly rooted in an intense life of prayer, must listen assiduously and humbly to the Word of God and participate frequently in the sacraments, so that they acquire a strong sense of belonging to the Church and a sound doctrinal formation, especially with regard to the Church's social doctrine in which they will find clear criteria and guidelines for giving a Christian light to the society in which they live.

Priests must have a special place in your pastoral concern. You are very closely bound to them by virtue of the Sacrament of Orders which they have received and by their participation in the same evangelizing mission. They deserve your best efforts and your closeness to each one of them, with knowledge of their personal situations, attention to all their spiritual and material needs and encouragement to persevere on their path of priestly holiness. In this, imitate the example of Jesus, who considered all who were with him his friends (cf. Jn 15:15). As the foundation and visible principle of unity in your particular Churches (cf. *Lumen Gentium*, no. 23), I encourage you to be promoters and models of communion in your own presbyterate and to recommend that all your priests live in harmony and union with one another and with their Bishop, as an expression of your affection as father and brother and without failing to correct irregular situations when necessary.

The priest's love for and fidelity to his vocation will be the best and most effective form of vocations promotion, as well as an example and incentive for your seminarians who are the heart of your dioceses. It is on them that you must expend your best resources and energies (cf. *Optatam Totius*, no. 5), for they are the hope of your Churches.

Also follow with attention the life and work of religious Institutes, esteeming and promoting in your diocesan communities the specific vocation and mission of the consecrated life (cf. *Lumen Gentium*, no. 44), and encouraging them to collaborate in diocesan pastoral activity in order to enrich "ecclesial communion by their presence and ministry" (*Pastores Gregis*, no. 50).

Although the challenges you face are enormous and seem to exceed your strength and capacity, know that you can turn with trust to the Lord, for whom nothing is impossible (cf. Lk 1:37), and open your hearts to the impulse of divine grace. In this constant, prayerful contact with Jesus, the Good Shepherd, your best pastoral projects will mature for your communities and you will truly be ministers of hope for all your brethren (cf. *Pastores Gregis*, no. 3), since Jesus is the One who brings to fruition your pastoral ministry, which in turn must be an authentic reflection of your pastoral charity in the image of the One who came "not to be served . . . and to give his life as a ransom for many" (Mk 10:45).

Dear Brothers, at the end of our meeting, I thank you once again for your generous devotion to the Church and accompany you with my prayers so that in all your pastoral challenges the Lord Jesus' words may fill you with hope and courage: "And lo, I am with you always, to the close of the age" (Mt 28:20). I clasp you to my heart in an embrace of peace in which I include the priests, men and women religious and lay people of your local Churches. Upon each one of you and your diocesan faithful I implore the constant protection of the Virgin Mary, Queen of Peace and Patroness of El Salvador, and at the same time I impart the Apostolic Blessing to you with deep affection.

Homily at Rome's San Lorenzo International Youth Center

I survived because "I knew I was expected"

On Sunday, March 9, the Fifth Sunday of Lent, the Holy Father visited San Lorenzo International Youth Center and celebrated Mass in the tiny Church of San

Lorenzo in Piscibus, close to the Vatican. The following is a translation of the Pope's Homily, given in Italian and part extemporaneously.

March 9, 2008

Your Eminences,
Venerable Brothers in the Episcopate and Priesthood,
Dear Brothers and Sisters,

It gives me great joy to commemorate together with you, in this beautiful Romanesque Church, the twenty-fifth anniversary of the San Lorenzo International Youth Center which Pope John Paul II wanted to be located in the vicinity of St. Peter's Basilica and which he inaugurated on March 13, 1983.

The Holy Mass celebrated here every Friday evening is an important spiritual event for many young people who have come from various parts of the world to study at the Roman Universities. It is also an important spiritual encounter and a significant opportunity to make contact with the Cardinals and Bishops of the Roman Curia as well as with Bishops from the five Continents as they pass through Rome on their ad limina visits.

As you have mentioned, I too came here often to celebrate the Eucharist when I was Prefect of the Congregation for the Doctrine of the Faith, and it was always a beautiful experience to meet boys and girls from all corners of the earth who find this Center an important and hospitable reference point.

And it is precisely to you, dear young people, that I first address my cordial greeting, while I thank you for your warm welcome. I also greet all of you who have desired to speak at this solemn and at the same time family celebration.

I greet in a special way the Cardinals and Prelates present. Among them, may I mention in particular Cardinal Paul Josef Cordes, the titular of this Church of San Lorenzo in Piscibus, and Cardinal Stanisław Ryłko, President of the Pontifical Council for the Laity, whom I thank for his kind words of welcome addressed to me at the beginning of Holy Mass, as well as to the two spokespersons for the young people.

I greet Bishop Josef Clemens, Secretary of the Pontifical Council, the youth team, priests and seminarians who animate this Center under the guidance of the Youth Section of this Dicastery, and all who in various capacities make their contribution.

I am referring to the Associations, Movements and Communities represented here, with a special mention to the Emmanuel Community which has coordinated the various initiatives for the past twenty years with great fidelity. It has also created a Mission School in Rome from which come several of the young people who are present here.

I also greet the chaplains and volunteers who for the past twenty-five years have worked at the service of youth. My affectionate greeting to each and every one.

Life, death: basic questions

We now come to today's Gospel, which is dedicated to an important, fundamental theme: what is life? What is death? How should one live? How should one die?

To enable us to understand better this mystery of life and Jesus' answer, St. John uses two different terms for this unique reality to suggest the different dimensions in this reality of "life"; the word *bíos* and the word *zoé*.

Bíos, as can easily be understood, means this great biocosmos, this biosphere that extends from individual, primitive cells to the most organized, most developed organisms; this great tree of life where all the possibilities of this reality, *bíos*, are developed. Man belongs to this tree of life; he is part of this living cosmos that begins with a miracle: in inert matter a vital center develops, the reality that we call an organism.

But although man is part of this great biocosmos, he transcends it, for he is also part of that reality which St. John calls *zoé*. It is a new level of life in which the being is open to knowledge. Of course, man is always man with all his dignity, even if he is in a comatose state, even if he is at the embryonic stage, but if he lives only biologically, the full potential of his being is not fulfilled. Man is called to open himself to new dimensions. He is a being who knows.

Certainly, animals know too, but only things that concern their biological life. Human knowledge goes further; the human being desires to know everything, all reality, reality in its totality; he wants to know what his being is and what the world is. He thirsts for knowledge of the infinite, he desires to arrive at the font of life, he desires to drink at this font, to find life itself.

Thus, we have touched on a second dimension: man is not only a being who knows; he also lives in a relationship of friendship, of love. In addition to the dimension of the knowledge of truth and being, and inseparable from it, exists the dimension of the relationship of love. And here the human being comes closer to the source of life from which he wants to drink in order to have life in abundance, to have life itself.

We could say that science, and medicine in particular, is one great struggle for life. In the end, medicine seeks to counter death; it is the search for immortality. But can we find a medicine that will guarantee us immortality? The question of today's Gospel is precisely this.

Spiritual immortality

Let us try to imagine that medicine succeeds in finding the recipe against death, the recipe for immortality. Even in this case it would always be a medicine that fitted into the biosphere, a useful medicine of course for our spiritual and human lives, but in itself confined to within this biosphere.

It is easy to imagine what would happen if the biological life of man lasted for ever; we would find ourselves in an ageing world, a world full of old people, a world that would no longer leave room for the young, for the renewal of life. We can therefore understand that this cannot be the type of immortality to which we aspire; this is not the possibility of drinking at the source of life for which we all long.

Precisely at this point, when on the one hand we realize that we cannot hope for biological life to be infinitely prolonged, yet on the other, we desire to drink from the very source of life to enjoy life without end, it is precisely at this point that the Lord intervenes.

He speaks to us in the Gospel, saying: "I am the resurrection and the life; he who believes in me, though he die, yet shall he live, and whoever lives and believes in me shall never die."

"I am the Resurrection": to drink from the source of life is to enter into communion with this infinite love which is the source of life. In encountering Christ, we enter into contact, indeed, into communion with life itself and we have already crossed the threshold of death because, beyond biological life, we are in touch with true life.

The Church Fathers have called the Eucharist a *drug of immortality*. And so it is, for in the Eucharist we come into contact, indeed, we enter into communion with the Risen Body of Christ, we enter the space of life already raised, eternal life. Let us enter into communion with this Body which is enlivened by immortal life and thus, from this moment and forever, we will dwell in the space of life itself.

In this way, this Gospel is also a profound interpretation of what the Eucharist is and invites us to live truly on the Eucharist, to be able thus to be transformed into the communion of love. This is true life. In John's Gospel the Lord says: "I came that they may have life, and have it abundantly."

Life in abundance is not as some think: to consume everything, to have all, to be able to do all that one wants. In that case we would live for inanimate things, we would live for death.

Life in abundance means being in communion with true life, with infinite love. It is in this way that we truly enter into the abundance of life and also become messengers of life for others.

On their return, prisoners of war who had been in Russia for ten years or more, exposed to cold and hunger, have said: "I was able to survive because I knew I was expected. I knew people were looking forward to my arrival, that I was necessary and awaited."

This love that awaited them was the effective medicine of life against all ills.

In reality, we are all awaited. The Lord waits for us and not only does he wait for us; he is present and stretches out his hand to us.

Let us take the Lord's hand and pray to him to grant that we may truly live, live the abundance of life and thus also be able to communicate true life to our contemporaries, life in abundance. Amen.

Address to the Bishops of Haiti on Their *Ad Limina* Visit

March 13, 2008

One of the concerns presented in your quinquennial reports is the situation of the family structure, rendered unstable by the crisis that has spread across the Country and also by the evolution of customs and the progressive loss of the meaning of marriage and the family by putting it on the same level as other forms of union. It is largely from the family that society and the Church develop.

Your attention to this aspect of pastoral life is therefore fundamental, for it is a question of the first place for the education of youth. "The Christian family springs from marriage, which is an image and a sharing in the partnership of love between Christ and the Church; it will show forth to all men Christ's living presence in the world and the authentic nature of the Church: by the love and generous fruitfulness of the spouses, by their unity and fidelity, and by the loving way in which all members of the family cooperate with each other" (*Gaudium et Spes*, no. 48). I therefore encourage you to support married couples and young families by giving them increasingly appropriate support and formation and thereby also teaching them respect for life.

Address to Members of the Twenty-Sixth General Chapter of the Salesian Congregation

March 31, 2008

In the education of youth it is extremely important that the family play an active role. Families frequently have difficulty in facing the challenges of education; they are often unable to make their own contribution or are absent. The special tenderness and commitment to young people that are characteristic of Don Bosco's charism must be expressed in an equal commitment to the involvement and formation of families. Your youth ministry, therefore, must be decisively open to family ministry. Caring for families does not mean taking people away from work for young people; on the contrary, it means making it more permanent and effective. I thus encourage you to deepen the forms of this commitment on which you have set out; this will prove advantageous to the education and evangelization of the young.

Address to the Bishops of the Antilles on Their *Ad Limina* Visit

April 7, 2008

To varying degrees, your shores have been battered by negative aspects of the entertainment industry, exploitative tourism and the scourge of the arms and drugs trade; influences which not only undermine family life and unsettle the foundations of traditional cultural values, but tend to affect negatively local politics.

Brothers, against this disturbing backdrop, stand tall as heralds of hope! . . .

Dear brothers, every one of you feels the great responsibility to do everything possible to support marriage and family life, the primary source for cohesion within the community and hence of capital importance in the eyes of the civil authorities. In this regard, the broad network of Catholic schools in your whole region makes a great contribution. The values rooted in the way of truth offered by Christ enlighten young people's minds and hearts and lead them to follow the way of fidelity, responsibility and true freedom. Good young Christians make good citizens! I am sure that everything possible will be done to encourage the specifically Catholic nature of your schools, which in the course of previous generations have rendered a great service to your people. For this reason, I have no doubts that the young adults of your dioceses will be able to discern what is urgently up to them to contribute to the economic and social development of the region, since this is an essential dimension of their Christian witness.*

---

*   This paragraph is an unofficial translation of the Italian.

Address at the Celebration of Vespers with the Bishops of the United States of America

April 16, 2008

A matter of deep concern to us all is the state of the family within society. Indeed, Cardinal George mentioned earlier that you have included the strengthening of marriage and family life among the priorities for your attention over the next few years. In this year's World Day of Peace Message I spoke of the essential contribution that healthy family life makes to peace within and between nations. In the family home we experience "some of the fundamental elements of peace: justice and love between brothers and sisters, the role of authority expressed by parents, loving concern for the members who are weaker because of youth, sickness or old age, mutual help in the necessities of life, readiness to accept others and, if necessary, to forgive them" (no. 3). The family is also the primary place for evangelization, for passing on the faith, for helping young people to appreciate the importance of religious practice and Sunday observance. How can we not be dismayed as we observe the sharp decline of the family as a basic element of Church and society? Divorce and infidelity have increased, and many young men and women are choosing to postpone marriage or to forego it altogether. To some young Catholics, the sacramental bond of marriage seems scarcely distinguishable from a civil bond, or even a purely informal and open-ended arrangement to live with another person. Hence we have an alarming decrease in the number of Catholic marriages in the United States together with an increase in cohabitation, in which the Christ-like mutual self-giving of spouses, sealed by a public promise to live out the demands of an indissoluble lifelong commitment, is simply absent. In such circumstances, children are denied the secure environment that they need in order truly to flourish as human beings, and society is denied the stable building blocks which it requires if the cohesion and moral focus of the community are to be maintained.

As my predecessor, Pope John Paul II taught, "The person principally responsible in the Diocese for the pastoral care of the family is the Bishop . . . he must devote to it personal interest, care, time, personnel and resources, but above all personal support for the families and for all those who . . . assist him in the pastoral care of the family" (*Familiaris Consortio*, no. 73). It is your task to proclaim boldly the arguments from faith and reason in favor of the institution of marriage, understood as a lifelong commitment between a man and a woman, open to the transmission of life. This message should resonate with people today, because it is essentially an unconditional and unreserved "yes" to life, a "yes" to love, and a "yes" to the aspirations at the heart of our common humanity, as we strive to fulfill our deep yearning for intimacy with others and with the Lord.

Among the countersigns to the Gospel of life found in America and elsewhere is one that causes deep shame: the sexual abuse of minors. Many of you have spoken to me of the enormous pain that your communities have suffered when clerics have betrayed their priestly obligations and duties by such gravely immoral behavior. As you strive to eliminate this evil wherever it occurs, you may be assured of the prayerful support of God's people throughout the world. Rightly, you attach priority to showing compassion and care to the victims. It is your God-given responsibility as pastors to bind up the wounds caused by every breach of trust, to foster healing, to promote reconciliation and to reach out with loving concern to those so seriously wronged.

Responding to this situation has not been easy and, as the President of your Episcopal Conference has indicated, it was "sometimes very badly handled." Now that the scale and gravity of the problem is more clearly understood, you have been able to adopt more focused remedial and disciplinary measures and to promote a safe environment that gives greater protection to young people. While it must be remembered that the overwhelming majority of clergy and religious in America do outstanding work in bringing the liberating message of the Gospel to the people entrusted to their care, it is vitally important that the vulnerable always be shielded from those who would cause harm. In this regard, your efforts to heal and protect are bearing great fruit not only for those directly under your pastoral care, but for all of society.

If they are to achieve their full purpose, however, the policies and programs you have adopted need to be placed in a wider context. Children deserve to grow up with a healthy understanding of sexuality and its proper place in human relationships. They should be spared the degrading manifestations and the crude manipulation of sexuality so prevalent today. They have a right to be educated in authentic moral values rooted in the dignity of the human person. This brings us back to our consideration of the centrality of the family and the need to promote the Gospel of life. What does it mean to speak of child protection when pornography and violence can be viewed in so many homes through media widely available today? We need to reassess urgently the values underpinning society, so that a sound moral formation can be offered to young people and adults alike. All have a part to play in this task—not only parents, religious leaders, teachers and catechists, but the media and entertainment industries as well. Indeed, every member of society can contribute to this moral renewal and benefit from it. Truly caring about young people and the future of our civilization means recognizing our responsibility to promote and live by the authentic moral values which alone enable the human person to flourish. It falls to you, as pastors modeled upon Christ, the Good Shepherd, to proclaim this message loud and clear, and thus to address the sin of abuse within the wider context of sexual *mores*. Moreover, by acknowledging and confronting the problem when it occurs in an ecclesial setting, you can give a lead to others, since this scourge is found not only within your Dioceses, but in every sector of society. It calls for a determined, collective response.

APOSTOLIC JOURNEY TO THE UNITED STATES OF
AMERICA AND VISIT TO THE UNITED NATIONS
ORGANIZATION HEADQUARTERS

Meeting with Representatives of Other Religions in the "Rotunda" Hall of the Pope John Paul II Cultural Center of Washington, DC

April 17, 2008

My dear friends,

I am pleased to have this occasion to meet with you today. I thank Bishop Sklba for his words of welcome, and I cordially greet all those in attendance representing various religions in the United States of America. Several of you kindly accepted the invitation to compose the reflections contained in today's program. For your thoughtful words on how each of your traditions bears witness to peace, I am particularly grateful. Thank you all.

This country has a long history of cooperation between different religions in many spheres of public life. Interreligious prayer services during the national feast of Thanksgiving, joint initiatives in charitable activities, a shared voice on important public issues: these are some ways in which members of different religions come together to enhance mutual understanding and promote the common good. I encourage all religious groups in America to persevere in their collaboration and thus enrich public life with the spiritual values that motivate your action in the world.

The place where we are now gathered was founded specifically for promoting this type of collaboration. Indeed, the Pope John Paul II Cultural Center seeks to offer a Christian voice to the "human search for meaning and purpose in life" in a world of "varied religious, ethnic and cultural communities" (*Mission Statement*). This institution reminds us of this nation's conviction that all people should be free to pursue happiness in a way consonant with their nature as creatures endowed with reason and free will.

Americans have always valued the ability to worship freely and in accordance with their conscience. Alexis de Tocqueville, the French historian and observer of American affairs, was fascinated with this aspect of the nation. He remarked that this is a country in which religion and freedom are "intimately linked" in contributing to a stable democracy that fosters social virtues and participation in the communal life of all its citizens. In urban areas, it is common for individuals from different cultural backgrounds and religions to engage with one another daily in commercial, social and educational settings. Today, in classrooms throughout the country, young Christians, Jews, Muslims, Hindus, Buddhists, and indeed children of all religions sit side-by-side, learning with one another and from one another. This diversity gives rise to new challenges that spark a deeper reflection on the core principles of a democratic society. May others take heart from your experience, realizing that a united society can indeed arise from a plurality of peoples—"*E pluribus unum*": "out of many, one"—provided that all recognize religious liberty as a basic civil right (cf. *Dignitatis Humanae*, no. 2).

The task of upholding religious freedom is never completed. New situations and challenges invite citizens and leaders to reflect on how their decisions respect this basic human right. Protecting religious freedom within the rule of law does not guarantee that peoples—particularly minorities—will be spared from unjust forms of discrimination and prejudice. This requires constant effort on the part of all members of society to ensure that citizens are afforded the opportunity to worship peaceably and to pass on their religious heritage to their children.

The transmission of religious traditions to succeeding generations not only helps to preserve a heritage; it also sustains and nourishes the surrounding culture in the present day. The same holds true for dialogue between religions; both the participants and society are enriched. As we grow in understanding of one another, we see that we share an esteem for ethical values, discernable to human reason, which are revered by all peoples of goodwill. The world begs for a common witness to these values. I therefore invite all religious people to view dialogue not only as a means of enhancing mutual understanding, but also as a way of serving society at large. By bearing witness to those moral truths which they hold in common with all men and women of goodwill, religious groups will exert a positive influence on the wider culture, and inspire neighbors, co-workers and fellow citizens to join in the task of strengthening the ties of solidarity. In the words of President Franklin Delano

Roosevelt: "no greater thing could come to our land today than a revival of the spirit of faith."

A concrete example of the contribution religious communities make to civil society is faith-based schools. These institutions enrich children both intellectually and spiritually. Led by their teachers to discover the divinely bestowed dignity of each human being, young people learn to respect the beliefs and practices of others, thus enhancing a nation's civic life.

What an enormous responsibility religious leaders have: to imbue society with a profound awe and respect for human life and freedom; to ensure that human dignity is recognized and cherished; to facilitate peace and justice; to teach children what is right, good and reasonable!

There is a further point I wish to touch upon here. I have noticed a growing interest among governments to sponsor programs intended to promote interreligious and intercultural dialogue. These are praiseworthy initiatives. At the same time, religious freedom, interreligious dialogue and faith-based education aim at something more than a consensus regarding ways to implement practical strategies for advancing peace. The broader purpose of dialogue is to discover the truth. What is the origin and destiny of mankind? What are good and evil? What awaits us at the end of our earthly existence? Only by addressing these deeper questions can we build a solid basis for the peace and security of the human family, for "wherever and whenever men and women are enlightened by the splendor of truth, they naturally set out on the path of peace" (*Message for the 2006 World Day of Peace*, no. 3).

We are living in an age when these questions are too often marginalized. Yet they can never be erased from the human heart. Throughout history, men and women have striven to articulate their restlessness with this passing world. In the Judeo-Christian tradition, the Psalms are full of such expressions: "My spirit is overwhelmed within me" (Ps 143:4; cf. Ps 6:6; 31:10; 32:3; 38:8; 77:3); "why are you cast down, my soul, why groan within me?" (Ps 42:5). The response is always one of faith: "Hope in God, I will praise him still; my Savior and my God" (Ps 42:5, 11; cf. Ps 43:5; 62:5). Spiritual leaders have a special duty, and we might say competence, to place the deeper questions at the forefront of human consciousness, to reawaken mankind to the mystery of human existence, and to make space in a frenetic world for reflection and prayer.

Confronted with these deeper questions concerning the origin and destiny of mankind, Christianity proposes Jesus of Nazareth. He, we believe, is the eternal *Logos* who became flesh in order to reconcile man to God and reveal the underlying reason of all things. It is he whom we bring to the forum of interreligious dialogue. The ardent desire to follow in his footsteps spurs Christians to open their minds and hearts in dialogue (cf. Lk 10:25-37; Jn 4:7-26).

Dear friends, in our attempt to discover points of commonality, perhaps we have shied away from the responsibility to discuss our differences with calmness and clarity. While always uniting our hearts and minds in the call for peace, we must also listen attentively to the voice of truth. In this way, our dialogue will not stop at identifying a common set of values, but go on to probe their ultimate foundation. We have no reason to fear, for the truth unveils for us the essential relationship between the world and God. We are able to perceive that peace is a "heavenly gift" that calls us to conform human history to the divine order. Herein lies the "truth of peace" (cf. *Message for the 2006 World Day of Peace*).

As we have seen then, the higher goal of interreligious dialogue requires a clear exposition of our respective religious tenets. In this regard, colleges, universities and study centers are important forums for a candid exchange of religious ideas. The Holy See, for its part, seeks to carry forward this important work through the Pontifical Council for Interreligious Dialogue, the Pontifical Institute for Arabic and Islamic Studies, and various Pontifical Universities.

Dear friends, let our sincere dialogue and cooperation inspire all people to ponder the deeper questions of their origin and destiny. May the followers of all religions stand together in defending and promoting life and religious freedom everywhere. By giving ourselves generously to this sacred task—through dialogue and countless small acts of love, understanding and compassion— we can be instruments of peace for the whole human family.

Peace upon you all!

APOSTOLIC JOURNEY TO THE
UNITED STATES OF AMERICA AND VISIT TO THE
UNITED NATIONS ORGANIZATION HEADQUARTERS

Homily at Votive Mass for the Universal Church, St. Patrick's Cathedral, New York

April 19, 2008

In this morning's second reading, St. Paul reminds us that spiritual unity— the unity which reconciles and enriches diversity—has its origin and supreme model in the life of the triune God. As a communion of pure love and infinite freedom, the Blessed Trinity constantly brings forth new life in the work of creation and redemption. The Church, as "a people made one by the unity of the Father, the Son and the Spirit" (cf. *Lumen Gentium*, no. 4), is called to proclaim the gift of life, to serve life, and to promote a culture of life. Here in this cathedral, our thoughts turn naturally to the heroic witness to the Gospel of life borne by the late Cardinals Cooke and O'Connor. The proclamation of life, life in abundance, must be the heart of the new evangelization. For true life—our salvation—can only be found in the reconciliation, freedom and love which are God's gracious gift.

This is the message of hope we are called to proclaim and embody in a world where self-centeredness, greed, violence, and cynicism so often seem to choke the fragile growth of grace in people's hearts. St. Irenaeus, with great insight, understood that the command which Moses enjoined upon the people of Israel: "Choose life!" (Dt 30:19) was the ultimate reason for our obedience to all God's commandments (cf. *Adv. Haer.* IV, 16, 2-5). Perhaps we have lost sight of this: in a society where the Church seems legalistic and "institutional" to many people, our most urgent challenge is to communicate the joy born of faith and the experience of God's love.

Homily at Mass for the Funeral of
Cardinal Alfonso López Trujillo

April 23, 2008

Dear Brothers and Sisters,

"Unless a grain of wheat falls into the earth and dies, it remains alone; but if it dies, it bears much fruit" (Jn 12:24). The Evangelist John thus foretold the glorification of Christ through the mystery of his death on the Cross. In this Easter Season, in the light of the mystery of the Resurrection itself, these words acquire an even deeper and more incisive eloquence. If it is true that a certain sorrow can be detected in them because of his imminent departure from his disciples, it is also true that Jesus pointed to the secret for defeating the power of death. Death does not have the last word, it is not the end of everything but, redeemed by the sacrifice of the Cross, it can henceforth be the passage to the joy of life without end. Jesus said, "He who loves his life loses it, and he who hates his life in this world will keep it for eternal life" (Jn 12:25). Thus, if we can die to our selfishness, if we refuse to withdraw into ourselves and make our life a gift to God and to our brethren, we too will be able to know the rich fruitfulness of love. And love does not die.

Here is the renewed message of hope that we gather from God's Word today, as we say our last farewell to our beloved Brother, Cardinal Alfonso López Trujillo. His death, which came just as he seemed to have recovered from a severe health crisis that began more than a year ago, has deeply distressed us all. In the United States, where I was on a Pastoral Visit, I immediately raised to God a prayer of suffrage for his soul and now, at the end of Holy Mass at which Cardinal Angelo Sodano, Dean of the College of Cardinals, has presided, I join you all with affection to recall the great generosity with which the late Cardinal served the Church and to thank the Lord for the many gifts with which he enriched the person and the ministry of our late Brother.

At the Consistory of February 2, 1983 Archbishop Alfonso López Trujillo was the youngest Cardinal on whom my Venerable Predecessor, Pope John Paul II, conferred a Cardinal's hat. He was born in Villahermosa in the Diocese of Ibagué, Colombia, in 1935, and while still a child moved with his family to the capital, Bogotá. Here, when he was a university student, he entered the Major Seminary. He continued his studies in Rome and was ordained a priest in November 1960. Having concluded his theological formation, he taught philosophy at the archdiocesan seminary and worked for many years at the service of the entire Church in Colombia. In 1971, the Servant of God Paul VI appointed him Auxiliary Bishop of Bogotá; in those same years he was also President of the Doctrinal Commission of the Colombian Bishops' Conference and was chosen shortly afterwards as Secretary General of CELAM, an office he carried out with recognized competence over a long period.

In 1978, again by Paul VI, he was entrusted with the office of Coadjutor Bishop of the Archdiocese of Medellín with the right of succession, and he later became its Pastor. His deep knowledge of the ecclesial situation in Latin America acquired during the long period in which he had worked as Secretary of CELAM led to his appointment as President of this important ecclesial body, which he directed wisely from 1979 to 1983. From 1987 to 1990 he was President of the Colombian Bishops' Conference. He also had opportunities to broaden his knowledge of the universal Church's problems, having taken part in the three Assemblies of the Synod of Bishops held in the Vatican: in 1974 on evangelization, in 1977 on catechesis and in 1980 on the family. Moreover, it was precisely to the family that he was called to be especially dedicated, from November 8, 1990 when John Paul II appointed him President of the Pontifical Council for the Family, an office that kept him in active service until the moment of his death.

On this occasion, how is it possible not to highlight the zeal and enthusiasm with which he worked during these approximately eighteen years, carrying out a tireless activity to safeguard and promote the family and Christian marriage? How can we fail to thank him for the courage with which he defended the non-negotiable values of human life? We have all admired his indefatigable activity. One result of his hard work is the *Lexicon*, which constitutes a precious text for the formation of pastoral workers and an instrument for dialogue with the contemporary world on the basic themes of Christian ethics. We can only be grateful to him for the tenacious battle he fought in defense of the "truth," family love and to spread the "Gospel of the family." The enthusiasm and determination with which he worked in this field were the fruit of his personal experience, linked in particular with the suffering his mother had to bear; she died at the age of forty-four from a very painful illness. "When in my work," he remarked, "I speak of the ideals of marriage and the family, it comes naturally to me to think of the family from which I come, because through my parents I have been able to understand how it is possible to fulfill both ideals."

The late Cardinal drew his love for the truth about man and for the Gospel of the family from the thought that every human being and every family reflect the mystery of God who is Love. His moving address to the Assembly of the Synod of Bishops in 1997 lives on, impressed in the minds of all: it was a true hymn to life. He presented a very practical spirituality to those who are involved in the implementation of the divine plan for the family. He emphasized that if knowledge does not concentrate on understanding and educating to life, it will lose the most crucial battle on the fascinating and mysterious ground of genetic engineering.

If Cardinal López Trujillo made the defense of and love for the family the characteristic commitment of his service in the Pontifical Council of which he was President, it was to the affirmation of the truth that he dedicated his whole life. He testifies to this in one of his writings in which he explains: "I have personally chosen the motto '*Veritas in Caritate*,' because all that concerns the truth is at the heart of my studies." And he added that truth in love has always been an "existential pole" for him, at first in Colombia, when he strove "to find the meaning of genuine liberation in the theological context," and later on, here in Rome, when he devoted himself "to deepening, proclaiming and spreading the Gospel of life and the Gospel of the family, as a collaborator of the Holy Father." He concluded: "I deeply believe in the value of this decisive battle for the Church and for humanity and I ask the Lord to give me the strength to be neither lazy nor cowardly."

To bring to completion the mission that Jesus entrusts to us, we must not be lazy or cowardly. In the Second Reading we heard how the Apostle Paul, a prisoner in Rome, urged his trusted disciple Timothy to take heart and to persevere in witnessing to Christ, even at the cost of being subjected to harsh persecution, ever strong in the certainty that: "if we have died with him, we shall also live with him; if we endure, we shall also reign with him" (2 Tm 2:11-12). May the late Cardinal's generosity, expressed in a multitude of charitable actions, especially for children in different parts of the world, be an encouragement to us to spend our physical and spiritual resources for the Gospel; may they spur us to work in defense of human life; help us to look constantly to the destination of our earthly pilgrimage. And St. John points out to us what this comforting destination is, offering for our contemplation in the passage of Revelation which has just been proclaimed the visions of a "new Heaven" and a "new earth" (21:1), and sketching before our eyes the prophetic lines of the "holy city," the "new Jerusalem . . . prepared as a bride adorned for her husband" (21:2).

Venerable Brothers and dear friends, let us never lift our eyes from this vision: let us look to eternity, anticipating, even among trials and tribulations, the joy of the future "dwelling place of God with men," where our Redeemer will wipe away our every tear and where "death shall be no more, neither shall there be mourning nor crying nor pain any more, for the former things have passed away" (cf. Rev 21:4). We like to think that beloved Cardinal Alfonso López Trujillo, for whom we still desire to pray, has already reached this dwelling place of light and joy. May Mary welcome him and may the angels and saints in Paradise accompany him: may his soul athirst for God at last be able to enter and to rest in peace for ever in the "shrine" of infinite Love. Amen!

Address to the Bishops of the Caucasus on Their *Ad Limina* Visit

April 24, 2008

Uphold the family, who are [the] living cells [of the Body of Christ]. Because of the mentality inculcated in society and inherited from the Communist period, families today meet with many difficulties and are scarred by the wounds and attacks on human life that are unfortunately recorded in many other parts of the world. May it be your task, as primarily responsible for the pastoral care of the family, to educate Christian spouses to "bear witness to the inestimable value of the indissolubility and fidelity of marriage [which] is one of the most precious and most urgent tasks of Christian couples in our time" (*Familiaris Consortio*, no. 20).

General Audience

April 30, 2008

I supported my Brothers in the Episcopate in their far from easy task of sowing the Gospel in a society marked by many contradictions, which even threaten the coherence of Catholics and the clergy themselves. I encouraged them to make their voice heard on the current moral and social issues and to form the lay faithful to be good "leaven" in the civil community, starting with the fundamental cell which is the family. In this regard I urged them to repropose the Sacrament of Matrimony as a gift and an indissoluble commitment between a man and a woman, the natural context for welcoming and raising children. The Church and the family, together with school, especially schools of Christian inspiration—must cooperate in order to offer young people a sound moral education, but in this task those who work in communications and entertainment also have a great responsibility.

Address to the Bishops of Cuba on Their *Ad Limina* Visit

May 2, 2008

In a special way I would like to entrust the pastoral care of marriage and the family to you. I know how concerned you are about the situation of the family whose stability is threatened by divorce and its consequences, the practice of abortion or financial difficulties, as well as the break-up of families caused by emigration or other reasons. I encourage you to redouble your efforts so that all, especially the young, may understand better and feel increasingly attracted by the beauty of the authentic values of marriage and the family. Likewise, it is necessary to encourage and to offer the appropriate means to ensure that families can exercise their responsibility and fundamental right to the religious and moral education of their children.

Address to the Bishops of Hungary on Their *Ad Limina* Visit

May 10, 2008

Dear and Venerable Brothers in the Episcopate,

I greet you all with great joy, Pastors of the Church in Hungary, on the occasion of your visit *ad limina Apostolorum*. I greet you with affection and I am grateful to Cardinal Péter Erdö for his words to me on behalf of the Bishops' Conference as a whole. In addition to expressing your fraternal sentiments to me, for which I warmly thank you, he has clearly outlined the salient characteristics of the Catholic Community and the society of your Country, summarizing the knowledge that I have been able to gain at the meetings with each one of you. Thus, dear Brothers, the people entrusted to you are now spiritually before you with their joys and plans, their sorrows, problems and hopes. And we pray first of all that through the intercession of Sts. Peter and Paul, and with the help of this Apostolic See which presides in charity, the faithful may find the strength to persevere on their way toward the fullness of the Kingdom of God.

Unfortunately, the long period of the Communist regime has so deeply scarred the Hungarian people that the consequences are still being felt today: in particular, many show a certain difficulty in trusting others, typical of those who have lived for a long time in an atmosphere of suspicion. Moreover, the feeling of insecurity, is accentuated by the difficult economic situation, which heedless consumerism does not help to improve. People, including Catholics, generally feel the "weakness" of thought and will that is very common in our day. As you yourselves have noted, today it is often difficult to initiate a serious theological and spiritual deepening because, on the one hand the necessary intellectual training is lacking and on the other, the objective reference to the truth of faith. In this context the Church must certainly be a teacher, but must always show herself first and foremost to be a mother, so as to foster growth in mutual trust and to encourage hope.

Unfortunately the family, which is going through a serious crisis in Hungary too, is the first to suffer from the widespread secularization. Its symptoms are the considerable decrease in the number of marriages and the striking rise in divorces, that are also very often premature. The so-called "de facto couples" are proliferating. You rightly criticized the public recognition of homosexual unions, because they are not only contrary to the Church's teaching but also to the Hungarian Constitution itself. This situation, together with the lack of subsidies for large families, has led to a drastic fall in the birth rate, made even more dramatic by the widespread practice of abortion. The family crisis is of course an enormous challenge to the Church. Conjugal fidelity and more in general the values on which society is founded are called into question. It is therefore obvious that after families it is youth who are affected by this problem. In the cities they are attracted by new forms of entertainment and in the villages are often left to themselves. I therefore express my deepest appreciation of the many initiatives that the Church promotes, even with the limited means at her disposal, to animate the world of youth with periods of formation and friendship that awaken their sense of responsibility. I am thinking, for example, of the activities of choirs, which fit into the praiseworthy commitment of parishes to encourage the spread of sacred music. Again, in the perspective of attention to the new generations, you offer praiseworthy support to Catholic schools, and in particular to the Catholic University of Budapest which I hope will always be able to preserve and develop its original identity. I encourage you to persevere in your efforts for the pastoral care of schools and universities, as well as, more generally, for the evangelization of culture which in our day also avails itself of the media; in this sector your Church has recently made important progress.

Address to the Members of Italy's Pro-Life Movement

May 12, 2008

Dear Brothers and Sisters,

With deep pleasure I welcome you today and I offer each one of you my cordial greeting. In the first place, I greet Bishop Michele Pennisi of Piazza Armerina, and the priests present. I address a special greeting to Hon. Carlo Carsini, President of the Pro-Life Movement and I warmly thank him for his kind words to me on your behalf. I greet the members of the National Management Committee and the Executive Board of the Pro-Life Movement, the Presidents of the Centers for Help to Life and those in charge of the various services, the "Progetto Gemma," the "Telefono Verde," "SOS Vita" and "Telefono Rosso." I also greet the representatives of the Pope John XXIII Association and several European pro-life movements. Through you who are present here I extend my affectionate thoughts to those who, although they are unable to be here in person are united with us in spirit. I am thinking in particular of the many volunteers who, with self-denial and generosity share with you the noble ideal of promoting and defending human life from its conception.

Your visit is taking place thirty years since the legalization of abortion in Italy and you are intending to suggest a profound reflection on the human and social effects this law has produced in the civil and Christian communities during this period. Looking at the past three decades and considering the current situation, it is impossible not to recognize that in practice defending human life today has become more difficult because a mindset has developed, entrusted to the opinion of the individual, which has gradually debased its value. One result of this has been the decrease in respect for the human person, a value at the root of all civil coexistence, over and above the faith professed.

The causes that lead to such painful decisions as abortion are of course many and complex. If, on the one hand, faithful to her Lord's commandment, the Church never tires of reaffirming that the sacred value of every human being's life originates in the Creator's plan, on the other hand, she encourages the promotion of every initiative in support of women and families in order to create the favorable conditions in which to welcome life, and the protection of the family institution founded on the marriage between a man and a woman. Not only has permitting recourse to the termination of pregnancy not solved the problems that afflict many women and a fair number of families, but it has also made another wound in our society, unfortunately, already burdened by deep suffering.

In recent years, there has been great dedication, and not only on the Church's part, in order to meet the needs and difficulties of families. However, we cannot conceal from ourselves that various problems continue to gnaw at today's society, preventing space from being given to the desire of so many young people to marry and to form a family, because of the unfavorable situation in which they live. The lack of steady employment, legislation that frequently does not provide for the protection of motherhood, the impossibility of guaranteeing adequate support for children, are some of the obstacles that seem to stifle the requirement of fertile love, while they open the door to a growing sense of distrust in the future. It is necessary, therefore, to join forces so that different Institutions may once again focus their action on the defense of human life and give priority attention to the family, in whose heart life is born and develops. It is necessary to help the family with every legislative means to facilitate its formation and its task of education in the difficult social context of today.

For Christians, in this fundamental context of society, an urgent and indispensable field for the apostolate and for Gospel witness is always open: to protect life with courage and love in all its stages. For this, dear brothers and sisters, I ask the Lord to bless the activity which, as the *Centro di Aiuto alla Vita* and the *Movimento per la Vita,* you carry out to prevent abortion, also in the case of difficult pregnancies, working at the same time in the contexts of education, culture and political debate. It is necessary to witness concretely that respect for life is the first form of justice to apply. For those who have the gift of faith this becomes a mandatory imperative, because the disciple of Christ is called to be increasingly a "prophet" of a truth that can never be eliminated: God alone is the Lord of life. Every person is known and loved, wanted and guided by him. Here alone lies the deepest and greatest unity of humanity: in the fact that every human being puts into practice God's one plan, originates in God's same creative idea. One thus understands why the Bible says: whoever profanes man, profanes the property of God (cf. Gn 9:5).

This year is the sixtieth anniversary of the Declaration of Human Rights whose merit is to have enabled different cultures, juridical forms and institutional models to converge around a fundamental nucleus of values, and hence, of rights. As I recently recalled during my Visit to the United Nations

Organization to the members of the U.N., "Human rights, then, must be respected as an expression of justice, and not merely because they are enforceable through the will of the legislators . . . . The promotion of human rights remains the most effective strategy for eliminating inequalities between countries and social groups, and for increasing security" (*Address to UN General Assembly*, New York, April 18, 2008). For this reason your commitment in the political arena, as a help and an incentive for Institutions so that proper recognition be given to the words "human dignity," is truly laudable. Your initiative with the Commission for Petitions of the European Parliament, in which you assert the fundamental values of the right to life from conception, of the family founded on the marriage of a man and a woman, of the right of every human being conceived to be born and brought up in a family by his parents, further confirms the solidity of your commitment and your full communion with the Magisterium of the Church, which has always proclaimed and defended these values as "non-negotiable."

Dear brothers and sisters, in meeting you on May 22, 1998, John Paul II urged you to persevere in your commitment of love and the defense of human life, and recalled that thanks to you, numerous children were able to experience the joy of the most precious gift of life. Ten years later, it is I who thank you for the service you have rendered to the Church and to society. How many human lives you have saved from death! Continue on this path and, in order that the smile of life may triumph on the lips of all children and their mothers, do not be afraid. I entrust each one of you, and the many people whom you meet at the Centers of help for life, to the motherly protection of the Virgin Mary, Queen of the family, and while I assure you of my remembrance in prayer, I warmly bless you and all those who belong to the Pro-Life Movements in Italy, in Europe and throughout the world.

Address to Participants in the Plenary Assembly of the Pontifical Council for the Pastoral Care of Migrants and Itinerant People

May 15, 2008

Your Eminences,
Venerable Brothers in the Episcopate and in the Priesthood,
Dear Brothers and Sisters,

I am pleased to welcome you on the occasion of the Plenary Assembly of the Pontifical Council for the Pastoral Care of Migrants and Itinerant People.

I greet in particular Cardinal Renato Raffaele Martino, President, whom I thank for the words with which he introduced our Meeting, illustrating the various facets of the interesting topic you have addressed in these days. I also greet Archbishop Agostino Marchetto, Secretary, the Undersecretary, the Officials and the Experts, the Members and the Consultors, I address a cordial thought of gratitude to all for the work achieved and for their dedication in putting into practice what has been discussed and planned in these days for the good of all families.

During my recent Visit to the United States of America, I was able to encourage that great Country to continue in its commitment to welcoming the brothers and sisters who arrive there, usually from poor countries. I pointed out in particular the serious problem of family reunion, a subject I had already treated in my *Message for the Ninety-Third World Day of Migrants and Refugees*, dedicated precisely to the theme. I wish to recall here that on various occasions I have presented the icon of the Holy Family as a model for migrant families, referring to the image presented by my Venerable Predecessor, Pope Pius XII, in the Apostolic Constitution *Exsul Familia*, which constitutes the *magna carta* of the pastoral care of migrants (cf. AAS 44, 1952, 649; *Erga Migrantes Caritas Christi*, no. 20: ORE, May 26, 2004, I). Moreover, in his Messages of 1980, 1986 and 1993, my Venerable Predecessor John Paul II intended to stress that ecclesial commitment is not only in favor of the individual migrant but also of his family, a community of love and a factor of integration.

First of all, I am pleased to reaffirm that the Church's concern for migrant families in no way diminishes her pastoral involvement with those on the move. Indeed, this commitment to preserving unity of vision and action between the two "wings" (migration and vagrancy) can help one understand the magnitude of the phenomenon, and at the same time be an incentive to all for a specific pastoral approach, encouraged by the Supreme Pontiffs and hoped for by the Second Vatican Ecumenical Council (cf. *Christus Dominus*, no. 18), and appropriately upheld by documents drafted by your Pontifical Council as well as by Congresses and Meetings. One must not forget that the family, even the migrant family and the itinerant family, constitutes the original cell of society which must not be destroyed but rather defended with courage and patience. It represents the community in which from infancy the child has been taught to worship and love God, learning the grammar of human and moral values and learning to make good use of freedom in the truth. Unfortunately, in many situations it is difficult for this to happen, especially in the case of those who are caught up in the phenomenon of human mobility.

Furthermore, in its action of welcome and dialogue with migrants and itinerant people, the Christian community has as a constant reference point, the Person of Christ our Lord. He has bequeathed to his disciples a golden rule to abide by in one's own life: the new commandment of love. Through the Gospel and the Sacraments, especially the Most Holy Eucharist, Christ continues to transmit to the Church the Love that he lived, even to death and death on a Cross. It is very significant, in this regard, that the Liturgy provides for the celebration of the Sacrament of Marriage in the heart of the Eucharistic celebration. This points to the profound bond that unites the two Sacraments. The spouses, in their daily life, must draw inspiration for their behavior from the example of Christ who "loved the Church and gave himself up for her" (Eph 5:25): this supreme act of love is represented in every Eucharistic celebration. It will thus be appropriate for the pastoral care of the family to stress this important sacramental fact as its fundamental reference point. Those who attend Mass—and it is also necessary to make the celebration of it easier for migrants and itinerant people—find in the Eucharist a very strong reference to their own family, to their own marriage, and are encouraged to live their situation in the perspective of faith, seeking in divine grace the necessary strength to succeed.

Lastly, it escapes no one that in today's globalized world human mobility represents an important frontier for the new evangelization. I encourage you, therefore, to persevere in your pastoral task with renewed zeal while, for my part, I assure you of my spiritual closeness. I accompany you with the prayer that the Holy Spirit will make your every initiative fruitful. To this end I invoke the maternal protection of Mary Most Holy, Our Lady of the Way, so that she may help every man and every woman to know her Son Jesus Christ and to receive from him the gift of salvation. With this hope, I cordially impart the Apostolic Blessing to you and your loved ones, as well as to all the migrants and itinerant people in this vast world and to their families.

Address to Participants in the Forum of Family Associations

May 16, 2008

Dear Brothers and Sisters,

Thank you for your visit which enables me to know the activities that your praiseworthy Associations carry out as part of the Forum of Family Associations and the European Federation of Catholic Family Associations. I offer a cordial greeting to each one of you who are present here and in the first place to Mr. Giovanni Giacobbe, President of the Forum, to whom I am grateful for his kind words on your behalf. This meeting is taking place on the occasion of the annual celebration of the *International Day of the Family* which was yesterday, May 15. To emphasize the importance of the occasion, you have wished to organize a special Congress with a timely theme: *"Alliance for the family in Europe: Associations in the leading role,"* in order to address the experiences of various forms of family associations and to sensitize government leaders and the public opinion concerning the central and irreplaceable role carried out by the family in our society.

In fact, as you rightly point out, any political policy that looks well into the future cannot fail to make the family the focus of its attention and planning. This year, as you know well, we are celebrating the fortieth anniversary of the Encyclical *Humanae Vitae* and the twenty-fifth anniversary of the promulgation of the *Charter of the Rights of the Family*, presented by the Holy See on October 22, 1983. These two Documents share a common inspiration since the former strongly reasserts the quality of spousal love, courageously going against the tide of the prevalent culture, selfless and open to life, the latter highlights those inalienable rights that permit the family, founded on the marriage of a man and a woman, to be the natural cradle of human life. The *Charter of the Rights of the Family* in particular, addressed primarily to Governments, offers all those who are invested with responsibility regarding the common good a model and a reference point for the elaboration of a sound legislation for family policies.

At the same time, the Charter is addressed to all families, inspiring them to join forces in the defense and promotion of their rights. And in this regard your associations are particularly well-adapted to implement the spirit of the above-mentioned Charter of the Rights of the Family in the best way.

The beloved Pontiff, John Paul II, also known and rightly so as the "Pope of the family," repeated that the "future of humanity passes by way of the family" (*Familiaris Consortio*, no. 86). He often emphasized the irreplaceable value of the family institution, in accordance with the plan of God the Creator and Father. Precisely at the beginning of my Pontificate, on June 6, 2005, in opening the Convention of the Diocese of Rome, dedicated specifically to the family, I too reaffirmed that the truth about marriage and the family is deeply rooted in the truth about the human being and comes to fulfillment in salvation history, at whose heart lie the words: "God loves his people." Indeed, biblical revelation is above all an expression of a love story, the story of God's Covenant with humankind. This is why the story of the union of life and love between a man and a woman in the covenant of marriage was used by God as a symbol of salvation history. For this very reason, the union of life and love based on the marriage between a man and a woman, which constitutes the family, is an indispensable good for society as a whole and must not be confused or likened to other types of union.

We are well aware of the many challenges facing families today, and we know how difficult it is, in current social conditions, to achieve the ideal of fidelity and solidarity in conjugal love, to bring up children, and to preserve the harmony of the family unit. While on the one hand—thanks be to God—there are shining examples of good families, open to the culture of life and love, on the other hand, sadly, an increasing number of marriages and families are in crisis. From so many families, in a worryingly precarious state, we hear a cry for help, often an unconscious one, which clamors for a response from civil authorities, from ecclesial communities and from the various educational agencies. Accordingly, there is an increasingly urgent need for a common commitment to support families by every means available, from the social and economic point of view, as well as the juridical and spiritual. In this context, I am pleased to recommend and encourage certain initiatives and proposals that have emerged in the course of your Conference. I am thinking, for example, of the laudable commitment to mobilize citizens in support of the initiative for "Family-friendly fiscal policy," urging Governments to promote family-related policies that give parents a real possibility of having children and bringing them up in the family.

For believers, the family, the cell of communion on which society is founded, resembles a "domestic church in miniature" called to reveal God's love to the world. Dear brothers and sisters, help families to be a visible sign of this truth, to defend the values inscribed in human nature itself, and therefore common to all humanity, that is: life, the family and education. These are not principles that derive from a confession of faith but rather from the application of justice that respects every person's rights. This is your mission, dear Christian families! May you never lack trust in the Lord and communion with him in prayer and in the constant reference to his Word. Thus, you will be witnesses of his Love, not merely relying on human resources, but firmly based on the rock that is God, enlivened by the power of his Spirit. May Mary, Queen of the Family, as a bright Star of hope guide the journey of all humanity's families. With these sentiments, I very gladly bless you who are present here and all who belong to the various Associations that you represent.

PASTORAL VISIT TO SAVONA AND GENOA (LIGURIA)

Homily at Mass in Piazza del Popolo, Savona

May 17, 2008

I am thinking of young families and I would like to ask them not to be afraid to adopt, from the first years of marriage, a simple style of domestic prayer, encouraged by the presence of small children who are often prompted to speak spontaneously to the Lord and to Our Lady. I urge parishes and associations to give time and space to prayer since activities are pastorally sterile if they are not constantly preceded, accompanied and sustained by prayer.

Address to the New Ambassador for Bangladesh to the Holy See*

May 29, 2008

Social progress and cohesion demand that everyone—individuals, families, elected officials, public officials and professionals—freely embrace their responsibility to contribute to the life of the community with integrity, honesty and a spirit of service (cfr. *Pacem in Terris*, no. 55; *Centesimus Annus*, no. 46).

. . . A vibrant educational system is essential to a strong democracy. Both the state and the Church have a role to play in helping families impart wisdom, knowledge and moral virtue to their children so that they come to recognize the dignity common to all men and women, include those who belong to cultures and religions different from their own. The Church seeks to contribute to that end by establishing schools that are concerned not only with the cognitive development of children but also with spiritual and moral development. To the degree in which these and other faith-based schools carry out the public service of forming young people in tolerance and respect, they should receive the support they need, including financial aid, for the good of the whole human family.

Address to the New Ambassador for Nigeria to the Holy See**

May 29, 2008

Your Excellency,

I am pleased to welcome you to the Vatican and to receive the Letters that accredit you as extraordinary and plenipotentiary Ambassador of the Federal

---

*   This text is an unofficial translation of the Italian.

**   This text is an unofficial translation of the Italian.

Republic of Nigeria to the Holy See. I thank you for the cordial greetings and sentiments of good will expressed in the name of the President of the Republic, Alhaji Umaru Musa Yar'Adua. I gladly offer my own in return and ask you kindly to pass along my personal gratitude and my good wishes to his Excellency, to the civil authorities and to the Nigerian people.

To help the needy is not merely a humanitarian obligation; it is also a source of joy. In fact, to assist others in a spirit of respect, integrity and impartiality is a rich and formative experience both for individuals and for societies. In this regard, the size, the population, the economic resources and the generosity of its people makes Nigeria one of the most influential countries on the continent and offers it the unique opportunity to support other African countries in achieving the wellbeing and stability they deserve. Your nation has contributed to the numerous efforts to bring social reconciliation to other lands through peace forces, material aid, and diplomatic efforts. I encourage Nigeria to continue to use its considerable human and material resources to guide neighboring countries to peace and prosperity. In fact, when this aid is offered with integrity and sacrifice it brings honor to a country's citizens and government.

Aid must be offered with this spirit at home and abroad to everyone who seeks to alleviate human suffering through research and concrete assistance. The Church has confidence in the fact that the services it offers in the educational sector, social programs and health assistance will continue to have a positive impact on the battle against poverty and disease. The Church always defends life from conception to natural death. As you know, the Church takes very seriously its own role in the campaign against the spread of HIV/AIDS by promoting programs that highlight fidelity in marriage and abstinence outside of marriage. Catholic personnel, including doctors, nurses, aides and teachers, will continue to exhort all men and women, especially the young, to reaffirm the value of the family and to act with moral courage based on faith in the battle against this disease and the conditions associated with it. At the same time, the Church is ready to offer assistance at the practical level to the innumerable sick people on your continent and in the rest of the world.

Mr. Ambassador, the people of Nigeria want full democracy and you have mentioned a number of priorities that your country has identified as necessary steps along the road to meaningful growth and sustainable development. Among these are a democratic government and a state of law, internal security and the efficient carriage of justice. As you know, your Excellency, good government requires that elections be considered unambiguously free, correct and transparent. It also depends on internal security, always based on the democratic ideal of respect for individual rights and for the state of law. Achieving this defining element of democracy requires that public officials first of all address the causes of social unrest and then form citizens in the virtues of respect and tolerance.

I know that in the past friction among different groups has caused concern. Conflicts of this type can often be attributed to a series of factors, including administrative errors, isolated grievances and ethnic tensions. In this regard, I am happy to observe that in the last few years the tensions seem to be less-ening. This can be taken as a real indicator of progress and a sign of hope for the future. By promoting understanding, reconciliation and good will among various groups, the Church continues to encourage a community spirit by seeking to uproot prejudice and supporting openness to all. The Church is particularly interested in promoting interreligious dialogue in the hope that a firm attitude of solidarity on the part of religious leaders will gradually be translated into popular expressions of peaceful acceptance, reciprocal under-standing and cooperation on the national level.

A troubling fact in many countries today is crime. Murder, kidnap-ping for extortion, and the exploitation of women, children, and foreign workers are a few of the worst manifestations of this intolerable practice. The insecurity, distress and aggression caused by the fragmentation of the family, unemployment, poverty and desperation are a few of the social and psychological factors that lie behind this phenomenon. An already fragile situation is exacerbated by a pervasive mentality of materialism and by a lack of respect for the human person. At times, the sense of desperation can lead people to seek deceptively simple solutions to their problems. In such circumstances, young people must be encouraged as much as possible to improve themselves through education, extra-curricular activities, vol-unteer assistance to others and, ideally, the opportunity of employment. In the wake of violent crime can come corruption, which has the effect of discouraging enterprise and investment and to undermine trust in a nation's political, judicial and economic institutions. The energy that Nigeria has injected into the battle against corruption and criminality and toward con-solidating the state of law are very important and ought to be encouraged and applied with equity and impartiality. I pray that politicians and social workers, professionals in economics, medicine and law, police officials, judges and everyone engaged in the struggle against criminality and corrup-tion will cooperate diligently to protect life and property, supported by the loyal cooperation of all the citizens. The Church will not fail to make its own specific contribution by offering holistic education based on honesty, integrity and the love of God and neighbor. The Church struggles to create opportunities for your people in difficult circumstances, always reminding them that "all serious and upright human conduct is hope in action" (*Spe Salvi*, no. 35).

Mr. Ambassador, I wish you every success in your mission and I assure you of the willing cooperation of the dicasteries of the Roman Curia. I recall with appreciation the generous welcome reserved for my predecessor, Pope John Paul II, on the occasion of his two visits to Nigeria. I pray that the sweet memory of that messenger of peace will continue to inspire the Nigerian people. May almighty God grant you, Excellency, your family, and the nation you represent abundant and enduring blessings of wellbeing and peace!

Address to Members of the Italian Episcopal Conference on the Occasion of the Fifty-Eighth General Assembly

May 29, 2008

In this context [of the integral formation of the human person,] how can one fail to say a word in favor of these specific places of formation which are the schools? In a democratic State, that is distinguished for its promotion of free initiative in every field, the exclusion of adequate support for the ecclesial institutions' commitment in the scholastic field does not seem justifiable. Indeed, it is legitimate to ask oneself whether the quality of teaching might not benefit from a lively comparison with the newly established formative centers, (with respect for the valid ministerial programs for all), and the multifaceted popular forces, (concerned to interpret the educational choices of each single family). It makes one think that a similar comparison would not fail to produce beneficial effects. Dear Italian Brother Bishops, not only in the very important area of education, but in a certain sense in one's own complex situation, Italy needs to come out of a difficult period, in which its economic and social dynamism seems to be weakening, its trust in the future diminishing whereas the sense of insecurity is growing due to the conditions of poverty of so many families, with the consequent tendency for each one to withdraw into itself. It is precisely the awareness of this context that with particular joy we perceive the signs of a new climate, more confident and more constructive. It is linked to the appearance of more serene relationships between political forces and institutions, in virtue of a more lively perception of the common responsibility of the Nation's future. And what gives comfort is that such a perception seems to be spreading in public feeling, in the territory and in social categories. In fact, the desire to continue the journey, to face and resolve together at least the most urgent and grave problems, to initiate a new season of economic, but also civil and moral growth, is spreading.

Message to Participants Attending the "High-Level Conference on World Food Security: The Challenges of Climate Change and Bioenergy" Organized by the UN Food and Agriculture Organization

June 2, 2008

The global increase in the production of agricultural products, however, can be effective only if production is accompanied by effective distribution and if it is primarily destined to satisfy essential needs. It certainly is not easy, but it would allow, among other things, to rediscover the value of the rural family: it would not be limited to preserving the transmission, from parents to children, of the cultivation methods, of conserving and distributing foodstuffs, but above all it would preserve a model of life, of education, of culture and of religiosity. Moreover, from the economic profile, it ensures an effective and loving attention to the weakest and, by virtue of the principle of subsidiarity, it could assume a direct role in the distribution chain and the trading of agricultural food products reducing the costs of intermediaries and favoring small scale production.

Address to the Bishops of Honduras on Their *Ad Limina* Visit

June 26, 2008

Likewise, a context that requires special pastoral attention is that of marriage and the family, whose solidity and stability so greatly benefit both the Church and society. In this respect, it is right to recognize the important step taken to include in your Country's Constitution an explicit recognition of marriage. Yet, you know well that possessing a good legislation does not suffice without the cultural work and catechesis required to illuminate the truth and beauty of marriage, a true perpetual covenant of life and love between a man and a woman.

Address at the Welcoming Celebration by the Young People at Barangaroo, Sydney Harbor

July 17, 2008

There is also something sinister which stems from the fact that freedom and tolerance are so often separated from truth. This is fuelled by the notion, widely held today, that there are no absolute truths to guide our lives. Relativism, by indiscriminately giving value to practically everything, has made "experience" all-important. Yet, experiences, detached from any consideration of what is good or true, can lead, not to genuine freedom, but to moral or intellectual confusion, to a lowering of standards, to a loss of self-respect, and even to despair.

Dear friends, life is not governed by chance; it is not random. Your very existence has been willed by God, blessed and given a purpose (cf. Gn 1:28)! Life is not just a succession of events or experiences, helpful though many of them are. It is a search for the true, the good and the beautiful. It is to this end that we make our choices; it is for this that we exercise our freedom; it is in this—in truth, in goodness, and in beauty—that we find happiness and joy. Do not be fooled by those who see you as just another consumer in a market of undifferentiated possibilities, where choice itself becomes the good, novelty usurps beauty, and subjective experience displaces truth.

Christ offers more! Indeed he offers everything! Only he who is the Truth can be the Way and hence also the Life. Thus the "way" which the Apostles brought to the ends of the earth is life in Christ. This is the life of the Church. And the entrance to this life, to the Christian way, is Baptism.

This evening I wish therefore to recall briefly something of our understanding of Baptism before tomorrow considering the Holy Spirit. On the day of your Baptism, God drew you into his holiness (cf. 2 Pt 1:4). You were adopted as a son or daughter of the Father. You were incorporated into Christ. You were made a dwelling place of his Spirit (cf. 1 Cor 6:19). Indeed, toward the conclusion of your Baptism, the priest turned to your parents and those gathered and, calling you by your name, said: "you have become a new creation" (Rite of Baptism, no. 99).

Dear friends, in your homes, schools and universities, in your places of work and recreation, remember that you are a new creation! As Christians you stand in this world knowing that God has a human face—Jesus Christ—the "way" who satisfies all human yearning, and the "life" to which we are called to bear witness, walking always in his light (cf. *Rite of Baptism*, no. 100).

The task of witness is not easy. There are many today who claim that God should be left on the sidelines, and that religion and faith, while fine for individuals, should either be excluded from the public forum altogether or included only in the pursuit of limited pragmatic goals. This secularist vision seeks to explain human life and shape society with little or no reference to the Creator. It presents itself as neutral, impartial and inclusive of everyone. But in reality, like every ideology, secularism imposes a world-view. If God is irrelevant to public life, then society will be shaped in a godless image. When God is eclipsed, our ability to recognize the natural order, purpose, and the "good" begins to wane. What was ostensibly promoted as human ingenuity soon manifests itself as folly, greed and selfish exploitation. And so we have become more and more aware of our need for humility before the delicate complexity of God's world.

PASTORAL VISIT TO CAGLIARI–SARDINIA
Address to the Young People of Sardinia

September 7, 2008

On October 20, 1985, John Paul II, meeting here in Cagliari young people from all over Sardinia, proposed three important values to build a society of fraternity and solidarity. They are suggestions that are still timely even today, which I willingly repeat, emphasizing in the first place the value of the family, to safeguard as an "ancient and sacred inheritance," the Pope said. You all have experienced the importance of family, as sons and daughters and as siblings; but the capacity to form a new one cannot be taken for granted. You must prepare yourselves for it. In the past traditional society helped to form and safeguard the family more. Today it is no longer so, or rather it is "on paper," but in actuality a different mentality dominates. Other forms of living together are permitted. Sometimes the term "family" is used for unions that, in reality, are not a family. Above all, in our context, the capacity for couples to defend the unity of the family nucleus is very reduced and at the cost of great sacrifice. Dear youth, recover the value of the family. Love it, not only as a tradition, but as a mature and conscious choice. Love the family in which you were born and prepare yourselves to love also those that with God's help you yourselves will make. I say "prepare yourselves," because real love does not happen suddenly. Beyond sentiment, love is made of responsibility, constancy and a sense of duty. One learns all of this through the prolonged practice of the Christian virtues of trust, purity, abandonment to Providence and prayer. In this commitment of growth toward a mature love the Christian community will always support you, because in it the family finds its highest dignity. The Second Vatican Council calls it a "little church" because Matrimony is a Sacrament, that is, a holy and efficacious sign of the love that God gives us in Christ through the Church.

Strictly connected to this first value I mentioned is the other value I wish to emphasize: *serious intellectual and moral formation*, indispensable in planning and building your future and that of society. The person who offers you a "discount" on this is not concerned for your good. In fact, how could one seriously plan a future if the natural desire that is in you to understand and to compare yourselves is neglected? The crisis of a society begins when it no longer knows how to hand down its cultural patrimony and its fundamental values to the new generations. I am not referring only and simply to the scholastic system. The issue is broader. There is, as we know, an educational emergency, which in order to be faced requires parents and teachers capable of sharing all the goodness and truth that they have experienced deeply firsthand. It requires young people who are open to their internal lives, curious to learn and to bring everything back to the fundamental needs and yearnings of the heart. You are truly free—in other words, impassioned for the truth. The Lord Jesus said: "the truth will set you free" (Jn 8:32). Modern nihilism instead preaches the opposite, that it is instead freedom which will make you true. Indeed, there are those who hold that no truth exists, thus opening the path to the disposal of the concepts of good and evil and even making them interchangeable. I was told that in the Sardinian culture there is this proverb: "It is better to want for bread than for justice." Man can indeed withstand and overcome the pangs of hunger, but he cannot live where justice and truth are banished. Material bread is not enough, it is not sufficient to live in a fully human way; another food for which to always hunger is necessary, food which nourishes one's personal growth and that of the family and of society.

This food, and it is the third great value, is *a sincere and deep faith*, which becomes the substance of your life. When the sense of the presence of God is lost, everything is "tasteless" and reduces to a single dimension. All the rest is "crushed" on the material level. When each thing is considered only for its usefulness, the essence of that which surrounds us is no longer perceived, and above all of the persons whom we meet. With the disappearance of the mystery of God the mystery of all that exists disappears too; things and people interest me in so much as they satisfy my needs, not for what they are. All of this constitutes a cultural fact that one breathes from birth and that produces permanent interior effects. Faith, in this sense, before being a religious belief, is a way of seeing reality, a way of thinking, an interior sensitivity that enriches the human person as such. Well, dear friends, Christ is also the

Teacher of this, because he has completely shared in our humanity and is contemporaneous with man of every epoch. This typically Christian reality is a stupendous grace! Being with Jesus, visiting him like a friend in the Gospel and in the Sacraments, you can all learn, in a new way, what society often is not able to give you, that is, a religious sense. And precisely because it is something new, discovering it is wonderful.

Dear friends, like the young St. Augustine, with all his problems on his difficult path, each one of you, every creature, hears the symbolic call from above; every beautiful creature is attracted back to the beauty of the Creator, who is effectively concentrated in the Face of Jesus Christ. When the soul experiences this, it exclaims, "Late have I loved you, o beauty ever ancient ever new, late have I loved you!" (*Conf.* X, 27.38). May each one of you rediscover God as the sense and foundation of every creature, light of truth, flame of charity, bond of unity, like the hymn of the *Agorà* of the Italian youth. May you be docile to the power of the Spirit! He, the Holy Spirit, the Protagonist of the World Youth Day at Sydney; he makes you witnesses of Christ. Not in word but in deed, with a new type of life. You will not be afraid any longer to lose your freedom, because you will live it fully by giving it away in love. You will no longer be attached to material goods, because you will feel within you the joy of sharing them. You will cease to be sad with the sadness of the world, but you will feel sorrow at evil and rejoice at goodness, especially for mercy and forgiveness. And if this happens, if you will have truly discovered God in the Face of Christ, you will no longer think of the Church as an institution external to you, but as your spiritual family, as we are living now, at this moment. This is the faith that your forefathers have handed down to you. This is the faith you are called to live today, in very different times.

Family, formation and faith. Here, dear young people of Cagliari and of the whole of Sardinia, I too, like Pope John Paul II, leave to you these three words, three values to make your own with the light and the strength of the Spirit of Christ. May Our Lady of Bonaria, First Patroness and sweet Queen of the Sardinian people, guide you, protect you and accompany you always! With affection I bless you, assuring you of a daily remembrance in prayer.

Address to the Bishops of
Paraguay on Their *Ad Limina* Visit

September 11, 2008

A significant aspect of the mission proper to lay people is their service to society through the exercise of politics. According to the Church's doctrinal ministry, "The direct duty to work for a just ordering of society, on the other hand, is proper to the lay faithful" (*Deus Caritas Est*, no. 29). Lay people must therefore be encouraged to live this important dimension of social charity with responsibility and dedication, so that the human community to which they belong with every right may progress in justice, rectitude and in the defense of true and authentic values—such as the protection of human life, marriage and the family—thereby contributing to the true human and spiritual good of all society.

APOSTOLIC JOURNEY TO FRANCE ON THE OCCASION OF
THE 150TH ANNIVERSARY OF THE APPARITIONS OF THE
BLESSED VIRGIN MARY AT LOURDES

Address to the French Episcopal Conference

September 14, 2008

What are the other areas that require particular attention? The answers probably vary from one diocese to another, but there is certainly one problem which arises with particular urgency everywhere: the situation of the family. We know that marriage and the family are today experiencing real turbulence. The words of the Evangelist about the boat in the storm on the lake may be applied to the family: "waves beat into the boat, so that the boat was already filling" (Mk 4:37). The factors which brought about this crisis are well known, and there is no need to list them here. For several decades, laws in different countries have been relativizing its nature as the primordial cell of society. Often they are seeking more to adapt to the *mores* and demands of particular individuals or groups, than to promote the common good of society. The stable union of a man and a women, ordered to building earthly happiness through the birth of children given by God, is no longer, in the minds of certain people, the reference point for conjugal commitment. However, experience shows that the family is the foundation on which the whole of society rests. Moreover, Christians know that the family is also the living cell of the Church. The more the family is steeped in the spirit and values of the Gospel, the more the Church herself will be enriched by them and the better she will fulfill her vocation. I recognize and encourage warmly the efforts you are making to support the various associations active in assisting families. You have reason to uphold firmly, even at the cost of opposing prevailing trends, the principles which constitute the strength and the greatness of the sacrament of marriage. The Church wishes to remain utterly faithful to the mandate entrusted to her by her Founder, her Master and Lord, Jesus Christ. She does not cease to repeat with him: "What God has joined together, let not man put asunder!" (Mt 19:6). The Church did not give herself this mission: she received it. To be sure, none can deny that certain families experience trials, sometimes very painful ones. Families in difficulty must be supported, they must be helped to understand the greatness of marriage, and encouraged not to relativize God's will and the laws of life which he has given us. A particularly painful situation, as you know, concerns those who are divorced and remarried. The Church, which cannot oppose the will of Christ, firmly maintains the principle of the indissolubility of marriage, while surrounding with the greatest affection those men and women who, for a variety of reasons, fail to respect it. Hence initiatives aimed at blessing irregular unions cannot be admitted. The Post-Synodal Apostolic Exhortation *Familiaris Consortio* has indicated a way open to the fruit of reflection carried out with respect for truth and charity.

Young people, I know well dear Brothers, are at the center of your concerns. You devote much of your time to them, and you are right to do so. As you know, I have recently encountered a great multitude of them in Sydney, in the course of World Youth Day. I appreciated their enthusiasm and their capacity to dedicate themselves to prayer. Even while living in a world which courts them and flatters their base instincts, and carrying, as they do, the heavy burdens handed down by history, the young retain a freshness of soul which has elicited my admiration. I appealed to their sense of responsibility by urging them always to draw support from the vocation given them by God on the day of their Baptism. "Our strength lies in what Christ wants from us," Cardinal Jean-Marie Lustiger used to say. In the course of his first journey to France, my venerable Predecessor delivered an address to the young people of your country which has lost none of its relevance, and which was received at the time with unforgettable fervor. "Moral permissiveness does not make people happy," he proclaimed at the *Parc des Princes*, amid thunderous applause. The good sense which inspired the healthy reaction of his hearers is still alive. I ask the Holy Spirit to speak to the hearts of all the faithful and, more generally, of all your compatriots, so as to give them—or to restore to them—the desire for a life lived in accordance with the criteria of true happiness.

Address to the Bishops of Panama on Their *Ad Limina* Visit

September 19, 2008

Many families in your homeland live the Christian ideal with self-denial amidst great difficulty that threaten the solidarity of conjugal love, responsible fatherhood and the harmony and stability of the domestic heart. The efforts made will never be enough to develop a lively pastoral care of the family that invites people to discover the beauty of the vocation to Christian marriage, to defend human life from its conception to its natural end and to build families in which children are raised in love for the truth of the Gospel and solid human values. In your country, as in other places, people are going through difficult times that give rise to hardship as well as situations that promise great hope. In the present situation, it is especially urgent that the Church in Panama does not cease to offer the illumination that contributes to the solution of the pressing human problems that exist, promoting a moral consensus of society based on the fundamental values.

Address to Participants in the
World Meeting of the Retrouvaille Movement

September 26, 2008

Your Eminence,
Venerable Brothers in the Episcopate and in the Priesthood,
Dear Brothers and Sisters,

I welcome you with joy today, on the occasion of the world meeting of the *Retrouvaille* Movement. I greet you all, married couples and priests, along with the international leaders of this association, which has worked with great dedication at the service of couples in difficulty for more than thirty years. I greet in particular Cardinal Ennio Antonelli, President of the Pontifical Council for the Family, and thank him for his courteous words, as well as for describing your Movement's goals to me.

I am impressed, dear friends, by your experience that brings you into contact with families marked by a marital crisis. In reflecting on your activity, once again I recognized God's "finger," that is, the action of the Holy Spirit who generates in the Church adequate responses to the needs and emergencies of every epoch. Of course, in our day, a very deeply felt emergency is that of separations and divorces. Thus, the insight of the Canadian couple Guy and Jeannine Beland in 1977 was providential, to help couples face serious crises with a special program geared to rebuilding their relationship—not as an alternative to psychotherapy but through a distinct and complementary process. You are not in fact professionals; you are married couples, many of whom have personally lived through the same difficulties, have overcome them with God's grace and the support of *Retrouvaille* and in turn have felt the desire to joyfully place your own experience at the service of others. There are various priests among you who guide couples on their way, breaking open the Word and the Bread of life for them. "You received without pay, give without pay" (Mt 10:8): you refer constantly to these words, which Jesus addressed to his disciples.

As your experience shows, a marital crisis—here we are speaking of serious and grave crises—constitutes a two-sided reality. One side of it, especially in its acute and more painful phase, presents itself as a failure, as the proof that the dream is over or has become a nightmare and that, unfortunately, "there is nothing left to be done." This is the negative side. There is another side, however, often unknown to us but that God sees. Every crisis, in fact—nature teaches us this—is a passage that leads to a new stage of life. Yet, if this happens automatically in inferior creatures, in the human being it involves freedom, the will, and therefore a "hope that is greater" than desperation. In the darkest moments, the spouses have lost hope. It is then that they are in need of others who preserve it, of a "we," of the company of true friends who, with the greatest respect and a sincere desire for good, are prepared to share a little of their own hope with those who have lost it—not in a sentimental or overly ambitious way, but in an organized and realistic one. Thus, at the moment of the break, you become for the couple the real possibility of having a positive reference, whom they can trust in their despair. In fact, when their relationship disintegrates, the husband and wife are plunged into loneliness, both individually and as a couple. They lose sight of the horizon of communion with God, with others and with the Church. It is then that your meetings offer them a "foothold" so as not to lose everything and to gradually get back on their feet. I like to think of you as custodians of a greater hope for married couples who have lost it.

Hence a crisis is a passage of growth. The account of the wedding feast at Cana can be interpreted from this perspective (Jn 2:1-11). The Virgin Mary realizes that the husband and wife "have no wine" and tells Jesus. This lack of wine brings to mind the moment in a couple's life when love ends, joy runs out and the enthusiasm of the marriage suddenly drains away. After Jesus had transformed the water into wine, the bridegroom received compliments because, they said, he had kept "the good wine" until that moment. This implies that Jesus' wine was better than the previous. We know that this "good wine" is a symbol of salvation, of the new nuptial covenant that Jesus came to make with humanity. Yet every Christian marriage, even the most wretched and insecure one, is a sacrament of precisely this and therefore can find in humility the courage to ask the Lord for help. When a husband and wife in difficulty or—as your experience shows—even already separated entrust themselves to Mary and turn to the One who made "one flesh" of two, they can be certain that, with the Lord's help, this crisis will become a passage of growth and that love will emerge from it purified, matured and strengthened. God alone can do this. He wants his disciples to serve as effective collaborators, to approach couples, listen to them and help them rediscover the hidden treasure of their marriage, the flame that has been buried under the ashes. It is he who revives this flame and brings it back to life; certainly not in the same way as falling in love, but in a different, more intense and profound manner; but it is always the same flame.

Dear friends, who have chosen to put yourselves at the service of others in such a delicate area, I assure you of my prayers that your commitment will not become merely an activity, but will remain always, at its roots, a witness of God's love. Yours is a service "against the tide." Today, in fact, when couples enter a crisis, they find many people ready to advise separation. Divorce is often proposed with ease even to spouses who are married in the Name of the Lord, in the forgetfulness that man cannot divide what God has united (cf. Mt 19:6; Mk 10:9). In order to carry out your mission you too need to nourish your spiritual life constantly, to put love into all that you do so that, when you encounter difficult situations, your hope will never run out or be reduced to a formula. May the Holy Family of Nazareth, to whom I entrust your service, especially the most difficult cases, help you in this delicate apostolic task. May Mary, Queen of the Family, be beside you, as I impart my heartfelt Apostolic Blessing to you and to all of the members of the *Retrouvaille* Movement.

Address to the Bishops of
Ecuador on Their *Ad Limina* Visit

October 16, 2008

In this regard, I would like to thank you for the effort you are making, not without great sacrifices, to attract the attention of society to those values that make human life more just and supportive. Although the Church's activity cannot be confused with political action (cf. *Deus Caritas Est*, no. 28), she must nevertheless make her contribution to the human community overall through reflection and moral judgments on those political issues that especially affect the dignity of the person (cf. *Gaudium et Spes*, no. 76). Among these should be pointed out, partly because of its importance for the future of your People, the promotion and stability of the family, founded on the bond of love between a man and a woman, the defense of human life from the moment of its conception to its natural end, and also the responsibility of parents for the moral education of their children, in which the important human and Christian values that forged the identity of your peoples are transmitted.

PASTORAL VISIT TO THE PONTIFICAL SHRINE OF POMPEII

Angelus

October 19, 2008

On this very day Louis Martin and Zélie Guérin, the parents of St. Thérèse of the Child Jesus whom Pius XI declared Patroness of Missions, are being beatified at Lisieux. These new Blesseds, accompanied and shared, with their prayers and their Gospel witness, the journey of their daughter, called by the Lord to consecrate herself to him without reserve within the walls of Carmel. It was there, in the concealment of the cloister, that the little St. Thérèse fulfilled her vocation: "In the heart of the Church, my mother, I will be love" (*Manuscripts Autobiographiques*, Lisieux, 1957, 229). In thinking of the beatification of the Martin couple, I am keen to recall another intention very dear to my heart: the family, whose role in teaching children a universal outlook that is both responsible and open to the world and its problems is fundamental, as it also is in the formation of vocations to missionary life. And then, so as to follow in spirit on the pilgrimage that so many families made a month ago to this Shrine, let us invoke the motherly protection of Our Lady of Pompeii upon all the families in the world, thinking already of the Fourth World Meeting of Families, scheduled to take place in Mexico City in January 2009.

Address After Holy Mass to Commemorate the Fiftieth Anniversary of the Election of Blessed Pope John XXIII

October 28, 2008

Allow me to place a special emphasis on the family, the central subject of ecclesial life, the womb of education in the faith and the irreplaceable cell of social life. In this regard the future Pope John wrote in a letter to his relatives: *"The education that leaves the deepest traces is always that provided at home. I have forgotten much of what I have read in books but I still remember very clearly all that I learned from my parents and from the elderly"* (December 20, 1932). In particular, in the family's daily life one learns to live the fundamental Christian precept of love. This is precisely why the Church counts on the family, whose mission it is to express everywhere, through her children, *"the fullness of Christian charity, than which nothing is more effective in eradicating the seeds of discord, nothing more efficacious in promoting concord, just peace and the brotherly unity of all"* (*Gaudet Mater Ecclesia*).

To conclude, returning to the parish, the theme of your Diocesan Synod, you are acquainted with Pope John XXIII's solicitude for this body that is so important in ecclesial life. With great confidence Pope Roncalli entrusted to the parish, the family of families, the task of nourishing sentiments of communion and brotherhood among the faithful. Formed by the Eucharist, the parish will be able to become he thought a leaven of healthy restlessness in the widespread consumerism and individualism of our time, reawakening solidarity and opening in faith the eye of the heart to recognize the Father, who is love freely given and who desires to share his own joy with his children.

Dear friends, the image of Our Lady that Pope John received as a gift on his visit to Loreto, a few days before the opening of the Council, has accompanied you to Rome. He wanted the statue to be set in his home diocese's Diocesan Seminary, named after him. I am glad to see there are many seminarians who are enthusiastic about their vocation. I willingly entrust to the Mother of God all the families and parishes, proposing to them the model of the Holy Family of Nazareth: may they be the first seminary and know how to develop in their own milieus vocations to the priesthood, to the mission, to religious consecration and to family life according to the Heart of Christ. In a famous Visit during the first months of his Pontificate, the Blessed asked those listening to him what they thought the meaning of the meeting was and he proceeded to answer his own question: *"The Pope's eyes have met yours and he has placed his heart beside your heart"* (On His First Christmas as Pope, 1958). I pray Pope John to grant us to experience the closeness of his gaze and his heart, so that we may truly feel like *God's family.*

Address to the New Ambassador of Lithuania to the Holy See

November 7, 2008

The Holy See values its diplomatic links with your country, marked as it is by centuries of Christian witness. Working together, we can help to forge a Europe in which priority is given to the defense of marriage and family life, to the protection of human life from conception to natural death, and to the promotion of sound ethical practices in medical and scientific research: practices which are truly respectful of the dignity of the human person.

Address to the New Ambassador of Argentina to the Holy See

December 5, 2008

The twenty-first century is showing ever more clearly the need to build a personal, family and social life in harmony with the indispensable values that uplift the person and the entire community. Among these values emphasis should be placed on: the endorsement of the family based on the marriage of a man and a woman, the inclination to a morality whose main traits are engraved in the depths of the human soul, the spirit of sacrifice and generous solidarity expressed especially when circumstances are particularly adverse, the defense of human life from its conception to its natural end, the eradication of poverty, promoting honesty, the fight against corruption, the adoption of means that help parents in their inalienable right to raise their children with their own ethical and religious convictions, as well as the promotion of young people so that they may be men and women of peace and reconciliation.

Message for the World Day of Peace

[January 1, 2009]

Fighting Poverty to Build Peace

December 8, 2008

5. A third area requiring attention in programs for fighting poverty, which once again highlights its intrinsic moral dimension, is *child poverty*. When poverty strikes a family, the children prove to be the most vulnerable victims: almost half of those living in absolute poverty today are children. To take the side of children when considering poverty means giving priority to those objectives which concern them most directly, such as caring for mothers, commitment to education, access to vaccines, medical care and drinking

water, safeguarding the environment, and above all, commitment to defense of the family and the stability of relations within it. When the family is weakened, it is inevitably children who suffer. If the dignity of women and mothers is not protected, it is the children who are affected most.

Address to the Bishops of Taiwan on Their *Ad Limina* Visit

December 12, 2008

Effective catechesis inevitably builds stronger families, which in turn give birth to new priestly vocations. Indeed, the family is that "domestic Church" where the Gospel of Jesus is first heard and the art of Christian living first practiced (cf. *Lumen Gentium*, no. 11). The Church, at every level, must cherish and foster the gift of priesthood so that young men will generously respond to the Lord's call to become laborers in the vineyard. Parents, pastors, teachers, parish leaders, and all the members of the Church must set before young people the radical decision to follow Christ, so that in finding him, they find themselves (cf. *Sacramentum Caritatis*, no. 25).

The family, as you know, is that "first and vital cell": the prototype for every level of society (cf. *Apostolicam Actuositatem*, no. 11). Your recent Pastoral Letter *Social Concern and Evangelization* underscores the Church's need to engage actively in the promotion of family life. Founded on an irrevocable covenant, the family leads people to discover goodness, beauty and truth, so that they may perceive their unique destiny and learn how to contribute to the building up of a civilization of love. Your deep concern for the good of families and society as a whole, my Brothers, moves you to assist couples in preserving the indissolubility of their marital promises. Never tire in promoting just civil legislation and policies that protect the sacredness of marriage. Safeguard this sacrament from all that can harm it, especially the deliberate taking of life in its most vulnerable stages.

General Audience

December 17, 2008

Because of the atmosphere that distinguishes it, Christmas is a universal celebration. In fact, even those who do not profess themselves to be believers can perceive in this annual Christian event something extraordinary and transcendent, something intimate that speaks to the heart. It is a Feast that praises the gift of life. The birth of a child must always be an event that brings joy; the embrace of a newborn baby usually inspires feelings of kindness and care, of emotion and tenderness. Christmas is the encounter with a newborn baby lying in a humble grotto. In contemplating him in the manger, how can we fail to think of all those children who continue to be born today in great poverty in many regions of the world? How can we fail to think of those newborn infants who are not welcomed, who are rejected, who do not manage to survive because of the lack of care and attention? How can we fail to think also of the families who long for the joy of a child and do not see their hope fulfilled? Unfortunately, under the influence of hedonist consumerism Christmas risks losing its spiritual meaning and being reduced to a mere commercial opportunity for purchases and the exchange of gifts! However, it is true that the difficulties, the uncertainties and the financial crisis itself that numerous families have had to come to terms with in recent months and which is affecting all humanity could be an incentive to rediscover the warmth of simplicity, friendship and solidarity: typical values of Christmas. Stripped of its consumerist and materialistic encrustations, Christmas can thus become an opportunity for welcoming, as a personal gift, the message of hope that emanates from the mystery of Christ's Birth.

Address to the New Ambassador of Luxembourg to the Holy See

December 18, 2008

I would also like to take the opportunity of our meeting to express to you my very deep concern about the text of the law on euthanasia and assisted suicide that is currently being discussed in Parliament. In practice, this text accompanied moreover and in a contradictory manner by another bill which contains felicitous legal measures for developing palliative care to make suffering more bearable in the final stages of illness and to encourage the appropriate humane care for the patient legitimizes the possibility of putting an end to life. Political leaders, who have the grave duty of serving the good of the human being, and likewise doctors and families, must remember that "the deliberate decision to deprive an innocent human being of his life is always morally evil and can never be licit" (*Evangelium Vitae*, no. 57). In truth, love and true compassion take a different path. The request that rises from the human heart, especially when a person is tempted to cede to discouragement and has reached the point of wishing to disappear, is above all a request for company and an appeal for greater solidarity and support in trial. This appeal may seem demanding but it is the only one worthy of the human being and gives access to new and deeper forms of solidarity which, ultimately, enrich and strengthen family and social ties. On this path of humanization all people of good will will be asked to cooperate and the Church, for her part, is determined to commit to it all her resources of attention and service. Faithful to their Christian and human roots and to the constant concern to further the common good, may every member of the population of Luxembourg always have at heart to reaffirm the greatness and inviolable character of human life!

Address to the New Ambassador of Belize to the Holy See

December 18, 2008

Essential to the future of any society are its families. In my *Message for the 2008 World Day of Peace*, I emphasized the unique role of the family as "the foundation of society and the first and indispensable teacher of peace" (no. 3). Strong families have long been a hallmark of your national life, and the Catholic community in Belize is committed to work with all people of good will in meeting responsibly the growing threats to the institutions of marriage and the family, especially by upholding the nature of marriage based on the life-long union of a man and woman, protecting the specific rights of the family, and respecting the inviolable dignity of all human life, from the moment of conception to natural death. This witness, aimed at informing public opinion and fostering wise, far-sighted family policies, is meant to contribute to the common good by defending an institution which has been, and continues to be, "an essential resource in the service of peace" and social progress (cf. ibid., no. 5).

Address to the New Ambassador of the Republic of Seychelles to the Holy See

December 19, 2008

However, this concern for education would be in vain if the family institution were to be excessively weakened. Families are constantly in need of the encouragement and support of public entities. A profound harmony exists between the tasks of the family and the duties of the state. To foster a successful synergy between them is to work effectively for a future of prosperity and social peace.

For her part, the local Church spares no effort to accompany families, offering them the light of the Gospel which sheds light on the full grandeur and beauty of the "mystery" of the family and helping them to assume their educational responsibilities. With regard to those in difficulty, she concerns herself with helping to bring peace to relationships and to foster reconciliation in hearts.

Angelus

December 28, 2008

Dear Brothers and Sisters,

On this Sunday following the Nativity of the Lord we are joyfully celebrating the Holy Family of Nazareth. It is a most suitable context because Christmas is the Feast of the family *par excellence*. This is demonstrated by numerous traditions and social customs, especially the practice of gathering together as a family for festive meals and for greetings and the exchange of gifts; and how can the hardship and suffering caused by certain family wounds which on these occasions are amplified go unnoticed? Jesus willed to be born and to grow up in a human family; he had the Virgin Mary as his mother and Joseph who acted as his father; they raised and educated him with immense love. Jesus' family truly deserves the title "Holy," for it was fully engaged in the desire to do the will of God, incarnate in the adorable presence of Jesus. On the one hand, it was a family like all others and as such, it is a model of conjugal love, collaboration, sacrifice and entrustment to divine Providence, hard work and solidarity in short, of all those values that the family safeguards and promotes, making an important contribution to forming the fabric of every society. At the same time, however, the Family of Nazareth was unique, different from all other families because of its singular vocation linked to the mission of the Son of God. With precisely this uniqueness it points out to every family and in the first place to Christian families God's horizon, the sweet and demanding primacy of his will, the prospect of Heaven to which we are all destined. For all this, today we thank God, but also the Virgin Mary and St. Joseph, who with much faith and willingness cooperated in the Lord's plan of salvation.

Thousands of people are meeting in Madrid today to express the beauty and value of the family. I would now like to speak to them in Spanish.

I now address a cordial greeting to the participants gathered at this moving celebration in Madrid to pray for the family and to commit with fortitude and hope to work in its favor. The family is certainly a grace of God through which transpires what God himself is: Love an entirely free love that sustains boundless fidelity, even in times of difficulty or dejection. These qualities are reflected eminently in the Holy Family in which Jesus came into the world, was raised and was filled with wisdom, with Mary's thoughtful care and St. Joseph's faithful custody. Dear families, do not let the love, openness to life and incomparable ties that unite your home weaken. Ask God for this constantly, pray together so that your resolutions may be enlightened by faith and strengthened by divine grace on the path to holiness. Thus, with the joy of sharing all things in love, you will give the world a beautiful witness to how important the family is for the human person and for society. The Pope is beside you, praying the Lord especially for those in every family who are most in need of health, work, comfort and company. In this *Angelus* prayer, I entrust you all to our Mother in Heaven, the Most Blessed Virgin Mary.

Dear brothers and sisters, in speaking of the family, I cannot then omit to recall that from January 14 to 18, 2009 the Sixth World Meeting of Families will be taking place in Mexico City. Let us pray from this moment for this important ecclesial event and entrust every family to the Lord, especially those families most sorely tried by life's difficulties and by the scourges of misunderstanding and division. May the Redeemer, born in Bethlehem, give to all of them serenity and the strength to walk united on the path of good.

After the *Angelus*

January 6, 2009

I address my fervent good wishes to our brothers and sisters of the Eastern Churches who, in accordance with the Julian Calendar, will be celebrating Holy Christmas tomorrow. May the memory of the Savior's birth kindle ever more brightly in their hearts the joy of being loved by God. The memory of these our brothers in the faith leads me in spirit to the Holy Land and to the Middle East. I continue to follow with lively apprehension the violent armed conflict in the Gaza Strip. As I reaffirm that hatred and the rejection of dialogue can only lead to war, I would like today to encourage the initiatives and efforts of all who, having peace at heart, are trying to help the Israelis and Palestinians to agree to sit down together and talk. May God sustain the endeavors of these courageous "peacemakers"!

In many countries, the Feast of the Epiphany is also the feast of children. I therefore address a special thought to all children, who are the wealth and blessing of the world, and above all to those who are denied a serene childhood. I wish, in particular, to draw attention to the dozens of children and youth who have been kidnapped in these recent months and over Christmas in the Eastern Province of the Democratic Republic of the Congo by armed bands that have attacked the villages, reaping a heavy toll of victims and injuring many. I appeal to the perpetrators of this inhuman brutality to restore the children to their families and to a secure future of development to which they, together with the beloved peoples in those places, are entitled. At the same time I express my spiritual closeness to the local Churches, whose people and institutions have also been struck, while I urge both Pastors and faithful to be strong and steadfast in hope.

The episodes of violence targeting children, which, unfortunately, are also happening in other parts of the world, appear even more deplorable given that the twentieth anniversary of the Convention of the Rights of the Child occurs in 2009, an engagement that the international community is called to renew in the defense, protection and promotion of children in the whole world. May the Lord help those and they are countless who work daily at the service of the new generations, helping them to be protagonists of their own future. In addition, the World Day of the Missionary Childhood, which is celebrated on today's Feast of the Epiphany, is an appropriate opportunity to emphasize that children and youth can play an important role in the dissemination of the Gospel and in acts of solidarity for their neediest peers. May the Lord reward them!

Address to the Members of the Diplomatic Corps

January 8, 2009

In this vast panorama embracing the whole world, I wish likewise to dwell for a moment on Latin America. There too, people desire to live in peace, liberated from poverty and able freely to exercise their fundamental rights. In this context, the needs of emigrants need to be taken into consideration by legislation which would make it easier to reunite families, reconciling the legitimate requirements of security with those of inviolable respect for the person. . . .

I return to my Message for the celebration of this year's World Day of Peace. There I recalled that the poorest human beings are unborn children (no. 3). But I cannot fail to mention, in conclusion, others who are poor, like the infirm, the elderly left to themselves, broken families and those lacking points of reference. Poverty is fought if humanity becomes more fraternal as a result of shared values and ideals, founded on the dignity of the person, on freedom joined to responsibility, on the effective recognition of the place of God in the life of man. In this perspective, let us fix our gaze on Jesus, the lowly infant lying in the manger. Because he is the Son of God, he tells us that fraternal solidarity between all men and women is the royal road to fighting poverty and to building peace.

Homily at Mass for the Feast of the Baptism of the Lord and for the Baptism of Young Children

January 11, 2009

Dear friends, I am truly glad that this year too, on this Feast day, I have been granted the opportunity to baptize these children. God's "favor" rests on them today. Ever since the Only-Begotten Son of the Father had himself baptized, the heavens are truly open and continue to open, and we may entrust every new life that begins into the hands of the One who is more powerful than the dark powers of evil. This effectively includes Baptism: we restore to God what came from him. The child is not the property of the parents but is entrusted to their responsibility by the Creator, freely and in a way that is ever new, in order that they may help him or her to be a free child of God. Only if the parents develop this awareness will they succeed in finding the proper balance between the claim that their children are at their disposal, as though they were a private possession, shaping them on the basis of their own ideas and desires, and the libertarian approach that is expressed in letting them grow in full autonomy, satisfying their every desire and aspiration, deeming this the right way to cultivate their personality. If, with this sacrament, the newly-baptized becomes an adoptive child of God, the object of God's infinite love that safeguards him and protects him from the dark forces of the evil one, it is necessary to teach the child to recognize God as Father and to be able to relate to him with a filial attitude. And therefore, when in accordance with the Christian tradition as we are doing today children are baptized and introduced into the light of God and of his teachings, no violence is done to them. Rather, they are given the riches of divine life in which is rooted the true freedom that belongs to the children of God a freedom that must be educated and modeled as the years pass to render it capable of responsible personal decisions.

Dear parents, dear godfathers and godmothers, I greet you all with affection and join in your joy for these little ones who today are reborn into eternal life. May you be aware of the gift received and never cease to thank the Lord who, with today's sacrament, introduces your children into a new family, larger and more stable, more open and more numerous than your own; I am referring to the family of believers, to the Church, to a family that has God as Father and in which all recognize one another as brothers and sisters in Jesus Christ. Today, therefore, you are entrusting your children to God's goodness, which is a force of light and love and they, even amid life's difficulties, will never feel abandoned if they stay united with him. Therefore, be concerned with educating them in the faith, teaching them to pray and grow as Jesus did and with his help, "in wisdom and in stature, and in favor with God and man" (Lk 2:52).

Angelus

January 11, 2009

Dear friends, how great is the gift of Baptism! If we were to take this fully into account our lives would become a continual "thank you." What a joy for Christian parents, who have seen a new creature come into being from their love, to carry the baby to the baptismal font and see him or her reborn from the womb of the Church, for a life without end! It is a gift, a joy, but also a responsibility! Parents, in fact, together with godparents, must educate their children in accordance with the Gospel. This makes me think of the theme of the *Sixth World Meeting of Families* which will be taking place in Mexico City in the next few days: "The family, teacher of human and Christian values." This great meeting of families, organized by the Pontifical Council for the Family, will be held in three stages: first, the Theological-Pastoral Congress, in which the theme will be deeply analyzed, also through an exchange of significant experiences. There will then be a moment for celebration and witness, which will bring out the beauty of a gathering of families from every part of the world, united by the same faith and by the same commitment. And finally, the solemn Eucharistic celebration as thanksgiving to the Lord for the gifts of marriage, the family and life. I have appointed Cardinal Tarcisio Bertone, Secretary of State, to represent me but I myself shall be following and taking an active part in the extraordinary event, accompanying it with prayer and intervening by video conference. From this moment, dear brothers and sisters, I ask you to implore an abundance of divine graces upon this important World Meeting of Families. Let us do so by invoking the motherly intercession of the Virgin Mary, Queen of the Family.

Address to the Administrators of the Region of Lazio and the Civil Authorities of Rome

January 12, 2009

I am thinking here of families, especially those with small children who have the right to a serene future, and of the elderly, many of whom live alone in conditions of hardship; I am thinking of the housing emergency; of the lack of employment and of the unemployment among the young; of the difficult coexistence between different ethnic groups; of the urgent question of immigration and itinerant people. . . .

In the face of the nihilism that increasingly pervades the world of youth, the Church asks everyone to devote themselves to young people seriously and not to leave them at their own mercy, exposed to the school of "bad teachers," but rather to involve them in serious initiatives that enable them to understand the value of life in a stable family founded on marriage. Only in this way are they given the possibility to plan their future with trust.

Greeting after the General Audience

January 14, 2009

Lastly, I address as usual the *young people*, the *sick* and the *newlyweds*. Yesterday the liturgy recalled St. Hilary, Bishop of Poitiers who "defended the divinity of Christ your Son" (cf. Liturgy), an ardent champion of the faith and teacher of truth. May his example sustain you, dear *young people*, in the constant and courageous search for Christ; may it encourage you, dear *sick people*, to offer up your sufferings so that the Kingdom of God may spread throughout the world; and may it help you, dear *newlyweds*, to be witnesses of Christ's love in family life. I ask you to join in my prayer to implore an abundance of divine graces on the Sixth World Meeting of Families that is taking place in these days in Mexico City. May this important ecclesial event express once again the beauty and value of the family, inspiring in it new energy for this irreplaceable fundamental cell of society and of the Church.

Message for the Seventeenth World Day of the Sick

February 2, 2009

Dear Brothers and Sisters,

The World Day of the Sick, which will be celebrated next February 11, the liturgical Memorial of Our Lady of Lourdes, will see the diocesan communities gathering with their Bishops at prayer meetings in order to reflect and decide on initiatives of sensitization concerning the reality of suffering.

The Pauline Year that we are celebrating is a favorable opportunity to pause and meditate with the Apostle Paul on the fact that "as we share abundantly in Christ's sufferings, so through Christ we share abundantly in comfort too" (2 Cor 1:5).

The spiritual connection with Lourdes also calls to mind the motherly concern of the Mother of Jesus for the brethren of her Son, "who still journey on earth surrounded by dangers and difficulties, until they are led into their blessed home" (*Lumen Gentium*, no. 62).

This year our attention focuses in particular on children, the weakest and most defenseless creatures, and on those of them who are sick and suffering. There are tiny human beings who bear in their bodies the consequences of incapacitating diseases, and others who are fighting illnesses that are still incurable today, despite the progress of medicine and the assistance of qualified researchers and health-care professionals.

There are children injured in body and in mind, subsequent to conflicts and wars, and other innocent victims of the insensate hatred of adults. There are "street" children, who are deprived of the warmth of a family and left to themselves, and minors defiled by degenerate people who violate their innocence, causing them psychological damage that will mark them for the rest of their lives.

Then we cannot forget the incalculable number of minors who die of thirst, hunger and the lack of medical help, as well as the small exiles and refugees who flee from their countries together with their parents in search of a better life. A silent cry of pain rises from all these children which questions our consciences as human beings and believers.

The Christian community, which cannot remain indifferent to such tragic situations, feels the impelling duty to intervene. Indeed, as I wrote in the Encyclical *Deus Caritas Est*, the Church "is God's family in the world. In this family no one ought to go without the necessities of life" (no. 25 b).

I therefore hope that the World Day of the Sick will offer the parish and diocesan communities an opportunity to be ever more aware that they are the "family of God" and will encourage them to make the love of the Lord, who asks that "within the ecclesial family no member should suffer through being in need," visible in villages, neighborhoods and cities (ibid).

The witness of charity is part of the very life of every Christian community. And from the outset the Church has expressed the Gospel principles in practical gestures, as we read in the Acts of the Apostles.

Today, given the changed conditions of health-care assistance, people are feeling the need for closer collaboration between health-care professionals who work in the various health-care institutions and the ecclesial communities present in the territory. In this perspective the value of an institution linked to the Holy See such as the Bambino Gesù Pediatric Hospital—this year celebrating its 140th anniversary—is confirmed in every way.

But this is not all. Since the sick child belongs to a family that frequently shares in his or her suffering with serious hardship and difficulties, Christian communities cannot but also feel duty-bound to help families afflicted by the illness of a son or daughter.

After the example of the "Good Samaritan," it is necessary to bend over the people so harshly tried and offer them the support of their concrete solidarity.

In this way the acceptance and sharing of suffering is expressed in the practical support of sick children's families, creating in them an atmosphere of serenity and hope and making them feel that they are in the midst of a larger family of brothers and sisters in Christ.

Jesus' compassion for the widow of Nain (cf. Lk 7:12-17) and for Jairus' supplication (cf. Lk 8:41-56) constitute, among others, useful reference points for learning to share in the moments of physical and moral suffering of the many sorely tried families.

All this implies disinterested and generous love, a reflection and a sign of the merciful love of God who never abandons his children in trial but always provides them anew with wonderful resources of heart and mind to equip them to face life's difficulties adequately.

The daily devotion and continuous commitment to serving sick children is an eloquent testimony of love for human life, particularly for the life of those who are weak and dependent on others in all things and for all things.

In fact, it is necessary to assert vigorously *the absolute and supreme dignity of every human life*. The teaching that the Church ceaselessly proclaims does not change with the passing of time: human life is beautiful and should be lived to the full, even when it is weak and enveloped in the mystery of suffering.

We must turn our gaze to the Crucified Jesus: in dying on the Cross he wished to share in the suffering of all humanity. We may discern in his suffering for love a supreme sharing in the plight of little ones who are ill and of their parents.

My venerable Predecessor John Paul II who offered a shining example of patient acceptance of suffering, particularly toward the end of his life, wrote: "On this Cross is the 'Redeemer of man,' the Man of Sorrows, who has taken upon himself the physical and moral sufferings of the people of all times, so that in love they may find the salvific meaning of their sorrow and valid answers to all of their questions" (*Salvifici Doloris*, no. 31).

I would like here to express my appreciation and encouragement to the international and national organizations which care for sick children, especially in the poor countries, and which with generosity and abnegation make their contribution to assuring them adequate and loving care.

At the same time, I address a heartfelt appeal to the leaders of nations that they will strengthen the laws and provisions for sick children and their families. For her part, the Church—always, but especially when a child's life is at stake—is prepared to offer cordial collaboration with the intention of transforming the whole human civilization into a "civilization of love" (*Salvifici Doloris*, no. 30).

To conclude, I would like to express my spiritual closeness to all of you, dear brothers and sisters who are suffering from an illness. I address an affectionate greeting to all those who assist you: the Bishops, priests, consecrated people, health-care workers, volunteers and all who devote themselves lovingly to treating and alleviating the sufferings of those who are grappling with illness.

Here is a special greeting for you, dear sick and suffering children: the Pope embraces you with fatherly affection together with your parents and relatives, and assures you of his special remembrance in prayer, as he asks you to trust in the maternal help of the Immaculate Virgin Mary who last Christmas we once again contemplated joyfully holding in her arms the Son of God who became a Child. As I invoke upon you and upon every sick person the motherly protection of the Blessed Virgin, Health of the Sick, I cordially impart to all a special Apostolic Blessing.

Address to the Ambassador of the Republic of Hungary to the Holy See

February 2, 2009

The experience of newly gained freedom has, at times, brought with it the risk that those same Christian and human values, so deeply rooted in the history and culture of individual peoples, and indeed of the whole continent of Europe, can be supplanted by others, based on unsound visions of man and his dignity and harmful to the development of a truly flourishing society. In my 2008 World Day of Peace Message, I stressed the primordial importance of the family for building peaceful community relations at every level. In much of modern Europe the vital cohesive role that the family has to play in human affairs is being called into question and even endangered as a result of misguided ways of thinking that at times find expression in aggressive social and political policies. It is my earnest hope that ways will be found of safeguarding this essential element of our society, which is the heart of every culture and nation. One of the specific ways government can support the family is by assuring that parents are allowed to exercise their fundamental right as the primary educators of their children, which would include the option to send their children to religious schools when they so desire.

Address After Mass for the Sick and Their Caregivers on the Feast of Our Lady of Lourdes

February 11, 2009

Dear brothers and sisters, we are increasingly realizing that human life is not a disposable good but a precious coffer to be preserved and looked after with every possible attention, from the moment of its origin to its ultimate natural end. Life is a mystery that in itself demands responsibility, love, patience and charity, on the part of each and every one.

Address to the Bishops of Nigeria on Their *Ad Limina* Visit

February 14, 2009

I would like to highlight the Bishop's task of sustaining the important social and ecclesial reality of marriage and family life. With the cooperation of well-prepared priests and lay people, experts and married couples, you will exercise with responsibility and zeal your solicitude in this area of pastoral priority (cf. *Familiaris Consortio*, no. 73). Courses for engaged couples, and general and specific catechetical teaching on the value of human life, marriage and the family will strengthen your faithful people for the challenges presented to them by changes in society. Likewise do not fail to encourage associations or movements that validly assist married couples in living their faith and marriage commitments.

Address to the Mayor and
Municipal Administrators of Rome

March 9, 2009

The Christian community, through the parishes and other charitable structures, is already involved in providing daily support for numerous families that are toiling to maintain a dignified standard of living and, as has recently happened, is ready to collaborate with the authorities responsible for the common good. In this case, too, the values of solidarity and generosity that are deeply rooted in the hearts of Romans can be sustained by the light of the Gospel, in order that all may reassume responsibility for the needs of those in the worst hardship, so that they may feel they belong to a single family. In fact, the greater each citizen's awareness is that he is personally responsible for the life and future of our City's inhabitants, the greater will be his confidence that he can surmount the difficulties of the present time.

And what can be said of families, children and youth? Thank you, Mr. Mayor, because on the occasion of my Visit, you have offered me as a gift a sign of hope for youth, giving it my name, that of an elderly Pontiff who looks trustingly to the young people and prays for them every day. Families and youth can hope in a better future to the extent that individualism leaves room for sentiments of fraternal collaboration among all the members of civil society and of the Christian community. May this new institution also be an incentive for Rome to weave a social fabric of acceptance and respect, where the encounter between culture and faith, between social life and religious testimony cooperates to form communities that are truly free and enlivened by sentiments of peace. The "Observatory for religious freedom" which you have just mentioned will also be able to make a unique contribution to this.

APOSTOLIC JOURNEY TO CAMEROON AND ANGOLA

Address to the Bishops of Cameroon

March 18, 2009

Among the many challenges facing you in your responsibility as Pastors, the situation of the family is of particular concern. The difficulties arising from the impact of modernity and secularization on traditional society inspire you to defend vigorously the essential values of the African family, and to give high priority to its thorough evangelization. In developing the pastoral care of the family, you are eager to promote a better understanding of the nature, dignity and role of marriage, which presupposes an indissoluble and stable union.

APOSTOLIC JOURNEY TO CAMEROON AND ANGOLA

Homily at Mass for the Publication of the *Instrumentum Laboris* of the Second Special Assembly for Africa of the Synod of Bishops

March 19, 2009

Dear Brother Bishops,
Dear Brothers and Sisters,

Praised be Jesus Christ who has gathered us in this stadium today that we may enter more deeply into his life!

Jesus Christ brings us together on this day when the Church, here in Cameroon and throughout the world, celebrates the Feast of St. Joseph, Husband of the Virgin Mary. I begin by wishing a very happy feast day to all those who, like myself, have received the grace of bearing this beautiful name, and I ask St. Joseph to grant them his special protection in guiding them toward the Lord Jesus Christ all the days of their life. I also extend cordial best wishes to all the parishes, schools, colleges, and institutions named after St. Joseph. I thank Archbishop Tonyé-Bakot of Yaoundé for his kind words, and I warmly greet the representatives of the African Episcopal Conferences who have come to Yaoundé for the promulgation of the *Instrumentum Laboris* of the Second Special Assembly for Africa of the Synod of Bishops.

How can we enter into the specific grace of this day? In a little while, at the end of Mass, the liturgy will remind us of the focal point of our meditation when it has us pray: "Lord, today you nourish us at this altar as we celebrate the feast of St. Joseph. Protect your Church always, and in your love watch over the gifts you have given us." We are asking the Lord to protect the Church always—and he does!—just as Joseph protected his family and kept watch over the child Jesus during his early years.

Our Gospel reading recalls this for us. The angel said to Joseph: "Do not be afraid to take Mary your wife into your home," (Mt 1:20) and that is precisely what he did: "he did as the angel of the Lord had commanded him" (Mt 1:24). Why was St. Matthew so keen to note Joseph's trust in the words received from the messenger of God, if not to invite us to imitate this same loving trust?

Although the first reading which we have just heard does not speak explic-itly of St. Joseph, it does teach us a good deal about him. The prophet Nathan, in obedience to God's command, tells David: "I will raise up your heir after you, sprung from your loins" (2 Sam 7:12). David must accept that he will die before seeing the fulfillment of this promise, which will come to pass "when (his) time comes" and he will rest "with (his) ancestors." We thus come to realize that one of mankind's most cherished desires—seeing the fruits of one's labors—is not always granted by God. I think of those among you who are mothers and fathers of families. Parents quite rightly desire to give the best of themselves to their children, and they want to see them achieve success. Yet make no mistake about what this "success" entails: what God asks David to do is to place his trust in him. David himself will not see his heir who will have a throne "firm for ever" (2 Sam 7:16), for this heir, announced under the veil of prophecy, is Jesus. David puts his trust in God. In the same way, Joseph trusts God when he hears his messenger, the Angel, say to him: "Joseph, son of David, do not be afraid to take Mary your wife into your home. For it is through the Holy Spirit that this child has been conceived in her" (Mt 1:20). Throughout all of history, Joseph is the man who gives God the greatest dis-play of trust, even in the face of such astonishing news.

Dear fathers and mothers here today, do you have trust in God who has called you to be the fathers and mothers of his adopted children? Do you accept that he is counting on you to pass on to your children the human and spiritual values that you yourselves have received and which will prepare them to live with love and respect for his holy name? At a time when so many people have no qualms about trying to impose the tyranny of materialism, with scant con-cern for the most deprived, you must be very careful. Africa in general, and Cameroon in particular, place themselves at risk if they do not recognize the True Author of Life! Brothers and sisters in Cameroon and throughout Africa, you who have received from God so many human virtues, take care of your souls! Do not let yourselves be captivated by selfish illusions and false ideals! Believe—yes!—continue to believe in God—Father, Son, and Holy Spirit—he alone truly loves you in the way you yearn to be loved, he alone can satisfy you, can bring stability to your lives. Only Christ is the way of Life.

God alone could grant Joseph the strength to trust the Angel. God alone will give you, dear married couples, the strength to raise your family as he wants. Ask it of him! God loves to be asked for what he wishes to give. Ask him for the grace of a true and ever more faithful love patterned after his own. As the Psalm magnificently puts it: his "love is established for ever, his loyalty will stand as long as the heavens" (Ps 88:3).

Just as on other continents, the family today—in your country and across Africa—is experiencing a difficult time; but fidelity to God will help see it through. Certain values of the traditional life have been overturned. Relationships between different generations have evolved in a way that no longer favors the transmission of accumulated knowledge and inherited wisdom. Too often we witness a rural exodus not unlike that known in many other periods of human history. The quality of family ties is deeply affected by this. Uprooted and fragile members of the younger generation who often—sadly—are without gainful employment, seek to cure their pain by living in ephemeral and man-made paradises which we know will never guarantee the human being a deep, abiding happiness. Sometimes the African people too are constrained to flee from themselves and abandon everything that once made up their interior richness. Confronted with the phenomenon of rapid urbanization, they leave the land, physically and morally: not as Abraham had done in response to the Lord's call, but as a kind of interior exile which alienates them from their very being, from their brothers and sisters, and from God himself.

Is this an irreversible, inevitable development? By no means! More than ever, we must "hope against all hope" (Rom 4:18). Here I wish to acknowledge with appreciation and gratitude the remarkable work done by countless associations that promote the life of faith and the practice of charity. May they be warmly thanked! May they find in the word of God renewed strength to carry out their projects for the integral development of the human person in Africa, especially in Cameroon!

The first priority will consist in restoring a sense of the acceptance of life as a gift from God. According to both Sacred Scripture and the wisest traditions of your continent, the arrival of a child is always a gift, a blessing from God. Today it is high time to place greater emphasis on this: every human being, every tiny human person, however weak, is created "in the image and likeness of God" (Gn 1:27). Every person must live! Death must not prevail over life! Death will never have the last word!

Sons and daughters of Africa, do not be afraid to believe, to hope, and to love; do not be afraid to say that Jesus is the Way, the Truth and the Life, and that we can be saved by him alone. St. Paul is indeed an inspired author given to the Church by the Holy Spirit as a "teacher of nations" (1 Tim 2:7) when he tells us that Abraham, "hoping against hope, believed that he should become the father of many nations; as he had been told, 'So shall your descendants be'" (Rom 4:18).

"Hoping against hope": is this not a magnificent description of a Christian? Africa is called to hope through you and in you! With Jesus Christ, who trod the African soil, Africa can become the continent of hope! We are all members of the peoples that God gave to Abraham as his descendants. Each and every one of us was thought, willed and loved by God. Each and every one of us has a role to play in the plan of God: Father, Son and Holy Spirit. If discouragement overwhelms you, think of the faith of Joseph; if anxiety has its grip on you, think of the hope of Joseph, that descendant of Abraham who hoped against hope; if exasperation or hatred seizes you, think of the love of Joseph, who was the first man to set eyes on the human face of God in the person of the Infant conceived by the Holy Spirit in the womb of the Virgin Mary. Let us praise and thank Christ for having drawn so close to us, and for giving us Joseph as an example and model of love for him.

Dear brothers and sisters, I want to say to you once more from the bottom of my heart: like Joseph, do not be afraid to take Mary into your home, that is to say do not be afraid to love the Church. Mary, Mother of the Church, will teach you to follow your pastors, to love your bishops, your priests, your deacons and your catechists; to heed what they teach you and to pray for their intentions. Husbands, look upon the love of Joseph for Mary and Jesus; those preparing for marriage, treat your future spouse as Joseph did; those of you who have given yourselves to God in celibacy, reflect upon the teaching of the Church, our Mother: "Virginity or celibacy for the sake of the Kingdom of God not only does not contradict the dignity of marriage but presupposes and confirms it. Marriage and virginity are two ways of expressing and living the one mystery of the Covenant of God with his people" (*Redemptoris Custos*, no. 20).

Once more, I wish to extend a particular word of encouragement to fathers so that they may take St. Joseph as their model. He who kept watch over the Son of Man is able to teach them the deepest meaning of their own fatherhood. In the same way, each father receives his children from God, and they are created in God's own image and likeness. St. Joseph was the spouse of Mary. In the same way, each father sees himself entrusted with the mystery of womanhood through his own wife. Dear fathers, like St. Joseph, respect and love your spouse; and by your love and your wise presence, lead your children to God where they must be (cf. Lk 2:49).

Finally, to all the young people present, I offer words of friendship and encouragement: as you face the challenges of life, take courage! Your life is priceless in the eyes of God! Let Christ take hold of you, agree to pledge your love to him, and—why not?—maybe even do so in the priesthood or in the consecrated life! This is the supreme service. To the children who no longer have a father, or who live abandoned in the poverty of the streets, to those forcibly separated from their parents, to the maltreated and abused, to those constrained to join paramilitary forces that are terrorizing some countries, I would like to say: God loves you, he has not forgotten you, and St. Joseph protects you! Invoke him with confidence.

May God bless you and watch over you! May he give you the grace to keep advancing toward him with fidelity! May he give stability to your lives so that you may reap the fruits he awaits from you! May he make you witnesses of his love here in Cameroon and to the ends of the earth! I fervently beg him to give you a taste of the joy of belonging to him, now and forever. Amen.

APOSTOLIC JOURNEY TO CAMEROON AND ANGOLA

Address to the Sick in the
Cardinal Paul Emile Léger Center, Yaoundé

March 19, 2009

We too can choose [St. Joseph] as a teacher of prayer, whatever our state of health, and all families can do the same. I am thinking especially of hospital staff, and all those who work in the field of health care. By accompanying those who suffer, through the care and attention you offer them, you accomplish an act of charity and love that God recognizes: "I was sick, and you visited me" (Mt 25:36). All of you, doctors and researchers, have the task of putting into practice every legitimate form of pain relief; you are called, in the first place, to protect human life, you are the defenders of life from conception to natural death. For every person, respect for life is a right and at the same time a duty, since all life is a gift from God. With you, I would like to give thanks to the Lord for all who, in one way or another, work in the service of the suffering. I encourage priests and those who visit the sick to commit themselves to an active and friendly presence in their hospital chaplaincy, or to assure an ecclesial presence in the home, for the comfort and spiritual support of the sick. In accordance with his promise, God will give you a just reward, and he will recompense you in heaven.

APOSTOLIC JOURNEY TO CAMEROON AND ANGOLA

Address to the Political and Civil
Authorities and Diplomatic Corps in Luanda

March 20, 2009

Friends, I wish to say that my visit to Cameroon and to Angola has stirred within me that profound human delight at being among families. Indeed I think that those who come from other continents can learn afresh from Africa that "the family is the foundation on which the social edifice is built"

(*Ecclesia in Africa*, no. 80). Yet the strains upon families, as we all know, are many indeed: anxiety and ignominy caused by poverty, unemployment, disease and displacement, to mention but a few. Particularly disturbing is the crushing yoke of discrimination that women and girls so often endure, not to mention the unspeakable practice of sexual violence and exploitation which causes such humiliation and trauma. I must also mention a further area of grave concern: the policies of those who, claiming to improve the "social edifice," threaten its very foundations. How bitter the irony of those who promote abortion as a form of "maternal" healthcare! How disconcerting the claim that the termination of life is a matter of reproductive health (cf. *Maputo Protocol*, art. 14)!

The Church, in accordance with the will of her divine founder, you will always find standing alongside the poorest of this continent. I wish to assure each of you that for her part, through diocesan initiatives, through the innumerable educational, healthcare and social works of Religious Orders, and through the development programs of Caritas and other agencies, the Church will continue to do all she can to support families—including those suffering the harrowing effects of HIV/Aids—and to uphold the equal dignity of women and men, realized in harmonious complementarity.

APOSTOLIC JOURNEY TO CAMEROON AND ANGOLA

Address to the Bishops of Angola and São Tomé

March 20, 2009

One such human reality, presently faced with numerous difficulties and threats, is the family. Families are particularly in need of evangelization and practical support, since, in addition to the fragility and lack of inner stability of so many conjugal unions, there is the widespread tendency in society and culture to call into question the unique nature and specific mission of the family based on marriage. In your pastoral concern, which extends to every human being, continue to raise your voice in defense of the sacredness of human life and the value of the institution of marriage, as well as in promotion of the family's proper role in the Church and in society, at the same time demanding economic and legislative measures to support the family in bearing and raising children.

APOSTOLIC JOURNEY TO CAMEROON AND ANGOLA

Address at the Meeting with
Catholic Movements for the Promotion of Women

March 22, 2009

Dear Brothers and Sisters,

"They have no more wine," said Mary, begging Jesus to intervene so that the wedding-feast could continue, as was only right and fitting: "As long as the wedding guests have the bridegroom with them, they cannot fast" (Mk 2:19). The Mother of Jesus turns to the servants and implores them: "Do whatever he tells you" (cf. Jn 2:1-5). Her maternal mediation thus made possible the "good wine," prefiguring a new covenant between divine omnipotence and the poor but receptive human heart. This, in fact, had already happened in the past when—as we heard in the first reading—"all the people answered together and said: 'all that the Lord has spoken, we will do'" (Ex 19:8).

These same words well up in the hearts of all gathered here today in St. Anthony's Church: a building which we owe to the commendable missionary efforts of the Capuchin Friars Minor, who wanted to provide a new Tent for the Ark of the Covenant, the sign of God's presence among his pilgrim people. To them, to those who work alongside them, and to all who benefit from their spiritual and social assistance, the Pope imparts his blessing with warm words of encouragement. I greet with affection all those present: Bishops, priests, religious men and women, and particularly the lay faithful who consciously embrace the duties of Christian commitment and witness that flow from the Sacrament of Baptism and also—in the case of spouses—from the Sacrament of Marriage. Moreover, given the main purpose of our gathering today, I extend greetings of great affection and hope to all women, to whom God has entrusted the wellsprings of life: I invite you to live and to put your trust in life, because the living God has put his trust in you! With gratitude in my heart I also greet the leaders and facilitators of ecclesial movements that have made the promotion of Angolan women a priority. I thank Archbishop José de Queirós Alves and your representatives for their kind words and for drawing attention to the aspirations and hopes of so many of the silent heroines among the women of this beloved nation.

I call everyone to an effective awareness of the adverse conditions to which many women have been—and continue to be—subjected, paying particular attention to ways in which the behavior and attitudes of men, who at times show a lack of sensitivity and responsibility, may be to blame. This forms no part of God's plan. In the Scripture reading, we heard that the entire people cried out together: "all that the Lord has spoken, we will do!" Sacred Scripture tells us that the divine Creator, looking upon all he had made, saw that something was missing: everything would have been fine if man had not been alone! How could one man by himself constitute the image and likeness of God who is one and three, God who is communion? "It is not good that the man should be alone; I will make him a helper fit for him" (Gn 2:18). God went to work again, fashioning for the man the helper he still lacked, and endowing this helper in a privileged way by incorporating the order of love, which had seemed under-represented in creation.

As you know, my dear friends, this order of love belongs to the intimate life of God himself, the Trinitarian life, the Holy Spirit being the personal *hypostasis* of love. As my predecessor Pope John Paul II once wrote, "in God's eternal plan, woman is the one in whom the order of love in the created world of persons takes first root" (*Mulieris Dignitatem*, no. 29). In fact, gazing upon the captivating charm that radiates from woman due to the inner grace God has given her, the heart of man is enlightened and he sees himself reflected in her: "This at last is bone of my bones and flesh of my flesh" (Gn 2:23). Woman is another "I" who shares in the same human nature. We must therefore recognize, affirm and defend the equal dignity of man and woman: they are both persons, utterly unique among all the living beings found in the world.

Man and woman are both called to live in profound communion through a reciprocal recognition of one another and the mutual gift of themselves, working together for the common good through the complementary aspects of masculinity and femininity. Who today can fail to recognize the need to make more room for the "reasons of the heart"? In a world like ours, dominated by technology, we feel the need for this feminine complementarity, so that the human race can live in the world without completely losing its humanity. Think of all the places afflicted by great poverty or devastated by war, and of all the tragic situations resulting from migrations, forced or otherwise. It is almost always women who manage to preserve human dignity, to defend the family and to protect cultural and religious values.

Dear brothers and sisters, history records almost exclusively the accomplishments of men, when in fact much of it is due to the determined, unrelenting and charitable action of women. Of all the many extraordinary women, allow me to mention two in particular: Teresa Gomes and Maria Bonino. The first, an Angolan, died in 2004 in the city of Sumbe after a happily married life in which she gave birth to seven children; she was a woman of unswerving Christian faith and exemplary apostolic zeal. This was particularly evident during the years 1975 and 1976 when fierce ideological and political propaganda invaded the parish of Our Lady of Grace of Porto Amboim, almost forcing the doors of the church to close. Teresa then became the leader of the faithful who refused to bend under pressure. Teresa offered support, courageously protecting the parish structures and trying every possible means to restore the celebration of Mass. Her love for the Church made her indefatigable in the work of evangelization, under the direction of the priests.

Maria Bonino was an Italian pediatrician who offered her expertise as a volunteer in several missions throughout this beloved African continent. She became the head of the pediatric ward in the provincial hospital at *Uíje* during the last two years of her life. Caring for the daily needs of thousands of children who were patients there, Maria paid the ultimate price for her service by sacrificing her life during the terrible epidemic of Marburg Haemorrhagic Fever, to which she herself succumbed. She was transferred to Luanda for treatment, but she died and was laid to rest here on March 24, 2005—the day after tomorrow is her fourth anniversary. Church and society have been—and continue to be—enormously enriched by the presence and virtues of women, and in a particular way by consecrated religious who, relying on the Lord's grace, have placed themselves at the service of others.

Dear Angolans, since the dignity of women is equal to that of men, no one today should doubt that women have "a full right to become actively involved in all areas of public life, and this right must be affirmed and guaranteed, also, where necessary, through appropriate legislation. This acknowledgment of the public role of women should not however detract from their unique role within the family. Here their contribution to the welfare and progress of society, even if its importance is not sufficiently appreciated, is truly incalculable" (*Message for the 1995 World Day of Peace*, no. 9). Moreover, a woman's personal sense of dignity is not primarily the result of juridically defined rights, but rather the direct consequence of the material and spiritual care she receives in the bosom of the family. The presence of a mother within the family is so important for the stability and growth of this fundamental cell of society, that it should be recognized, commended and supported in every possible way. For the same reason, society must hold husbands and fathers accountable for their responsibilities toward their families.

Dear families, you have undoubtedly noticed that no human couple, alone and on its own strength, can adequately offer children love and a genuine understanding of life. In fact, in order to say to someone, "your life is good even though you don't know what the future will bring," there needs to be a higher and more trustworthy authority than parents alone can offer. Christians know that this higher authority has been given to the larger family which God, through his Son Jesus Christ and the gift of the Holy Spirit, has established within human history, namely the Church. We find at work here the eternal and indestructible love which guarantees to each of us that our life will always have meaning, even if we do not know what the future will bring. For this reason, the building up of every Christian family takes place within the larger family, the Church, which sustains the domestic family and holds it close to her heart, giving it the assurance that it is protected, now and in the future, by the "yes" of the Creator.

"They have no more wine"—Mary says to Jesus. Dear women of Angola, accept Mary as your advocate with the Lord. This is precisely how we see her at the wedding-feast of Cana: a tender woman, full of motherly care and courage, a woman who recognizes the needs of others and, wanting to help, places those needs before the Lord. If we stay close to her, we can all—men and women alike—recover that sense of serenity and deep trust that makes us feel blessed by God and undaunted in our struggle for life. May Our Lady of Muxima be the guiding star of your lives. May she keep all of you united in the great family of God. Amen.

Message to Participants in the International Conference on "Life, Family, and Development: The Role of Women in the Promotion of Human Rights"

March 20, 2009

To my Venerable Brother,
Cardinal Renato Raffaele Martino,

I am pleased to extend cordial greetings to you and to all those taking part in the International Conference on the theme "Life, Family and Development: the Role of Women in the Promotion of Human Rights." This event, sponsored by the Pontifical Council for Justice and Peace, with the cooperation of the World Women's Alliance for Life and Family, the World Union of Catholic Women's Organizations and other associations, is an exemplary response to my predecessor Pope John Paul II's call for a "new feminism" with the power to transform culture, imbuing it with a decisive respect for life (cf. *Evangelium Vitae*, nos. 98-99).

Every day we learn of further ways in which life is compromised, particularly in its most vulnerable stages. While justice demands that these be decried as a violation of human rights, they must also evoke a positive and proactive response. The recognition and appreciation of God's plan for women in the transmission of life and the nurturing of children is a constructive step in this direction. Beyond this, and given the distinctive influence of women in society, they must be encouraged to embrace the opportunity to uphold the dignity of life through their involvement in education and their participation in political and civic life. Indeed, because they have been gifted by the Creator with a unique "capacity for the other," women have a crucial part to play in the promotion of human rights, for without their voice the social fabric of society would be weakened (cf. *Letter to the Bishops of the Catholic Church on the Collaboration of Men and Women in the Church and in the World*, Congregation for the Doctrine of the Faith, 13).

As you reflect on the role of women in the promotion of human rights, I invite you to keep in mind a task to which I have drawn attention on several occasions: namely, to correct any misconception that Christianity is simply a collection of commandments and prohibitions. The Gospel is a message of joy which encourages men and women to delight in spousal love; far from stifling it, Christian faith and ethics make it healthy, strong and truly free. This is the exact meaning of the Ten Commandments: they are not a series of "nos" but a great "yes" to love and to life (cf. *Address to the Participants at the Ecclesial Convention of the Diocese of Rome*, June 5, 2006).

It is my sincere hope that your discussions over these next two days will translate into concrete initiatives that safeguard the indispensable role of the family in the integral development of the human person and of society as a whole. The genius of women to mobilize and organize endows them with the skills and motivation to develop ever-expanding networks for sharing experiences and generating new ideas. The accomplishments of WWALF and the UMOFC/WUCWO are an outstanding example of this, and I encourage their members to persevere in their generous service to society. May the sphere of your influence continue to grow at regional, national and international levels for the advancement of human rights based on the strong foundation of marriage and family.

I once more extend best wishes for the success of this conference and my prayers for the continuing mission of the participating organizations. Invoking the intercession of Mary, "the symbol and the most perfect realization of the Church" (CCC, no. 570), I cordially impart my Apostolic Blessing.

PASTORAL VISIT TO THE PARISH CHURCH OF
"SANTO VOLTO DI GESÙ" IN MAGLIANA, ROME

Homily at Mass

March 29, 2009

I know what great care you devote to liturgical formation, making the most of every resource of your community: the readers, the choir and all those who are dedicated to enlivening the celebrations. It is important to put always personal and liturgical prayer first in our life. I am aware of the great commitment you devote to catechesis to ensure that it lives up to the expectations of the children, both those preparing to receive the sacraments of

First Communion and Confirmation and those who attend the After-School Prayer and Recreation Center. You are also anxious to provide a suitable catechesis for parents, whom you invite to take a course of Christian formation together with their children. In this way you seek to help families to live the sacramental events together, educating and being educated in the faith "in the family," which must be the first and natural "school" of Christian life for all its members. I congratulate you on your open and welcoming parish. It is motivated and enlivened by a sincere love for God and for all the brethren, in imitation of St. Maximilian Mary Kolbe to whom it was originally dedicated.

PILGRIMAGE TO THE HOLY LAND

Homily at Holy Mass in International Stadium, Amman

May 10, 2009

In today's second reading, St. John invites us to "think of the love that the Father has lavished on us" by making us his adopted children in Christ. Hearing these words should make us grateful for the experience of the Father's love which we have had in our families, from the love of our fathers and mothers, our grandparents, our brothers and sisters. During the celebration of the present Year of the Family, the Church throughout the Holy Land has reflected on the family as a mystery of life-giving love, endowed in God's plan with its own proper calling and mission: to radiate the divine Love which is the source and the ultimate fulfillment of all the other loves of our lives. May every Christian family grow in fidelity to its lofty vocation to be a true school of prayer, where children learn a sincere love of God, where they mature in self-discipline and concern for the needs of others, and where, shaped by the wisdom born of faith, they contribute to the building of an ever more just and fraternal society. The strong Christian families of these lands are a great legacy handed down from earlier generations. May today's families be faithful to that impressive heritage, and never lack the material and moral assistance they need to carry out their irreplaceable role in service to society.

An important aspect of your reflection during this Year of the Family has been the particular dignity, vocation and mission of women in God's plan. How much the Church in these lands owes to the patient, loving and faithful witness of countless Christian mothers, religious Sisters, teachers, doctors and nurses! How much your society owes to all those women who in different and at times courageous ways have devoted their lives to building peace and fostering love! From the very first pages of the Bible, we see how man and woman, created in the image of God, are meant to complement one another as stewards of God's gifts and partners in communicating his gift of life, both physical and spiritual, to our world. Sadly, this God-given dignity and role of women has not always been sufficiently understood and esteemed. The Church, and society as a whole, has come to realize how urgently we need what the late Pope John Paul II called the "prophetic charism" of women (cf. *Mulieris Dignitatem*, no. 29) as bearers of love, teachers of mercy and artisans of peace, bringing warmth and humanity to a world that all too often judges the value of a person by the cold criteria of usefulness and profit. By its public witness of respect for women, and its defense of the innate dignity of every human person, the Church in the Holy Land can make an important contribution to the advancement of a culture of true humanity and the building of the civilization of love.

Address at the Welcoming Ceremony at Ben Gurion International Airport, Tel Aviv

May 11, 2009

To the Catholic bishops and faithful here present, I offer a special word of greeting. In this land, where Peter received his commission to feed the Lord's sheep, I come as Peter's successor to minister among you. It will be my special joy to join you for the concluding celebrations of the Year of the Family, due to take place in Nazareth, home of the Holy Family of Jesus, Mary and Joseph. As I said in my Message for the World Day of Peace last year, the family is the "first and indispensable teacher of peace" (no. 3), and hence it has a vital role to play in healing divisions in human society at every level. To the Christian communities in the Holy Land, I say: by your faithful witness to him who preached forgiveness and reconciliation, by your commitment to uphold the sacredness of every human life, you can make a particular contribution to ending the hostilities that for so long have afflicted this land. I pray that your continuing presence in Israel and the Palestinian Territories will bear much fruit in promoting peace and mutual respect among all the peoples who live in the lands of the Bible.

Address During the Courtesy Visit to the Two Chief Rabbis of Jerusalem

May 12, 2009

Our encounter today is a most fitting occasion to give thanks to the Almighty for the many blessings which have accompanied the dialogue conducted by the Bilateral Commission, and to look forward with expectation to its future sessions. The willingness of the delegates to discuss openly and patiently not only points of agreement, but also points of difference, has already paved the way to more effective collaboration in public life. Jews and Christians alike are concerned to ensure respect for the sacredness of human life, the central-ity of the family, a sound education for the young, and the freedom of religion and conscience for a healthy society. These themes of dialogue represent only the initial phases of what we trust will be a steady, progressive journey toward an enhanced mutual understanding.

An indication of the potential of this series of meetings is readily seen in our shared concern in the face of moral relativism and the offences it spawns against the dignity of the human person. In approaching the most urgent ethical questions of our day, our two communities are challenged to engage people of good will at the level of reason, while simultaneously pointing to the religious foundations which best sustain lasting moral values. May the dialogue that has begun continue to generate ideas on how Christians and Jews can work together to heighten society's appreciation of the distinctive contribution of our religious and ethical traditions. Here in Israel, given that Christians constitute only a small portion of the total population, they partic-ularly value opportunities for dialogue with their Jewish neighbors.

Address at the Caritas Baby Hospital

May 13, 2009

Dear Friends,

I affectionately greet you in the name of our Lord Jesus Christ "who died, was raised from the dead, and now sits at the right hand of God to intercede for us" (cf. Rom 8:34). May your faith in his Resurrection and his promise of new life through Baptism fill your hearts with joy in this Easter season!

I am grateful for the warm welcome extended to me on your behalf by Father Michael Schweiger, President of the Kinderhilfe Association, Mr. Ernesto Langensand, who is completing his term as Chief Administrator of the Caritas Baby Hospital, and Mother Erika Nobs, Superior of this local com-munity of the Elizabettine Franciscan Sisters of Padua. I also cordially greet Archbishop Robert Zollitsch and Bishop Kurt Koch, representing respec-tively the German and Swiss Episcopal Conferences, which have advanced the mission of Caritas Baby Hospital by their generous financial assistance.

God has blessed me with this opportunity to express my appreciation to the administrators, physicians, nurses and staff of Caritas Baby Hospital for the invaluable service they have offered—and continue to offer—to children in the Bethlehem region and throughout Palestine for over fifty years. Father Ernst Schnydrig founded this facility upon the conviction that innocent children deserve a safe haven from all that can harm them in times and places of conflict. Thanks to the dedication of Children's Relief Bethlehem, this institution has remained a quiet oasis for the most vulnerable, and has shone as a beacon of hope that love can prevail over hatred and peace over violence.

To the young patients and the members of their families who benefit from your care, I wish simply to say: "the Pope is with you"! Today he is with you in person, but he spiritually accompanies you each and every day in his thoughts and prayers, asking the Almighty to watch over you with his tender care.

Father Schnydrig described this place as "one of the smaller bridges built for peace." Now, having grown from fourteen cots to eighty beds, and caring for the needs of thousands of children each year, this bridge is no longer small! It brings together people of different origins, languages and religions, in the name of the Reign of God, the Kingdom of Peace (cf. Rom 14:17). I heartily encourage you to persevere in your mission of showing charity to all the sick, the poor and the weak.

On this Feast of Our Lady of Fatima, I would like to conclude by invoking Mary's intercession as I impart my Apostolic Blessing to the children and all of you. Let us pray:

Mary, Health of the Sick, Refuge of Sinners, Mother of the Redeemer: we join the many generations who have called you "Blessed." Listen to your children as we call upon your name. You promised the three children of Fatima that "in the end, my Immaculate Heart will triumph." May it be so! May love triumph over hatred, solidarity over division, and peace over every form of violence! May the love you bore your Son teach us to love God with all our heart, strength and soul. May the Almighty show us his mercy, strengthen us with his power, and fill us with every good thing (cf. Lk 1:46-56). We ask your Son Jesus to bless these children and all children who suffer throughout the world. May they receive health of body, strength of mind, and peace of soul. But most of all, may they know that they are loved with a love which knows no bounds or limits: the love of Christ which surpasses all understanding (cf. Eph 3:19). Amen.

Homily at Holy Mass on the Mount of Precipice, Nazareth

May 14, 2009

Dear Brothers and Sisters,

"May the peace of the Risen Christ reign in your hearts, for as members of the one body you have been called to that peace!" (Col 3:15). With these words of the Apostle Paul, I greet all of you with affection in the Lord. I rejoice to have come to Nazareth, the place blessed by the mystery of the Annunciation, the place which witnessed the hidden years of Christ's growth in wisdom, age and grace (cf. Lk 2:52). I thank Archbishop Elias Chacour for his kind words of welcome, and I embrace with the sign of peace my brother Bishops, the priests and religious, and all the faithful of Galilee, who, in the diversity of their rites and traditions, give expression to the universality of Christ's Church. In a special way I wish to thank all those who have helped to make this celebration possible, particularly those involved in the planning and construction of this new theatre with its splendid panorama of the city.

Here in the home town of Jesus, Mary and Joseph, we have gathered to mark the conclusion of the Year of the Family celebrated by the Church in the Holy Land. As a sign of hope for the future I will bless the first stone of an International Center for the Family to be built in Nazareth. Let us pray that the Center will promote strong family life in this region, offer support and assistance to families everywhere, and encourage them in their irreplaceable mission to society.

This stage of my pilgrimage, I am confident, will draw the whole Church's attention to this town of Nazareth. All of us need, as Pope Paul VI said here, to return to Nazareth, to contemplate ever anew the silence and love of the Holy Family, the model of all Christian family life. Here, in the example of Mary, Joseph and Jesus, we come to appreciate even more fully the sacredness of the family, which in God's plan is based on the lifelong fidelity of a man and a woman consecrated by the marriage covenant and accepting of God's gift of new life. How much the men and women of our time need to reappropriate this fundamental truth, which stands at the foundation of society, and how important is the witness of married couples for the formation of sound consciences and the building of a civilization of love!

In today's first reading, drawn from the book of Sirach (3:3-7, 14-17), the word of God presents the family as the first school of wisdom, a school which trains its members in the practice of those virtues which make for authentic happiness and lasting fulfillment. In God's plan for the family, the love of husband and wife bears fruit in new life, and finds daily expression in the loving efforts of parents to ensure an integral human and spiritual formation for their children. In the family each person, whether the smallest child or the oldest relative, is valued for himself or herself, and not seen simply as a means to some other end. Here we begin to glimpse something of the essential role of the family as the first building-block of a well-ordered and welcoming society. We also come to appreciate, within the wider community, the duty of the

State to support families in their mission of education, to protect the institution of the family and its inherent rights, and to ensure that all families can live and flourish in conditions of dignity.

The Apostle Paul, writing to the Colossians, speaks instinctively of the family when he wishes to illustrate the virtues which build up the "one body" which is the Church. As "God's chosen ones, holy and beloved," we are called to live in harmony and peace with one another, showing above all forbearance and forgiveness, with love as the highest bond of perfection (cf. Col 3:12-14). Just as in the marriage covenant, the love of man and woman is raised by grace to become a sharing in, and an expression of, the love of Christ and the Church (cf. Eph 5:32), so too the family, grounded in that love, is called to be a "domestic church," a place of faith, of prayer and of loving concern for the true and enduring good of each of its members.

As we reflect on these realities here, in the town of the Annunciation, our thoughts naturally turn to Mary, "full of grace," the mother of the Holy Family and our Mother. Nazareth reminds us of our need to acknowledge and respect the God-given dignity and proper role of women, as well as their particular charisms and talents. Whether as mothers in families, as a vital presence in the work force and the institutions of society, or in the particular vocation of following our Lord by the evangelical counsels of chastity, poverty and obedience, women have an indispensable role in creating that "human ecology" (cf. *Centesimus Annus*, no. 39) which our world, and this land, so urgently needs: a milieu in which children learn to love and to cherish others, to be honest and respectful to all, to practice the virtues of mercy and forgiveness.

Here too, we think of St. Joseph, the just man whom God wished to place over his household. From Joseph's strong and fatherly example Jesus learned the virtues of a manly piety, fidelity to one's word, integrity and hard work. In the carpenter of Nazareth he saw how authority placed at the service of love is infinitely more fruitful than the power which seeks to dominate. How much our world needs the example, guidance and quiet strength of men like Joseph!

Finally, in contemplating the Holy Family of Nazareth, we turn to the child Jesus, who in the home of Mary and Joseph grew in wisdom and understanding, until the day he began his public ministry. Here I would simply like to leave a particular thought with the young people here. The Second Vatican Council teaches that children have a special role to play in the growth of their parents in holiness (cf. *Gaudium et Spes*, no. 48). I urge you to reflect on this, and to let the example of Jesus guide you, not only in showing respect for your parents, but also helping them to discover more fully the love which gives our lives their deepest meaning. In the Holy Family of Nazareth, it was Jesus who taught Mary and Joseph something of the greatness of the love of God his heavenly Father, the ultimate source of all love, the Father from whom every family in heaven and on earth takes its name (cf. Eph 3:14-15).

Dear friends, in the Opening Prayer of today's Mass we asked the Father to "help us to live as the Holy Family, united in respect and love." Let us reaffirm here our commitment to be a leaven of respect and love in the world around us. This Mount of the Precipice reminds us, as it has generations of pilgrims, that our Lord's message was at times a source of contradiction and conflict with his hearers. Sadly, as the world knows, Nazareth has experienced tensions in recent years which have harmed relations between its Christian and Muslim communities. I urge people of good will in both communities to repair the damage that has been done, and in fidelity to our common belief in one God, the Father of the human family, to work to build bridges and find the way to a peaceful coexistence. Let everyone reject the destructive power of hatred and prejudice, which kills men's souls before it kills their bodies!

Allow me to conclude with a word of gratitude and praise for all those who strive to bring God's love to the children of this town, and to educate new generations in the ways of peace. I think in a special way of the local Churches, particularly in their schools and charitable institutions, to break down walls and to be a seedbed of encounter, dialogue, reconciliation and solidarity. I encourage the dedicated priests, religious, catechists and teachers, together with parents and all concerned for the good of our children, to persevere in bearing witness to the Gospel, to be confident in the triumph of goodness and truth, and to trust that God will give growth to every initiative which aims at the extension of his Kingdom of holiness, solidarity, justice and peace. At the same time I acknowledge with gratitude the solidarity which so many of our brothers and sisters throughout the world show toward the faithful of the Holy Land by supporting the praiseworthy programs and activities of the Catholic Near East Welfare Association.

"Let it be done to me according to your word" (Lk 1:38). May our Lady of the Annunciation, who courageously opened her heart to God's mysterious plan, and became the Mother of all believers, guide and sustain us by her prayers. May she obtain for us and our families the grace to open our ears to that word of the Lord which has the power to build us up (cf. Acts 20:32), to inspire courageous decisions, and to guide our feet into the path of peace!

General Audience

May 20, 2009

Yet the Church continues on her way, supported by the power of faith and witnessing to love with concrete works of service to the brethren such as, for example, the Caritas Baby Hospital in Bethlehem, supported by the Dioceses of Germany and Switzerland, and humanitarian action in the refugee camps. In the camp that I visited I wished to assure the families that are housed there of the closeness and encouragement of the universal Church and I invited everyone to seek peace with nonviolent methods, after the example of St. Francis of Assisi. I celebrated the third and last Mass with the people last Thursday, in Nazareth, the town of the Holy Family. We prayed for all the families that they might rediscover the beauty of marriage and family life, the value of domestic spirituality and of education, attention to children who are entitled to grow up in peace and serenity. In addition, in the Basilica of the Annunciation, together with all the Pastors, consecrated people, ecclesial movements and lay people involved in Galilee, we sang our faith in the creative and transforming power of God. There, where the Word was made flesh in the womb of the Virgin Mary, flows an inexhaustible source of hope and joy that does not cease to bring life to the heart of the Church, a pilgrim through history.

Address to the New Ambassador of Burkina Faso to the Holy See

May 29, 2009

Mr. Ambassador, as you emphasized, through her work in the fields of health care, education and social action, the Catholic Church is profoundly committed to Burkinabè society. Through her service to the population, the Church hopes to contribute, keeping within her own province, to responding to the numerous and difficult challenges that families are facing. Indeed, the safeguard of family values must be an important concern for everyone because the family is the main pillar of the social structure. Thus, signs of the break-down of family cohesion cannot but lead to situations of which children and young people will often be victims. The education and formation of the young generations are also of primordial importance for the nation's future. In the face of life's difficulties, society must give its youngest members reasons to live and to hope.

Encyclical Letter *Caritas in Veritate,* On Integral Human Development in Charity and Truth

June 29, 2009

2. Charity is at the heart of the Church's social doctrine. Every responsibility and every commitment spelt out by that doctrine is derived from charity which, according to the teaching of Jesus, is the synthesis of the entire Law

(cf. Mt 22:36-40). It gives real substance to the personal relationship with God and with neighbor; it is the principle not only of micro-relationships (with friends, with family members or within small groups) but also of macro-relationships (social, economic and political ones). . . .

7. Another important consideration is the common good. To love someone is to desire that person's good and to take effective steps to secure it. Besides the good of the individual, there is a good that is linked to living in society: the common good. It is the good of "all of us," made up of individuals, families and intermediate groups who together constitute society (cf. *Gaudium et Spes*, no. 26). . . .

44. The notion of rights and duties in development must also take account of the problems associated with *population growth*. This is a very important aspect of authentic development, since it concerns the inalienable values of life and the family (cf. Paul VI, *Populorum Progressio*, nos. 36-37). To consider population increase as the primary cause of underdevelopment is mistaken, even from an economic point of view. Suffice it to consider, on the one hand, the significant reduction in infant mortality and the rise in average life expectancy found in economically developed countries, and on the other hand, the signs of crisis observable in societies that are registering an alarming decline in their birth rate. Due attention must obviously be given to responsible procreation, which among other things has a positive contribution to make to integral human development. The Church, in her concern for man's authentic development, urges him to have full respect for human values in the exercise of his sexuality. It cannot be reduced merely to pleasure or entertainment, nor can sex education be reduced to technical instruction aimed solely at protecting the interested parties from possible disease or the "risk" of procreation. This would be to impoverish and disregard the deeper meaning of sexuality, a meaning which needs to be acknowledged and responsibly appropriated not only by individuals but also by the community. It is irresponsible to view sexuality merely as a source of pleasure, and likewise to regulate it through strategies of mandatory birth control. In either case materialistic ideas and policies are at work, and individuals are ultimately subjected to various forms of violence. Against such policies, there is a need to defend the primary competence of the family in the area of sexuality (cf. *Populorum Progressio*, no. 37), as opposed to the State and its restrictive policies, and to ensure that parents are suitably prepared to undertake their responsibilities.

Morally responsible openness to life represents a rich social and economic resource. Populous nations have been able to emerge from poverty thanks not least to the size of their population and the talents of their people. On the other hand, formerly prosperous nations are presently passing through a phase of uncertainty and in some cases decline, precisely because of their falling birth rates;

this has become a crucial problem for highly affluent societies. The decline in births, falling at times beneath the so-called "replacement level," also puts a strain on social welfare systems, increases their cost, eats into savings and hence the financial resources needed for investment, reduces the availability of qualified laborers, and narrows the "brain pool" upon which nations can draw for their needs. Furthermore, smaller and at times miniscule families run the risk of impoverishing social relations, and failing to ensure effective forms of solidarity. These situations are symptomatic of scant confidence in the future and moral weariness. It is thus becoming a social and even economic necessity once more to hold up to future generations the beauty of marriage and the family, and the fact that these institutions correspond to the deepest needs and dignity of the person. In view of this, States are called to *enact policies promoting the centrality and the integrity of the family* founded on marriage between a man and a woman, the primary vital cell of society (cf. *Apostolicam Actuositatem*, no. 11), and to assume responsibility for its economic and fiscal needs, while respecting its essentially relational character. . . .

51. . . . In order to protect nature, it is not enough to intervene with economic incentives or deterrents; not even an apposite education is sufficient. These are important steps, but *the decisive issue is the overall moral tenor of society*. If there is a lack of respect for the right to life and to a natural death, if human conception, gestation and birth are made artificial, if human embryos are sacrificed to research, the conscience of society ends up losing the concept of human ecology and, along with it, that of environmental ecology. It is contradictory to insist that future generations respect the natural environment when our educational systems and laws do not help them to respect themselves. The book of nature is one and indivisible: it takes in not only the environment but also life, sexuality, marriage, the family, social relations: in a word, integral human development. Our duties toward the environment are linked to our duties toward the human person, considered in himself and in relation to others. It would be wrong to uphold one set of duties while trampling on the other. Herein lies a grave contradiction in our mentality and practice today: one which demeans the person, disrupts the environment and damages society.

Letter to the Prime Minister of Italy on the Occasion of the G8 Summit

July 1, 2009

I am therefore keen to remind the distinguished participants of the G8 that the measure of technical efficacy of the provisions to adopt in order to emerge from the crisis coincides with the measure of its ethical value. In other words, it is necessary to bear in mind practical human and family needs. I refer, for example, to the effective creation of positions for all, that enable workers to provide fittingly for their family's needs and to fulfill their primary responsibility as educators of their children and protagonists in the community to which they belong. "A society in which this right is systematically denied," John Paul II wrote, "in which economic policies do not allow workers to reach satisfactory levels of employment, cannot be justified from an ethical point of view, nor can that society attain social peace" (*Centesimus Annus*, no. 43; cf. *Laborem Exercens*, no. 18).

Address to Participants in the European Congress on the Pastoral Care of Vocations

July 4, 2009

Dear Brothers and Sisters,

I meet you with great pleasure, aware of the precious pastoral service that you carry out in the context of the promotion, animation and discernment of vocations. You have come to Rome to take part in a congress of reflection, comparison and sharing among the Churches of Europe on the theme: *"Sowers of the Gospel of Vocation: a word that calls and sends forth"* and it aims to imbue your commitment to vocations with new dynamism. The fostering of vocations is a pastoral priority for every diocese which assumes even greater value in the context of the Year for Priests that has just begun. I therefore warmly greet the Bishops Delegate for the pastoral care of vocations of the various Bishops' Conferences, as well as the directors of the national Vocations Centers, their collaborators and all of you present.

At the heart of your labors is the Gospel Parable of the Sower. The Lord scatters the seed of the word of God freely and with abundance but knowing that it may fall on poor soil, which will not allow a seed to mature because of dryness, or that its vital force may be extinguished, choked by thorn bushes. Yet the sower does not lose heart, for he knows that part of this seed is destined to find "good soil," namely, ardent hearts capable of receiving the word with willingness to help it mature through perseverance and yield fruit generously for the benefit of many.

The image of the soil can evoke the reality of the family, on the whole good; the sometimes arid and harsh environment of work; the days of suffering and tears. The earth is above all the heart of every person, especially of youth, to whom you address your service of listening and guidance: a heart that is often confused and disoriented, yet capable of containing unimaginable powers of generosity. It is like a bud ready to open to a life spent for the love of Jesus, able to follow him with the totality and the certainty that comes from having found the greatest treasure that exists. It is always and only the Lord who sows in human hearts. Only after the abundant and generous sowing of the word of God can one progress further along the paths of companionship and education, of formation and discernment. All this is linked to that tiny seed, the mysterious gift of divine Providence which releases from within an extraordinary force. In fact, it is the Word of God who brings about in himself what he says and desires.

Address to the New Ambassador of Mexico to the Holy See

July 10, 2009

The celebration of the *World Meeting of Families in Mexico City* several months ago has further highlighted the importance of this institution, so highly esteemed by the Mexican People. In fact, the family, a community of life and love founded on indissoluble marriage between a man and a woman, is the fundamental nucleus of the entire social fabric. Accordingly, it is of supreme importance that it be given satisfactory assistance so that homes do not cease to be schools of respect and mutual understanding, seedbeds of human virtues and a cause of hope for the rest of society. In this context, I would like to repeat to you how pleased I am with the fruits of this important ecclesial meeting, as once again I thank the Authorities of your country and all Mexicans for the visible hard work they devoted to its organization.

Angelus

July 19, 2009

Dear Brothers and Sisters,

I have come to your beautiful town and your beautiful Church with great joy; it is the native town of my most important collaborator, Cardinal Tarcisio Bertone, Secretary of State, with whom I formerly worked for years at the Congregation for the Doctrine of the Faith. As you see, because of my accident, my movements are somewhat limited, but I am wholeheartedly present and among you with great joy!

At this moment I would like to say "thank you" with all my heart to you all. Many people have expressed their closeness, sympathy and affection for me and have prayed for me in this situation, and so the network of prayer that unites us in every part of the world has been strengthened. I would like first of all to thank the doctors and the medical personnel of Aosta who treated me with such care, with such competence and friendship and, in the end we hope! with success. I would also like to say "thank you" to the State and Church Authorities and to all the rest who have written to me or who have shown me their affection and closeness. Lastly, I would especially like to greet your Bishop and likewise Bishop Luigi Bettazzi, Bishop emeritus of this diocese. I greet the Mayor, who has given me a very beautiful gift, and the civil and military Authorities; I greet the parish priest and the other priests, the men and women religious, the leaders of the ecclesial associations and movements and all the citizens, with a special thought for the children, young people, families, the sick and the needy. To you all, each and every one, I extend my most heartfelt gratitude for making me so welcome in this short stay with you.

This morning you celebrated the Eucharist and Cardinal Tarcisio Bertone must certainly have explained to you the word of God which the liturgy offers for our meditation on this Sixteenth Sunday of Ordinary Time. Just as the Lord asks the disciples to stay apart to listen to him in private, so I too would like to speak with you, recalling that it was precisely by listening to and welcoming the Gospel that your municipal community whose name recalls Canavese's 2,000-year-old links with Rome came to life. As your Bishop said, very early on your region was bathed in the blood of martyrs, including St. Solutor. I must confess that until now I had never heard his name, but I am always grateful to become acquainted with new intercessor saints after whom, together with St. Peter the Apostle, your church is named. Your impressive parish church is an eloquent testimony of a long history of faith. It dominates a large part of the area of Canavese, whose people are well known for their predilection for hard work. Currently, however, I know that here too, in the district of Ivrea, many families are experiencing financial difficulty because of unemployment. I have spoken of this problem on various occasions, as your Bishop also mentioned, and I have now addressed it more deeply in the Encyclical *Caritas in Veritate*. I hope that this will mobilize positive efforts to renew the world!

Dear friends, do not be downhearted! Providence always helps those who do good and who strive for justice. Providence helps all who think not only of themselves but also of those in worse situations. And you know this well, because lack of work also obliged your grandparents to emigrate. Then, however, financial development led to well-being and others immigrated here, from

Italy and from abroad. The basic values of the family and respect for human life, sensitivity to social justice, the capacity to confront fatigue and sacrifice, the strong bond with Christian faith through parish life and especially participation in Holy Mass have been your real strength down the centuries. It will be these same values that enable today's generations to build their future with hope, giving life to a truly supportive and fraternal society, in which all the various contexts, the institutions and the economy are imbued with a Gospel spirit. I address the youth in particular, whose educational prospective we must take into account. Dear young people, here, as everywhere, it is necessary to ask yourselves what type of culture is being presented to you, what examples and models are recommended to you, and to evaluate them to see whether they encourage you to follow the paths of the Gospel and of authentic freedom. Youth is resourceful but must be helped to overcome the temptations of easy and deceptive ways in order to find the road to a true and full life.

Angelus

July 26, 2009

A second point for reflection comes from today's liturgical commemoration of Saints Joachim and Anne, parents of Our Lady, and therefore, grandparents of Jesus. This occasion makes us think of the subject of education which has an important place in the pastoral work of the Church. In particular, it invites us to pray for grandparents, who, in the family, are the depositories and often witnesses of the fundamental values of life. The educational task of grandparents is always very important, and it becomes even more so when, for various reasons, the parents are unable to provide their children with an adequate presence while they are growing up. I entrust to the protection of St. Anne and St. Joachim all the grandparents of the world and bestow on them a special blessing. May the Virgin Mary who according to a beautiful iconography—learned to read the Sacred Scriptures at her mother Anne's knee, help them always to nourish their faith and hope at the sources of the Word of God.

Homily at Mass with His Former University Students

August 30, 2009

All this is found in greater depth in the passage from the *Letter of James* that the Church presents to us today. I especially like the *Letter of St. James*

because it gives us an idea of the devotion of Jesus' family. It was an observant family. Observant in the sense that it lived the joy at God's closeness,
described in Deuteronomy and which is given to us in his Word and in his
Commandment. It is quite a different kind of observance from what we
encounter in the Pharisees of the Gospel, who had made it into an exteri-
orized and enslaving system. Moreover it is a kind of observance unlike that
which Paul, as a rabbi, had learned: that was as we see from his Letters the
observance of an expert who knew everything; who was proud of his knowledge and of his righteousness but nevertheless suffered under the burden of
the Law's prescriptions, so that the Law no longer appeared as a joyous guide
to God but rather as an exigency which, ultimately, it was impossible to fulfill.

In the *Letter of St. James* we find that observance which does not look
inwards but turns joyfully toward the caring God who gives us his closeness
and points out to us the right way. Thus the *Letter of St. James* speaks of the
perfect Law of freedom that perseveres to reach a new and deeper understanding of the Law given to us by the Lord. For James the Law is not a requirement that demands too much of us, which stands before us and can never be
satisfied. He is thinking in the perspective that we find in a sentence of Jesus'
farewell discourse: "No longer do I call you servants, for the servant does not
know what his master is doing; but I have called you friends, for all that I
have heard from my Father I have made known to you" (Jn 15:15). The one
to whom all is revealed is part of the family; he is no longer a servant but is
free precisely because he himself belongs to the household. A similar, initial
introduction into the thought of God himself happened in Israel on Mount
Sinai. It happened again in a definitive and grand way at the Last Supper
and, generally through the work, the life, the Passion and the Resurrection of
Jesus; in him God told us everything, he manifested himself completely. We
are no longer servants, but friends. And the Law is no longer a prescription
for people who are not free but is contact with God's love being introduced
to become part of the family, an act that makes us free and "perfect." It is in
this sense that James says in today's Reading that the Lord has created us by
means of his Word, that he planted his Word deep within us as a life force.
Here he also speaks of "pure religion" which consists in love for our neighbor
particularly for orphans and widows who are needier than we are and in freedom from the ways of the world that contaminate us. The Law, like a word of
love, is not a contradiction of freedom but a renewal from within by means of
friendship with God. Something similar occurs when Jesus, in the discourse
on the vine, says to the disciples: "You are already made clean by the word
which I have spoken to you" (Jn 15:3). And the same thing appears again in
the Priestly Prayer: sanctify them in the truth (cf. Jn 17:17-19). Thus we now
find the right structure for the process of purification and of purity: we do not
create what is good that would be mere moralism but Truth comes to us. He

himself is Truth, Truth in person. Purity happens through dialogue. It begins with the fact that he comes to us he who is Truth and Love he takes us by the hand and penetrates our being. Insofar as we allow him to touch us, insofar as the encounter becomes friendship and love, we ourselves, on the basis of his purity, become pure people and then people who love with his love, people who introduce others to his purity and his love.

Angelus

August 30, 2009

Dear Brothers and Sisters,

Three days ago, on August 27, we celebrated the liturgical Memorial of St. Monica, Mother of St. Augustine, considered the model and patroness of Christian mothers. We are provided with a considerable amount of information about her by her son in his autobiography, *Confessions*, one of the widest read literary masterpieces of all time. In them we learn that St. Augustine drank in the name of Jesus with his mother's milk, and that his mother brought him up in the Christian religion whose principles remained impressed upon him even in his years of spiritual and moral dissipation. Monica never ceased to pray for him and for his conversion and she had the consolation of seeing him return to the faith and receive Baptism. God heard the prayers of this holy mother, of whom the Bishop of Tagaste had said: "the son of so many tears could not perish." In fact, St. Augustine not only converted but decided to embrace the monastic life and, having returned to Africa, founded a community of monks. His last spiritual conversations with his mother in the tranquility of a house at Ostia, while they were waiting to embark for Africa, are moving and edifying. By then St. Monica had become for this son of hers, "more than a mother, the source of his Christianity." For years her one desire had been the conversion of Augustine, whom she then saw actually turning to a life of consecration at the service of God. She could therefore die happy, and in fact she passed away on August 27, 387, at the age of fifty-six, after asking her son not to trouble about her burial but to remember her, wherever he was, at the Lord's altar. St. Augustine used to say that his mother had "conceived him twice."

The history of Christianity is spangled with innumerable examples of holy parents and authentic Christian families who accompanied the life of generous priests and pastors of the Church. Only think of St. Basil the Great and St. Gregory of Nazianzus, both of whom belonged to families of saints. Let us think of Luigi Beltrame Quattrocchi and Maria Corsini, a husband and wife, very close to us, who lived at the end of the nineteenth century until the middle of the twentieth and whose beatification by my Venerable Predecessor John Paul II in October 2001 coincided with the twentieth anniversary of the Apostolic Exhortation *Familiaris Consortio*. In addition to illustrating the value of marriage and the tasks of the family, this Document urged spouses to be especially committed to the path of sanctity which, drawing grace and strength from the Sacrament of Marriage, accompanies them throughout their life (cf. no. 56). When married couples devote themselves generously to the education of children, guiding them and orienting them to the discovery of God's plan of love, they are preparing that fertile spiritual ground from which vocations to the priesthood and to the consecrated life spring up and develop. This reveals how closely connected they are, and marriage and virginity illumine each other on the basis of their common roots in the spousal love of Christ.

Dear brothers and sisters, in this Year for Priests, let us pray "through the intercession of the Holy Curé d'Ars, [that] Christian families become churches in miniature in which all vocations and all charisms, given by the Holy Spirit, are welcomed and appreciated" (from the Prayer for the Year for Priests). May the Blessed Virgin, whom we shall now invoke together, obtain this grace for us.

PASTORAL VISIT TO VITERBO AND BAGNOREGIO

Prayer to Our Lady of the Oak Tree

September 6, 2009

Virgin of Nazareth,
Queen of the family,
make our Christian families
schools of evangelical life,
enriched by the gift of many vocations
to the priesthood and
to the consecrated life.
Keep intact the unity of our families,
today so threatened from all sides,
making them hearths of serenity and
of harmony, where patient dialogue
dispels difficulties and differences.
Above all, watch over those
who are divided and in crisis,
Mother of forgiveness
and reconciliation.

Address to Bishops of Brazil
(Regions 1 and 4) on Their *Ad Limina* Visit

September 25, 2009

Dear Brothers in the Episcopate,

Welcome! With great pleasure I receive you in this house and I hope with all my heart that your *ad limina* visit will give you the comfort and encouragement that you are expecting. I thank you for the cordial welcome you have just addressed to me through Dom José, Archbishop of Fortaleza, testifying to the sentiments of affection and communion that unite your particular Churches to the See of Rome, and to the determination with which you have assumed the urgent mission to rekindle the light and grace of Christ on your people's paths through life.

Today I would like to speak of the first of these paths: the family based on marriage, "the intimate union of marriage, as a mutual giving of two persons . . . a man and a woman" (cf. *Gaudium et Spes*, no. 48). As a natural institution confirmed by the divine law, the family is ordered to the good of the spouses and the education of the offspring, and it is in them that it finds its crowning glory (cf. ibid.). All this is being called into question by forces and voices in contemporary society that seem determined to demolish the natural cradle of human life. Your reports and our individual conversations have repeatedly touched on this situation of the family under siege, whose life is drained by numerous battles; however, it is encouraging to perceive that despite all the negative influences the people of your North East Regions I and IV, sustained by their characteristic religious piety and a deep sense of fraternal solidarity, continue to be open to the Gospel of Life.

Since we know that the image and likeness proper to the human being can only come from God (Gn 1:27), as happened in the Creation the generation and continuation of Creation with you and with your faithful, *"I bow my knees before the Father, from whom every family in heaven and on earth is named, that according to the riches of his glory he may grant you to be strengthened with might through his Spirit in the inner man"* (Eph 3:14-16). May the father and mother in every home, intimately fortified by the power of the Holy Spirit, continue united to be God's Blessing in their own family, seeking the eternity of their love in the sources of grace entrusted to the Church which is *"a people brought into unity from the unity of the Father, the Son and the Holy Spirit"* (Lumen Gentium, no. 4).

However, whereas the Church compares human life with the life of the Blessed Trinity the first unity of life in the plurality of the Persons and never tires of teaching that the family is founded on marriage and on God's plan; much of the secularized world experiences the deepest uncertainty in this regard, especially since Western societies legalized divorce. The only recognized foundation seems to be sentiment or individual subjectivity which is expressed in the desire to live together. In this situation, the number of marriages is dwindling, because no one pledges their life on such a frail and inconstant premise, and so de facto unions and divorces are increasing. The drama of so many children who are deprived of the support of their parents, victims of uneasiness and neglect is played out in this instability, and social disorder spreads.

The Church cannot be indifferent to the separation of spouses and to divorce, facing the break-up of homes and the consequences for the children that divorce causes. If they are to be instructed and educated, children need extremely precise and concrete reference points, in other words parents who are determined and reliable who contribute in quite another way to their upbringing. Nor, it is this principle that the practice of divorce is undermining and jeopardizing with the so-called "extended" family that multiplies "father" and "mother" figures and explains why today the majority of those who feel "orphans" are not children without parents but children who have too many. This situation, with the inevitable interference and the intersection of relationships, cannot but give rise to inner conflict and confusion, contributing to creating and impressing upon children an erroneous typology of the family, which in a certain sense can be compared to cohabitation, because of its precariousness.

The Church is firmly convinced that the true solution to the current problems that husbands and wives encounter and that weaken their union lies in a return to the stable Christian family, an environment of mutual trust, reciprocal giving, respect for freedom and education in social life. It is important to remember that: "the love of the spouses requires, of its very nature, the unity and indissolubility of the spouses' community of persons, which embraces their entire life" (CCC, no. 1644). In fact, Jesus said clearly "what therefore God has joined together, let not man put asunder" (Mk 10:9) and added, "whoever divorces his wife and marries another, commits adultery against her; and if she divorces her husband and marries another, she commits adultery" (Mk 10:11-12). With all the understanding that the Church can show in these situations, there are no spouses of the second marriage but only of the first: this is an irregular and dangerous situation which it is necessary to resolve, in fidelity to Christ and with the help of a priest, finding a possible way to save all those involved.

To help families, I urge you to propose to them with conviction the virtues of the Holy Family: prayer, the cornerstone of every domestic hearth faithful to its own identity and mission; hard work, the backbone of every mature and responsible marriage; silence, the foundation of every free and effective activity. In this way, I encourage your priests and the pastoral centers of your dioceses to accompany families, so that they are not disappointed or seduced by certain relativistic lifestyles that the cinema and other forms of media promote. I trust in the witness of those families that draw their energy from the sacrament of marriage; with them it becomes possible to overcome the trial that befalls them, to be able to forgive an offence, to accept a suffering child, to illumine the life of the other, even if he or she is weak or disabled, through the beauty of love. It is on the basis of families such as these that the fabric of society must be restored.

Dear Brothers, these are a few thoughts that I leave you at the end of your *ad limina* visit full of comforting information but also anxiety for the future features that your beloved nation could acquire. Work with intelligence and zeal, spare no effort in training active communities aware of their faith, to consolidate the features of the North Eastern population in accordance with the example of the Holy Family of Nazareth. These are my wishes which I strengthen with the Apostolic Blessing which I impart to you all, extending it to the Christian families and to the various ecclesial communities with their pastors, as well as to all the faithful of your beloved dioceses.

APOSTOLIC VISIT TO THE CZECH REPUBLIC

Greeting Given at the "Holy Infant of Prague" Statue in the Church of Our Lady Victorious, Prague

September 26, 2009

Dear Cardinals,
Your Excellencies,
Dear Brothers and Sisters,
Dear Children,

I greet all of you warmly and I want you to know what joy it gives me to visit this Church, dedicated to Our Lady of Victory, where the faithful venerate the statue of the Infant Jesus, known throughout the world as the "Holy Infant of Prague." I thank Archbishop Jan Graubner, President of the Episcopal Conference, for his words of welcome spoken on behalf of all the Bishops. I offer respectful greetings to the Mayor and to the other civil and religious authorities present at this gathering. I greet you, dear families, who have come in such large numbers to be here with me.

The image of the Child Jesus calls to mind the mystery of the Incarnation, of the all-powerful God who became man and who lived for thirty years in the lowly family of Nazareth, entrusted by Providence to the watchful care of Mary and Joseph. My thoughts turn to your own families and to all the families in the world, in their joys and difficulties. Our reflections should lead us to prayer, as we call upon the Child Jesus for the gift of unity and harmony for all families. We think especially of young families who have to work so hard to offer their children security and a decent future. We pray for families in difficulty, struggling with illness and suffering, for those in crisis, divided or torn apart by strife or infidelity. We entrust them all to the Holy Infant of Prague, knowing how important their stability and harmony is for the true progress of society and for the future of humanity.

The figure of the Child Jesus, the tender infant, brings home to us God's closeness and his love. We come to understand how precious we are in his eyes, because it is through him that we in our turn have become children of God. Every human being is a child of God and therefore our brother or sister, to be welcomed and respected. May our society grasp this truth! Every human person would then be appreciated not for what he has, but for who he is, since in the face of every human being, without distinction of race or culture, God's image shines forth.

This is especially true of children. In the Holy Infant of Prague we contemplate the beauty of childhood and the fondness that Jesus Christ has always shown for little ones, as we read in the Gospel (cf. Mk 10:13-16). Yet how many children are neither loved, nor welcomed nor respected! How many of them suffer violence and every kind of exploitation by the unscrupulous! May children always be accorded the respect and attention that are due to them: they are the future and the hope of humanity!

Dear children, I now want to say a special word to you and to your families. You have come here in large numbers to meet me, and for this I thank you most warmly. You are greatly loved by the Child Jesus, and you should return his love by following his example: be obedient, good and kind. Learn to be, like him, a source of joy to your parents. Be true friends of Jesus, and always turn to him in trust. Pray to him for yourselves, for your parents, relations, teachers and friends, and pray also for me. Thank you once again for your welcome. I bless you from my heart and I invoke upon all of you the protection of the Holy Infant Jesus, his Immaculate Mother and St. Joseph.

APOSTOLIC VISIT TO THE CZECH REPUBLIC

Message to Young People at the End of Mass on the Esplanade, Melnik, Starà Boleslav

September 28, 2009

As he did with Augustine, so the Lord comes to meet each one of you. He knocks at the door of your freedom and asks to be welcomed as a friend.

He wants to make you happy, to fill you with humanity and dignity. The Christian faith is this: encounter with Christ, the living Person who gives life a new horizon and thereby a definitive direction. And when the heart of a young person opens up to his divine plans, it is not difficult to recognize and follow his voice. The Lord calls each of us by name, and entrusts to us a specific mission in the Church and in society. Dear young people, be aware that by Baptism you have become children of God and members of his Body, the Church. Jesus constantly renews his invitation to you to be his disciples and his witnesses. Many of you he calls to marriage, and the preparation for this Sacrament constitutes a real vocational journey. Consider seriously the divine call to raise a Christian family, and let your youth be the time in which to build your future with a sense of responsibility. Society needs Christian families, saintly families!

General Audience

September 30, 2009

The love of Christ first revealed itself in the face of a Child. In fact, on my arrival in Prague I made my first stop at the Church of Our Lady of Victory where the Infant Jesus, known precisely as the "Infant of Prague," is venerated. This image refers to the mystery of God made man, to the "close God," the foundation of our hope. Before the "Infant of Prague," I prayed for all children, for parents and for the future of the family. The true "victory" for which we ask Mary today is the victory of love and life in the family and in society!

Address to the New Ambassador of the Kingdom of the Netherlands to the Holy See

October 2, 2009

Even more basic than schools in this regard [of supporting human dignity] are families built on the foundation of a stable and fruitful marriage between a man and a woman. Nothing can equal or replace the formative value of growing up in a secure family environment, learning to respect and foster the personal dignity of others, acquiring the capacity for "acceptance, encounter and dialogue, disinterested availability, generous service and deep solidarity"

(*Familiaris Consortio*, no. 43; cf. *Compendium of the Social Doctrine of the Church*, no. 221)—in short, learning to love. A society, on the other hand, which encourages alternative models of domestic life for the sake of a supposed diversity, is likely to store up social consequences that are not conducive to integral human development (cf. *Caritas in Veritate*, nos. 44, 51). The Catholic Church in your country is eager to play its part in supporting and promoting stable family life, as the Dutch Bishops' Conference stated in its recent document on the pastoral care of young people and the family. It is my earnest hope that the Catholic contribution to ethical debate will be heard and heeded by all sectors of Dutch society, so that the noble culture that has distinguished your country for centuries may continue to be known for its solidarity with the poor and the vulnerable, its promotion of authentic freedom and its respect for the dignity and inestimable value of every human life.

Homily at Mass for the Opening of the Second Special Assembly for Africa of the Synod of Bishops

October 4, 2009

As regards the subject of marriage, the text of chapter 2 of the Book of Genesis has recalled the perennial foundation that Jesus himself confirmed: "Therefore a man leaves his father and his mother and cleaves to his wife, and they become one flesh" (Gn 2:24). How is it possible not to recall the wonderful cycle of catecheses that the Servant of God John Paul II dedicated to this subject, based on a particularly deeply studied exegesis of this biblical text? Today, in proposing it to us again at the opening of the Synod, the liturgy offers us the superabundant light of the truth revealed and incarnate in Christ with which it is possible to consider the complex topic of marriage in the African ecclesial and social context. On this point too, however, I would like briefly to mention a thought that precedes any reflection or indication of a moral order, and which is nevertheless still connected to the primacy of the meaning of the sacred and of God. Marriage, as the Bible presents it to us, does not exist outside the relationship with God. Conjugal life between a man and a woman, and hence the life of the family that results from it, is inscribed in communion with God and, in the light of the New Testament, becomes an icon of Trinitarian Love and the sacrament of Christ's union with the Church. To the extent in which it preserves and develops its faith, Africa will be able to draw on immense resources for the benefit of the family founded on marriage.

Address to the New Ambassador of Panama to the Holy See

October 30, 2009

In this sense it is appropriate to acknowledge the numerous activities of human and social advancement that are carried out in Panama by the dioceses, parishes, religious communities, lay associations and apostolic movements, contributing decisively to enlivening the present time and to kindling the longing for a better future for the country. Of particular importance is the presence of the Church in the field of education and aid to the poor, the sick, the imprisoned and the emigrants, as well as in the defense of fundamental aspects such as: the commitment to social justice, the fight against corruption, the work of promoting peace, the inviolability of the right to human life from the moment of conception to that of natural death, as well as the safeguarding of the family founded on the marriage of a man and a woman. These are irreplaceable elements in the creation of a healthy social fabric and a thriving society, precisely thanks to the sound moral values that sustain it, ennoble it and give it dignity.

PLENARY ASSEMBLY OF THE CONGREGATION FOR
THE EVANGELIZATION OF PEOPLES ON THE THEME:
"ST. PAUL AND THE NEW AREOPAGI"

Message to Cardinal Ivan Dias, Prefect of the Congregation for the Evangelization of Peoples

November 13, 2009

It is necessary to look at the "new areopagi" in this spirit [of transmitting Gospel values]; some of them, in today's globalization, have become common, whereas others remain specific to certain continents, as was also seen at the recent Special Assembly for Africa of the Synod of Bishops. Missionary activity should therefore be oriented to these nerve centers of society in the third millennium. Nor should the influence of a widespread relativistic culture be underestimated, more often than not lacking in values, which is permeating the sanctuary of the family and infiltrating the field of education and other social contexts and contaminating them, manipulating consciences, especially of the young. At the same time, however, in spite of these snares, the Church knows that the Holy Spirit is always active. Indeed, new doors are opening to the Gospel and the longing for authentic spiritual and apostolic renewal is spreading in the world. As in other periods of change, the pastoral priority is to show the true Face of Christ, the Lord of history and the one Redeemer of humankind. This requires every Christian community and the Church in her entirety to offer a witness of fidelity to Christ, patiently building the unity he desired and for which he prayed for all his disciples. Christian unity will in fact facilitate evangelization and the confrontation with the cultural, social and religious challenges of our time.

Address to the Bishops of Brazil
(Regions III and IV) on Their *Ad Limina* Visit

December 5, 2009

May the Catholic School, in a convinced synergy with families and with the ecclesial community, promote that unity between faith, culture and life that constitutes the fundamental objective of Christian education.

Catholic schools too, in various forms and ways, may be helped in their educational task by the presence of teachers who are believers in the first place, but not exclusively, Catholic teachers of religion and by students who have had a Christian formation, as well as by the collaboration of families and of the Christian community itself. In fact, a healthy secularism at school implies the denial of transcendence nor mere neutrality in the face of those prerequisites and moral values, including religious education, that are found at the root of an authentic formation of the person.

The Catholic school cannot be considered as existing separate or apart from other educational institutions. It is at the service of society: it carries out a public role and a service of public usefulness that is not reserved exclusively to Catholics but open to all who wish to avail themselves of a good education. The problem of its juridical and financial parity with the State school may be correctly understood only if we start by recognizing the primary role of families and the subsidiary role of the other educational institutions. Article 26, 3 of the Universal Declaration of Human Rights says: "Parents have a prior right to choose the kind of education that shall be given to their children." The centuries-old commitment of the Catholic school is set in this direction, impelled by an even more radical force, that is, by the power that makes Christ the center of the educational process.

After the *Angelus**

December 6, 2009

I greet with affection the Italian-speaking pilgrims, in particular the "National Association of Large Families" whose motto is, "More babies, more future." Dear friends, I pray for you that Providence may always be with you in the midst of the joys and the difficulties and I hope that effective political measures in support of families, especially families, with more children, will be developed everywhere. I greet the faithful from Bergamo, Bracciano and Catania, the young people from Petosino and from Gràssina, the Association of Volunteers for International Cooperation from Cesena and the group of "Seekers of the Holy Grail." I will you all a good Sunday.

Message for the World Day of Peace

[January 1, 2010]

If You Want to Cultivate Peace, Protect Creation

December 8, 2009

12. *The Church has a responsibility toward creation,* and she considers it her duty to exercise that responsibility in public life, in order to protect earth, water and air as gifts of God the Creator meant for everyone, and above all to save mankind from the danger of self-destruction. The degradation of nature is closely linked to the cultural models shaping human coexistence: consequently, "when 'human ecology' is respected within society, environmental ecology also benefits" (*Caritas in Veritate,* no. 51). Young people cannot be asked to respect the environment if they are not helped, within families and society as a whole, to respect themselves. The book of nature is one and indivisible; it includes not only the environment but also individual, family and social ethics (cf. *Caritas in Veritate,* nos. 15, 51). Our duties toward the environment flow from our duties toward the person, considered both individually and in relation to others.

Hence I readily encourage efforts to promote a greater sense of ecological responsibility which, as I indicated in my Encyclical *Caritas in Veritate,*

---

*   Text is an unofficial translation of the Italian.

would safeguard an authentic "human ecology" and thus forcefully reaffirm the inviolability of human life at every stage and in every condition, the dignity of the person and the unique mission of the family, where one is trained in love of neighbor and respect for nature (cf. *Caritas in Veritate*, nos. 28, 51, 61; John Paul II, *Centesimus Annus*, nos. 38, 39). There is a need to safeguard the human patrimony of society. This patrimony of values originates in and is part of the natural moral law, which is the foundation of respect for the human person and creation.

Angelus

December 13, 2009

We have now reached the Third Sunday of Advent. Today in the liturgy the Apostle Paul's invitation rings out: "Rejoice in the Lord always; again I will say, Rejoice. . . . The Lord is at hand!" (Phil 4:4-5). While Mother Church accompanies us toward Holy Christmas she helps us rediscover the meaning and taste of Christian joy, so different from that of the world. On this Sunday, according to a beautiful tradition, the children of Rome come to have the Pope bless the Baby Jesus figurines that they will put in their cribs. And in fact, I see here in St. Peter's Square a great number of children and young people, together with their parents, teachers and catechists. Dear friends, I greet you all with deep affection and thank you for coming. It gives me great joy to know that the custom of creating a crib scene has been preserved in your families. Yet it is not enough to repeat a traditional gesture, however important it may be. It is necessary to seek to live in the reality of daily life that the crib represents, namely, the love of Christ, his humility, his poverty. This is what St. Francis did at Greccio: he recreated a live presentation of the nativity scene in order to contemplate and worship it, but above all to be better able to put into practice the message of the Son of God who for love of us emptied himself completely and made himself a tiny child.

The blessing of the "Bambinelli" [Baby Jesus figurines] as they are called in Rome, reminds us that the crib is a school of life where we can learn the secret of true joy. This does not consist in having many things but in feeling loved by the Lord, in giving oneself as a gift for others and in loving one another. Let us look at the crib. Our Lady and St. Joseph do not seem to be a very fortunate family; their first child was born in the midst of great hardship; yet they are full of deep joy, because they love each other, they help each other and, especially, they are certain that God, who made himself present in the little Jesus, is at work in their story. And the shepherds? What did they have to rejoice about?

That Newborn Infant was not to change their condition of poverty and marginalization. But faith helped them recognize the "babe wrapped in swaddling clothes and lying in a manger" as a "sign" of the fulfillment of God's promises for all human beings, "with whom he is pleased" (Lk 2:12, 14).

This, dear friends, is what true joy consists in: it is feeling that our personal and community existence has been visited and filled by a great mystery, the mystery of God's love. In order to rejoice we do not need things alone, but love and truth: we need a close God who warms our hearts and responds to our deepest expectations. This God is manifested in Jesus, born of the Virgin Mary. Therefore that "Bambinello" which we place in a stable or a grotto is the center of all things, the heart of the world. Let us pray that every person, like the Virgin Mary, may accept as the center of his or her life the God who made himself a Child, the source of true joy.

Angelus

December 27, 2009

Dear Brothers and Sisters,

Today is Holy Family Sunday. We can still identify ourselves with the shepherds of Bethlehem who hastened to the grotto as soon as they had received the Angel's announcement and found "Mary and Joseph, and the Babe lying in the manger" (Lk 2:16). Let us too pause to contemplate this scene and reflect on its meaning. The first witnesses of Christ's birth, the shepherds, found themselves not only before the Infant Jesus but also a small family: mother, father and newborn son. God had chosen to reveal himself by being born into a human family and the human family thus became an icon of God! God is the Trinity, he is a communion of love; so is the family despite all the differences that exist between the Mystery of God and his human creature, an expression that reflects the unfathomable Mystery of God as Love. In marriage the man and the woman, created in God's image, become "one flesh" (Gn 2:24), that is a communion of love that generates new life. The human family, in a certain sense, is an icon of the Trinity because of its interpersonal love and the fruitfulness of this love.

Today's Liturgy presents the famous Gospel episode of the twelve-year-old Jesus who stays behind in the Temple in Jerusalem unbeknown to his parents who, surprised and anxious, discover him three days later conversing with the teachers. Jesus answers his Mother who asks for an explanation that he must "be in his Father's house" that is God's house (cf. Lk 2:49). In this episode the boy Jesus appears to us full of zeal for God and for the Temple. Let us ask ourselves: from whom did Jesus learn love for his Father's affairs? As Son he certainly had an intimate knowledge of his Father, of God, and a profound and permanent relationship with him but, in his own culture he had of course learned prayers and love for the Temple and for the Institutions of Israel from his parents. We may therefore say that Jesus' decision to stay on at the Temple was above all the result of his close relationship with the Father, but it was also a result of the education he had received from Mary and Joseph. Here we can glimpse the authentic meaning of Christian education: it is the fruit of a collaboration between educators and God that must always be sought. The Christian family is aware that children are a gift and a project of God. Therefore it cannot consider that it possesses them; rather, in serving God's plan through them, the family is called to educate them in the greatest freedom, which is precisely that of saying "yes" to God in order to do his will. The Virgin Mary is the perfect example of this "yes." Let us entrust all families to her, praying in particular for their precious educational mission.

And I now address in Spanish all those who are taking part in the Feast of the Holy Family in Madrid.

I cordially greet the Pastors and faithful who have gathered in Madrid to celebrate joyfully the Sacred Family of Nazareth. How is it possible not to remember the true meaning of this feast? Having come into the world, into the heart of a family, God shows that this institution is a sure path on which to encounter and come to know him, as well as an ongoing call to work for the unity of all people centered on love. Hence one of the greatest services that we Christians can render our fellow human beings is to offer them our serene and unhesitating witness as a family founded on the marriage of a man and a woman, safeguarding and promoting the family, since it is of supreme importance for the present and future of humanity. Indeed, the family is the best school at which to learn to live out those values which give dignity to the person and greatness to peoples. In the family sorrows and joys are shared, since all feel enveloped in the love that prevails at home, a love that stems from the mere fact of belonging to the same family. I ask God that in your homes you may always breathe this love of total self-giving and faithfulness which Jesus brought to the world with his birth, nurturing and strengthening it with daily prayer, the constant practice of the virtues, reciprocal understanding and mutual respect. I then encourage you so that, trusting in the motherly intercession of Mary Most Holy, Queen of Families, and under the powerful protection of St. Joseph, her spouse, you may dedicate yourselves tirelessly to this beautiful mission which the Lord has placed in your hands. In addition you may count on my closeness and affection, and I ask you to convey to your loved ones who are in the greatest need or find themselves in difficulty a very special greeting from the Pope. I warmly bless you all.

After the Angelus*

Dear French-speaking pilgrims, on this Feast of the Holy Family of Jesus, Mary and Joseph I am pleased to greet all of you families, and my prayers go out especially to those in difficulties. With you, I thank God for the Holy Family of Nazareth: Mary and Joseph did not only provide the Infant Jesus with earthly bread; they gave him an authentic testimony of faith and love. May their example guide all families and be an inexhaustible source of joy and happiness! I wish you all a peaceful New Year's eve!

I am happy to greet all the English-speaking visitors present at this *Angelus* prayer. Today we celebrate with joy the Feast of the Holy Family, who shared with us this fundamental human experience. I pray that the Lord may bless all Christian families and assist them in living their daily life in mutual love and in generosity to others, after the example of Jesus, Mary and Joseph. May Almighty God continue to bless you all with peace and joy during this Christmas Season! Best wishes to all!

I welcome all the German-speaking pilgrims and visitors with Christmas joy. On this Sunday, we celebrate the Feast of the Holy Family. On this occasion we look to the Family of Nazareth who experienced worries and dangers as every family does. As the Gospel tells us, Mary and Joseph understood next to nothing about why their son did not go with them but returned and remained in the Temple. Jesus' words, however, that he 'must be in his Father's house' (Lk 2:49), allow them and us to understand that the living relationship with God and love strengthen each other. I wish you and your families a happy Christmas season.

I warmly greet the Spanish-speaking pilgrims taking part in this Marian prayer. On this Sunday of the Holy Family, I invite everyone to turn their eyes to the home of Nazareth, the peerless school of human and Christian virtues, in order to learn from Jesus, Joseph and Mary how to live them personally and to give an example of them to those around you with humility and conviction. During this Christmas season I wish once again that the joy of the Lord Jesus born in Bethlehem may be your strength. In His Name I bless you with great affection.

I extend a cordial greeting to the Poles. Today is the Sunday of the Holy Family. May the love that united Mary and Joseph and surrounded the Baby Jesus unite all Christian families. May mutual respect between spouses, concern for every new life and for the happy development of future generations be born from this love. I commend all Polish families to the care of Mary and Joseph and implore the Divine Blessing for them.

---

*	The five paragraphs greeting French-, German-, Spanish-, Polish-, and Italian-speaking pilgrims are an unofficial translation of the Italian.

I greet the Italian-speaking pilgrims, particularly the group of faithful from Atri. On this Sunday of the Holy Family I extend a warm greeting to all the families in Rome and in Italy, with a special prayer for those who are encountering serious difficulties. May the Lord bless you! My best wishes to all of you!

Homily at Mass for the Solemnity of Mary, Mother of God

January 1, 2010

It is important to be taught respect for others, even when they are different from us, from an early age. Increasingly today classes in schools consist of children of various nationalities but even when this is not the case their faces are a prophecy of the humanity we are called to form: a family of families and peoples. The smaller these children are, the more they awaken in us tenderness and joy at an innocence and brotherhood that seem obvious to us despite their differences, they cry and laugh in the same way, they have the same needs, they communicate spontaneously, they play together. . . . Children's faces are like a reflection of God's gaze on the world. So why extinguish their smiles? Why poison their hearts? Unfortunately the icon of the Mother of the God of Tenderness finds its tragic opposite in the sorrowful images of so many children and their mothers at the mercy of war and violence, refugees, asylum seekers and forced migrants. Faces hollowed by hunger and disease, faces disfigured by suffering and desperation and the faces of little innocents are a silent appeal to our responsibility: before their helpless plight, all the false justifications of war and violence fall away. We must simply convert to projects of peace, lay down every kind of weapon and strive all together to build a world that is worthier of the human being.

Address to the Administrators of the Region of Lazio and the Civil Authorities of Rome

January 14, 2010

I wish to express my appreciation of the efforts made by these Administrations to meet the needs of the weakest and most marginalized classes, with a view to promoting a more just and solidary society. In this regard I would like to ask you to do your utmost to ensure that the centrality of the human being and of the family may be the inspiring principle behind all your decisions. It is particularly necessary to bear this in mind when establishing new urban districts, so that the inhabited complexes springing up may not be solely dormer towns. To this end it is opportune to plan structures designed to encourage socialization. This will prevent the growth and increase of withdrawal into individualism and exclusive attention to personal interests, damaging to all forms of human coexistence. With respect for the civil authorities' competences, the Church is willing to make her own contribution to ensuring that these neighborhoods have a social life worthy of the human person. I know that this has already happened in various areas on the city's outskirts, thanks to the hard work of the Municipal Administration in establishing important institutions and I hope that these needs will be kept in mind everywhere. I am grateful for the consolidated collaboration that exists between the Administrations you head and the Vicariate, particularly with regard to the building of new parish complexes which, in addition to being reference points for Christian life, also play a fundamental educational and social role.

Such collaboration has made it possible to achieve significant objectives. In this regard, I would like to recall that in certain new quarters, inhabited in particular by young families with small children, the ecclesial communities have set up "children's prayer and recreation centers," aware that openness to life is the heart of true human development (cf. ibid., no. 28). These useful structures enable children to spend the day there while their parents are at work. I am confident that an ever more fruitful synergy between the different institutions will permit the creation of similar structures that help young parents in their educational task, both in the suburbs and in the rest of the City. I likewise hope that further provisions for families will be adopted, especially for those that are numerous, so that the entire City may enjoy the irreplaceable function of this fundamental institution, the first and indispensable cell of society.

As part of the promotion of the common good, the education of the new generations that constitute the future of our Region is a predominant concern that Government Administrators share with the Church and with all other educational organizations. For several years the Dioceses of Rome and Lazio have been committed to making their contribution in order to face the ever more urgent requests coming from the world of youth that demand appropriate, high-profile educational responses. The urgent need to help the young plan their lives in accordance with authentic values that refer to a "lofty" vision of the human being is clear to everyone and the Christian religious and cultural patrimony is one of its most sublime expressions. Today the new generations are asking to know who the human being is and what is the human destiny. They seek responses that can point out to them the way to take in order to found their lives on the perennial values. In particular, in the education that is proposed on the great themes of affectivity and sexuality, so important for life, it is essential not to present adolescents and young people with approaches that encourage the trivialization of these fundamental dimensions of human existence. To this end, the Church requests the collaboration of all, especially those who work in schools, in order to teach a lofty vision of love and of human sexuality. In this regard I would like to ask everyone to understand that in pronouncing her "nos," in reality the Church is saying "yes" to life, to love lived in the truth of the gift of self to the other, to love that is open to life and is not locked into a narcissistic vision of the couple. She is convinced that these decisions alone can lead to a model of life in which happiness is a shared good. On these themes, as well as on those of the family founded on marriage and on respect for life, from its conception to its natural end, the ecclesial community cannot but be faithful to the truth "which alone is the guarantee of freedom and of the possibility of integral human development" (ibid., no. 9).

Lastly, I cannot but urge the competent authorities to pay constant and consistent attention to the world of sickness and suffering. May the health-care structures so numerous in Rome and in Lazio that offer an important service to the community be places in which one may always find an attentive and responsible management of government, professional skill and generous dedication to the sick, whose acceptance and treatment must be the supreme criterion of all who work in this sphere. For centuries Rome and Lazio have seen the presence of structures of Catholic inspiration that work for large sections of the population, flanking the public health-care structures. Catholic institutions seek to combine professional competence and attention to the sick with the truth and love of Christ. Indeed, by drawing inspiration from the Gospel they strive to be close to the suffering with love and hope, also supporting them in their search for meaning and seeking to provide answers to the questions that inevitably arise in the hearts of those who are experiencing the difficult dimension of illness and pain. In fact the human being needs to be treated in the unity of his spiritual and physical being. I therefore trust that despite the on-going financial problems, these structures may be adequately supported in their precious service.

Distinguished Authorities, as I express my deep gratitude for your courteous and welcome visit, I assure you of my cordial closeness and my prayers for you, for the lofty responsibilities with which you have been entrusted and for those within your administrative scope. May the Lord support you, guide you and fulfill the expectations of good present in the heart of each one.

With these sentiments, I impart the Apostolic Blessing with affection and benevolence, and cordially extend it to your families and to all who live and work in Rome, in its Province and throughout Lazio.

Address to the Members of the
Congregation of the Faith for the
Plenary Assembly

January 15, 2010

In this context a response is likewise given to the widespread mentality that presents faith as an obstacle to scientific freedom and research, because it presumes that faith is made up of a pattern of prejudices that hinder the objective understanding of reality. Faced with this attitude that strives to replace truth with a consensus that is fragile and easy to manipulate, the Christian faith, instead, makes a real contribution in the ethical and philosophical context. It does not provide pre-constituted solutions to concrete problems like bio-medical research and experimentation, but rather proposes reliable moral perspectives within which human reason can seek and find valid solutions.

There are in fact specific contents of Christian revelation that cast light on bioethical problems: the value of human life, the relational and social dimension of the person, the connection between the unitive and the procreative aspects of sexuality, and the centrality of the family founded on the marriage of a man and a woman. These matters engraved in the human heart are also rationally understandable as an element of natural moral law and can be accepted also by those who do not identify with the Christian faith.

The natural moral law is neither exclusively nor mainly confessional, even if the Christian Revelation and the fulfillment of Man in the mystery of Christ fully illumines and develops its doctrine. As the *Catechism of the Catholic Church* says, it "states the first and essential precepts which govern the moral life" (no. 1955). Established in human nature itself and accessible to every rational creature, the natural moral law thus determines the basis for initiating dialogue with all who seek the truth and, more generally, with civil and secular society. This law, engraved in every human being's heart, touches on one of the essential problems of reflection on law and likewise challenges the conscience and responsibility of legislators.

As I encourage you to persevere in your demanding and important service, I would also like on this occasion to express my spiritual closeness to you, as a pledge of my affection and gratitude, as I warmly impart the Apostolic Blessing to you all.

Address at the Synagogue of Rome

January 17, 2010

6. In particular, the Decalogue the "Ten Words" or Ten Commandments (cf. Ex 20:1-17; Dt 5:1-21) which comes from the *Torah* of Moses, is a shining light for ethical principles, hope and dialogue, a guiding star of faith and morals for the people of God, and it also enlightens and guides the path of Christians. It constitutes a beacon and a norm of life in justice and love, a "great ethical code" for all humanity. The "Ten Commandments" shed light on good and evil, on truth and falsehood, on justice and injustice, and they match the criteria of every human person's right conscience. Jesus himself recalled this frequently, underlining the need for active commitment in living the way of the Commandments: "If you wish to enter into life, observe the Commandments" (Mt 19:17). From this perspective, there are several possible areas of cooperation and witness. I would like to recall three that are especially important for our time.

The "Ten Commandments" require that we recognize the one Lord, against the temptation to construct other idols, to make golden calves. In our world there are many who do not know God or who consider him superfluous, without relevance for their lives; hence, other new gods have been fabricated to whom man bows down. Reawakening in our society openness to the transcendent dimension, witnessing to the one God, is a precious service which Jews and Christians can and must offer together.

The "Ten Commandments" call us to respect life and to protect it against every injustice and abuse, recognizing the worth of each human person, created in the image and likeness of God. How often, in every part of the world, near and far, the dignity, the freedom and the rights of human beings are trampled upon! Bearing witness together to the supreme value of life against all selfishness, is an important contribution to a new world where justice and peace reign, a world marked by that "shalom" which the lawgivers, the prophets and the sages of Israel longed to see.

The "Ten Commandments" call us to preserve and to promote the sanctity of the family, in which the personal and reciprocal, faithful and definitive "Yes" of man and woman makes room for the future, for the authentic humanity of each, and makes them open, at the same time, to the gift of new life. To witness that the family continues to be the essential cell of society and the basic environment in which human virtues are learned and practiced is a precious service offered in the construction of a world with a more human face.

Angelus

February 7, 2010

After the Angelus

Today the Church in Italy is observing the *Day for Life* on the theme: "The Power of Life, a Challenge in Poverty." In the present period of financial difficulty the mechanisms that harm and offend life, targeting in particular the weakest and the most defenseless people by producing poverty and creating strong social inequalities, are becoming even more dramatic.

This situation thus engages us to encourage integral human development to surmount poverty and neediness and, especially, reminds us that the human goal is not wellbeing but God himself, and that human life must be defended at every stage.

Indeed, no one is master of his own life. Rather we are all called to treasure life and to respect it from the moment of conception to its natural end.

As I express my appreciation of those who work more directly at the service of children, the sick and the elderly, I greet affectionately the many faithful of Rome who are gathered here, led by the Cardinal Vicar and by several Auxiliary Bishops.

The Diocese of Rome pays special attention to the Day for Life and extends it in the Week for Life and for the Family. I wish this initiative success and encourage the activities of the consultants, associations and movements, as well as of the university professors who are committed to supporting life and the family.

In this context, I would like to remind you that in the morning of February 11, the Memorial of Our Lady of Lourdes and the World Day of the Sick, I shall celebrate Mass with the sick at St. Peter's Basilica.

Address to the Bishops of Romania on Their *Ad Limina* Visit

February 12, 2010

The flourishing of priestly and religious vocations largely depends on the moral and religious health of Christian families. Unfortunately, today there are many pitfalls for the family institution in our secularized and disoriented society. Catholic families in your country which during the time of trial, gave witness of faithfulness to the Gospel sometimes paying dearly for it are not immune to the scourges of abortion, corruption, alcoholism, and drugs, as well as birth control using methods contrary to the dignity of the human person. To combat these challenges, it is necessary to promote parish counselors who can assure an adequate preparation for conjugal and family life, and who can better organize the pastoral care of youth. More necessary than anything else is a decisive commitment to encouraging the presence of the Christian values in society, developing centers for formation where young people may learn the authentic values, enriched by the genius of your countries' culture, so as to be able to witness to these values in the areas in which they live. The Church wants to make her crucial contribution to building a reconciled and supportive society, able to confront the process of secularization that is under way. The transformation of the industrial and agricultural system, the financial crisis and emigration abroad have not encouraged the preservation of traditional values; these must therefore be proposed anew and reinforced.

In this context it is particularly important to witness to brotherhood between Catholics and Orthodox. This witness must prevail over division and dissent and open hearts to reconciliation.

I am aware of the difficulties that the Catholic communities have to face in this sphere; I hope they will be able to find adequate solutions in that spirit of justice and charity which will animate relations between brothers and sisters in Christ. In May 2009, you commemorated the tenth anniversary of Venerable Pope John Paul II's historic visit to Romania. On that occasion Divine Providence gave the Successor of Peter the chance to make an Apostolic Visit to a nation with an Orthodox majority, where an important Catholic community has been present for centuries. May the desire for unity inspired by that Visit nourish prayer as well as the commitment to dialogue in charity and truth and to the promotion of common initiatives. An area of collaboration between Orthodox and Catholics that is particularly important today concerns the defense of the Christian roots of Europe and of the Christian values as well as the common testimony on issues such as the family, bioethics, human rights, honesty in public life and ecology. A joint commitment to these subjects will make an important contribution to society's moral and civil development. A constructive dialogue between Orthodox and Catholics will not fail to be a leaven of unity and harmony not only for your countries but also for the whole of Europe.

At the end of our Meeting, my thoughts turn to your Communities. Please convey to your priests, men and women religious and to all the faithful of Romania and of the Republic of Moldova, my greetings and encouragement, assuring them of my affection and my prayers. As I invoke the intercession of the Mother of God and of the Saints of your lands, I cordially impart my blessing to you and to all the members of the People of God entrusted to your pastoral care.

Homily at Mass in the
Parish of St. John of the Cross, Rome

March 7, 2010

Dear Christian families, dear young people who live in this neighborhood and attend the parish, let the wish to proclaim the Gospel of Jesus Christ to all involve you more and more. Do not wait for others to come and bring you other messages that do not lead to life; rather, make yourselves missionaries of Christ for your brothers and sisters, where they live, work and study or merely spend their leisure time. Here too, start a far-reaching and thorough vocations ministry, consisting of the education of families and young people in prayer and in living life as a gift that comes from God.

Message to Cardinal Stanisław Ryłko for the
Tenth International Youth Forum

March 20, 2010

I would also like to encourage the young delegates to discover the greatness and beauty of Marriage: the relationship between the man and the woman reflects divine love in a quite special way; therefore the conjugal bond acquires an immense dignity. Through the Sacrament of Marriage the spouses are united to God and with their relationship express the love of Christ who gave his life for the salvation of the world. In a cultural context in which many people consider Marriage as a temporary contract that may be violated, it is vitally important to understand that true love is faithful, it is the definitive gift of self. Since Christ consecrates the love of Christian spouses and is committed to and with them, this fidelity is not only possible but is the way by which to enter into ever greater charity. Thus, in the daily life of the couple and of the family, the spouses learn to love as Christ loves. To measure up to this vocation a serious educational process is necessary and this *Forum* also fits into this perspective.

Address to the Bishops of Scandinavia on Their *Ad Limina* Visit

March 25, 2010

Dear Brother Bishops,

I welcome you to Rome on the occasion of your visit "to the threshold of the Apostles" and I thank Bishop Arborelius for the words he has addressed to me on your behalf. You exercise pastoral governance over the Catholic faithful in the far north of Europe and you have travelled here to express and renew the bonds of communion between the people of God in those lands and the Successor of Peter at the heart of the universal Church. Your flock is small in number, and scattered over a wide area. Many have to travel great distances in order to find a Catholic community in which to worship. It is most important for them to realize that every time they gather around the altar for the Eucharistic sacrifice, they are participating in an act of the universal Church, in communion with all their fellow Catholics throughout the world. It is this communion that is both exercised and deepened through the quinquennial visits of bishops to the Apostolic See.

I am pleased to note that a Congress on the Family is due to be held at Jönköping in May of this year. One of the most important messages that the people of the Nordic lands need to hear from you is a reminder of the centrality of the family for the life of a healthy society. Sadly, recent years have seen a weakening of the commitment to the institution of marriage and the Christian understanding of human sexuality that for so long served as the foundation of personal and social relations in European society. Children have the right to be conceived and carried in the womb, brought into the world and brought up within marriage: it is through the secure and recognized relationship to their own parents that they can discover their identity and achieve their proper human development (cf. *Donum Vitae*, February 22, 1987). In societies with a noble tradition of defending the rights of all their members, one would expect this fundamental right of children to be given priority over any supposed right of adults to impose on them alternative models of family life and certainly over any supposed right to abortion. Since the family is "the first and indispensable teacher of peace" (*Message for the 2008 World Day of Peace*), the most reliable promoter of social cohesion and the best school of the virtues of good citizenship, it is in the interests of all, and especially of governments, to defend and promote stable family life.

While the Catholic population of your territories constitutes only a small percentage of the total, it is nevertheless growing, and at the same time a good number of others listen with respect and attention to what the Church has to say. In the Nordic lands, religion has an important role in shaping public opinion and influencing decisions on matters concerning the common good. I urge you, therefore, to continue to convey to the people of your respective countries the Church's teaching on social and ethical questions, as you do through such initiatives as your 2005 pastoral letter "The Love of Life" and the forthcoming Congress on the Family. The establishment of the Newman Institute in Uppsala is a most welcome development in this regard, ensuring that Catholic teaching is given its rightful place in the Scandinavian academic world, while also helping new generations to acquire a mature and informed understanding of their faith.

Within your own flock, pastoral care of families and young people needs to be pursued with vigor, and with particular care for the many who have experienced difficulties in the wake of the recent financial crisis. Due sensitivity should be shown to the many married couples in which only one partner is Catholic. The immigrant component among the Catholic population of the Nordic lands has needs of its own, and it is important that your pastoral outreach to families should include them, with a view to assisting their integration into society. Your countries have been particularly generous to refugees from the Middle East, many of whom are Christians from Eastern Churches. For your part, as you welcome "the stranger who sojourns with you" (Lv 19:34), be sure to help these new members of your community to deepen their knowledge and understanding of the faith through apposite programs of catechesis—in the process of integration within their host country, they should be encouraged not to distance themselves from the most precious elements of their own culture, particularly their faith.

In this Year for Priests, I ask you to give particular priority to encouraging and supporting your priests, who often have to work in isolation from one another and in difficult circumstances in order to bring the sacraments to the people of God. As you know, I have proposed the figure of St. John Vianney to all the priests of the world as a source of inspiration and intercession in this year devoted to exploring more deeply the meaning and indispensable role of the priesthood in the Church's life. He expended himself tirelessly in order to be a channel of God's healing and sanctifying grace to the people he served, and all priests are called to do likewise: it is your responsibility, as their Ordinaries, to see that they are well prepared for this sacred task. Ensure too that the lay faithful appreciate what their priests do for them, and that they offer them the encouragement and the spiritual, moral and material support that they need.

I would like to pay tribute to the enormous contribution that men and women religious have made to the life of the Church in your countries over many years. The Nordic lands are also blessed with the presence of a number of the new ecclesial movements, which bring fresh dynamism to the Church's mission. In view of this wide variety of charisms, there are many ways in which young people may be attracted to devote their lives to the service of the Church through a priestly or religious vocation. As you carry out your responsibility to foster such vocations (cf. *Christus Dominus*, no. 15), be sure to address yourselves to both the native and the immigrant populations. From the heart of any healthy Catholic community, the Lord always calls men and women to serve him in this way. The fact that more and more of you, the Bishops of the Nordic lands, originate from the countries in which you serve is a clear sign that the Holy Spirit is at work among the Catholic communities there. I pray that his inspiration will continue to bear fruit among you and those to whom you have dedicated your lives.

With great confidence in the life-giving power of the Gospel, commit your energies to promoting a new evangelization among the people of your territories. Part and parcel of this task is continued attention to ecumenical activity, and I am pleased to note the numerous tasks in which Christians from the Nordic lands come together to present a united witness before the world.

With these sentiments, I commend all of you and your people to the intercession of the Nordic saints, especially St. Bridget, co-patron of Europe, and I gladly impart my Apostolic Blessing as a pledge of strength and peace in the Lord.

Address to the Youth of Rome and Lazio in Preparation for World Youth Day

March 25, 2010

Holy Father, the young man of the Gospel asked Jesus: "Good Teacher, what must I do to inherit eternal life?" I do not even know what eternal life is. I cannot even imagine it, but I know one thing: I don't want to waste my life, I want to live it to the full and not alone. I'm afraid this mightn't happen, I am afraid of thinking only of myself, of making a mess of everything and of finding myself without a goal to attain, living from one day to the next. Is it possible to make something beautiful and great of my life?

Dear young people,

Before answering the question I would like to express my heartfelt thanks to you all for coming, for this marvelous witness of faith, for wanting to live in communion with Jesus, for your enthusiasm in following Jesus and for living well. Thank you!

And now for the question. You have said that you do not know what eternal life is and cannot imagine it. None of us can imagine eternal life because
it is outside our experience. Yet, we can begin to understand what eternal life
is and I think that, with your question, you have given us a description of the
essential of eternal life, that is, of true life: not to waste life, to live it in depth,
not to live for oneself, not to live from one day to the next, but truly to live
life in its riches and in its totality. And how can we do this? This is the big
question which the rich young man of the Gospel came to ask the Lord (cf.
Mk 10:17). At first sight the Lord's response seems somewhat dry. In sum, he
tells the young man to observe the Commandments (cf. Mk 10:19). Yet, if
we think carefully, if we listen carefully to the Lord, we find throughout the
Gospel the great wisdom of the Word of God, of Jesus. The Commandments,
according to another of Jesus' sayings, are summed up in this one alone: love
God with all your heart, with all your mind, with all your life, and love your
neighbor as yourself. Loving God implies knowing God, recognizing God.
and this is the first step we must take: to seek to know God. And thus we
know that our life does not exist by chance, it is not an accident. My life
has been willed by God since eternity. I am loved, I am necessary. God has
a plan for me in the totality of history: he has a plan specifically for me. My
life is important and also necessary. Eternal love created me in depth and
awaits me. So this is the first point: to know, to seek to know God and thus to
understand that life is a gift, that it is good to be alive. Then the essential is
love. To love this God who has created me, who has created this world, who
governs among all the difficulties of man and of history and who accompanies
me. It means loving my neighbor.

The Ten Commandments to which Jesus refers in his answer are only to
clarify the commandment of love. They are, so to speak, rules of love, they
indicate the way of love with these essential points; the family, as a foundation of society; life, to be respected as a gift of God; the order of sexuality, of
relations between man and woman; the social order and, finally, truth. These
essential elements describe the route of love, they explain how really to love
and how to find the right route. Hence there is a fundamental will of God
for us all, which is identical for us all. However its application is different in
every life, for God has a specific project for each person. St. Francis de Sales
once said: perfection, that is, being good, living faith and love, is substantially
one but comes in many different forms. The holiness of a Carthusian and of
a politician, of a scientist or of a peasant, and so forth, is very different. Thus
God has a plan for every person and I must find, in my own circumstances,
my way of living this one and, at the same time, common will of God whose
great rules are indicated in these explanations of love. Consequently I must
seek to do what is the essence of love, that is, not to live selfishly, but to give

life; not to "possess" life but to make life a gift, not to seek for myself but to give to others. This is the essential. And it entails sacrifices, that is, it means coming out of myself and not seeking myself. And it is precisely by not seeking myself but by giving myself for important and true things that I find true life. Thus each person will find different possibilities in his life: he may devote himself to volunteer work in a community of prayer, in a movement or in the activity of his parish, in his own profession. Finding my vocation and living it everywhere is important and fundamental, whether I am a great scientist or a farmer. Everything is important in God's eyes: life is beautiful if it is lived to the full with that love which really redeems the world.

Lastly I would like to tell a little story about Josephine Bakhita, the small African Saint who found God and Christ in Italy and who never fails to make a great impression on me. She was a Sister in an Italian convent; one day, the local Bishop visited that monastery, saw this little African sister, about whom it seems nothing was known, and said, "Sister, what are you doing here?" And Bakhita answered him: "the same thing as you, Your Excellency." The Bishop, visibly irritated, said: "But Sister, do you do the same as me? How come?" "Yes," the Sister said, "we both want to do God's will, don't we?" In the end, this is the essential: knowing, with the help of the Church, of the Word of God and of friends, the will of God, both in its broad lines that are common to all and in the concreteness of my personal life. Thus life becomes not too easy, perhaps, but beautiful and happy. Let us pray the Lord to help us always to discover his will and to do it joyfully.

Homily at Mass in St. Peter's Square for the Twenty-Fifth World Youth Day

March 28, 2010

What is important is to point out that with the term "Law" [St. Paul] does not mean the Ten Commandments but rather the complex way of life Israel had adopted to protect itself against the temptations of paganism. Now, however, Christ has brought God to the pagans. This form of distinction was not imposed upon them. They were given as the Law Christ alone. However, this means love of God and of neighbor and of everything that this entails. The Commandments, interpreted in a new and deeper way starting from Christ, are part of this love, those Commandments are none other than the fundamental rules of true love: first of all, and as a fundamental principle, the worship of God, the primacy of God, which the first three Commandments express. They say: "without God nothing succeeds correctly. Who this God is and how he is we know from the person of Jesus Christ. Next come the holiness of the family (Fourth Commandment), the holiness of life (Fifth Commandment), the order of marriage (Sixth Commandment), the social order (Seventh Commandment), and lastly the inviolability of the truth (Eighth Commandment). Today all this is of the greatest timeliness and precisely also in St. Paul's meaning if we read all his Letters. "Bear fruit with good works": at the beginning of Holy Week let us pray the Lord to grant us this fruit in ever greater abundance.

Homily at Mass in Turin, Italy

May 2, 2010

The First Reading we have heard presents to us precisely a special way of glorifying Jesus: the apostolate and its fruits. Paul and Barnabas, at the end of their first apostolic voyage, return to the cities they have already visited and give fresh courage to the disciples, exhorting them to remain firm in the faith for, as they say, "through many tribulations we must enter the kingdom of God" (Acts 14:22). Christian life, dear brothers and sisters, is not easy; I know that difficulties, problems and anxieties abound in Turin: I am thinking in particular of those who currently live in precarious conditions, because of the scarcity of work, uncertainty about the future, physical and moral suffering. I am thinking of families, of young people, of elderly people who often live alone, of the marginalized and of immigrants. Yes, life leads to confrontation with many difficulties, many problems, but it is precisely the certainty that comes from faith, the certainty that we are not alone, that God loves each one without distinction and is close to everyone with his love, that makes it possible to face, live through and surmount the effort of dealing with daily problems. It was the universal love of the Risen Christ that motivated the Apostles to come out of themselves, to disseminate the word of God, to spend themselves without reserve for others, with courage, joy and serenity. The Risen One has a power of love that overcomes every limit, that does not stop in front of any obstacle. And the Christian community, especially in the most pastorally demanding situations, must be a concrete instrument of this love of God.

I urge families to live the Christian dimension of love in simple everyday actions in family relationships, overcoming divisions and misunderstandings; in cultivating the faith, which makes communion even stronger. Nor, in the rich and diverse world of the university and of culture, should there be a lack of the witness to love of which today's Gospel speaks in the capacity for attentive listening and humble dialogue in the search for Truth, in the certainty that Truth itself will come to us and catch hold of us. I would also like to encourage the frequently difficult endeavors of those called to administer public affairs: collaboration in order to achieve the common good and to make the City ever more human and livable is a sign that Christian thought on man is never contrary to his freedom but favors a greater fullness that can only find its fulfillment in a "civilization of love."

I wish to say to all, and especially to the young: never lose hope, the hope that comes from the Risen Christ, from God's victory over sin, hatred and death.

General Audience

May 5, 2010

I send cordial greetings to all who will be taking part in the Congress on the Family in Jönköping, Sweden, later this month. Your message to the world is truly a message of joy, because God's gift to us of marriage and family life enables us to experience something of the infinite love that unites the three divine persons—Father, Son and Holy Spirit. Human beings, made in the image and likeness of God, are made for love—indeed at the core of our being, we long to love and to be loved in return. Only God's love can fully satisfy our deepest needs, and yet through the love of husband and wife, the love of parents and children, the love of siblings for one another, we are offered a foretaste of the boundless love that awaits us in the life to come. Marriage is truly an instrument of salvation, not only for married people but for the whole of society. Like any truly worthwhile goal, it places demands upon us, it challenges us, it calls us to be prepared to sacrifice our own interests for the good of the other. It requires us to exercise tolerance and to offer forgiveness. It invites us to nurture and protect the gift of new life. Those of us fortunate enough to be born into a stable family discover there the first and most fundamental school for virtuous living and the qualities of good citizenship. I encourage all of you in your efforts to promote a proper understanding and appreciation of the inestimable good that marriage and family life offer to human society. May God bless all of you.

Homily at the Celebration of the Word with Social Pastoral Care Organizations in Fátima, Portugal

May 13, 2010

The services you provide, and your educational and charitable activities, must all be crowned by projects of freedom whose goal is human promotion and universal fraternity. Here we can locate the urgent commitment of Christians in defense of human rights, with concern for the totality of the human person in its various dimensions. I express my deep appreciation for all those social and pastoral initiatives aimed at combating the socio-economic and cultural mechanisms which lead to abortion, and are openly concerned to defend life and to promote the reconciliation and healing of those harmed by the tragedy of abortion. Initiatives aimed at protecting the essential and primary values of life, beginning at conception, and of the family based on the indissoluble marriage between a man and a woman, help to respond to some of today's most insidious and dangerous threats to the common good. Such initiatives represent, alongside numerous other forms of commitment, essential elements in the building of the civilization of love.

General Audience

April 21, 2010

From that shipwreck, or rather from Paul's subsequent stay in Malta, a fervent and solid Christian community came into being. After 2,000 years it is still faithful to the Gospel and strives to combine it with the complex questions of the contemporary age. This of course is not easy, nor must it be taken for granted, but the Maltese People know how to find in the Christian outlook responses to the new challenges. For example, one sign of this is the fact that they have kept intact their profound respect for unborn life and for the sacredness of marriage, opting to refrain from introducing abortion and divorce into the Country's legislation.

Address to the Sixty-First General Assembly of the Italian Episcopal Conference

May 27, 2010

The task of educating, that you have chosen as your priority, makes use of signs and traditions, in which Italy is rich. It has need of trustworthy references: the family above all, with its distinctive and inalienable role; the school, a common horizon beyond membership of any ideological choice; the parish, "the village fountain," a place and an experience which initiates the faith in the fabric of everyday relationships. The quality of our testimony remains a decisive factor in each of these areas, a privileged path for the ecclesiastical mission. The acceptance of the Christian proposal takes place, in fact, through relationships of closeness, loyalty and trust. In a time in which the great tradition of the past risks becoming a dead letter, we are called on to stand beside each young person with an ever new availability, accompanying him/her on the journey of discovery and the personal assimilation of the truth. By doing this we too can discover anew the fundamental realities in a new way.

Address to Participants in the Plenary Assembly of the Pontifical Council for the Pastoral Care of Migrants and Itinerant People

May 28, 2010

The fundamental rights of the person can be the focal point in the commitment to responsibility by international institutions. This, then, is closely linked to "openness to life, which is at the center of true development," as I confirmed in the Encyclical *Caritas in Veritate* (cf. no. 28), where I also appealed to States to promote policies for the centrality and the integrity of the family (cf. no. 44). On the other hand, it is evident that openness to life and to the rights of the family must conform to the different contexts, because "in an increasingly globalized society, the common good and the effort to obtain it cannot fail to assume the dimensions of the whole human family, that is to say, the community of peoples and nations" (no. 7). The future of our societies rests upon the meeting between peoples, upon dialogue between cultures with respect for identity and legitimate differences. In this scenario, the family retains its fundamental role. Therefore, the Church with the proclamation of the Gospel of Christ in every sector of existence, carries forward "the commitment . . . in favor not only of the individual migrant, but also of his family, which is a place and resource of the culture of life and a factor for the integration of values," as I affirmed in the *Message for the Ninety-Third World Day of Migrants and Refugees*, October 18, 2006, celebrated in 2007.

Address at the Opening of the Ecclesial Convention of the Diocese of Rome

June 15, 2010

The very nature of love demands definitive and irrevocable choices of life. I address you in particular, dear young people: do not be afraid to choose love as the supreme rule of life. Do not be afraid to love Christ in the priesthood and, if in your heart you become aware of the Lord's call, follow him in this extraordinary adventure of love, abandoning yourselves to him with trust! Do not be afraid to form Christian families who live faithful and indissoluble love that is open to life! Bear witness that love, as Christ lived it and as the Church's Magisterium teaches, takes nothing from our happiness but on the contrary provides that profound joy that Christ promised his disciples.

Letter to Cardinal Stanisław Ryłko on the Occasion of the Congress of Asian Catholic Laity

August 10, 2010

If the lay faithful are to take up this mission [of proclaiming the Gospel], they need to become ever more conscious of the grace of their Baptism and the dignity which is theirs as sons and daughters of God the Father, sharers in the death and resurrection of Jesus his Son, and anointed by the Holy Spirit as members of Christ's mystical Body which is the Church. In union of mind and heart with their Pastors, and accompanied at every step of their journey of faith by a sound spiritual and catechetical formation, they need to be encouraged to cooperate actively not only in building up their local Christian communities but also in making new pathways for the Gospel in every sector of society. Vast horizons of mission are now opening up before the lay men and women of Asia in their efforts to bear witness to the truth of the Gospel; I think especially of the opportunities offered by their example of Christian married love and family life, their defense of God's gift of life from conception to natural death, their loving concern for the poor and the oppressed, their willingness to forgive their enemies and persecutors, their example of justice, truthfulness and solidarity in the workplace, and their presence in public life.

The increasing numbers of committed, trained and enthusiastic lay persons is thus a sign of immense hope for the future of the Church in Asia. Here I wish to single out with gratitude the outstanding work of the many catechists who bring the riches of the Catholic faith to young and old alike, drawing individuals, families and parish communities to an ever deeper encounter with the Risen Lord. The apostolic and charismatic movements are also a special gift of the Spirit, since they bring new life and vigor to the formation of the laity, particularly families and young people. The associations and ecclesial movements devoted to the promotion of human dignity and justice concretely demonstrate the universality of the Gospel message of our adoption as children of God.

Address to the New Ambassador of
Germany to the Holy See

September 13, 2010

Mr. Ambassador,

I am pleased to take the opportunity of the solemn presentation of the Letters of Credence accrediting you as Ambassador Extraordinary and Plenipotentiary of the Federal Republic of Germany to the Holy See to welcome you and to express my best wishes for your lofty mission. I cordially thank you for your kind words addressed to me, also on behalf of the Federal President, Mr. Christian Wulff, and of the Federal Government. I willingly extend my Greeting and Blessing to the Head of State, to the Members of Government and to all the citizens of Germany, in the hope that the good relations between the Holy See and the Federal Republic of Germany may endure and be further developed in the future.

Many Christians in Germany are turning their full attention to the imminent celebration of the beatifications of various priests martyred under the Nazi regime. Next Sunday, September 19, Gerhard Hirschfelder will be beatified in Münster. The Beatifications of Georg Häfner in Würzburg, as well as of Johannes Prassek, Hermann Lange and of Eduard Müller in Lübeck, will take place in the coming year. The Evangelical Pastor Karl Friedrich Stellbrink will also be commemorated, together with the Chaplains of Lübeck. The attested friendship of four clerics is an impressive testimony of the ecumenism of prayer and suffering which flourished in various places during the dark period of Nazi terror. We can look to these witnesses as luminous indicators for our common ecumenical journey.

In contemplating these martyrs it appears ever more clearly and as an example that on the basis of their Christian conviction some people are prepared to give their life for their faith, for the right to practice what they believe freely, for freedom of speech, for peace and for human dignity. Today, fortunately, we live in a free and democratic society. Yet, at the same time, we note that many of our contemporaries are not strongly attached to religion, as was the case with these witnesses of faith. One might ask whether there are still Christians today who guarantee their faith without compromises. On the contrary, generally many people show an inclination for more permissive religious concepts, also for themselves. A supreme, mysterious and indeterminate being who only has a hazy relationship with the personal life of the human person is succeeding the personal God of Christianity who reveals himself in the Bible.

These conceptions are increasingly stimulating discussion in society, especially in the area of justice and legislation. Yet, if someone abandons the faith in a personal God, the alternative arises of a "god" that does not know, does not hear and does not speak; and, especially, of one that has no will. If God has no will of his own, in the end good and evil are no longer distinguishable; good and evil are no longer in contradiction but in an opposition in which the one would be a complement to the other. In this way human beings lose their moral and spiritual strength which is essential for the person's overall development. Social action is increasingly dominated by private interests or the calculations of power, to the detriment of society. Instead, if God is a Person and the order of creatures, as likewise the presence of so many convinced Christians in society is a sign of this it follows that an order of values is legitimate. There are signs, that can also be traced in recent times, that attest to the development of new relations between the State and religion, even superseding the great Christian Churches that up to now have determined. In this situation, therefore, it is the task of Christians to follow this development positively and critically. They must also refine its meaning for the fundamental and lasting importance of Christianity in laying the foundations and forming the structures of our culture.

However, the Church sees with concern the growing endeavor to eliminate the Christian concept of marriage and family from society's conscience. Marriage is manifested as a lasting union of love between a man and a woman, which also always aspires to the transmission of human life. One of its conditions is the willingness of the spouses to refer to each other forever. This requires a certain maturity of the person and a fundamental existential and social attitude: a "culture of the person," as my Predecessor John Paul II once said. The existence of this culture of the person also depends on social developments. It can happen that the culture of the person in a society diminishes; paradoxically, this often derives from a rise in the standard of living. In the preparation and guidance of married couples it is necessary to create the basic conditions to sustain and develop this culture. At the same time, we must be aware that the success of marriages depends on all of us and on the personal culture of each individual citizen. In this regard, the Church cannot approve legislative initiatives that entail a re-evaluation of alternative models to married and family life. They contribute to weakening the principles of natural law and hence to the relativization of all legislation, as well as to the confusion about values in society.

It is a principle of Christian faith, anchored to natural law, that the human being should be protected, precisely in situations of weakness; the human person always takes priority over other aims. The new possibilities of biotechnology and medicine frequently put us in situations as difficult as walking on the razor's edge. It is our duty to study diligently to what point these methods may be helpful to the human being and where, instead, it is a matter of the manipulation of the human being or a violation of human integrity and dignity. We cannot refuse such developments but we must also be attentive. When people begin to make distinctions and often this is already done in the maternal womb between a life that is worthy and one that is unworthy of living, no other phases of life will be spared, especially not old age and infirmity.

Building a human society requires fidelity to the truth. In this context, certain phenomena active in the context of the public media are ultimately food for thought. Being in ever greater competition, the media believe they are impelled to attract the greatest possible attention. In addition, it is contrast that makes the news in general, even at the expense of the report's veracity. This becomes particularly problematic when authoritative people take a stance in this regard publicly, without being able to verify adequately all the aspects. Let us accept favorably the intention of the Federal Government to do its utmost in such cases, in a compensatory and reconciliatory manner.

Mr. Ambassador, I offer you my best wishes for your work and for the contacts you will have with the representatives of the Roman Curia, with the Diplomatic Corps and also with the priests, religious and lay faithful involved in ecclesial activities who live here in Rome. I warmly implore for you, for your distinguished wife and for your collaborators at the Embassy an abundance of divine Blessings.

Post-Synodal Apostolic Exhortation
Verbum Domini, On the Word of God in the
Life and Mission of the Church

September 30, 2010

73. Furthermore, as was brought out during the Synod sessions, it is good that pastoral activity also favor the growth of *small communities*, "formed by families or based in parishes or linked to the different ecclesial movements and new communities" (*Propositio* 21), which can help to promote formation, prayer and knowledge of the Bible in accordance with the Church's faith. . . .

d) *The word of God and the lay faithful*

84. The Synod frequently spoke of the laity and thanked them for their generous activity in spreading the Gospel in the various settings of daily life, at work and in the schools, in the family and in education (cf. *Propositio* 30).

This responsibility, rooted in Baptism, needs to develop through an ever more conscious Christian way of life capable of "accounting for the hope" within us (cf. 1 Pt 3:15). In the *Gospel of Matthew*, Jesus points out that "the field is the world, and the good seed are the children of the Kingdom" (13:38). These words apply especially to the Christian laity, who live out their specific vocation to holiness by a life in the Spirit expressed "in a particular way by their *engagement in temporal matters* and by their *participation in earthly activities*" (John Paul II, *Christifideles Laici*, no. 17). The laity need to be trained to discern God's will through a familiarity with his word, read and studied in the Church under the guidance of her legitimate pastors. They can receive this training at the school of the great ecclesial spiritualities, all of which are grounded in sacred Scripture. Wherever possible, dioceses themselves should provide an opportunity for continuing formation to lay persons charged with particular ecclesial responsibilities (cf. *Propositio* 33).

e) The word of God, marriage and the family

85. The Synod also felt the need to stress the relationship between the word of God, marriage and the Christian family. Indeed, "with the proclamation of the word of God, the Church reveals to Christian families their true identity, what it is and what it must be in accordance with the Lord's plan" (John Paul II, *Familiaris Consortio*, no. 49). Consequently, it must never be forgotten that *the word of God is at the very origin of marriage* (cf. Gn 2:24) and that Jesus himself made marriage one of the institutions of his Kingdom (cf. Mt 19:4-8), elevating to the dignity of a sacrament what was inscribed in human nature from the beginning. "In the celebration of the sacrament, a man and a woman speak a prophetic word of reciprocal self-giving, that of being 'one flesh,' a sign of the mystery of the union of Christ with the Church (cf. Eph 5:31-32)" (*Propositio* 20). Fidelity to God's word leads us to point out that nowadays this institution is in many ways under attack from the current mentality. In the face of widespread confusion in the sphere of affectivity, and the rise of ways of thinking which trivialize the human body and sexual differentiation, the word of God re-affirms the original goodness of the human being, created as man and woman and called to a love which is faithful, reciprocal and fruitful.

The great mystery of marriage is the source of the essential *responsibility of parents toward their children*. Part of authentic parenthood is to pass on and bear witness to the meaning of life in Christ: through their fidelity and the unity of family life, spouses are the first to proclaim God's word to their children. The ecclesial community must support and assist them in fostering family prayer, attentive hearing of the word of God, and knowledge of the Bible. To this end the Synod urged that *every household have its Bible*, to be kept in a worthy place and used for reading and prayer. Whatever help is needed in this regard can be provided by priests, deacons and a well-prepared laity. The Synod also recommended the formation of small communities of families, where common prayer and meditation on passages of Scripture can be cultivated (cf. *Propositio* 21). Spouses should also remember that "the Word of God is a precious support amid the difficulties which arise in marriage and in family life" (*Propositio* 20). . . .

The word of God and Marian prayer

88. . . . The Synod also recommended that the faithful be encouraged to pray the *Angelus*. This prayer, simple yet profound, allows us "to commemorate daily the mystery of the Incarnate Word" (*Propositio* 55). It is only right that the People of God, families and communities of consecrated persons, be faithful to this Marian prayer traditionally recited at sunrise, midday and sunset. In the *Angelus* we ask God to grant that, through Mary's intercession, we may imitate her in doing his will and in welcoming his word into our lives. This practice can help us to grow in an authentic love for the mystery of the incarnation. . . .

Dialogue with other religions

119. Here too I wish to voice the Church's respect for the ancient religions and spiritual traditions of the various continents. These contain values which can greatly advance understanding between individuals and peoples (cf. *Propositio* 50). Frequently we note a consonance with values expressed also in their religious books, such as, in Buddhism, respect for life, contemplation, silence, simplicity; in Hinduism, the sense of the sacred, sacrifice and fasting; and again, in Confucianism, family and social values. We are also gratified to find in other religious experiences a genuine concern for the transcendence of God, acknowledged as Creator, as well as respect for life, marriage and the family, and a strong sense of solidarity.

Address at the Meeting with Young People and Families of Sicily

October 3, 2010

Dear Young People and Families of Sicily,

I greet you with great affection and great joy! Thank you for your joy and for your faith! This encounter with you is the last meeting of my Visit to Palermo today but in a certain sense it is the central one. In fact, it is this occasion that prompted you to invite me: your Regional Meeting of Young People and Families. So today I must begin here, with this event; and I do so first of all by thanking Bishop Mario Russotto of Caltanissetta, who is the Delegate for the pastoral care of youth and the family at the regional level, and then, also, the two young people, Giorgia and David. Dear friends, yours was more than a greeting, it was a sharing of faith and hope. I warmly thank you. The Bishop of Rome goes everywhere to strengthen Christians in the faith, but he then goes home strengthened by your faith, by your joy and by your hope!

Therefore, young people and families, we must take seriously this gathering, this get-together, which cannot be solely an occasional or functional event. It has a meaning, a human, Christian and ecclesial value. And I do not want to start with a discussion but with a testimonial, a true and very timely life story. I believe you know that last Saturday, September 25, a young Italian girl, called Chiara, Chiara Badano, was declared Blessed in Rome. I invite you to become acquainted with her. Her life was a short one but it is a wonderful message. Chiara was born in 1971 and died in 1990 from an incurable disease. Nineteen years full of life, love and faith. Her last two years were also full of pain, yet always of love and light, a light that shone around her, that came from within: from her heart filled with God! How was this possible? How could a seventeen- or eighteen-year-old girl live her suffering in this way, humanly without hope, spreading love, serenity, peace and faith? This was obviously a grace of God, but this grace was prepared and accompanied by human collaboration as well: the collaboration of Chiara herself, of course, but also of her parents and friends.

In the first place her parents, her family. Today I want to emphasize this in a special way. Bl. Chiara Badano's parents are alive, they were in Rome for the Beatification. I myself met them and they are witnesses of the fundamental fact that explains everything: their daughter was overflowing with God's light! And this light, which comes from faith and love, was first lit by them: father and mother kindled that little flame of faith in their daughter's soul and helped Chiara to keep it constantly alight, even in the difficult times of growing up and above all during her great and long trial of suffering, as was the case for Venerable Maria Carmelina Leone, who died at the age of seventeen. This, dear friends, is the first message that I would like to leave you: the relationship between parents and children as you know is fundamental; but not only due to a just tradition I know that this is keenly felt by Sicilians. It is something more, which Jesus himself taught us: it is the torch of faith that is passed on from one generation to the next; that flame which is also present in the rite of Baptism, when the priest says: "Receive the light of Christ . . . [a sign of Easter] . . . this light is entrusted to you to be kept burning brightly."

The family is fundamental because that is where the first awareness of the meaning of life germinates in the human soul. It germinates in the relationship with the mother and with the father, who are not the masters of their children's lives but are God's primary collaborators in the transmission of life and faith. This happened in an exemplary and extraordinary way in Bl. Chiara Badano's family; but it also happens in many families. In Sicily too there are splendid examples of young people who have grown up like beautiful, vigorous plants, after germinating in the family with the Lord's grace and human collaboration. I am referring to Bl. Pina Suriano, Venerable Maria Carmelina Leone and Maria Magno Magro, a great teacher; to the Servants of God Rosario Livatino, Mario Giuseppe Restivo and to many young people whom you know! Often their activities do not make the headlines because evil is more newsworthy, but they are the strength and future of Sicily! The image of a tree is very significant for representing the human person. The Bible uses it, for example, in the Psalms. Psalm 1 says blessed is the man who meditates on the law of the Lord: "He is like a tree planted by streams of water, / that yields its fruit in its season" (v. 3). These "streams of water" could be the "river" of tradition, the "river" of the faith from which to draw the vital sap. Dear young people of Sicily, be trees that sink their roots in the "river" of good! Do not be afraid of opposing evil! Together you will be like a forest that grows, silent perhaps, but capable of yielding fruit, of bringing life and of deeply renewing your land! Do not give in to the suggestions of the Mafia, which is a path to death incompatible with the Gospel, as our Bishops have so often said and say!

The Apostle Paul takes up this image in his Letter to the Colossians, where he urges Christians to be "rooted and built up in him [Christ] and established in the faith" (cf. Col 2:7). You young people know that these words are the theme of my Message for next year's World Youth Day in Madrid. The image of the tree tells us that each one of us needs fertile ground in which to sink our own roots, a ground rich with nutritious substances that make a person grow: these are values, but above all they are love and faith, the knowledge of God's true face, the awareness that he loves us infinitely, faithfully, patiently, to the point of giving his life for us. In this sense the family is a "Church in miniature" because it transmits God, it transmits Christ's love, by virtue of the sacrament of Matrimony. Divine love, which unites a man and a woman and makes them become parents, is capable of generating in the hearts of their children the seed of faith, that is, the light of the deep meaning of life.

And here we come to the next important passage, which I can only outline: the family, to be this "Church in miniature," must be properly inserted in the "great Church," that is, in the family of God that Christ came to form. Bl. Chiara Badano also witnessed to this, as did all the other young saints and blesseds; that together with the family they were born into, the great family of the Church is fundamental, encountered and experienced in the parish community and in the diocese. For Bl. Pina Suriano it was Catholic Action, widespread in this region; for Bl. Chiara Badano, the Focolare Movement. In fact, ecclesial movements and associations do not serve themselves but Christ and the Church.

Dear Friends, I know your difficulties in today's social context. They are the difficulties of the young people and families of today, particularly in the south of Italy. And I also know the commitment with which you seek to react to and face these problems, supported by your priests who are authentic fathers and brothers in the faith to you, as was Fr. Pino Puglisi. I thank God for having met you, because wherever there are young people and families who choose the path of the Gospel there is hope. And you are a sign of hope, not only for Sicily but also for all Italy. I have brought you a testimony of holiness and you offer me your own: the faces of the many young people of this land who have loved Christ with Gospel radicalism; your own faces resemble a mosaic! This is the greatest gift we have received: to be Church, to be in Christ a sign and instrument of unity, of peace, of true freedom. No one can take this joy from us! No one can take this power from us! Courage, dear young people and families of Sicily! Be holy! At the school of Mary, our Mother, make yourselves fully available to God. Let yourselves be molded by his Word and his Spirit and you will be even more, and increasingly, the salt and light of this beloved land of yours. Thank you!

Message to Cardinal Angelo Bagnasco on the Occasion of the Fourty-Sixth Social Week of Italian Catholics[*]

October 12, 2010

All of this takes on a more meaningful prominence in the socio-economic juncture we are currently crossing. At the national level, the most obvious consequence of the recent global financial crisis lies in the rising unemployment and uncertainty that often prevents young people—especially in parts of Southern Italy—from putting down roots in their own territory and taking a leading role in development. For everyone, however, such difficulties represent a roadblock to the realization of their own ideals of life and give

---

[*]   Text is an unofficial translation of the Italian.

rise to the temptation to retreat and confusion. Discouragement is easily transformed into resignation, diffidence, disaffection and withdrawal, at the expense of legitimate investment in the future.

On closer inspection, the problem is not merely economic but primarily cultural, borne out particularly in the demographic crisis, in the difficulty with giving full value to the role of women, in the struggle of so many adults to imagine and to apply themselves as educators. Even more, the irreplaceable social function of the family as the heart of affective and relational life and as the place that ensures aid, care, solidarity, and the ability to pass on inherited values to new generations better than any other, needs to be recognized and energetically supported. Thus, it is necessary that every institutional and social agency be committed to guaranteeing the family effective measures of support, supplying it with adequate resources and allowing for a fair accommodation regarding working hours.

Catholics certainly do not lack an awareness of the fact that such expectations should find a place today within the complex and delicate transformations that involve all humanity. As I had occasion to point out in the Encyclical *Caritas in Veritate* "The risk for our time is that the *de facto* interdependence of people and nations is not matched by ethical interaction of consciences and minds" (no. 9). That demands "a clear vision of all economic, social, cultural and spiritual aspects" (ibid., no. 31) of development.

To confront these current problems while at the same time protecting human life from conception to its natural end, defending the dignity of the person, safeguarding the environment and promoting peace is no easy task but neither is it impossible if trust in human ability remains firm, the concept of reason and its use is broadened, and everyone assumes their proper responsibilities. In fact, it would be misleading to leave the search for solutions exclusively to public authorities: politicians, the business world, unions, social workers and all citizens, as individuals and as groups, are called to develop a strong capacity for analysis, foresight and participation.

Address to the New Ambassador of Ecuador to the Holy See

October 22, 2010

Mr. Ambassador, although there have been times of difficulty and anxiety in the past of your beloved nation, so dear to the Pope's heart, they have not diminished the human and Christian virtues of your people. Nor have they diminished the desire to overcome them with sacrifices that recall useful teachings whose ongoing care is entrusted to the people of today with a view to planning a serene and encouraging future.

The Ecuadorian Authorities will render an important service to the country if they increase this outstanding human and spiritual heritage. In it can be found the energy and inspiration to continue to build the pillars of every human community worthy of this name.

These pillars include the defense of life from its conception to its natural end, religious freedom, the free expression of thought, and also the other civil freedoms. The latter constitute the authentic condition for real social justice. This, in turn, can only be affirmed on the basis of the support and protection, in both juridical and economic terms, of the primary cell of society: which is nothing other than the family based on the matrimonial union of a man and a woman.

Programs intended to uproot unemployment, violence, impunity, illiteracy, and corruption will also be of fundamental importance. In achieving these praiseworthy goals, the Church's Pastors are aware that they must not intervene in the political debate by proposing practical solutions or imposing their own conduct.

Yet they cannot and must not remain neutral in the face of the great problems or aspirations of the human being. Nor must they be inactive when the time comes to fight for justice. Rather, with due respect for the plurality of legitimate options their role consists in illuminating the minds and wills of the faithful with the Gospel and with the Church's social teaching. Thus they will make responsible decisions for building a more harmonious and well-ordered society.

APOSTOLIC JOURNEY TO SANTIAGO DE
COMPOSTELA AND BARCELONA

Interview with Journalists
During the Flight to Spain

November 6, 2010

Fr. Lombardi: And now let us shift our gaze to Barcelona. What significance can the consecration of a church like the Sagrada Família have at the beginning of the twenty-first century? And is there some specific aspect of Gaudí's vision that has struck you in particular?

The Holy Father: In fact this cathedral itself is also a sign for our time. In Gaudí's vision moreover I perceive three elements above all. . . . Lastly—the third point—this cathedral was born from the typical devotion of the nineteenth century: St. Joseph, the Holy Family of Nazareth, the mystery of Nazareth. Yet this devotion of the past, one could say, is itself very up to date because the problem of the family, of the renewal of the family as a fundamental cell of society, is the great theme today and points out to us where we can go, in both the construction of society and in the unity between faith and life, between religion and society. Family is the fundamental theme expressed here; it says that God made himself a son in a family and calls us to build the family and experience family life.

Homily at Mass in Barcelona, Spain, with the Dedication of the Church of the Sagrada Familia and of the Altar

November 7, 2010

Dear Brothers and Sisters in the Lord,

"This day is holy to the Lord your God; do not mourn or weep. . . . The joy of the Lord is your strength" (Neh 8:9-11). With these words from the first reading that we have proclaimed, I wish to greet all of you taking part in this celebration. I extend an affectionate greeting to their Majesties the King and Queen of Spain who have graciously wished to be with us. I extend a thankful greeting to Cardinal Luís Martínez Sistach, Archbishop of Barcelona, for his words of welcome and for his invitation to me to dedicate this Church of the Sagrada Familia, a magnificent achievement of engineering, art and faith. I also greet Cardinal Ricardo María Carles Gordó, Archbishop Emeritus of Barcelona, the other Cardinals present and my brother bishops, especially the auxiliary bishop of this local church, and the many priests, deacons, seminarians, religious men and women, and lay faithful taking part in this solemn ceremony. I also extend a respectful greeting to the national, regional and local authorities present, as well as to the members of other Christian communities, who share in our joy and our grateful praise of God.

Today marks an important step in a long history of hope, work and generosity that has gone on for more than a century. At this time I would like to mention each and every one of those who have made possible the joy that fills us today, from the promoters to the executors of this work, the architects and the workers, all who in one way or another have given their priceless contribution to the building of this edifice. We remember of course the man who was the soul and the artisan of this project, Antoni Gaudí, a creative architect and a practicing Christian who kept the torch of his faith alight to the end of his life, a life lived in dignity and absolute austerity. This event is also in a certain sense the high point of the history of this land of Catalonia which, especially since the end of the nineteenth century, has given an abundance of saints and founders, martyrs and Christian poets. It is a history of holiness, artistic and poetic creation, born from the faith, which we gather and present to God today as an offering in this Eucharist.

The joy which I feel at presiding at this ceremony became all the greater when I learned that this shrine, since its beginnings, has had a special relationship with St. Joseph. I have been moved above all by Gaudí's confidence when, in the face of many difficulties, filled with trust in divine Providence, he would exclaim, "St. Joseph will finish this church." So it is significant that it is also being dedicated by a Pope whose baptismal name is Joseph.

What do we do when we dedicate this church? In the heart of the world, placed before God and mankind, with a humble and joyful act of faith, we raise up this massive material structure, fruit of nature and an immense achievement of human intelligence which gave birth to this work of art. It stands as a visible sign of the invisible God, to whose glory these spires rise like arrows pointing toward absolute light and to the One who is Light, Height and Beauty itself.

In this place, Gaudí desired to unify that inspiration which came to him from the three books which nourished him as a man, as a believer and as an architect: the book of nature, the book of sacred Scripture and the book of the liturgy. In this way he brought together the reality of the world and the history of salvation, as recounted in the Bible and made present in the liturgy. He made stones, trees and human life part of the church so that all creation might come together in praise of God, but at the same time he brought the sacred images outside so as to place before people the mystery of God revealed in the birth, passion, death and resurrection of Jesus Christ. In this way, he brilliantly helped to build our human consciousness, anchored in the world yet open to God, enlightened and sanctified by Christ. In this he accomplished one of the most important tasks of our times: overcoming the division between human consciousness and Christian consciousness, between living in this temporal world and being open to eternal life, between the beauty of things and God as beauty. Antoni Gaudí did this not with words but with stones, lines, planes, and points. Indeed, beauty is one of mankind's greatest needs; it is the root from which the branches of our peace and the fruits of our hope come forth. Beauty also reveals God because, like him, a work of beauty is pure gratuity; it calls us to freedom and draws us away from selfishness.

We have dedicated this sacred space to God, who revealed and gave himself to us in Christ so as to be definitively God among men. The revealed Word, the humanity of Christ and his Church are the three supreme expressions of his self-manifestation and self-giving to mankind. As says St. Paul in the second reading: "Let each man take care how he builds. For no other foundation can anyone lay than that which is laid, which is Jesus Christ" (1 Cor 3:10-11). The Lord Jesus is the stone which supports the weight of the world, which maintains the cohesion of the Church and brings together in ultimate unity all the achievements of mankind. In him, we have God's word and presence and from him the Church receives her life, her teaching and her mission. The Church of herself is nothing; she is called to be the sign and instrument of Christ, in pure docility to his authority and in total service to his mandate. The one Christ is the foundation of the one Church. He is the rock on which our faith is built. Building on this faith, let us strive together to show the world the face of God who is love and the only one who can respond to our yearning for fulfillment. This is the great task before us: to show everyone that God is a God of peace not of violence, of freedom not of coercion, of harmony not of discord. In this sense, I consider that the dedication of this church of the Sagrada Familia is an event of great importance, at a time in which man claims to be able to build his life without God, as if God had nothing to say to him. In this masterpiece, Gaudí shows us that God is the true measure of man; that the secret of authentic originality consists, as he himself said, in returning to one's origin which is God. Gaudí, by opening his spirit to God, was capable of creating in this city a space of beauty, faith and hope which leads man to an encounter with him who is truth and beauty itself. The architect expressed his sentiments in the following words: "A church [is] the only thing worthy of representing the soul of a people, for religion is the most elevated reality in man."

This affirmation of God brings with it the supreme affirmation and protection of the dignity of each and every man and woman: "Do you not know that you are God's temple? . . . God's temple is holy, and you are that temple" (1 Cor 3:16-17). Here we find joined together the truth and dignity of God and the truth and dignity of man. As we consecrate the altar of this church, which has Christ as its foundation, we are presenting to the world a God who is the friend of man and we invite men and women to become friends of God. This is what we are taught in the case of Zacchaeus, of whom today's gospel speaks (Lk 19:1-10), if we allow God into our hearts and into our world, if we allow Christ to live in our hearts, we will not regret it: we will experience the joy of sharing his very life, as the object of his infinite love.

This church began as an initiative of the Association of the Friends of St. Joseph, who wanted to dedicate it to the Holy Family of Nazareth. The home formed by Jesus, Mary and Joseph has always been regarded as a school of love, prayer and work. The promoters of this church wanted to set before the world love, work and service lived in the presence of God, as the Holy Family lived them. Life has changed greatly and with it enormous progress has been made in the technical, social and cultural spheres. We cannot simply remain content with these advances. Alongside them, there also need to be moral advances, such as in care, protection and assistance to families, inasmuch as the generous and indissoluble love of a man and a woman is the effective context and foundation of human life in its gestation, birth, growth and natural end. Only where love and faithfulness are present can true freedom come to birth and endure. For this reason the Church advocates adequate economic and social means so that women may find in the home and at work their full development, that men and women who contract marriage and form a family receive decisive support from the state, that life of children may be defended as sacred and inviolable from the moment of their conception, that the reality of birth be given due respect and receive juridical, social and legislative support. For this reason the Church resists every form of denial of human life and gives its support to everything that would promote the natural order in the sphere of the institution of the family.

As I contemplate with admiration this sacred space of marvelous beauty, of so much faith-filled history, I ask God that in the land of Catalonia new witnesses of holiness may rise up and flourish, and present to the world the great service that the Church can and must offer to humanity: to be an icon of divine beauty, a burning flame of charity, a path so that the world may believe in the One whom God has sent (cf. Jn 6:29).

Dear brothers and sisters, as I dedicate this splendid church, I implore the Lord of our lives that, from this altar, which will now be anointed with holy oil and upon which the sacrifice of the love of Christ will be consumed, there may be a flood of grace and charity upon the city of Barcelona and its people, and upon the whole world. May these fruitful waters fill with faith and apostolic vitality this archdiocesan Church, its pastors and its faithful.

[In Catalan:] Finally, I wish to commend to the loving protection of the Mother of God, Mary Most Holy, April Rose, Mother of Mercy, all who enter here and all who in word or deed, in silence and prayer, have made this possible this marvel of architecture. May Our Lady present to her divine Son the joys and tribulations of all who come in the future to this sacred place so that here, as the Church prays when dedicating religious buildings, the poor may find mercy, the oppressed true freedom and all men may take on the dignity of the children of God. Amen.

General Audience

November 10, 2010

While I was in Barcelona, I prayed intensely for families, the vital cells and hope of society and of the Church. I also remembered those who are suffering, especially in these times of serious financial difficulty. At the same time, I kept in mind the young people—who accompanied me throughout my Visits to Santiago and Barcelona with their enthusiasm and their joy—that they might discover the beauty, value and commitment of Marriage, in which a man and a woman form a family that is generously open to life and nurtures it from its conception until its natural end. Everything done to support marriage and the family, to help the neediest people, everything that increases the greatness of the human being and his inviolable dignity contributes to perfecting society. In this regard no effort is in vain.

Prayer for Unborn Life

November 27, 2010

Lord Jesus,
You who faithfully visit and fulfil with your Presence
the Church and the history of men;
You who in the miraculous Sacrament of your Body and Blood
render us participants in divine Life
and allow us a foretaste of the joy of eternal Life;
We adore and bless you.

Prostrated before You, source and lover of Life,
truly present and alive among us, we beg you.

Reawaken in us respect for every unborn life,
make us capable of seeing in the fruit of the maternal womb
the miraculous work of the Creator,
open our hearts to generously welcoming every child
that comes into life.

Bless all families,
sanctify the union of spouses,
render fruitful their love.

Accompany the choices of legislative assemblies
with the light of your Spirit,
so that peoples and nations may recognise and respect
the sacred nature of life, of ever human life.

Guide the work of scientists and doctors,
so that all progress contributes to the integral well-being of the person,
and no-one endures suppression or injustice.

Gift creative charity to administrators and economists,
so they may realise and promote sufficient conditions
so that young families can serenely embrace
the birth of new children

Console the married couples who suffer
because they are unable to have children
and in Your goodness provide for them.

Teach us all to care for orphaned or abandoned children,
so they may experience the warmth of your Charity,
the consolation of your divine Heart.

Together with Mary, Your Mother, the great believer,
in whose womb you took on our human nature,
we wait to receive from You, our Only True Good and Savior,
the strength to love and serve life,
in anticipation of living forever in You,
in communion with the Blessed Trinity.

Address to the New Ambassador of
Hungary to the Holy See

December 2, 2010

The Holy See also notes with interest the efforts the political authorities are making to introduce a change in the Constitution. It has expressed its intention to make a reference to the Christian heritage in the Preamble. It is likewise to be hoped that the new Constitution will be inspired by the Christian values, particularly as regards the place of marriage and the family in society and the protection of life.

Marriage and the family constitute a decisive foundation for the healthy development of civil society, countries and peoples. Marriage as a basic form of ordering the relationship between a man and a woman and, at the same time, as a founding cell of the State community has continued to be modeled on biblical faith. In this way, marriage has given Europe its particular aspect and its humanism, also and precisely because it has meant continuously learning and achieving the characteristic of fidelity and self-denial that this implies. Europe would no longer be Europe if this basic cell of the social fabric were to disappear or to be substantially transformed.

We all know how endangered marriage and the family are today—on the one hand because of the erosion of their most intimate values of stability and indissolubility, due to the increasing liberalization of divorce laws and the ever more widespread custom of men and women of cohabiting without legal sanction and the protection of marriage, and, on the other, because of the different forms of union that have no basis in the history of culture and law in Europe. The Church cannot approve legislative initiatives that imply the support of alternative models of life for couples and the family. They contribute to the weakening of the principles of natural law and thus to the relativization of all legislation, as well as of the awareness of values in society.

Message for the World Day of Peace

[January 1, 2011]

Religious Freedom, the Path to Peace

December 8, 2010

A sacred right to life and to a spiritual life

2. *The right to religious freedom is rooted in the very dignity of the human person* (cf. *Dignitatis Humanae*, no. 2), whose transcendent nature must not be ignored or overlooked. God created man and woman in his own image and likeness (cf. Gn 1:27). For this reason each person is endowed with the *sacred right* to a full life, also from a spiritual standpoint. Without the acknowledgement of his spiritual being, without openness to the transcendent, the human person withdraws within himself, fails to find answers to the heart's deepest questions about life's meaning, fails to appropriate lasting ethical values and principles, and fails even to experience authentic freedom and to build a just society (cf. *Caritatis in Veritate*, no. 78).

Sacred Scripture, in harmony with our own experience, reveals the profound value of human dignity: "When I look at your heavens, the work of your fingers, the moon and the stars which you have established, what is man that you are mindful of him, and the son of man, that you care for him? Yet you have made him little less than God, and crowned him with glory and honor. You have given him dominion over the works of your hands; you have put all things under his feet" (Ps 8:3-6).

Contemplating the sublime reality of human nature, we can experience the same amazement felt by the Psalmist. Our nature appears as openness to the Mystery, a capacity to ask deep questions about ourselves and the origin of the universe, and a profound echo of the supreme Love of God, the beginning and end of all things, of every person and people (cf. *Nostra Aetate*, no. 1). The transcendent dignity of the person is an essential value of Judeo-Christian wisdom, yet thanks to the use of reason, it can be recognized by all. This dignity, understood as a capacity to transcend one's own materiality and to seek truth, must be acknowledged as a universal *good*, indispensable for the building of a society directed to human fulfillment. Respect for essential elements of human dignity, such as the right to life and the right to religious freedom, is a condition for the moral legitimacy of every social and legal norm.

Religious freedom and mutual respect

3. *Religious freedom is at the origin of moral freedom.* Openness to truth and perfect goodness, openness to God, is rooted in human nature; it confers full dignity on each individual and is the guarantee of full mutual respect between persons. Religious freedom should be understood, then, not merely as immunity from coercion, but even more fundamentally as an ability to order one's own choices in accordance with truth.

Freedom and respect are inseparable; indeed, "in exercising their rights, individuals and social groups are bound by the moral law to have regard for the rights of others, their own duties to others and the common good of all" (*Dignitatis Humanae*, no. 7).

A freedom which is *hostile* or *indifferent* to God becomes self-negating and does not guarantee full respect for others. A will which believes itself radically incapable of seeking truth and goodness has no objective reasons or motives for acting save those imposed by its fleeting and contingent interests; it does not have an "identity" to safeguard and build up through truly free and conscious decisions. As a result, it cannot demand respect from other "wills," which are themselves detached from their own deepest being and thus capable of imposing other "reasons" or, for that matter, no "reason" at all. The illusion that moral relativism provides the key for peaceful coexistence is actually the origin of divisions and the denial of the dignity of human beings. Hence we can see the need for recognition of a twofold dimension within the unity of the human person: a *religious* dimension and a *social* dimension. In this regard, "it is inconceivable that believers should have to suppress a part of themselves—their faith—in order to be active citizens. It should never be necessary to deny God in order to enjoy one's rights" (Benedict XVI, *Address to the General Assembly of the United Nations* [April 18, 2008]).

The family, the school of freedom and peace

4. If religious freedom is the path to peace, *religious education* is the highway which leads new generations to see others as their brothers and sisters, with whom they are called to journey and work together so that all will feel that they are living members of the one human family, from which no one is to be excluded.

The family founded on marriage, as the expression of the close union and complementarity between a man and a woman, finds its place here as the first school for the social, cultural, moral and spiritual formation and growth of children, who should always be able to see in their father and mother the first witnesses of a life directed to the pursuit of truth and the love of God. Parents must be always free to transmit to their children, responsibly and without constraints, their heritage of faith, values and culture. The family, the first cell of human society, remains the primary training ground for harmonious relations at every level of coexistence, human, national and international. Wisdom suggests that this is the road to building a strong and fraternal social fabric, in which young people can be prepared to assume their proper responsibilities in life, in a free society, and in a spirit of understanding and peace.

Address to the Ambassador of Andorra to the Holy See

December 16, 2010

In the words that you addressed to me, Mr. Ambassador, you mentioned the recent demographical development of your country. This shows the attraction that your country exerts on the young generations. It is above all a case of young Andorrans returning to their country.

Furthermore, your nation also welcomes new peoples. This openness brings with it the need for awareness and an increased sense of responsibility on the part of the institutions and of each individual. Indeed, the social harmony that could well be thrown off balance is linked not only to a correct and adapted legislative framework but also to the moral quality of each citizen, for "solidarity is seen therefore under two complementary aspects: that of a social principle and that of a moral virtue" (*Compendium of the Social Doctrine of the Church*, no. 193).

Solidarity attains the rank of a social virtue when it can rely at the same time on structures of solidarity and also on the firm and persevering determination of each person to work for the common good, because we are all responsible for all. Moral virtue, in turn, is expressed through decisions and laws that are in conformity with ethical principles. These principles consolidate democracy and permit Andorrans to live according to positive values, thousands of years old and steeped in Christianity, and to cultivate and preserve their identity which is so marked.

The education of young people is certainly the best way of awakening a permanent sense of the solidarity that I have just mentioned. Whatever his degree of responsibility, I encourage each person to show creativity in this sphere, to invest in it the necessary means and to sow generously for the future, mindful of giving it the necessary ethical foundations.

Along with education, it is also right to give the family the support which it deserves. As the basic cell of society, the family carries out its mission when it is encouraged and promoted by the public authorities as the first place where an apprenticeship in social life takes place. Granting to all the members of the family the aid they need will effectively facilitate harmony and social cohesion. The Church can make a positive contribution to the consolidation of the family, weakened by the contemporary culture.

Angelus

December 26, 2010

Dear Brothers and Sisters,

The Gospel according to Luke recounts that when the shepherds of Bethlehem had received the Angel's announcement of the Messiah's birth "they went with haste, and found Mary and Joseph, and the babe lying in a manger" (2:16). The first eyewitnesses of Jesus' birth therefore beheld a family scene: a mother, a father and a newborn son. For this reason the Liturgy has us celebrate the Feast of the Holy Family on the First Sunday after Christmas. This year it occurred the very day after Christmas, and, taking precedence over the Feast of St. Stephen, invites us to contemplate this "icon" in which the little Jesus appears at the center of his parents' affection and care.

In the poor grotto of Bethlehem—the Fathers of the Church wrote—shines a very bright light, a reflection of the profound mystery which envelopes that Child, which Mary and Joseph cherish in their hearts and which can be seen in their expression, in their actions, and especially in their silence. Indeed, they preserve in their inmost depths the words of the Angel's Annunciation to Mary: "the Child to be born will be called holy, the Son of God" (Lk 1:35).

Yet every child's birth brings something of this mystery with it! Parents who receive a child as a gift know this well and often speak of it in this way. We have all heard people say to a father and a mother: "this child is a gift, a miracle!" Indeed, human beings do not experience procreation merely as a reproductive act but perceive its richness and intuit that every human creature who is born on earth is the "sign" par excellence of the Creator and Father who is in Heaven.

How important it is, therefore, that every child coming into the world be welcomed by the warmth of a family! External comforts do not matter: Jesus was born in a stable and had a manger as his first cradle, but the love of Mary and of Joseph made him feel the tenderness and beauty of being loved. Children need this: the love of their father and mother. It is this that gives them security and, as they grow, enables them to discover the meaning of life. The Holy Family of Nazareth went through many trials, such as the "massacre of the innocents"—as recounted in the Gospel according to Matthew—which obliged Joseph and Mary to flee to Egypt (cf. 2:13-23). Yet, trusting in divine Providence, they found their stability and guaranteed Jesus a serene childhood and a sound upbringing.

Dear friends, the Holy Family is of course unique and unrepeatable, but at the same time it is a "model of life" for every family because Jesus, true man, chose to be born into a human family and thereby blessed and consecrated it. Let us therefore entrust all families to Our Lady and to St. Joseph, so that they do not lose heart in the face of trials and difficulties but always cultivate conjugal love and devote themselves with trust to the service of life and education.

After the *Angelus*[*]

January 2, 2011

I greet with affection the many Pastors and faithful gathered in Plaza de Colón in Madrid to celebrate with joy the value of marriage and the family under the motto: "The Christian family, hope for Europe." Dear brothers and sisters, I ask you to be strong in love and to contemplate with humility the mystery of the Nativity, which continues to speak to our hearts and transforms itself into a school of family and fraternal life. The maternal gaze of the Virgin Mary, the loving protection of St. Joseph and the sweet presence of the Baby Jesus are a shining image of what every Christian family ought to be: an authentic sanctuary of fidelity, respect and understanding where faith

---

[*]   This text is an unofficial translation of the Italian.

is also handed on, hope is strengthened and charity is enkindled. I encourage everyone to live out the Christian vocation in the family with renewed enthusiasm, as authentic servants of the love that welcomes, befriends and defends life. Make your home a real seed bed of virtue, a serene space where trust shines forth, in which, guided by God's grace, the call of the Lord can be wisely discerned as he continues to invite us to follow Him. With these sentiments, I fervently commend to the Holy Family of Nazareth the proposals and the results of this meeting, that joy, reciprocal self-gift and generosity may reign in an ever-growing number of families. May God always bless you!

Address to Children Recovering in Rome's Agostino Gemelli Hospital

January 5, 2011

Now, before concluding, I cannot but extend a cordial greeting to all the personnel and patients of this large hospital. I encourage the various initiatives of good and of voluntary work, as well as the institutions which give quality to the commitment to the service of life, I am thinking in particular in this circumstance, of the Paul VI International Scientific Institute, which aims at promoting responsible procreation.

Homily at Mass on the Feast of the Baptism of the Lord with the Administration of the Sacrament of Baptism

January 9, 2011

The Church, which welcomes [these newly baptized infants] among her children must take charge of them, together with their parents and godparents, to accompany them on this journey of growth.

Collaboration between the Christian community and the family is especially necessary in the contemporary social context in which the family institution is threatened on many sides and finds itself having to face numerous difficulties in its role of raising children in the faith. The lack of stable cultural references and the rapid transformation to which society is constantly subjected, truly make the commitment to bring them up arduous. Parishes must therefore do their utmost increasingly to sustain families, small domestic churches, in their task of passing on the faith.

Dear parents, together with you I thank the Lord for the gift of the Baptism of your little sons and daughters; in raising our prayers for them, let us invoke in abundance the gift of the Holy Spirit, who today consecrates them in the image of Christ the Priest, King and Prophet. As I entrust them to the motherly intercession of Mary Most Holy, let us ask for life and health for them, so that they may grow and mature in the faith and with their lives bear fruits of holiness and of love. Amen!

Address to the Members of the Diplomatic Corps

January 10, 2011

Acknowledging religious freedom also means ensuring that religious communities can operate freely in society through initiatives in the social, charitable or educational sectors. Throughout the world, one can see the fruitful work accomplished by the Catholic Church in these areas. It is troubling that this service which religious communities render to society as a whole, particularly through the education of young people, is compromised or hampered by legislative proposals which risk creating a sort of state monopoly in the schools; this can be seen, for example, in certain countries in Latin America. Now that many of those countries are celebrating the second centenary of their independence—a fitting time for remembering the contribution made by the Catholic Church to the development of their national identity—I exhort all governments to promote educational systems respectful of the primordial right of families to make decisions about the education of their children, systems inspired by the principle of subsidiarity which is basic to the organization of a just society.

Continuing my reflection, I cannot remain silent about another attack on the religious freedom of families in certain European countries which mandate obligatory participation in courses of sexual or civic education which allegedly convey a neutral conception of the person and of life, yet in fact reflect an anthropology opposed to faith and to right reason.

Address to the Administrators of the Region of Lazio and the Civil Authorities of Rome

January 14, 2011

The unique vocation of Rome, the center of Catholicism and the capital of the Italian State, requires our City to be an example of fruitful and profitable collaboration between the public institutions and the ecclesial community. This collaboration with regard to our mutual skills is particularly urgent today because of the new challenges that are looming on the horizon. The Church, especially through the work of the lay faithful and Catholic associations, wishes to make her contribution through the promotion of the common good and through authentic human progress.

The original cell of society is the family, founded on the marriage of a man and a woman. It is in the family that children learn the human and Christian values which enable them to have a constructive and peaceful coexistence. It is in the family that they learn solidarity between the generations, respect for rules, forgiveness and how to welcome others. It is in their own home that young people, experiencing their parents' affection, discover what love is and learn how to love. Therefore the family must be supported by administrative policies that are not limited to proposing solutions to contingent problems, but aim to consolidate and develop the family and are accompanied by adequate education.

However sometimes violent acts occur and certain aspects of the family crisis, caused by the rapid social and cultural changes, are aggravated. Even the approval of certain forms of union which distort the essence and purpose of the family end by penalizing those who, not without effort, work to live out stable emotional ties, legally guaranteed and publically recognized. In this perspective the Church sees favorably those initiatives which aim at teaching young people to live love in the logic of the gift of self with a high altruistic vision of sexuality. An educational convergence between the various members of society serves this purpose, so that human love is not reduced to a consumer object but may be perceived and lived as a fundamental experience that gives meaning and a purpose to life.

The mutual giving of husband and wife brings openness to procreation: indeed the desire for fatherhood and motherhood is engraved in the human heart. Many couples would like to welcome the gift of new children but are compelled to wait. It is therefore necessary to give motherhood concrete support as well as to guarantee women with a profession the possibility to reconcile family and work.

All too often, in fact, women are faced with the need to choose between the two. The development of appropriate policies for assistance, as well as structures destined for infants, day nurseries and those run by families, can help ensure that a child is not seen as a problem but rather as a gift and a great joy.

Furthermore, since "openness to life is at the center of true development" (*Caritas in Veritate*, no. 28), the increased number of abortions that occur in our Region should not leave us indifferent. The Christian community, through the many "Case Famiglia" [foster homes] and "Centri di Aiuto alla Vita" [centers that offer support to mothers and families in difficulty because of a new pregnancy], and other such initiatives, is committed to accompanying and supporting women who find it difficult to welcome a new life. May public institutions understand how to offer their support so that family counselors are in a position to help these women overcome the causes that can induce them to terminate pregnancy. In this regard, I express my appreciation of the law in force in the Lazio Region which provides for the so-called "family quotient" and considers the conceived child as part of the family; and I hope this legislation will be fully implemented. I am pleased that the City of Rome has already committed itself to this.

At the other end of life is the ageing of the population. Elderly people are a great treasure for society. Their knowledge, experience and wisdom are a patrimony for young people, who need teachers of life. While many of the elderly can count on the support and closeness of their own family, the number of those who are alone and in need of medical and health-care assistance is growing.

The Church, in our Region too, has always been close to those who find themselves in fragile conditions because of age or unstable health. While I rejoice in the existing synergy with the large Catholic health centers—such as, for example, in the pediatric sector, with the Bambino Gesù Hospital and the public institutions—I hope that these institutions will continue to collaborate with the local entities to assure their service to those who turn to them. I renew the invitation to promote a culture that respects life until its natural end, in the awareness that "the true measure of humanity is essentially determined in relationship to suffering and to the sufferer" (Encyclical *Spe Salvi*, no. 38).

In recent times the serenity of our families is threatened by a serious and persistent economic crisis and many families can no longer guarantee their children an adequate standard of living. Our parishes, through *Caritas*, are doing their utmost to come to the aid of these families as far as possible, alleviating hardship and responding to basic needs. I trust that appropriate measures can be adopted which aim to support low-income families, especially large families which are all too often penalized.

Then there is an additional problem which is every day more dramatic. I am referring to the serious question of work. Young people in particular, who after years of training see few job opportunities and possibilities for social integration or for planning for the future; they often feel disappointed and are tempted to reject society itself. The continuation of such situations causes social tensions that are exploited by organized crime for illegal activities. It is therefore urgent, even in a difficult period, to make every effort to promote employment policies that can guarantee work and a decent livelihood, an indispensable condition for giving life to new families.

Dear Authorities, there are multiple problems which demand solutions. Your duty as administrators who strive to collaborate for the good of the community is always to consider human beings as an end, so that they may live in an authentically human way.

As Bishop of this City I would therefore like to invite you all to find in the word of God the source of inspiration for your political and social action, through "work for the true common good in respecting and promoting the dignity of every person" (Post-Synodal Apostolic Exhortation *Verbum Domini*, no. 101).

I assure you all that I will remember you in my prayers, especially those who are beginning their service to the common good today; and as I invoke the maternal protection of the Virgin Mary, *Salus Populi Romani*, on your work, I cordially impart my Blessing, which I willingly extend to the inhabitants of Rome, of the Province and of all Lazio.

Angelus

January 16, 2011

Dear Brothers and Sisters,

This Sunday is World Day of Migrants and Refugees, which every year invites us to reflect on the experience of numerous men and women and a great many families who leave their homeland in search of a better standard of living.

Migration is sometimes voluntary and at other times, unfortunately, is forcefully imposed by war or persecution and often happens—as we know—in dramatic circumstances. The Office of the United Nations High Commissioner for Refugees (UNHCR) was set up sixty years ago for this reason.

On the Feast of the Holy Family, straight after Christmas, we recalled that Jesus' parents were also obliged to flee from their country and seek refuge in Egypt, to save the life of their Child: the Messiah, the Son of God was a refugee.

The Church herself has always experienced migration internally. Unfortunately, Christians at times feel forced, with distress, to leave their land, thereby impoverishing the countries in which their ancestors lived.

Yet the voluntary moving of Christians, for various reasons, from one city to another, from one country to another, from one continent to another, is an opportunity to increase the missionary drive of the Word of God. It ensures a broader circulation of the witness of faith within the Mystical Body of Christ through peoples and cultures, reaching new frontiers and new environments.

Address to the Members of the Neocatechumenal Way

January 17, 2011

Today I am particularly glad to be able to send more than 200 new families to different parts of the world. They have made themselves available with great generosity and are leaving for the mission, joining in spirit the almost 600 families that are already working on the five continents.

Dear families, may the faith you have received as gift be the light that is placed on the lampstand, which can show people the way to Heaven. With the same sentiment, I shall send out thirteen new *"missiones ad gentes,"* which will be called to create a new ecclesial presence in the highly secularized milieus of various countries and in places where Christ's message has not yet arrived. May you always be aware of the living presence of the Risen Lord and of the company of so many brothers and sisters beside you, as well as of the Pope's prayers.

Address to Members of the United Evangelical Lutheran Church of Germany

January 24, 2011

I am pleased to say that in Germany the international Lutheran-Catholic dialogue on the topic: "Baptism and growing ecclesial communion," has been flanked by a bilateral commission for dialogue, since 2009, between the Bishops' Conference and the United Evangelical Lutheran Church of Germany, which has resumed its activity on the topic: "God and the dignity of man." This thematic context also includes in particular the problems that have recently arisen in relation to the protection and dignity of human life, as well as urgent questions on the family, marriage and sexuality, which cannot be silenced or neglected merely to avoid endangering the ecumenical consensus attained so far. We hope that in these important questions related to life, new confessional differences will not emerge but rather that we will be able together to testify to the world and to men what the Lord has shown us and is showing us.

Address to the New Ambassador of Austria to the Holy See

February 3, 2011

A further important requirement of the Holy See is for a balanced family policy. The family occupies a place in society that concerns the foundations of human life. The social order finds essential support in the spousal union of a man and a woman which is also oriented to procreation. For this reason marriage and the family also require the special protection of the State. For all their members they are a school of humanity with positive effects for individuals as well as for society.

Indeed, families are called to live and safeguard reciprocal love and truth, respect and justice, faithfulness and collaboration, service and willingness to help others, especially the weakest. Yet families with many children are often at a disadvantage. The problems in these families, such as, for example, a high potential for conflictuality, low standard of living, difficult access to education, indebtedness and an increase in divorce, give rise to the thought of their deeper causes which must be uprooted from society. Furthermore, it is regrettable that the life of unborn children does not receive adequate protection and that, on the contrary, recognition of their right to life is only secondary to the parents' right to decide on it freely.

Address to Members of the Emmanuel Community for the Twentieth Anniversary of the Death of Their Founder, Ven. Pierre Goursat

February 3, 2011

Today, the urgent need for this proclamation is making itself felt, particularly in families that so often fall apart, among young people and in intellectual milieus. May you help to renew the apostolic dynamism of parishes from within by developing their spiritual and missionary approaches! I further encourage you to be attentive to people who return to the Church and who have not had the benefit of a sound catechesis. Help them to root their faith in an authentically theological, sacramental and ecclesial life! Especially the work carried out by FIDESCO witnesses to your commitment to the people of the least privileged countries. May your charity be radiant with Christ's love everywhere and thus become a force for building a more just and fraternal world!

Angelus

February 27, 2011

Faith in Providence does not in fact dispense us from the difficult struggle for a dignified life but frees us from the yearning for things and from fear of the future.

It is clear that although Jesus' teaching remains ever true and applicable for all it is practiced in different ways according to the different vocations: a Franciscan friar will be able to follow it more radically while a father of a family must bear in mind his proper duties to his wife and children. In every case, however, Christians are distinguished by their absolute trust in the heavenly Father, as was Jesus. It was precisely Christ's relationship with God the Father that gave meaning to the whole of his life, to his words, to his acts of salvation until his Passion, death and Resurrection. Jesus showed us what it means to live with our feet firmly planted on the ground, attentive to the concrete situations of our neighbor yet at the same time keeping our heart in Heaven, immersed in God's mercy.

Address to the Bishops of the Philippines on Their *Ad Limina* Visit

March 3, 2011

Regarding "those of the household of the faith" who require your apostolic care, the Church in your respective regions naturally shares many of the pastoral challenges confronting the rest of the country. Among them, one of the most important is the task of ongoing catechetical formation. The deep personal piety of your people needs to be nourished and supported by a profound understanding of and appreciation for the teachings of the Church in matters of faith and morals. Indeed, these elements are required in order for the human heart to give its full and proper response to God. As you continue to strengthen catechesis in your dioceses, do not fail to include in it an outreach to families, with particular care for parents in their role as the first educators of their children in the faith. This work is already evident in your support of the family in the face of influences which would diminish or destroy its rights and integrity. I appreciate that providing this kind of catechetical formation is no small task, and I take the opportunity to salute the many religious sisters and lay catechists who assist you in this important work.

Message to the President of
Italy on the 150th Anniversary of the
Unification of Italy

March 17, 2011

The experience that matured during the years in which the new measures of the pact have been in force has once again seen the Church and Catholics committed in various ways to the "promotion of the human person and the good of the country" which, in respect for the independence and sovereignty of both parties, is a principal inspiration and orientation of the Concordat now in effect (art. 1).

The Church is not only aware of the contribution she makes to civil society for the common good, but also of what she receives from civil society, as the Second Vatican Council affirms: "whoever promotes the human community at the family level, culturally, in its economic, social and political dimensions, both nationally and internationally, such a one, according to God's design, is contributing greatly to the Church as well, to the extent that she depends on things outside herself" (*Gaudium et Spes*, no. 44).

Homily at Mass for the
Dedication of the New Parish of
St. Corbinian in Rome

March 20, 2011

Yours is a young community, consisting largely of newly married couples who have come to live in the neighborhood; there are many children and young people. I know the dedication and attention that are given to families and to the guidance of young couples: may you be able to start a pastoral service for families, marked by open and cordial hospitality to the new family nuclei, which will be able to foster reciprocal knowledge, so that the parish community may always be, increasingly, a "family of families" able to share with them, alongside the joys, the inevitable initial difficulties.

I rejoice in all you do to prepare children and young people for the sacraments of Christian life, and I urge you to take an increasing interest in their parents too, especially those who have small children; the Parish is striving to propose to them too, at convenient times and in suitable ways, prayer and formation meetings, especially for the parents of children who must receive Baptism and the other sacraments of Christian initiation.

May you also treat with special care and attention families in difficulty or in an irregular or precarious condition. Do not leave them on their own, but be lovingly close to them, helping them to understand God's authentic plan for marriage and the family.

The Pope wishes to address a special word of affection and friendship also to you, dear children and young people who are listening to me, and to your peers who live in this parish. The present and the future of the ecclesial and civil community are entrusted in a special way to you. The Church expects much from your enthusiasm, from your ability to look ahead and from your wish for firm in the choices in life.

*Angelus**

March 20, 2011

Greetings after the Angelus to Polish- and Italian-speaking pilgrims:

I cordially greet all the Poles. Yesterday we celebrated the Solemnity of St. Joseph, Head of the Holy Family, Patron of the Church and my patron saint as well. I sincerely thank everyone who has prayed for me during our spiritual retreat in the Vatican and on yesterday's solemnity. May St. Joseph intercede from heaven on behalf of us all and may he assist your families to be diligent in the face of life's adversities. I bless you from my heart and the start of this new week of Lent.

Finally I greet with affection the Italian-speaking pilgrims, particularly the faithful from Venice, the promoters of the campaign "Adopt a father in the southern hemisphere" which was launched on the occasion of the feast of St. Joseph, the members of the Movement of Christian Life from Salerno, the Palagonia Institute of Higher Learning and the other student groups. I wish you all a good Sunday and a good week. Thanks to all of you. A good Sunday.

---

*   This text is an unofficial translation of the Italian.

Address to the Bishops of the Episcopal Conference of the Syro-Malabar Church on Their *Ad Limina* Visit

April 7, 2011

Within this mystery of loving communion, a privileged expression of sharing in the divine life is through sacramental marriage and family life. The rapid and dramatic changes which are a part of contemporary society throughout the world bring with them not only serious challenges, but new possibilities to proclaim the liberating truth of the Gospel message to transform and elevate all human relationships. Your support, dear Brother Bishops, and that of your priests and communities for the sound and integral education of young people in the ways of chastity and responsibility will not only enable them to embrace the true nature of marriage, but will also benefit Indian culture as a whole. Unfortunately, the Church can no longer count on the support of society at large to promote the Christian understanding of marriage as a permanent and indissoluble union ordered to procreation and the sanctification of the spouses. Have your families look to the Lord and his saving word for a complete and truly positive vision of life and marital relations, so necessary for the good of the whole human family. Let your preaching and catechesis in this field be patient and constant.

Address to the New Ambassador of Croatia to the Holy See

April 11, 2011

There is no shame in remembering and in supporting the truth, rejecting, if necessary, what is contrary to it. I am certain that your country will be able to defend its identity with conviction and pride, avoiding the new stumbling blocks which crop up and, which, under the pretext of a badly understood religious freedom, are contrary to the natural law, to the family and, quite simply, to morals.

Address to the New Ambassador of
Spain to the Holy See

April 16, 2011

You are beginning your lofty responsibility, Madam Ambassador, in a situation of great global financial difficulty, which is also besetting Spain with truly disturbing results, especially in the area of unemployment. This gives rise to discouragement and frustration, especially among young people and the less privileged families. I keep all citizens present in my mind and I ask the Almighty to enlighten all who have public responsibilities so that they may bravely seek the path to a recovery that benefits the whole of society. In this regard, I would like to point out with pleasure the praiseworthy work of the Catholic institutions which provide prompt aid to the neediest, while I ask all for an increasing readiness in this commitment to solidarity. . . .

In her concern for all human beings, in all their dimensions, the Church keeps watch over their fundamental rights in frank dialogue with all who help to make them effective and not to restrict them. She watches over the right to human life from its beginning to its natural end, because life is sacred and no one may arbitrarily dispose of it. She supervises protection and aid to the family, and supports financial, social and juridical measures, so that the man and woman who contract marriage and form a family may have the necessary support to fulfill their mission of being a shrine of love and life.

The Church also supports an education that integrates moral and religious values, in accordance with the beliefs of the parents, as is their right and as befits the integral development of young people; and for the same reason, the teaching of Catholicism at all the centers they may choose, as sanctioned in the proper juridical order.

Address to Participants in
the Seventeenth Assembly of
the European Broadcasting Union

April 30, 2011

In today's society, the basic values for the good of humanity are at stake, and public opinion, in the formation of which your work has great importance, is often disoriented and divided. You well know what the concerns of the Church are on respect for human life, the defense of the family, the recognition of the authentic rights and the just aspirations of peoples. Her concerns over the imbalances caused by underdevelopment and hunger in many parts of the world, the reception of immigrants, of unemployment and of social security, the new forms of poverty and social marginalization, discrimination and the violations of religious freedom, disarmament and the search for a peaceful solution to conflicts. I have mentioned many of these issues in the Encyclical *Caritas in Veritate*.

Address at the Second Ecclesial Convention of Aquileia

May 7, 2011

The primary mission that God entrusts to you today, renewed by a personal encounter with him, is to bear witness to God's love for man. You are called to do this first and foremost with works of love and life decisions in favor of real people, starting with those most vulnerable, frail, helpless, and dependent, such as the poor, the elderly, the sick, the disabled, what St. Paul calls the weak parts of the Body of the Church (cf. 1 Cor 12:15-27).

New Ideas and achievements in the approach to longevity, such a precious asset for human relations, are a beautiful and innovative witness to evangelical charity projected into the social dimension. Be sure to put at the center of your attention the family, the cradle of love and life, the fundamental cell of society and the ecclesial community; this pastoral commitment is made more urgent by the growing crisis of married life and the declining birth rate. In all your pastoral activities make sure that you reserve a very special care for young people: they, who today look to the future with great uncertainty, often live in a state of unease, insecurity and fragility, but who carry in their hearts a great hunger and thirst for God, which calls for a constant attention and response!

Also in this context of yours, Christian faith today must face new challenges: the often exacerbated search for economic well-being in a period of serious economic and financial crisis, the practical materialism, the prevailing subjectivism. It is within the complexity of these situations that you are called to promote the Christian meaning of life through the explicit proclamation of the Gospel, brought with gentle pride and great joy to the various milieus of daily life.

From faith lived with courage, today as in the past, flows a rich culture of love for life, from conception until its natural end, the promotion of human dignity, of the elevation of the importance of the family based on faithful marriage and open to life, and of the commitment to justice and solidarity. The cultural changes taking place are asking you to be committed Christians, "Always be prepared to make a defense to anyone who calls you to account for the hope" (1 Pt 3:15), able to face up to new cultural challenges, in a respectful confrontation which is both constructive and mindful with all those who live in this society.

Regina Caeli

May 15, 2011

My Predecessor's felicitous insight was based on the conviction that vocations grow and mature in the particular Churches, facilitated by a healthy family background and fortified by a spirit of faith, charity and devotion.

Homily at Mass in San Marino

June 19, 2011

Nor should we forget the crisis into which many families have been plunged, aggravated by the widespread psychological and spiritual fragility of couples, as well as the struggle experienced by many educators in offering formative continuity to young people, who are conditioned by various types of instability, and in the first place that of their social role and work opportunities.

Address at the Official Meeting with Members of the Government, Congress, and the Diplomatic Corps in San Marino, Italy

June 19, 2011

The Church, respecting the legitimate autonomy which the civil authority must enjoy, collaborates with it at the service of man, to defend his fundamental rights, those ethical requirements that are engraved in human nature itself.

For this reason the Church strives to ensure that civil legislation always promotes and protects human life, from conception until its natural end. She also asks for due recognition of the family, as well as effective support. In fact, we know well that in the present context the family institution is being called into question, as if in the attempt to ignore its inalienable value. Those that suffer the consequences are the weakest social categories, especially the young generations that are more vulnerable and so more easily exposed to disorientation, situations of self-marginalization and the slavery of dependence. It is sometimes difficult for educational institutes to provide youth with adequate responses and when family support is lacking they often find natural insertion into the social fabric difficult. For this reason too it is important to recognize that the family, as God made it, is the milieu that best encourages harmonious growth and helps free and responsible individuals to develop, trained in the deep and enduring values.

Address to Participants in the Thirty-Seventh Conference of the Food and Agriculture Organization of the United Nations

July 1, 2011

Thus the chosen projects must also be supported by the international community as a whole, in order to rediscover the value of the rural family business and to support its central role in order to achieve stable food security. Indeed, in the rural world the traditional family nucleus is endeavoring to promote agricultural production through the wise transmission by parents to their children not only of systems of cultivation or of the preservation and distribution of food, but also of lifestyles, principles of education, culture, the religious sense, and the conception of the sacredness of the person in all the stages of his or her existence. The rural family is not only a work model, but a model of living and a concrete expression of solidarity, in which the essential role of women is confirmed.

Mr. President, Ladies and Gentlemen, the aim of food security is an authentically human requirement, as we are aware. To guarantee it to the present generations and to those that are to come also means protecting natural resources from frenzied exploitation, since the consumer race and consequent waste appear to pay no attention at all to the genetic patrimony and biological differences that are so important for agricultural activities. Moreover, the idea of an exclusive appropriation of these resources is opposed to the call that God addresses to men and women, so that by tilling the earth and preserving it (cf. Gn 2:8-17) they may encourage participation in the use of the goods of Creation, an aim that international multilateral activity and legislation can certainly contribute to achieve.

In our era when, in addition to the numerous problems that besiege agricultural work there are new opportunities to contribute to resolving the drama of famine, you can strive to ensure that by guaranteeing the food that corresponds to their needs, each and every one may develop in accordance with their true dimension as creatures made in the likeness of God.

This is the wish I would like to express, as I invoke upon you and upon your work an abundance of divine blessings.

Homily at Mass for the Conclusion of the Twenty-Fifth Italian National Eucharistic Congress in Ancona, Italy

September 11, 2011

The 2,000-year-old history of the Church is spangled with saints whose existence is an eloquent sign of how in communion with the Lord and from the Eucharist a new and intense assumption of responsibility comes into being at all the levels of community life; thus a new positive social development is born which is centered on the person, especially when he or she is poor, sick or in need. Being nourished by Christ is the way not to be foreign or indifferent to the fate of the brethren, but rather to enter into the same logic of love and of the gift of the sacrifice of the Cross; anyone who can kneel before the Eucharist, who receives the Body of the Lord, cannot but be attentive in the ordinary daily routine to situations unworthy of the human being; anyone who can bend over the needy in the first person, who can break his own bread with the hungry and share water with the thirsty, who can clothe the naked and visit the sick person and the prisoner (cf. Mt 25:34-36).

This person will be able to see in every individual that same Lord who did not hesitate to give the whole of himself for us and for our salvation. A Eucharistic spirituality, then, is the true antidote to the individualism and selfishness that often mark daily life. It leads to the rediscovery of giving freely, to the centrality of relationships, starting with the family, and pays special attention to alleviating the wounds of broken families.

A Eucharistic spirituality is the soul of an ecclesial community which surmounts divisions and antagonism and appreciates the diversity of charisms and ministries, putting them at the service of the Church, of her vitality and mission. A Eucharistic spirituality is the way to restore dignity to the days of human beings, hence to their work, in the quest for its reconciliation with the times of celebration and of the family, and in the commitment to overcome the uncertainty of precarious situations and the problem of unemployment.

A Eucharistic spirituality will also help us to approach the different forms of human frailty, aware that they do not dim the value of a person but require closeness, acceptance and help. A renewed educational ability will draw strength from the Bread of Life, attentive to witnessing to the fundamental values of existence, of knowledge of the spiritual and cultural heritage; its vitality will enable us to dwell in the human city with the readiness to expend ourselves on the horizon of the common good in order to build a fairer and more brotherly society.

Address at the Meeting with Families and Priests in Ancona, Italy

September 11, 2011

Dear Priests and Dear Married Couples,

The hill on which this cathedral is built gives us a very beautiful view of the city and of the sea, but in passing through its majestic portal the mind is fascinated by the harmony of the Romanesque style, enriched by an interweaving of Byzantine with Gothic elements

In your presence too—priests and married couples from different Italian dioceses—we perceive the beauty of the harmony and complementarity of your different vocations. In sharing the same faith, your mutual knowledge and esteem lead to an appreciation of each other's charism and to recognizing that we are in the one "spiritual house" (1 Pt 2:5) which, with Jesus Christ himself as cornerstone, develops in a well-ordered way to become a holy temple in the Lord (cf. Eph 2:20-21). So I thank you for this meeting: and I thank dear Archbishop Edoardo Menichelli—also for the words with which he has introduced it—and each one of you.

I would like to reflect briefly on the need to lead Sacred Orders and Matrimony back to the one Eucharistic source. Indeed, both these states of life share the same root in the love of Christ who gives himself for humanity's salvation. They are called to a common mission: to witness to and make present this love at the service of the community in order to build up the People of God (cf. CCC, no. 1534).

First of all, this perspective makes it possible to overcome a reductive vision of the family, which sees it merely as the object of pastoral action. It is true that in these difficult times families require special attention. This is not a reason for the family's identity to be diminished or for its specific responsibility to be humiliated. The family is a source of wealth for married couples, an irreplaceable good for children, an indispensable foundation of society and a vital community for the journey of the Church.

At the ecclesial level appreciating the family means recognizing its importance in pastoral action. The ministry that is born from the Sacrament of Matrimony is important for the life of the Church: the family is the privileged place of human and Christian education and remains, for this end, as the closest ally of the priestly ministry. It is a precious gift for the edification of the community.

The priest's closeness to the family helps it in its turn to become aware of its own profound reality and its own mission, fostering the development of a strong ecclesial sensitivity. No vocation is a private matter, and even less so is the vocation to marriage, because its horizon is the entire Church. Thus an effort should be made in pastoral action to integrate and harmonize the priestly ministry with "the authentic Gospel of marriage and of the family" (cf. Direttorio di pastorale familiare, Italian Episcopal Conference, July 25, 1993, no. 8) for an effective and fraternal communion. And the Eucharist is the center and source of this unity that enlivens the whole of the Church's action.

Dear priests, because of the gift you have received in Ordination, you are called to serve as Pastors the ecclesial community, which is the "family of families," and therefore to love each one with a paternal heart, with genuine detachment from yourselves, with full, continuous and faithful dedication. You are a living sign that refers to Jesus Christ, the one Good Shepherd. Conform yourselves to him, to his style of life, with that total and exclusive service of which celibacy is an expression.

The priest also has a spousal dimension: to identify himself with the heart of Christ the Bridegroom, who gives his life for the Church his Bride (cf. Sacramentum Caritatis, no. 24). Cultivate deep familiarity with the Word of God, a light on your way.

May the daily and faithful celebration of the Eucharist be the place in which to find the strength to give yourselves in the ministry every day and to live constantly in God's presence. He is your dwelling place and your heritage. You must be witnesses of this to the family and to every person whom the Lord sets on your path, even in the most difficult circumstances (cf. Sacramentum Caritatis, nos. 79-80).

Encourage married couples, share their educational responsibilities, help them to renew continually the grace of their marriage. Make the family play the lead in pastoral action. Be welcoming and compassionate also to those who find it harder to fulfill the commitments taken on with the bond of marriage, and to all those who, unfortunately, have failed in it.

Dear married couples, your marriage is rooted in the belief that "God is love" (1 Jn 4:8), and that following Christ means "abiding in love" (cf. Jn 15:9-10). Your union—as the Apostle St. Paul teaches—is a sacramental sign of the love of Christ for the Church (cf. Eph 5:32), a love that culminates in the Cross and is "signified and made present in the Eucharist" (*Sacramentum Caritatis*, no. 29).

May the Eucharistic mystery have an ever deeper effect on your daily life; draw inspiration and strength from this sacrament for your conjugal relationship and for the educational mission to which you are called. Build your families in unity, a gift that comes from on high and nourishes your commitment in the Church and in promoting a just and fraternal world. Love your priests, tell them of your appreciation of the generous service they carry out. May you also be able to be supportive despite their limitations, without ever giving up asking them to be exemplary ministers among you who speak to you of God and lead you to God. Your brotherliness is a precious spiritual help to them and a support in the trials of life.

Dear priests and dear married couples, may you always be able to find in Holy Mass the strength to live belonging to Christ and to his Church in forgiveness, in the gift of yourselves and in gratitude. May the origin and center of your daily activity be sacramental communion so that all things may be done for the glory of God.

In this way Christ's sacrifice of love will transform you, until it makes you in him "one body and one spirit" (cf. Eph 4:4-6). Educating the new generations in the faith also passes through your consistent witness. Bear witness to them of the demanding beauty of Christian life with the trust and patience of those who know the potential of the seed scattered on the ground.

As in the Gospel episode that we heard (Mk 5:21-24, 35-43), may you be to all those entrusted to your responsibility a sign of Jesus' kindness and tenderness. In him it was visible that the God who loves life is not foreign or remote from human affairs but is the Friend who never abandons us. And in moments when the temptation creeps in to consider every educational commitment vain, draw from the Eucharist the light to reinforce your faith, in the certainty that the grace and power of Jesus Christ can reach the human being in every situation, even the most difficult.

Dear friends, I entrust you all to the protection of Mary, venerated in this cathedral by the title: "Queen of all the Saints." Tradition links this to the image of the *ex voto* given by a sailor in thanksgiving to her for saving his son, who emerged unharmed from a storm at sea. May the motherly gaze of Mary also accompany your steps in holiness on the way toward a landing-place of peace. Many thanks.

Address to Young Couples in Ancona, Italy

September 11, 2011

Dear Engaged Couples,

I am pleased to end this intense day, the culmination of the National Eucharistic Congress by meeting you, almost as if I wanted to entrust to your young lives the legacy of this event of grace. Moreover, the Eucharist, Christ's gift for the salvation of the world, indicates and contains the truest horizon of the experience you are living: Christ's love as the fulfillment of human love. I thank Archbishop Edoardo Menichelli of Ancona-Osimo for his cordial and profound greeting and all of you for this lively participation; I also thank you for the questions you have put to me and which I welcome, trusting in the presence among us of the Lord Jesus. He alone has the words of eternal life, words of life for you and for your future!

The questions you are asking acquire even greater importance in the present social context. I would like to offer you just a few guidelines by way of an answer. In certain ways our times are far from easy, especially for you, the young. The table is laden with so many delectable things, but it seems, as in the Gospel episode of the wedding at Cana, that the wine of the celebration has run out. Above all the difficulty of finding a steady job veils the future with uncertainty. This condition contributes to postponing definitive decisions and has a negative influence on the growth of society, which fails to fully appreciate the wealth of energy, competence and creativity of your generation.

A culture that tends to ignore clear moral criteria also lacks the festive wine: in the confusion everyone is urged to act in an individual, autonomous manner, often solely on the perimeter of the present. The fragmentation of the community fabric is reflected in a relativism that corrodes essential values; the harmony of feelings, of spiritual states and emotions seems more important than sharing a plan for life. Even basic decisions then become fragile, exposed as they are to the possibility of revocation that is often considered an expression of freedom, whereas in fact it points to the lack of it. The exaltation of the body, which in reality banalizes sexuality and tends to make it live outside the communal context of life and love, also belongs to this culture which also lacks the wine of the feast.

Dear young people, do not fear to face these challenges! Never lose hope. Be brave, even in difficulties, remaining steadfast in your faith. You may be certain that in every circumstance you are cherished and protected by the love of God, who is our strength. God is good. For this reason it is important that the encounter with God, especially in personal and community prayer, should be constant and faithful, as is the development of your love: loving God and feeling that he loves me. Nothing can separate us from God's love!

Rest assured, therefore, that the Church too is close to you, supports you and never ceases to look at you with great trust. She knows that you are thirsting for values, true values on which it is worthwhile to build your home! They are the values of faith, of the person, of the family, of human relations and of justice.

Do not lose heart in the face of these shortages that seem to extinguish the joy on the table of life. When there was no more wine at the wedding in Cana Mary told the servants to turn to Jesus and gave them a precise order: "Do whatever he tells you" (Jn 2:5). Treasure these words, the last to be spoken by Mary as recorded in the Gospels, as it were, a spiritual testament of hers, and you will always have the joy of the celebration: Jesus is the wine of the feast!

As engaged couples, you find yourselves living a unique season that opens you to the wonder of the encounter and enables you to discover the beauty of existence and of being precious to someone, of being able to say to each other: you are important to me. Live this journey intensely, gradually and truthfully. Do not give up following a high ideal of love, a reflection and testimony of God's love! But how should you live this stage of your life and bear witness to love in the community? I would like to tell you first of all to avoid shutting yourselves into intimist, falsely reassuring relationships; rather, endeavor to make your relationship become a leaven of active and responsible presence in the community.

Then do not forget that if it is to be genuine, love too requires a process of maturation: from the initial attraction and from that "feeling good" with the other, learn to "love" the other and "to want the best" for the other. Love lives by giving freely, by self-sacrifice, by forgiveness and by respect for the other.

Dear friends, all human love is a sign of the eternal Love that created us and whose grace sanctifies the decision made by a man and a woman to give each other reciprocal life in marriage. Live the period of your engagement in the trusting expectation of this gift, which should be received while following a path of knowledge, respect and care, which you should never lose: only on this condition will the language of love remain significant, despite the passage of time. Consequently educate yourselves from this moment in the freedom of fidelity that leads you to look after each other, to the point of living for each other.

Prepare yourselves to choose with conviction the "forever" which connotes love; indissolubility, before being a condition, is a gift to be desired, asked for and lived out, over and above any other changeable human situation. And do not imagine, in accordance with a widespread idea, that coexistence is a guarantee for the future.

Precipitating matters ends by "missing out" on love, which instead needs to respect timing and to be gradual in its expression; it needs to make room for Christ, who can make human love faithful, happy and indissoluble. The fidelity and continuity of your love for each other will also enable you to be open to life, to be parents: the permanence of your union in the sacrament of Matrimony will allow the children God bestows upon you to grow up trusting in the goodness of life. Fidelity, indissolubility and the transmission of life are the pillars of every family, the true common good, a precious patrimony of society as a whole. From now on found your journey toward marriage on these pillars and witness to this among your peers, too: such a service is precious! Be grateful to those who guide you in your formation with commitment, competence and availability: they are a sign of the Christian community's attention and care for you. You are not alone: be the first to seek and welcome the Church's company!

I would like to go back over an essential point: the experience of love contains the quest for God. True love promises the Infinite! Therefore make this period of your preparation for marriage an itinerary of faith: rediscover for your life as a couple the centrality of Jesus Christ and of walking with the Church.

Mary teaches us that the good of each one depends on listening with docility to her Son's words. In those who trust in him, the water of everyday life is changed into the wine of love that makes life good, beautiful and fruitful. Indeed, Cana is the announcement and anticipation of the gift of the new wine of the Eucharist, the sacrifice and banquet in which the Lord comes to us and renews and transforms us. And do not underestimate the vital importance of this meeting: may the Sunday liturgical assembly find you fully participating: the Christian meaning of existence and a new way of life flows from the Eucharist (cf. *Sacramentum Caritatis*, nos. 72-73).

You will then have no fear in assuming the demanding responsibility of deciding to marry; you will not fear to enter into this "great mystery" in which "two shall become one" (cf. Eph 5:31-32).

Dear young people, I entrust you to the protection of St. Joseph and Mary Most Holy; by following the Virgin Mother's invitation—"Do whatever he tells you"—you will certainly enjoy the real feast and will know how to offer the best "wine," the wine Christ gives for the Church and for the world. I would like to say that I too am close to you and to all those who, like you, are living this marvelous journey of love. I bless you with all my heart!

Homily at Mass in Lamezia Terme, Italy

October 9, 2011

I would also like to encourage and bless the efforts of all those, priests and lay people, who are involved in the preparation of Christian couples for marriage and the family, in order to give an evangelical and competent response to the many contemporary challenges in the area of the family and of life. . . .

To you, lay faithful, young people and families I say: do not be afraid to live and to witness to faith in the different sectors of society, in the many contexts of human life! You have every reason to show you are strong, confident and courageous, and this is thanks to the light of faith and the power of love. And when you encounter opposition from the world, make the Apostle's words your own: "I can do all things in him who strengthens me" (Phil 4:13). This is how the saints behaved that blossomed down the centuries throughout Calabria. May it be they who keep you ever united and nourish in each one the desire to proclaim, with words and with works, the presence and love of Christ. May the Mother of God, whom you so deeply venerate, help you and lead you to profound knowledge of her Son. Amen!

Address to the Participants in a Congress Promoted by the "Centesimus Annus–Pro Pontifice" Foundation

October 15, 2011

Venerable Brothers in the Episcopate and in the Priesthood,
Dear Brothers and Sisters,

I am very glad to welcome you on the occasion of the Annual Congress of the *Centesimus Annus–Pro Pontifice* Foundation which has brought you together for two study days on the theme of the relationship between the family and business. I thank Mr. Domingo Sugranyes Bickel for his courteous word and I cordially greet you all.

This year, as was mentioned, is the twentieth anniversary of the Encyclical *Centesimus Annus* of Blessed John Paul II, published one hundred years after *Rerum Novarum*. It is also the thirtieth anniversary of the Apostolic Exhortation *Familiaris Consortio*. This double commemoration makes your well-chosen theme ever more timely. In the past 120 years of the development of the Church's social teaching great changes have occurred in the world that were not even imaginable at the time of Pope Leo's historic Encyclical.

Yet, the inner patrimony of the social Magisterium that has always promoted the human person and the family, in the context of their life and business, has not changed with the changing external conditions. The Second Vatican Council spoke of the family in terms of the *domestic Church* as the "intangible sanctuary" where a person's affections, solidarity and spirituality mature. Even economics, with its laws, must always *take into account* and *safeguard* this primary cell of society; the etymological origin of the very word "economics" contains a reference to the family's importance: *oikia* and *nomos*, the law of the home.

In his Apostolic Exhortation *Familiaris Consortio*, Bl. John Paul II pointed out four tasks for the family institution which I should like to recall briefly: forming a community of persons; serving life; participating in the development of society; and sharing in the life and mission of the Church. All these tasks are based on love and it is love that teaches and forms the family.

"The love," the Venerable Pontiff started, "between husband and wife and, in a derivatory and broader way, the love between members of the same family—between parents and children, brothers and sisters and relatives and members of the household—is given life and sustenance by an unceasing inner dynamism leading the family to ever deeper and more intense communion, which is the foundation and soul of the community of marriage and the family" (no. 18). In the same way, love is at the root of the service to life, founded on the cooperation that the family gives to the continuity of creation, to the procreation of man made in God's image and likeness.

Moreover the family is the first place where one learns that the right approach in the social context and also in the world of work, economics and business, must be guided by *caritas*, in the logic of "free giving" giving, of solidarity, and of responsibility for each other. "The relationships between the members of the family community," Bl. John Paul II wrote further, "are inspired and guided by the law of 'free giving.' By respecting and fostering personal dignity in each and every one as the only basis for value, this free giving takes the form of heartfelt acceptance, encounter and dialogue, disinterested availability, generous service and deep solidarity" (no. 43).

In this perspective, from being a mere object, the family becomes an active subject that is able to remember the "human countenance" which the world of economics must present. If this applies to society in general, in the ecclesial community it assumes an even greater importance. Indeed, the family also has an important role in evangelization, as I recently mentioned in Ancona: it is not simply on the receiving end of pastoral action but plays the lead in it. It is called to take part in evangelization in its own original way, placing its being and action as "an 'intimate community of life and love' at the service of the Church and of society" (cf. *Familiaris Consortio*, no. 50). Family and work are privileged places in which to realize the vocation of human beings to collaborate with God's creative work today.

As you pointed out in your reports, in the difficult situation in which we live we are unfortunately witnessing a crisis of work and of the economy which is accompanied by a crisis of the family: the conflict within the couple, between generations and between the time for family and for work, as well as the employment crisis, are creating a complex situation of unease that has a negative influence on life in society itself. A new, harmonious synthesis between family and work is therefore necessary, to which the Church's social doctrine can make its own precious contribution.

In the Encyclical *Caritas in Veritate* I wished to stress that the family model of the logic of love, of free giving and of reciprocal gift, should be extended to a universal dimension. Commutative justice—"giving in order to acquire"—and distributive justice—"giving through duty" [no. 39], are not sufficient to build up society. In order for true justice to exist it is necessary to add free giving and solidarity.

"Solidarity is first and foremost a sense of responsibility on the part of everyone with regard to everyone and it cannot therefore be delegated to the State alone. While in the past it was possible to argue that justice had to come first and that gratuitousness could complement it afterwards, today one must say that without gratuitousness, there can be no justice in the first place . . . . Charity in truth, in this case, requires that shape and structure be given to those types of economic initiative which, without rejecting profit, aim at a higher goal than the mere logic of the exchange of equivalents, of profit as an end in itself" (cf. *Caritas in Veritate*, no. 38).

"The market of gratuitousness does not exist, and attitudes of gratuitousness cannot be established by law. Yet both the market and politics need individuals who are open to reciprocal gift" (*Caritas in Veritate*, no. 39). It is not up to the Church to define ways to face the current crisis. Yet Christians are duty bound to report evils, to witness to and to keep alive the values on which the person's dignity is founded and to promote those forms of solidarity that encourage the common good so that humanity may become increasingly a family of God.

Dear friends, I hope that the considerations which arose at your Congress will help you to assume ever more actively your role in the spread and application of the Church's social teaching, without forgetting that "development needs Christians with their arms raised toward God in prayer, Christians moved by the knowledge that truth-filled love, *caritas in veritate*, from which authentic development proceeds, is not produced by us, but given to us" (no. 79).

With this wish, as I entrust you to the intercession of the Virgin Mary, I warmly impart to all of you and to your dear ones a special Apostolic Blessing.

Address to the Bishops of Angola, São Tomé, and Príncipe on Their *Ad Limina* Visit

October 29, 2011

Christians truly breathe the spirit of their time and suffer from the pressure of the customs of the society in which they live. But, through the grace of Baptism, they are called to reject the prevalent damaging tendencies and to swim against the tide, guided by the spirit of the Beatitudes. With this in mind, I would like to talk about three reefs on which has run aground the will of many people of Angola and São Tomé e Príncipe, who have clung to Christ. The first is the so-called "amigamento" or concubinage which contradicts God's plan for procreation and the human family. The reduced number of Catholic marriages in your communities points to the difficulties that weigh on the family, whose stability in the social fabric we know is of irreplaceable value. Aware of this problem, your Bishops' Conference has chosen marriage and the family as pastoral priorities for the current three years. May God reward the initiatives for the positive outcome of this cause! Help married couples to acquire the human and spiritual maturity necessary to assume responsibly their mission as spouses and Christian parents, reminding them that married love should be one and indissoluble, as the covenant between Christ and his Church. This precious treasure should be safeguarded at all costs.

Post-Synodal Apostolic Exhortation *Africae Munus*, On the Church in Africa in Service to Reconciliation, Justice, and Peace

"You are the salt of the earth . . . You are the light of the world."
(Mt 5:13-14)

November 19, 2011

Introduction

7. The Exhortation *Ecclesia in Africa* made its own the idea of "the Church as God's Family," which the Synod Fathers "acknowledged . . . as an expression of the Church's nature particularly appropriate for Africa. For this

image emphasizes care for others, solidarity, warmth in human relationships, acceptance, dialogue and trust" (John Paul II, *Ecclesia in Africa*, no. 43). The Exhortation invited Christian families in Africa to become "domestic churches" (cf. *Ecclesia in Africa*, no. 92; *Lumen Gentium*, no. 11; *Apostolicam Actuositatem*, no. 11; *Familiaris Consortio*, no. 21) so as to help their respective communities to recognize that they belong to one single Body. This image is important not only for the Church in Africa, but also for the universal Church at a time when the family is under threat from those who seek to banish God from our lives. To deprive the African continent of God would be to make it die a slow death, by taking away its very soul.

8. Within the Church's living tradition and following the desire expressed in the Exhortation *Ecclesia in Africa* (cf. no. 63), to see the Church as a family and a fraternity is to recover one aspect of her heritage. In this community where Jesus Christ, "the first-born among many brethren" (Rom 8:29), reconciled all people with God the Father (cf. Eph 2:14-18) and bestowed the Holy Spirit (cf. Jn 20:22), the Church for her part becomes the bearer of the Good News that every human person is a child of God. She is called to transmit this message to all humanity by proclaiming the salvation won for us by Christ, by celebrating our communion with God and by living in fraternal solidarity. . . .

II. Living in harmony

A. *The family*

42. The family is the "sanctuary of life" and a vital cell of society and of the Church. It is here that "the features of a people take shape; it is here that its members acquire basic teachings. They learn to love inasmuch as they are unconditionally loved, they learn respect for others inasmuch as they are respected, they learn to know the face of God inasmuch as they receive a first revelation of it from a father and a mother full of attention in their regard. Whenever these fundamental experiences are lacking, society as a whole suffers violence and becomes in turn the progenitor of more violence" (Congregation for the Doctrine of the Faith, *Letter to the Bishops of the Catholic Church on the Collaboration of Men and Women in the Church and in the World*, no. 13).

43. The family is the best setting for learning and applying the culture of forgiveness, peace and reconciliation. "In a healthy family life we experience some of the fundamental elements of peace: justice and love between brothers and sisters, the role of authority expressed by parents, loving concern for the members who are weaker because of youth, sickness or old age, mutual

help in the necessities of life, readiness to accept others and, if necessary, to forgive them. For this reason, the family is the first and indispensable teacher of peace" (Benedict XVI, *Message for the 2008 World Day of Peace*, no. 3). By virtue of its central importance and the various threats looming over it—distortion of the very notion of marriage and family, devaluation of maternity and trivialization of abortion, easy divorce and the relativism of a "new ethics"—the family needs to be protected and defended (cf. *Propositio* 38), so that it may offer society the service expected of it, that of providing men and women capable of building a social fabric of peace and harmony.

44. I therefore strongly encourage families to draw inspiration and strength from the sacrament of the Eucharist, so as to live the radical newness brought by Christ into the heart of everyday life, leading each person to be a radiant witness in his or her working environment and in the whole of society. "The love between man and woman, openness to life, and the raising of children are privileged spheres in which the Eucharist can reveal its power to transform life and give it its full meaning" (*Sacramentum Caritatis*, no. 79). It is clear that participation in the Sunday Eucharist is both demanded by the Christian conscience and at the same time serves to form it (cf. *Sacramentum Caritatis*, no. 73).

45. Moreover, to give prayer—individual and communal—its rightful place within the family is to respect an essential principle of the Christian vision of life: the primacy of grace. Prayer constantly reminds us of Christ's primacy and, linked to this, the primacy of the interior life and holiness. Dialogue with God opens the heart to streams of grace and allows the word of Christ to be channeled through us with all its strength. For this, assiduous listening and attentive reading of sacred Scripture within families is necessary (cf. John Paul II, *Novo Millennio Ineunte*, nos. 38, 39).

46. In addition, "the educational mission of the Christian family" is "a true ministry through which the Gospel is transmitted and radiated, so that family life itself becomes an itinerary of faith and in some way a Christian initiation and a school of following Christ. In the family conscious of this gift, as Pope Paul VI noted, 'all the members evangelize and are evangelized.' By virtue of their ministry of educating, parents are, through the witness of their lives, the first heralds of the Gospel for their children . . . they become fully parents, in that they are begetters not only of bodily life but also of the life that through the Spirit's renewal flows from the Cross and Resurrection of Christ" (*Familiaris Consortio*, no. 39; cf. Paul VI, *Evangelii Nuntiandi*, no. 71).

B. The elderly

47. In Africa, the elderly are held in particular veneration. They are not banished from families or marginalized as in other cultures. On the contrary, they are esteemed and perfectly integrated within their families, of which they are indeed the pinnacle. This beautiful African appreciation of old age should inspire Western societies to treat the elderly with greater dignity. Sacred Scripture speaks frequently of the elderly. "Rich in experience is the crown of the aged, and their boast is the fear of the Lord" (Sir 25:6). Old age, despite the frailty which seems to accompany it, is a gift that should be lived each day in serene openness to God and neighbor. It is also a time of wisdom, since length of years teaches one the grandeur and the fragility of life. As a man of faith, the elderly Simeon with joy and wisdom offers not a sorrowful farewell to life but rather a song of thanksgiving to the Savior of the world (cf. Lk 2:25-32).

48. It is because of this wisdom, sometimes obtained at a high price, that the elderly can influence the family in a variety of ways. Their experience naturally leads them not only to bridge the generation gap, but also to affirm the need for mutual support. They are an enrichment for all elements of the family, especially for young couples and for children who find in them understanding and love. Not only have they given life, but they contribute by their actions to building up their family (cf. Ti 2:2-5), and by their prayer and their life of faith, they spiritually enrich every member of their family and community.

49. In Africa, stability and social order are still frequently entrusted to a council of elders or traditional chiefs. Through this structure, the elderly can contribute effectively to the building of a more just society which evolves, not on the basis of whatever experiences happen to come its way, but gradually and with a prudent equilibrium. The elderly are thus able to participate in the reconciliation of individuals and communities through their wisdom and experience.

50. The Church regards the elderly with great esteem. Echoing the words of Blessed John Paul II, let me repeat that "the Church needs you! . . . But civil society also needs you! . . . May you be able to use generously the time you have at your disposal and the talents God has granted to you . . . Help proclaim the Gospel . . . Devote time and energy to prayer" (John Paul II, *Homily for the Jubilee of the Elderly*, no. 5; cf. *Letter to the Elderly*, October 1, 1999).

C. Men

51. In the family, men have received a particular mission. In their role as husbands and fathers, they exercise the noble responsibility of giving society the values it needs through marriage and the raising of children.

52. In union with the Synod Fathers, I encourage Catholic men, within their families, to make a real contribution to the human and Christian upbringing of their children, and to the welcoming and protection of life from the moment of conception (cf. *Final Message*, no. 26). I invite them to adopt a Christian style of life, rooted and grounded in love (cf. Eph 3:17). With St. Paul, I exhort them once more: "Love your wives, as Christ loved the Church and gave himself up for her . . . husbands should love their wives as their own bodies. He who loves his wife loves himself. For no man ever hates his own flesh, but nourishes and cherishes it, as Christ does the Church" (Eph 5:25, 28). Do not be afraid to demonstrate tangibly that there is no greater love than to lay down one's life for those one loves (cf. Jn 15:13), that is to say, first and foremost, for one's wife and children. Cultivate a serene atmosphere of joy in your home! Marriage is a "gift from the Lord," in the words of St. Fulgentius of Ruspe (*Epistula* 1, 11: *PL* 65, 306C). Your witness to the inviolable dignity of every human person will serve as an effective antidote to traditional practices which are contrary to the Gospel and oppressive to women in particular.

53. In manifesting and in living on earth God's own fatherhood (cf. Eph 3:15), you are called to guarantee the personal development of all members of the family, which is the cradle and most effective means for humanizing society, and the place of encounter for different generations (cf. *Familiaris Consortio*, nos. 25, 4). By the creative dynamic of the word of God itself (cf. *Propositio* 45), may your sense of responsibility grow to the point where you make concrete commitments in the Church. She needs convinced and effective witnesses of the faith who will promote reconciliation, justice and peace (cf. *Final Message*, no. 26), and will offer their enthusiastic and courageous contribution to the transformation of their own milieu and of society as a whole. You are these witnesses through your work, which enables you constantly to provide for yourselves and for your families. What is more, by offering this work to God, you are associated with the redemptive work of Jesus Christ who gave an eminent dignity to labor by the work of his own hands at Nazareth (cf. *Gaudium et Spes*, no. 67).

54. The quality and impact of your Christian lives depend on a life of profound prayer, nourished by the word of God and the sacraments. So be vigilant in

keeping alive this essential dimension of your Christian commitment; it is there that your witness of faith in everyday tasks and your participation in ecclesial movements find their source! In the process, you also become models whom the young will want to imitate, and so you will be able to help them embark upon a responsible adult life. Do not be afraid to speak to them about God and to introduce them, by your own example, to the life of faith and to commitment in social or charitable activities, and in this way lead them to discover that they are truly created in the image and likeness of God. "The signs of this divine image in man can be recognized, not in the form of the body, which is subject to corruption, but in the prudence of intelligence, in justice, moderation, courage, wisdom, education" (Origen, *De Principiis*, IV, 4, 10, SC 268, 427).

D. Women

55. Women in Africa make a great contribution to the family, to society and to the Church by their many talents and unique gifts. As John Paul II said: "woman is the one in whom the order of love in the created world of persons takes first root" (John Paul II, *Mulieris Dignitatem*, no. 29; cf. Benedict XVI, *Meeting with Catholic Movements for the Promotion of Women*, Luanda, March 22, 2009). The Church and society need women to take their full place in the world "so that the human race can live in the world without completely losing its humanity" (Benedict XVI, *Meeting with Catholic Movements for the Promotion of Women*, Luanda, March 22, 2009).

56. While it is undeniable that in certain African countries progress has been made toward the advancement of women and their education, it remains the case that, overall, women's dignity and rights as well as their essential contribution to the family and to society have not been fully acknowledged or appreciated. Thus women and girls are often afforded fewer opportunities than men and boys. There are still too many practices that debase and degrade women in the name of ancestral tradition. With the Synod Fathers, I urge all Christians to combat all acts of violence against women, speaking out and condemning them (cf. *Propositio* 47). In this area, the conduct of the members of the Church ought to be a model for society as a whole.

57. When I visited Africa, I insisted that: "we must recognize, affirm and defend the equal dignity of man and woman: they are both persons, utterly unique among all the living beings found in the world" (Benedict XVI, *Meeting with Catholic Movements for the Promotion of Women*, Luanda, March 22, 2009). Unfortunately, the evolution of ways of thinking in this area is much too slow. The Church has the duty to contribute to the recognition and

liberation of women, following the example of Christ's own esteem for them (cf. Mt 15:21-28; Lk 7:36-50; 8:1-3; 10:38-42; Jn 4:7-42). Giving women opportunities to make their voice heard and to express their talents through initiatives which reinforce their worth, their self-esteem and their uniqueness would enable them to occupy a place in society equal to that of men—without confusing or conflating the specific character of each—since both men and women are the "image" of the Creator (cf. Gn 1:27). Bishops should encourage and promote the formation of women so that they may assume "their proper share of responsibility and participation in the community life of society and . . . of the Church" (Second Ordinary General Assembly of the Synod of Bishops, *Justitia in Mundo*, no. 45; cf. *Ecclesia in Africa*, no. 121). Women will thus contribute to the humanization of society.

58. You, Catholic women, carry on the Gospel tradition of those women who assisted Jesus and the apostles (cf. Lk 8:3). In the local Churches, you are a kind of "backbone" (*Final Message*, no. 25), because your numbers, your active presence and your organizations are a great support for the Church's apostolate. When peace is under threat, when justice is flouted, when poverty increases, you stand up to defend human dignity, the family and the values of religion. May the Holy Spirit unceasingly call forth holy and courageous women in the Church, who can make their precious spiritual contribution to the growth of our communities!

59. Dear daughters of the Church, sit constantly at the school of Christ, like Mary of Bethany, and learn to recognize his word (cf. Lk 10:39). Grow in knowledge of the catechism and the Church's social teaching, so as to acquire for yourselves the principles that will assist you in acting as true disciples. Thus you will be able to engage with discernment in the various projects involving women. Continue to defend life, for God has made you channels of life. The Church will always support you. Help young girls by your counsel and example, so that they may approach adult life serenely. Support one another! Show respect to the elderly in your midst. The Church counts on you to create a "human ecology" (Benedict XVI, *Message for the 2010 World Day of Peace*, no. 11; cf. *Caritas in Veritate*, no. 51) through your sympathetic love, your friendly and thoughtful demeanor, and finally through mercy, values that you know how to instill in your children, values that the world so badly needs. In this way, by the wealth of your specifically feminine gifts (cf. *Mulieris Dignitatem*, no. 31; *Letter to Women*, no. 12), you will foster the reconciliation of individuals and communities.

E. *Young people*

60. Young people make up the majority of Africa's population. This youthfulness is a gift and a treasure from God for which the whole Church is grateful to the Lord of life (cf. *Final Message*, no. 27-28). Young people should be loved, esteemed and respected. "Whatever their possible ambiguities, [they] have a profound longing for those genuine values which find their fullness in Christ. Is not Christ the secret of true freedom and profound joy of heart? Is not Christ the supreme friend and the teacher of all genuine friendship? If Christ is presented to young people as he really is, they experience him as an answer that is convincing and they can accept his message, even when it is demanding and bears the mark of the Cross" (*Novo Millennio Ineunte*, no. 9).

61. As I said on the subject of young people in the Post-Synodal Apostolic Exhortation *Verbum Domini*: "Youth is a time when genuine and irrepressible questions arise about the meaning of life and the direction our own lives should take. Only God can give the true answer to these questions. Concern for young people calls for courage and clarity in the message we proclaim; we need to help young people to gain confidence and familiarity with sacred Scripture so it can become a compass pointing out the path to follow. Young people need witnesses and teachers who can walk with them, teaching them to love the Gospel and to share it, especially with their peers, and thus to become authentic and credible messengers" (no. 104).

62. In his Rule, St. Benedict asks the abbot of the monastery to listen to the youngest monks. As he says: "It is often to a younger brother that the Lord reveals the best course" (*Rule* III, 3; cf. *Novo Millennio Ineunte*, no. 45). So we should make every effort to involve young people directly in the life of society and of the Church, so that they do not fall prey to feelings of frustration and rejection in the face of their inability to shape their own future, especially in those situations where young people are vulnerable due to lack of education, unemployment, political exploitation and various kinds of addiction (cf. *Propositio* 48).

63. Dear young people, enticements of all kinds may tempt you: ideologies, sects, money, drugs, casual sex, violence . . . Be vigilant: those who propose these things to you want to destroy your future! In spite of difficulties, do not be discouraged and do not give up your ideals, your hard work and your commitment to your human, intellectual and spiritual formation! In order to grow in discernment, along with the strength and the freedom needed to resist these pressures, I encourage you to place Jesus Christ at the center of your lives through prayer, but also through the study of sacred Scripture,

frequent recourse to the sacraments, formation in the Church's social teaching, and your active and enthusiastic participation in ecclesial groups and movements. Cultivate a yearning for fraternity, justice and peace. The future is in the hands of those who find powerful reasons to live and to hope. If you want it, the future is in your hands, because the gifts that the Lord has bestowed upon each one of you, strengthened by your encounter with Christ, can bring genuine hope to the world! (cf. Benedict XVI, *Message for the XXV World Youth Day*, no. 7; *Verbum Domini*, no. 104).

64. When it comes to making life choices, when you find yourselves considering the question of a total consecration to Christ—in the ministerial priesthood or the consecrated life—turn to him, take him as your model, and listen to his word by meditating regularly. During the homily of the inaugural Mass of my pontificate, I spoke words to you that I want to repeat now, for they remain timely: "If we let Christ into our lives, we lose nothing, nothing, absolutely nothing of what makes life free, beautiful and great. No! Only in this friendship are the doors of life opened wide. Only in this friendship is the great potential of human existence truly revealed . . . Dear young people: Do not be afraid of Christ! He takes nothing away, and he gives you everything. When we give ourselves to him, we receive a hundredfold in return. Yes, open, open wide the doors to Christ—and you will find true life" (*AAS* 97 [2005], 712).

F. Children

65. Like young people, children are a gift of God to humanity, and they must be the object of particular concern on the part of their families, the Church, society and governments, for they are a source of hope and renewed life. God is particularly close to them and their lives are precious in his eyes, even when circumstances seem difficult or impossible (cf. Gn 17:17-18; 18:12, Mt 18:10).

66. Indeed, "as far as the right to life is concerned, every innocent human being is absolutely equal to all others. This equality is the basis of all authentic social relationships which, to be truly such, can only be founded on truth and justice, recognizing and protecting every man and woman as a person and not as an object to be used" (*Evangelium Vitae*, no. 57).

67. This being the case, how can we fail to deplore and forcefully denounce the intolerable treatment to which so many children in Africa are subjected? (The Synod Fathers referred to different situations, including those involving: children killed before birth, unwanted children, orphans, albinos, street

children, abandoned children, child soldiers, child prisoners, children forced into labor, children ill-treated on account of physical or mental handicap, children said to be witches or warlocks, children said to be serpents, children sold as sex slaves, traumatized children without any future prospects, etc. Cf. *Propositio* 49.) The Church is Mother and could never abandon a single one of them. It is our task to let Christ's light shine in their lives by offering them his love, so that they can hear him say to them: "You are precious in my eyes, and honored, and I love you" (Is 43:4). God wants every child to be happy and to smile, and his favor rests upon them, "for to such belongs the kingdom of God" (Mk 10:14).

68. Christ Jesus always manifested his preferential love for the little ones (cf. Mk 10:13-16). The Gospel itself is deeply permeated by the truth about children. What, indeed, is meant by these words: "unless you turn and become like children, you will never enter the kingdom of heaven" (Mt 18:3)? Does not Jesus make the child a model, even for adults? The child has something which must never be lacking in those who would enter the kingdom of heaven. Heaven is promised to all who are simple, like children, to all who, like them, are filled with a spirit of trusting abandonment, pure and rich in goodness. They alone can find in God a Father and become, through Jesus, children of God. Sons and daughters of our parents, God wants us all to become his adopted children by grace! (cf. John Paul II, *Letter to Children* [December 13, 1994]). . . .

III. The African vision of life

A. *The protection of life*

70. Among the initiatives aimed at protecting human life on the African continent, the Synod members took into consideration the efforts expended by international institutions to promote certain aspects of development (cf. *Final Message*, no. 30). Yet they noted with concern a lack of ethical clarity at international meetings, and specifically the use of confusing language conveying values at odds with Catholic moral teaching. The Church is perennially concerned for the integral development of "every man and the whole man," as Pope Paul VI put it (*Populorum Progressio*, no. 14; cf. *Caritas in Veritate*, no. 18). That is why the Synod Fathers took pains to emphasize the questionable elements found in certain international documents, especially those concerned with women's reproductive health. The Church's position on the matter of abortion is unambiguous. The child in his or her mother's womb is a human life which must be protected. Abortion, which is the destruction of an innocent unborn child, is contrary to God's will, for the value and dignity of

human life must be protected from conception to natural death. The Church in Africa and the neighboring islands must be committed to offering help and support to women and couples tempted to seek an abortion, while remaining close to those who have had this tragic experience and helping them to grow in respect for life. She acknowledges the courage of governments that have legislated against the culture of death—of which abortion is a dramatic expression—in favor of the culture of life (cf. *Propositio* 20).

71. The Church knows that many individuals, associations, specialized groups and states reject sound teaching on this subject. "We must not fear hostility or unpopularity, and we must refuse any compromise or ambiguity which might conform us to the thinking of this world (cf. Rom 12:2). We must be *in the world but not of the world* (cf. Jn 15:19; 17:16), drawing our strength from Christ, who by his death and resurrection has overcome the world (cf. Jn 16:33)" (*Evangelium Vitae*, no. 82).

72. Serious threats loom over human life in Africa. Here, as elsewhere, one can only deplore the ravages of drug and alcohol abuse which destroy the continent's human potential and afflict young people in particular (cf. *Propositio* 53). Malaria (cf. *Propositio* 52), as well as tuberculosis and AIDS, decimate the African peoples and gravely compromise their socio-economic life. The problem of AIDS, in particular, clearly calls for a medical and pharmaceutical response. This is not enough, however: the problem goes deeper. Above all, it is an ethical problem. The change of behavior that it requires—for example, sexual abstinence, rejection of sexual promiscuity, fidelity within marriage—ultimately involves the question of integral development, which demands a global approach and a global response from the Church. For if it is to be effective, the prevention of AIDS must be based on a sex education that is itself grounded in an anthropology anchored in the natural law and enlightened by the word of God and the Church's teaching.

73. In the name of life—which it is the Church's duty to defend and protect—and in union with the Synod Fathers, I offer an expression of renewed encouragement and support to all the Church's institutions and movements that are working in the field of healthcare, especially with regard to AIDS. You are doing wonderful and important work. I ask international agencies to acknowledge you and to offer you assistance, respecting your specific character and acting in a spirit of collaboration. Once again, I warmly encourage those institutes and programs of therapeutic and pharmaceutical research which seek to eradicate pandemics. Spare no effort to arrive at results as swiftly as possible, out of love for the precious gift of life (cf. *Propositio* 51). May you discover solutions and provide everyone with access to treatments

and medicines, taking account of uncertain situations! The Church, indeed, has been pleading for a long time for high quality medical treatment to be made available at minimum cost to all concerned (cf. *Final Message*, no. 31).

74. The defense of life also entails the elimination of ignorance through literacy programs and quality education that embraces the whole person. Throughout her history, the Catholic Church has shown particular concern for education. She has always raised awareness among parents, providing them with encouragement and assistance in carrying out their responsibility as the first educators of their children in life and in faith. In Africa, the Church's teaching establishments—her schools, colleges, high schools, professional schools, universities and so forth—place tools for learning at people's disposal without discrimination on the basis of origin, financial means or religion. The Church makes her own contribution by recognizing and making fruitful the talents that God has placed in the heart of each person. Many religious congregations were founded with this end in view. Countless holy men and women understood that leading people to holiness first entailed promoting their dignity through education.

75. The Synod members noted that Africa, like the rest of the world, is experiencing a crisis of education (cf. *Propositio* 19). They stressed the need for educational programs combining faith and reason so as to prepare children and young people for adult life. These solid foundations will be able to help them address the daily decisions arising in every adult life on the affective, social, professional and political plane. . . .

D. Migrants, displaced persons and refugees

84. . . . Migration inside and outside the continent thus becomes a complex drama which seriously affects Africa's human capital, leading to the destabilization or destruction of families.

85. The Church remembers that Africa offered a place of refuge for the Holy Family when they were fleeing the murderous political power of Herod (cf. Benedict XVI, *Address to Members of the Special Council for Africa of the Synod of Bishops*, Yaoundé, March 19, 2009), in search of a land that could offer them security and peace. The Church will continue to make her voice heard and to campaign for the defense of all people (cf. *Caritas in Veritate*, no. 62). . . .

IV. Dialogue and communion among believers

88. . . . Families must be educated in attentive listening, fraternity and respect without fear of the other (cf. *Propositiones* 10, 11, 12, 13). . . .

91. Various syncretistic movements and sects have sprung up in Africa in recent decades. Sometimes it is hard to discern whether they are of authentically Christian inspiration or whether they are simply the fruit of sudden infatuation with a leader claiming to have exceptional gifts. Their nomenclature and vocabulary easily give rise to confusion, and they can lead people in good faith astray. These many sects take advantage of an incomplete social infrastructure, the erosion of traditional family solidarity and inadequate catechesis in order to exploit people's credulity, and they offer a religious veneer to a variety of heterodox, non-Christian beliefs. They shatter the peace of couples and families through false prophecies and visions. They even seduce political leaders. The Church's theology and pastoral care must determine the causes of this phenomenon, not only in order to stem the hemorrhage of the faithful from the parishes to the sects, but also in order to lay the foundations of a suitable pastoral response to the attraction that these movements and sects exert. Once again, this points to the need for a profound evangelization of the African soul.

B. Interreligious dialogue

1. Traditional African religions

92. The Church lives daily alongside the followers of traditional African religions. With their reference to ancestors and to a form of mediation between man and Immanence, these religions are the cultural and spiritual soil from which most Christian converts spring and with which they continue to have daily contact. It is worth singling out knowledgeable individual converts, who could provide the Church with guidance in gaining a deeper and more accurate knowledge of the traditions, the culture and the traditional religions. This would make it easier to identify points of real divergence. It would also help to clarify the vital distinction between culture and cult and to discard those magical elements which cause division and ruin for families and societies. In this regard, the Second Vatican Council taught that the Church "urges her sons and daughters to enter with prudence and charity into discussion and collaboration with members of other religions. Let Christians, while witnessing to their own faith and way of life, acknowledge, preserve and encourage the spiritual and moral truths found among non-Christians, together with their life and culture" (Declaration on the Relation of the Church to Non-Christian Religions, *Nostra Aetate*, no. 2; cf. *Propositiones* 3 and 13). It would help to manifest the treasures of the Church's sacramental life and spirituality in all their depth and to pass them on more effectively in catechesis, if the Church were to carry out a theological study of those elements of the traditional African cultures in conformity with Christ's teaching. . . .

VII. Catechists

127. Dear catechists, remember that for many communities you are the first embodiment of the zealous disciple and a model of Christian life. I encourage you to proclaim, by your example, that family life merits great esteem, that a Christian upbringing prepares young people to live in society as persons who are honest and trustworthy in their dealings with others. Be welcoming to all without discrimination: rich and poor, native and foreign, Catholic and non-Catholic (cf. Jas 2:1). Do not show partiality (cf. Acts 10:34; Rom 2:11; Gal 2:6; Eph 6:9). By your own assimilation of sacred Scripture and the teachings of the magisterium you will be able to offer solid catechesis, guide prayer groups and propose *lectio divina* to the communities in your care. Your activity will then become consistent, persevering and a source of inspiration. As I gratefully evoke the glorious memories of your predecessors, I salute all of you and I encourage you to toil today with the same selflessness, the same apostolic courage and the same faith. By striving to be faithful to your mission, you will contribute not only to your own holiness, but also in an effective way, to building up the Body of Christ, the Church.

APOSTOLIC JOURNEY TO BENIN

Address at the Welcome Ceremony at Cardinal Bernardin Gantin International Airport

November 18, 2011

Modernity need not provoke fear, but neither can it be constructed by neglecting the past. It needs to be accompanied by prudence for the good of all in order to avoid the pitfalls which exist on the African continent and elsewhere, such as unconditional surrender to the law of the market or that of finance, nationalism or exaggerated and sterile tribalism which can become destructive, a politicization of interreligious tensions to the detriment of the common good, or finally the erosion of human, cultural, ethical and religious values. The transition to modernity must be guided by sure criteria based on recognized virtues, which are listed in your national motto, but equally which are firmly rooted in the dignity of the person, the importance of the family and respect for life. All of these values exist in view of the common good which must take first place, and which must constitute the primary concern of all in positions of responsibility. God trusts in man and desires his good. It is our task to respond, in honesty and justice, to his high expectations.

APOSTOLIC JOURNEY TO BENIN

Address at the Meeting with Government Members, Representatives of State Institutions, Diplomatic Corps and Major Religions at the Presidential Palace of Cotonou, Benin

November 19, 2011

These general ideas may be applied especially to Africa. In your continent, there are many families whose members profess different beliefs, and yet these families remain united. This is not just a unity wished by culture, but it is a unity cemented by a fraternal affection. Sometimes, of course, there are failures, but there are also many successes. In this area, Africa can offer all of us food for thought and thus become a source of hope.

APOSTOLIC JOURNEY TO BENIN

Address to Priests, Seminarians, Men and Women Religious, and the Lay Faithful in Ouidah, Benin

November 19, 2011

Dear lay faithful here present, you who are at the heart of the daily realities of life, you are called to be *the salt of the earth and the light of the world*, I urge you to renew yourselves and your work for justice, peace and reconciliation. This mission requires first of all a faith in your family built according to the design of God and in fidelity to his plan for Christian marriage. He also demands of you to be true *domestic churches*. Thanks to the power of prayer, "personal and family life is transformed, gradually improved and enriched with dialogue, faith is transmitted to the children, the pleasure of being together grows and the home is further united and consolidated" without ceasing (*Message for the Sixth World Day of Families*, Mexico, January 17, 2009, 3). By having love and forgiveness reign in your families, you will contribute to the upbuilding of a Church which is beautiful and strong, and to the advent of greater justice and peace in the whole of society. In this way, I encourage you, dear parents, to have a profound respect for life and to bear witness to human and spiritual values before your children. And I am pleased to recall that, ten years ago, Pope John Paul II founded at Cotonou a section for French-speaking Africa of the Institute which bears his name, to contribute to theological and pastoral reflection on marriage and the family. Lastly, I exhort especially the catechists, those valiant missionaries at the heart of the most humble realities, to offer them always, with an unshakable hope and determination, an outstanding and absolutely necessary contribution to the spread of the faith through fidelity to the teaching of the Church (cf. *Ad Gentes*, no. 17).

APOSTOLIC JOURNEY TO BENIN

Address at the Basilica of the Immaculate Conception in Ouidah, Benin, for the Signing of the Post-Synodal Apostolic Exhortation

November 19, 2011

The Second Special Assembly for Africa of the Synod of Bishops benefited from the Post-Synodal Apostolic Exhortation *Ecclesia in Africa* of Blessed John Paul II, which emphasized the urgent need to evangelize this continent, an activity which cannot be separated from the work of human promotion. The Exhortation also developed the concept of *the Church as God's Family*. This concept has borne many spiritual fruits for the Catholic Church and for the activity of evangelization and human promotion which she has carried out in African society as a whole. The Church is called to see herself increasingly as a family.

APOSTOLIC JOURNEY TO BENIN

Angelus

November 20, 2011

Dear Brothers and Sisters,

At the conclusion of this solemn Eucharistic celebration, having been made one in Christ, let us turn with confidence to his Mother and pray the *Angelus*. Now that I have consigned the Apostolic Exhortation *Africae Munus*, I wish to entrust to the Virgin Mary, Our Lady of Africa, the new chapter now opening for the Church on this continent, asking her to accompany the future evangelization of Africa as a whole and, in particular, of this land of Benin.

Mary joyfully accepted the Lord's invitation to become the Mother of Jesus. May she show us how to respond to the mission which God entrusts to us today! Mary is that earthly woman who received the privilege of becoming the Mother of the Savior of the world. Who better than she knows the value and beauty of human life? May we never cease to be amazed before the gift of life! Who better than she knows our needs as men and women who are still pilgrims on this earth? At foot of the Cross, united to her crucified Son, she is the Mother of Hope. This hope enables us to take up our daily lives with the power bestowed by the truth which is made known in Jesus.

Dear Brothers and Sisters of Africa, this land which sheltered the Holy Family, may you continue to cultivate Christian family values. At a time when so many families are separated, in exile, grief-stricken as a result of unending conflicts, may you be artisans of reconciliation and hope. With Mary, Our Lady of the Magnificat, may you always abide in joy. May this joy remain deep within hearts of your families and your countries!

In the words of the *Angelus*, let us now turn to our beloved Mother. Before her let us place the intentions of our hearts. Let us now pray to her for Africa and for the whole world.

Message for the World Day of Peace

[January 1, 2012]

Educating Young People in Justice and Peace

December 8, 2011

The concerns expressed in recent times by many young people around the world demonstrate that they desire to look to the future with solid hope. At the present time, they are experiencing apprehension about many things: they want to receive an education which prepares them more fully to deal with the real world, they see how difficult it is to form a family and to find stable employment; they wonder if they can really contribute to political, cultural and economic life in order to build a society with a more human and fraternal face.

It is important that this unease and its underlying idealism receive due attention at every level of society. The Church looks to young people with hope and confidence; she encourages them to seek truth, to defend the common good, to be open to the world around them and willing to see "new things" (Is 42:9; 48:6). . . .

Educators

2. Education is the most interesting and difficult adventure in life. Educating—from the Latin *educere*—means leading young people to move beyond themselves and introducing them to reality, toward a fullness that leads to growth. This process is fostered by the encounter of two freedoms, that of adults and that of the young. It calls for responsibility on the part of the learners, who must be open to being led to the knowledge of reality, and on the part of educators, who must be ready to give of themselves. For this reason, today more than ever we need authentic witnesses, and not simply people who parcel out rules and facts; we need witnesses capable of seeing farther than others because their life is so much broader. A witness is someone who first lives the life that he proposes to others.

Where does true education in peace and justice take place? First of all, in the family, since parents are the first educators. The family is the primary cell of society; "it is in the family that children learn the human and Christian values which enable them to have a constructive and peaceful coexistence. It is in the family that they learn solidarity between the generations, respect for rules, forgiveness and how to welcome others" (Benedict XVI, *Address to Administrators of Lazio Region and of the Municipality and Province of Rome* [January 14, 2011]). The family is the first school in which we are trained in justice and peace.

We are living in a world where families, and life itself, are constantly threatened and not infrequently fragmented. Working conditions which are often incompatible with family responsibilities, worries about the future, the frenetic pace of life, the need to move frequently to ensure an adequate livelihood, to say nothing of mere survival—all this makes it hard to ensure that children receive one of the most precious of treasures: the presence of their parents. This presence makes it possible to share more deeply in the journey of life and thus to pass on experiences and convictions gained with the passing of the years, experiences and convictions which can only be communicated by spending time together. I would urge parents not to grow disheartened! May they encourage children by the example of their lives to put their hope before all else in God, the one source of authentic justice and peace.

I would also like to address a word to those in charge of educational institutions: with a great sense of responsibility may they ensure that the dignity of each person is always respected and appreciated. Let them be concerned that every young person be able to discover his or her own vocation and helped to develop his or her God-given gifts. May they reassure families that their children can receive an education that does not conflict with their consciences and their religious principles.

Every educational setting can be a place of openness to the transcendent and to others; a place of dialogue, cohesiveness and attentive listening, where young people feel appreciated for their personal abilities and inner riches, and can learn to esteem their brothers and sisters. May young people be taught to savor the joy which comes from the daily exercise of charity and compassion toward others and from taking an active part in the building of a more humane and fraternal society.

I ask political leaders to offer concrete assistance to families and educational institutions in the exercise of their right and duty to educate. Adequate support should never be lacking to parents in their task. Let them ensure that no one is ever denied access to education and that families are able freely to choose the educational structures they consider most suitable for their children. Let them be committed to reuniting families separated by the need to earn a living. Let them give young people a transparent image of politics as a genuine service to the good of all.

Address to Members of the Confederation of Italian Cooperatives and of the Italian Federation of Cooperative Credit Banks

December 10, 2011

The importance of Catholic cooperation in Italy is well known. It came into being following Pope Leo XIII's Encyclical *Rerum Novarum*, the 120th anniversary of whose promulgation we are celebrating this year. It encouraged the fertile presence of Catholics in Italian society through the promotion of cooperatives and mortgage loan companies, the development of social businesses and many other institutions of public interest. This activity has always aimed to provide material support for the population and to pay constant attention to families, drawing inspiration from the Magisterium of the Church. . . .

I would like very briefly to recall certain elements for which your action is invaluable. First of all, you are called to make a contribution with your specific professionalism and tenacious commitment, so that the economy and the market are never devoid of solidarity. In addition, you are called to promote the culture of life and of the family and to encourage the formation of new families that can count on dignified work respectful of the creation that God has entrusted to our responsible care.

May you be able always to appreciate human beings in their wholeness, over and above any difference of race, language or religious affiliation, paying attention to their real needs and also to their initiative capacity. It is particularly important moreover to remember what characterizes Catholic cooperatives: the Christian inspiration that must constantly direct them. Stay faithful to the Gospel, therefore, and to the Church's teaching. Keep in mind and encourage the various initiatives of experimentation that draw on the content of the social Magisterium of the Church, as in the case of social consortiums for development, micro-credit experiences and an economy animated by the logic of communion and brotherhood.

Homily at Mass for the Solemnity of Our Lady of Guadalupe

December 12, 2011

At this time, as various parts of Latin America are commemorating the bicentenary of their Independence, the process of integration in this beloved continent is progressing, while at the same time it is playing a new role on the world scene. In these circumstances it is important that its diverse people can safeguard the rich treasure of faith and their historical-cultural dynamism, always being the defenders of human life from conception to natural end and promoters of peace; they must likewise care for the family in this genuine nature and mission, at the same time intensifying a vast grass-roots educational campaign that correctly prepares individuals and makes them aware of their capacities in such a way that they can face their destiny with responsibility and dignity. They are likewise called to foster ever more proven initiatives and effective programs that promote reconciliation and fraternity, increase solidarity and care for the environment, at the same time intensifying efforts to overcome poverty, illiteracy and corruption, and to eradicate every form of injustice, violence, criminality, civic unrest, drug trafficking and extortion.

Message for the "Mass for Families"*

December 27, 2011

To My Venerable Brother,
Antonio María Cardinal Rouco Varela,
Archbishop of Madrid,

I am pleased to give a warm welcome to Your Eminence, as well as to those participating in the solemn Eucharist being celebrated in the center of Madrid

---

* This text is an unofficial translation of the Spanish in the Italian compendium.

with the purpose both of thanking God for this great mystery that enlightens every Christian home and of manifesting hope and joy to all humanity. I invite everyone to consider this Eucharistic celebration as a continuation of Christmas. Jesus became man to bring God's goodness and love to the world, and he did so right where the human being is most disposed to wanting the best for others, to doing one's best for others, and to placing love above any other interest and ambition.

And so he came to a family pure of heart who did not put on airs but were rather filled with the kind of affection that is worth more than anything else. According to the Gospel, the shepherds, the first people from our world who went to see Jesus, "found Mary and Joseph, and the child lying in the manger" (Lk 2:16). That family is, so to speak, the gateway on Earth for the Savior of Humankind, who, at the same time, gives the life of love and family communion the greatness of being a privileged reflection of the Trinitarian mystery of God.

This greatness is at the same time a splendid vocation and a decisive commitment for the family, which my venerable predecessor, Blessed John Paul II, described thirty years ago as sharing both "actively and responsibly in the mission of the Church in a way that is original and specific, by placing itself, what it is and what it does as an 'intimate community of life and love,' at the service of the Church and of society" (Familiaris Consortio, no. 50).

I urge you, then, and especially you families participating in this celebration, to be conscious of having God at your side. Always call upon him to receive from him the help you need to overcome your difficulties: a sure help, founded on the grace of the sacrament of matrimony.

Let yourselves be guided by the Church, to whom Christ has entrusted the mission of spreading the good news of salvation throughout the ages, without giving in to the many worldly forces that threaten the great treasure of the family, which you should guard every day.

The Child Jesus, who grew in stature and strength, full of wisdom, in the intimacy of the household of Nazareth (cf. Lk 2:40), also learned there in some way how to live as a human being.

This leads us to consider the family's necessary educative dimension; here one learns to live with others, the faith is passed on, values are strengthened and freedom is channeled in order that one day the children may have full awareness of their own vocation and dignity, as well as of that of others. The warmth and exemplary behavior of the home, is capable of teaching many more things than can be said in words.

This educative dimension of the family can be especially encouraged during the Year of the Faith, which will begin in a few months. For this reason, I invite you to revitalize the faith in your homes and to be more conscious of the Creed we profess.

When I think back with unforgettable emotion on the joy of the young people gathered in Madrid for the World Youth Day, I ask God, through the intercession of Jesus, Mary and Joseph, that they will unceasingly give thanks for the gift of the family, that they will be grateful to their parents, and that they will commit themselves to defend and to make radiant the authentic dignity of this institution, which is fundamental for society and so vital for the Church. With these sentiments, I cordially impart to you the Apostolic Blessing.

General Audience

December 28, 2011

The Prayer and the Holy Family of Nazareth

Dear Brothers and Sisters,

Today's meeting is taking place in the atmosphere of Christmas, imbued with deep joy at the Birth of the Savior. We have just celebrated this Mystery whose echo ripples through the Liturgy of all these days. It is a Mystery of Light that all people in every era can relive with faith and prayer. It is through prayer itself that we become capable of drawing close to God with intimacy and depth.

Therefore, bearing in mind the theme of prayer that I am developing in the Catecheses in this period, I would therefore like to invite you to reflect today on the way that prayer was part of the life of the Holy Family of Nazareth. Indeed, the house of Nazareth is a school of prayer where one learns to listen, meditate on and penetrate the profound meaning of the manifestation of the Son of God, following the example of Mary, Joseph and Jesus.

The Discourse of the Servant of God Paul VI during his Visit to Nazareth is memorable. The Pope said that at the school of the Holy Family we "understand why we must maintain a spiritual discipline, if we wish to follow the teaching of the Gospel and become disciples of Christ." He added: "In the first place it teaches us silence. Oh! If only esteem for silence, a wonderful and indispensable spiritual atmosphere, could be reborn within us! Whereas we are deafened by the din, the noise and discordant voices in the frenetic, turbulent life of our time. O silence of Nazareth! Teach us to be steadfast in good thoughts, attentive to our inner life, ready to hear God's hidden inspiration clearly and the exhortations of true teachers" (*Discourse in Nazareth*, January 5, 1964).

We can draw various ideas for prayer and for the relationship with God and with the Holy Family from the Gospel narratives of the infancy of Jesus. We can begin with the episode of the Presentation of Jesus in the Temple. St. Luke tells how "when the time came for their purification according to the law of Moses," Mary and Joseph "brought him up to Jerusalem to present him to the Lord" (2:22). Like every Jewish family that observed the law, Jesus' parents went to the Temple to consecrate their first-born son to God and to make the sacrificial offering. Motivated by their fidelity to the precepts of the Law, they set out from Bethlehem and went to Jerusalem with Jesus who was only forty days old. Instead of a year-old lamb they presented the offering of simple families, namely, two turtle doves. The Holy Family's pilgrimage was one of faith, of the offering of gifts—a symbol of prayer—and of the encounter with the Lord whom Mary and Joseph already perceived in their Son Jesus.

Mary was a peerless model of contemplation of Christ. The face of the Son belonged to her in a special way because he had been knit together in her womb and had taken a human likeness from her. No one has contemplated Jesus as diligently as Mary. The gaze of her heart was already focused on him at the moment of the Annunciation, when she conceived him through the action of the Holy Spirit; in the following months she gradually became aware of his presence, until, on the day of his birth, her eyes could look with motherly tenderness upon the face of her son as she wrapped him in swaddling clothes and laid him in the manger.

Memories of Jesus, imprinted on her mind and on her heart, marked every instant of Mary's existence. She lived with her eyes fixed on Christ and cherished his every word. St. Luke says: "Mary kept all these things, pondering them in her heart" (2:19) and thus describes Mary's approach to the Mystery of the Incarnation which was to extend throughout her life: keeping these things, pondering on them in her heart. Luke is the Evangelist who acquaints us with Mary's heart, with her faith (cf. 1:45), her hope and her obedience (cf. 1:38) and, especially, with her interiority and prayer (cf. 1:46-56), her free adherence to Christ (cf. 1:55).

And all this proceeded from the gift of the Holy Spirit who overshadowed her (cf. 1:35), as he was to come down on the Apostles in accordance with Christ's promise (cf. Acts 1:8). This image of Mary which St. Luke gives us presents Our Lady as a model for every believer who cherishes and compares Jesus' words with his actions, a comparison which is always progress in the knowledge of Jesus. After Bl. Pope John Paul II's example (cf. Apostolic Letter *Rosarium Virginis Mariae*) we can say that the prayer of the Rosary is modeled precisely on Mary, because it consists in contemplating the mysteries of Christ in spiritual union with the Mother of the Lord.

Mary's ability to live by God's gaze, is so to speak, contagious. The first to experience this was St. Joseph. His humble and sincere love for his betrothed and his decision to join his life to Mary's attracted and introduced him, "a just man," (Mt 1:19), to a special intimacy with God. Indeed, with Mary and later, especially, with Jesus, he began a new way of relating to God, accepting him in his life, entering his project of salvation and doing his will. After trustfully complying with the Angel's instructions "Do not fear to take Mary your wife" (Mt 1:20)—he took Mary to him and shared his life with her; he truly gave the whole of himself to Mary and to Jesus and this led him to perfect his response to the vocation he had received.

As we know, the Gospel has not recorded any of Joseph's words: his is a silent and faithful, patient and hard-working presence. We may imagine that he too, like his wife and in close harmony with her, lived the years of Jesus' childhood and adolescence savoring, as it were, his presence in their family.

Joseph fulfilled every aspect of his paternal role. He must certainly have taught Jesus to pray, together with Mary. In particular Joseph himself must have taken Jesus to the Synagogue for the rites of the Sabbath, as well as to Jerusalem for the great feasts of the people of Israel. Joseph, in accordance with the Jewish tradition, would have led the prayers at home both every day—in the morning, in the evening, at meals—and on the principal religious feasts. In the rhythm of the days he spent at Nazareth, in the simple home and in Joseph's workshop, Jesus learned to alternate prayer and work, as well as to offer God his labor in earning the bread the family needed.

And lastly, there is another episode that sees the Holy Family of Nazareth gathered together in an event of prayer. When Jesus was twelve years old, as we have heard, he went with his parents to the Temple of Jerusalem. This episode fits into the context of pilgrimage, as St. Luke stresses: "His parents went to Jerusalem every year at the feast of the Passover. And when he was twelve years old, they went up according to custom" (2:41-42).

Pilgrimage is an expression of religious devotion that is nourished by and at the same time nourishes prayer. Here, it is the Passover pilgrimage, and the Evangelist points out to us that the family of Jesus made this pilgrimage every year in order to take part in the rites in the Holy City. Jewish families, like Christian families, pray in the intimacy of the home but they also pray together with the community, recognizing that they belong to the People of God, journeying on; and the pilgrimage expresses exactly this state of the People of God on the move. Easter is the center and culmination of all this and involves both the family dimension and that of liturgical and public worship.

In the episode of the twelve-year-old Jesus, the first words of Jesus are also recorded: "How is it that you sought me? Did you not know that I must be in my Father's house?" (2:49). After three days spent looking for him his parents found him in the temple, sitting among the teachers, listening to them and asking them questions (cf. 2:46). His answer to the question of why he had done this to his father and mother was that he had only done what the Son should do, that is, to be with his Father.

Thus he showed who is the true Father, what is the true home, and that he had done nothing unusual or disobedient. He had stayed where the Son ought to be, that is, with the Father, and he stressed who his Father was.

The term "Father" therefore dominates the tone of this answer and the Christological mystery appears in its entirety. Hence, this word unlocks the mystery, it is the key to the Mystery of Christ, who is the Son, and also the key to our mystery as Christians who are sons and daughters in the Son. At the same time Jesus teaches us to be children by being with the Father in prayer. The Christological mystery, the mystery of Christian existence, is closely linked to, founded on, prayer. Jesus was one day to teach his disciples to pray, telling them: when you pray say "Father." And, naturally, do not just say the word say it with your life, learn to say it meaningfully with your life. "Father"; and in this way you will be true sons in the Son, true Christians.

It is important at this point, when Jesus was still fully integrated in the life of the Family of Nazareth, to note the resonance that hearing this word "Father" on Jesus' lips must have had in the hearts of Mary and Joseph. It is also important to reveal, to emphasize, who the Father is, and, with his awareness, to hear this word on the lips of the Only-Begotten Son who, for this very reason, chose to stay on for three days in the Temple, which is the "Father's house."

We may imagine that from this time the life of the Holy Family must have been even fuller of prayer since from the heart of Jesus the boy—then an adolescent and a young man—this deep meaning of the relationship with God the Father would not cease to spread and to be echoed in the hearts of Mary and Joseph.

This episode shows us the real situation, the atmosphere of being with the Father. So it was that the Family of Nazareth became the first model of the Church in which, around the presence of Jesus and through his mediation, everyone experiences the filial relationship with God the Father which also transforms interpersonal, human relationships.

Dear friends, because of these different aspects that I have outlined briefly in the light of the Gospel, the Holy Family is the icon of the domestic Church, called to pray together. The family is the domestic Church and must be the first school of prayer. It is in the family that children, from the tenderest age, can learn to perceive the meaning of God, also thanks to the teaching and example of their parents: to live in an atmosphere marked by God's presence. An authentically Christian education cannot dispense with the experience of prayer. If one does not learn how to pray in the family it will later be difficult to bridge this gap. And so I would like to address to you the invitation to pray together as a family at the school of the Holy Family of Nazareth and thereby really to become of one heart and soul, a true family. Many thanks.

Greetings:*

Finally, I send an affectionate thought to the young people, to those who are ill and to newlyweds. The feast of the Holy Family that we will celebrate shortly is an auspicious occasion for thinking about our relationships and our affections. Dear young people, look to the Holy Family and imitate them, allowing yourselves to be formed by the love of God which is the model for human love. Dear infirm people, with the help of Mary always trust in the Lord who knows your sufferings and, joining them to His own, offers them for the salvation of the world. And you, dear newlyweds who desire to build your dwelling on the solid rock of God's Word, make your home a welcoming place, full of love, of understanding and of forgiveness in imitation of that house in Nazareth.

Best wishes to everyone!

Homily at *Te Deum* and First Vespers of the Solemnity of Mary, Mother of God

December 31, 2011

Within this framework, at the Diocesan Conference held last June, the Diocese of Rome launched a program which sets out to explore more deeply the meaning of Christian initiation and the joy of bringing new Christians into the faith. To proclaim faith in the Word made flesh is, after all, at the heart of the Church's mission, and the entire ecclesial community needs to rediscover this indispensable task with renewed missionary zeal. Young generations have an especially keen sense of the present disorientation, magnified by the crisis in economic affairs which is also a crisis of values, and so they in particular need to recognize in Jesus Christ "the key, the center and the purpose of the whole of human history" (*Gaudium et Spes*, no. 10).

Parents are the first educators in faith of their children, starting from a most tender age, and families must therefore be supported in their educational mission by appropriate initiatives. At the same time it is desirable that the baptismal journey, the first stage along the formative path of Christian initiation, in addition to fostering conscious and worthy preparation for the

---

*   This text is an unofficial translation of the Italian.

celebration of the Sacrament, should devote adequate attention to the years following Baptism, with appropriate programs that take account of the life conditions that families must address. I therefore encourage parish communities and other ecclesial groupings to engage in continuing reflection on ways to promote a better understanding and reception of the sacraments, by which man comes to share in the very life of God. May the Church of Rome have no shortage of lay faithful who are ready to make their own contribution to building living communities that allow the Word of God to burst forth in the hearts of those who have not yet known the Lord or have moved away from him. At the same time, it is appropriate to create opportunities to encounter the City, giving rise to fruitful dialogue with those who are searching for Truth.

Dear friends, ever since God sent his only-begotten Son, so that we might obtain adoptive sonship (cf. Gal 4:5), we can have no greater task than to be totally at the service of God's plan. And so I would like to encourage and thank all the faithful from the Diocese of Rome who feel a responsibility to restore our society's soul. Thank you, Roman families, the first and fundamental cells of society! Thank you, members of the many Communities, Associations and Movements that are committed to animating the Christian life of our City.

PART III

Documents and Teachings of
the Roman Curia

CHAPTER I

Congregation for the Doctrine of the Faith

Considerations Regarding Proposals to Give Legal Recognition to Unions Between Homosexual Persons

Introduction

1. In recent years, various questions relating to homosexuality have been addressed with some frequency by Pope John Paul II and by the relevant Dicasteries of the Holy See.[1] Homosexuality is a troubling moral and social phenomenon, even in those countries where it does not present significant legal issues. It gives rise to greater concern in those countries that have granted or intend to grant—legal recognition to homosexual unions, which may include the possibility of adopting children. The present Considerations do not contain new doctrinal elements; they seek rather to reiterate the essential points on this question and provide arguments drawn from reason which could be used by Bishops in preparing more specific interventions, appropriate to the different situations throughout the world, aimed at protecting and promoting the dignity of marriage, the foundation of the family, and the stability of society, of which this institution is a constitutive element. The present Considerations are also intended to give direction to Catholic politicians by indicating the approaches to proposed legislation in this area which would be consistent with Christian conscience.[2] Since this question relates to the natural moral law, the arguments that follow are addressed not only to those who believe in Christ, but to all persons committed to promoting and defending the common good of society.

I. The Nature of Marriage and Its Inalienable Characteristics

2. The Church's teaching on marriage and on the complementarity of the sexes reiterates a truth that is evident to right reason and recognized as such by all the major cultures of the world. Marriage is not just any relationship between human beings. It was established by the Creator with its own nature, essential properties and purpose.[3] No ideology can erase from the human spirit the certainty that marriage exists solely between a man and a woman, who by mutual personal gift, proper and exclusive to themselves, tend toward the communion of their persons. In this way, they mutually perfect each other, in order to cooperate with God in the procreation and upbringing of new human lives.

3. The natural truth about marriage was confirmed by the Revelation contained in the biblical accounts of creation, an expression also of the original human wisdom, in which the voice of nature itself is heard. There are three fundamental elements of the Creator's plan for marriage, as narrated in the Book of Genesis.

In the first place, man, the image of God, was created "male and female" (Gn 1:27). Men and women are equal as persons and complementary as male and female. Sexuality is something that pertains to the physical-biological realm and has also been raised to a new level—the personal level—where nature and spirit are united.

Marriage is instituted by the Creator as a form of life in which a communion of persons is realized involving the use of the sexual faculty. "That is why a man leaves his father and mother and clings to his wife and they become one flesh" (Gn 2:24).

Third, God has willed to give the union of man and woman a special participation in his work of creation. Thus, he blessed the man and the woman with the words "Be fruitful and multiply" (Gn 1:28). Therefore, in the Creator's plan, sexual complementarity and fruitfulness belong to the very nature of marriage.

Furthermore, the marital union of man and woman has been elevated by Christ to the dignity of a sacrament. The Church teaches that Christian marriage is an efficacious sign of the covenant between Christ and the Church (cf. Eph 5:32). This Christian meaning of marriage, far from diminishing the profoundly human value of the marital union between man and woman, confirms and strengthens it (cf. Mt 19:3-12; Mk 10:6-9).

4. There are absolutely no grounds for considering homosexual unions to be in any way similar or even remotely analogous to God's plan for marriage and family. Marriage is holy, while homosexual acts go against the natural moral law. Homosexual acts "close the sexual act to the gift of life. They do

not proceed from a genuine affective and sexual complementarity. Under no circumstances can they be approved."[4]

Sacred Scripture condemns homosexual acts "as a serious depravity" (cf. Rom 1:24-27; 1 Cor 6:10; 1 Tm 1:10). "This judgment of Scripture does not of course permit us to conclude that all those who suffer from this anomaly are personally responsible for it, but it does attest to the fact that homosexual acts are intrinsically disordered."[5] This same moral judgment is found in many Christian writers of the first centuries[6] and is unanimously accepted by Catholic Tradition.

Nonetheless, according to the teaching of the Church, men and women with homosexual tendencies "must be accepted with respect, compassion and sensitivity. Every sign of unjust discrimination in their regard should be avoided."[7] They are called, like other Christians, to live the virtue of chastity.[8] The homosexual inclination is however "objectively disordered"[9] and homosexual practices are "sins gravely contrary to chastity."[10]

II. Positions on the Problem of Homosexual Unions

5. Faced with the fact of homosexual unions, civil authorities adopt different positions. At times they simply tolerate the phenomenon; at other times they advocate legal recognition of such unions, under the pretext of avoiding, with regard to certain rights, discrimination against persons who live with someone of the same sex. In other cases, they favor giving homosexual unions legal equivalence to marriage properly so-called, along with the legal possibility of adopting children.

Where the government's policy is *de facto* tolerance and there is no explicit legal recognition of homosexual unions, it is necessary to distinguish carefully the various aspects of the problem. Moral conscience requires that, in every occasion, Christians give witness to the whole moral truth, which is contradicted both by approval of homosexual acts and unjust discrimination against homosexual persons. Therefore, discreet and prudent actions can be effective; these might involve: unmasking the way in which such tolerance might be exploited or used in the service of ideology; stating clearly the immoral nature of these unions; reminding the government of the need to contain the phenomenon within certain limits so as to safeguard public morality and, above all, to avoid exposing young people to erroneous ideas about sexuality and marriage that would deprive them of their necessary defenses and contribute to the spread of the phenomenon. Those who would move from tolerance to the legitimization of specific rights for cohabiting homosexual persons need to be reminded that the approval or legalization of evil is something far different from the toleration of evil.

In those situations where homosexual unions have been legally recognized or have been given the legal status and rights belonging to marriage, clear and emphatic opposition is a duty. One must refrain from any kind of formal cooperation in the enactment or application of such gravely unjust laws and, as far as possible, from material cooperation on the level of their application. In this area, everyone can exercise the right to conscientious objection.

III. Arguments from Reason Against Legal Recognition of Homosexual Unions

6. To understand why it is necessary to oppose legal recognition of homosexual unions, ethical considerations of different orders need to be taken into consideration.

From the order of right reason

The scope of the civil law is certainly more limited than that of the moral law,[11] but civil law cannot contradict right reason without losing its binding force on conscience.[12] Every humanly-created law is legitimate insofar as it is consistent with the natural moral law, recognized by right reason, and insofar as it respects the inalienable rights of every person.[13] Laws in favor of homosexual unions are contrary to right reason because they confer legal guarantees, analogous to those granted to marriage, to unions between persons of the same sex. Given the values at stake in this question, the State could not grant legal standing to such unions without failing in its duty to promote and defend marriage as an institution essential to the common good.

It might be asked how a law can be contrary to the common good if it does not impose any particular kind of behavior, but simply gives legal recognition to a *de facto* reality which does not seem to cause injustice to anyone. In this area, one needs first to reflect on the difference between homosexual behavior as a private phenomenon and the same behavior as a relationship in society, foreseen and approved by the law, to the point where it becomes one of the institutions in the legal structure. This second phenomenon is not only more serious, but also assumes a more wide-reaching and profound influence, and would result in changes to the entire organization of society, contrary to the common good. Civil laws are structuring principles of man's life in society, for good or for ill. They "play a very important and sometimes decisive role in influencing patterns of thought and behavior."[14] Lifestyles and the underlying presuppositions these express not only externally shape the life of society, but also tend to modify the younger generation's perception and evaluation of forms of behavior. Legal recognition of homosexual unions

would obscure certain basic moral values and cause a devaluation of the institution of marriage.

From the biological and anthropological order

7. Homosexual unions are totally lacking in the biological and anthropological elements of marriage and family which would be the basis, on the level
of reason, for granting them legal recognition. Such unions are not able to
contribute in a proper way to the procreation and survival of the human
race. The possibility of using recently discovered methods of artificial reproduction, beyond involving a grave lack of respect for human dignity,[15] does
nothing to alter this inadequacy.

Homosexual unions are also totally lacking in the conjugal dimension,
which represents the human and ordered form of sexuality. Sexual relations
are human when and insofar as they express and promote the mutual assistance of the sexes in marriage and are open to the transmission of new life.

As experience has shown, the absence of sexual complementarity in these
unions creates obstacles in the normal development of children who would
be placed in the care of such persons. They would be deprived of the experience of either fatherhood or motherhood. Allowing children to be adopted
by persons living in such unions would actually mean doing violence to these
children, in the sense that their condition of dependency would be used to
place them in an environment that is not conducive to their full human
development. This is gravely immoral and in open contradiction to the principle, recognized also in the United Nations Convention on the Rights of the
Child, that the best interests of the child, as the weaker and more vulnerable
party, are to be the paramount consideration in every case.

From the social order

8. Society owes its continued survival to the family, founded on marriage.
The inevitable consequence of legal recognition of homosexual unions would
be the redefinition of marriage, which would become, in its legal status, an
institution devoid of essential reference to factors linked to heterosexuality;
for example, procreation and raising children. If, from the legal standpoint,
marriage between a man and a woman were to be considered just one possible
form of marriage, the concept of marriage would undergo a radical transformation, with grave detriment to the common good. By putting homosexual
unions on a legal plane analogous to that of marriage and the family, the
State acts arbitrarily and in contradiction with its duties.

The principles of respect and non-discrimination cannot be invoked to
support legal recognition of homosexual unions. Differentiating between persons or refusing social recognition or benefits is unacceptable only when it is

contrary to justice.[16] The denial of the social and legal status of marriage to forms of cohabitation that are not and cannot be marital is not opposed to justice; on the contrary, justice requires it.

Nor can the principle of the proper autonomy of the individual be reasonably invoked. It is one thing to maintain that individual citizens may freely engage in those activities that interest them and that this falls within the common civil right to freedom; it is something quite different to hold that activities which do not represent a significant or positive contribution to the development of the human person in society can receive specific and categorical legal recognition by the State. Not even in a remote analogous sense do homosexual unions fulfill the purpose for which marriage and family deserve specific categorical recognition. On the contrary, there are good reasons for holding that such unions are harmful to the proper development of human society, especially if their impact on society were to increase.

From the legal order

9. Because married couples ensure the succession of generations and are therefore eminently within the public interest, civil law grants them institutional recognition. Homosexual unions, on the other hand, do not need specific attention from the legal standpoint since they do not exercise this function for the common good.

Nor is the argument valid according to which legal recognition of homosexual unions is necessary to avoid situations in which cohabiting homosexual persons, simply because they live together, might be deprived of real recognition of their rights as persons and citizens. In reality, they can always make use of the provisions of law—like all citizens from the standpoint of their private autonomy—to protect their rights in matters of common interest. It would be gravely unjust to sacrifice the common good and just laws on the family in order to protect personal goods that can and must be guaranteed in ways that do not harm the body of society.[17]

IV. Positions of Catholic Politicians with Regard to Legislation in Favor of Homosexual Unions

10. If it is true that all Catholics are obliged to oppose the legal recognition of homosexual unions, Catholic politicians are obliged to do so in a particular way, in keeping with their responsibility as politicians. Faced with legislative proposals in favor of homosexual unions, Catholic politicians are to take account of the following ethical indications.

When legislation in favor of the recognition of homosexual unions is proposed for the first time in a legislative assembly, the Catholic law-maker has a moral duty to express his opposition clearly and publicly and to vote against it. To vote in favor of a law so harmful to the common good is gravely immoral.

When legislation in favor of the recognition of homosexual unions is already in force, the Catholic politician must oppose it in the ways that are possible for him and make his opposition known; it is his duty to witness to the truth. If it is not possible to repeal such a law completely, the Catholic politician, recalling the indications contained in the Encyclical Letter *Evangelium vitae*, "could licitly support proposals aimed at limiting the harm done by such a law and at lessening its negative consequences at the level of general opinion and public morality," on condition that his "absolute personal opposition" to such laws was clear and well known and that the danger of scandal was avoided.[18] This does not mean that a more restrictive law in this area could be considered just or even acceptable; rather, it is a question of the legitimate and dutiful attempt to obtain at least the partial repeal of an unjust law when its total abrogation is not possible at the moment.

Conclusion

11. The Church teaches that respect for homosexual persons cannot lead in any way to approval of homosexual behavior or to legal recognition of homosexual unions. The common good requires that laws recognize, promote and protect marriage as the basis of the family, the primary unit of society. Legal recognition of homosexual unions or placing them on the same level as marriage would mean not only the approval of deviant behavior, with the consequence of making it a model in present-day society, but would also obscure basic values which belong to the common inheritance of humanity. The Church cannot fail to defend these values, for the good of men and women and for the good of society itself.

The Sovereign Pontiff John Paul II, in the Audience of March 28, 2003, approved the present Considerations, adopted in the Ordinary Session of this Congregation, and ordered their publication.

Rome, from the Offices of the Congregation for the Doctrine of the Faith, June 3, 2003, Memorial of St. Charles Lwanga and his Companions, Martyrs.

Joseph Card. Ratzinger
Prefect

Angelo Amato, SDB
Titular Archbishop of Sila
Secretary

Notes

1 Cf. John Paul II, *Angelus Messages* of February 20, 1994, and of June 19, 1994; *Address to the Plenary Meeting of the Pontifical Council for the Family* (March 24, 1999); *Catechism of the Catholic Church*, nos. 2357-2359, 2396; Congregation for the Doctrine of the Faith, Declaration *Persona Humana* (December 29, 1975), 8; *Letter on the Pastoral Care of Homosexual Persons* (October 1, 1986); *Some Considerations Concerning the Response to Legislative Proposals on the Non-discrimination of Homosexual Persons* (July 24, 1992); Pontifical Council for the Family, *Letter to the Presidents of the Bishops' Conferences of Europe on the Resolution of the European Parliament Regarding Homosexual Couples* (March 25, 1994); *Family, Marriage and "De Facto" Unions* (July 26, 2000), 23.

2 Cf. Congregation for the Doctrine of the Faith, *Doctrinal Note on Some Questions Regarding the Participation of Catholics in Political Life* (November 24, 2002), 4.

3 Cf. Second Vatican Council, Pastoral Constitution *Gaudium et Spes*, 48.

4 Catechism of the Catholic Church, no. 2357.

5 Congregation for the Doctrine of the Faith, Declaration *Persona Humana* (December 29, 1975), 8.

6 Cf., for example, St. Polycarp, *Letter to the Philippians*, V, 3; St. Justin Martyr, *First Apology*, 27, 1-4; Athenagoras, *Supplication for the Christians*, 34.

7 *Catechism of the Catholic Church*, no. 2358; cf. Congregation for the Doctrine of the Faith, *Letter on the Pastoral Care of Homosexual Persons* (October 1, 1986), 10.

8 Cf. *Catechism of the Catholic Church*, no. 2359; cf. Congregation for the Doctrine of the Faith, *Letter on the Pastoral Care of Homosexual Persons* (October 1, 1986), 12.

9 Catechism of the Catholic Church, no. 2358.

10 Ibid., no. 2396.

11 Cf. John Paul II, Encyclical Letter *Evangelium Vitae* (March 25, 1995), 71.

12 Cf. ibid., 72.

13 Cf. St. Thomas Aquinas, *Summa Theologiae*, I-II, q. 95, a. 2.

14 John Paul II, Encyclical Letter *Evangelium Vitae* (March 25, 1995), 90.

15 Cf. Congregation for the Doctrine of the Faith, Instruction *Donum Vitae* (February 22, 1987), II. A. 1-3.

16 Cf. St. Thomas Aquinas, *Summa Theologiae*, II-II, q. 63, a.1, c.

17 It should not be forgotten that there is always "a danger that legislation which would make homosexuality a basis for entitlements could actually encourage a person with a homosexual orientation to declare his homosexuality or even to seek a partner in order to exploit the provisions of the law" (Congregation for the Doctrine of the Faith, *Some Considerations Concerning the Response to Legislative Proposals on the Non-discrimination of Homosexual Persons* [July 24, 1992], 14).

18 John Paul II, Encyclical Letter *Evangelium Vitae* (March 25, 1995), 73.

Letter to the Bishops of the Catholic Church on the Collaboration of Men and Women in the Church and in the World

Introduction

1. The Church, expert in humanity, has a perennial interest in whatever concerns men and women. In recent times, much reflection has been given to the question of the dignity of women and to women's rights and duties in the different areas of civil society and the Church. Having contributed to a deeper understanding of this fundamental question, in particular through the teaching of John Paul II,[1] the Church is called today to address certain currents of thought which are often at variance with the authentic advancement of women.

After a brief presentation and critical evaluation of some current conceptions of human nature, this document will offer reflections—inspired by the doctrinal elements of the biblical vision of the human person that are indispensable for safeguarding his or her identity—on some of the essentials of a correct understanding of active collaboration, in recognition of the difference between men and women in the Church and in the world. These reflections are meant as a starting point for further examination in the Church, as well as an impetus for dialogue with all men and women of good will, in a sincere search for the truth and in a common commitment to the development of ever more authentic relationships.

I. The Question

2. Recent years have seen new approaches to women's issues. A first tendency is to emphasize strongly conditions of subordination in order to give rise to antagonism: women, in order to be themselves, must make themselves the adversaries of men. Faced with the abuse of power, the answer for women is to seek power. This process leads to opposition between men and women, in which the identity and role of one are emphasized to the disadvantage of the other, leading to harmful confusion regarding the human person, which has its most immediate and lethal effects in the structure of the family.

A second tendency emerges in the wake of the first. In order to avoid the domination of one sex or the other, their differences tend to be denied, viewed as mere effects of historical and cultural conditioning. In this perspective, physical difference, termed *sex*, is minimized, while the purely cultural element, termed *gender*, is emphasized to the maximum and held to be primary. The obscuring of the difference or duality of the sexes has enormous consequences on a variety of levels. This theory of the human person, intended to promote prospects for equality of women through liberation from biological determinism, has in reality inspired ideologies which, for example, call into question the family, in its natural two-parent structure of mother and father, and make homosexuality and heterosexuality virtually equivalent, in a new model of polymorphous sexuality.

3. While the immediate roots of this second tendency are found in the context of reflection on women's roles, its deeper motivation must be sought in the human attempt to be freed from one's biological conditioning.[2] According to this perspective, human nature in itself does not possess characteristics in an absolute manner: all persons can and ought to constitute themselves as they like, since they are free from every predetermination linked to their essential constitution.

This perspective has many consequences. Above all it strengthens the idea that the liberation of women entails criticism of Sacred Scripture, which would be seen as handing on a patriarchal conception of God nourished by an essentially male-dominated culture. Second, this tendency would consider as lacking in importance and relevance the fact that the Son of God assumed human nature in its male form.

4. In the face of these currents of thought, the Church, enlightened by faith in Jesus Christ, speaks instead of *active collaboration* between the sexes precisely in the recognition of the difference between man and woman.

To understand better the basis, meaning and consequences of this response it is helpful to turn briefly to the Sacred Scriptures, rich also in human wisdom, in which this response is progressively manifested thanks to God's intervention on behalf of humanity.[3]

II. Basic Elements of the Biblical Vision of the Human Person

5. The first biblical texts to examine are the first three chapters of Genesis. Here we "enter into the setting of the biblical 'beginning.' In it the revealed truth concerning the human person as 'the image and likeness' of God constitutes the immutable *basis of all Christian anthropology*."[4]

The first text (Gn 1:1-2:4) describes the creative power of the Word of God, which makes distinctions in the original chaos. Light and darkness appear, sea and dry land, day and night, grass and trees, fish and birds, "each according to its kind." An ordered world is born out of differences, carrying with them also the promise of relationships. Here we see a sketch of the framework in which the creation of the human race takes place: "God said 'Let us make man in our image, after our likeness'" (Gn 1:26). And then: "God created man in his own image, in the image of God he created him; male and female he created them" (Gn 1:27). From the very beginning therefore, humanity is described as articulated in the male-female relationship. This is the humanity, sexually differentiated, which is explicitly declared "the image of God."

6. The second creation account (Gn 2:4-25) confirms in a definitive way the importance of sexual difference. Formed by God and placed in the garden which he was to cultivate, the man, who is still referred to with the generic expression *Adam*, experienced a loneliness which the presence of the animals is not able to overcome. He needs a *helpmate* who will be his partner. The term here does not refer to an inferior, but to a vital helper.[5] This is so that *Adam's* life does not sink into a sterile and, in the end, baneful encounter with himself. It is necessary that he enter into relationship with another being on his own level. Only the woman, created from the same "flesh" and cloaked in the same mystery, can give a future to the life of the man. It is therefore above all on the ontological level that this takes place, in the sense that God's creation of woman characterizes humanity as a relational reality. In this encounter, the man speaks words for the first time, expressive of his wonderment: "This at last is bone of my bones and flesh of my flesh" (Gn 2:23).

As the Holy Father has written with regard to this text from Genesis, ". . . woman is another 'I' in a common humanity. From the very beginning they appear as a 'unity of the two,' and this signifies that the original solitude is overcome, the solitude in which man does not find 'a helper fit for him' (Gn 2:20). Is it only a question here of a 'helper' in activity, in 'subduing the earth' (cf. Gn 1:28)? Certainly it is a matter of a life's companion with whom, as a wife, the man can unite himself, becoming with her 'one flesh' and for this reason leaving 'his father and his mother' (cf. Gn 2:24)."[6]

This vital difference is oriented toward communion and was lived in peace, expressed by their nakedness: "And the man and his wife were both naked, yet they felt no shame" (Gn 2:25). In this way, the human body, marked with the sign of masculinity or femininity, "includes right from the beginning the nuptial attribute, that is, *the capacity of expressing love, that love in which the person becomes a gift* and—by means of this gift—fulfills the meaning of his being and his existence."[7] Continuing his commentary on these verses of Genesis, the Holy Father writes: "In this peculiarity, the body is the expression of the spirit and is called, in the mystery of creation, to exist in the communion of persons in the image of God."[8]

Through this same spousal perspective, the ancient Genesis narrative allows us to understand how woman, in her deepest and original being, exists "for the other" (cf. 1 Cor 11:9): this is a statement which, far from any sense of alienation, expresses a fundamental aspect of the similarity with the Triune God, whose Persons, with the coming of Christ, are revealed as being in a communion of love, each for the others. "In the 'unity of the two,' man and woman are called from the beginning not only to exist 'side by side' or 'together,' but they are also called to exist mutually 'one for the other' . . . The text of Genesis 2:18-25 shows that marriage is the first and, in a sense, the fundamental dimension of this call. But it is not the only one. The whole of human history unfolds within the context of this call. In this history, on the basis of the principle of mutually being 'for' the other in interpersonal 'communion,' there develops in humanity itself, in accordance with God's will, the integration of what is 'masculine' and what is 'feminine.'"[9]

The peaceful vision which concludes the second creation account recalls the "indeed it was very good" (Gn 1:31) at the end of the first account. Here we find the heart of God's original plan and the deepest truth about man and woman, as willed and created by him. Although God's original plan for man and woman will later be upset and darkened by sin, it can never be abrogated.

7. Original sin changes the way in which the man and the woman receive and live the Word of God as well as their relationship with the Creator. Immediately after having given them the gift of the garden, God gives them a positive command (cf. Gn 2:16), followed by a negative one (cf. Gn 2:17), in which the essential difference between God and humanity is implicitly expressed. Following enticement by the serpent, the man and the woman deny this difference. As a consequence, the way in which they live their sexual difference is also upset. In this way, the Genesis account establishes a relationship of cause and effect between the two differences: when humanity considers God its enemy, the relationship between man and woman becomes distorted. When this relationship is damaged, their access to the face of God risks being compromised in turn.

God's decisive words to the woman after the first sin express the kind of relationship which has now been introduced between man and woman: "your desire shall be for your husband, and he shall rule over you" (Gn 3:16). It will be a relationship in which love will frequently be debased into pure self-seeking, in a relationship which ignores and kills love and replaces it with the yoke of domination of one sex over the other. Indeed the story of humanity is continuously marked by this situation, which recalls the three-fold concupiscence mentioned by St. John: the concupiscence of the flesh, the concupiscence of the eyes and the pride of life (cf. 1 Jn 2:16). In this tragic situation, the equality, respect and love that are required in the relationship of man and woman according to God's original plan, are lost.

8. Reviewing these fundamental texts allows us to formulate some of the principal elements of the biblical vision of the human person.

Above all, the fact that human beings are persons needs to be underscored: "*Man is a person, man and woman equally so*, since both were created in the image and likeness of the personal God."[10] Their equal dignity as persons is realized as physical, psychological and ontological complementarity, giving rise to a harmonious relationship of "uni-duality," which only sin and "the structures of sin" inscribed in culture render potentially conflictual. The biblical vision of the human person suggests that problems related to sexual difference, whether on the public or private level, should be addressed by a relational approach and not by competition or retaliation.

Furthermore, the importance and the meaning of sexual difference, as a reality deeply inscribed in man and woman, needs to be noted. "Sexuality characterizes man and woman not only on the physical level, but also on the psychological and spiritual, making its mark on each of their expressions."[11] It cannot be reduced to a pure and insignificant biological fact, but rather "is a fundamental component of personality, one of its modes of being, of manifestation, of communicating with others, of feeling, of expressing and of living human love."[12] This capacity to love—reflection and image of God who is Love—is disclosed in the spousal character of the body, in which the masculinity or femininity of the person is expressed.

The human dimension of sexuality is inseparable from the theological dimension. The human creature, in its unity of soul and body, is characterized therefore, from the very beginning, by the relationship with the other-beyond-the-self. This relationship is presented as still good and yet, at the same time, changed. It is good from its original goodness, declared by God from the first moment of creation. It has been changed however by the disharmony between God and humanity introduced by sin. This alteration does not correspond to the initial plan of God for man and woman, nor to the truth of the relationship between the sexes. It follows then that the relationship is good, but wounded and in need of healing.

What might be the ways of this healing? Considering and analyzing the problems in the relationship between the sexes solely from the standpoint of the situation marked by sin would lead to a return to the errors mentioned above. The logic of sin needs to be broken and a way forward needs to be found that is capable of banishing it from the hearts of sinful humanity. A clear orientation in this sense is provided in the third chapter of Genesis by God's promise of a Savior, involving the "woman" and her "offspring" (cf. Gn

3:15). It is a promise which will be preceded by a long preparation in history before it is realized.

9. An early victory over evil is seen in the story of Noah, the just man, who guided by God, avoids the flood with his family and the various species of animals (cf. Gn 6-9). But it is above all in God's choice of Abraham and his descendants (cf. Gn 12:1ff.) that the hope of salvation is confirmed. God begins in this way to unveil his countenance so that, through the chosen people, humanity will learn the path of divine likeness, that is, the way of holiness, and thus of transformation of heart. Among the many ways in which God reveals himself to his people (cf. Heb 1:1), in keeping with a long and patient pedagogy, there is the recurring theme of the covenant between man and woman. This is paradoxical if we consider the drama recounted in Genesis and its concrete repetition in the time of the prophets, as well as the mixing of the sacred and the sexual found in the religions which surrounded Israel. And yet this symbolism is indispensable for understanding the way in which God loves his people: God makes himself known as the Bridegroom who loves Israel his Bride.

If, in this relationship, God can be described as a "jealous God" (cf. Ex 20:5; Nah 1:2) and Israel denounced as an "adulterous" bride or "prostitute" (cf. Hos 2:4-15; Ez 16:15-34), it is because of the hope, reinforced by the prophets, of seeing Jerusalem become the perfect bride: "For as a young man marries a virgin so shall your creator marry you, and as the bridegroom rejoices over the bride, so shall your God rejoice over you" (Is 62:5). Recreated "in righteousness and in justice, in steadfast love and in mercy" (Hos 2:21), she who had wandered far away to search for life and happiness in false gods will return, and "shall respond as in the days of her youth" (Hos 2:17) to him who will speak to her heart; she will hear it said: "Your bridegroom is your Creator" (Is 54:5). It is substantially the same reality which is expressed when, parallel to the mystery of God's action through the male figure of the suffering Servant, the Book of the prophet Isaiah evokes the feminine figure of Zion, adorned with a transcendence and a sanctity which prefigure the gift of salvation destined for Israel.

The Song of Songs is an important moment in the use of this form of revelation. In the words of a most human love, which celebrate the beauty of the human body and the joy of mutual seeking, God's love for his people is also expressed. The Church's recognition of her relationship to Christ in this audacious conjunction of language about what is most human with language about what is most divine, cannot be said to be mistaken.

In the course of the Old Testament, a story of salvation takes shape which involves the simultaneous participation of male and female. While having an evident metaphorical dimension, the terms bridegroom and bride—and covenant as well—which characterize the dynamic of salvation, are much more than simple metaphors. This spousal language touches on the very nature of the relationship which God establishes with his people, even though that relationship is more expansive than human spousal experience. Likewise, the same concrete conditions of redemption are at play in the way in which prophetic statements, such as those of Isaiah, associate masculine and feminine roles in proclaiming and prefiguring the work of salvation which God is about to undertake. This salvation orients the reader both toward the male figure of the suffering Servant as well as to the female figure of Zion. The prophetic utterances of Isaiah in fact alternate between this figure and the Servant of God, before culminating at the end of the book with the mystical vision of Jerusalem, which gives birth to a people in a single day (cf. Is 66:7-14), a prophecy of the great new things which God is about to do (cf. Is 48:6-8).

10. All these prefigurations find their fulfillment in the New Testament. On the one hand, Mary, the chosen daughter of Zion, in her femininity, sums up and transfigures the condition of Israel/Bride waiting for the day of her salvation. On the other hand, the masculinity of the Son shows how Jesus assumes in his person all that the Old Testament symbolism had applied to the love of God for his people, described as the love of a bridegroom for his bride. The figures of Jesus and Mary his mother not only assure the continuity of the New Testament with the Old, but go beyond it, since—as St. Irenaeus wrote—with Jesus Christ "all newness" appears.[13]

This aspect is particularly evident in the Gospel of John. In the scene of the wedding feast at Cana, for example, Jesus is asked by his mother, who is called "woman," to offer, as a sign, the new wine of the future wedding with humanity (cf. Jn 2:1-12). This messianic wedding is accomplished on the Cross when, again in the presence of his mother, once again called "woman," the blood/wine of the New Covenant pours forth from the open heart of the crucified Christ (cf. Jn 19:25-27, 34).[14] It is therefore not at all surprising that John the Baptist, when asked who he is, describes himself as "the friend of the bridegroom," who rejoices to hear the bridegroom's voice and must be eclipsed by his coming: "He who has the bride is the bridegroom; the friend of the bridegroom, who stands and hears him, rejoices greatly at the bridegroom's voice; therefore this joy of mine is now full. He must increase, but I must decrease" (Jn 3:29-30).[15]

In his apostolic activity, Paul develops the whole nuptial significance of the redemption by seeing Christian life as a nuptial mystery. He writes to the Church in Corinth, which he had founded: "I feel a divine jealousy for you, for I betrothed you to Christ to present you as a chaste virgin to her one husband" (2 Cor 11:2).

In the Letter to the Ephesians, the spousal relationship between Christ and the Church is taken up again and deepened in its implications. In the New

Covenant, the beloved bride is the Church, and as the Holy Father teaches in his *Letter to Families*: "This bride, of whom the Letter to the Ephesians speaks, is present in each of the baptized and is like one who presents herself before her Bridegroom: 'Christ loved the Church and gave himself up for her . . . , that he might present the Church to himself in splendor, without spot or wrinkle or any such thing, that she might be holy and without blemish' (Eph 5:25-27)."[16]

Reflecting on the unity of man and woman as described at the moment of the world's creation (cf. Gn 2:24), the Apostle exclaims: "this mystery is a profound one, and I am saying that it refers to Christ and the Church" (Eph 5:32). The love of a man and a woman, lived out in the power of baptismal life, now becomes the sacrament of the love between Christ and his Church, and a witness to the mystery of fidelity and unity from which the "New Eve" is born and by which she lives in her earthly pilgrimage toward the fullness of the eternal wedding.

11. Drawn into the Paschal mystery and made living signs of the love of Christ and his Church, the hearts of Christian spouses are renewed and they are able to avoid elements of concupiscence in their relationship, as well as the subjugation introduced into the life of the first married couple by the break with God caused by sin. For Christian spouses, the goodness of love, for which the wounded human heart has continued to long, is revealed with new accents and possibilities. It is in this light that Jesus, faced with the question about divorce (cf. Mt 19:3-9), recalls the demands of the covenant between man and woman as willed by God at the beginning, that is, before the eruption of sin which had justified the later accommodations found in the Mosaic Law. Far from being the imposition of a hard and inflexible order, these words of Jesus are actually the proclamation of the "good news" of that faithfulness which is stronger than sin. The power of the resurrection makes possible the victory of faithfulness over weakness, over injuries and over the couple's sins. In the grace of Christ which renews their hearts, man and woman become capable of being freed from sin and of knowing the joy of mutual giving.

12. "For all of you who have been baptized into Christ have put on Christ . . . there is neither male nor female," writes St. Paul to the Galatians (3:27-28). The Apostle Paul does not say that the distinction between man and woman, which in other places is referred to the plan of God, has been erased. He means rather that in Christ the rivalry, enmity and violence which disfigured the relationship between men and women can be overcome and have been overcome. In this sense, the distinction between man and woman is reaffirmed more than ever; indeed, it is present in biblical revelation up to the very end. In the final hour of present history, the Book of Revelation of St. John, speaking of "a new heaven and a new earth" (Rev 21:1), presents the vision of a

feminine Jerusalem "prepared as a bride adorned for her husband" (Rev 21:2). Revelation concludes with the words of the Bride and the Spirit who beseech the coming of the Bridegroom, "Come, Lord Jesus!" (Rev 22:20).

Male and female are thus revealed as *belonging ontologically to creation* and destined therefore *to outlast the present time*, evidently in a transfigured form. In this way, they characterize the "love that never ends" (1 Cor 13:8), although the temporal and earthly expression of sexuality is transient and ordered to a phase of life marked by procreation and death. Celibacy for the sake of the Kingdom seeks to be the prophecy of this form of future existence of male and female. For those who live it, it is an anticipation of the reality of a life which, while remaining that of a man and a woman, will no longer be subject to the present limitations of the marriage relationship (cf. Mt 22:30). For those in married life, celibacy becomes the reminder and prophecy of the completion which their own relationship will find in the face-to-face encounter with God.

From the first moment of their creation, man and woman are distinct, and will remain so for all eternity. Placed within Christ's Paschal mystery, they no longer see their difference as a source of discord to be overcome by denial or eradication, but rather as the possibility for collaboration, to be cultivated with mutual respect for their difference. From here, new perspectives open up for a deeper understanding of the dignity of women and their role in human society and in the Church.

III. The Importance of Feminine Values in the Life of Society

13. Among the fundamental values linked to women's actual lives is what has been called a "capacity for the other." Although a certain type of feminist rhetoric makes demands "for ourselves," women preserve the deep intuition of the goodness in their lives of those actions which elicit life, and contribute to the growth and protection of the other.

This intuition is linked to women's physical capacity to give life. Whether lived out or remaining potential, this capacity is a reality that structures the female personality in a profound way. It allows her to acquire maturity very quickly, and gives a sense of the seriousness of life and of its responsibilities. A sense and a respect for what is concrete develop in her, opposed to abstractions which are so often fatal for the existence of individuals and society. It is women, in the end, who even in very desperate situations, as attested by history past and present, possess a singular capacity to persevere in adversity, to keep life going even in extreme situations, to hold tenaciously to the future, and finally to remember with tears the value of every human life.

Although motherhood is a key element of women's identity, this does not mean that women should be considered from the sole perspective of physical procreation. In this area, there can be serious distortions, which extol biological fecundity in purely quantitative terms and are often accompanied by dangerous disrespect for women. The existence of the Christian vocation of virginity, radical with regard to both the Old Testament tradition and the demands made by many societies, is of the greatest importance in this regard.[17] Virginity refutes any attempt to enclose women in mere biological destiny. Just as virginity receives from physical motherhood the insight that there is no Christian vocation except in the concrete gift of oneself to the other, so physical motherhood receives from virginity an insight into its fundamentally spiritual dimension: it is in not being content only to give physical life that the other truly comes into existence. This means that motherhood can find forms of full realization also where there is no physical procreation.[18]

In this perspective, one understands the irreplaceable role of women in all aspects of family and social life involving human relationships and caring for others. Here what John Paul II has termed *the genius of women* becomes very clear.[19] It implies first of all that women be significantly and actively present in the family, "the primordial and, in a certain sense sovereign society,"[20] since it is here above all that the features of a people take shape; it is here that its members acquire basic teachings. They learn to love inasmuch as they are unconditionally loved, they learn respect for others inasmuch as they are respected, they learn to know the face of God inasmuch as they receive a first revelation of it from a father and a mother full of attention in their regard. Whenever these fundamental experiences are lacking, society as a whole suffers violence and becomes in turn the progenitor of more violence. It means also that women should be present in the world of work and in the organization of society, and that women should have access to positions of responsibility which allow them to inspire the policies of nations and to promote innovative solutions to economic and social problems.

In this regard, it cannot be forgotten that the interrelationship between these two activities—family and work—has, for women, characteristics different from those in the case of men. The harmonization of the organization of work and laws governing work with the demands stemming from the mission of women within the family is a challenge. The question is not only legal, economic and organizational; it is above all a question of mentality, culture, and respect. Indeed, a just valuing of the work of women within the family is required. In this way, women who freely desire will be able to devote the totality of their time to the work of the household without being stigmatized by society or penalized financially, while those who wish also to engage in other work may be able to do so with an appropriate work-schedule, and not have to choose between relinquishing their family life or enduring continual stress, with negative consequences for one's own equilibrium and the harmony of the family. As John Paul II has written, "it will redound to the credit of society to make it possible for a mother—without inhibiting her freedom, without psychological or practical discrimination and without penalizing her as compared with other women—to devote herself to taking care of her children and educating them in accordance with their needs, which vary with age."[21]

14. It is appropriate however to recall that the feminine values mentioned here are above all human values: the human condition of man and woman created in the image of God is one and indivisible. It is only because women are more immediately attuned to these values that they are the reminder and the privileged sign of such values. But, in the final analysis, every human being, man or woman, is destined to be "for the other." In this perspective, that which is called "femininity" is more than simply an attribute of the female sex. The word designates indeed the fundamental human capacity to live for the other and because of the other.

Therefore, the promotion of women within society must be understood and desired as a humanization accomplished through those values, redis-covered thanks to women. Every outlook which presents itself as a conflict between the sexes is only an illusion and a danger: it would end in segregation and competition between men and women, and would promote a solipsism nourished by a false conception of freedom.

Without prejudice to the advancement of women's rights in society and the family, these observations seek to correct the perspective which views men as enemies to be overcome. The proper condition of the male-female relationship cannot be a kind of mistrustful and defensive opposition. Their relationship needs to be lived in peace and in the happiness of shared love.

On a more concrete level, if social policies—in the areas of education, work, family, access to services and civic participation—must combat all unjust sexual discrimination, they must also listen to the aspirations and identify the needs of all. The defense and promotion of equal dignity and common personal values must be harmonized with attentive recognition of the difference and reciprocity between the sexes where this is relevant to the realization of one's humanity, whether male or female.

IV. The Importance of Feminine Values in the Life of the Church

15. In the Church, woman as "sign" is more than ever central and fruitful, fol-lowing as it does from the very identity of the Church, as received from God and accepted in faith. It is this "mystical" identity, profound and essential,

which needs to be kept in mind when reflecting on the respective roles of men and women in the Church.

From the beginning of Christianity, the Church has understood herself to be a community, brought into existence by Christ and joined to him by a relationship of love, of which the nuptial experience is the privileged expression. From this it follows that the Church's first task is to remain in the presence of this mystery of God's love, manifested in Jesus Christ, to contemplate and to celebrate it. In this regard, the figure of Mary constitutes the fundamental reference in the Church. One could say metaphorically that Mary is a mirror placed before the Church, in which the Church is invited to recognize her own identity as well as the dispositions of the heart, the attitudes and the actions which God expects from her.

The existence of Mary is an invitation to the Church to root her very being in listening and receiving the Word of God, because faith is not so much the search for God on the part of human beings, as the recognition by men and women that God comes to us; he visits us and speaks to us. This faith, which believes that "nothing is impossible for God" (cf. Gn 18:14; Lk 1:37), lives and becomes deeper through the humble and loving obedience by which the Church can say to the Father: "Let it be done to me according to your word" (Lk 1:38). Faith continually makes reference to Jesus: "Do whatever he tells you" (Jn 2:5) and accompanies Jesus on his way, even to the foot of the Cross. Mary, in the hour of darkness, perseveres courageously in faithfulness, with the sole certainty of trust in the Word of God.

It is from Mary that the Church always learns the intimacy of Christ. Mary, who carried the small child of Bethlehem in her arms, teaches us to recognize the infinite humility of God. She who received the broken body of Jesus from the Cross shows the Church how to receive all those in this world whose lives have been wounded by violence and sin. From Mary, the Church learns the meaning of the power of love, as revealed by God in the life of his beloved Son: "he has scattered the proud in the thoughts of their heart . . . he has lifted up the lowly" (Lk 1:51-52). From Mary, the disciples of Christ continually receive the sense and the delight of praise for the work of God's hands: "The Almighty has done great things for me" (Lk 1:49). They learn that they are in the world to preserve the memory of those "great things," and to keep vigil in expectation of the day of the Lord.

16. To look at Mary and imitate her does not mean, however, that the Church should adopt a passivity inspired by an outdated conception of femininity. Nor does it condemn the Church to a dangerous vulnerability in a world where what count above all are domination and power. In reality, the way of Christ is neither one of domination (cf. Phil 2:6) nor of power as understood by the world (cf. Jn 18:36). From the Son of God one learns that this "passivity" is

in reality the way of love; it is a royal power which vanquishes all violence; it is "passion" which saves the world from sin and death and recreates humanity. In entrusting his mother to the Apostle John, Jesus on the Cross invites his Church to learn from Mary the secret of the love that is victorious.

Far from giving the Church an identity based on a historically conditioned model of femininity, the reference to Mary, with her dispositions of listening, welcoming, humility, faithfulness, praise and waiting, places the Church in continuity with the spiritual history of Israel. In Jesus and through him, these attributes become the vocation of every baptized Christian. Regardless of conditions, states of life, different vocations with or without public responsibilities, they are an essential aspect of Christian life. While these traits should be characteristic of every baptized person, women in fact live them with particular intensity and naturalness. In this way, women play a role of maximum importance in the Church's life by recalling these dispositions to all the baptized and contributing in a unique way to showing the true face of the Church, spouse of Christ and mother of believers.

In this perspective one understands how the reservation of priestly ordination solely to men[22] does not hamper in any way women's access to the heart of Christian life. Women are called to be unique examples and witnesses for all Christians of how the Bride is to respond in love to the love of the Bridegroom.

Conclusion

17. In Jesus Christ all things have been made new (cf. Rev 21:5). Renewal in grace, however, cannot take place without conversion of heart. Gazing at Jesus and confessing him as Lord means recognizing the path of love, triumphant over sin, which he sets out for his disciples.

In this way, man's relationship with woman is transformed, and the three-fold concupiscence described in the First Letter of John (1 Jn 2:16) ceases to have the upper hand. The witness of women's lives must be received with respect and appreciation, as revealing those values without which humanity would be closed in self-sufficiency, dreams of power and the drama of violence. Women too, for their part, need to follow the path of conversion and recognize the unique values and great capacity for loving others which their femininity bears. In both cases, it is a question of humanity's conversion to God, so that both men and women may come to know God as their "helper," as the Creator full of tenderness, as the Redeemer who "so loved the world that he gave his only begotten Son" (Jn 3:16).

Such a conversion cannot take place without humble prayer to God for that penetrating gaze which is able to recognize one's own sin and also the grace which heals it. In a particular way, we need to ask this of the Blessed Virgin Mary, the woman in accord with the heart of God, she who is "blessed among women" (cf. Lk 1:42), chosen to reveal to men and women the way of love. Only in this way, can the "image of God," the sacred likeness inscribed in every man and woman, emerge according to the specific grace received by each (cf. Gn 1:27). Only thus can the path of peace and wonderment be recovered, witnessed in the verses of the Song of Songs, where bodies and hearts celebrate the same jubilee.

The Church certainly knows the power of sin at work in individuals and in societies, which at times almost leads one to despair of the goodness of married couples. But through her faith in Jesus crucified and risen, the Church knows even more the power of forgiveness and self-giving in spite of any injury or injustice. The peace and wonderment which she trustfully proposes to men and women today are the peace and wonderment of the garden of the resurrection, which have enlightened our world and its history with the revelation that "God is love" (1 Jn 4:8, 16).

The Sovereign Pontiff John Paul II, in the Audience granted to the undersigned Cardinal Prefect, approved the present Letter, adopted in the Ordinary Session of this Congregation, and ordered its publication.

Rome, from the Offices of the Congregation for the Doctrine of the Faith, May 31, 2004, the Feast of the Visitation of the Blessed Virgin Mary.

+ Joseph Card. Ratzinger
Prefect

+ Angelo Amato, SDB
Titular Archbishop of Sila
Secretary

Notes

1   Cf. John Paul II, Post-Synodal Apostolic Exhortation *Familiaris Consortio* (November 22, 1981): AAS 74 (1982), 81-191; Apostolic Letter *Mulieris Dignitatem* (August 15, 1988): AAS 80 (1988), 1653-1729; *Letter to Families* (February 2, 1994): AAS 86 (1994), 868-925; *Letter to Women* (June 29, 1995): AAS 87 (1995), 803-812; *Catechesi sull'amore umano* (1979-1984): *Insegnamenti* II (1979)—VII (1984): English translation in *The Theology of the Body* (Boston: Pauline Books Media, 1997); Congregation for Catholic Education, *Educational Guidance in Human Love* (November 1, 1983); Pontifical Council for the Family, *The Truth and Meaning of Human Sexuality: Guidelines for Education Within the Family* (December 8, 1995).

2   On the complex question of *gender*, see also The Pontifical Council for the Family, *Family, Marriage and "De Facto" Unions* (July 26, 2000), 8.

3   Cf. John Paul II, Encyclical Letter *Fides et Ratio* (September 14, 1998), 21: AAS 91
     (1999), 22: "This opening to the mystery, which came to him [biblical man] through
     Revelation, was for him, in the end, the source of true knowledge. It was this which
     allowed his reason to enter the realm of the infinite where an understanding for
     which until then he had not dared to hope became a possibility."

4   John Paul II, Apostolic Letter *Mulieris Dignitatem* (August 15, 1988), 6: AAS 80
     (1988), 1662; cf. St. Irenaeus, *Adversus Haereses*, 5,6,1; 5, 16, 2-3: SC 153, 72-81;
     216-221; St. Gregory of Nyssa, *De hominis opificio*, 16: PG 44, 180; *In Canticum hom-
     ilia*, 2: PG 44, 805-808; St. Augustine, *Enarratio in Psalmum*, 4, 8: CCL 38, 17.

5   The Hebrew word *ezer* which is translated as "helpmate" indicates the assistance
     which only a person can render to another. It carries no implication of inferiority or
     exploitation if we remember that God too is at times called *ezer* with regard to human
     beings (cf. Ex 18:4; Ps10:14).

6   John Paul II, Apostolic Letter *Mulieris Dignitatem* (August 15, 1988), 6: AAS 80
     (1988), 1664.

7   John Paul II, General Audience of January 16, 1980, reprinted in *The Theology of the
     Body*, (Boston: Pauline Books Media, 1997), 63.

8   John Paul II, General Audience of July 23, 1980, reprinted in *The Theology of the
     Body*, (Boston: Pauline Books Media, 1997), 125.

9   John Paul II, Apostolic Letter *Mulieris Dignitatem* (August 15, 1988), 7: AAS 80
     (1988), 1666.

10   Ibid., 6, *l.c.*, 1663.

11   Congregation for Catholic Education, *Educational Guidance in Human Love*
     (November 1, 1983), 4.

12   Ibid.

13   *Adversus Haereses*, 4, 34, 1: SC 100, 846: "*Omnem novitatem attulit semetipsum afferens.*"

14   The ancient exegetical tradition sees in Mary at Cana the "*figura Synagogae*" and the
     "*inchoatio Ecclesiae.*"

15   Here the Fourth Gospel presents in a deeper way an element found also in the Synoptic
     Gospels (cf. Mt 9:15 and parallel texts). On the theme of Christ the Bridegroom, see
     John Paul II, *Letter to Families* (February 2, 1994), 18: AAS 86 (1994), 906-910.

16   John Paul II, *Letter to Families* (February 2, 1994), 19: AAS 86 (1994), 911; cf.
     Apostolic Letter *Mulieris Dignitatem* (August 15, 1988), 23- 25: AAS 80 (1988),
     1708-1715.

17   Cf. John Paul II, Post-Synodal Apostolic Exhortation *Familiaris Consortio* (November
     22, 1981), 16: AAS 74 (1982), 98-99.

18   Ibid., 41, *l.c.*, 132-133; Congregation for the Doctrine of the Faith, Instruction
     Donum Vitae (February 22, 1987), II, 8: AAS 80 (1988), 96-97.

19   Cf. John Paul II, *Letter to Women* (June 29, 1995), 9-10: AAS 87 (1995), 809-810.

20   John Paul II, *Letter to Families* (February 2, 1994), 17: AAS 86 (1994), 906.

21 Encyclical Letter *Laborem Exercens* (September 14, 1981), 19: *AAS* 73 (1981), 627.

22 Cf. John Paul II, Apostolic Letter *Ordinatio Sacerdotalis* (May 22, 1994): *AAS* 86 (1994), 545-548; Congregation for the Doctrine of the Faith, *Responsum Ad Dubium* regarding the doctrine of the Apostolic Letter *Ordinatio Sacerdotalis* (October 28, 1995): *AAS* 87 (1995), 1114.

Instruction *Dignitas Personae*, On Certain Bioethical Questions

Introduction

1. The dignity of a person must be recognized in every human being from conception to natural death. This fundamental principle expresses *a great "yes" to human life* and must be at the center of ethical reflection on biomedical research, which has an ever greater importance in today's world. The Church's Magisterium has frequently intervened to clarify and resolve moral questions in this area. The Instruction *Donum Vitae* was particularly significant.[1] And now, twenty years after its publication, it is appropriate to bring it up to date.

The teaching of *Donum Vitae* remains completely valid, both with regard to the principles on which it is based and the moral evaluations which it expresses. However, new biomedical technologies which have been introduced in the critical area of human life and the family have given rise to further questions, in particular in the field of research on human embryos, the use of stem cells for therapeutic purposes, as well as in other areas of experimental medicine. These new questions require answers. The pace of scientific developments in this area and the publicity they have received have raised expectations and concerns in large sectors of public opinion. Legislative assemblies have been asked to make decisions on these questions in order to regulate them by law; at times, wider popular consultation has also taken place.

These developments have led the Congregation for the Doctrine of the Faith to prepare *a new doctrinal Instruction* which addresses some recent questions in the light of the criteria expressed in the Instruction *Donum Vitae* and which also examines some issues that were treated earlier, but are in need of additional clarification.

2. In undertaking this study, the Congregation for the Doctrine of the Faith has benefited from the analysis of the Pontifical Academy for Life and has

consulted numerous experts with regard to the scientific aspects of these questions, in order to address them with the principles of Christian anthropology. The Encyclicals *Veritatis Splendor*[2] and *Evangelium Vitae*[3] of John Paul II, as well as other interventions of the Magisterium, offer clear indications with regard to both the method and the content of the examination of the problems under consideration.

In the current multifaceted philosophical and scientific context, a considerable number of scientists and philosophers, in the spirit of the *Hippocratic Oath*, see in medical science a service to human fragility aimed at the cure of disease, the relief of suffering and the equitable extension of necessary care to all people. At the same time, however, there are also persons in the world of philosophy and science who view advances in biomedical technology from an essentially eugenic perspective.

3. In presenting principles and moral evaluations regarding biomedical research on human life, the Catholic Church draws upon *the light both of reason and of faith* and seeks to set forth an integral vision of man and his vocation, capable of incorporating everything that is good in human activity, as well as in various cultural and religious traditions which not infrequently demonstrate a great reverence for life.

The Magisterium also seeks to offer a word of support and encouragement for the perspective on culture which considers *science an invaluable service to the integral good of the life and dignity of every human being*. The Church therefore views scientific research with hope and desires that many Christians will dedicate themselves to the progress of biomedicine and will bear witness to their faith in this field. She hopes moreover that the results of such research may also be made available in areas of the world that are poor and afflicted by disease, so that those who are most in need will receive humanitarian assistance. Finally, the Church seeks to draw near to every human being who is suffering, whether in body or in spirit, in order to bring not only comfort, but also light and hope. These give meaning to moments of sickness and to the experience of death, which indeed are part of human life and are present in the story of every person, opening that story to the mystery of the Resurrection. Truly, the gaze of the Church is full of trust because "Life will triumph: this is a sure hope for us. Yes, life will triumph because truth, goodness, joy and true progress are on the side of life. God, who loves life and gives it generously, is on the side of life."[4]

The present Instruction is addressed to the Catholic faithful and to all who seek the truth.[5] It has three parts: the first recalls some anthropological, theological and ethical elements of fundamental importance; the second addresses new problems regarding procreation; the third examines new procedures involving the manipulation of embryos and the human genetic patrimony.

First Part: Anthropological, Theological and Ethical Aspects of Human Life and Procreation

4. In recent decades, medical science has made significant strides in understanding human life in its initial stages. Human biological structures and the process of human generation are better known. These developments are certainly positive and worthy of support when they serve to overcome or correct pathologies and succeed in re-establishing the normal functioning of human procreation. On the other hand, they are negative and cannot be utilized when they involve the destruction of human beings or when they employ means which contradict the dignity of the person or when they are used for purposes contrary to the integral good of man.

The body of a human being, from the very first stages of its existence, can never be reduced merely to a group of cells. The embryonic human body develops progressively according to a well-defined program with its proper finality, as is apparent in the birth of every baby.

It is appropriate to recall the *fundamental ethical criterion* expressed in the Instruction *Donum Vitae* in order to evaluate all moral questions which relate to procedures involving the human embryo: "Thus the fruit of human generation, from the first moment of its existence, that is to say, from the moment the zygote has formed, demands the unconditional respect that is morally due to the human being in his bodily and spiritual totality. The human being is to be respected and treated as a person from the moment of conception; and therefore from that same moment his rights as a person must be recognized, among which in the first place is the inviolable right of every innocent human being to life."[6]

5. This ethical principle, which reason is capable of recognizing as true and in conformity with the natural moral law, should be the basis for all legislation in this area.[7] In fact, it presupposes a *truth of an ontological character*, as *Donum Vitae* demonstrated from solid scientific evidence, regarding the continuity in development of a human being.

If *Donum Vitae*, in order to avoid a statement of an explicitly philosophical nature, did not define the embryo as a person, it nonetheless did indicate that there is an intrinsic connection between the ontological dimension and the specific value of every human life. Although the presence of the spiritual soul cannot be observed experimentally, the conclusions of science regarding the human embryo give "a valuable indication for discerning by the use of reason a personal presence at the moment of the first appearance of a human life: how could a human individual not be a human person?"[8] Indeed, the reality of the human being for the entire span of life, both before and after birth, does not allow us to posit either a change in nature or a gradation in moral value, since it possesses *full anthropological and ethical status*. The human embryo has, therefore, from the very beginning, the dignity proper to a person.

6. Respect for that dignity is owed to every human being because each one carries in an indelible way his own dignity and value. *The origin of human life has its authentic context in marriage and in the family,* where it is generated through an act which expresses the reciprocal love between a man and a woman. Procreation which is truly responsible vis-à-vis the child to be born "must be the fruit of marriage."[9]

Marriage, present in all times and in all cultures, "is in reality something wisely and providently instituted by God the Creator with a view to carrying out his loving plan in human beings. Thus, husband and wife, through the reciprocal gift of themselves to the other—something which is proper and exclusive to them—bring about that communion of persons by which they perfect each other, so as to cooperate with God in the procreation and raising of new lives."[10] In the fruitfulness of married love, man and woman "make it clear that at the origin of their spousal life there is a genuine 'yes,' which is pronounced and truly lived in reciprocity, remaining ever open to life . . . Natural law, which is at the root of the recognition of true equality between persons and peoples, deserves to be recognized as the source that inspires the relationship between the spouses in their responsibility for begetting new children. The transmission of life is inscribed in nature and its laws stand as an unwritten norm to which all must refer."[11]

7. It is the Church's conviction that what is human is not only received and respected by *faith,* but is also purified, elevated and perfected. God, after having created man in his image and likeness (cf. Gn 1:26), described his creature as "very good" (Gn 1:31), so as to be assumed later in the Son (cf. Jn 1:14). In the mystery of the Incarnation, the Son of God confirmed the dignity of the body and soul which constitute the human being. Christ did not disdain human bodiliness, but instead fully disclosed its meaning and value: "In reality, it is only in the mystery of the incarnate Word that the mystery of man truly becomes clear."[12]

By becoming one of us, the Son makes it possible for us to become "sons of God" (Jn 1:12), "sharers in the divine nature" (2 Pt 1:4). This new dimension does not conflict with the dignity of the creature which everyone can recognize by the use of reason, but elevates it into a wider horizon of life which is proper to God, giving us the ability to reflect more profoundly on human life and on the acts by which it is brought into existence.[13]

The respect for the individual human being, which reason requires, is further enhanced and strengthened in the light of these truths of faith: thus, we see that there is no contradiction between the affirmation of the dignity and the affirmation of the sacredness of human life. "The different ways in which God, acting in history, cares for the world and for mankind are not mutually exclusive; on the contrary, they support each other and intersect. They have their origin and goal in the eternal, wise and loving counsel whereby God predestines men and women 'to be conformed to the image of his Son' (Rom 8:29)."[14]

8. By taking the interrelationship of these two dimensions, *the human and the divine*, as the starting point, one understands better why it is that man has unassailable value: *he possesses an eternal vocation* and *is called to share in the trinitarian love of the living God*.

This value belongs to all without distinction. By virtue of the simple fact of existing, every human being must be fully respected. The introduction of discrimination with regard to human dignity based on biological, psychological, or educational development, or based on health-related criteria, must be excluded. At every stage of his existence, man, created in the image and likeness of God, reflects "the face of his Only-begotten Son . . . This boundless and almost incomprehensible love of God for the human being reveals the degree to which the human person deserves to be loved in himself, independently of any other consideration—intelligence, beauty, health, youth, integrity, and so forth. In short, human life is always a good, for it '*is a manifestation of God in the world, a sign of his presence, a trace of his glory*' (*Evangelium Vitae*, no. 34)."[15]

9. These two dimensions of life, the natural and the supernatural, allow us to understand better the sense in which *the acts that permit a new human being to come into existence*, in which a man and a woman give themselves to each other, *are a reflection of trinitarian love*. "God, who is love and life, has inscribed in man and woman the vocation to share in a special way in his mystery of personal communion and in his work as Creator and Father."[16]

Christian marriage is rooted "in the natural complementarity that exists between man and woman, and is nurtured through the personal willingness of the spouses to share their entire life-project, what they have and what they are: for this reason such communion is the fruit and the sign of a profoundly human need. But in Christ the Lord, God takes up this human need, confirms it, purifies it and elevates it, leading it to perfection through the sacrament of matrimony: the Holy Spirit who is poured out in the sacramental celebration offers Christian couples the gift of a new communion of love that is the living and real image of that unique unity which makes of the Church the indivisible Mystical Body of the Lord Jesus."[17]

10. The Church, by expressing an ethical judgment on some developments of recent medical research concerning man and his beginnings, does not intervene in the area proper to medical science itself, but rather calls everyone to ethical and social responsibility for their actions. She reminds them that the ethical value of biomedical science is gauged in reference to both the *unconditional respect owed to every human being* at every moment of his or her existence, and the *defense of the specific character of the personal act which transmits life*. The intervention of the Magisterium falls within its mission of *contributing to the formation of conscience*, by authentically teaching the truth which is Christ and at the same time by declaring and confirming authoritatively the principles of the moral order which spring from human nature itself.[18]

Second Part: New Problems Concerning Procreation

11. In light of the principles recalled above, certain questions regarding procreation which have emerged and have become more clear in the years since the publication of *Donum Vitae* can now be examined.

Techniques for assisting fertility

12. With regard to the *treatment of infertility*, new medical techniques must respect three fundamental goods: a) the right to life and to physical integrity of every human being from conception to natural death; b) the unity of marriage, which means reciprocal respect for the right within marriage to become a father or mother only together with the other spouse;[19] c) the specifically human values of sexuality which require "that the procreation of a human person be brought about as the fruit of the conjugal act specific to the love between spouses."[20] Techniques which assist procreation "are not to be rejected on the grounds that they are artificial. As such, they bear witness to the possibilities of the art of medicine. But they must be given a moral evaluation in reference to the dignity of the human person, who is called to realize his vocation from God to the gift of love and the gift of life."[21]

In light of this principle, all techniques of heterologous artificial fertilization,[22] as well as those techniques of homologous artificial fertilization[23] which substitute for the conjugal act, are to be excluded. On the other hand, techniques which act *as an aid to the conjugal act and its fertility* are permitted. The Instruction *Donum vitae* states: "The doctor is at the service of persons and of human procreation. He does not have the authority to dispose of them or to decide their fate. A medical intervention respects the dignity of persons when it seeks to assist the conjugal act either in order to facilitate its performance or in order to enable it to achieve its objective once it has been normally performed."[24] And, with regard to homologous artificial insemination, it states: "Homologous artificial insemination within marriage cannot be admitted except for those cases in which the technical means is not a substitute for the conjugal act, but serves to facilitate and to help so that the act attains its natural purpose."[25]

13. Certainly, techniques aimed at removing obstacles to natural fertilization, as for example, hormonal treatments for infertility, surgery for endometriosis, unblocking of fallopian tubes or their surgical repair, are licit. All these techniques may be considered *authentic treatments* because, once the problem causing the infertility has been resolved, the married couple is able to engage in conjugal acts resulting in procreation, without the physician's action directly interfering in that act itself. None of these treatments replaces the conjugal act, which alone is worthy of truly responsible procreation.

In order to come to the aid of the many infertile couples who want to have children, *adoption* should be encouraged, promoted and facilitated by appropriate legislation so that the many children who lack parents may receive a home that will contribute to their human development. In addition, research and investment directed at the *prevention of sterility* deserve encouragement.

In vitro fertilization and the deliberate destruction of embryos

14. The fact that the process of *in vitro* fertilization very frequently involves the deliberate destruction of embryos was already noted in the Instruction *Donum Vitae*.[26] There were some who maintained that this was due to techniques which were still somewhat imperfect. Subsequent experience has shown, however, that all techniques of *in vitro* fertilization proceed as if the human embryo were simply a mass of cells to be used, selected and discarded.

It is true that approximately a third of women who have recourse to artificial procreation succeed in having a baby. It should be recognized, however, that given the proportion between the total number of embryos produced and those eventually born, *the number of embryos sacrificed is extremely high.*[27] These losses are accepted by the practitioners of *in vitro* fertilization as the price to be paid for positive results. In reality, it is deeply disturbing that research in this area aims principally at obtaining better results in terms of the percentage of babies born to women who begin the process, but does not manifest a concrete interest in the right to life of each individual embryo.

15. It is often objected that the loss of embryos is, in the majority of cases, unintentional or that it happens truly against the will of the parents and physicians. They say that it is a question of risks which are not all that different from those in natural procreation; to seek to generate new life without running any risks would in practice mean doing nothing to transmit it. It is

true that not all the losses of embryos in the process of *in vitro* fertilization have the same relationship to the will of those involved in the procedure. But it is also true that in many cases the abandonment, destruction and loss of embryos are foreseen and willed.

Embryos produced *in vitro* which have defects are directly discarded. Cases are becoming ever more prevalent in which couples who have no fertility problems are using artificial means of procreation in order to engage in genetic selection of their offspring. In many countries, it is now common to stimulate ovulation so as to obtain a large number of oocytes which are then fertilized. Of these, some are transferred into the woman's uterus, while the others are frozen for future use. The reason for multiple transfer is to increase the probability that at least one embryo will implant in the uterus. In this technique, therefore, the number of embryos transferred is greater than the single child desired, in the expectation that some embryos will be lost and multiple pregnancy may not occur. In this way, the practice of multiple embryo transfer implies *a purely utilitarian treatment of embryos*. One is struck by the fact that, in any other area of medicine, ordinary professional ethics and the healthcare authorities themselves would never allow a medical procedure which involved such a high number of failures and fatalities. In fact, techniques of *in vitro* fertilization are accepted based on the presupposition that the individual embryo is not deserving of full respect in the presence of the competing desire for offspring which must be satisfied.

This sad reality, which often goes unmentioned, is truly deplorable: the "various techniques of artificial reproduction, which would seem to be at the service of life and which are frequently used with this intention, actually open the door to new threats against life."[28]

16. The Church moreover holds that it is ethically unacceptable to *dissociate procreation from the integrally personal context of the conjugal act:*[29] human procreation is a personal act of a husband and wife, which is not capable of substitution. The blithe acceptance of the enormous number of abortions involved in the process of *in vitro* fertilization vividly illustrates how the replacement of the conjugal act by a technical procedure—in addition to being in contradiction with the respect that is due to procreation as something that cannot be reduced to mere reproduction—leads to a weakening of the respect owed to every human being. Recognition of such respect is, on the other hand, promoted by the intimacy of husband and wife nourished by married love.

The Church recognizes the legitimacy of the desire for a child and understands the suffering of couples struggling with problems of fertility. Such a desire, however, should not override the dignity of every human life to the point of absolute supremacy. The desire for a child cannot justify the "production" of offspring, just as the desire not to have a child cannot justify the abandonment or destruction of a child once he or she has been conceived.

In reality, it seems that some researchers, lacking any ethical point of reference and aware of the possibilities inherent in technological progress, surrender to the logic of purely subjective desires[30] and to economic pressures which are so strong in this area. In the face of this manipulation of the human being in his or her embryonic state, it needs to be repeated that "God's love does not differentiate between the newly conceived infant still in his or her mother's womb and the child or young person, or the adult and the elderly person. God does not distinguish between them because he sees an impression of his own image and likeness (Gn 1:26) in each one. . . Therefore, the Magisterium of the Church has constantly proclaimed the sacred and inviolable character of every human life from its conception until its natural end."[31]

Intracytoplasmic sperm injection (ICSI)

17. Among the recent techniques of artificial fertilization which have gradually assumed a particular importance is *intracytoplasmic sperm injection*.[32] This technique is used with increasing frequency given its effectiveness in overcoming various forms of male infertility.[33]

Just as in general with *in vitro* fertilization, of which it is a variety, ICSI is intrinsically illicit: it causes *a complete separation between procreation and the conjugal act*. Indeed ICSI takes place "outside the bodies of the couple through actions of third parties whose competence and technical activity determine the success of the procedure. Such fertilization entrusts the life and identity of the embryo into the power of doctors and biologists and establishes the domination of technology over the origin and destiny of the human person. Such a relationship of domination is in itself contrary to the dignity and equality that must be common to parents and children. Conception *in vitro* is the result of the technical action which presides over fertilization. Such fertilization is neither in fact achieved nor positively willed as the expression and fruit of a specific act of the conjugal union."[34]

Freezing embryos

18. One of the methods for improving the chances of success in techniques of *in vitro* fertilization is the multiplication of attempts. In order to avoid repeatedly taking oocytes from the woman's body, the process involves a single intervention in which multiple oocytes are taken, followed by cryopreservation of a considerable number of the embryos conceived *in vitro*.[35] In this way, should the initial attempt at achieving pregnancy not succeed, the procedure can be repeated or additional pregnancies attempted at a later date. In some cases, even the embryos used in the first transfer are frozen because the hormonal

ovarian stimulation used to obtain the oocytes has certain effects which lead physicians to wait until the woman's physiological conditions have returned to normal before attempting to transfer an embryo into her womb.

Cryopreservation is *incompatible with the respect owed to human embryos*; it presupposes their production *in vitro*; it exposes them to the serious risk of death or physical harm, since a high percentage does not survive the process of freezing and thawing; it deprives them at least temporarily of maternal reception and gestation; it places them in a situation in which they are sus-ceptible to further offense and manipulation.[36]

The majority of embryos that are not used remain "orphans." Their par-ents do not ask for them and at times all trace of the parents is lost. This is why there are thousands upon thousands of frozen embryos in almost all countries where *in vitro* fertilization takes place.

19. With regard to the large number of *frozen embryos already in existence* the question becomes: what to do with them? Some of those who pose this question do not grasp its ethical nature, motivated as they are by laws in some countries that require cryopreservation centers to empty their storage tanks periodically. Others, however, are aware that a grave injustice has been per-petrated and wonder how best to respond to the duty of resolving it.

Proposals to *use these embryos for research* or *for the treatment of disease* are obviously unacceptable because they treat the embryos as mere "biological material" and result in their destruction. The proposal to thaw such embryos without reactivating them and use them for research, as if they were normal cadavers, is also unacceptable.[37]

The proposal that these embryos could be put at the disposal of infertile couples as a *treatment for infertility* is not ethically acceptable for the same rea-sons which make artificial heterologous procreation illicit as well as any form of surrogate motherhood;[38] this practice would also lead to other problems of a medical, psychological and legal nature.

It has also been proposed, solely in order to allow human beings to be born who are otherwise condemned to destruction, that there could be a form of *"prenatal adoption."* This proposal, praiseworthy with regard to the intention of respecting and defending human life, presents however various problems not dissimilar to those mentioned above.

All things considered, it needs to be recognized that the thousands of abandoned embryos represent a *situation of injustice which in fact cannot be resolved*. Therefore John Paul II made an "appeal to the conscience of the world's scientific authorities and in particular to doctors, that the produc-tion of human embryos be halted, taking into account that there seems to be no morally licit solution regarding the human destiny of the thousands and thousands of 'frozen' embryos which are and remain the subjects of essential rights and should therefore be protected by law as human persons."[39]

The freezing of oocytes

20. In order to avoid the serious ethical problems posed by the freezing of embryos, the freezing of oocytes has also been advanced in the area of techniques of *in vitro* fertilization.[40] Once a sufficient number of oocytes has been obtained for a series of attempts at artificial procreation, only those which are to be transferred into the mother's body are fertilized while the others are frozen for future fertilization and transfer should the initial attempts not succeed.

In this regard it needs to be stated that cryopreservation of oocytes for the purpose of being used in artificial procreation is to be considered morally unacceptable.

The reduction of embryos

21. Some techniques used in artificial procreation, above all the transfer of multiple embryos into the mother's womb, have caused a significant increase in the frequency of multiple pregnancy. This situation gives rise in turn to the practice of so-called embryo reduction, a procedure in which embryos or fetuses in the womb are directly exterminated. The decision to eliminate human lives, given that it was a human life that was desired in the first place, represents a contradiction that can often lead to suffering and feelings of guilt lasting for years.

From the ethical point of view, *embryo reduction is an intentional selective abortion*. It is in fact the deliberate and direct elimination of one or more innocent human beings in the initial phase of their existence and as such it always constitutes a grave moral disorder.[41]

The ethical justifications proposed for embryo reduction are often based on analogies with natural disasters or emergency situations in which, despite the best intentions of all involved, it is not possible to save everyone. Such analogies cannot in any way be the basis for an action which is directly abortive. At other times, moral principles are invoked, such as those of the lesser evil or double effect, which are likewise inapplicable in this case. It is never permitted to do something which is intrinsically illicit, not even in view of a good result: *the end does not justify the means*.

Preimplantation diagnosis

22. Preimplantation diagnosis is a form of prenatal diagnosis connected with techniques of artificial fertilization in which embryos formed *in vitro* undergo genetic diagnosis before being transferred into a woman's womb. Such

diagnosis is done *in order to ensure that only embryos free from defects or having the desired sex or other particular qualities are transferred.*

Unlike other forms of prenatal diagnosis, in which the diagnostic phase is clearly separated from any possible later elimination and which provide therefore a period in which a couple would be free to accept a child with medical problems, in this case, the diagnosis before implantation is immediately followed by the elimination of an embryo suspected of having genetic or chromosomal defects, or not having the sex desired, or having other qualities that are not wanted. Preimplantation diagnosis—connected as it is with artificial fertilization, which is itself always intrinsically illicit—is directed toward the *qualitative selection and consequent destruction of embryos,* which constitutes an act of abortion. Preimplantation diagnosis is therefore the expression of a *eugenic mentality* that "accepts selective abortion in order to prevent the birth of children affected by various types of anomalies. Such an attitude is shameful and utterly reprehensible, since it presumes to measure the value of a human life only within the parameters of 'normality' and physical well-being, thus opening the way to legitimizing infanticide and euthanasia as well."[42]

By treating the human embryo as mere "laboratory material," *the concept itself of human dignity is also subjected to alteration and discrimination.* Dignity belongs equally to every single human being, irrespective of his parents' desires, his social condition, educational formation or level of physical development. If at other times in history, while the concept and requirements of human dignity were accepted in general, discrimination was practiced on the basis of race, religion or social condition, today there is a no less serious and unjust form of discrimination which leads to the non-recognition of the ethical and legal status of human beings suffering from serious diseases or disabilities. It is forgotten that sick and disabled people are not some separate category of humanity; in fact, sickness and disability are part of the human condition and affect every individual, even when there is no direct experience of it. Such discrimination is immoral and must therefore be considered legally unacceptable, just as there is a duty to eliminate cultural, economic and social barriers which undermine the full recognition and protection of disabled or ill people.

New forms of interception and contragestation

23. Alongside methods of preventing pregnancy which are, properly speaking, contraceptive, that is, which prevent conception following from a sexual act, there are other technical means which act after fertilization, when the embryo is already constituted, either before or after implantation in the uterine wall. Such methods are *interceptive* if they interfere with the embryo

before implantation and *contragestative* if they cause the elimination of the embryo once implanted.

In order to promote wider use of interceptive methods,[43] it is sometimes stated that the way in which they function is not sufficiently understood. It is true that there is not always complete knowledge of the way that different pharmaceuticals operate, but scientific studies indicate that *the effect of inhibiting implantation is certainly present,* even if this does not mean that such interceptives cause an abortion every time they are used, also because conception does not occur after every act of sexual intercourse. It must be noted, however, that anyone who seeks to prevent the implantation of an embryo which may possibly have been conceived and who therefore either requests or prescribes such a pharmaceutical, generally intends abortion.

When there is a delay in menstruation, a contragestative is used,[44] usually one or two weeks after the non-occurrence of the monthly period. The stated aim is to re-establish menstruation, but what takes place in reality is the *abortion of an embryo which has just implanted.*

As is known, abortion is "the deliberate and direct killing, by whatever means it is carried out, of a human being in the initial phase of his or her existence, extending from conception to birth."[45] Therefore, the use of means of interception and contragestation fall within the *sin of abortion* and are gravely immoral. Furthermore, when there is certainty that an abortion has resulted, there are serious penalties in canon law.[46]

Third Part: New Treatments Which Involve the Manipulation of the Embryo or the Human Genetic Patrimony

24. Knowledge acquired in recent years has opened new perspectives for both regenerative medicine and for the treatment of genetically based diseases. In particular, *research on embryonic stem cells* and its possible future uses have prompted great interest, even though up to now such research has not produced effective results, as distinct from *research on adult stem cells*. Because some maintain that the possible medical advances which might result from research on embryonic stem cells could justify various forms of manipulation and destruction of human embryos, a whole range of questions has emerged in the area of gene therapy, from cloning to the use of stem cells, which call for attentive moral discernment.

Gene therapy

25. *Gene therapy* commonly refers to techniques of genetic engineering applied to human beings for therapeutic purposes, that is to say, with the aim

of curing genetically based diseases, although recently gene therapy has been attempted for diseases which are not inherited, for cancer in particular.

In theory, it is possible to use gene therapy on two levels: somatic cell gene therapy and germ line cell therapy. *Somatic cell gene therapy* seeks to eliminate or reduce genetic defects on the level of somatic cells, that is, cells other than the reproductive cells, but which make up the tissue and organs of the body. It involves procedures aimed at certain individual cells with effects that are limited to a single person. *Germ line cell therapy* aims instead at correcting genetic defects present in germ line cells with the purpose of transmitting the therapeutic effects to the offspring of the individual. Such methods of gene therapy, whether somatic or germ line cell therapy, can be undertaken on a fetus *before his or her birth* as gene therapy in the uterus or *after birth* on a child or adult.

26. For a moral evaluation the following distinctions need to be kept in mind. *Procedures used on somatic cells for strictly therapeutic purposes are in principle morally licit.* Such actions seek to restore the normal genetic configuration of the patient or to counter damage caused by genetic anomalies or those related to other pathologies. Given that gene therapy can involve significant risks for the patient, the ethical principle must be observed according to which, in order to proceed to a therapeutic intervention, it is necessary to establish beforehand that the person being treated will not be exposed to risks to his health or physical integrity which are excessive or disproportionate to the gravity of the pathology for which a cure is sought. The informed consent of the patient or his legitimate representative is also required.

The moral evaluation of *germ line cell therapy* is different. Whatever genetic modifications are effected on the germ cells of a person will be transmitted to any potential offspring. Because the risks connected to any genetic manipulation are considerable and as yet not fully controllable, *in the present state of research, it is not morally permissible to act in a way that may cause possible harm to the resulting progeny.* In the hypothesis of gene therapy on the embryo, it needs to be added that this only takes place in the context of *in vitro* fertilization and thus runs up against all the ethical objections to such procedures. For these reasons, therefore, it must be stated that, in its current state, germ line cell therapy in all its forms is morally illicit.

27. *The question of using genetic engineering for purposes other than medical treatment also calls for consideration.* Some have imagined the possibility of using techniques of genetic engineering to introduce alterations with the presumed aim of improving and strengthening the gene pool. Some of these proposals exhibit a certain dissatisfaction or even rejection of the value of the human being as a finite creature and person. Apart from technical difficulties and

the real and potential risks involved, such manipulation would promote a eugenic mentality and would lead to indirect social stigma with regard to people who lack certain qualities, while privileging qualities that happen to be appreciated by a certain culture or society; such qualities do not constitute what is specifically human. This would be in contrast with the fundamental truth of the equality of all human beings which is expressed in the principle of justice, the violation of which, in the long run, would harm peaceful coexistence among individuals. Furthermore, one wonders who would be able to establish which modifications were to be held as positive and which not, or what limits should be placed on individual requests for improvement since it would be materially impossible to fulfill the wishes of every single person. Any conceivable response to these questions would, however, derive from arbitrary and questionable criteria. All of this leads to the conclusion that the prospect of such an intervention would end sooner or later by harming the common good, by favoring the will of some over the freedom of others. Finally it must also be noted that in the attempt to create *a new type of human being* one can recognize *an ideological element* in which man tries to take the place of his Creator.

In stating the ethical negativity of these kinds of interventions which imply *an unjust domination of man over man*, the Church also recalls the need to return to an attitude of care for people and of education in accepting human life in its concrete historical finite nature.

Human cloning

28. Human cloning refers to the asexual or agametic reproduction of the entire human organism in order to produce one or more "copies" which, from a genetic perspective, are substantially identical to the single original.[47]

Cloning is proposed for two basic purposes: *reproduction*, that is, in order to obtain the birth of a baby, and *medical therapy* or research. In theory, reproductive cloning would be able to satisfy certain specific desires, for example, control over human evolution, selection of human beings with superior qualities, pre-selection of the sex of a child to be born, production of a child who is the "copy" of another, or production of a child for a couple whose infertility cannot be treated in another way. Therapeutic cloning, on the other hand, has been proposed as a way of producing embryonic stem cells with a predetermined genetic patrimony in order to overcome the problem of immune system rejection; this is therefore linked to the issue of the use of stem cells.

Attempts at cloning have given rise to genuine concern throughout the entire world. Various national and international organizations have expressed negative judgments on human cloning and it has been prohibited in the great majority of nations.

Human cloning is intrinsically illicit in that, by taking the ethical negativity of techniques of artificial fertilization to their extreme, it seeks to *give rise to a new human being without a connection to the act of reciprocal self-giving between the spouses* and, more radically, *without any link to sexuality*. This leads to manipulation and abuses gravely injurious to human dignity.[48]

29. If cloning were to be done for *reproduction*, this would impose on the resulting individual a predetermined genetic identity, subjecting him—as has been stated—to a form of *biological slavery*, from which it would be difficult to free himself. The fact that someone would arrogate to himself the right to determine arbitrarily the genetic characteristics of another person represents *a grave offense to the dignity of that person as well as to the fundamental equality of all people*.

The originality of every person is a consequence of the particular relationship that exists between God and a human being from the first moment of his existence and carries with it the obligation to respect the singularity and integrity of each person, even on the biological and genetic levels. In the encounter with another person, we meet a human being who owes his existence and his proper characteristics to the love of God, and only the love of husband and wife constitutes a mediation of that love in conformity with the plan of the Creator and heavenly Father.

30. From the ethical point of view, so-called therapeutic cloning is even more serious. To create embryos with the intention of destroying them, even with the intention of helping the sick, is completely incompatible with human dignity, because it makes the existence of a human being at the embryonic stage nothing more than a means to be used and destroyed. It is *gravely immoral to sacrifice a human life for therapeutic ends*.

The ethical objections raised in many quarters to therapeutic cloning and to the use of human embryos formed *in vitro* have led some researchers to propose new techniques which are presented as capable of producing stem cells of an embryonic type without implying the destruction of true human embryos.[49] These proposals have been met with questions of both a scientific and an ethical nature regarding above all the ontological status of the "product" obtained in this way. Until these doubts have been clarified, the statement of the Encyclical *Evangelium Vitae* needs to be kept in mind: "what is at stake is so important that, from the standpoint of moral obligation, the mere probability that a human person is involved would suffice to justify an absolutely clear prohibition of any intervention aimed at killing a human embryo."[50]

The therapeutic use of stem cells

31. Stem cells are undifferentiated cells with two basic characteristics: a) the prolonged capability of multiplying themselves while maintaining the

undifferentiated state; b) the capability of producing transitory progenitor cells from which fully differentiated cells descend, for example, nerve cells, muscle cells and blood cells.

Once it was experimentally verified that when stem cells are transplanted into damaged tissue they tend to promote cell growth and the regeneration of the tissue, new prospects opened for regenerative medicine, which have been the subject of great interest among researchers throughout the world.

Among the sources for human stem cells which have been identified thus far are: the embryo in the first stages of its existence, the fetus, blood from the umbilical cord and various tissues from adult humans (bone marrow, umbilical cord, brain, mesenchyme from various organs, etc.) and amniotic fluid. At the outset, studies focused on *embryonic stem cells*, because it was believed that only these had significant capabilities of multiplication and differentiation. Numerous studies, however, show that *adult stem cells* also have a certain versatility. Even if these cells do not seem to have the same capacity for renewal or the same plasticity as stem cells taken from embryos, advanced scientific studies and experimentation indicate that these cells give more positive results than embryonic stem cells. Therapeutic protocols in force today provide for the use of adult stem cells and many lines of research have been launched, opening new and promising possibilities.

32. With regard to the ethical evaluation, it is necessary to consider the methods of obtaining stem cells as well as the risks connected with their clinical and experimental use.

In these methods, the origin of the stem cells must be taken into consideration. Methods which do not cause serious harm to the subject from whom the stem cells are taken are to be considered licit. This is generally the case when tissues are taken from: (a) an adult organism; (b) the blood of the umbilical cord at the time of birth; (c) fetuses who have died of natural causes. The obtaining of stem cells from a living human embryo, on the other hand, invariably causes the death of the embryo and is consequently gravely illicit: "research, in such cases, irrespective of efficacious therapeutic results, is not truly at the service of humanity. In fact, this research advances through the suppression of human lives that are equal in dignity to the lives of other human individuals and to the lives of the researchers themselves. History itself has condemned such a science in the past and will condemn it in the future, not only because it lacks the light of God but also because it lacks humanity."[51]

The use of embryonic stem cells or differentiated cells derived from them—even when these are provided by other researchers through the destruction of embryos or when such cells are commercially available—presents serious problems from the standpoint of cooperation in evil and scandal.[52]

There are no moral objections to the clinical use of stem cells that have been obtained licitly; however, the common criteria of medical ethics need to be respected. Such use should be characterized by scientific rigor and prudence, by reducing to the bare minimum any risks to the patient and by facilitating the interchange of information among clinicians and full disclosure to the public at large.

Research initiatives involving the use of adult stem cells, since they do not present ethical problems, should be encouraged and supported.[53]

Attempts at hybridization

33. Recently animal oocytes have been used for reprogramming the nuclei of human somatic cells—this is generally called *hybrid cloning*—in order to extract embryonic stem cells from the resulting embryos without having to use human oocytes.

From the ethical standpoint, such procedures represent an offense against the dignity of human beings on account of *the admixture of human and animal genetic elements capable of disrupting the specific identity of man*. The possible use of the stem cells, taken from these embryos, may also involve additional health risks, as yet unknown, due to the presence of animal genetic material in their cytoplasm. To consciously expose a human being to such risks is morally and ethically unacceptable.

The use of human "biological material" of illicit origin

34. For scientific research and for the production of vaccines or other products, cell lines are at times used which are the result of an illicit intervention against the life or physical integrity of a human being. The connection to the unjust act may be either mediate or immediate, since it is generally a question of cells which reproduce easily and abundantly. This "material" is sometimes made available commercially or distributed freely to research centers by governmental agencies having this function under the law. All of this gives rise to *various ethical problems with regard to cooperation in evil and with regard to scandal*. It is fitting therefore to formulate general principles on the basis of which people of good conscience can evaluate and resolve situations in which they may possibly be involved on account of their professional activity.

It needs to be remembered above all that the category of abortion "is to be applied also to the recent forms of *intervention on human embryos* which, although carried out for purposes legitimate in themselves, inevitably involve the killing of those embryos. This is the case with *experimentation on embryos*, which is becoming increasingly widespread in the field of biomedical research and is legally permitted in some countries . . . [T]he use of human embryos or fetuses as an object of experimentation constitutes a crime against their dignity as human beings who have a right to the same respect owed to a child once born, just as to every person."[54] These forms of experimentation always constitute a grave moral disorder.[55]

35. A different situation is created when researchers use "biological material" of illicit origin which has been produced apart from their research center or which has been obtained commercially. The Instruction *Donum Vitae* formulated the general principle which must be observed in these cases: "The corpses of human embryos and fetuses, whether they have been deliberately aborted or not, must be respected just as the remains of other human beings. In particular, they cannot be subjected to mutilation or to autopsies if their death has not yet been verified and without the consent of the parents or of the mother. Furthermore, the moral requirements must be safeguarded that there be no complicity in deliberate abortion and that the risk of scandal be avoided."[56]

In this regard, *the criterion of independence as it has been formulated by some ethics committees is not sufficient.* According to this criterion, the use of "biological material" of illicit origin would be ethically permissible provided there is a clear separation between those who, on the one hand, produce, freeze and cause the death of embryos and, on the other, the researchers involved in scientific experimentation. The criterion of independence is not sufficient to avoid a contradiction in the attitude of the person who says that he does not approve of the injustice perpetrated by others, but at the same time accepts for his own work the "biological material" which the others have obtained by means of that injustice. When the illicit action is endorsed by the laws which regulate healthcare and scientific research, it is necessary to distance oneself from the evil aspects of that system in order not to give the impression of a certain toleration or tacit acceptance of actions which are gravely unjust.[57] Any appearance of acceptance would in fact contribute to the growing indifference to, if not the approval of, such actions in certain medical and political circles.

At times, the objection is raised that the above-mentioned considerations would mean that people of good conscience involved in research would have the duty to oppose actively all the illicit actions that take place in the field of medicine, thus excessively broadening their ethical responsibility. In reality, the duty to avoid cooperation in evil and scandal relates to their ordinary professional activities, which they must pursue in a just manner and by means of which they must give witness to the value of life by their opposition to gravely unjust laws. Therefore, it needs to be stated that there is a duty to refuse to use such "biological material" even when there is no close connection between the researcher and the actions of those who performed the artificial fertilization or the abortion, or when there was no prior agreement with the centers in which the artificial fertilization took place. This duty springs from the necessity to *remove oneself*, within the area of one's own research, *from a gravely unjust legal situation and to affirm with clarity the value of human life*. Therefore, the above-mentioned criterion of independence is necessary, but may be ethically insufficient.

Of course, within this general picture there exist *differing degrees of responsibility*. Grave reasons may be morally proportionate to justify the use of such "biological material." Thus, for example, danger to the health of children could permit parents to use a vaccine which was developed using cell lines of illicit origin, while keeping in mind that everyone has the duty to make known their disagreement and to ask that their healthcare system make other types of vaccines available. Moreover, in organizations where cell lines of illicit origin are being utilized, the responsibility of those who make the decision to use them is not the same as that of those who have no voice in such a decision.

In the context of the urgent need to *mobilize consciences in favor of life*, people in the field of healthcare need to be reminded that "their responsibility today is greatly increased. Its deepest inspiration and strongest support lie in the intrinsic and undeniable ethical dimension of the health-care profession, something already recognized by the ancient and still relevant *Hippocratic Oath*, which requires every doctor to commit himself to absolute respect for human life and its sacredness."[58]

Conclusion

36. There are those who say that the moral teaching of the Church contains too many prohibitions. In reality, however, her teaching is based on the recognition and promotion of all the gifts which the Creator has bestowed on man: such as life, knowledge, freedom and love. Particular appreciation is due not only to man's intellectual activities, but also to those which are practical, like work and technological activities. By these, in fact, he participates in the creative power of God and is called to transform creation by ordering its many resources toward the dignity and wellbeing of all human beings and of the human person in his entirety. In this way, man acts as the steward of the value and intrinsic beauty of creation.

Human history shows, however, how man has abused and can continue to abuse the power and capabilities which God has entrusted to him, giving rise to *various forms of unjust discrimination and oppression* of the weakest and most defenseless: the daily attacks on human life; the existence of large regions of poverty where people are dying from hunger and disease, excluded from the intellectual and practical resources available in abundance in many countries; technological and industrial development which is creating the real risk of a collapse of the ecosystem; the use of scientific research in the areas of physics, chemistry and biology for purposes of waging war; the many conflicts which still divide peoples and cultures; these sadly are only some of the most obvious signs of how man can make bad use of his abilities and become his own worst enemy by losing the awareness of his lofty and specific vocation to collaborate in the creative work of God.

At the same time, human history has also shown real *progress in the understanding and recognition of the value and dignity of every person* as the foundation of the rights and ethical imperatives by which human society has been, and continues to be structured. Precisely in the name of promoting human dignity, therefore, practices and forms of behavior harmful to that dignity have been prohibited. Thus, for example, there are legal and political—and not just ethical—prohibitions of racism, slavery, unjust discrimination and marginalization of women, children, and ill and disabled people. Such prohibitions bear witness to the inalienable value and intrinsic dignity of every human being and are a sign of genuine progress in human history. In other words, the legitimacy of every prohibition is based on the need to protect an authentic moral good.

37. If initially human and social progress was characterized primarily by industrial development and the production of consumer goods, today it is distinguished by developments in information technologies, research in genetics, medicine and biotechnologies for human benefit, which are areas of great importance for the future of humanity, but in which there are also evident and unacceptable abuses. "Just as a century ago it was the working classes which were oppressed in their fundamental rights, and the Church courageously came to their defense by proclaiming the sacrosanct rights of the worker as person, so now, when another category of persons is being oppressed in the fundamental right to life, the Church feels in duty bound to speak out with the same courage on behalf of those who have no voice. Hers is always the evangelical cry in defense of the world's poor, those who are threatened and despised and whose human rights are violated."[59]

In virtue of the Church's doctrinal and pastoral mission, the Congregation for the Doctrine of the Faith has felt obliged to reiterate both the dignity and the fundamental and inalienable rights of every human being, including those in the initial stages of their existence, and to state explicitly the need for protection and respect which this dignity requires of everyone.

The fulfillment of this duty implies courageous opposition to all those practices which result in grave and unjust discrimination against unborn human beings, who have the dignity of a person, created like others in the image of God. *Behind every "no"* in the difficult task of discerning between good and evil, there shines a *great "yes" to the recognition of the dignity and inalienable value of every single and unique human being called into existence.*

The Christian faithful will commit themselves to the energetic promotion of a new culture of life by receiving the contents of this Instruction with the religious assent of their spirit, knowing that God always gives the grace necessary to observe his commandments and that, in every human being, above all in the least among us, one meets Christ himself (cf. Mt 25:40). In addition, all persons of good will, in particular physicians and researchers open to dialogue and desirous of knowing what is true, will understand and agree with these principles and judgments, which seek to safeguard the vulnerable condition of human beings in the first stages of life and to promote a more human civilization.

The Sovereign Pontiff Benedict XVI, in the Audience granted to the undersigned Cardinal Prefect on June 20, 2008, approved the present Instruction, adopted in the Ordinary Session of this Congregation, and ordered its publication.

Rome, from the Offices of the Congregation for the Doctrine of the Faith, September 8, 2008, Feast of the Nativity of the Blessed Virgin Mary.

William Card. Levada
Prefect

+ Luis F. Ladaria, SI
Titular Archbishop of Thibica
Secretary

Notes

1   Congregation for the Doctrine of the Faith, Instruction *Donum Vitae* on Respect for Human Life at its Origin and on the Dignity of Procreation (February 22, 1987): AAS 80 (1988), 70-102.

2   John Paul II, Encyclical Letter *Veritatis Splendor* Regarding Certain Fundamental Questions of the Church's Moral Teaching (August 6, 1993): AAS 85 (1993), 1133-1228.

3   John Paul II, Encyclical Letter *Evangelium Vitae* on the Value and Inviolability of Human Life (March 25, 1995): AAS 87 (1995), 401-522.

4   John Paul II, Address to the Participants in the Seventh Assembly of the Pontifical Academy of Life (March 3, 2001), 3: AAS 93 (2001), 446.

5   Cf. John Paul II, Encyclical Letter *Fides et Ratio* on the Relationship Between Faith and Reason (September 14, 1998), 1: AAS 91 (1999), 5.

6   Congregation for the Doctrine of the Faith, Instruction *Donum Vitae*, I, 1: AAS 80 (1988), 79.

7   Human rights, as Pope Benedict XVI has recalled, and in particular the right to life of every human being "are based on the natural law inscribed on human hearts and present in different cultures and civilizations. Removing human rights from this context would mean restricting their range and yielding to a relativistic conception, according to which the meaning and interpretation of rights could vary and their universality would be denied in the name of different cultural, political, social and even religious outlooks. This great variety of viewpoints must not be allowed to obscure the fact that not only rights are universal, but so too is the human person, the subject of those rights" (Address to the General Assembly of the United Nations [April 18, 2008]: AAS 100 [2008], 334).

8   Congregation for the Doctrine of the Faith, Instruction *Donum Vitae*, I, 1: AAS 80 (1988), 78-79.

9   Congregation for the Doctrine of the Faith, Instruction *Donum Vitae*, II, A, 1: AAS 80 (1988), 87.

10   Paul VI, Encyclical Letter *Humanae Vitae* (July 25, 1968), no. 8: AAS 60 (1968), 485-486.

11   Benedict XVI, Address to the Participants in the International Congress organized by the Pontifical Lateran University on the Fortieth Anniversary of the Encyclical *Humanae Vitae*, May 10, 2008: *L'Osservatore Romano*, May 11, 2008, 1; cf. John XXIII, Encyclical Letter *Mater et Magistra* (May 15, 1961), III: AAS 53 (1961), 447.

12   Second Vatican Council, Pastoral Constitution *Gaudium et Spes*, no. 22.

13   Cf. John Paul II, Encyclical Letter *Evangelium Vitae*, no. 37-38: AAS 87 (1995), 442-444.

14   John Paul II, Encyclical Letter *Veritatis Splendor*, no. 45: AAS 85 (1993), 1169.

15   Benedict XVI, Address to the General Assembly of the Pontifical Academy for Life and International Congress on "The Human Embryo in the Pre-implantation Phase" (February 27, 2006): AAS 98 (2006), 264.

16   Congregation for the Doctrine of the Faith, Instruction *Donum Vitae*, Introduction, 3: AAS 80 (1988), 75.

17   John Paul II, Apostolic Exhortation *Familiaris Consortio* on the Role of the Christian Family in the Modern World (September 22, 1981), 19: AAS 74 (1982), 101-102.

18   Cf. Second Vatican Council, Declaration *Dignitatis Humanae*, no. 14.

19   Cf. Congregation for the Doctrine of the Faith, Instruction *Donum Vitae*, II, A, 1: AAS 80 (1988), 87.

20   Congregation for the Doctrine of the Faith, Instruction *Donum Vitae*, II, B, 4: AAS 80 (1988), 92.

21   Congregation for the Doctrine of the Faith, Instruction *Donum Vitae*, Introduction, 3: AAS 80 (1988), 75.

22   The term *heterologous artificial fertilization or procreation* refers to "techniques used to obtain a human conception artificially by the use of gametes coming from at least one

donor other than the spouses who are joined in marriage" (Instruction *Donum Vitae*, II: AAS 80 [1988], 86).

23   The term *homologous artificial fertilization or procreation* refers to "the technique used to obtain a human conception using the gametes of the two spouses joined in marriage" (Instruction *Donum Vitae*, II: AAS 80 [1988], 86).

24   Congregation for the Doctrine of the Faith, Instruction *Donum Vitae*, II, B, 7: AAS 80 (1988), 96; cf. Pius XII, Address to Those Taking Part in the Fourth International Congress of Catholic Doctors (September 29, 1949): AAS 41 (1949), 560.

25   Congregation for the Doctrine of the Faith, Instruction *Donum Vitae*, II, B, 6: AAS 80 (1988), 94.

26   Cf. Congregation for the Doctrine of the Faith, Instruction *Donum Vitae*, II: AAS 80 (1988), 86.

27   Currently the number of embryos sacrificed, even in the most technically advanced centers of artificial fertilization, hovers above 80 percent.

28   John Paul II, Encyclical Letter *Evangelium Vitae*, 14: AAS 87 (1995), 416.

29   Cf. Pius XII, Address to the Second World Congress in Naples on Human Reproduction and Sterility (May 19, 1956): AAS 48 (1956), 470; Paul VI, Encyclical Letter *Humanae Vitae*, no. 12: AAS 60 (1968), 488-489; Congregation for the Doctrine of the Faith, Instruction *Donum Vitae*, II, B, 4-5: AAS 80 (1988), 90-94.

30   An increasing number of persons, even those who are unmarried, are having recourse to techniques of artificial reproduction in order to have a child. These actions weaken the institution of marriage and cause babies to be born in environments which are not conducive to their full human development.

31   Benedict XVI, Address to the General Assembly of the Pontifical Academy for Life and International Congress on "The Human Embryo in the Pre-implantation Phase" (February 27, 2006): AAS 98 (2006), 264.

32   *Intracytoplasmic sperm injection* is similar in almost every respect to other forms of *in vitro* fertilization with the difference that in this procedure fertilization in the test tube does not take place on its own, but rather by means of the injection into the oocyte of a single sperm, selected earlier, or by the injection of immature germ cells taken from the man.

33   There is ongoing discussion among specialists regarding the health risks which this method may pose for children conceived in this way.

34   Congregation for the Doctrine of the Faith, Instruction *Donum Vitae*, II, B, 5: AAS 80 (1988), 93.

35   Cryopreservation of embryos refers to freezing them at extremely low temperatures, allowing long term storage.

36   Cf. Congregation for the Doctrine of the Faith, Instruction *Donum Vitae*, I, 6: AAS 80 (1988), 84-85.

37   Cf. numbers 34-35 below.

38 Cf. Congregation for the Doctrine of the Faith, Instruction *Donum Vitae*, II, A, 1-3: *AAS* 80 (1988), 87-89.

39 John Paul II, Address to the participants in the Symposium on *"Evangelium Vitae* and Law" and the Eleventh International Colloquium on Roman and Canon Law (May 24, 1996), 6: *AAS* 88 (1996), 943-944.

40 Cryopreservation of oocytes is also indicated in other medical contexts which are not under consideration here. The term oocyte refers to the female germ cell (gametocyte) not penetrated by the spermatozoa.

41 Cf. Second Vatican Council, Pastoral Constitution *Gaudium et spes*, no. 51; John Paul II, Encyclical Letter *Evangelium Vitae*, no. 62: *AAS* 87 (1995), 472.

42 John Paul II, Encyclical Letter *Evangelium Vitae*, no. 63: *AAS* 87 (1995), 473.

43 The interceptive methods which are best known are the IUD (intrauterine device) and the so-called "morning-after pills."

44 The principal means of contragestation are RU-486 (Mifepristone), synthetic prostaglandins or Methotrexate.

45 John Paul II, Encyclical Letter *Evangelium Vitae*, no. 58: *AAS* 87 (1995), 467.

46 Cf. CIC, c. 1398 and CCEO, c. 1450 § 2; cf. also CIC, c. 1323-1324. The Pontifical Commission for the Authentic Interpretation of the *Code of Canon Law* declared that the canonical concept of abortion is "the killing of the fetus in whatever way or at whatever time from the moment of conception" (*Response* of May 23, 1988: *AAS* 80 [1988], 1818).

47 In the current state of knowledge, the techniques which have been proposed for accomplishing human cloning are two: artificial embryo twinning and cell nuclear transfer. *Artificial embryo twinning* consists in the artificial separation of individual cells or groups of cells from the embryo in the earliest stage of development. These are then transferred into the uterus in order to obtain identical embryos in an artificial manner. *Cell nuclear transfer,* or cloning properly speaking, consists in introducing a nucleus taken from an embryonic or somatic cell into a denucleated oocyte. This is followed by stimulation of the oocyte so that it begins to develop as an embryo.

48 Cf. Congregation for the Doctrine of the Faith, Instruction *Donum Vitae*, I, 6: *AAS* 80 (1988), 84; John Paul II, Address to Members of the Diplomatic Corps accredited to the Holy See (January 10, 2005), 5: *AAS* 97 (2005), 153.

49 The new techniques of this kind are, for example, the use of human parthenogenesis, altered nuclear transfer (ANT) and oocyte assisted reprogramming (OAR).

50 John Paul II, Encyclical Letter *Evangelium Vitae*, no. 60: *AAS* 87 (1995), 469.

51 Benedict XVI, Address to the participants in the Symposium on the topic: "Stem Cells: what is the future for therapy?" organized by the Pontifical Academy for Life (September 16, 2006): *AAS* 98 (2006), 694.

52 Cf. numbers 34-35 below.

53   Cf. Benedict XVI, Address to the participants in the Symposium on the topic: "Stem
     Cells: what is the future for therapy?" organized by the Pontifical Academy for Life
     (September 16, 2006): AAS 98 (2006), 693-695.

54   John Paul II, Encyclical Letter *Evangelium Vitae*, no. 63: AAS 87 (1995), 472-473.

55   Cf. John Paul II, Encyclical Letter *Evangelium Vitae*, no. 62: AAS 87 (1995), 472.

56   Congregation for the Doctrine of the Faith, Instruction *Donum Vitae*, I, 4: AAS 80
     (1988), 83.

57   Cf. John Paul II, Encyclical Letter *Evangelium Vitae*, no. 73: AAS 87 (1995), 486:
     "Abortion and euthanasia are thus crimes which no human law can claim to legiti-
     mize. There is no obligation in conscience to obey such laws; instead there is a *grave
     and clear obligation to oppose them by conscientious objection.*" The right of conscientious
     objection, as an expression of the right to freedom of conscience, should be protected
     by law.

58   John Paul II, Encyclical Letter *Evangelium Vitae*, no. 63: AAS 89 (1995), 502.

59   John Paul II, Letter to all the Bishops on "The Gospel of Life" (May 19, 1991): AAS
     84 (1992), 319.

Clarification on Procured Abortion

L'Osservatore Romano

July 11, 2009

Recently a number of letters have been sent to the Holy See, some of them
from prominent figures in political and ecclesial life, explaining the confusion that has been created in various countries, especially in Latin America,
following the manipulation and exploitation of an article by His Excellency
Archbishop Rino Fisichella, President of the Pontifical Academy for Life,
on the sad affair of the "Brazilian girl." In this article, which appeared in
"L'Osservatore Romano" on March 15, 2009, the doctrine of the Church was
presented, while still keeping in mind the dramatic situation of the aforementioned girl, who—as could be demonstrated afterward—had been accompanied with all pastoral delicacy, in particular by the Archbishop of Olinda and
Recife at the time, His Excellency Archbishop José Cardoso Sobrinho. In
this regard, the Congregation for the Doctrine of the Faith reiterates that the
Church's teaching on procured abortion has not changed, nor can it change.
This teaching has been presented in numbers 2270-2273 in the Catechism of
the Catholic Church, in these terms:

"Human life must be respected and protected absolutely from the moment
of conception. From the first moment of his existence, a human being must

be recognized as having the rights of a person—among which is the inviolable right of every innocent being to life "Before I formed you in the womb I knew you, and before you were born I consecrated you" (Jer 1:5). "My frame was not hidden from you, when I was being made in secret, intricately wrought in the depths of the earth" (Ps 139:15).

"Since the first century the Church has affirmed the moral evil of every procured abortion. This teaching has not changed and remains unchangeable. Direct abortion, that is to say, abortion willed either as an end or a means, is gravely contrary to the moral law: "You shall not kill the embryo by abortion and shall not cause the newborn to perish" (Didaché, 2:2). "God, the Lord of life, has entrusted to men the noble mission of safeguarding life, and men must carry it out in a manner worthy of themselves. Life must be protected with the utmost care from the moment of conception: abortion and infanticide are abominable crimes" (*Gaudium et Spes*, no. 51).

"Formal cooperation in an abortion constitutes a grave offense. The Church attaches the canonical penalty of excommunication to this crime against human life. "A person who procures a completed abortion incurs excommunication *latae sententiae*" (CIC, c. 1398), "by the very commission of the offense" (CIC, c. 1314) and subject to the conditions provided by Canon Law (cf. CIC, c. 1323-1324). The Church does not thereby intend to restrict the scope of mercy. Rather, she makes clear the gravity of the crime committed, the irreparable harm done to the innocent who is put to death, as well as to the parents and the whole of society.

"The inalienable right to life of every innocent human individual is a constitutive element of a civil society and its legislation: "The inalienable rights of the person must be recognized and respected by civil society and the political authority. These human rights depend neither on single individuals nor on parents; nor do they represent a concession made by society and the state; they belong to human nature and are inherent in the person by virtue of the creative act from which the person took his origin. Among such fundamental rights one should mention in this regard every human being's right to life and physical integrity from the moment of conception until death . . . The moment a positive law deprives a category of human beings of the protection which civil legislation ought to accord them, the state is denying the equality of all before the law. When the state does not place its power at the service of the rights of each citizen, and in particular of the more vulnerable, the very foundations of a state based on law are undermined. . . . As a consequence of the respect and protection which must be ensured for the unborn child from the moment of conception, the law must provide appropriate penal sanctions for every deliberate violation of the child's rights." (Congregation for the Doctrine of the Faith, Instruction *Donum Vitae*, III)

In the encyclical *Evangelium Vitae*, Pope John Paul II reaffirmed this teaching with his authority as Supreme Pastor of the Church: "By the authority which Christ conferred upon Peter and his Successors, in communion with the Bishops—who on various occasions have condemned abortion and who in the aforementioned consultation, albeit dispersed throughout the world, have shown unanimous agreement concerning this doctrine—I declare that direct abortion, that is, abortion willed as an end or as a means, always constitutes a grave moral disorder, since it is the deliberate killing of an innocent human being. This doctrine is based upon the natural law and upon the written Word of God, is transmitted by the Church's Tradition and taught by the ordinary and universal Magisterium. No circumstance, no purpose, no law whatsoever can ever make licit an act which is intrinsically illicit, since it is contrary to the Law of God which is written in every human heart, knowable by reason itself, and proclaimed by the Church" (no. 62).

As for abortion procured in certain difficult and complex situations, the clear and precise teaching of Pope John Paul II applies: "It is true that the decision to have an abortion is often tragic and painful for the mother, insofar as the decision to rid herself of the fruit of conception is not made for purely selfish reasons or out of convenience, but out of a desire to protect certain important values such as her own health or a decent standard of living for the other members of the family. Sometimes it is feared that the child to be born would live in such conditions that it would be better if the birth did not take place. Nevertheless, these reasons and others like them, however serious and tragic, can never justify the deliberate killing of an innocent human being" (*Evangelium Vitae*, no. 58).

As for the problem of specific medical treatments intended to preserve the health of the mother, it is necessary to make a strong distinction between two different situations: on the one hand, a procedure that directly causes the death of the fetus, sometimes inappropriately called "therapeutic" abortion, which can never be licit in that it is the direct killing of an innocent human being; on the other hand, a procedure not abortive in itself that can have, as a collateral consequence, the death of the child: "If, for example, saving the life of the future mother, independently of her condition of pregnancy, urgently required a surgical procedure or another therapeutic application, which would have as an accessory consequence, in no way desired or intended, but inevitable, the death of the fetus, such an action could not be called a direct attack on the innocent life. In these conditions, the operation can be considered licit, as can other similar medical procedures, always provided that a good of high value, like life, is at stake, and that it is not possible to postpone it until after the birth of the child, or to use any other effective remedy" (Pius XII, *Speech to the Fronte della Famiglia and the Associazione Famiglie numerose*, November 27, 1951).

As for the responsibility of medical workers, the words of Pope John Paul II must be recalled: "Their profession calls for them to be guardians and servants of human life. In today's cultural and social context, in which science and the practice of medicine risk losing sight of their inherent ethical dimension, health-care professionals can be strongly tempted at times to become manipulators of life, or even agents of death. In the face of this temptation their responsibility today is greatly increased. Its deepest inspiration and strongest support lie in the intrinsic and undeniable ethical dimension of the health-care profession, something already recognized by the ancient and still relevant Hippocratic Oath, which requires every doctor to commit himself to absolute respect for human life and its sacredness" (*Evangelium Vitae*, no. 89).

Note on the Banalization of Sexuality Regarding Certain Interpretations of "Light of the World"

December 22, 2010

Following the publication of the interview-book *Light of the World* by Benedict XVI, a number of erroneous interpretations have emerged which have caused confusion concerning the position of the Catholic Church regarding certain questions of sexual morality. The thought of the Pope has been repeatedly manipulated for ends and interests which are entirely foreign to the meaning of his words—a meaning which is evident to anyone who reads the entire chapters in which human sexuality is treated. The intention of the Holy Father is clear: to rediscover the beauty of the divine gift of human sexuality and, in this way, to avoid the cheapening of sexuality which is common today.

Some interpretations have presented the words of the Pope as a contradiction of the traditional moral teaching of the Church. This hypothesis has been welcomed by some as a positive change and lamented by others as a cause of concern—as if his statements represented a break with the doctrine concerning contraception and with the Church's stance in the fight against AIDS. In reality, the words of the Pope—which specifically concern a gravely disordered type of human behavior, namely prostitution (cf. *Light of the World*, 117-119)—do not signify a change in Catholic moral teaching or in the pastoral practice of the Church.

As is clear from an attentive reading of the pages in question, the Holy Father was talking neither about conjugal morality nor about the moral norm concerning contraception. This norm belongs to the tradition of the Church and was summarized succinctly by Pope Paul VI in paragraph

14 of his Encyclical Letter *Humanae Vitae*, when he wrote that "also to be excluded is any action which either before, at the moment of, or after sexual intercourse, is specifically intended to prevent procreation—whether as an end or as a means." The idea that anyone could deduce from the words of Benedict XVI that it is somehow legitimate, in certain situations, to use condoms to avoid an unwanted pregnancy is completely arbitrary and is in no way justified either by his words or in his thought. On this issue the Pope proposes instead—and also calls the pastors of the Church to propose more often and more effectively (cf. *Light of the World*, 147)—humanly and ethically acceptable ways of behaving which respect the inseparable connection between the unitive and procreative meaning of every conjugal act, through the possible use of natural family planning in view of responsible procreation.

On the pages in question, the Holy Father refers to the completely different case of prostitution, a type of behavior which Christian morality has always considered gravely immoral (cf. *Gaudium et Spes*, no. 27; CCC, no. 2355). The response of the entire Christian tradition—and indeed not only of the Christian tradition—to the practice of prostitution can be summed up in the words of St. Paul: "Flee from fornication" (1 Cor 6:18). The practice of prostitution should be shunned, and it is the duty of the agencies of the Church, of civil society and of the State to do all they can to liberate those involved from this practice.

In this regard, it must be noted that the situation created by the spread of AIDS in many areas of the world has made the problem of prostitution even more serious. Those who know themselves to be infected with HIV and who therefore run the risk of infecting others, apart from committing a sin against the sixth commandment are also committing a sin against the fifth commandment—because they are consciously putting the lives of others at risk through behavior which has repercussions on public health. In this situation, the Holy Father clearly affirms that the provision of condoms does not constitute "the real or moral solution" to the problem of AIDS and also that "the sheer fixation on the condom implies a banalization of sexuality" in that it refuses to address the mistaken human behavior which is the root cause of the spread of the virus. In this context, however, it cannot be denied that anyone who uses a condom in order to diminish the risk posed to another person is intending to reduce the evil connected with his or her immoral activity. In this sense the Holy Father points out that the use of a condom "with the intention of reducing the risk of infection, can be a first step in a movement toward a different way, a more human way, of living sexuality." This affirmation is clearly compatible with the Holy Father's previous statement that this is "not really the way to deal with the evil of HIV infection."

Some commentators have interpreted the words of Benedict XVI according to the so-called theory of the "lesser evil." This theory is, however, susceptible to proportionalistic misinterpretation (cf. John Paul II, Encyclical Letter *Veritatis Splendor*, nos. 75-77). An action which is objectively evil, even if a lesser evil, can never be licitly willed. The Holy Father did not say—as some people have claimed—that prostitution with the use of a condom can be chosen as a lesser evil. The Church teaches that prostitution is immoral and should be shunned. However, those involved in prostitution who are HIV positive and who seek to diminish the risk of contagion by the use of a condom may be taking the first step in respecting the life of another—even if the evil of prostitution remains in all its gravity. This understanding is in full conformity with the moral theological tradition of the Church.

In conclusion, in the battle against AIDS, the Catholic faithful and the agencies of the Catholic Church should be close to those affected, should care for the sick and should encourage all people to live abstinence before and fidelity within marriage. In this regard it is also important to condemn any behavior which cheapens sexuality because, as the Pope says, such behavior is the reason why so many people no longer see in sexuality an expression of their love: "This is why the fight against the banalization of sexuality is also part of the struggle to ensure that sexuality is treated as a positive value and to enable it to have a positive effect on the whole of man's being" (*Light of the World*, 119).

CHAPTER II

Pontifical Biblical Commission

The Bible and Morality:
Biblical Roots of Christian Conduct

May 11, 2008

Preface

The yearning for happiness, the desire to achieve a fully satisfying life, is forever deeply rooted in the human heart. The realization of this desire depends mainly on our behavior, which agrees, but sometimes clashes with that of others. In which way is it possible to arrive at an effective decision regarding the just behavior that leads individuals, communities and entire nations toward a successful life, in other words, toward happiness?

For Christians Holy Scripture is not only a source of revelation on which to ground one's faith, it is also an indispensable reference point for morality. They are convinced that in the bible they can find indications and norms of right behavior to attain fullness of life.

Such a conviction encounters various objections. The first difficulty is the instinctive refusal of norms, obligations and commandments within the human person, particularly strong in our own days. Equally cogent in contemporary society is the desire to attain full happiness together with unlimited liberty, that is, freedom to act in accordance with one's whims, without the constraint of any norms. For some people such an unlimited freedom is in fact essential for the attainment of true happiness. Within this frame of mind human dignity itself demands that it not be subjected to externally imposed norms: each human person should freely and autonomously decide for himself what he deems just and acceptable. Hence the normative complex present in the Scriptures, the development of Tradition and the Magisterium of the Church that interprets and actualizes these norms appear as obstacles to happiness of which we must free ourselves.

A second difficulty derives from Sacred Scripture itself: biblical writings were redacted at least nineteen hundred years ago and belong to distant epochs in which life conditions were very different from those of today. Many actual situations and problems were completely unknown in these writings and therefore one may think that they can offer no appropriate answers to these problems. Consequently even if the fundamental value of the bible as an inspired text is acknowledged some people retain a strong skeptical attitude and maintain that Scripture is of no use for offering solutions to the numerous problems of our times. Present humanity is confronted every day with delicate moral problems continually presented by the sciences and by globalization; even convinced believers have the impression that many of our past certainties have been annulled; just think about such themes as violence, terrorism, war, immigration, distribution of wealth, respect for natural resources, life, work, sexuality, genetic research, the family and community life. Faced by such complex problems one is tempted to marginalize, totally or partially, Sacred Scripture. In this case too, though for a variety of motives, the sacred text is laid aside and solutions to the grave and urgent problems of today are sought elsewhere.

Already in 2002 the Pontifical Biblical Commission, at the behest of the then President Card. Joseph Ratzinger, set about to examine the problem of the relationship between the bible and morality by posing itself the question: what is the value and the significance of the inspired text for today's morality, regarding which the above mentioned difficulties cannot be neglected?

In the bible we find many norms, commandments, laws, collections of codices, etc. An attentive reading, however, draws attention to the fact that such norms are never found by themselves in isolation, they always belong to a definite context. It can be stated that in biblical anthropology the primary and basic factor is God's action, forestalling human behavior: his gifts of grace, his call to communion. The normative complex is consequential; it shows the proper way to accept and live out God's gift. At the root of this biblical concept is the view of the human person as created by God, it is never an isolated, autonomous being, detached from everything and from everyone; it stands in a radical and essential relationship with God and with a brotherly community. God created mankind in his own image, its very existence is the first and basic gift received from God. In biblical perspective a discourse on moral norms cannot treat them in isolation and in a restricted fashion, but it needs to insert them into the context of the entire biblical view of human existence.

The first part of the document therefore sets out to present this characteristic biblical concept in which anthropology and theology intertwine.
Following the canonical order of the bible the human person first appears as
a creature to whom God had donated life itself, it then appears as a member
of the chosen people with whom God had entered a special covenant, and
finally, as brother and sister of Jesus, incarnate Son of God.

The second part of the document stresses the fact that direct solutions to
the numerous outstanding problems cannot be found in Sacred Scripture.
However, although the bible does not offer prefabricated solutions, it does
present some criteria whose application is certainly of help in finding valid
solutions for human behavior. Two basic criteria are presented in the first
place, conformity with the biblical concept of the human being and conformity with the example of Jesus. These are followed by other more particular
criteria. From Holy Scripture as a whole at least six strong lines of reasoning emerge that can lead to making solid moral decisions with a Scriptural
foundation: (1) opening up to various cultures, hence a certain ethical uni-
versalism (criterion of convergence); (2) a firm stand against incompatible
values (criterion of opposition); (3) a process of refinement of the human
conscience which can be observed within each of the two Testaments (criterion of progress); (4) a rectification of the tendency to leave moral decisions
to the subjective, individual sphere alone (criterion of community dimension); (5) an aperture toward the absolute future of the world and of history
that enables us to mark out clearly the goal and the motivations of human
behavior (criterion of finality); (6) an attentive evaluation, in each case, of
the relative or absolute value of moral principles and precepts in the bible
(criterion of discernment).

All these criteria, whose listing is only representative not exhaustive, are
deeply rooted in the bible; their application can certainly be of help to the
believer. They show which points biblical revelation offers to help us, in our
own day, in the delicate process of correct moral discernment.

I wish to express my thanks to the members of the Pontifical Biblical
Commission for their patient and demanding work. I hope that the present
text will be of help in discovering ever more the fascinating values of a genuine Christian life, and to consider the bible as an inexhaustible treasure, ever
actual for determining just behavior, on which the attainment of happiness
in its fullness by individuals and by the entire human community depends.

William Cardinal Levada
President

. . .

3) Discovering values in obligations

30. . . . Translated into a terminology of values the precepts of the Decalogue point to the following values: the Absolute, religious homage, time, the family, life, the stability of the male and female couple, freedom (the Hebrew verb *gnb* probably refers to abduction not to the theft of material objects), good reputation, the household, the house and its material belongings.

Each of these values opens a "program," a moral demand that is never complete. The following propositions, each introduced by a verb, illustrate the dynamic to which each of these values gives rise. . . .

Seven horizontal values regarding the relationships between human persons.

1. to honor the family
2. to further the right to life
3. to safeguard the union of the couple, man and wife
4. to defend the right of each person to respect for his or her personal liberty and dignity
5. to safeguard the reputation of other people
6. to respect every individual (members of a household, family or group)
7. to leave to others their material goods.

The ten values seen in the Decalogue are presented in decreasing order of value, from the most to the least important, God in the first place and material goods in the last. Within human relationships family, life, and a stable marriage head the list.

This analysis therefore offers humanity in search of autonomy a legal and moral support that can prove both fruitful and stable. In our present situation, however, it may seem unattractive, as the popular scale of values commonly followed in today's world runs contrary to the biblical proposal. It puts human beings before God. Indeed, material goods, economics in a certain sense, may stand at the head of the list. When a political and social system is founded, openly or not, on false basic values (or uncertainty about values), when commerce and consumerism are considered more important than personal relationships, that system is fractured from its very beginning, and doomed, sooner or later, to collapse.

By contrast, the Decalogue opens up a broad way toward a liberating morality, giving first place to God's sovereignty over the world (value nos. 1 and 2), offering every individual the possibility of dedicating time to God and of managing time in a constructive manner (no. 3), broadening the opportunities of family life (no. 4), defending life, even an apparently unproductive life of suffering, against arbitrary decisions of the system and subtle manipulations of public opinion (no. 5), neutralizing the seeds of division that render married life so fragile, especially in our days (no. 6), preventing all forms of exploitation of the body, of the heart and of ideas (no. 7), protecting personal reputations from attack (no. 8) and from all kinds of deception, of exploitation, abuse and coercion (nos. 9 and 10).

4) Juridical Consequences

31. The ten values underlying the Decalogue offer a clear foundation for a charter of rights and of freedom to the whole of humanity:

1. the right to a religious rapport with God,
2. right to the respect for beliefs and religious symbols,
3. the right to freedom of worship and secondly to leisure, to free time and to quality of life,
4. the right of families to just and protective policies, of children to support from their parents and to a training in work and social values, the right of elderly parents to respect and to support from their children,
5. the right to life (to be born), to respect for life (to live and die a natural death), to education,
6. the right of persons to free choice of a spouse, the right of the couple to respect, encouragement and support from the state and from society at large, the right of children to stability (emotional, affective, financial) from their parents,
7. the right to civil liberties (physical integrity, choice of life and career, freedom of movement and of expression),
8. the right to a good reputation, and secondly to respect for private life and unbiased information,
9. the right to domestic and professional security and tranquility, and further to freedom of activity,
10. the right to private property, including the certainty of civil protection of material goods.

In the context of a "revealed morality" however, these inalienable human rights are fully subordinated to the divine right, to God's universal sovereignty. The Decalogue begins with the words: "I am the LORD your God, who led you out of the land of Egypt." (Ex 20:2; Dt 5:6). This divine sovereignty, as it manifests itself in the founding event of the exodus, is exercised not according to an authoritarian and despotic manner, as so often occurs in the human control of rights and liberty, but rather in view of personal and community freedom. From the human side it implies, among other things, exclusive worship, a time devoted to personal and common prayer, the acknowledgement of God's supreme authority to order the lives of his creatures, to govern individuals and peoples, to exercise judgment. Finally, the biblical view of divine sovereignty propounds a world vision in which not merely the Church, but the cosmos, the environment and the totality of earthly goods belong, in the last resort, to God alone.

In short, building on the fundamental values contained in the Decalogue, moral theology and the consequent catechetical teaching are able to propose to today's humanity a balanced ideal that, on one hand never privileges duties to the detriment of rights or vice-versa, and, on the other hand, avoids the stumbling-block of a purely secular ethic that disregards the relationship of human beings to God. . . .

The Book of Qoheleth

. . . Nothing that can be obtained in this world has an enduring value: wisdom, richness, pleasure, labor, youth, life itself. People may or may not receive what they deserve. Everything yields to the specter of death, the only inevitable factor of life which no one can escape. Notwithstanding the inconsistencies and vicissitudes of life, human beings must accept their proper role in relation to God. This is the sense of Qoheleth's admonition: "Fear God" (5:7). . . .

The Book of Ben Sirach

. . . Wisdom is also at work in developing family relationships: duties of children toward their parents (3:1-16; 7:27-28), of parents toward their children (7:23-25; 16:1-14); relationship with women: wives (7:19; 23:22-26; 25:12–26:18), daughters (7:24-26; 22:4-5), and women in general (9:1-9). . . .

The First Letter of Peter

. . . Believers should not adapt themselves to the godless society in which they live, in which they are 'aliens and exiles' (2:11). They shall abstain from 'the evil desires of the flesh' (2:11), from the godless way of life (cf. 4:3), and rather lead the godless, by means of good works, to the point of 'glorifying God when he manifests himself' (2:12). Despite their differences from it, they are called to enter into the society in which they live, and to subject themselves 'to all human authority for love of the Lord' (2:13). The same attentive participation in society may be seen in the rules regarding various relationships of life: state, family, marriage (2:13–3:12). . . .

Biblical Criteria for Moral Reflection

Introduction

92. The first part of this document had the purpose of indicating the principal anthropological and theological biblical guidelines that constitute the foundations of reflection about morality, and to point out their moral consequences.

The second part will take into consideration the modern situation. Our contemporaries, both individually and collectively, are confronted every day by delicate moral problems. These arise from the development of science as well as from the globalization of communications, constantly presented in such a way that even convinced believers have the impression that some certainties of the past no longer hold. Think of the various ways of dealing with the ethics of violence, terrorism, war, immigration, distribution of wealth, respect for natural resources, life itself, work, sexuality, research in the genetic field, the family and community life. Faced by these complex problems, the temptation arose in these latest decades to put aside the Scriptures, either wholly or in part. What is to be done when the Bible provides no satisfying answers? How can we integrate biblical data into a moral discourse on problems that need the light of theological reflection, reason and the sciences for their solution? This is our present project.

It is certainly a delicate project, the reason being that the biblical canon is a complex collection of inspired texts, a collection of books by different authors dating back to very diverse epochs; they express a multitude of theological views, at times in a context of legislation or of prescriptive dicta; at other times they are narratives illustrating the revelation of the history of salvation; they also present concrete examples of moral conduct, whether positive or negative. Moreover, in the course of time they betray a diversified evolution and refinement of moral sensitivity and motivation.

All these factors render necessary the formation of some methodological criteria that will allow us to refer to Sacred Scripture in moral matters. At the same time we must take into account the theological contents of these writings, the complexity of their literary composition and finally their canonical dimension. In this regard we must pay particular attention to the re-reading of the Old Testament in the New, and apply to it with maximum possible rigor the categories of continuity, discontinuity, and advance that qualify the relationship between the two Testaments. . . .

1.1. First fundamental criterion, conformity with the biblical concept of human nature

95. It is suggested that, since much of what is contained in Scripture can also be found in other cultures and that believers do not have the monopoly of good deeds, biblical morality is not really original. Hence the main insights to be used in these matters should be sought in the field of reason. . . .

a. Life*

"You shall not kill" (Ex 20:13; Dt 5:17). On the basis of this negative formulation the prohibition implies a non-action: not to commit a serious attack against life (in this context, human life). Jesus will amplify and refine the field of abstention: not to hurt one's "own brother" by anger or verbal abuse (Mt 5:21-22). Therefore, in a certain sense, it is possible to kill without guns or bombs or arsenic inasmuch as there is something more precious in man. The tongue can become a mortal weapon (Jas 3:8-10). The same holds true for hate (1 Jn 3:15).

b. The couple**

"You shall not commit adultery" (Ex 20:14; Dt 5:18). The original commandment looked primarily toward a social goal: to ensure the stability of the clan and the family. Is it necessary to say that this goal has not lost any of its timeliness and urgency? In this case too, Jesus expands the extent of the prohibition to the point of ruling out every desire for marital infidelity, even when not acted out, and practically rendering the mosaic ordinance about divorce inoperative (Mt 5:27-32).

1.1.3 Implications for Today's World

a. Life

98. A transposition of this precept into an axiological key opens it up to a broader perspective.

1. As we have already observed when speaking of Jesus' preaching, this transposition compels us to refine the concept of 'respect for life.' The value in

---

*   This paragraph is an unofficial translation of the Italian.

**   This paragraph is an unofficial translation of the Italian.

question does not refer to the body alone, it also applies to everything that affects human dignity, social integration and spiritual growth.

2. Even with respect to the biological aspect it forbids us to claim power over life, whether ours or that of others. So the Church understands 'you shall not kill' in the Scripture as a prohibition of willingly causing the death of any human being, be it an embryo, a fetus, a handicapped person, the terminally diseased or individuals who are considered as socially or economically unproductive. The Church's serious reservations concerning genetic engineering are to be understood in the same way.

3. In the course of history and of the development of civilization, the Church too, meditating on the Scriptures, has refined her moral stance on the death penalty and on war, which is now becoming more and more absolute. Underlying this stance, which may seem radical, is the same anthropological basis, the fundamental dignity of the human person, created in the image of God.

4. With reference to the global problem of the ecology of our planet the moral horizon opened up by the value 'respect for life' may well go beyond the interests of humanity alone to the point of warranting a new reflection on the preservation of animal and plant species. The biblical narrative of the origins could well invite us to do so. Before the Fall the first couple receive four charges: to be fruitful, to multiply, to fill the earth and to subdue it, following a vegetarian regime (Gn 1:28-29). In Gn 9:1-4 Noah, a new Adam, ensures the repopulation of the earth after the deluge, but he is given only the first three assignments, which tends to limits his powers; he is authorized to eat flesh and fish, but is told to abstain from blood, the symbol of life. This ethic of respect for life is based on two themes of biblical theology, the fundamental 'goodness' of the whole of creation (Gn 1:4, 10, 12, 18, 21, 25, 31) and the extension of the covenant to include all living beings (Gn 9:12-16).

What is it in biblical thought that explains, in the last resort, such respect for life? None other than its divine origin. The gift of life to humanity is described symbolically as the act of 'breathing' on God's part (Gn 2:7). Moreover, this 'immortal spirit is in all things,' it 'has filled the world' (Wis 12:1; 1:7).

b. The couple

99. The negative manner in which the duties of the couple are expressed (avoid, abstain from, do not . . .) does not exhaust their ethical message. The moral horizon opened by the commandment is expressed, among other things, in terms of personal, mutual responsibility and of solidarity: for

example, it is the task of both partners to take seriously the duty of constantly renewing his and her initial pledge. Both must take into account the other's psychology, rhythm, tastes and spiritual progress (1 Pt 3:1-2, 7); both must cultivate mutual respect and selfless love (Eph 5:21-22, 28, 33); they must resolve conflicts or divergent points of view and develop harmonious relationships. Moreover the couple as such must take responsible decisions in matters of family planning, contribution to society and spiritual advance. The ritual celebration of Christian marriage implies essentially a dynamic task, not fulfilled once for all, to become ever more fully a sacramental couple that witnesses and symbolizes, in the heart of a world of relationships that are so often ephemeral and superficial, the stability, permanence, and fruitfulness of God's loving pledge toward humanity and of Christ's toward the Church.

It is therefore understandable that the Church, because of her commitment to remain unyieldingly faithful to the Word, has always extolled the greatness of the male-female couple, both in its radical dignity as 'God's image' (creation) and in the bond of mutual pledge before God and with God (covenant). In constantly and untiringly recalling the importance and sanctity of marriage, the Church does not limit herself to denouncing moral laxity, but defends the full significance of the reality of marriage in God's purpose. . . .

2.4.2. Implications for today's world

135. The community is a fundamental datum of moral life according to the Bible. It is founded on that love which surpasses individual interests and holds all human beings together. This love is ultimately rooted in the life of the Holy Trinity itself, is manifested by the dynamic power of the Holy Spirit and is, at the same time, the source and aim of any authentic Christian community.

a. Various types of community

Communities are to be found on the various levels of human life, each with their own dynamic and specific moral requirements. The family is the most fundamental human community, decisive for the social and moral formation of the individual. The Church too is a community, for whom the gift of faith is essential. The Church is entered by means of baptism, and Christian love constitutes her intimate unitive bond. Moral duties derive from membership of the civil community, both local and national. Moreover, modern society today is ever more conscious of the global dimension of the human community and of the moral obligations for the economic, social and political well-being of the entire family of nations. In the social teaching of the Church the Popes have, for over a century, underlined the moral duties that derive from membership of a community at various levels.

CHAPTER III

International Theological Commission

Communion and Stewardship:
Human Persons Created in the Image of God

July 23, 2004

36. The Bible lends no support to the notion of a natural superiority of the masculine over the feminine sex. Their differences notwithstanding, the two sexes enjoy an inherent equality. As Pope John Paul II wrote in *Familiaris Consortio*: "Above all it is important to underline the equal dignity and responsibility of women with men. This equality is realized in a unique manner in that reciprocal self-giving by each one to the other and by both to the children which is proper to marriage and the family. . . .In creating the human race 'male and female,' God gives man and woman an equal personal dignity, endowing them with the inalienable rights and responsibilities proper to the human person" (no. 22). Man and woman are equally created in God's image. Both are persons, endowed with intelligence and will, capable of orienting their lives through the exercise of freedom. But each does so in a manner proper and distinctive to their sexual identity, in such wise that the Christian tradition can speak of a reciprocity and complementarity. These terms, which have lately become somewhat controversial, are nonetheless useful in affirming that man and woman each needs the other in order to achieve fullness of life.

37. To be sure, the original friendship between man and woman was deeply impaired by sin. Through his miracle at the wedding feast of Cana (Jn 2:1ff.),

our Lord shows that he has come to restore the harmony that God intended in the creation of man and woman.

38. The image of God, which is to be found in the nature of the human person as such, can be realized in a special way in the union between human beings. Since this union is directed to the perfection of divine love, Christian tradition has always affirmed the value of virginity and celibacy which foster chaste friendship among human persons at the same time that they point to the eschatological fulfillment of all created love in the uncreated love of the Blessed Trinity. In this very connection, the Second Vatican Council drew an analogy between the communion of the divine persons among themselves, and that which human beings are invited to establish on earth (cf. *Gaudium et Spes*, no. 24). While it is certainly true that union between human beings can be realized in a variety of ways, Catholic theology today affirms that marriage constitutes an elevated form of the communion between human persons and one of the best analogies of the Trinitarian life. When a man and a woman unite their bodies and spirits in an attitude of total openness and self-giving, they form a new image of God. Their union as one flesh does not correspond simply to a biological necessity, but to the intention of the Creator in leading them to share the happiness of being made in his image. The Christian tradition speaks of marriage as an eminent way of sanctity. "God is love, and in himself he lives a mystery of personal loving communion. Creating man and woman in his image . . . , God inscribed in the humanity of man and woman the vocation, and thus the capacity and responsibility of love and communion" (CCC, no. 2331). The Second Vatican Council also underlined the profound significance of marriage: "Christian spouses, in virtue of the sacrament of matrimony, signify and partake of the mystery of that unity and fruitful love which exists between Christ and His Church (cf. Eph. 5:32). The spouses thereby help each other to attain to holiness in their married life and by the rearing of their children" (*Lumen Gentium*, no. 11; cf. *Gaudium et Spes*, no. 48).

3. Person and community

40. Persons created in the image of God are bodily beings whose identity as male or female orders them to a special kind of communion with one another. As Pope John Paul II has taught, the nuptial meaning of the body finds its realization in the human intimacy and love that mirror the communion of the Blessed Trinity whose mutual love is poured out in creation and redemption. This truth is at the center of Christian anthropology. Human beings are created in the *imago Dei* precisely as persons capable of a knowledge and love

that are personal and interpersonal. It is of the essence of the *imago Dei* in them that these personal beings are relational and social beings, embraced in a human family whose unity is at once realized and prefigured in the Church.

41. When one speaks of the person, one refers both to the irreducible identity and interiority that constitutes the particular individual being, and to the fundamental relationship to other persons that is the basis for human community. In the Christian perspective, this personal identity that is at once an orientation to the other is founded essentially on the Trinity of divine Persons. God is not a solitary being, but a communion of three Persons. Constituted by the one divine nature, the identity of the Father is his paternity, his relation to the Son and the Spirit; the identity of the Son is his relation to the Father and the Spirit; the identity of the Spirit is his relation to the Father and the Son. Christian revelation led to the articulation of the concept of person, and gave it a divine, Christological, and Trinitarian meaning. In effect, no person is as such alone in the universe, but is always constituted with others and is summoned to form a community with them.

42. It follows that personal beings are social beings as well. The human being is truly human to the extent that he actualizes the essentially social element in his constitution as a person within familial, religious, civil, professional, and other groups that together form the surrounding society to which he belongs. While affirming the fundamentally social character of human existence, Christian civilization has nonetheless recognized the absolute value of the human person as well as the importance of individual rights and cultural diversity. In the created order, there will always be a certain tension between the individual person and the demands of social existence. In the Blessed Trinity there is a perfect harmony between the Persons who share the communion of a single divine life.

43. Every individual human being as well as the whole human community are created in the image of God. In its original unity—of which Adam is the symbol—the human race is made in the image of the divine Trinity. Willed by God, it makes its way through the vicissitudes of human history toward a perfect communion, also willed by God, but yet to be fully realized. In this sense, human beings share the solidarity of a unity that both already exists and is still to be attained. Sharing in a created human nature and confessing the triune God who dwells among us, we are nonetheless divided by sin and await the victorious coming of Christ who will restore and recreate the unity God wills in a final redemption of creation (cf. Rom 8:18-19). This unity of the human family is yet to be realized eschatologically. The Church is the sacrament of salvation and of the kingdom of God: catholic, in bringing together

man of every race and culture; one, in being the vanguard of the unity of the human community willed by God; holy, sanctified herself by the power of the Holy Spirit, and sanctifying all men through the Sacraments; and, apostolic, in continuing the mission of the men chosen by Christ to accomplish progressively the divinely willed unity of the human race and the consummation of creation and redemption.

The Hope of Salvation for Infants Who Die Without Being Baptized

April 19, 2007

Introduction

1. St. Peter encourages Christians to be always ready to give an account of the hope that is in them (cf. 1 Pt 3:15-16). This document deals with the hope that Christians can have for the salvation of unbaptized infants who die. It indicates how such a hope has developed in recent decades and what its grounds are, so as to enable an account of that hope to be given. Though at first sight this topic may seem to be peripheral to theological concerns, questions of great depth and complexity are involved in its proper explication, and such an explication is called for today by pressing pastoral needs.

2. In these times, the number of infants who die unbaptized is growing greatly. This is partly because of parents, influenced by cultural relativism and religious pluralism, who are non-practicing, but it is also partly a consequence of *in vitro* fertilization and abortion. Given these developments, the question of the destiny of such infants is raised with new urgency. In such a situation, the ways by which salvation may be achieved appear ever more complex and problematic. The Church, faithful guardian of the way of salvation, knows that salvation can be achieved only in Christ, by the Holy Spirit. Yet, as mother and teacher, she cannot fail to reflect on the destiny of all human beings, created in the image of God (cf. International Theological Commission, *Communion and Stewardship: Human Persons Created in the Image of God*, Vatican City, 2005), and especially of the weakest. Being endowed with reason, conscience and freedom, adults are responsible for their own destiny in so far as they accept or reject God's grace. Infants, however, who do not yet have the use of reason, conscience and freedom, cannot decide for themselves. Parents experience great grief and feelings of guilt when they do not have the moral assurance

of the salvation of their children, and people find it increasingly difficult to accept that God is just and merciful if he excludes infants, who have no personal sins, from eternal happiness, whether they are Christian or non-Christian. From a theological point of view, the development of a theology of hope and an ecclesiology of communion, together with a recognition of the greatness of divine mercy, challenge an unduly restrictive view of salvation. In fact, the universal salvific will of God and the correspondingly universal mediation of Christ mean that all theological notions that ultimately call into question the very omnipotence of God, and his mercy in particular, are inadequate. . . .

3.4. The Church and the Communion of Saints

97. St. Paul teaches that the unbelieving husband or wife of a Christian believer is "consecrated" through their wife or husband, respectively, and moreover that their children too are "holy" (1 Cor 7:14). This is a remarkable indication that the holiness that resides in the Church reaches out to people outside the visible bounds of the Church by means of the bonds of human communion, in this case the family bonds between husband and wife in marriage and parents and children. St. Paul implies that the spouse and the child of a believing Christian have by that very fact at least a connection to membership of the Church and to salvation; their family situation "involves a certain introduction to the Covenant" (Y. Congar, *Vaste monde ma paroisse*, 171). His words give no assurance of salvation for the unbaptized spouse (cf. 1 Cor 7:16) or child, but surely, once again, grounds for hope.

In Search of a Universal Ethic:
A New Look at the Natural Law

May 20, 2009

Chapter 1: Convergences

1.6. The Magisterium of the Church and natural law

35. . . . In the third place, facing an aggressive secularism that wants to exclude believers from public debate, the Church points out that the interventions of Christians in public life on subjects that regard natural law (the defense of the rights of the oppressed, justice in international relations, the defense of life and of the family, religious freedom and freedom of education), are not in themselves of a confessional nature, but derive from the care which every

citizen must have for the common good of society. In the fourth place, facing the threats of the abuse of power, and even of totalitarianism, which juridical positivism conceals and which certain ideologies propagate, the Church recalls that civil laws do not bind in conscience when they contradict natural law, and asks for the acknowledgment of the right to conscientious objection, as well as the duty of disobedience in the name of obedience to a higher law (cf. John Paul II, Encyclical *Evangelium Vitae*, no. 73–74). The reference to natural law, far from producing conformism, guarantees personal freedom and defends the marginalized and those oppressed by social structures which do not take the common good into account. . . .

Chapter 2: The Perception of Common Moral Values

2.1. The role of society and culture

38. The human person only progressively comes to moral experience and becomes capable of expressing to himself the precepts that should guide his action. The person attains this to degree to which he is inserted in a network of human relationships from birth, beginning with the family, relationships which allow him, little by little, to become aware of himself and of reality around him. This is done in particular by the learning of a language—one's mother tongue—which teaches the person to name things and allows him to become a subject aware of himself. Oriented by the persons who surround him, permeated by the culture in which he is immersed, the person recognizes certain ways of behaving and of thinking as values to pursue, laws to observe, examples to imitate, visions of the world to accept. The social and cultural context thus exercises a decisive role in the education in moral values. There is, however, no contradiction between such conditioning and human freedom. Rather, it makes freedom possible, since it is through such conditioning that the person is able to come to moral experience, which will eventually allow him to review some of the "obvious facts" that he had interiorized in the course of his moral apprenticeship. Moreover, in the present context of globalization, societies and cultures themselves must inevitably practice sincere dialogue and exchange, based on the co-responsibility of all in regard to the common good of the planet: they must leave aside particular interests to attain the moral values that all are called to share.

Chapter 4: Natural Law and the City

4.1. The person and the common good

84. The person is at the center of the political and social order because he is an end and not a means. The person is a social being by nature, not by choice

or in virtue of a pure contractual convention. In order to flourish as a person, he needs the structure of relations that he forms with other persons. He thus finds himself at the center of a network formed by concentric circles: the family, the sphere of life and work, the neighborhood community, the nation, and finally humanity (78). The person draws from each of these circles the elements necessary for his own growth, and at the same time he contributes to their perfection.

4.4. The norm of natural justice and positive law

92. The norms of natural justice are thus the measures of human relationships prior to the will of the legislator. They are given from the moment that human beings live in society. They express what is naturally just, prior to any legal formulation. The norms of natural justice are expressed in a particular way in the subjective rights of the human person, such as the right to respect for one's own life, the right to the integrity of one's person, the right to religious liberty, the right to freedom of thought, the right to start a family and to educate one's children according to one's convictions, the right to associate with others, the right to participate in the life of the community, etc. These rights, to which contemporary thought attributes great importance, do not have their source in the fluctuating desires of individuals, but rather in the very structure of human beings and their humanizing relations. The rights of the human person emerge therefore from the order of justice that must reign in relations among human beings. To acknowledge these natural rights of man means to acknowledge the objective order of human relations based on the natural law.

CHAPTER IV

Pontifical Academy for Life

Proposal of an Ethical Commitment for Researchers in the Biomedical Field

Introductory Note

The following "manifesto" is published as an appendix to the Final Communiqué of the Nineth General Assembly of the Pontifical Academy for Life. It is a concrete result of the Assembly's deliberations, whose theme this year was "Ethics of biomedical research. For a Christian vision," *offered as an open proposal to be freely supported.*

The invitation for a personal adherence is addressed to all researchers and those involved in research in the biomedical field and also to researchers in bioethics. . . .

Premise

The scientific developments of recent decades have brought about important cultural and social transformations, modifying in a qualitative way many aspects of human life. Indeed, the advance of scientific progress in many sectors has given rise to great hopes of concrete improvements for the life and future of the human person. However, in certain sectors of scientific research problems and/or doubts of an ethical and religious nature have arisen; they have demonstrated unequivocally the real need for constant dialogue/integration between the experimental sciences and the broader human sciences and philosophy in terms of operating in a more ample perspective so that the acquisition of greater knowledge may effectively serve the true good of the human person.

Human life and human nature appear to be realities too complex to be exhaustively evaluated from a single perspective; a multidisciplinary approach therefore appears indispensable for a better understanding of the human being in his integrity and contribute to a meaningful growth of a science that would truly be *for* the human being.

Moreover, such an interdisciplinary dialogue, by re-focusing attention on the centrality of the human person, would make the scientists more aware of the ethical implications of their work, and, conversely, would incite those involved in philosophical and theological anthropology to assume toward the scientists a mission of dialogue, collaboration and practical support, with the mutual intention of developing cognitive and applied tools for the service of the human community.

In this perspective, the reference to human values, and finally, to an anthropological and ethical vision, is an indispensable premise for a correct scientific research, that recognizes the person's responsibility to himself and to others.

In fact, without reference to ethics, science and technology can be used either to kill or to save human lives, to manipulate or to promote, to destroy or to build. It is therefore necessary that, through responsible management, research be addressed toward the true common good, a good that transcends any merely private interest, going beyond the geographical and cultural boundaries of nations and keeping one's vision directed toward the good of future generations.

For science to be really placed at the service of the human being, it is necessary that it goes "beyond matter," intuiting in the corporeal dimension of the individual the expression of a greater spiritual good.

Scientists should understand the human body as the tangible dimension of a unitary personal reality, which is at the same time corporeal and spiritual. The spiritual soul of the human being, although not in itself tangible, it is always the root of his existential and tangible reality, of his relationship with the rest of the world, and consequently, of his specific and inalienable value.

Only such a vision can make scientific research effectively respectful of the human person, considered in his complex corporeal-spiritual unity, every time he/she becomes the object of investigation, with particular reference to those events that constitute the beginning and the end of the individual human life.

For this reason, emerges a strong need to offer to young researchers formative programs that put the accent not only on the scientific preparation, but also on the acquisition of the fundamental notions of anthropology and ethics. The expression of such programs could, then, crystallize in the elaboration of a true and proper *Deontological Code* for researchers, to which each researcher could safely refer in his work, and which, at the same time, would represent a sign of hope and commitment for a truly "humanized" medicine in the new millennium.

A first indication of the way to take, might concern the manner in which the researchers should behave and the norms they should observe in order to direct their research toward the objective just recalled above. It is our desire to propose such ethical indications, to which we firmly adhere, to all others who are involved in the world of biomedical research; somehow, they delineate the principal features of the researcher's "moral personality."

Commitment

— I commit myself to adhere to a methodology of research characterized by scientific rigor and a high quality of the information that is furnished.

— I will not take part in research projects in which I could be subject of a conflict of interests, from the personal, professional or economic point of view.

— I recognize that science and technology must be at the service of the human person, fully respecting his dignity and rights.

— I recognize and respect all researches and their applications which are based on the principle of "moral goodness" and referring to the correct vision of the corporeal and spiritual dimensions of the human being.

— I recognize that every human being, from the first moment of his existence (process of fertilization) up to the moment of his natural death, is to be guaranteed the full and unconditional respect due to every human person by virtue of his peculiar dignity.

— I recognize, because of my duty to safeguard human life and health, the usefulness and the obligation of a serious and responsible experimentation on animals, carried out according to determined ethical guidelines, before applying new diagnostic and therapeutic methodologies to human beings. I also recognize that the passage from the experiments with animals to the clinical experimental stage (on man) should take place only when the evidences resulting from the experiments with animals sufficiently demonstrate the harmlessness or the acceptability of the possible harms and risks that such experiments might involve.

— I recognize the legitimacy of clinical experiments on the human being, but only under precise conditions, including, in the first place, the safeguarding of the life and physical integrity of human beings who are involved. Then, there is the need that the experiments be always preceded by proper, correct and complete information regarding the significance and developments of the same experiments. I will treat each person who submits to an experiment as a free and responsible subject and never as a mere means to achieve other ends. I will never let a person be involved in an experiment unless he/she has given his/her free and informed consent.

PONTIFICAL ACADEMY FOR LIFE AND THE WORLD
FEDERATION OF CATHOLIC MEDICAL ASSOCIATIONS

International Congress on "Life-Sustaining Treatments and Vegetative State: Scientific Advances and Ethical Dilemmas"

Joint Statement on the Vegetative State

April 18, 2004

At the conclusion of four days of study and intense debate in the course of the International Congress "Life-Sustaining Treatments and Vegetative State. Scientific Advances and Ethical Dilemmas" (Rome, March 17-20, 2004), after listening to the presentations of several eminent scholars in the field who evaluated the question from scientific, anthropological and ethical perspectives, and after reflection on the message of the Holy Father to participants in the Congress, the World Federation of Catholic Medical Associations (FIAMC) and the Pontifical Academy for Life offer to everyone employed in health services and to society at large the following.*

Scientific and Ethical Problems Related to the Vegetative State

1. Vegetative State (VS) is a state of unresponsiveness, currently defined as a condition marked by: a state of vigilance, some alternation of sleep/wake cycles, absence of signs of awareness of self and surroundings, lack of behavioral responses to stimuli from the environment, maintenance of autonomic and other brain functions.

---

*   This paragraph is an unofficial translation of the Italian.

2. VS must be clearly distinguished from: encephalic death, coma, "locked-in" syndrome, minimally conscious state. VS cannot be simply equated with cortical death either, considering that in VS patients islands of cortical tissue which may even be quite large can continue functioning.

3. In general, VS patients do not require any technological support in order to maintain their vital functions.

4. VS patients cannot in any way be considered terminal patients, since their condition can be stable and enduring.

5. VS diagnosis is still clinical in nature and requires careful and prolonged observation, carried out by specialized and experienced personnel using specific assessment standardized for VS patients in an optimum-controlled environment. Medical literature, in fact, shows diagnostic errors in a substantially high proportion of cases. For this reason, when needed, all available modern technologies should be used to substantiate the diagnosis.

6. Modern neuroimaging techniques have demonstrated the persistence of cortical activity and response to certain kinds of stimuli, including painful stimuli, in VS patients. Although it is not possible to determine the subjective quality of such perceptions, some elementary discriminatory processes between meaningful and neutral stimuli seem to be nevertheless possible.

7. No single investigation method available today allows us to predict, in individual cases, who will recover and who will not among VS patients.

8. Until today, statistical prognostic indexes regarding VS have been obtained from studies quite limited as to number of cases considered and duration of observation. Therefore, the use of misleading terms like "permanent" referred to VS should be discouraged, by indicating only the cause and duration of VS.

9. We acknowledge that every human being has the dignity of a human person, without any discrimination based on race, culture, religion, health conditions or socio-economic conditions. Such a dignity, based on human nature itself, is a permanent and intangible value that cannot depend on specific circumstances of life and cannot be subordinated to anyone's judgment.

We recognize the search for the best possible quality of life for every human being as an intrinsic duty of medicine and society, but we believe that it cannot and must not be the ultimate criterion used to judge the value of a human being's life.

We acknowledge that the dignity of every person can also be expressed in the practice of autonomous choices; however, personal autonomy can never justify decisions or actions against one's own life or that of others: in fact, the exercise of freedom is impossible outside of life.

10. Based on these premises, we feel the duty to state that VS patients are human persons, and as such, they need to be fully respected in their fundamental rights. The first of these rights is the right to life and to the safeguard of health. In particular, VS patients have the right to:

— correct and thorough diagnostic evaluation, in order to avoid possible mistakes and to orient rehabilitation in the best way;
— basic care, including hydration, nutrition, warming and personal hygiene;
— prevention of possible complications and monitoring for any possible signs of recovery;
— adequate rehabilitative processes, prolonged in time, favoring the recovery and maintenance of all progress achieved;
— be treated as any other patients with reference to general assistance and affective relationships.

This requires that any decision of abandonment based on a probability judgment be discouraged, considering the insufficiency and unreliability of prognostic criteria available to date. The possible decision of withdrawing nutrition and hydration, necessarily administered to VS patients in an assisted way, is followed inevitably by the patients' death as a direct consequence. Therefore, it has to be considered a genuine act of euthanasia by omission, which is morally unacceptable.

At the same time, we refuse any form of therapeutic obstinacy in the context of resuscitation, which can be a substantial cause of post-anoxic VS.

11. To the rights of VS patients corresponds the duty of health workers, institutions and societies in general to guarantee what is needed for their safeguard, and the allocation of sufficient financial resources and the promotion of scientific research aimed to the understanding of cerebral physiopathology and of the mechanisms on which the plasticity of the central nervous system is based.

12. Particular attention has to be paid to families having one of their members affected by VS. We are sincerely close to their daily suffering, and we reaffirm their right to obtain help from all health workers and full human,

psychological and financial support, which enables them to overcome isolation and feel part of a network of human solidarity.

13. In addition, it is necessary for institutions to organize models of assistance, specialized with reference to the care of these patients (awakening centers and specialized rehabilitation centers), sufficiently spread over the territory. Institutions should also promote the training of competent personnel.

14. VS patients cannot be considered as "burdens" for society; rather, they should be viewed as a "challenge" to implement new and more effective models of health care and of social solidarity.

Moral Reflections on Vaccines Prepared from Cells Derived from Aborted Human Fetuses*

June 5, 2005

The question to be examined is whether it is licit to produce, distribute and use certain vaccines whose manufacture is connected with acts of procured abortion. It concerns vaccines containing live viruses that have been prepared from human cell lines of fetal origin, using tissue from aborted human fetuses as the source of such cells. The best known, and perhaps the most important since is it widely distributed and used almost universally, is the vaccine against rubella (German measles).

Rubella and Its Vaccine

Rubella (German measles)[1] is a viral disease caused by a togavirus of the genus *rubivirus* and is characterized by a maculopapular rash. An infection common in infancy, it is self-limiting and usually benign and has no clinical manifestations in one out of two cases. Nevertheless, the German measles virus is one of the most pathologically infective agents for the embryo and fetus. When the infection is contracted during pregnancy, especially during the first trimester, the risk of fetal infection is very high (around 95 percent). The virus replicates itself in the placenta and infects the fetus, causing the constellation of abnormalities identified as *Congenital Rubella Syndrome*. For example, the severe epidemic of German measles that struck a large part of the United

---

*   This text is an unofficial translation of the Italian.

States in 1964, caused 20,000 cases of congenital rubella,[2] resulting in 11,250 abortions (spontaneous or surgical), 2,100 neonatal deaths, 11,600 cases of deafness, 3,580 cases of blindness and 1,800 cases of mental retardation. It was this epidemic that prompted the development and marketing of a successful vaccine against German measles which would enable an effective prophylaxis against the infection.

The severity of congenital rubella and the handicaps it causes justify universal vaccination against the disease. It is difficult if not impossible to avoid infecting a pregnant woman even if the illness of an infected person is diagnosed on the first day of eruption of the rash. Early immunization of all children (universal vaccination) is therefore an attempt to prevent transmission by suppressing the reservoir of infection represented by unvaccinated children. Such universal vaccination has resulted in a serious decline in the incidence of congenital rubella, with a general incidence reduced to fewer than 5 cases per 100,000 live births. This progress remains fragile nonetheless. In the United States, for example, after a spectacular decline in the incidence of congenital rubella to a few cases annually (fewer than 0.1 per 100,000 live births) a new epidemic surge appeared in 1991, with an incidence that rose to 0.8/100,000. Such waves of resurgence of German measles were also seen in 1997 and 2000. These periodic episodes of recrudescence are evidence that the virus continues to circulate among young adults as a result of insufficient vaccination coverage. This allows a significant proportion of susceptible subjects to remain as the source of periodic epidemics that put unimmunized women of childbearing age at risk. Therefore, reducing congenital rubella to the point of elimination is considered a priority in public health care.

Vaccines Currently Produced Using Human Cell Lines from Aborted Fetuses

To date, there are two human diploid cell lines originally prepared (1964 and 1970) from the tissue of aborted fetuses that are for preparing vaccines based on live attenuated virus. The first is the WI-38 line (Winstar Institute 38) with human diploid lung fibroblasts derived from a female fetus that was aborted because the family felt they already had too many children (G. Sven et al., 1969). It was prepared and developed by Leonard Hayflick in 1964 (L. Hayflick, 1965; G. Sven et al., 1969)[3]; ATCC number CCL-75. WI-38 was used in the preparation of the historic vaccine against German measles RA 27/3 (S. A. Plotkin et al., 1965).[4] The second human cell line is MRC-5 (Medical Research Council 5) (embryonic human lung) (ATCC number CCL-171), with human lung fibroblasts from a fourteen-week male fetus aborted for "psychiatric reasons" from a twenty-seven-year old woman in the United Kingdom. MRC-5 was prepared and developed by J. P. Jacobs in 1966 (J. P. Jacobs et al.,

1970).[5] Other human cell lines have been developed for pharmaceutical needs but are not involved in the vaccines currently available.[6]

The current vaccines that are implicated in using the human cell lines WI-38 and MRC-5 obtained from aborted fetuses are the following:[7]

A) *Live vaccines against rubella*[8]

- the monovalent vaccines against rubella: Meruvax®II (Merck, USA), Rudivax® (Sanofi Pasteur, France), and Ervevax® (RA 27/3) (GlaxoSmithKline, Belgium);
- the combined vaccine MR against rubella and measles: marketed under the names M-R-VAX® II (Merck, USA) and Rudi-Rouvax® (AVP, France);
- the combined vaccine against rubella and mumps marketed under the name Biavax®II (Merck, USA),
- the combined vaccine MMR (*measles, mumps, rubella*) against measles, mumps and rubella, marketed under the name M-M-R® II (Merck, USA), R.O.R.®, Trimovax® (Sanofi Pasteur, France), and Priorix® (GlaxoSmithKline UK).

B) *Other vaccines, also prepared using human cell lines from aborted fetuses:*

- two vaccines against hepatitis A, one produced by Merck (VAQTA), the other one produced by GlaxoSmithKline (HAVRIX), both prepared using MRC-5;
- one vaccine against chicken pox, Varivax®, produced by Merck using WI-38 and MRC-5;
- one vaccine against poliomyelitis, the inactivated polio virus vaccine Poliovax® (Aventis-Pasteur, France) using MRC-5;
- one vaccine against rabies, Imovax®, produced by Aventis Pasteur, harvested from infected human diploid cells of the MRC-5 strain;
- one vaccine against smallpox, AC AM 1000, prepared by Acambis using MRC-5, still under trial.

Posing the Ethical Problem Linked with These Vaccines

From the perspective of preventing viral diseases such as German measles, mumps, measles, chicken pox and hepatitis A, it is clear that perfecting

vaccines effective against such diseases and using them in the fight to eradicate these infections by means of mandatory immunization of every at risk
demographic undoubtedly represents a milestone in man's worldly battle
against infectious and contagious diseases.

However, because these same vaccines are prepared from viruses collected
in the tissue of fetuses that were infected and voluntarily aborted, viruses that
were then attenuated and cultivated from human cell lines which likewise
come from procured abortions, they do not avoid raising important ethical
problems. The need to articulate a moral reflection on the matter in question
emerges primarily from the connection that exists between the preparation
of the above-mentioned vaccines and the procured abortions from which the
biological material necessary for such preparation was obtained.

If someone rejects every form of voluntary abortion of human fetuses,
would he not contradict himself by allowing the use of these vaccines of live
attenuated viruses on their children? Would it not be a case of real (and illicit)
cooperation in evil, even though this evil had been carried out forty years ago?

Prior to considering the specific case we must briefly recall the principles
assumed in classical moral doctrine regarding the problem of cooperation in
evil,[9] a problem that arises every time a moral agent perceives the existence
of connection between his own acts and an evil act committed by others.

The Principle of Licit Cooperation in Evil

First, there is a fundamental distinction between formal and material cooperation. Formal cooperation occurs when the moral agent cooperates with
the immoral action of another while sharing in the latter's evil intention.
On the other hand, when a moral agent cooperates with the immoral action
of another person without sharing in the latter's evil intention, it is a case of
material cooperation.

Material cooperation can be further distinguished as immediate (direct)
or mediate (indirect), depending on whether there is cooperation in carrying
out the evil act as such or whether one acts to create the conditions or to supply the instruments or products that make it possible to carry out the evil act.
Next, on the basis of the "distance" (whether temporal or in terms of material
connection) between the act of cooperation and the evil act carried out by
another, we can distinguish proximate cooperation from remote cooperation.
Immediate material cooperation is always proximate while indirect material
cooperation can be proximate or remote.

Formal cooperation is always morally illicit because it involves a form of
direct and intentional participation in the evil action of another.[10] Material
cooperation can sometimes be licit (based on the conditions of "double

effect" or "indirect voluntary act") but when it assumes the dimensions of immediate material cooperation in a serious attack against human life it must always be considered illicit, given the precious nature of the value at stake.[11]

Classical moral theology makes a further distinction between active (or positive) cooperation in evil and passive (or negative) cooperation in evil. The first refers to performing an act of cooperation in a sinful action carried out by another person; the second to the lack of an act of denouncing or impeding an evil act committed by another, to the degree that there was a moral duty to do what failed to be done.[12] Passive cooperation can also be formal or material, immediate or mediate, proximate or remote. Obviously every type of formal passive cooperation is to be considered illicit but even passive material cooperation should generally be avoided, although it is admitted (by many authors) that there is no strict obligation to avoid it when it would be seriously difficult to do so.

Application to the Use of Vaccines Prepared from Cells Derived from Embryos or Fetuses Aborted Voluntarily

In the specific case under examination, three categories of people are involved in cooperating in evil, namely, the evil represented by the act of a voluntary abortion performed by others: (a) those who prepare the vaccines using human cell lines derived from voluntary abortions; (b) those who participate in the marketing of such vaccines; (c) those who need to use them for reasons of health.

First of all, one must consider morally illicit every form of formal cooperation (sharing the evil intention) in the action of those who have performed a voluntary abortion, which in turn has enabled the retrieval of fetal tissue needed to prepare the vaccines. Therefore, anyone—regardless of the category to which he or she belongs—who cooperates in some way in the performance of a voluntary abortion and shares that intention with the goal of producing the vaccines in question would actually be participating in the very same moral evil as the person who carries out such an abortion. Such participation would likewise occur whenever someone who shares the intention to abort simply refrains from denouncing or opposing such an illicit act (formal passive cooperation), since they have the moral duty to do so.

Whenever there is no such formal sharing in the evil intention of the one who performed the abortion, any form of cooperation would be material with the following stipulations:

With regard to the preparation, distribution and marketing of vaccines produced by using biological material whose origin is connected with cells coming from voluntarily aborted fetuses, it must be stated that, as a matter of principle, such a process is morally illicit since it can actually work toward encouraging other abortions for the sake of producing such vaccines. Still, it must be recognized that, the moral responsibility of the various cooperating agents in the chain of production-distribution-marketing can be different.

Another aspect to consider, however, is the material passive cooperation that is incurred by the producers of these vaccines whenever they do not publicly denounce and reject the original evil act (the voluntary abortion) and do not work together in research and promotion of alternative forms of producing the same vaccines without the moral evil. Such material passive cooperation is also illicit whenever it occurs.

As for the person who needs to use such vaccines for health reasons, it must be specified that, excluding all formal cooperation, doctors or parents who resort to using such vaccines even when they know their origin (voluntary abortion), generally commit a very remote and therefore very weak form of mediate material cooperation in producing an abortion, a mediate material cooperation regarding marketing of cells coming from abortions and immediate cooperation regarding the marketing of vaccines produced from such cells. There is stronger cooperation on the part of authorities and national health systems that accept the use of the vaccines.

What stands out most in this situation, however, is the aspect of passive cooperation. It is up to the faithful and citizens of upright conscience (parents, doctors, etc.) to oppose even to the point of conscientious objection, the ever more widespread attacks against life and the "culture of death" that undergirds them. From this point of view the use of vaccines whose production is connected with procured abortion constitutes at least a mediate remote passive material cooperation with the abortion and an immediate passive material cooperation with their marketing. Moreover, on a cultural level, the use of such vaccines contributes to the creation of a broad social consent to the practices of the pharmaceutical industries that produces them in an immoral manner.

Therefore, doctors and parents have a duty to make use of alternative vaccines[13] (if they exist), exerting pressure on political authorities and healthcare systems to make available other vaccines that are not morally problematic. If necessary, they should invoke conscientious objection[14] to the use of vaccines produced by means of cell lines originating in aborted human fetuses. By the same token, they should oppose by every means (in writing, through various organizations, mass media, etc.) vaccines that do not yet have morally acceptable alternatives, creating pressure for the preparation of alternative vaccines and requesting strict legal oversight of the pharmaceutical industries that produce them.

In the case of diseases against which there are no available alternative vaccines that are morally acceptable, there is a duty to abstain from using these vaccines only if it can be done without causing significant health risks to the children and, indirectly, to the population in general. However if these are exposed to significant health risks, even vaccines that are morally problematic may be used provisionally. The moral reasoning is that the obligation to avoid passive material cooperation does not hold if there is a grave difficulty. Moreover, in such a case, we find a proportionate reason to accept the use of these vaccines where there is danger of encouraging the spread of the pathological agent by not vaccinating children. This is especially true in the case of vaccination against rubella.[15]

In every instance, there remains a moral duty to continue to fight and to employ every licit means of making life difficult for pharmaceutical industries that act without ethical scruples. But the burden of this important battle certainly cannot and should not fall on innocent children and on the health of the population in general—particularly pregnant women.

In summary, it must be reaffirmed that

— there exists a serious duty to use alternative vaccines and to express conscientious objection to those that are morally problematic.

— regarding vaccines for which there are no alternatives, while the duty to fight for the production of other vaccines remains, it is also licit to make use of the former in the meantime to the degree necessary to avoid grave danger not just for one's own children but also, and perhaps especially, for the public health situation in general and especially for pregnant women.

— the lawful use of these vaccines should not be interpreted as a declaration of the lawfulness of their production, marketing and use, but rather as passive (and, in a weaker and more remote sense, also active) material cooperation that is morally justified as an extreme measure by reason of the duty to see to the good of one's own children and of persons coming into contact with them (pregnant women).

— such cooperation happens in a context of moral constraint of the parents' conscience, who must choose between acting contrary to conscience or putting at risk the health of their own children and of the population at large. This is an unjust alternative that must be eliminated as soon as possible.

Notes

1   J. E. Banatvala and D.W.G. Brown, "Rubella," *The Lancet*, 363, no. 9415 (April 3, 2004): 1127-1137.

2   "Rubella," Morbidity and Mortality Weekly Report 13 (1964): 93. S. A. Plotkin, "Virologic Assistance in the Management of German Measles in Pregnancy," JAMA, 190 (October 26, 1964): 265-268.

3   L. Hayflick, "The Limited *In Vitro* Lifetime of Human Diploid Cell Strains,"
     Experimental Cell Research 37:3 (March 1965): 614-636. G. Sven, S. Plotkin, K.
     McCarthy, "Gamma Globulin Prophylaxis; Inactivated Rubella Virus; Production
     and Biological Control of Live Attenuated Rubella Virus Vaccines," *American Journal
     of Diseases of Children* 118:2 (August 1969): 372-381.

     G. Sven, S. Plotkin, K. McCarthy, "Gamma Globulin Prophylaxis; Inactivated
     Rubella Virus; Production and Biological Control of Live Attenuated Rubella Virus
     Vaccines," *American Journal of Diseases of Children* 118:2 (August 1969): 372-381.

4   S. A. Plotkin, D. Cornfeld, Th. H. Ingalls, "Studies of Immunization with Living
     Rubella Virus, Trials in Children with a Strain Coming from an Aborted Fetus,"
     American Journal of Diseases in Children 110:4 (October 1965): 381-389.

5   J. P. Jacobs, C. M. Jones, J. P. Bailie, "Characteristics of a Human Diploid Cell
     Designated MRC-5," *Nature* 277 (July 11, 1970): 168-170.

6   Two other permanent human cell lines, HEK 293 an aborted fetal cell line from pri-
     mary human embryonic kidney cells transformed by sheared adenovirus type 5 (the
     fetal kidney material was probably obtained from an aborted fetus in 1972), and PER.
     C6, a fetal cell line created using retinal tissue from a baby aborted at eighteen weeks
     of gestation, have been developed for the pharmaceutical manufacture of adenovi-
     rus vectors (for gene therapy). They have not been involved in making any of the
     attenuated live viruses vaccines presently in use because of their capacity to develop
     tumorigenic cells in the recipient. However some vaccines against the Ebola virus,
     still at the developmental stage, (Crucell, N.V. and the Vaccine Research Center of
     the National Institutes of Health's Allergy and Infectious Diseases, NIAID), HIV
     (Merck), influenza (MedImmune, Sanofi Pasteur), and Japanese encephalitis (Crucell
     N.V. and Rhein Biotech N.V.) are prepared using PER.C6® cell line (Crucell N.V.,
     Leiden, The Netherlands).

7   There are some alternative vaccines against these various infectious diseases that are
     prepared using animal cells or tissue and are therefore ethically acceptable. Their
     availability depends on the country in question. In the particular case of the United
     States, there are currently no options for the vaccination against rubella, chicken-
     pox and hepatitis A other than the vaccines offered by Merck, prepared using the
     human cell lines WI-38 and MRC-5. There is a vaccine against smallpox prepared
     with the Vero cell line (derived from the kidney of an African green monkey),
     ACAM2000 (Acambis-Baxter) (a second-generation smallpox vaccine, stockpiled,
     not approved in the US), which therefore offers an alternative to the Acambis
     1000. There are alternative vaccines against mumps (Mumpsvax, Merck, measles
     (Attenuvax, Merck), rabies (RabAvert, Chiron therapeutics), prepared from chicken
     embryos (although serious allergies have occurred with such vaccines), poliomyeli-
     tis (IPOL, Aventis-Pasteur, prepared with monkey kidney cells) and smallpox (a
     third-generation smallpox vaccine MVA, Modified Vaccinia Ankara, Acambis-
     Baxter). In Europe and Japan, there are other vaccines available against rubella and
     hepatitis A, produced using non-human cell lines. The Kitasato Institute produces
     four vaccines against rubella, called Takahashi, TO-336 and Matuba, prepared with

cells from rabbit kidney, and one (Matuura) prepared with cells from a quail embryo. The Chemo-sero-therapeutic Research Institute Kaketsuken produces another vaccine against hepatitis A, called Ainmugen, prepared with cells from monkey kidney. The only remaining problem is with the vaccine Varivax® against chicken pox, for which there is no alternative.

8   The vaccine against rubella using the strain Wistar RA27/3 of live attenuated rubella virus, adapted and propagated in WI-38 human diploid lung fibroblasts, is at the center of the current controversy regarding the morality of the use of vaccines prepared with the help of human cell lines coming from aborted fetuses.

9   D. M. Prummer OP, "*De cooperatione ad malum.*" In *Manuale Theologiae Moralis secundum Principia S. Thomae Aquinatis*, Tomus I, (Friburgi Brisgoviae: Herder & Co., 1923), Pars I, Tract. IX, Caput III, no. 2, pp. 429-434. K. H. Peschke, "Cooperation in the Sins of Others." In *Christian Ethics: Moral Theology in the Light of Vatican II; Volume 1: General Moral Theology* (Alcester, Warwickshire: C. Goodliffe Neale Ltd., 1986), 320-324.

10 A. Fisher, "Cooperation in Evil," *Catholic Medical Quarterly* (1994): 15-22. D. Tettamanzi, "Cooperazione." In *Dizionario di Bioetica*, edited by S. Leone and S. Privitera (Istituto Siciliano di Bioetica, EDB-ISB: 1994), 194-198. L. Melina, "La cooperazione con azioni moralmente cattive contra la vita umana." In *Commentario Interdisciplinare alia "Evangelium Vitae,"* edited by E. Sgreccia and Ramon Luca Lucas. (Libreria Editrice Vaticana: 1997), 467-490. E. Sgreccia, *Manuale di Bioetica: Volume 1.* (Milan: Vita e Pensiero, 1999), 362-363.

11 Cf. John Paul II, *Evangelium Vitae*, no. 74.

12 CCC, no. 1868.

13 The alternative vaccines in question are those that are prepared by means of cell lines which are not of human origin; for example, the Vero cell line (from monkeys; D. Vinnedge), the kidney cells of rabbits or monkeys, or the cells of chicken embryos. However, it should be noted that serious forms of allergy have occurred with some of the vaccines prepared in this way. The use of recombinant DNA technology could lead to the development of new vaccines in the near future which will no longer require the use of cultures of human diploid cells for the attenuation of the virus and its growth since such vaccines will not be prepared on the basis of an attenuated virus but from the genome of the virus and from the antigens thus developed (G. C. Woodrow, W. M. McDonnell and F. K. Askari). Some experimental studies have already been done using vaccines developed from DNA derived from the genome of the German measles virus. Moreover, some Asian researchers are trying to use the Varicella virus as a vector for the insertion of genes that codify the viral antigens of Rubella. These studies are still in a preliminary phase and the refinement of vaccine preparations which can be used in clinical practice will require a long period of time and will be quite costly. D. Vinnedge, "The Smallpox Vaccine," *The National Catholic Bioethics Quarterly*, 2:1 (Spring 2000): 12. G. C. Woodrow, "An Overview of Biotechnology as Applied to Vaccine Development." In *New Generation Vaccines*, edited by G. C. Woodrow, M. M. Levine (New York and Basel: Marcel

Dekker Inc., 1990), 32-37. W. M. McDonnell, F. K. Askari, "Immunization," *JAMA* 278:2 (December 10, 1997): 2000-2007, see 2005-2006.

14   Such a duty may, as a consequence, lead to invoking an "objection of conscience" when the action recognized as illicit is an act permitted or even encouraged by the laws of the country and poses a threat to human life. The Encyclical Letter *Evangelium Vitae* underlined this "obligation to oppose" the laws which permit abortion or euthanasia "by conscientious objection" (no. 73).

15   This is particularly true in the case of vaccination against German measles, because of the danger of Congenital Rubella Syndrome. This could occur, causing grave congenital malformations in the fetus, when a pregnant woman enters into contact, however brief, with children who have not been immunized and are carriers of the virus. In this case, the parents who did not accept the vaccination of their own children become responsible for the malformations in question and for the subsequent abortion of fetuses when they have been discovered to be malformed.

PONTIFICAL ACADEMY FOR LIFE

The Pre-Implantation Human Embryo: Scientific Aspects and Bioethical Considerations[*]

June 8, 2006

Foreword

On February 27 and 28, 2006, the Pontifical Academy for Life, on the occasion of its twelfth Assembly, organized a Scientific Congress entitled "The Pre-Implantation Human Embryo," with presentations by embryologists, philosophers, ethicists and jurists, to shed light on the identity and anthropological value of the human being in this earliest phase of its existence.

The interest and timeliness already present for years in the bioethical debate regarding the human embryo has been further intensified in recent times on account of the problems raised by the possibility of freezing the fertilized ovum (actually an embryo in the earliest phase of development), by the practice of experimenting on the embryo itself, by the use of the so called *morning after pill*, as well as by the spread of pre-implantation diagnosis.

As is customary, the Proceedings of the Congress include all the presentations made in their entirety with the necessary documentation. We have, however, thought it useful to publish an organic synthesis of the subject in

---

[*]   This text is an unofficial translation of the Italian.

comprehensible language as a service to those who need to have the essential content and also to meet the need of informing the wider public.

And so this synthesis can remain relevant beyond the specific circumstances that brought it about, to the benefit of providing ever more updated information about essential themes that touch on life, reaching ever more deeply into both the political debate and the catechesis of the Church.

Msgr. Elio Sgreccia
President

Msgr. Ignacio Carrasco De Paula
Chancellor

Introduction[1]

The question of prenatal human life has been and remains one of the most discussed themes in the scientific realm and in ethical, political and legal debate.

Among the liveliest periods for this topic we must recall the debates surrounding campaigns in favor of the legalization of abortion in the 1970s, those which followed the employment of artificial fertilization beginning in the 1980s, and, more recently, those born out of the possibility of using embryonic stem cells for therapeutic purposes and/or to obtain a new human life through means other than fertilization such as cloning.

These periods have defined a profound cultural change in the perception of prenatal life and have brought to light the possibility of using the human embryo in the phase before implantation as a valuable technological tool.

Scientific Aspects[2]

The Embryo Before Implantation

The term "pre-implantation embryo"[3] refers to the embryo in its development from the zygote to what precedes implantation in the mother's womb, at which point the embryo is termed a blastocyst. During this period, which includes important stages of development and cellular differentiation, the embryo travels along the female genital tract implanting itself in the uterus, establishing an intense *molecular dialogue* with the maternal environment.

The Process of Fertilization[4]

What science currently knows about the beginning of human life and the first phases of its embryonic development is the fruit of the gains made by developmental biology, which brings together the insights of embryology, physiology and anatomy with the most recent data supplied by research in the area of developmental biology (molecular, cellular and immunological).

The Protagonists in the Process of Fertilization:
The Spermatozoon and the Ovum

Fertilization in mammals is a complex, highly regulated process unfolding over various stages that occur in a necessary order. The protagonists of the process of fertilization are the mature male and female gametes, which possess half of the complete set of chromosomes. They blend together to create the beginnings of a new individual with a genetically complete set of forty-six chromosomes derived from both parents.

In humans, the mature male and female gametes, the *spermatozoa* and *ova* respectively, derive from prior elements, the *primordial germinal cells*, which undergo a complex process of maturation and differentiation called *gameto-genesis*. The maturation enables halving the chromosomal inheritance of the germinal cells by means of a special process of nuclear division called *meiosis* and the subsequent morphological maturation of the gametes. In the male, meiotic divisions begin at puberty, while in the female the maturation of the gametes begins earlier, during fetal life.

The *mature spermatozoon* of a mammal is a highly specialized epithelial cell, elongated in form, whose structure and definitive organization enable the spermatozoon to penetrate the egg cell. Two segments are differenti-ated in the mature spermatozoon: the *head* that encloses the nucleus capped by a vesicle called *acrosome*, and the *tail*, which is endowed with structures enabling motion.

The length of the human spermatozoon including the tail, is about fifty microns; the distance the spermatozoa must travel from the testicles to the tubes to reach the ovulum is more than seven meters or more than 100,000 times their length. During this long journey through the male and then the female genital tracts (vagina, uterus and oviduct), the spermatozoon under-goes basic maturational and selective processes in order to fertilize the oocyte efficiently and specifically. Of particular relevance is the so-called *capacitation process*, which involves removing from the spermatozoon's outermost mem-brane a glycoprotein called *acrosome stabilizing factor*. Capacitation initiates *the activation processes of the spermatozoon* that allow encounter and contact with the oocyte to occur. The movement of the spermatozoa through the female genital tract is associated with both physical and chemical stimuli that allow them to be directed to the oocyte without veering off course. If fertiliza-tion does not occur, the spermatozoon survives along the female genital tract only a few days.

Mature oocytes are very large cells compared not only to the spermatozoa but also to other types of bodily cells; in humans the oocyte can reach 150 microns. All the matter necessary for the start of growth and development of the embryo must be present in the oocyte (amino acids and proteins, ribosomes and transport RNA, morphogenetic factors, etc.). Within this voluminous mass of cytoplasm is found the nucleus whose meiotic maturation is completed only if the spermatozoon penetrates the oocyte. The egg cell is covered by a thick glycoprotein membrane called the *zona pellucida* (ZP), which is essential to the species-specific bonding of the spermatozoon (spermatozoa of the human species recognize only oocytes of their own species through the ZP) and for the first stages of the pre-implanted embryo's development and differentiation, during which it undergoes biochemical and structural changes.

At the moment of expulsion from the ovary, the oocyte in mammals is surrounded by a layer of cells called the corona radiata, which is made up of follicular cells. The oocyte extruded from the ovary is caught in the canal of the tube (also called the oviduct) which it awaits a possible meeting with the spermatozoon.

The Stages of the Fertilization Process

Fertilization is the fundamental event that initiates the development of a new organism and implies a highly coordinated series of events and cellular interactions that enable the meeting of spermatozoon and oocyte to form a new activated cell, the *zygote* or *single cell embryo, a new organism of the human species*.

If fertilization does not occur, the spermatozoon and oocyte degrade rapidly; hence, these two highly differentiated cells cannot live alone for long.

In describing the events that characterize the fertilization process, a distinction can be drawn between the stages that precede the *fusion of the gametes* and the modifications that follow immediately, preparing the embryo for its first cellular division. The events of the fertilization process can therefore be organized in three main stages:

1. The *acrosomal reaction* that enables the spermatozoon to pass through the layers that surround the oocyte and the bond to the zona pellucida.
2. The *fusion of the gametes* or *syngamy that determines the activation of the fertilized oocyte's metabolism by initiating embryonic development* and the *cortical reaction* to regulate the entrance of the spermatozoon into the oocyte.
3. The *formation of male and female pronuclei and the beginning of the mitotic process of segmentation*.

Recent experimental studies have made it possible to individuate the complex molecular interaction between the spermatozoon and the egg cell, highlighting the precision and elegance of these mechanisms.

1. The *acrosomal reaction* consists in releasing from the acrosomal vesicle of the spermatozoon lytic enzymes capable of dispersing the cells of the corona radiata. One of these enzymes, hyaluronidase (pH-20) digests the hyaluronic acid found in the extracellular matrix surrounding the cell while the *corona-dispersing enzyme* disrupts contact among the cells. These enzymes enable the spermatozoon to open a path to reach the zona pellucida (ZP). On the surface of the ZP are found particular proteins that bond with specific receptors found on the surface of the spermatozoon. The fusion of spermatozoon and ZP induces activation and release of acrosin, another acrosomal enzyme that facilitates the penetration of the spermatozoon through the zona pellucida by creating a channel that allows it to reach the plasma membrane that encloses the oocyte.

   The spermatozoon that penetrates the zona pellucida fastest bonds and fuses with the oocyte's plasma membrane; the equatorial segment of the head of the spermatozoon attaches itself to the surface of the oocyte by means of a receptor-bond mechanism and only the head of the spermatozoon is embedded in the egg cell. The nucleus and centriole[5] of the spermatozoon are incorporated into the oocyte.[6]

2. Gamete fusion is an irreversible process that signals the beginning of a new organism: the zygote or single cell embryo. The first consequence of gamete fusion is the variation in the ionic composition of the fertilized oocyte and, in particular, the sudden and temporary increase in the intracellular concentration of Ca2+, which causes an ionic wave called a *calcium wave*[7]; this signals the beginning of the *activation* of the zygote and embryonic development, doing away with the inhibiting phenomena that had caused a reduced metabolic activity in the oocyte after its expulsion from the ovary. In fact, the metabolism of the oocyte abates and results in the death of the cell whenever fertilization does not occur within twelve to twenty-four hours after ovulation.

Thus Begins the Development of a New Individual Presenting the Genetic and Molecular Pattern of the Human Species

The increased concentration of cytoplasmic Ca2+ induces what is called the *cortical reaction*, which, through a hardening of the *zona pellucida* and the inactivation of the receptor molecules for the spermatozoa, impedes the bonding and entry of other spermatozoa (polyspermia) and enables the protection of the new individual whose life cycle has begun.

Gender determination of the new individual occurs with the penetration of the oocyte by the spermatozoon: the zygote will be male if the fertilizing spermatozoon carries the Y sex chromosome and female if it carries the X sex chromosome.

3. *Formation of the pronuclei* occurs at the same time. Within a few hours of the spermatozoon's penetration, the nucleus originating in the female completes its maturation and is called, in this phase, *female pronucleus*. Meanwhile, the male nucleus which, at the moment of its introduction into the oocyte, was silent, that is, inert to the mechanisms of transcription which enable reading and translating the genetic information contained in the nucleus, is transformed into a functionally active nucleus, the *male pronucleus*, by means of profound biochemical and structural modifications which prepare it to interact with molecular elements originating in the mother. During this so-called *pronuclear phase*, the two pronuclei approach the center of the cell and as they move toward each other their genetic information is read in order to guide the development. Today, we know many of the genes active at this stage of the new human genome, some of which play a key role in the successive development of the embryo.

The Information of the New Genome Therefore Guides Embryonic Development from the Single-Cell Stage

Around the fifteenth hour after fertilization, the two pronuclei meet and their envelopes are broken open, causing the paternal and maternal chromosomes to mingle, which is necessary to prepare the single-cell embryo for its first cellular division.

It is important to emphasize that, as has been described, the coordinated activation of the new genome precedes and does not depend upon the meeting of the pronuclei and the apposition of the chromosomes.

At this point the centrosome originating from the father divides and, beginning with the pronuclei, the mitotic spindle is arranged; the duplicated male and female chromosomes group together at the equator of the common mitotic spindle to prepare for the first cellular division. At the end of this first cellular division two cells are formed, each endowed with a copy of the whole genome, and they remain united with each other to form a *two-cell embryo*. In mammals, the diploid genome is enclosed in its own nuclear envelope for the first time at the two-cell stage.

From the moment of gamete fusion, through a complete and coordinated exchange, the elements originating from the father and the mother contribute to the activity of a new organism at the single-cell level.

The Constitution of the Axes of the Development of the Embryo[8]

Recent complex and refined experiments in developmental biology have shown that that the axes of embryonic development begin to be defined in the minutes and hours that follow the gamete fusion. These studies are very important because, until a few years ago, it was held that precocious human embryos were "bundles of featureless cells" until the moment of formation of the embryonic disk, the structure that defines the general design of the body and begins the shaping of the various organs and tissues.

This conviction was supported by a variety of evidence: above all, the oocytes of mammals, unlike many other animal species, do not display a clear polarity evincing the definition of a pattern of bodily development. Moreover, the cells that make up the embryo in the first stages of division are totipotent, undifferentiated cells capable of developing into any type of embryonic or extra-embryonic cell whatsoever (if, for example, the cells of a mouse embryo are separated at the two-cell stage, each of them will form two normal mice), endowing them with an impressive ability to compensate for damage. Finally, only 15 percent of the cells in the blastocyst (those residing in the internal cellular mass) contribute to the formation of the general bodily plan, while the others are involved in the formation of extra-embryonic appendages.

Recent experiments on mammals seem to have revolutionized this paradigm by showing that the position of the second polar globule or the spermatozoon's point of entry into the oocyte and the form of the fertilized oocyte are key elements influencing the orientation of the axis along which the first cellular division occurs. This, in turn, permits prediction of the structuration and polarization of the blastocyst.

It has further been demonstrated that the orientation of the second cellular division can influence the fate of the resulting cells: the precursors of the embryo derive mainly from one cell while the precursors contributing to the formation of the placenta (extra-embryonic tissue) derive mostly from the other.

Finally, studies on mouse chimeras have demonstrated that blastomeres can already be differentiated among themselves at the embryonic stage of four cells, thus already losing their totipotence at this stage.

These results confirm that, if the axes of embryonic development and their cellular fate begin to be defined rather early, then there is no room for the idea that early embryos are a "bundle of featureless cells."[9]

This evidence can seem to contradict the demonstrated cellular totipotence and the plasticity of development in early embryos; actually, these properties do not imply indeterminacy in growth but rather reveal the possibility of compensating for damage or errors in the embryonic program of evolution. The early human embryo is a harmonious system in which all the potentially independent parts work together to form a single organism.

The recent discoveries about early determination of the axes of embryonic development and cell fate also reveal how potentially harmful interventions on the early embryo can be for its further development. It raises questions, for example, about the advisability of employing certain technologies of assisted reproduction (such as ICSI, *intracytoplasmic sperm injection*), inasmuch as they have the potential to destroy the delicate processes that permit the establishment of bodily axes. Genetic tests carried out on the embryo prior to implantation (pre-implantation genetic diagnosis), in which two cells are removed from an embryo at the stage of only eight cells, is likewise shown to be an area for real concern.[10]

The Development of the Embryo Prior to Implantation in the Mother's Uterus[11]

Beginning with the formation of the zygote, during a period of around five days the embryo undergoes a series of cellular divisions regulated in a particular manner under the control of a large number of genes. This period of cellular proliferation is called *segmentation*. While the embryo is being segmented it is transported through the fallopian tube, moved along by the cilia, and enters the uterus.

The divisions of segmentation are not accompanied by cell growth and so they subdivide the large zygote into many smaller cells called *blastomeres*. The dimensions of the embryo as a whole do not change and it remains enclosed in the zona pellucida that protects it and keeps it from adhering to the tube walls. In mice, the rate of segmentation is controlled by the PED (*pre-implantation embryo development*) gene, also found in humans.

The result of these divisions is the formation of the *morula*, from the Latin *morum*, meaning mulberry, so called because of its resemblance to that fruit. In this phase, the embryo is composed of loosely connected cells. At the stage of eight to sixteen cells, the morula undergoes the process of *compaction*, when the cells suddenly draw together to form a compact sphere while undergoing profound metabolic and structural changes.

The embryo is held tightly together by *tight connections* that form among the exterior cells of the sphere, while the interior cells communicate among themselves by means of particular structures called *gap junctions* which enable the exchange of substances and molecules to regulate and coordinate cellular division in this phase of development. The cells that make up the outermost layer are destined to become the *trophoblast* which will form the tissue of the chorion, the embryonic part of the placenta, while the more interior cells are destined to form the ICM (*internal cell mass*) that gives rise to the properly embryonic tissue and the associated extra-embryonic tissues (the vitelline sac, the amnios and the allantoides).

At first the morula does not have an internal cavity, even though the majority of the cells are located on the outer layer and only a few are on the inner one. At the fourth day of development the morula is transformed into a blastocyst that does exhibit a large cavity called the blastocoel and the internal cellular mass appears as a small compact mass of cells gathered on one site of the cavity adhering to the cells of the trophoblast (arranged to form a thin, single layer epithelium).[12] The formation of the cavity in the blastocyst and the formation of the cellular polarity are guided by the expression of specific genetic sets comprising the *tight junction gene family*, the *NaK-ATPase gene family* and the *aquaporin gene family*.

The important morphological and differential changes taking place in this period are connected with metabolic and energetic variations. The substances providing energy to the developing embryo vary over the different phases of this period, reflecting the organism's differing energetic needs.

Processes of apoptosis, programmed cell death needed to remove genetically anomalous or mutated cells and to play a protective role can also be observed during the development of the pre-implantation embryo. The rate of apoptosis (particularly elevated at the blastocyst stage) cannot exceed a certain level without destroying the embryonic homeostasis thereby ending development.

Growth factors, hormones, amino acids, carbohydrates and proteins produced by the pre-implantation embryo regulate its development, reaffirming the leading role the embryo has in guiding its own development. An important example of embryonic self-regulation is the PAF (platelet activating factor), a soluble factor synthesized immediately after fertilization and persisting until the implant phase in all species of mammals studied to date. The release of PAF plays a relevant part in stimulating the embryo's metabolism, in the progress of the cellular cycle and in the embryo's migration while also bringing about important changes in the maternal environment, as will be explained below.

During the period prior to implantation the embryo is carried from the tube, also called the oviduct, to the uterus. On the seventh day after fertilization the blastocyst is implanted in the uterine mucosa (endometrium).

The Embryo-Maternal Dialogue and Preparation for Implantation[13]

The tube where mature gametes meet has an active role in the maturation of spermatozoa, in the process of fertilization, in the development of the early embryo and in its transportation toward the uterus. The oviduct is therefore no simple canal of passage but a reproductive organ whose secretional and transportational activities are needed for the early events of reproduction. Along with the uterus, the tube supplies a series of molecules needed to create the most adequate environment for embryonic development. The embryo, for its part, produces hormones and other important molecules in its interaction with the maternal environment. This *molecular communication* between mother and pre-implantation embryo is called *cross talk*.

Since the embryo is covered by the zona pellucida until just before the implantation, all the maternal-embryonic signals must pass through this thick glyco-protein membrane. As embryonic development proceeds, proteins secreted by the oviduct and uterus are incorporated into the zona pellucida along with embryonic proteins, altering their morphological and biochemical properties. The zona pellucida is like a mailbox that receives and selects these messages. Depending on their biochemical properties they will either be incorporated into the zona pellucida, pass through it or be rejected by it.

The tube's epithelium supplies proteins, cytokines and growth factors in a transudate made up of serum and other fluids but also leaves behind protein through an intense biosynthetic process regulated by estrogens. One of the proteins synthesized *de novo* in the tube is the glycoprotein OSP (*oviductal secretory glycoprotein*), which is conserved in many different mammalian species. This protein seems to play an important role in improving capacitation and the efficiency of the bond and penetration of the spermatozoon in the oocyte and in influencing embryonic development.

Additionally, there are secretions of protease inhibitors whose role is to protect the integrity first of the oocyte and then of the embryo and to promote embryonic development, for example, by improving the rate of segmentation and preventing the degradation of the embryo. The epithelium of the maternal uterus also produces a number of important factors for embryonic development, such as the *granulocyte-macrophage colony stimulating factor* which, stimulated by estrogens, seems to regulate the number of cells in the internal cellular mass.

This intense biochemical conversation undertaken with the mother prepares the embryo for implantation. The blastocyst reaches the uterus by the third or fourth day of development, on the fifth day exits the zona pellucida that had protected the developing embryo and prevented it from adhering to the tubal walls. This process is called *hatching*. The blastocyst can thus freely adhere to the endometrium, usually in the upper part of back wall of the uterus, and so begin the *process of implantation*. The process of implantation is subject to endocrine regulation by the estrogens and progesterone produced in the ovaries. The hormones of the ovaries control the female menstrual cycle that, through a series of morphological and biochemical processes, prepares the uterus for the implantation of the blastocyst. The uterine mucosa (endometrium) is made receptive by these hormones for a limited period termed the *window of implantation,* outside of which the endometrium is unable to receive the embryo and may even be hostile to it.

The uterus is readied for implantation by the synthesis of steroid-sensitive proteins, enzymes such as peptidase, glycosidase and esterase are used to disgregate the zona pellucida and modify the endometrium and trophoblast to facilitate implantation; other proteins are employed to protect the fetus from the mother's immune reaction (immune tolerance) and to regulate embryonic development, especially growth factors (EGF, TGF, IGF, FGF), the *leukemia inhibitory factor* (LIF) and the *corticotropin releasing hormone* (CRH), whose expression is induced by factors originating in the embryo.

The embryo for its part, immediately after implantation or very likely even before, secretes hormones, cytokines, growth factors, angiogenic factors, apoptical factors and adhesion molecules which function as recognition signals to the mother for accurate preparation for implantation. *Human chorionic gonadotrophine* (HCG) is also produced which alters the maternal organism and is expressed at high levels during the window of implantation; as well as the PAF factor which is involved with immunosuppression in the mother.

Another important factor which may influence the embryo's transportation through the tube and its implantation in the uterus is the uterus' ability to contract, which is controlled of ovarian hormones.

Implantation begins with apposition and entwining of the microvilli of the uterine epithelium with those of the trophoblast. Their interaction requires reorganization of the cells, which is mediated by a family of transmembrane receptors called *integrins,* which are expressed by both the mother and the embryo.

The phases of apposition and adhesion are also characterized by a complex biochemical dialogue between embryo and uterus, consisting in an exchange of chemokines, interleukins, adhesion molecules, chemotactic factors and lymphocyte activation factors.

The intense and complex interaction between mother and embryo is extremely important for proper development of the pre-implantation embryo: *the mother-child relationship that is begun at the moment of fertilization will continue throughout the course of the pregnancy thanks to biochemical, hormonal and immunological communication.* This indivisible relationship will mark the later development of the individual and there will be an enduring "memory" of the biological contact and channels of communication that exist during pregnancy.

Prenatal Diagnosis and Pre-Implantation Diagnosis[14]

Prenatal diagnosis broadly includes all those methods of diagnosis before birth that seek to evaluate the well-being of the fetus and to identify any possible pathologies. By this definition, prenatal diagnosis includes all the technologies that make it possible to identify illnesses due to anomalies of the chromosomes, the mutation of one or more genes (polygenic syndromes) or other cases of congenital diseases or deformities whether infectious or determined by teratogenic agents although the main indication for recourse to a prenatal diagnosis is the identification of genetic diseases. The various technologies are classified according to the type of diagnostic information they provide or on the basis of the degree of invasiveness.

In tandem with the development of prenatal diagnosis, the progress made by fetal medicine has opened a new area of extremely promising research, the fetal therapy that has made it possible to resolve a number of diseases by treating the embryo in the same way as a patient already born or an adult. Unfortunately, however, most of the diseases that can be diagnosed remain without therapeutic treatment, thus creating an imbalance between the ability to diagnose and the possibility of effective therapies. This limitation has given rise to questions about the goal sought by recourse to prenatal diagnosis, bearing in mind as well the associated risks.

Invasive Prenatal Diagnosis

Invasive technologies involve obtaining fetal cells via the amniotic cavity for analysis. Among technologies that are already entrenched we might mention chorionic villus sampling, performed between the tenth and fourteenth weeks of gestation, and analysis of amniotic fluid, performed at the fifteenth or sixteenth weeks of gestation. Less common methods include cordocentesis, normally carried out after the eighteenth week of gestation and early amniocentesis, performed between the eleventh and fourteenth weeks of gestation.

The invasiveness of these technologies for obtaining samples is responsible for an elevated *risk* of losing the fetus (for villocentesis from 1-3 percent and for amniocentesis from 0.5-1.0 percent) and a good percentage of premature births. Earlier diagnoses are associated with a greater risk of spontaneous abortion which later ones have the disadvantage of requiring ten to fourteen days from sampling to providing results in the more advanced stages of prenatal development.

Some 190,000 amniocenteses are performed annually in the USA, around 80,000 in France while in Italy some 100,000 were performed in 2003 alone. Considering the risk of abortion connected with the invasiveness of the technique, we can estimate that, in Italy in the course of a year, between 500 and 1000 pregnancies of healthy babies end in abortion due to the technique. These data should not be overlooked when considering that recourse to ever earlier prenatal diagnoses is becoming part of the normal process of monitoring pregnancy even in the absence of a clear medical indication.

It has recently been demonstrated that the invasiveness of these diagnostic tests causes noteworthy fetal stress and suffering. Obtaining amniotic fluid or a fetal blood sample changes the composition of the liquid itself and ultrasound reveals that the fetus "recoils" and its cardiac rhythm increases at the moment of sampling.

Non-Invasive Prenatal Diagnosis

For some time now, in order to eliminate the quota of risks linked to the invasiveness of prenatal technologies, there have been attempts to develop non-invasive approaches by drawing a sample of the mother's blood (in which free-floating embryonic cells or fetal DNA can be isolated by using specific membrane or cytoplasmic markers). From these samples one can then isolate embryonic/fetal cells on which cytogenic testing can be done to reveal the possible presence of anomalies in the chromosomes or molecular testing on DNA extracted to bring to light the existence of gene mutation thus allowing for a diagnosis and sometimes also a prognosis. The greatest limitation imposed on these technologies is the rarity of the embryonic/fetal cells in the maternal blood sample and the possibility of contamination from maternal cells, which could lead to false results. Non-invasive methods also include ultrasonic echographic and ultrasonographic technologies that, when performed by experts, make it possible to identify even the slightest deformities.

If on one hand the introduction of non-invasive diagnostic technologies which can even be performed very early (eighth to tenth week of gestation) eliminates the risk to the health or life of the fetus, on the other hand, precisely because the test is much simpler and less invasive, it can be more frequently requested with less attention to the presence of a real medical indication, leading to a possible unjustifiably higher perception of risk in the conceived child and hence encouraging abortion as the only way to remove this risk.

Pre-Implantation Diagnosis

Recourse to extracorporeal artificial reproduction has led to the development of *pre-implantation diagnosis*. Refined specifically to increase the efficiency of *in vitro* fertilization technology, allowing the selection of the human embryos most fit for transfer and the elimination of those that carry determined genetic or chromosomal anomalies or in any case those embryos that do not have a high *implant potential*.

Pre-implantation genetic diagnosis (PGD) consists in genetic analysis of individual cells taken from the embryo around three days after *in vitro* fertilization or of the polar body taken from the maternal oocyte. The goal of these technologies is to determine any alterations caused by a single gene (SGD, *single gene disease*) or by chromosomal anomalies that could result in the expression of serious or grave illnesses or syndromes.

PGD technology, which takes advantage of known methods of molecular biology for genetic analysis, now makes it possible to identify more than forty hereditary illnesses connected with single genes, such as sickle-cell anemia or cystic fibrosis; possible chromosomal aneuploidy connected with known illnesses such as Down's Syndrome (trisomy 21) or Turner's Syndrome; or other anomalies that can cause spontaneous abortion or failure of *in vitro* fertilization. Also available nowadays is chromosomal screening to determine categories of patients considered at risk of transmitting possible hereditary illnesses. Diagnoses are also made to reveal the mere probability of developing a specific disease such as Alzheimer's Syndrome, Huntington's Chorea or breast cancer linked to a particular mutation of the BRCA gene.

Pre-implantation genetic diagnosis raises serious problems, however, on both the technical and ethical levels. The first serious technical problem regards the elevated rate of diagnostic error ranging between 5 percent and 10 percent depending on the centers, due especially to the phenomenon of mosaicism, which accounts for the elimination of a high percentage of healthy embryos. The second problem regards the invasiveness of a diagnosis performed on at least one blastomere of an eight-cell embryo, elevating the risk of destroying the delicate processes that allow the correct corporeal pattern of the embryo to be established and consequently of damaging their later development; the extent of these risks is still little known today due to a lack of follow up studies. The elevated rate of diagnostic error, which fluctuates between 5 percent and 10 percent depending on the centers, also needs to be considered.

Despite the risks connected with PGD and its high costs (between $1,500 and $3,500 in the United States, depending on the test performed and excluding the cost of *in vitro* fertilization), recourse to pre-implantation diagnosis seems to be increasing continually.

Beyond the risks to the development of the embryo that will eventually be transferred to the uterus, the reasons for which these technologies are employed raise a series of ethical questions because pre-implantation diagnosis is currently being used to select diseased embryos (and is therefore seen as an alternative form of voluntary abortion) or to make a social choice about gender, or even to select embryos that are immunologically apt to be tissue or organ donors for siblings suffering from some disease.

The programmed destruction of human embryos according to a eugenic and selective mindset represents an obvious abuse of the human embryo, selected, left to die or suppressed in response to determined qualitative or *pseudo-therapeutic* parameters.

One risk that is common to the various technologies of prenatal diagnosis described so far is certainly the *psychological risk* of the search for a *perfect child*, burdened with too many parental expectations. According to some recent studies, a real *interruption* of the affective relationship between mother and child is created while awaiting the results of the test and the report of even the slightest abnormality in the child creates a sense of anguish and rejection disproportionate to the real seriousness of the situation. It has been shown that maternal emotions (joy, suffering, etc.) have a certain influence in the development of the embryo, just as nutritional support and the quality of the exchange between the fetus and the placenta do. These psychological mechanisms can leave indelible traces even when the child turns out to be healthy.[15]

Finally, mention should be made of the risk of losing *prenatal privacy*: to know in advance information about the sex or health of the embryo, even about its predisposition to diseases that could manifest themselves at a more advanced age can lead to a choice for eugenics, to discrimination and to violate the right of the subject not to know.

The reasons which drive the increasing request for prenatal genetic diagnosis today are often as much cultural as medical. It is the search for a child in the best state of health, a consequence of a change in the perception of pregnancy, seen not as something that happens but rather as something that is *chosen*, a kind of *self-actualization for the couple*.

Bioethical Considerations

Even though clarification of biological aspects regarding the moment when life begins and the characteristics of early embryonic development cannot in and of itself provide ontological answers to the nature of the human person in the initial phases of development, it is nevertheless a necessary step in an objective approach to the complex bioethical debate about the nature and dignity of human life at the beginnings of its existence.

The Bioethical Debate over the Human Embryo[16]

At the heart of bioethical discussions on the theme of incipient human life lies the question of the value and dignity to be ascribed to a human being at the dawn of its existence; from this flows consideration of the modes and levels of respect and protection due to it. The various theories that have emerged in the current debate are mutually contradictory inasmuch as they reflect the plurality of anthropological viewpoints that characterize the contemporary cultural panorama. The various theoretical perspectives have pointed out different moments in human embryonic development and linked the dignity of the human person to different standards, basing themselves with reference to different *criteria*.

Extrinsic Criteria

Criteria considered *extrinsic* are based on factors outside the human embryo. Some authors point to recognition by others as the basic standard for attributing personal dignity: personhood is a social status conferred by others; it has a relational character because a being is a person only if recognized as such by other human individuals; a person only exists in relation to other persons. Others subordinate the embryo's attribute of personhood to the *procreative intention* of the parents at the moment when the activity leading to conception took place; consequently, an undesired embryo or one conceived as a result of sexual assault would not be considered a human person.

Critics of these positions note that they lead to the paradox that a human being could both be considered a person if, for example, his father so regarded him and, at the same time, not be considered one if another individual, such as his mother, refused to consider him so.

According to other positions, an embryo becomes a *fully human* person only if recognized as such by positive law; the embryo's status must therefore be defined by democratic consensus.

These extrinsic criteria and others like them prove to be inadequate for attributing a moral and ontological *status* to the human embryo, since every possible judgment ends up by basing itself on entirely conventional and arbitrary factors.

Intrinsic Criteria

Intrinsic criteria on the other hand, refer to specific stages in development, to defined characteristics acquired by the embryo that are considered to be significant for attributing the dignity of personhood.

Some of these theses center around the *concept of individuality* and accentuate the events that would determine the origin of human biological individuality because the ontological and moral *status* of personhood is attributed along with this, whether implicitly or explicitly; a personal existence and consequently full human dignity and full claim to human rights would not be possible in the absence of a recognized individual existence. The new human subject has a dignity that must be respected and protected from the moment when it acquires a *stable biological individuality*. Some authors trace the concept of individuality back to the classical understanding of the individual as *subsistens distinctum aut indivisum in se, divisum a quolibet alio*, which points to the double characteristic of *internal unity* and *difference* from other individuals or *unity and unicity*.[17] Other authors, however, interpret the concept of individuality more restrictively in a purely analytical manner as *indivisibility* and *separateness*.

The *theory of cellular totipotence* is one example. Until the embryo reaches the eight-cell stage its cells are called totipotent, meaning that they have the capacity to develop into any embryonic or extra-embryonic cellular element whatsoever since the information contained in their genetic code is still completely accessible. If totipotent cells are separated from the developing embryo by way of experiment, they can be used to begin a new and complete individual.

According to some authors, this evidence rules out the affirmation of a fully constituted individual. Related to this is the *theory of monozygotic twins*: during early embryogenesis it can happen, although rarely, that some cells of the developing individual are separated, causing the independent development of a new organism. This phenomenon can occur from the two-cell stage to around the fourteenth day of development and, in very rare cases, even beyond this period (Siamese twins); therefore it is held that the presence of an individual human cannot be recognized so long as the developing being has the ability to become two or more individuals.

The first reply to these arguments is that they deal with events that are statistically quite rare. Next, the phenomenon of twins is explained by the theory that the embryonic individual already established by fertilization, provides the origin for another individual who begins an independent life process with an identical genetic inheritance.

Moreover, a proper analysis of the scientific data shows that the destiny of an organism is defined from the moment of fertilization. The cellular plasticity and malleability of early embryonic development do not cancel out the individuality established by gamete fusion; if anything, they highlight the essential role of the new organism in providing, for example, the ability to compensate for any damage or errors in the embryo's evolutionary program.

Other arguments are based on the presence of an *adequate development of the organs needed to exercise reason*. Since reason is what distinguishes human beings from other animals, the presence of a human person can be affirmed only when a certain level of development of the organs involved in intellectual functions is attested. The minimum level of development for these organs required for recognizing the personhood of a human being is still highly debated.

Taking the biological reality as a point of departure, however, it must be emphasized that the development of the brain, like the birth of the sensory world, begins to be constructed by an uninterrupted progression of events initiated at the moment when the gametes fuse. Once the zygote has been formed by gamete fusion it is always the same individual biological human that continues to evolve until the end of its life cycle.

Some authors who embrace Thomist thought, basing their arguments on the theory of *successive animation*, raise questions about the moment at which the body becomes sufficiently organized to be able to receive a rational soul. The rational soul can only be present in a body that is ready to carry out spiritual activities and the requisite condition for this, some would hold, is the presence of the cerebral cortex.

Consequently, the biological organism formed at fertilization (capable only of biological and not rational actions), cannot be ready to receive a rational soul.

This position has come under pointed criticism from some branches of Thomistic thought who claim that the theory of delayed animation held by Aristotle and then by St. Thomas is not a logical consequence of the hylomorphic theory but rather depends essentially on the limited knowledge of biology available when the two authors were writing; an adequate application of the principles in the light of up to date scientific information would lead to upholding the theory of immediate animation and therefore to affirming the full humanity of the newly formed human being.

The Substantialist View

According to a *substantialist* interpretation of the concept of personhood, that is one that refers to actual human nature as such, personhood is revealed by its abilities and expressed in its behavior although it cannot be limited, much less reduced, to these two features. Hence the fact that specific characteristics or behaviors are not yet present (as is inevitable in the case of prenatal human life) does not equal the absence of personhood. The person exists prior to and beyond the expression of his abilities and behaviors.

The classic hylomorphic theory according to which the intellective soul is the substantial form of the body and its organizing principle also falls within the context of substantialism. Because of the presence of the intellective soul, the body is defined, organized and differentiated. The intellective soul is the ontological condition for carrying out both lower and higher human activities, although it is not reducible to them.

The presence of an ontological foundation guarantees the personal human being's internal unity and continuity within time, right from the moment of his constitution as an organism. According to this view, there is no "anonymous" human life lacking a subject and there can be no continuous, gradual transition from "something" to "someone." One cannot think of a human life without thinking of the life of a specific human being.

In support of this observation it should be observed that the theory of immediate animation applied to every human being that comes into existence shows itself to be completely coherent with the biological reality. From the very first moment, there is a disposition in the human embryo capable of gradually guiding the emergence of differentiation according to the plan for the human species; any interruption or alteration of the process depends on accidental causes that may be genetic or may derive from external agents. This view does not contradict St. Thomas' fundamental metaphysical principles.

The possibility of overlapping the concepts of human being and personhood lead to a clear position on the beginning of human life: from the moment in which human biological individuality is observed we are dealing with a person; when there is a human being, a biological organism of the human species, there is a person. The formation of a new human organism constitutes the qualitative leap at both the biological and ontological levels which endures until the end of its life cycle. At every stage of its development, it remains the same human individual with its own internal unity, from the very first moment of its constitution, so as to be capable of directing its own development in a self-sufficient manner (even if, in the first phases of growth, it depends on the relationship with its mother and the external environment); so as to be, therefore, a "substance," a subsistent subject, thus "existing in and of itself." As a substance, its structural characteristic and specificity is rationality, regardless of the actual capacity to exercise it.

Ethical and Legal Considerations[18]

Ethical Aspects

The ethical aspects regarding the pre-implantation human embryo (both more general questions and the more concrete ones relating, for example, to discussions of the possibility of using it for experiments or as a cell and tissue donor) are closely connected with the ontological question about identifying the true nature of the human embryo. There is a close relationship between the ethical and ontological questions because the respect due to the being depends on its *value* and *preciousness*. The term *value* does not refer to market value but the *objective worth which, in the case of a human being, comes from the fact of having a rational nature.* The term *dignity* was coined precisely to indicate the specific value and the preciousness of man; *persona significant id quod est perfectissimum in tota natura, scilicet subsistens in rationali natura* (St. Thomas Aquinas, *Summa theologiae* I, q. 29, a. 3) ["person signifies the most perfect thing in all of nature; namely, subsisting in a rational nature"].

Here the dignity of the person finds powerful ontological support: someone who is maximally perfect cannot fail to be recognized and respected unconditionally in his life and in his integrity. In this view, the dignity of man takes on an unconditional and ontologically based value.

We must emphasize, however, that the moral question does not depend solely on ontology as the Instruction *Donum Vitae* expressed it meaningfully. This document asserts that every human being must be respected as a person from the moment of conception, basing this assertion on three arguments that do not address the theme of the human embryo's personal identity.

Instead, these arguments are based on three different points:

1. *The biological argument*: The data provided today by embryology and genetics allow us to affirm that from the first stages of embryonic development we are in the presence of a human biological individuality.
2. *The biographical argument*: Destroying a human embryo obviously means impeding the birth of a human being.
3. *The ethical argument*: A general moral principle affirms that it is never permissible to act with a doubtful conscience. Where there is doubt about the human embryo being a human person the embryo must be respected as if it were a person; otherwise one accepts the risk of committing homicide.

From the moral viewpoint, therefore, the simple fact of being in the presence of a human being demands full respect for its integrity and dignity. Every behavior that might in any way constitute a threat or offense against its fundamental rights, above all the right to life, must be considered gravely immoral.

Juridical Aspects

This perspective, which recognizes the being and dignity of the human embryo as absolute values, gives rise to full respect for its inviolability and protection of its free expression, above all on the level of human rights; a respect that demands always seeking the true and whole good of the person, defending the autonomy and freedom of every human being and avoiding every form of exploitation and discrimination against them.

Recognition that the embryo is a human being from the moment its life cycle begins also means recognizing its extreme vulnerability, and this vulnerability demands taking responsibility for one who is weak, an attention that must be guaranteed by the ethical conduct of scientists and doctors and by appropriate national and international legislation.

The attempts to deny the subjectivity of the embryo that are taking place today in the fields of medicine and science have repercussions for all of society, causing a devaluation of the human individual above all at the moments when he or she is weakest and most defenseless. Unless human beings are guaranteed real protection especially in the situations where they are at their weakest, how can every human being be protected always and in every circumstance?

Notes

1   This present work summarizes the most significant points that emerged during the International Congress "The Pre-Implantation Human Embryo: Scientific Aspects and Bioethical Considerations" (Vatican City, February 27-28, 2006) organized by the Pontifical Academy for Life on the occasion of its Twelfth General Assembly. For further study of the themes treated, see the *Atti della XII Assemblea della PAV*. Edited by Elio Sgreccia and Ignacio Carrasco De Paula (Vatican City" Libreria Editrice Vaticana, 2007). English translation: *www.academiavita.org/_pdf/assemblies/12/human_embryo_before_implantation.pdf*.

2   For further bibliography on the topic, see the individual presentations from this part of the Proceedings and the bibliography they contain.

3   The descriptive term "pre-implantation embryo" or "embryo before implantation" should not be confused with the qualitative term "pre-embryo." The latter was introduced for the first time by the scholar Clifford Grobstein in an article published in the journal *Scientific American* in 1979 in order to deny the individual character of the embryo in its first days of development. C. Grobstein, "External Human Fertilization," *Scientific American* 240: 6 (1979): 33-43.

4   What takes place in the process of fertilization is described at the molecular level in the paper "Dalla gametogenesi alla fecondazione" by Prof. R. Colombo.

5   The centriole is a tiny, cylindrical organ that plays an important role in the formation of the mitotic spindle at whose equator the chromosomes line up at the moment of the first cellular division.

6   As has recently been demonstrated, at the moment of fertilization RNA messenger molecules contained in the spermatozoon are also incorporated which, despite their paternal origin, can have a role in the initial phases of embryonic development.

7   These processes are triggered by a series of enzymatic reactions. A few of the proteins present in the spermatozoon that are involved in the propagation of the calcium wave have been isolated for some time now.

8   The topic is discussed in the paper by M. Zernicka-Goetz, "*Genetica ed epigenetica nello sviluppo dell' embrione preimpiantatorio*," which describes the results of important experiments conducted in her laboratory.

9   "What is clear is that developmental biologists will no longer dismiss early mammalian embryos as featureless bundles of cells," H. Pearson, "Developmental Biology: Your Destiny from Day One," *Nature* 418 (2002): 14-15.

10   Ibid., 15.

11   This topic is explored in the paper by G. Sica, "The Development of Pre-Implantation Embryo." (sic)

12 The exterior cells contain a sodium potassium pump (NaK-ATPase) that carries sodium ions inside the central cavity of the blastocyst, called the blastocoel. This accumulation of sodium ions triggers a flow of water that accumulates in the blastocoelic cavity increasing its volume.

13 This section was explored in depth in the paper by G. Sica, "The Embryo-Maternal Dialogue and Preparation for Implantation."

14 The scientific aspects and some ethical considerations regarding the theme of prenatal and pre-implantation diagnosis are addressed in two papers: C. Bellieni, "Pre-Implantation Diagnosis, Prenatal Diagnosis" and K. Fitzgerald, "Pre-Implantation Diagnosis: Bio-Medical Insights and Ethical Considerations."

15 On this point, in addition to the report of Professor. C. Bellieni, see the article by M. Vial, Benoit A., Schneider Z. et al., *Ann Pediatr* (1996): 446-455.

16 The bioethical and philosophical debate about the beginnings of human life is addressed in the following papers: W. J. Ejik, "The criteria of overall individuality and the bio-anthropological status of the embryo before implantation"; M. Pangallo, "The philosophy of Saint Thomas on the human embryo"; and P. Ide, "Is the human embryo a person? *Status quaestionis and determination.*" Some aspects of an ontological nature are also treated in the following papers: A. Gil Lopes, "The pre-implantation embryo between biology and philosophy: the individual being"; I. Carrasco De Paula, "The embryo before implantation: between nature and person"; and R. Spaemann, "When does the human begin to be a person?"

17 Obviously the concept of individuality does not exclude the ability to reproduce.

18 Aspects of ethics and law were addressed in an interesting Round Table which included the following papers: A. Gil Lopes, "The Pre-Implantation Embryo Between Biology and Philosophy: The Individual Being"; I. Carrasco de Paula, "The Embryo Before Implantation: Between Nature and Person"; R. Spaeman, "When Does the Human Being Cease to Be a Person?"; Jean-Marie Le Méne, "Why Is It a Duty to Protect by Law the Pre-Implantation Embryo?"

CHAPTER V

Pontifical Council for Culture

Where Is Your God? Responding to the Challenge of Unbelief and Religious Indifference Today

Concluding Document of the 2006 Plenary Assembly

I. New Forms of Unbelief and Religiosity

2.5. New Factors

A Rupture in the Process of Handing on the Faith

One consequence of the process of secularization is the growing difficulty faced in handing on the faith through catechesis, through the school, the family and the homily. These traditional channels for the handing on of the faith struggle to fulfill their fundamental role.

The Family. There is a real problem in the handing on of the faith within traditionally Christian families, especially in the cities. The causes are manifold: the rhythm and pace of work, the fact that both parents often work long hours away from the home, the secularization of the social fabric, the influence of television. The transformation of living and working conditions and the meager size of apartments has led to separation of the nuclear family from grandparents, who are now often excluded from the important processes of handing on both faith and culture. Moreover, in many countries children spend little time in the family home as they spend long hours at school and in extracurricular activities such as sport, music, and various associations; at home they are often immersed in and isolated by the computer, by video games, and by the television, leaving little space for constructive dialogue with their parents. In traditionally Catholic countries, the growing instability of family life, the rise in the number of so-called "civil marriages" and the increasingly prevalent so-called "common law marriage" accelerate and amplify this process. This does not of course mean that parents have become non-believers, for often they ask for the baptism of their children and wish for them to make their first holy communion, but beyond these sacred rites of passage the faith does not seem to have any role in the family setting, hence the question: if the parents have no living faith, what will they hand over to their children in an environment that has become indifferent to the Gospel values and, as it were, deaf to the proclamation of the saving message?

In other countries, for example in Africa and parts of Latin America some of the content of the faith and a certain religious sentiment is handed on, but the lived-experience of the faith which requires a personal and living relationship with Jesus Christ is often faulty. Christian rites are followed, but are perceived only as cultural expressions.

Catholic Schools. In various countries some Catholic schools have had to close as a result of a lack of resources and personnel, while a weakening, or a rupture in the handing on of the faith in some schools and even Catholic universities, results from a growing number of teachers void of commitment and a solid formation. Too often teaching in these schools has little to do with the faith and Christian morality. The phenomenon of migration also destabilizes schools when the large non-Christian presence is used as an excuse to justify abandoning an explicit teaching of the faith, rather than to seize on this opportunity to propose the faith, as has long been the tradition of Church's missionary activity. . . .

II. Concrete Proposals

2.2. In the Family

If for some, unbelief is an abstract theory, it becomes real for parents when they see their children abandon the faith and live as though God did not exist. This causes acute pain. There is a need to help parents hand on, together with their cultural heritage, the inheritance of the faith and experience of God. The assistance offered to couples during their period of engagement, in preparation to marriage and after it is more than ever necessary. The experience of the Équipes Notre-Dame is important, as Christian homes offer each other help as they grow in their faith lives, by sharing the daily difficulties and joys and by deepening together their faith. There where the Gospel is written on the hearts of the youth by their families and teachers, the problems of adolescence become surmountable. The family, first school of the Gospel, is a key place where a lived-out faith can be transmitted, and can take form in concrete expressions which become part of daily Christian experience: in the proper celebration of religious feasts, in family prayer in the evening, at bedtime and at mealtime, in the recitation of the rosary, in the visiting of churches, and in the setting aside time for lectio divina. Within the naturally enriching experience of family life, where trials, joys and tribulations nurture Christian virtues, by physically accompanying offspring to church-based liturgical activity and by being a family in prayer, parents and guardians are the first evangelizers of their children and build up solid roots on which to offer the special support needed at the time of preparation to receive the sacraments and to form a Christian conscience. Hereby they live a fuller version of family and ecclesial life. "Family catechesis" are one example, where the parents themselves, and particularly the fathers, exercise their parental responsibility in the proclamation of the Gospel.

The family is a place of culture, of life and for life, where each member learns from the other the fundamental values of community living, in appreciating each other's diversity and riches. In order to install in Christian families the "criteria of judgment, determining values, points of interest, lines of thought, sources of inspiration and models of life" (*Evangelii Nuntiandi*, no. 19), i.e., a culture inspired by faith, it is important to dedicate more time to family life. In this way can be born a new way of seeing and of living, of understanding, of acting and of preparing the future, and of being promoters of a new culture. Moreover, in an image-driven culture, it is important to educate the children to control their use of the television, to watch it together with them, discuss its content and answer their questions with availability and love. Otherwise, television might steal the time necessary for interpersonal relationships that are so important for the handing on of the faith.

CHAPTER VI

Pontifical Council for Legislative Texts

Instruction *Dignitas Connubii* to Be Observed by Diocesan and Interdiocesan Tribunals in Handling Causes of the Nullity of Marriage

The dignity of marriage, which between the baptized "is the image of and the participation in the covenant of love between Christ and the Church,"[1] demands that the Church with the greatest pastoral solicitude promote marriage and the family founded in marriage, and protect and defend them with all the means available.

The Second Vatican Council not only presented the doctrine on the dignity of marriage and the family[2] using new concepts and renewed terminology, and developed it by exploring more deeply their Christian and properly human aspects, but also prepared a correct path for further doctrinal perspectives and laid renewed foundations upon which the revision of the Code of Canon Law could be based.

These new perspectives, which are commonly called "personalist," offered much for the progressive development of certain values in a doctrine which was commonly accepted and quite often proposed by the Magisterium in a variety of ways, values which by their nature offer much to assist the institution of marriage and the family in attaining those highest ends which were destined for it by God the Creator by a marvelous plan and given to it by Christ the Redeemer with a spousal love.[3]

It is evident that marriage and the family is not a private matter that each person can construct at will. The Council itself, which so extols whatever pertains to the dignity of the human person, aware that the social dimension of man belongs to this dignity, does not fail to point out that marriage by its nature is an institution founded by the Creator and endowed by his laws,[4] and that its essential properties are unity and indissolubility, "which in a Christian marriage by reason of the sacrament obtain a particular firmness" (c. 1056).

From all this it follows that the juridic dimension of marriage is not and cannot be conceived as something "juxtaposed as something foreign to the *interpersonal reality* of marriage, but constitutes *a truly intrinsic dimension of it*,"[5] as is affirmed explicitly in the doctrine of the Church beginning with St. Paul, as St. Augustine observes: "The Apostle attributes so much of a right to this fidelity [of the covenant of marriage] that he calls it a power, saying 'a wife does not have power over her own body but rather her husband does, likewise a husband does not have power over his body, but rather his wife does' (1 Cor 7:4)."[6] Therefore, as John Paul II affirms, "in a vision of authentic personalism, the Church's teaching implies the affirmation that marriage can be established as an *indissoluble bond* between the persons of the spouses, a bond essentially ordered to the good of the spouses themselves and of their children."[7]

To this doctrinal progress in the understanding of the institution of marriage there is added in our day a progress in the human sciences, especially the psychological and psychiatric ones which, since they offer a deeper understanding of the human person, can offer much help for a fuller understanding of those things which are required in the human person in order that he or she be capable of entering the conjugal covenant. The Roman Pontiffs, since Pius XII,[8] while they called attention to the dangers to be encountered if in this area mere hypotheses, not scientifically proved, were to be taken for scientifically acquired data, always encouraged and exhorted scholars of matrimonial canonical law and ecclesiastical judges not to hesitate to transfer for the advantage of their own science certain conclusions, founded in a sound philosophy and Christian anthropology, which those sciences had offered in the course of time.[9]

The new Code promulgated on January 25, 1983 attempted not only to translate "into 'canonical' language"[10] the renewed vision of marriage and the family which the Council presented, but also to gather together the legislative, doctrinal and jurisprudential progress which in the meanwhile had taken place in both substantial and procedural law, of which is especially relevant here the Apostolic Letter given *Motu proprio* of Paul VI, *Causas matrimoniales* of March 28, 1971, which, "while a fuller reform of matrimonial procedure was awaited" provided some norms by which the process itself was rendered more rapid,[11] which norms for the most part were incorporated into the promulgated Code.

However, the new Code followed the same method as the Code of 1917, in regard to the matrimonial process for the declaration of nullity. In the special part *De processibus matrimonialibus*, it gathers together in one chapter the particular norms proper to this process (cc. 1671-1691), while the other prescriptions which govern the entire process are found in the general part *De iudicibus in genere* (cc. 1400-1500) and *De iudicio contentioso* (cc. 1501-1655), with the result that the procedural path which the judges and ministers of the tribunal are bound to follow in causes for the declaration of the nullity of marriage is not found in one and the same continuous tract. The difficulties which follow from this in handling causes of this nature are obvious in themselves and judges admit to experiencing them continuously, all the more so because the canons on trials in general and on the ordinary contentious trial are only to be applied "unless the nature of the matter prevents this" and also "without prejudice to the special norms concerning causes of the status of persons and causes concerning the public good" (c. 1691).

In regard to the Code of 1917, since these difficulties were encountered, the Sacred Congregation for the Discipline of the Sacraments issued the instruction *Provida Mater* on August 15, 1936,[12] with the stated intention "of providing for the same causes to be instructed and decided more quickly and more securely." In regard to the method and the criteria employed, the instruction organized the material by gathering together the canons, the jurisprudence and the praxis of the Roman Curia.

After the Code was promulgated in 1983, there appeared a pressing need to prepare an Instruction which, following the footsteps of *Provida Mater*, would be helpful to judges and other ministers of tribunals in properly understanding and applying the renewed matrimonial law, all the more so because the number of causes of the nullity of marriage had increased while, in contrast, the judges and ministers of tribunals were often found to be fewer and entirely unequal to the task of carrying on the work. Nonetheless it also seemed necessary that some time would be allowed to pass before that instruction would be prepared, as had happened after the promulgation of the 1917 Code, so that in preparing the instruction account could be taken of the application of the new matrimonial law in the light of experience, of any authentic interpretations that might be given by the Pontifical Council for Legislative Texts, and also of both doctrinal development and the evolution of jurisprudence, especially that of the Supreme Tribunal of the Apostolic Signatura and the Tribunal of the Roman Rota.

Once such a suitable period of time had elapsed, the Supreme Pontiff John Paul II, on February 24, 1996, judged it opportune that an interdicasterial Commission be established to prepare, using the same criteria and the same method as in the Instruction *Provida Mater*, an instruction by which judges and ministers of tribunals might be led by the hand, as it were, in carrying out this sort of work of great importance, namely, in processing causes which pertain to the declaration of the nullity of marriage, avoiding the difficulties which can emerge in the course of a trial even from the manner in which the norms of this process have been distributed throughout the Code.

The first and second drafts of this instruction were prepared through the cooperation of the Dicasteries concerned, namely, the Congregation for the Doctrine of the Faith, the Congregation for Divine Worship and the Discipline of the Sacraments, the Supreme Tribunal of the Apostolic Signatura, the Tribunal of the Roman Rota and the Pontifical Council for Legislative Texts; Conferences of Bishops were heard as well.

After he had studied the work carried out by the Commission, the Roman Pontiff, with a letter dated February 4, 2003, determined that this Pontifical Council, taking into consideration the two drafts previously mentioned, would prepare and publish the definitive text of an instruction concerning the norms in force. This was carried out with the help of a new interdicasterial Commission and in consultation with the Congregations and Apostolic Tribunals concerned.

The Instruction then has been drafted and published with the intention that it be a help to judges and other ministers of the tribunals of the Church, to whom the sacred ministry of hearing the causes of the nullity of marriage has been entrusted. Thus, the procedural laws of the Code of Canon Law for the declaration of the nullity of marriage remain in their full force and reference is always to be made to them in interpreting the Instruction. However, keeping in mind the proper nature of this kind of process, it is especially important to avoid both a juridical formalism, which is entirely foreign to the spirit of the laws of the Church, and a way of acting that indulges in too great a subjectivism in interpreting and applying both the substantive and the procedural norms.[13] Furthermore, in order to achieve in the Church that fundamental unity of jurisprudence which matrimonial causes demand, it is necessary that the tribunals of a lower level look to the Apostolic Tribunals, namely to the Tribunal of the Roman Rota, to which it pertains "to provide for the unity of jurisprudence" and "through its sentences, to be of assistance to lower tribunals" (*Pastor Bonus*, art. 126), and to the Supreme Tribunal of the Apostolic Signatura, to which it pertains, "besides the function which it exercises of a Supreme Tribunal," to provide "that justice in the Church is properly administered" (*Pastor Bonus*, art. 121).

It must be stated that the observation which *Provida Mater* made is still valid today and is even more urgent now than when that Instruction was issued, namely, "However it must be observed that such rules will be insufficient to achieve their stated purpose unless diocesan judges know the sacred canons thoroughly and are well prepared through an experience of tribunal work."[14]

For this reason it falls to the Bishops, and this should weigh heavily on their consciences, to see to it that suitable ministers of justice for their tribunals are trained in canon law appropriately and in a timely manner, and are prepared by suitable practice to instruct causes of marriage properly and decide them correctly.

Therefore, the following norms are to be observed by diocesan and inter-diocesan tribunals in handling causes of the nullity of marriage:

Art. 1—§ 1. This Instruction concerns only the tribunals of the Latin Church (cf. c. 1).

§ 2. All tribunals are regulated by the procedural law of the Code of Canon Law and by this Instruction, without prejudice to the proper laws of the tribunals of the Apostolic See (cf. c. 1402; *Pastor Bonus*, artt. 125; 130).

§ 3. Dispensation from procedural laws is reserved to the Apostolic See (cf. c. 87; *Pastor Bonus*, art. 124, no. 2).

Art. 2—§ 1. A marriage between Catholics, even if only one party is a Catholic, is governed not only by divine law but also by canon law, without prejudice to art. 3, § 3 (cf. c. 1059).

§ 2. A marriage between a Catholic party and a baptized non-Catholic party is governed also:

1° by the proper law of the church or ecclesial community to which the non-Catholic party belongs, if that community has its own marriage law;

2° by the law used by the ecclesial community to which the non-Catholic party belongs, if that community lacks its own marriage law.

Art. 3—§ 1. The matrimonial causes of the baptized pertain by right to the ecclesiastical judge (c. 1671).

§ 2. However, an ecclesiastical judge hears only those causes of the nullity of marriage of non-Catholics, whether baptized or unbaptized, in which it is necessary to establish the free state of at least one party before the Catholic Church, without prejudice to art. 114.

§ 3. Causes concerning the merely civil effects of marriage belong to the civil magistrate, unless particular law provides that those same causes, if they are to be treated incidentally and subordinately, can be heard and decided by an ecclesiastical judge.

Art. 4—§ 1. Whenever an ecclesiastical judge must decide about the nullity of a marriage of baptized non-Catholics:

1° in regard to the law by which the parties were bound at the time of the celebration of the marriage, art. 2, § 2 is to be observed;

2° in regard to the form of celebration of marriage, the Church recognizes any form prescribed or accepted in the Church or ecclesial community to which the parties belonged at the time of the marriage, provided that, if at least one party is a member of a non-Catholic Eastern Church, the marriage was celebrated with a sacred rite.

§ 2. Whenever an ecclesiastical judge must decide about the nullity of a marriage contracted by two unbaptized persons:

1° the cause of nullity is heard according to canonical procedural law;

2° however, the question of the nullity of the marriage is decided, without prejudice to divine law, according to the law by which the parties were bound at the time of the marriage.

Art. 5—§ 1. Causes of the nullity of marriage can be decided only through the sentence of a competent tribunal.

§ 2. However, the Apostolic Signatura enjoys the faculty of deciding by decree cases of the nullity of marriage in which the nullity appears evident; but if they require a more detailed study or investigation the Signatura is to remit them to a competent tribunal or another tribunal, if need be, which is to handle the cause according to the ordinary procedure of the law.

§ 3. However, in order to establish the free state of those who, while bound to observe the canonical form of marriage according to canon 1117, attempted marriage before a civil official or non-Catholic minister, it is sufficient to use the prematrimonial investigation in accordance with canons 1066-1071.[15]

Art. 6—§ 1. Causes for the declaration of the nullity of marriage cannot be handled through the oral process (cf. c. 1690).

Art. 7—§ 1. This Instruction is concerned only with the process for the declaration of the nullity of marriage, and not with the processes for obtaining the dissolution of the marriage bond (cf. cc. 1400, § 1, no. 1; 1697-1706).

§ 2. Therefore the distinction between the declaration of the nullity of a marriage and the dissolution of a marriage must be kept clearly in mind also in regard to terminology.

TITLE I

The Competent Forum

Art. 8—§ 1. It is the right of the Roman Pontiff alone to judge causes of the nullity of the marriage of those who hold the highest office of governance of a state, as well as other causes of the nullity of marriage which the same Roman Pontiff has called to his own judgment (cf. c. 1405, § 1, nos. 1, 4).

§ 2. In the causes mentioned in § 1, the incompetence of other judges is absolute (cf. c. 1406, § 2).

Art. 9—§ 1. The incompetence of a judge is also absolute:

1° if the cause is legitimately pending before another tribunal (cf. c. 1512, no. 2);

2° if competence by reason of grade or by reason of matter is not observed (cf. c. 1440).

§ 2. Thus the incompetence of a judge is absolute by reason of grade if the same cause, after a definitive sentence has been issued, is heard again in the same instance, unless the sentence happens to have been declared null; it is absolute by reason of matter if a cause of nullity of marriage is heard by a tribunal which is able to judge only causes of another type.

§ 3. In the case mentioned in § 1, no. 2, the Apostolic Signatura for a just cause can entrust the hearing of the cause to a tribunal otherwise absolutely incompetent (cf. *Pastor Bonus*, art. 124, no. 2).

Art. 10—§ 1. In causes of the nullity of marriage which are not reserved to the Apostolic See and have not been called to it, the following tribunals are competent in the first grade of jurisdiction:

1° the tribunal of the place in which the marriage was celebrated;

2° the tribunal of the place in which the respondent party has a domicile or quasi-domicile;

3° the tribunal of the place in which the petitioning party has a domicile, as long as both parties live in the territory of the same Conference of bishops and the Judicial Vicar of the domicile of the respondent party has given his consent; before doing so, he is to ask the respondent party whether he has any objection to make;

4° the tribunal of the place in which *de facto* the greater part of the proofs are to be collected, as long as the Judicial Vicar of the domicile of the respondent party has given his consent; before doing so, he is to ask the respondent party whether he has any objection to make (cf. c. 1673).

§ 2. The incompetence of a judge who does not enjoy any of these titles of competence is called relative, without prejudice however to the prescriptions regarding absolute incompetence (cf. c. 1407, § 2).

§ 3. If no exception of relative incompetence is filed before the concordance of the doubt, the judge becomes competent *ipso iure*, but without prejudice to c. 1457, § 1.

§ 4. In a case of relative incompetence the Apostolic Signatura for a just cause can grant an extension of competence (cf. *Pastor Bonus*, art. 124, no. 3).

Art. 11—§ 1. In order to verify the canonical domicile of the parties and especially their quasi-domicile, as treated in canons 102-107, in case of doubt a simple declaration of the parties does not suffice, but suitable documents are required, whether civil or ecclesiastical, or if these are lacking, other means of proof.

§ 2. If it is claimed that a quasi-domicile has been acquired by a stay in the territory of some parish or diocese, combined with the intention of remaining there for at least three months, particular care is to be taken to see whether the requirements of canon 102, § 2 have truly been fulfilled.

§ 3. A spouse separated for whatever reason either permanently or for an indefinite time does not follow the domicile of the other spouse (cf. c. 104).

Art. 12—Once a cause is pending, a change of the domicile or quasi-domicile of the spouses does not remove or suspend the competence of the tribunal (cf. c. 1512, nos. 2, 5).

Art. 13—§ 1. Until the conditions stated in art. 10, § 1, nos. 3-4, have been fulfilled, the tribunal cannot proceed legitimately.

§ 2. In these cases there must be written proof of the consent of the Judicial Vicar of the domicile of the respondent party; such consent cannot be presumed.

§ 3. The prior hearing of the respondent party by his Judicial Vicar can be done either in writing or orally; if done orally, the Vicar is to draw up a document attesting to this.

§ 4. Before giving his consent, the Judicial Vicar of the domicile of the respondent party is to consider carefully all the circumstances of the cause, especially the difficulties of the respondent party in defending himself before the tribunal of the place in which the petitioning party has a domicile or in which the greater part of the proofs are to be collected.

§ 5. The Judicial Vicar of the domicile of the respondent party in this case is not the judicial vicar of an interdiocesan tribunal but rather the diocesan judicial vicar; if in a particular case there is no such Vicar, it is the Diocesan Bishop.[16]

§ 6. If the conditions stated in the preceding paragraphs cannot be observed because, after a diligent investigation, it is not known where the respondent party lives, this must be documented in the acts.

Art. 14—In weighing the question of whether some tribunal is truly that of the place in which the greater part of the proofs is to be collected, one must take into consideration not only those proofs which it is expected that the two parties will propose but also those which should be collected *ex officio*.

Art. 15—When a marriage is being challenged because of several different grounds of nullity, those grounds, by reason of connection, are to be considered by one and the same tribunal in the same process (cf. cc. 1407, § 1; 1414).

Art. 16—§ 1. A tribunal of the Latin Church, without prejudice to artt. 8-15, can hear the cause of the nullity of the marriage of Catholics of another Church *sui iuris*:

1° *ipso iure* in a territory where, besides the local Ordinary of the Latin Church, there is no other local Hierarch of any other Church *sui iuris*, or where the pastoral care of the faithful of the Church *sui iuris* in question has been entrusted to the local Ordinary of the Latin Church by designation of the Apostolic See or at least with its assent (cf. c. 916, § 5, CCEO);

2° in other cases by reason of an extension of competence granted by the Apostolic Signatura whether stably or *ad casum*.

§ 2. In such case, the tribunal of the Latin Church must proceed according to its own procedural law, but the question of the nullity of marriage is to be decided according to the laws of the Church *sui iuris* to which the parties belong.

Art. 17—In regard to the competence of tribunals in the second or higher grade of jurisdiction, articles 25 and 27 are to be observed (cf. cc. 1438-1439; 1444, § 1; 1632, § 2; 1683).

Art. 18—By reason of prevention, if two or more tribunals are equally competent, the right to hear the cause pertains to the tribunal which first legitimately cited the respondent party (c. 1415).

Art. 19—§ 1. Once an instance has finished through abatement (*peremptio*) or renunciation, a party who wishes to introduce the cause anew or pursue it can approach any tribunal which is competent at the time of resumption.[17]

§ 2. If the abatement or renunciation or desertion (*desertio*) took place, however, before the Roman Rota, a cause which was either entrusted to that same Apostolic Tribunal or was brought there through a legitimate appeal can be resumed only before the Rota.[18]

Art. 20—A conflict of competence between tribunals subject to the same tribunal of appeal is to be resolved by that tribunal; if they are not subject to the same tribunal of appeal it is to be resolved by the Apostolic Signatura (c. 1416).

Art. 21—If an exception is proposed against the competence of a tribunal, articles 78-79 are to be observed.

TITLE II

Tribunals

Chapter I: Judicial power in general and tribunals

Art. 22—§ 1. In each diocese the judge of first instance for causes of nullity of marriage not expressly excepted by law is the Diocesan Bishop, who can exercise judicial power personally or through others, in accordance with the law (cf. c. 1419, § 1).

§ 2. Nonetheless, it is expedient that, unless special causes demand it, he not do this personally.

§ 3. Therefore all Bishops must establish a diocesan tribunal for their respective dioceses.

Art. 23—§ 1. Several Diocesan Bishops, however, with the approval of the Apostolic See, can by common agreement establish a single tribunal of first instance for their dioceses, in accordance with c. 1423, in place of the diocesan tribunals described in canons 1419-1421.

§ 2. In such case, a Bishop can establish in his own diocese an "instructional" section, with one or more auditors and a notary, for the purpose of collecting the proofs and communicating judicial acts.

Art. 24—§ 1. If it is entirely impossible to establish a diocesan or interdiocesan tribunal, a Diocesan Bishop can request from the Apostolic Signatura an extension of competence for another nearby tribunal, with the consent of the Bishop Moderator of that tribunal.

§ 2. The Bishop Moderator is understood to be the Diocesan Bishop in regard to a diocesan tribunal and the designated Bishop, mentioned in art. 26, in regard to an interdiocesan tribunal.

Art. 25—§ 1. In regard to tribunals of second instance, without prejudice to art. 27 and any indults granted by the Apostolic See:

1°   from the tribunal of a suffragan Bishop appeal is made to the tribunal of the Metropolitan, without prejudice to the prescriptions of nos. 3-4 (cf. c. 1438, no. 1);

2°   in causes judged in first instance before the tribunal of the Metropolitan appeal is made to the tribunal which he, with the approval of the Apostolic See, has stably designated (cf. c. 1438, no. 2);

3°   if a single tribunal of first instance has been established for several dioceses, in accordance with art. 23, the Conference of Bishops must establish a tribunal of appeal, with the approval of the Apostolic See, unless the dioceses are all suffragans of the same archdiocese (cf. c. 1439, § 1);

4°   the Conference of Bishops can, with the approval of the Apostolic See, establish one or more tribunals of second instance even apart from the cases mentioned in no. 3 (cf. c. 1439, § 2).

Art. 26—In regard to the tribunal mentioned in art. 23, the *coetus* of Bishops, and in regard to the tribunals mentioned in art. 25, nos. 3-4, the Conference of Bishops, or the Bishop designated by either body, has all the powers which pertain to a Diocesan Bishop in regard to his own tribunal (cf. cc. 1423, § 1; 1439, § 3).

Art. 27—§ 1. The Roman Rota is an appeal tribunal of second instance concurrent with the tribunals mentioned in art. 25; therefore all causes judged in first instance at any tribunal whatsoever can be brought to the Roman Rota by legitimate appeal (cf. c. 1444, § 1, no. 1; *Pastor Bonus*, art. 128, no. 1).

§ 2. Without prejudice to particular laws issued by the Apostolic See or indults granted by it, the Roman Rota is the only tribunal of third and higher instance (cf. c. 1444, § 1, no. 2; *Pastor Bonus*, art. 128, no. 2).

Art. 28—Apart from a legitimate appeal to the Roman Rota in accordance with art. 27, a referral of a cause (*provocatio*) made to the Apostolic See does not suspend the exercise of jurisdiction by a judge who has already begun to hear that cause; therefore he can continue the trial through to the definitive sentence, unless the Apostolic See has notified the judge that it has called the cause to itself (cf. c. 1417 § 2).

Art. 29—§ 1. Any tribunal has the right to call upon another tribunal for help in instructing a cause or in communicating acts (c. 1418).

§ 2. If need be, rogatorial letters can be sent to the diocesan bishop so that he can take care of the matter.

Art. 30—§ 1. Causes of the nullity of marriage are reserved to a collegial tribunal of three judges, without prejudice to artt. 295, 299 (cf. c. 1425, § 1), with any custom to the contrary being reprobated.

§ 2. The Bishop Moderator can entrust more difficult or more important causes to the judgment of five judges (cf. c. 1425, § 2).

§ 3. In the first grade of trial, if it happens that a college cannot be formed, the Conference of Bishops, as long as this impossibility persists, can permit a Bishop Moderator to entrust causes to a single clerical judge who, when this can be done, is to employ an assessor and an auditor; to the same single judge, unless it is determined otherwise, pertain those things attributed to a college, *praeses* or *ponens* (cf. c. 1425, § 4).

§ 4. A tribunal of second instance is formed in the same way as a tribunal of first instance; but for validity that tribunal must always be collegial (cf. cc. 1441; 1622, no. 1).

Art. 31—Whenever a tribunal must proceed collegially, it is bound to make its decisions by a majority of votes (cf. c. 1426, § 1).

Art. 32—§ 1. The judicial power enjoyed by judges or judicial colleges is to be exercised in the manner prescribed by law and it may not be delegated except for the purpose of carrying out acts preparatory to some decree or sentence (c. 135, § 3).

§ 2. Judicial power is to be exercised in one's proper territory, without prejudice to art. 85.

Chapter II: The ministers of the tribunal

1. Ministers of justice in general

Art. 33—In light of the seriousness and the difficulty of causes of the nullity of marriage, it is the responsibility of Bishops to see to it:

1°   that suitable ministers of justice are prepared for their tribunals;
2°   that those selected for this ministry each fulfill their respective functions diligently and in accordance with the law.

Art. 34—§ 1. Ministers of a diocesan tribunal are named by the Diocesan Bishop; ministers of an interdiocesan tribunal, unless otherwise expressly determined, are named by the *coetus* of Bishops or, as the case may be, by the Conference of Bishops.

§ 2. In an urgent case the ministers of an interdiocesan tribunal may be named by the Bishop Moderator until the *coetus* or Conference provides.

Art. 35—§ 1. All who make up the tribunal or assist it must take an oath to carry out their function properly and faithfully (c. 1454).

§ 2. In order to exercise their respective functions properly, judges, defenders of the bond and promoters of justice are to be diligent in continuing to deepen their knowledge of matrimonial and procedural law.

§ 3. With particular reason it is necessary that they study the jurisprudence of the Roman Rota, since it is responsible to promote the unity of jurisprudence and, through its own sentences, to be of assistance to lower tribunals (cf. *Pastor Bonus*, art.126).

Art. 36—§ 1. The Judicial Vicar, Adjunct Judicial Vicars, other judges, defenders of the bond and promoters of justice are not to exercise the same function or any other of these functions in a stable manner in two tribunals which are connected by reason of appeal.

§ 2. The same officials are not to exercise simultaneously two functions in a stable manner in the same tribunal, without prejudice to art. 53, § 3.

§ 3. It is not permitted for the ministers of the tribunal to exercise, at the same tribunal or at another tribunal connected with it by reason of appeal, the function of advocate or procurator, whether directly or through an intermediate person.

Art. 37—No other minister of the tribunal can be established besides those listed in the Code.

2. Ministers of justice in particular

a) The Judicial Vicar, the Adjunct Judicial Vicars and other Judges

Art. 38—§ 1. Every Diocesan Bishop is bound to appoint for his tribunal one Judicial Vicar or Officialis with the ordinary power of judging; he is to be distinct from the Vicar General, unless the smallness of the diocese or the scarcity of causes suggests otherwise (cf. c. 1420, § 1).

§ 2. The Judicial Vicar forms one tribunal with the Bishop, but he cannot judge causes which the Bishop reserves to himself (cf. c. 1420, § 2).

§ 3. Without prejudice to those things which pertain to himself by right, especially freedom in passing judgment, the Judicial Vicar is bound to render an account concerning the state and activity of the tribunal to the Bishop, who is responsible for monitoring the proper administration of justice.

Art. 39—A Judicial Vicar is also to be appointed for each interdiocesan tribunal; to him those things concerning the diocesan Judicial Vicar are to be applied in an appropriate manner.

Art. 40—Judicial Vicars are bound by the obligation of making personally, before the Bishop Moderator of the tribunal or his delegate, the profession of faith and oath of fidelity, according to the formula approved by the Apostolic See (cf. c. 833, no. 5).[19]

Art. 41—§ 1. The Judicial Vicar can be given assistants, called Adjunct Judicial Vicars or Vice-Officiales (c. 1420, § 3).

§ 2. Without prejudice to their freedom in judging, the Adjunct Judicial Vicars are bound to act under the direction of the Judicial Vicar.

Art. 42—§ 1. Both the Judicial Vicar and the Adjunct Judicial Vicars must be priests or bishops (*sacerdotes*), of unimpaired reputation, having a doctorate or at least a licentiate in canon law, and not less than thirty years of age (c. 1420, § 4).

§ 2. It is strongly recommended that no one lacking experience of tribunal work be appointed a Judicial Vicar or Adjunct Judicial Vicar.

§ 3. The same officials do not cease from office during the vacancy of the see nor can they be removed by the diocesan administrator; however, when the new Bishop arrives they need confirmation (c. 1420, § 5).

Art. 43—§ 1. Judges are to be appointed for both diocesan and interdiocesan tribunals; they are to be clerics (cf. c. 1421, § 1).

§ 2. The Conference of Bishops can permit even lay judges to be named; when necessary, one of these can be chosen in order to form a college (c. 1421, § 2).

§ 3. Judges are to be of unimpaired reputation and to have a doctorate or at least a licentiate in canon law (cf. c. 1421, § 3).

§ 4. It is also recommended that no one be named a judge who has not already carried out another function in the tribunal for a suitable period of time.

Art. 44—The Judicial Vicar, the Adjunct Judicial Vicars and the other judges are named for a definite period of time, without prejudice to what is prescribed by art. 42, § 3, nor can they be removed except for a legitimate and grave cause (cf. c. 1422).

Art. 45—§ 1. It pertains to a collegial tribunal:

1°   to decide the principal cause (cf. art. 30, §§ 1, 3);

2°   to hear an exception of incompetence (cf. art. 78);

3°   to hear a recourse proposed to it against the rejection of a *libellus* (cf. art. 124, § 1);

4°   to hear a recourse proposed to it against a decree of the *praeses* or *ponens* by which the formulation of the doubt or doubts was set (cf. art. 135, § 4);

5°   to decide the question *expeditissime* if a party insists that a rejected proof be admitted (cf. art. 158, § 1);

6°   to decide incidental questions according to artt. 217- 228;

7°   to grant, for a grave reason, a period longer than a month for the drawing up of the sentence (cf. art. 249, § 5);

8°   to impose a *vetitum*, if need be (cf. artt. 250, no. 3; 251);

9°   to determine the judicial expenses and to hear a recourse against a decision regarding expenses and remunerations (cf. artt. 250, no. 4; 304, § 2):

10° to correct a material error in a sentence (cf. art. 260);

11° in the grade of appeal to confirm expeditiously by decree a sentence in favor of the nullity of marriage given in the first grade of trial or to admit it to an ordinary examination in the new grade, in accordance with art. 265;

12° to hear questions about the nullity of a sentence (cf. artt. 269; 274, § 1; 275; 276, § 2; 277, § 2);

13° to issue other procedural acts which the college has reserved to itself or which have been deferred to it.

Art. 46—§ 1. The collegial tribunal is to be presided over by the Judicial Vicar or Adjunct Judicial Vicar or, if this cannot be done, by a cleric from the college designated by either one of them (cf. c. 1426, § 2).

§ 2. It pertains to the *praeses* of the college:

1°   to designate the *ponens* or to replace the *ponens* with another for a just cause (cf. art. 47);

2°   to designate an auditor or for a just cause to delegate a suitable person *ad actum* to interrogate a party or witness (cf. artt. 50, § 1; 51);

3°   to hear an exception against the defender of the bond, the promoter of justice, or other officials of the tribunal (cf. art. 68, § 4);

4°   to discipline those taking part in the trial in accordance with cc. 1457, § 2; 1470, § 2; 1488-1489 (cf. artt. 75, § 1; 87; 111, § 1; 307, § 3);

5°   to admit or designate a guardian (*curator*) (cf. artt. 99, § 1; 144, § 2);

6° to provide for the ministry of a procurator or advocate in accordance with artt. 101, §§ 1, 3; 102; 105, § 3; 106, § 2; 109; 144, § 2);

7° to admit or reject the *libellus* and to summon the respondent party to the trial in accordance with artt. 119- 120; 126;

8° to see that the decree of citation is communicated immediately and, if need be, to convoke the parties and the defender of the bond with a new decree (cf. artt. 126, § 1; 127, § 1);

9° to decree that the *libellus* is not to be communicated to the respondent party before that party has given a deposition in the trial (cf. art. 127, § 3);

10° to propose and set the formulation of the doubt or doubts (cf. artt. 127, § 2; 135, § 1);

11° to arrange and carry out the instruction of the cause (cf. artt. 137; 155ff.; 239);

12° to declare the respondent party absent from the trial and to try to get him to participate (cf. artt. 138; 142);

13° to proceed in accordance with art. 140 if the petitioner does not respond to the citation (cf. art 142);

14° to declare the instance abated or to admit a renunciation (cf. artt. 146- 147; 150, § 2);

15° to name experts and, if need be, to accept reports already made by other experts (cf. art. 204);

16° to reject at the outset (*in limine*) a petition to introduce an incidental cause, in accordance with art. 120, or to revoke a decree issued by himself that has been challenged (cf. art. 221, § 2);

17° by mandate of the college to decide an incidental question by decree in accordance with art. 225;

18° to decree the publication of the acts and the conclusion in the cause and to oversee its discussion (cf. artt. 229-245);

19° to schedule the session of the college for deciding the cause and to lead the discussion of the college (cf. art. 248);

20° to provide in accordance with art. 225 if a judge is not able to affix his signature to the sentence;

21° in the process mentioned in art. 265, to provide by his decree that the acts are to be sent to the defender of the bond for his *votum* and that the parties are advised to propose their observations, if they wish;

22° to grant free legal representation (cf. artt. 306-307);

23° to place other procedural acts which have not been reserved to the college by the law itself or by an act of the college.

Art. 47—§ 1. The *ponens*, or presenter, designated by the *praeses* from among the judges of the college, is to present the cause in the meeting of the judges, to write down the decision in the form of a response to the proposed doubt, as well as to draw up in writing the sentence and decrees in incidental causes (cf. c. 1429; artt. 248, §§ 3, 6; 249, § 1).

§ 2. Once the *libellus* has been admitted, the powers of the *praeses*, mentioned in art. 46, § 2, nos. 8-16, 18, 21, *ipso iure* belong to the *ponens*, or presenter, without prejudice to the faculty of the *praeses* to reserve some matters to himself.

§ 3. For a just cause the *praeses* can replace the *ponens* with another (cf. c. 1429).

Art. 48—§ 1. The Judicial Vicar is to assign judges in order by panels to judge each individual cause or, as the case may be, to assign a single judge according to a pre-established order (cf. c. 1425, § 3).

§ 2. In individual cases the Bishop Moderator can determine otherwise (cf. c. 1425, § 3).

Art. 49—Once they have been assigned the Judicial Vicar is not to replace judges except for a very serious cause to be expressed in the decree (cf. c. 1425, § 5).

b) Auditors and Assessors

Art. 50—§ 1. The *praeses* of the tribunal can designate an auditor to carry out the instruction of the cause, selecting him either from among the judges of the tribunal or from among the persons approved by the Diocesan Bishop for this function (cf. c. 1428, § 1).

§ 2. The Diocesan Bishop can approve for his diocese for the function of auditor clerics or laypersons who are outstanding for their upright life, prudence and learning (cf. c. 1428, § 2).

§ 3. It pertains to the auditor, according to the mandate of the judge, only to collect the proofs and give them to the judge; however, unless the mandate of the judge provides otherwise, he can also decide in the interim what proofs are to be collected and how they are to be collected, if the question should happen to arise while he is carrying out this function (cf. can 1428, § 3).

§ 4. At any point in the trial the auditor can be removed for a just cause by the one who appointed him (cf. c. 193, § 3).

Art. 51—The *praeses*, *ponens* and, without prejudice to art. 50, § 3, an auditor for a just cause can delegate *ad actum* a suitable person who, especially if a party or witness cannot come to the seat of the tribunal without grave inconvenience, is to question them according to the mandate received (cf. cc. 1558, § 3; 1561).

Art. 52—An assessor, who is assumed as a consultant to a single judge in accordance with art. 30, § 3, is to be chosen from among those clergy or laypersons approved for this function by the Bishop Moderator (cf. c. 1424).

c) The Defender of the Bond and the Promoter of Justice

Art. 53—§ 1. For all causes of the nullity of marriage, there must be appointed in each diocesan or interdiocesan tribunal at least one defender of the bond and promoter of justice, with due observance of art. 34 concerning their nomination (cf. cc. 1430; 1432).

§ 2. However, others may be appointed for individual causes, with due observance of art. 34, to carry out the function of defender of the bond or promoter of justice (cf. c. 1436, § 2).

§ 3. The same person, but not in the same cause, can carry out the office of defender of the bond and promoter of justice (cf. c. 1436, § 1).

§ 4. The defender of the bond and the promoter of justice can be removed, for a just cause, by those who appointed them (cf. c. 1436, § 2).

Art. 54—The defender of the bond and the promoter of justice are to be clerics or laypersons, of unimpaired reputation, having a doctorate or at least a licentiate in canon law, and of proven prudence and zeal for justice (cf. c. 1435).

Art. 55—The Judicial Vicar can name substitutes for the defender of the bond and promoter of justice from among those named in accordance with art. 53, §§ 1-2; this is to be done by a decree to be mentioned in the acts, and can be done either from the beginning of the process or during it. The substitutes are to stand in for those who were originally named whenever the latter are impeded.

Art. 56—§ 1. In causes of the nullity of marriage the presence of the defender of the bond is always required.

§ 2. The defender must participate from the beginning of the process and during its course, in accordance with the law.

§ 3. In every grade of trial, the defender is bound by the obligation to propose any kind of proofs, responses and exceptions that, without prejudice to the truth of the matter, contribute to the protection of the bond (cf. c. 1432).

§ 4. In causes concerning the incapacities described in canon 1095, it pertains to the defender to see whether the questions proposed in a clear fashion to the expert are relevant to the matter and do not go beyond the limits of the expert's competence; it pertains to the defender to observe whether the expert opinions are rooted in a Christian anthropology and have been drawn up according to a scientific method, pointing out to the judge anything he has found in the reports that is to be advanced in favor of the bond; in case of an affirmative sentence, before the tribunal of appeal it pertains to the defender to indicate clearly if anything in the expert reports was not correctly evaluated by the judges to the detriment of the bond.

§ 5. The defender can never act in favor of the nullity of marriage; if in a special case he has nothing that can be reasonably proposed or argued in favor of the bond, the defender can remit himself to the justice of the court.

§ 6. At the appellate level, after having carefully considered all the acts, even though the defender can refer back to the observations in favor of the bond proposed in the prior instance, he nonetheless must always propose his own observations, especially in regard to a supplementary instruction, if one has been carried out.

Art. 57—§ 1. The promoter of justice must take part when he challenges a marriage in accordance with art. 92, no. 2.

§ 2. The promoter of justice, by virtue of a decree issued by the judge, whether ex officio or at the instance of the defender of the bond or a party, must take part when it is a matter of safeguarding a procedural law, especially when the question concerns the nullity of the acts or exceptions.

§ 3. If in a preceding instance of a principal or incidental cause the promoter of justice took part, his participation is presumed to be necessary in a higher grade of the same cause (cf. c. 1431, § 2).

Art. 58—In causes in which the promoter of justice has challenged a marriage in accordance with art. 57, § 1, the promoter enjoys the same rights as a petitioning party, unless something else is determined by the nature of the matter or a prescription of the law.

Art. 59—§ 1. Unless something else has been expressly provided:

1° whenever the law prescribes that the judge is to hear the parties or one of them, the defender of the bond and the promoter of justice, if he is taking part in the trial, are to be heard as well;

2° whenever a request by a party is required in order for the judge to be able to deliberate on a matter, a request by the defender of the bond or the promoter of justice, if he is taking part in the trial, has the same force (cf. c. 1434).

Art. 60—If the defender of the bond or the promoter of justice, if his presence is required, have not been cited, the acts are invalid unless the same persons, even though not cited, actually took part, or at least, having examined the acts, were each able to perform their proper function before the sentence (cf. c. 1433).

d) The Head of the Tribunal Chancery and the Other Notaries

Art. 61—§ 1. It pertains to the head of the tribunal chancery, who is automatically a notary for tribunal acts, to see that the acts of the tribunal are properly drawn up and sent, according to the mandate of the judge, and are preserved in the archive (cf. c. 482).

§ 2. Therefore, unless otherwise determined, it pertains to this person: to record in the protocol book all the acts which arrive at the tribunal; to note in the protocol book the beginning, the progress and the end of causes; to receive documents exhibited by the parties; to send citations and letters; to see to the preparation of the *summaria* of processes and their distribution to the judges; to safeguard the acts of each cause; to send an authenticated copy of the acts to the tribunal of appeal if an appeal is filed or *ex officio*; to keep the original copy of acts and documents in the archive; to authenticate a copy of any act or document at the legitimate request of an interested party; finally, to return documents in accordance with art. 91, §§ 1-2;

§ 3. The head of the chancery is to abstain carefully from any kind of intervention in a cause apart from those things which pertain to his function.

§ 4. If the head of the chancery is absent or impeded, another notary for judicial acts is to take care of all these matters.

Art. 62—§ 1. A notary must take part in every process, so that acts (*acta*) which have not been signed by the same are null (cf. c. 1437, § 1).

§ 2. Acts which notaries draw up in the exercise of their function, having observed the formalities required by law, warrant public trust (cf. cc. 1437, § 2; 1540, § 1).

§ 3. A notary can be given a substitute to stand in for him when the notary is impeded; this appointment is to be made by a decree to be mentioned in the acts.

§ 4. For a just reason, a substitute can be named *ad actum* by the judge or his delegate or the auditor, especially when a party or a witness is to be questioned outside the seat of the tribunal.

Art. 63—The head of the chancery and the notaries must be of unimpaired reputation and above all suspicion (cf. c. 483, § 2).

Art. 64—In the diocesan tribunal they can be removed from office in accordance with canon 485 and in an interdiocesan tribunal by the Bishop Moderator.

TITLE III

The Discipline to Be Observed in Tribunals

Chapter I: The duty of the judge and the other ministers of the tribunal

Art. 65—§ 1. A judge, before he accepts a cause and whenever he perceives the hope of a good outcome, is to employ pastoral means to convince the spouses, if this can be done, to convalidate the marriage and reestablish conjugal life (c. 1676).

§ 2. If this cannot be done, the judge is to urge the spouses to work together sincerely, putting aside any personal desire and living the truth in charity, in order to arrive at the objective truth, as the very nature of a marriage cause demands.

§ 3. If, however, the judge observes that the spouses are affected by a spirit of mutual animosity, he is to urge them strongly to observe mutual courtesy, graciousness, and charity within the process, avoiding any hostility.

Art. 66—§ 1. One who has taken part in a cause as a judge cannot afterwards in another instance validly decide the same cause as a judge or carry out the function of assessor (cf. c. 1447).

§ 2. One who has taken part in a cause as a defender of the bond, promoter of justice, procurator, advocate, witness or expert cannot in the same or another instance validly decide the same cause as a judge or carry out the function of assessor (cf. c. 1447).

Art. 67—§ 1. A judge is not to take up a cause in which he has some interest by reason of consanguinity or affinity in any degree in the direct line and up to the fourth degree in a collateral line, or by reason of guardianship or tutelage, close personal relationship, great hostility, gain to be made or damage to be avoided, or in which any other sort of founded suspicion of favoritism could fall upon him (cf. c. 1448, § 1).

§ 2. In the same circumstances the defender of the bond, promoter of justice, assessor and auditor, and the other ministers of the tribunal must abstain from exercising their office (cf. c. 1448, § 2).

Art. 68—§ 1. In those cases mentioned in art. 67, unless the judge, defender of the bond, promoter of justice or other tribunal minister abstains, a party can object to them (cf. c. 1449, § 1).

§ 2. The Judicial Vicar hears an objection (*exceptio*) against a judge; if the objection is against himself, the Bishop Moderator is to deal with the matter (cf. c. 1449, § 2).

§ 3. If the Bishop is the judge and the objection is filed against him, he is to abstain from judging (cf. c. 1449, § 3).

§ 4. If the objection is filed against the defender of the bond, the promoter of justice or other ministers of the tribunal, the question is heard by the *praeses* in a collegial court or by the judge himself, if he is a single judge (cf. c. 1449, § 4).

§ 5. Without prejudice to art. 67, § 1, an objection filed because of acts legitimately placed by a judge or other minister of the tribunal cannot be considered to have any foundation.

Art. 69—§ 1. If the objection is admitted, the persons must be changed, but not the grade of the trial (c. 1450).

§ 2. If the tribunal cannot take the cause due to a lack of other ministers and there is no other competent tribunal, the matter is to be deferred to the Apostolic Signatura so that it may designate another tribunal to handle the cause.

Art. 70—§ 1. The question of an objection is to be decided *expeditissime*, after the parties have been heard, as well as the defender of the bond and the promoter of justice, if taking part in the process, unless they themselves have been recused (cf. c. 1451, § 1).

§ 2. Acts placed by the judge before an objection was made against him are valid; those taken after an objection was filed must be rescinded if a party so requests within ten days of the admission of the objection (cf. c. 1451, § 2).

Art. 71—§ 1. Once a cause of the nullity of marriage has been legitimately introduced, the judge can and must proceed not only at the request of the parties but even *ex officio* (cf. c. 1452, § 1).

§ 2. Therefore the judge can and must supply for the parties' negligence in presenting proofs and placing exceptions, whenever he deems it necessary in order to avoid an unjust sentence, without prejudice to the requirements of art. 239 (cf. c. 1452, § 2).

Art. 72—Judges and tribunals are to see that all causes are finished as soon as possible, while safeguarding justice, and that they not be prolonged beyond one year in a tribunal of first instance and beyond six months in a tribunal of second instance (c. 1453).

Art. 73—§ 1. Judges and other ministers of the tribunal and assistants are bound to keep the secret of office (cf. c. 1455, § 1).

§ 2. Judges are bound in a special way to maintain secrecy concerning the discussion among themselves prior to issuing a sentence, as well as concerning the various votes and opinions expressed therein, without prejudice to art. 248, § 4 (cf. c. 1455, § 2).

§ 3. Whenever the nature of the cause or of the proofs is such that from the divulgation of the acts and proofs the reputation of others could suffer, an occasion could be given for disagreements, or a scandal or other inconveniences of this type could arise, the judge can bind the witnesses, experts, parties and their advocates or procurators to secrecy by a special oath or, as the case may be, at least a promise, without prejudice to artt. 159, 229-230 (cf. c. 1455, § 3).

Art. 74—The judge and all ministers of the tribunal are prohibited from accepting any gifts on the occasion of their acting in a trial (c. 1456).

Art. 75—§ 1. Judges and other ministers of the tribunal who commit an offense against the office entrusted to them are to be punished in accordance with the law (cf. cc. 1386; 1389; 1391; 1457; 1470, § 2).

§ 2. When the correct administration of justice is impeded because of negligence, incompetence or abuses, the Bishop Moderator or the *coetus* of Bishops is to address the matter by apt means, not excluding removal from office, as the case may require.

§ 3. Whoever illegitimately causes harm to another by a juridic act, indeed by any other act placed maliciously or negligently, is bound by the obligation to repair the damage (c. 128).

Chapter II: The order of proceeding

Art. 76—§ 1. Causes are to be judged in the order in which they were presented and inscribed in the case register (cf. c. 1458).

§ 2. However if some cause demands a quicker handling ahead of others, that is to be ordered by a special decree containing the reasons (cf. c. 1458).

Art. 77—§ 1. At any stage or grade of trial, defects by which the nullity of a sentence can occur can be proposed as an exception and likewise declared by the judge *ex officio* (c. 1459, § 1).

§ 2. Apart from the cases mentioned in § 1, dilatory exceptions, especially those which pertain to persons and the manner of trial, are to be proposed before the formulation of the doubt is set, unless they emerge after the doubt has been set, and are to be decided as quickly as possible (cf. c. 1459, § 2).

Art. 78—§ 1. If an exception is proposed against the competence of the tribunal, the college must hear the question, without prejudice to art. 30, § 3 (cf. c. 1460, § 1).

§ 2. In case of an exception of relative incompetence, if the college declares itself competent, its decision does not admit an appeal, but a complaint of nullity, treated in artt. 269-278, is not prohibited, nor is a *restitutio in integrum*, treated in cc. 1645-1648 (cf. c. 1460, § 2).

§ 3. But if the college declares itself incompetent, a party who considered himself injured can have recourse to the tribunal of appeal within fifteen canonical days (cf. c. 1460, § 3).

Art. 79—A tribunal which at any stage of the cause realizes that is absolutely incompetent must declare its incompetence (cf. c. 1461).

Art. 80—Questions regarding the deposit to be made against the expenses of the trial or concerning the granting of gratuitous legal assistance, when this was requested from the very beginning, and other such questions are normally to be heard before the formulation of the doubt has been set (cf. c. 1464).

Chapter III: Time limits and delays

Art. 81—§ 1. The so-called *fatalia legis*, that is, the time limits established by the law by which rights expire, cannot be extended, nor can they be validly shortened except at the request of the parties (c. 1465, § 1).

§ 2. Judicial or conventional time limits, that is, those established by the judge on his own initiative or with the agreement of the parties, can be extended for a just cause by the judge before their expiration, after the parties have been heard or at their request, but they can never be validly shortened without their consent (cf. c. 1465, § 2).

§ 3. Nonetheless the judge is to take care lest the handling of the cause become too prolonged as a result of this extension (cf. c. 1465, § 3).

Art. 82—When the law does not set time limits for carrying out procedural acts, the judge must set them beforehand, having taken into account the nature of each act (c. 1466).

Art. 83—If the tribunal is closed on the day set for a judicial act, the time limit is understood to be extended to the first subsequent day which is not a holiday (c. 1467).

Chapter IV: The place of the trial

Art. 84—The seat of each tribunal is to be a stable one, inasmuch as possible, which is open at set times (c. 1468).

Art. 85—§ 1. A judge expelled by force from his territory or impeded from exercising his jurisdiction there, can exercise his jurisdiction and issue a sentence outside his territory; however the Diocesan Bishop of the place has to be informed of this (c. 1469, § 1).

§ 2. Apart from the case mentioned in § 1, a judge, for a just cause and having heard the parties, can go even outside his territory for the purpose of acquiring proofs, but with the permission of the Diocesan Bishop of the place in question and in a place designated by the same (c. 1469, § 2).

Chapter V: Persons to be admitted to the courtroom and the manner of preparing and conserving the acts

Art. 86—While causes are being conducted at the tribunal, only those persons are to be present in the courtroom whom the law or the judge has determined are necessary for the carrying out of the process (cf. c. 1470, § 1).

Art. 87—The judge can call to task all those taking part in the trial who are gravely lacking in the respect and obedience due the tribunal; furthermore he can even suspend advocates and procurators from exercising their function in the cause (cf. c. 1470, § 2).

Art. 88—§ 1. Judicial acts, both those which concern the merits of the question, that is, the acts of the cause, and those which pertain to the formalities of the procedure, that is, the acts of the process, must be put into written form (cf. c. 1472, § 2).

§ 2. The individual pages of the acts are to be numbered and authenticated (c. 1472, § 2).

Art. 89—Whenever the signature of parties or witnesses is required on judicial acts, if the party or witness is unable or unwilling to sign, that fact is to be noted on the acts themselves. At the same time, the judge and notary are to certify that the act itself was read verbatim to the party or witness and that the party or witness was unable or unwilling to sign (c. 1473).

Art. 90—§ 1. If the cause is to be heard at the tribunal of appeal, a copy of the acts, whose authenticity and completeness has been certified by the notary, is to be sent to the higher tribunal (cf. c. 1474, § 1).

§ 2. If the acts are drawn up in a language unknown to the higher tribunal, they are to be translated into a language known to that tribunal, with due precautions having been taken to verify the fidelity of the translation (c. 1474, § 2).

Art. 91—§ 1. When the trial has finished, documents belonging to private individuals are to be returned, but a copy of them authenticated by a notary is to be retained (cf. c. 1475, § 2).

§ 2. Without the mandate of the judge, the head of the chancery and the notaries are prohibited from giving out a copy of the judicial acts and of documents which were acquired for the process (cf. c. 1475, § 2).

TITLE IV

The Parties in the Cause

Chapter I: The right to challenge a marriage

Art. 92—§ 1. The following have the ability to challenge a marriage:

1° the spouses, whether Catholics or non-Catholics (cf. cc. 1674, no. 1; 1476; art. 3, § 2);

2° the promoter of justice, when the nullity of the marriage has been revealed and the marriage cannot be convalidated or this would not be expedient (cf. c. 1674, no. 2).

Art. 93—A marriage which was not challenged when both spouses were living can be challenged after the death of one or both spouses by one for whom the cause of the nullity of the marriage would be prejudicial to the resolution of a controversy in canonical or civil court (cf. c. 1675, § 1).

Art. 94—If a spouse dies while the cause is pending, art. 143 is to be observed (cf. c. 1675, § 2).

Chapter II: The spouses as parties in the cause

Art. 95—§ 1. In order for the truth to be more easily discovered and for the right of defense to be more aptly safeguarded, it is most expedient that both spouses take part in a process of the nullity of marriage.

§ 2. Therefore a spouse legitimately summoned to the trial must respond (cf. c. 1476).

Art. 96—Even when a spouse has named a procurator or advocate, he is still bound to take part in the trial when so prescribed by the law or the judge (cf. c. 1477).

Art. 97—§ 1. Those who are deprived of the use of reason can stand trial only through a guardian (cf. c. 1478, § 1).

§ 2. Those who at the beginning of the process, or in its course, are of impaired mind can stand trial for themselves only at the prescription of the judge; in other matters they must act and respond through their guardians (cf. c. 1478, § 4).

§ 3. Minors can act and respond on their own behalf without the permission of parents or guardian, without prejudice to §§ 1-2 (cf. c. 1478, § 3).

Art. 98—Whenever there is a guardian appointed by the civil authorities, the same can be admitted by the judge, who is first to hear, if possible, the Diocesan Bishop of the one for whom the guardian is appointed; if there is none, or it appears that the existing one is not to be admitted, the judge himself will designate a guardian for the cause (cf. c. 1479).

Art. 99—§ 1. It pertains to the *praeses* to admit or designate a guardian by a decree which indicates the reasons and which is to be kept in the acts.

§ 2. The decree in question is to be communicated to all interested parties, including the spouse who was given a guardian, unless a grave cause should prevent this, with the right of defense nonetheless remaining intact.

Art. 100—§ 1. The guardian is bound by office to protect the rights of the person to whom he was given.

Chapter III: Procurators and advocates

Art. 101—§ 1. Without prejudice to the right of the parties to defend themselves personally, the tribunal is bound by the obligation to provide that each spouse is able to defend his rights with the help of a competent person, most especially when it concerns causes of a special difficulty.

§ 2. If in the judgment of the *praeses* the ministry of a procurator or advocate is necessary and the party has not so provided within a prescribed time limit, the *praeses* is to name them, as the case requires, but they remain in function only as long as the party has not named others.

§ 3. If gratuitous legal assistance has been granted, it pertains to the tribunal *praeses* himself to name the procurator or advocate.

§ 4. In any case, the appointment of a procurator or advocate by decree is to be communicated to the parties and the defender of the bond.

Art. 102—If both parties are seeking a declaration of the nullity of the marriage, they can name for themselves a common procurator or advocate.

Art. 103—§ 1. The parties can name a procurator separate from the advocate.

§ 2. Each person can name only one procurator for himself, who cannot appoint another in his place unless the express faculty has been given to him to do so (c. 1482, § 1).

§ 3. If, however, for a just cause several have been appointed by the same person, they are to be so designated that prevention is operative among them (c. 1482, § 2).

§ 4. Several advocates can still be named at the same time (c. 1482, § 3).

Art. 104—§ 1. The advocate and procurator are bound according to their function to protect the rights of the party and to keep the secret of office.

§ 2. It pertains to the procurator to represent the party, to present the libellus or recourses to the tribunal, to receive its notifications, and to inform the party of the state of the cause; but those things pertaining to defense are always reserved to the advocate.

Art. 105—§ 1. The procurator and advocate must be of good reputation; in addition the advocate must be a Catholic, unless the Bishop Moderator allows otherwise, and a doctor in canon law, or otherwise truly expert, and approved by the same Bishop (cf. c. 1483).

§ 2. Those who have the diploma of Rotal Advocate do not need this approval; however the Bishop Moderator for a grave cause can prohibit them from practicing in his tribunal; in such case, recourse can be had to the Apostolic Signatura.

§ 3. The *praeses* because of special circumstances can approve as procurator *ad casum* someone who does not reside in the territory of the tribunal.

Art. 106—§ 1. Before a procurator and advocate can take up their function, they must deposit an authentic mandate at the tribunal (c. 1484, § 1).

§ 2. Nonetheless, in order to prevent the extinction of a right, the *praeses* can admit a procurator even before the mandate has been exhibited, with a suitable guarantee having been offered, if the matter so warrants; any act lacks force, however, if the procurator does not properly present an authentic mandate within the peremptory time limit to be set by the same *praeses* (cf. c. 1484, § 2).

Art. 107—§ 1. Unless he has a special mandate, a procurator cannot validly renounce an action, an instance, or judicial acts, nor in general do those things for which the law requires a special mandate (cf. c. 1485).

§ 2. Once a definitive sentence has been issued, the procurator retains the right and duty to appeal, unless the mandating party declines (c. 1486, § 2).

Art. 108—Advocates and procurators can be removed at any stage in the cause by the person who named them, without prejudice to the obligation of paying the remuneration due them for the work they have done; in order for the removal to take effect, however, it is necessary that it be communicated to them and, if the doubt has already been established, that the judge and the other party be informed of the removal (cf. c. 1486, § 1).

Art. 109—Both the procurator and the advocate can be rejected by the *praeses*, by a decree containing motives, either *ex officio* or at the instance of a party, but only for a grave cause (cf. c. 1487).

Art. 110—Advocates and procurators are forbidden:

1°   to renounce their mandate without a just reason while the cause is pending;
2°   to contract for an excessive fee for themselves: if they should do so, the agreement is null;
3°   to betray their duty because of gifts, promises or another reason;
4°   to withdraw causes from competent tribunals or to act *in fraudem legis* in any way whatsoever (cf. cc. 1488-1489).

Art. 111—§ 1. Advocates and procurators who commit an offense against the responsibility entrusted to them are to be punished in accordance with the law (cf. cc. 1386; 1389; 1391, no. 2; 1470, § 2; 1488-1489).

§ 2. If however they were found to be unequal to their duty because of incompetence, a loss of good reputation, negligence or abuses, the Bishop Moderator or *coetus* of Bishops is to provide for the matter using appropriate means, not excluding, if need be, a prohibition from practicing in their tribunal.

§ 3. Whoever has harmed another by any act illegitimately placed, either maliciously or through negligence, is bound by the obligation to repair the harm (cf. c. 128).

Art. 112—§ 1. It pertains to the Bishop Moderator to publish an index or directory in which there are listed the advocates admitted before his tribunal and the procurators who usually represent parties there.

§ 2. The advocates inscribed in the directory are bound, by a mandate of the Judicial Vicar, to provide gratuitous legal assistance to those to whom the tribunal has granted this benefit (cf. art. 307).

Art. 113—§ 1. At every tribunal there is to be an office or a person available so that anyone can freely and quickly obtain advice about the possibility of, and procedure for, the introduction of their cause of nullity of marriage, if such should be the case.

§ 2. If this office should happen to be carried out by the ministers of the tribunal, they cannot have the part of judge or defender of the bond in the cause.

§ 3. In each tribunal, to the extent possible, there are to be stable advocates designated, receiving their salary from the tribunal itself, who can carry out the function described in § 1, and who are to exercise the function of advocate or procurator for the parties who prefer to choose them (cf. c. 1490).

§ 4. If the function described in § 1 is entrusted to a stable advocate, he cannot take on the defense of the cause except as a stable advocate.

TITLE V

The Introduction of the Cause

Chapter I: The introductory *libellus* of the cause

Art. 114—A judge cannot hear a cause unless a petition has been proposed by one who in accordance with artt. 92-93 enjoys the right to challenge the marriage (cf. c. 1501).

Art. 115—§ 1. One who wishes to challenge a marriage must present a *libellus* to a competent tribunal (cf. c. 1502).

§ 2. An oral petition can be admitted, whenever the petitioner is impeded from presenting a *libellus*, in which case the Judicial Vicar is to order the notary to draw up the act in writing, which is then to be read to the petitioner to be approved, and which then takes the place of a *libellus* written by the petitioner, for all legal effects (cf. c. 1503).

Art. 116—§ 1. A *libellus* by which a cause in introduced must:

1°   express the tribunal before which the cause is to be introduced;
2°   describe the object of the cause, that is, specify the marriage in question, present a petition for a declaration of nullity, and propose—although not necessarily in technical terms—the reason for petitioning, that is, the ground or grounds of nullity on which the marriage is being challenged;
3°   indicate at least in a general way the facts and proofs on which the petitioner is relying in order to demonstrate what is being asserted;

4° be signed by the petitioner or his procurator, indicating also the day, month and year, as well as the place in which the petitioner or his advocate live, or declare they reside for the purpose of receiving acts;

5° indicate the domicile or quasi-domicile of the other spouse (cf. c. 1504).

§ 2. There should be attached to the *libellus* an authentic copy of the marriage certificate and, if need be, a document of the civil status of the parties.

§ 3. It is not permissible to require expert reports at the time when the petition is being exhibited.

Art. 117—If proof through documents is being proposed, these, inasmuch as possible, are to be submitted with the petition; if, however, proof through witnesses is being proposed, their names and domicile are to be indicated. If other proofs are being proposed, there should be indicated, at least in general, the facts or indications from which they are to be brought to light. Nothing however prevents further proofs of any kind from being brought forth in the course of the trial.

Art. 118—§ 1. Once a *libellus* has been exhibited, the Judicial Vicar must constitute a tribunal as soon as possible by his decree in accordance with artt. 48-49.

§ 2. The names of the judges and the defender of the bond must be communicated to the petitioner immediately.

Art. 119—§ 1. The *praeses*, once he has seen both that the matter is within the competence of his tribunal and that the petitioner does not lack legitimate standing in the trial, must either admit or reject the *libellus* by his decree as soon as possible (cf. c. 1505, § 1).

§ 2. It is advisable that the *praeses* hear the defender of the bond first.

Art. 120—§ 1. The *praeses* can and must, if the case requires, institute a preliminary investigation regarding the question of the tribunal's competence and of the petitioner's legitimate standing in the trial.

§ 2. In regard to the merits of the cause he can only institute an investigation in order to admit or reject the *libellus*, if the *libellus* should seem to lack any basis whatsoever; he can do this only in order to see whether it could happen that some basis could appear from the process.

Art. 121—§ 1. The *libellus* can be rejected only:

1°   if the tribunal is incompetent;
2°   if the petition is without a doubt presented by one who does not have
      the right to challenge the marriage (cf. artt. 92- 93; 97, §§ 1-2; 106,
      § 2);
3°   if the prescriptions of art. 116, § 1, nos. 1-4 have not been observed;
4°   if it is certainly apparent from the *libellus* that the petition lacks any
      basis, and that it could not happen that some basis could appear from
      the process (cf. c. 1505, § 2).

§ 2. The decree must express at least in a summary manner the reasons for
the rejection and must be communicated as soon as possible to the petitioning party and, if need be, to the defender of the bond (cf. c. 1617).

Art. 122—There is no basis for the admission of the *libellus* if the fact upon
which the challenge is based, even if completely true, is nonetheless entirely
incapable of making the marriage null or else, even if the fact is such that it
would make the marriage null, the untruth of the assertion is obvious.

Art. 123—If the *libellus* is rejected because of defects that can be remedied,
these defects are to be indicated in the decree of rejection and the petitioner
is to be invited to present a new *libellus* properly drafted (cf. c. 1505, § 3).

Art. 124—§ 1. The party always has the right to present a recourse, indicating reasons, against the rejection of the *libellus* within the canonical time
period of ten days to the college, if the *libellus* was rejected by the *praeses*, otherwise to the tribunal of appeal: in either case the question of the rejection is
to be decided *expeditissime* (cf. c. 1505, § 4).

§ 2. If the tribunal of appeal admits the *libellus*, the cause is to be judged
by the tribunal *a quo*.

§ 3. If the recourse was presented to the college, it cannot be proposed
again to the tribunal of appeal.

Art. 125—If within a month of the *libellus* having been presented the judge
does not issue a decree by which the *libellus* is accepted or rejected, the interested party can insist that the judge carry out his duty; if the judge nonetheless should remain silent, once ten days from the presentation of the request
have passed without a response the *libellus*, if it had been presented legitimately, is considered to have been admitted (cf. c. 1506).

Chapter II: The citation and the communication of judicial acts

1. The first citation and its communication

Art. 126—§ 1. In the decree by which the *libellus* of the petitioner is admitted, the *praeses* must summon or cite to the trial the respondent party, stating whether he must respond in writing or, at the request of the petitioner, appear before the tribunal for the concordance of the doubt(s). If from the written response it appears necessary to convoke the parties and the defender of the bond, the *praeses* or *ponens* is to state this by a new decree and is to see that it is communicated to them (cf. cc. 1507, § 1; 1677, § 2).

§ 2. If the *libellus* is considered admitted in accordance with art. 125, the decree of citation to the trial is to be issued within twenty days of the request mentioned in the same article (cf. c. 1507, § 2).

§ 3. If the respondent party in fact appears before the judge to take part in the cause, there is no need for that party's citation, but the notary is to signify in the acts that the party was present in the trial (cf. c. 1507, § 3).

§ 4. If the marriage is being challenged by the promoter of justice in accordance with art. 92, no. 2, both parties are to be cited.

Art. 127—§ 1. The *praeses* or *ponens* is to see that the decree of citation to the trial is communicated immediately to the respondent party and at the same time made known to the petitioning party and the defender of the bond (cf. cc. 1508, § 1; 1677, § 1).

§ 2. It is advisable that the *praeses* or *ponens*, together with these communications, propose to the parties the formulation of the doubt or doubts based on the *libellus* so that they may respond.

§ 3. The introductory *libellus* is to be attached to the citation, unless the *praeses* or *ponens* for grave reasons decrees, with a decree indicating reasons, that the *libellus* is not to be communicated to the respondent party before that party has given his judicial deposition. In this case, however, it is required that the respondent party be notified of the object of the cause and the ground(s) proposed by the petitioner (cf. c. 1508, § 2).

§ 4. Together with the decree of citation the names of the judges and defender of the bond are to be communicated to the respondent party.

Art. 128—If the citation does not contain those things which are necessary in accordance with art. 127, § 3 or if it was not legitimately communicated to the respondent party, the acts of the process are null, without prejudice to the prescriptions of artt. 60; 126, § 3; 131 and with the prescriptions of art. 270, nos. 4, 7 remaining in force (cf. c. 1511).

Art. 129—When the citation has been legitimately communicated to the respondent party or that same party has appeared before the judge to participate in the cause, the instance begins to be pending and becomes proper to the tribunal, otherwise competent, before which the action was instituted (cf. c. 1512, nos. 2-3, 5).

2. Those things to be observed in citations and communications

Art. 130—§ 1. The communication of citations, decrees, sentences and other judicial acts is to be done through the postal service or by another means which is very secure, having observed the requirements established by particular law (c. 1509, § 1).

§ 2. There must be proof in the acts of the fact of communication and of the manner in which it was carried out (c. 1509, § 2).

Art. 131—§ 1. If a party lacks the use of reason or is of impaired mind, the citations and communications are to be made to the guardian (cf. c. 1508, § 3).

§ 2. A party who has a procurator is to be informed of citations and communications through that person.

Art. 132—§ 1. Whenever, after a diligent investigation has been made, it is still unknown where a party lives who is to be cited or to whom some act is to be communicated, the judge can proceed further, but there must be proof in the acts of the diligent investigation that was made.

§ 2. Particular law can establish that in this sort of case the citation or communication can be made by edict (cf. c. 1509, § 1).

Art. 133—One who refuses to receive a citation or other judicial communication, or who prevents it from reaching himself, is to be considered to have been cited legitimately or to have been legitimately informed of the matter that was to have been communicated (cf. c. 1510).

Art. 134—§ 1. To those parties who are taking part in the tribunal either personally or through a procurator, all those acts shall be communicated which by law must be communicated.

§ 2. To those parties who entrust themselves to the justice of the court, there must be communicated the decree by which the formulation of the doubt is determined, any new petition which might have been made, the decree of publication of the acts, and all decisions of the college.

§ 3. To a party who has been declared absent from the trial, there shall be communicated the formulation of the doubt and the definitive sentence, without prejudice to art. 258, § 3.

§ 4. To a party absent in accordance with art. 132 because the place of residence is unknown, no communication of acts is made.

Chapter III: The formulation of the doubt

Art. 135—§ 1. When fifteen days have passed from the communication of the decree of citation, the *praeses* or *ponens*, unless one or another of the parties or the defender of the bond has requested a session for the determination of the formulation of the doubt, is to set by his decree within ten days the formulation of the doubt or doubts, taken from the petitions and responses of the parties (cf. c. 1677, § 2).

§ 2. The petitions and responses of the parties, in addition to the introductory *libellus*, can be expressed either in the response to the citation or in declarations made orally before the judge (cf. c. 1513, §§ 1-2).

§ 3. The formulation of the doubt must determine by which ground or grounds the validity of the marriage is being challenged.

§ 4. The decree of the *praeses* or *ponens* is to be communicated to the parties, who, unless they have already agreed to it, can have recourse to the college within ten days to have it changed; the question however is to be decided *expeditissime* by the decree of the college itself (cf. c. 1513, § 3).

Art. 136—Once the formulation of the doubt has been set, it cannot be validly changed unless by a new decree, for a grave reason, at the request of a party, with the other party and the defender of the bond having been heard and their reasons considered (cf. c. 1514).

Art. 137—After ten days from the communication of the decree, if the parties have not offered any opposition, the *praeses* or *ponens* is to order by a new decree the instruction of the cause (c. 1677, § 4).

Chapter IV: Parties who do not appear

Art. 138—§ 1. If the respondent party is properly cited but neither appears nor offers a suitable excuse for the absence or does not respond in accordance with art. 126, § 1, the *praeses* or *ponens* is to declare that party absent from the trial and decree that the cause, with due observance of those things to be observed, is to proceed through to the definitive sentence (cf. c. 1592, § 1).

§ 2. However, the *praeses* or *ponens* is to make an effort to have the party withdraw from the absence.

§ 3. Before the decree mentioned in § 1 is to be issued, there must be proof, even through a new citation if needed, that the citation, made legitimately, reached the respondent party in sufficient time (cf. c. 1592, § 2).

Art. 139—§ 1. If the respondent party then appears in the trial or gives a response before the decision of the cause, he can offer conclusions and proofs, without prejudice to art. 239; the judge however is to see that the trial is not deliberately drawn out into longer and unnecessary delays (cf. c. 1593, § 1).

§ 2. Even if the party did not appear or give a response before the decision in the cause, he can use the means of challenging the sentence; if the party proves that he was detained by a legitimate impediment, which he through no fault was unable to demonstrate earlier, that party can use a complaint of nullity in accordance with art. 272, no. 6 (cf. c. 1593, § 2).

Art. 140—If at the day and hour set for the concordance of the formula of the doubt the petitioner does not appear either personally nor through a procurator, nor offers a suitable excuse:

1° the *praeses* or *ponens* is to cite that party again;
2° if the petitioner does not appear in response to the new citation, the cause will be declared deserted by the *praeses*, unless the respondent party or the promoter of justice, in accordance with art. 92, no. 2, continues for the nullity of the marriage;
3° if the petitioner later wishes to take part in the process, art. 139 is to be observed (cf. c. 1594).

Art. 141—Art. 134, § 3, is to be observed in regard to a party who was declared absent from the trial by the judge.

Art. 142—The norms on the declaration of absence of a party from the trial are also to be observed, with suitable adaptations, if a party must be declared absent during the process.

TITLE VI

The Ending of the Instance

Chapter I: The suspension, abatement and renunciation of the instance

Art. 143—§ 1. If a spouse dies during the process:

1° if the cause has not yet been concluded, the instance is suspended until the other spouse or another interested party insists on its prosecution; in the latter case it must be proved that there is a legitimate interest;
2° if the cause has been concluded in accordance with art. 237, the judge must proceed further, having cited the procurator, if there is

one, or else the heir or successor of the deceased person (cf. cc. 1518; 1675, § 2).

Art. 144—§ 1. If a guardian or procurator, whose presence is necessary in accordance with art. 101, § 2, should cease his function, the instance is suspended for the moment (cf. c. 1519, § 1).

§ 2. The *praeses* or *ponens* is to name another guardian as soon as possible; he can even name a procurator if the party neglects to do so within a brief time limit set by the same judge (cf. c. 1519, § 2).

Art. 145—§ 1. The progress of the principal cause is also suspended whenever a question must first be resolved on which depends the continuation of the instance or the very resolution of the principal cause.

§ 2. This sort of suspension takes place when a complaint of nullity is pending against a definitive sentence or if, in a cause concerning the impediment of a prior bond, the existence of the prior bond is being called into question at the same time.

Art. 146—If no procedural act is placed by the parties for six months, while no obstacle is preventing this, the instance is abated; however, the tribunal is not to neglect to inform a party beforehand of an act that must be placed. Particular law can establish other peremptory time limits (cf. c. 1520).

Art. 147—Abatement (*peremptio*) takes place by virtue of the law itself and must even be declared *ex officio* (cf. c. 1521).

Art. 148—Abatement extinguishes the acts of the process, not however the acts of the cause, which retain the same force in a new instance for the declaration of the nullity of the same marriage (cf. c. 1522).

Art. 149—The expenses of the abated instance which each of the parties incurred, are to be borne by the same party, unless the judge for a just cause has decided otherwise (cf. c. 1523).

Art. 150—§ 1. In any state or grade of the trial the petitioner can renounce the instance; likewise both the petitioner and the respondent party can renounce all or some of the acts of the process which they themselves had requested (cf. c. 1524, § 1).

§ 2. In order to be valid, the renunciation must be made in writing, must be signed by the party or by the party's procurator who has a special mandate to do so, must be communicated to the other party, must be accepted by that party or at least not challenged, and must be admitted by the *praeses* or *ponens* (cf. c. 1524, § 3).

§ 3. The defender of the bond is to be informed of the renunciation, without prejudice to art. 197.

Art. 151—A renunciation admitted by the judge has the same effect, for the acts which were renounced, as the abatement of the instance and likewise obliges the renouncing party to pay any expenses already incurred, unless the judge for a just cause has decided otherwise (cf. c. 1525).

Art. 152—In case of abatement or renunciation, the cause can be resumed in accordance with canon 19.

Chapter II: The suspension of the cause in case of a doubt about non-consummation

Art. 153—§ 1. If in the course of the instruction of the cause a very probable doubt has arisen about the non-consummation of the marriage, the tribunal, with the consent of the parties and at the request of one or both parties, can suspend the cause by decree and begin a process concerning marriage which is *ratum et non consummatum* (cf. c. 1681).

§ 2. In such case, the tribunal is to complete the instruction for a dispensation *super rato* (cf. cc. 1681; 1702-1704).[20]

§ 3. When the instruction has been completed, the acts are to be sent to the Apostolic See together with the petition for the dispensation, as well as the observations of the defender of the bond and the *votum* of the tribunal and the Bishop (cf. c. 1681).

§ 4. If either party refuses to give the consent mentioned in § 1, that party is to be warned of the juridic consequences of that refusal.

Art. 154—§ 1. If the cause of nullity has been instructed in an interdiocesan tribunal, the *votum* mentioned in art. 153, § 3 is to be drawn up by the Bishop Moderator of the tribunal, who is to confer with the Bishop of the party requesting the dispensation, at least concerning the advisability of granting the requested dispensation.[21]

§ 2. In preparing its *votum* the tribunal is to explain the fact of inconsummation and the just cause for the dispensation.

§ 3. In regard to the *votum* of the Bishop, there is no reason why he cannot follow the *votum* of the tribunal by putting his signature to it, as long as the existence of the just and proportionate cause for the favor of the dispensation and the absence of scandal on the part of the faithful have been verified.[22]

TITLE VII

Proofs

Art. 155—§ 1. The following norms are to be observed in collecting the proofs.

§ 2. Unless something else is apparent or required by the nature of the matter, the term "judge" in this title refers to the *praeses* or *ponens*, the judge of the tribunal which is called to assist by virtue of art. 29, their delegate and the auditor, without prejudice to art. 158, § 2.

Art. 156—§ 1. The burden of proof lies on the one making an assertion (c. 1526, § 1).

§ 2. Those things which are presumed by the law itself have no need of proof (cf. c. 1526, § 2, no. 1).

Art. 157—§ 1. Proofs of any kind which seem useful for understanding the cause and are licit can be brought forward. Proofs which are illicit, whether in themselves or in the manner in which they are acquired, are neither to be brought forward nor admitted (cf. c. 1527, § 1).

§ 2. Proofs are not to be admitted under secrecy, unless for a grave reason and as long as their communication with the advocates of the parties has been guaranteed, without prejudice to artt. 230 and 234 (cf. c. 1598, § 1).

§ 3. The judge is to restrain an excessive number of witnesses and other proofs, and likewise is not to admit proofs brought forward in order to cause delays in the process (cf. c. 1553).

Art. 158—§ 1. If a party insists that a rejected proof be admitted, the college itself is to decide the matter *expeditissime* (cf. c. 1527, § 2).

§ 2. The auditor in accordance with art. 50, § 3 can decide only in the interim, if a question of admitting a proof should happen to arise.

Art. 159—§ 1. It is the right of the defender of the bond and the advocates of the parties:

1° to be present for the examination of the parties, the witnesses and the experts, unless the judge, in regard to advocates, decides that because of the circumstances and persons involved, the proceeding should be done in secret;

2° to view the judicial acts, even if not yet published, and to inspect documents produced by the parties (cf. cc. 1678, § 1; 1559).

§ 2. The parties cannot be present at the examination mentioned in § 1, no. 1 (c. 1678, § 2).

Art. 160—Without prejudice to art. 120, the tribunal is not to proceed to collecting the proofs before the formulation of the doubt has been set in accordance with art. 135, except for a grave reason, since the formulation of the doubt is to delimit those things which are to be investigated (cf. c. 1529).

Art. 161—§ 1. If a party or witness refuses to submit to a judicial examina-tion in accordance with the following articles, it is permitted to hear them through a suitable person designated by the judge, or to ask for their decla-ration to be made before a notary public or in any other legitimate manner (cf. c. 1528).

§ 2. Whenever the following articles cannot be observed in collecting the proofs, precautions must always be taken so that there is proof of their authen-ticity and integrity, avoiding any danger of fraud, collusion or corruption.

Chapter I: The judicial examination

Art. 162—§ 1. The parties, the witnesses, and as the case may be, the experts are to be examined in the seat of the tribunal, unless the judge for a just rea-son thinks otherwise (cf. c. 1558, § 1).

§ 2. Cardinals, Patriarchs, Bishops and those who by the law of their own state enjoy a similar favor are to be heard in a place of their choosing (c. 1558, § 2).

§ 3. The judge is to decide where persons are to be heard for whom it would be impossible or difficult to come to the seat of the tribunal because of distance, illness or other impediment, without prejudice to the prescriptions of artt. 29; 51; 85 (cf. c. 1558, § 3).

Art. 163—§ 1. The summons to the judicial examination is to be made by a decree of the judge legitimately communicated to the person to be ques-tioned (cf. c. 1556).

§ 2. The one who has been duly summoned is to appear or inform the judge without delay of the reason for his absence (cf. c. 1557).

Art. 164—The parties, either personally or through their advocates, and the defender of the bond are to exhibit, within a time limit set by the judge, the specific points of the matters about which the interrogation of the par-ties, witnesses or experts is being sought, without prejudice to art. 71 (cf. c. 1552, § 2).

Art. 165—§ 1. The parties, witnesses and experts are each to be questioned individually and apart from one another (cf. c. 1560, § 1).

§ 2. If however they disagree with one another in a grave matter, the judge can have the disagreeing parties discuss or confer between themselves, while avoiding disagreements and scandal as much as possible (cf. c. 1560, § 2).

Art. 166—The examination is to be carried out by the judge who must be assisted by a notary; therefore, without prejudice to art. 159, the defender of the bond or the advocates who are present for the examination, if they have further questions to be asked, are to propose them to the judge or the one taking the judge's place, so that he may put the questions, unless particular law provides otherwise (cf. c. 1561).

Art. 167—§ 1. The judge is to remind the parties and the witnesses about their duty to speak the whole truth and only the truth, without prejudice to art. 194, § 2 (cf. c. 1562, § 1).[23]

§ 2. The judge is also to have them take an oath to tell the truth, or at least an oath about the truth of the things they have already said, unless a grave cause would suggest otherwise; if someone should refuse to take an oath he is to make a promise to tell the truth (cf. cc. 1532; 1562, § 2).

§ 3. The judge can also administer to them an oath, or if need be, a promise to keep secrecy.

Art. 168—The judge is first to establish the identity of the person to be questioned; he is to inquire what is his relationship with the parties and, when he is asking specific questions about the object of the cause, he is also to ask for the sources of this knowledge and in what specific moment of time the person came to know of what he is now asserting (cf. c. 1563).

Art. 169—The questions are to be brief, adapted to the capacity of the person being questioned, not involving several matters at the same time, not confusing, not tricky, not suggesting a response, avoiding any offensiveness, and pertinent to the cause in question (c. 1564).

Art. 170—§ 1. The questions are not to be communicated in advance to the persons to be questioned (cf. c. 1565, § 1).

§ 2. However, if it is a matter of things which are so remote from memory that they certainly cannot be affirmed unless they are first recalled, the judge can give the persons some advance notice, if he thinks that this can be done without danger (cf. c. 1565, § 2).

Art. 171—The persons being questioned are to respond orally and are not to read anything written, unless it is a matter of explaining an expert report; in such case, the expert can consult the notes which he has brought with him (cf. c. 1566).

Art. 172—If the person to be questioned uses a language unknown to the judge, a sworn interpreter designated by the judge is to be employed. The declarations are still to be written down in the original language and the translation added. An interpreter is also to be used if a person with a speech or hearing impairment must be questioned, unless the judge should prefer that the questions which he proposes be answered in writing (cf. c. 1471).

Art. 173—§ 1. The answer is to be written down immediately by the notary under the direction of the judge, and must relate the very words of the deposition, at least in regard to those things which directly touch on the matter of the trial (cf. c. 1567, § 1).

§ 2. The use of a recording machine or a similar device can be admitted, as long as the responses are then put into writing and, if this can be done, signed by those giving the deposition (cf. c. 1567, § 2).

Art. 174—The notary is to make mention in the acts of the oath taken, postponed or refused, or the promise taken, postponed or refused, of the presence of the defender of the bond and advocates, of the questions added *ex officio* and in general of all things worthy of remembrance that may have happened during the examination (cf. c. 1568).

Art. 175—§ 1. At the end of the examination, there must be read to the questioned person what the notary wrote down about his deposition, or the person must be made to listen to what was recorded concerning the deposition, giving him the faculty of adding, deleting, correcting and changing (cf. c. 1569, § 1).

§ 2. Without prejudice to art. 89, the questioned person, the judge and the notary must sign the act, as must the defender of the bond and, if they are present, the promoter of justice and the advocates (cf. c. 1569, § 2).

§ 3. If the device mentioned in art. 173, § 2 is used, an act attesting to this is to be drawn up with the signatures mentioned in § 2. The notary is also to authenticate the recording, taking care that it is preserved safely and intact.

Art. 176—The questioned person, although already interrogated, can be called again for an examination at the request of the defender of the bond or a party or *ex officio*, if the judge deems this necessary or useful, as long as there is no danger whatsoever of collusion or corruption (cf. c. 1570).

Chapter II: Specific proofs

1. The declarations of the parties

Art. 177—In order to arrive better at the truth, the judge is to see that the parties are questioned (cf. c. 1530).

Art. 178—A party who has been legitimately questioned must respond and speak the truth wholly. If he refuses to respond, it pertains to the judge to evaluate what can be concluded from this for the purpose of proving the facts (cf. cc. 1531; 1534; 1548, § 2).

Art. 179—§ 1. In accordance with c. 1535, an assertion about some fact, made in writing or orally before a competent judge by a party concerning the matter itself of the trial, whether spontaneously or at the questioning of the judge, and made against oneself, is a judicial confession.

§ 2. However, in causes of the nullity of marriage a judicial confession is understood to be a declaration, made in writing or orally, before a competent judge, spontaneously or at the questioning of the judge, by which a party asserts a fact regarding oneself that is opposed to the validity of the marriage.

Art. 180—§ 1. Confessions and other judicial declarations of the parties can have probative force, to be evaluated by the judge together with the other circumstances of the cause, but the force of full proof cannot be attributed to them, unless there are present other elements of proof that entirely corroborate them (cf. c. 1536, § 2).

§ 2. Unless full means of proof are present from other sources, the judge, in order to evaluate the depositions of the parties, is to use witnesses to the credibility of the parties, if possible, in addition to other indications and helps (cf. c. 1679).

Art. 181—In regard to extrajudicial confessions of the parties against the validity of the marriage and other extrajudicial declarations of theirs introduced into the trial, it pertains to the judge, having considered all the circumstances, to evaluate how much to make of them (cf. c. 1537).

Art. 182—A confession or any other declaration of the party lacks all force whatsoever, if it is determined that it was made on the basis of an error of fact or that it was extorted by force or grave fear (c. 1538).

2. Proof by documents

Art. 183—In causes of the nullity of marriage proof by documents, both public and private, is also admitted (c. 1539).

Art. 184—§ 1. Public ecclesiastical documents are those which a public person has created in the exercise of his function in the Church, having observed the formalities prescribed by law (c. 1540, § 1).

§ 2. Public civil documents are those which according to the laws of each place are considered in law to be such (c. 1540, § 2).

§ 3. Other documents are private (c. 1540, § 3).

Art. 185—§ 1. Unless something else is proven by contrary and evident arguments, public documents are to be trusted concerning all things which are directly and principally affirmed in them (c. 1541).

§ 2. The certification of a private document, done by a notary having observed those things which must be observed, is indeed public, but the document itself remains private.

§ 3. In causes of nullity of marriage any written document purposely prepared in advance in order to prove the nullity of marriage obtains only the probative force of a private document, even if it was deposited with a notary public.

Art. 186—§ 1. Among private documents, letters which the engaged parties before marriage or the spouses after marriage, but *tempore non suspecto*, gave to one another or to other persons, can be of no little value as long as there is manifest proof of their authenticity and of the time when they were written.

§ 2. Letters, like other private documents, have that weight which can be attributed to them in light of the circumstances, especially the time when they were written.

Art. 187—A private document examined in the presence of a judge has the same probative force as a confession or a declaration made outside the trial (cf. c. 1542).

Art. 188—So-called anonymous letters and other anonymous documents of any kind whatsoever, per se cannot be considered even an indication, unless they describe facts which can be verified from other sources, and only to the extent that they can be so verified.

Art. 189—If documents are shown to have been erased, corrected, added to or tainted by any other defect, it pertains to the judge to evaluate how much, if anything, can be made of this kind of document (c. 1543).

Art. 190—Documents do not have the force of proof in a trial unless they are original or exhibited in a certified copy and deposited at the chancery of the tribunal so that they can be examined by the judge, the defender of the bond, the parties and their advocates (cf. c. 1544).

Art. 191—The judge can order that a document common to both parties, or which affects both parties, is to be exhibited in the process (cf. c. 1545).

Art. 192—§ 1. No one is bound to exhibit documents, even if they are common, which cannot be exhibited without danger of harm in accordance with art. 194, § 2, no. 3, or without danger of the violation of a secret (cf. c. 1546, § 1).

§ 2. However, if at least some portion of the document can be described and exhibited in a copy without the aforementioned dangers, the judge can decree that it be produced (c. 1546, § 2).

3. Witnesses

Art. 193—Proof through witnesses is to be carried out under the direction of the judge in accordance with artt. 162-176 (c. 1547).

Art. 194—§ 1. Witnesses must speak the truth to a judge who is legitimately questioning them (cf. c. 1548, § 1).

§ 2. Without prejudice to the prescription of art. 196, § 2, no. 2, the following are exempted from the obligation to respond:

1°   clerics, in regard to those things which have been revealed to them by reason of the sacred ministry;

2°   magistrates of the state, physicians, midwives, advocates, notaries and others who are bound to secrecy of office even by reason of advice given, in regard to matters subject to this secrecy;

3°   those who fear that from their testifying there could result dishonor, dangerous harassments, or other grave evils for themselves, their spouse or those closely related to them by blood or marriage (cf. c. 1548, § 2).

Art. 195—All persons may be witnesses, unless expressly excluded completely or partially by the law (c. 1549).

Art. 196—§ 1. Minors under fourteen years of age and those of impaired mind are not to be admitted to give testimony; nonetheless they can be heard in virtue of a decree of the judge declaring that this is expedient (c. 1550, § 1).

§ 2. The following are considered incapable of testifying:

1°   those who are parties in the cause or who are participating in the trial in the name of the parties, the judge and his assistants, the advocate and others who are assisting or had assisted the parties in the same cause; therefore care should be taken lest these functions be assumed by persons who through their testimony could make a contribution toward ascertaining the truth;

2°   priests, in regard to all those things which have been made known to them in a sacramental confession, even if the penitent should ask for the revelation of those things; indeed those things heard by anyone in any manner whatsoever on the occasion of a confession cannot be admitted, not even as an indication of the truth (cf. c. 1550, § 2).

Art. 197—A party who has proposed a witness can renounce the examination of the witness; but the other party or the defender of the bond can ask that the witness be examined anyway (cf. c. 1551).

Art. 198—When the hearing of witnesses is requested, their names and domicile or place of residence are to be indicated to the tribunal (cf. c. 1552, § 1).

Art. 199—Before the witnesses are examined, their names are to be communicated to the parties; if this, in the prudent estimation of the judge, cannot be done without grave difficulty, it is to be done at least before the publication of the testimonies (c. 1554).

Art. 200—Without prejudice to the requirement of art. 196, a party can request that a witness be excluded, if a just cause for the exclusion is demonstrated before the questioning of the witness (cf. c. 1555).

Art. 201—§ 1. In evaluating the testimonies, the judge, having sought, if necessary, testimonial letters, is to consider:

1°   what is the condition of the person and whether he is honest;

2°   whether he is testifying from his own knowledge, especially from what he has seen and heard, or rather from his opinion, from a rumor, or from what he has heard from others;

3°   when he came to know what he is asserting, especially whether it was *tempore non suspecto*, that is, when the parties had not yet considered introducing the cause;

4°   whether the witness is consistent and firmly coherent with himself, or rather changeable, uncertain or wavering;

5° whether there are other witnesses to what is testified, or whether or not it is confirmed by other elements of proof (cf. c. 1572).

Art. 202—The deposition of one witness cannot provide full proof, unless it is a matter of a qualified witness who is testifying concerning matters carried out *ex officio*, or unless circumstances of things or persons suggest otherwise (c. 1573).

4. Experts

Art. 203—§ 1. In causes concerning impotence or a defect of consent because of a *mentis morbum* or because of the incapacities described in canon 1095, the judge is to employ the assistance of one or more experts, unless from the circumstances this would appear evidently useless (cf. c. 1680).[24]

§ 2. In other causes the assistance of experts is to be employed whenever, according to the prescription of the judge, their study and expert opinion, based on the precepts of their art or science, are required in order to establish some fact or to ascertain the true nature of something, as when an investigation of the authenticity of some written document is to be made (cf. cc. 1574; 1680).

Art. 204—§ 1. It pertains to the *praeses* or the *ponens* to appoint experts and, as the case may be, to accept reports already made by other experts (cf. c. 1575).

§ 2. The appointment of an expert is to be communicated to the parties and the defender of the bond, without prejudice to art. 164.

Art. 205—§ 1. For the role of expert there are to be chosen those who not only have obtained a testimonial of their suitability, but are outstanding for their knowledge and experience of their art, and commended for their religiosity and honesty.

§ 2. In order that the assistance of experts in causes concerning the incapacities mentioned in canon 1095 may be truly useful, special care is to be taken that experts are chosen who adhere to the principles of Christian anthropology.

Art. 206—Experts can be excluded or exception can be taken to them for the same reasons as witnesses (cf. c. 1576).

Art. 207—§ 1. The judge, taking into account those things which might have been brought forward by the parties or the defender of the bond, is to define by his decree the individual points about which the assistance of the expert is to be concerned (cf. c. 1577, § 1).

§ 2. The expert is to be given the acts of the cause and other documents and aids which he could need in order to carry out his task properly and faithfully (c. 1577, § 2).

§ 3. The judge, having heard the expert himself, is to set the time period within which the examination is to be carried out and the report presented, taking care, however, that the cause not suffer useless delays (cf. c. 1577, § 3).

Art. 208—In causes of impotence the judge is to ask of the expert the nature of the impotence and whether it is absolute or relative, antecedant or subsequent, perpetual or temporary, and, if curable, by what means.

Art. 209—§ 1. In causes of incapacity, according to the understanding of canon 1095, the judge is not to omit asking the expert whether one or both parties suffered from a particular habitual or transitory anomaly at the time of the wedding; what was its seriousness; and when, from what cause and in what circumstances it originated and manifested itself.

§ 2. Specifically:

1° in causes of *defectus usus rationis*, he is to ask whether the anomaly seriously disturbed the use of reason at the time of the celebration of the marriage; and with what intensity and by what symptoms it manifested itself;

2° in causes of *defectus discretionis iudicii*, he is to ask what was the effect of the anomaly on the critical and elective faculty for making serious decisions, particularly in freely choosing a state in life;

3° finally, in causes of incapacity to assume the essential obligations of marriage, he is to ask what was the nature and gravity of the psychic cause on account of which the party would labor not only under a serious difficulty but even the impossibility of sustaining the actions inherent in the obligations of marriage.

§ 3. The expert in his opinion is to respond to the individual points defined in the decree of the judge according to the precepts of his own art and science; he is to take care lest he exceed the limits of his task by giving forth judgments which pertain to the judge (cf. cc. 1577, § 1; 1574).

Art. 210—§ 1. Each individual expert is to prepare his own report distinct from the others, unless the judge orders that one report be signed by all the experts; if this is done, then differences of opinion, should there be any, are to be carefully noted (c. 1578, § 1).

§ 2. The experts must indicate clearly by which documents or other suitable means they verified the identity of the persons or things; by what path and method they proceeded to carry out the task entrusted to them; and, most especially, which arguments form the basis for the conclusions reached in the report and what degree of certainty those conclusions enjoy (cf. c. 1578, § 2).

Art. 211—The expert can be called by the judge in order to confirm his conclusions and to supply further explanations which seem necessary (cf. c. 1578, § 3).

Art. 212—§ 1. The judge is to weigh carefully not only the conclusions of the experts, even if they are in agreement, but also the other circumstances of the cause (c. 1579, § 1).

§ 2. When he gives the reasons for his decision, he must express by which arguments he was moved to accept or reject the conclusions of the experts (c. 1579, § 2).

Art. 213—§ 1. The parties can designate private experts to be approved by the judge (c. 1581, § 1).

§ 2. These experts, if the judge so admits, can examine the acts of the cause, if need be, and be present at the carrying out of the expert examination; moreover they can always exhibit their own report (cf. c. 1581, § 2).

5. Presumptions

Art. 214—A presumption is a probable conjecture about an uncertain matter; one kind is a presumption of law (*iuris*), which is established by the law itself, the other is a presumption of an individual (*hominis*), which is made by the judge (c. 1584).

Art. 215—One who has a presumption of law in his favor is freed from the burden of proof, which falls on the other party (cf. c. 1585).

Art. 216—§ 1. The judge is not to make presumptions, which are not established by law, unless from a certain and determined fact, which is directly connected with the object of the controversy (c. 1586).

§ 2. Likewise the judge is not to make presumptions which are contrary to those developed in the jurisprudence of the Roman Rota.

TITLE VIII

Incidental Causes

Art. 217—An incidental cause arises whenever, after the instance of the trial has begun through the citation, a question is proposed which, even though it is not contained in the *libellus* which introduced the principal cause, none-theless pertains to the principal cause in such a way that for the most part it must be resolved before the principal cause is decided (cf. c. 1587).

Art. 218—In causes of matrimonial nullity, given the nature of the principal cause, incidental questions are not to be lightly proposed or admitted, and if they are admitted, particular care is to be taken so that they are resolved as soon as possible.[25]

Art. 219—An incidental question is to be proposed in writing or orally, indi-cating the connection between it and the principal cause, before the judge competent to decide the principal cause (c. 1588).

Art. 220—If the petition does not pertain to the principal cause or appears evidently devoid of any basis, the *praeses* or *ponens* can reject it at the outset, without prejudice to art. 221.

Art. 221—§ 1. Unless something else is expressly provided for, an interested party or the defender of the bond can have recourse to the college against a decree of the *praeses*, *ponens* or auditor which is not merely procedural, in order to institute an incidental cause. However, the recourse is to be placed within the period of ten days from the communication of the decree; otherwise the parties and the defender of the bond are considered to have acquiesced to the decree.

§ 2. The recourse is to be proposed before the author of the decree, who, unless he has decided that the decree issued by him is to be revoked, is to defer to the matter to the college without delay.

Art. 222—§ 1. The college, having received the petition and having heard the defender of the bond and the parties, is to decree whether the proposed incidental question seems to have a basis and a connection with the principal cause, or whether it is to be rejected at the outset; if it admits the question, it is also to decree whether it must be resolved with observance of the full form of trial, and thus with the proposition of doubts, or rather through briefs and then by decree (cf. c. 1589, § 1).

§ 2. Those things prescribed in § 1 are to be carried out without delay and *expeditissime*, that is, excluding any appeal and not allowing any recourse (cf. cc. 1589, § 1; 1629, no. 5).

§ 3. If the college decides that the incidental question is not to be resolved before the definitive sentence, it likewise is to decree *expeditissime* that it is to be taken into account when the principal cause is decided (cf. c. 1589, § 2).

Art. 223—The college, at the request of a party or the defender of the bond or *ex officio*, can request the intervention of the promoter of justice, even if he has not yet taken part in the process, if the nature or difficulty of the incidental question recommends this.

Art. 224—§ 1. If the incidental question must be solved by a sentence of the college, cc. 1658-1670 on the oral contentious process are to be observed, unless, in light of the gravity of the matter, it appears otherwise to the college (cf. c. 1590, § 1).

§ 2. Nonetheless, the college can by its decree, containing reasons, derogate from those procedural norms mentioned in § 1 which are not required *ad validitatem*, in order to provide for speed, without detriment to justice (cf. c. 1670).

Art. 225—If the question must be decided by decree, a time limit is to be given as soon as possible to the parties and the defender of the bond, within which they are to present their reasons in a written brief or memorial; the college can also entrust the matter to an auditor or the *praeses*, unless something to the contrary is evident or is required by the nature of the matter (cf. c. 1590, § 2).

Art. 226—Before the principal cause is finished, and unless it concerns a decision having the force of a definitive sentence, the college can revoke or change an interlocutory decree or sentence, if there should be a just cause, either at the request of a party or the defender of the bond, or *ex officio*, having heard the parties and the defender of the bond (cf. c. 1591).

Art. 227—If a single judge is deciding the cause, he himself, with the appropriate adaptations, is to hear incidental questions.

Art. 228—There is no appeal against a decision by which an incidental question is decided and which does not have the force of a definitive sentence, unless it is joined with an appeal from the definitive sentence (cf. c. 1629, no. 4).

TITLE IX

The Publication of the Acts, the Conclusion in the Cause, and the Discussion of the Cause

Chapter I: The publication of the acts

Art. 229—§ 1. After the proofs have been acquired, the judge is to proceed, before the discussion of the cause, to the publication of the acts (cf. c. 1598, § 1).

§ 2. The publication of the acts is carried out by a decree of the judge by which the parties and their advocates are given the faculty of examining the acts.

§ 3. Therefore the judge by the same decree must permit the parties and their advocates to examine the acts not yet known to them, without prejudice to art. 230, at the chancery of the tribunal (cf. c. 1598, § 1).

§ 4. In this Title, the term judge is understood to mean the *praeses* or the *ponens*, unless otherwise is evident or is required by the nature of the matter.

Art. 230—In order to avoid very serious dangers, the judge can decree that some act is not to be shown to the parties, with due care taken however that the right of defense remains intact (cf. c. 1598, § 1).

Art. 231—The violation of the prescription given in art. 229, § 3, brings with it the remediable nullity of the sentence, but in a case in which the right of defense was actually denied it brings irremediable nullity (cf. cc. 1598, § 1; 1620, no. 7; 1622, no. 5).

Art. 232—§ 1. Before the examination of the acts, the judge can require the parties to take an oath or, as the case may be, a promise, that they will use the knowledge gained through this inspection of the acts only for their legitimate defense in the canonical forum (cf. c. 1455, § 3).

§ 2. But if a party refuses to take an oath or, as the case may be, make a promise, he will be considered to have renounced the faculty of examining the acts, unless particular law establishes otherwise.

Art. 233—§ 1. The examination of the acts is to be done at the chancery of the tribunal which is hearing the cause, within the time limit set in the decree of the judge.

§ 2. But if a party lives far away from the seat of this tribunal, he can inspect the acts at the seat of the tribunal in the place where he now lives, or else in another suitable place, in order that his right of defense remains intact.

Art. 234—If the judge thinks that in order to avoid very serious dangers some act is not to be shown to the parties, the advocates of the parties, having first taken an oath or made a promise to observe secrecy, may study the same act.

Art. 235—§ 1. The judge can hand over a copy of the acts to advocates requesting this (cf. c. 1598, § 1).

§ 2. The advocates however are bound by the serious obligation not to hand over a copy of the acts, whether whole or in part, to other persons, including the parties.

Art. 236—When the publication of the acts has been completed, the parties and the defender of the bond, in order to complete the proofs, can propose others to the judge; when these have been acquired, if the judge thinks it necessary, it is again an occasion for the decree mentioned in art. 229, § 3 (cf. c. 1598, § 2).

Chapter II: The conclusion in the cause

Art. 237—§ 1. When all those things pertaining to the production of the proofs have been completed, it is time for the conclusion in the cause (c. 1599, § 1).

§ 2. This conclusion takes place either when the parties and the defender of the bond declare that they have nothing else to be added, or when the useful time period set by the judge for proposing proofs has elapsed, or when the judge has declared that he considers the cause to have been sufficiently instructed (cf. c. 1599, § 2).

§ 3. The judge is to issue a decree declaring the conclusion in the cause to have taken place, in whatever way this has happened (cf. c. 1599, § 3).

Art. 238—Nonetheless the judge is to take care not to issue the decree of the conclusion in the cause if he thinks that something else is still to be sought in order that the cause might be sufficiently instructed. In such case, having heard the defender of the bond, if this is expedient, he is to order that those things which are lacking be provided.

Art. 239—§ 1. After the conclusion in the cause, the judge can still call the same or other witnesses or provide for other proofs which had not been sought earlier:

1° whenever it is likely that, unless the new proof is admitted, the sentence will be unjust for the reasons given in canon 1645, § 2, nos. 1-3;
2° in other cases, provided that the parties have been heard, that there is a grave reason, and that any danger of fraud or subornation is removed (cf. c. 1600, § 1).

§ 2. Furthermore, the judge can order or allow to be exhibited a document which, without the fault of the interested party, was not able to be exhibited before (c. 1600, § 2).

§ 3. The new proofs are to be published, with due observance of artt. 229-235 (cf. c. 1600, § 3).

Chapter III: The discussion of the cause

Art. 240—§ 1. When the conclusion in the cause has taken place, the judge is to set a suitable period of time for the preparation of the summary of the acts, if needed, and for exhibiting defenses and observations in writing (cf. c. 1601).

§ 2. The regulations of the tribunal are to be observed in regard to the preparation of the summary and the writing of the defenses and observations, the number of copies, and other things of this nature (cf. c. 1602).

Art. 241—It is entirely forbidden that information given to the judge by the parties or their advocates or even other persons remain outside the acts of the cause (c. 1604, § 1).

Art. 242—§ 1. When the defenses and observations have been mutually exchanged, each party is permitted to exhibit responses within a short time period set by the judge (c. 1603, § 1).

§ 2. This right is to be given to the parties only once, unless it seems to the judge that for a grave cause it is to be granted again; then, however, a concession granted to one party is considered to have been granted to the other as well (c. 1603, § 2).

Art. 243—§ 1. It is always the right of the defender of the bond to be heard last (cf. c. 1603, § 3).

§ 2. If the defender of the bond offers no response within the brief time limit set by the judge, he is presumed to have nothing to be added to his observations, and it is permitted to go forward.

Art. 244—§ 1. After the discussion of the cause has been carried out in writing, the judge can allow a moderate debate to take place orally before the tribunal in session, in order to clarify some questions (cf. c. 1604, § 2).

§ 2. A notary is to be present at this oral debate so that, if the judge orders or a party of the defender of the bond requests and the judge consents, he may immediately make a record of the points debated and the conclusions reached (cf. c. 1605).

Art. 245—§ 1. If the advocates neglect to prepare their defenses within the time given them, the parties are to be informed of this and advised to take care of the matter within the time period set by the judge, either themselves or through a new advocate legitimately designated.

§ 2. But if the parties do not take care of this within the time period given, or if they entrust themselves to the knowledge and conscience of the judge, the judge, if he has a full understanding of the matter from the acts and proofs, having received the written observations of the defender of the bond, can pronounce his sentence immediately (cf. c. 1606).

TITLE X

The Pronouncements of the Judge

Art. 246—The principal cause is decided by the judge by means of a definitive sentence, without prejudice to art. 265, § 1; an incidental cause by means of an interlocutory sentence, without prejudice to the requirement of art. 222, § 1 (cf. c. 1607).

Art. 247—§ 1. In order to declare the nullity of a marriage there is required in the mind of the judge moral certainty of its nullity (cf. c. 1608, § 1).

§ 2. In order to have the moral certainty necessary by law, a preponderance of the proofs and indications is not sufficient, but it is required that any prudent positive doubt of making an error, in law or in fact, is excluded, even if the mere possibility of the contrary remains.

§ 3. The judge must derive this certainty from those things which have been carried out and proven in the process (*ex actis et probatis*) (c. 1608, § 2).

§ 4. The judge must weigh the proofs according to his conscience, without prejudice to the prescriptions of the law regarding the efficacy of certain proofs (c. 1608, § 3).

§ 5. The judge who, after a diligent study of the cause, is not able to arrive at this certainty, is to rule that the nullity of the marriage has not been proven, without prejudice to art. 248, § 5 (cf. cc. 1608, § 4; 1060).

Art. 248—§ 1. Once the discussion of the cause has been finished, the *praeses* of a collegial tribunal is to determine on what day and at what hour the judges must convene for the deliberation, without the presence of any ministers of the tribunal whatsoever; this meeting, unless a particular cause recommends otherwise, is to be held in the seat of the tribunal itself (cf. c. 1609, § 1; art. 31).

§ 2. On the day assigned for the meeting, the individual judges are to bring their written opinions on the merits of the cause, with the reasons both in law and in fact by which they each reached their conclusions (cf. c. 1609, § 2).

§ 3. After the invocation of the Divine Name, and after the individual opinions have been presented in order of precedence, always beginning, however, with the *ponens* or presenter of the cause, a discussion is to be carried out under the guidance of the *praeses* of the tribunal, chiefly in order to establish what is to be determined in the dispositive part of the sentence (cf. c. 1609, § 3).

§ 4. In the discussion, however, each one is permitted to withdraw from his original opinion, with a notation of this withdrawal being made on the opinion itself. But a judge who does not wish to agree to the decision of the others can demand that his opinion be sent *sub secreto* to the higher tribunal.

§ 5. But if the judges in the first discussion are not willing or able to arrive at a sentence, the decision can be deferred to another meeting to be set in writing, but not beyond a week, unless the instruction of the cause is to be completed, in accordance with art. 239, in which case the judges must decree: *dilata et compleantur acta* (cf. c. 1609, § 5).

§ 6. When a decision has been agreed upon, the *ponens* is to write it in the form of an affirmative or negative response to the doubt proposed, then sign it together with the other judges and attach it to the dossier of the acts.

§ 7. The opinions of the individual judges are to be added to the acts in a closed envelope to be kept secret (cf. c. 1609, § 2).

Art. 249—§ 1. In a collegial tribunal, it pertains to the *ponens* or presenter to draw up the sentence, unless in the discussion it appeared that for a just cause this task was to be entrusted to another of the judges (cf. c. 1610, § 2).

§ 2. The one drawing up the sentence is to take the reasons from those things which the individual judges brought up in the discussion, unless the motives to be set forth had already been determined by a majority of the judges (cf. c. 1610, § 2).

§ 3. The sentence is then to be submitted for the approval of the individual judges (cf. c. 1610, § 2).

§ 4. If there is a single judge, he will draw up the sentence (c. 1610, § 1).

§ 5. The sentence is to be issued not longer than a month after the day when the cause was decided, unless, in a collegial tribunal, the judges for a grave reason had given a longer time period (cf. c. 1610, § 3).

Art. 250—§ 1. The sentence must:

1°   decide the question being debated before the tribunal, with an appropriate response given to each of the doubts;
2°   present the arguments or reasons, in law and in fact, on which the dispositive part of the sentence is based;
3°   add, if need be, the *vetitum* mentioned in art. 251;
4°   make a determination about the judicial expenses (cf. c. 1611).

Art. 251—§ 1. If a party in the process was found to be absolutely impotent or incapable of marriage by reason of a permanent incapacity, a *vetitum* is to be added to the sentence, by which the party is prohibited to enter a new marriage unless the same tribunal which issued the sentence has been consulted.

§ 2. But if a party was the cause of the nullity of the marriage by deception or by simulation, the tribunal is bound to see whether, having considered all the circumstances of the case, a *vetitum* should be added to the sentence, by which the party is prohibited to enter a new marriage unless the Ordinary of the place in which the marriage is to be celebrated has been consulted.

§ 3. If a lower tribunal added a *vetitum* to the sentence, the tribunal of appeal is to see whether it is to be confirmed.

Art. 252—In the sentence the parties are to be warned about the moral obligations or even civil ones by which they may be bound in regard to the other party or offspring concerning support and education to be provided (c. 1689).

Art. 253—§ 1. The sentence, after the invocation of the Divine Name, must express in order the following: who is the judge or tribunal; who is the petitioner, the respondent party, the procurator, with name and domicile properly indicated; and who is the defender of the bond and the promoter of justice, if he had had taken part in the process (cf. c. 1612, § 1).

§ 2. Then it must present briefly the facts with the positions of the parties and the formulation of the doubts (c. 1612, § 2).

§ 3. The dispositive part of the sentence follows these things, preceded by the reasons both in law and in fact on which it is based (cf. c. 1612, § 3).

§ 4. It is to be concluded with the indication of the place, the day, the month and the year in which it was given, and with the signatures of all the judges, or of the single judge, and the notary (cf. c. 1612, § 4).

§ 5. There is to be added, moreover, information about whether the sentence can be executed immediately, about the way in which it can be challenged and, as the case may be, information about the transmission *ex officio* to the tribunal of appeal (cf. cc. 1614; 1682, § 1).

Art. 254—§ 1. The sentence, avoiding both an excessive brevity and an excessive length, must be clear in explaining the reasons in law and in fact and must be based *in actis et probatis*, so that it is apparent by what path the judges arrived at their decision and how they applied the law to the facts.

§ 2. The presentation of the facts, however, as the nature of the matter requires, is to be done prudently and cautiously, avoiding any offense to the parties, the witnesses, the judges and the other ministers of the tribunals.

Art. 255—But if a judge, by reason of death, grave illness or other impediment is not able to add his signature to the sentence, it is sufficient that the *praeses* of the college or the judicial vicar declares this, attaching an authentic copy of the dispositive part of the sentence signed by the judge on the day of the decision according to art. 248, § 6.

Art. 256—The rules set out above concerning a definitive sentence are also to be adapted to an interlocutory sentence (c. 1613).

Art. 257—§ 1. The sentence is to be published as soon as possible, and it has no force before the publication, even if the dispositive part, by permission of the judge, is made known to the parties (cf. c. 1614).

§ 2. If there is the possibility for an appeal, information is to be provided at the time of the publication of the sentence regarding the way in which an appeal is to be placed and pursued, with explicit mention being made of the faculty to approach the Roman Rota besides the local tribunal of appeal (cf. c. 1614).

Art. 258—§ 1. The publication or communication of the sentence is to be made either by giving a copy of the sentence to the parties or their procurators, or by sending it to them in accordance with art. 130 (cf. c. 1615).

§ 2. The sentence must always be communicated in the same way to the defender of the bond and to the promoter of justice, if he took part in the process.

§ 3. But if a party has declared that he does not want any notice at all about the cause, he is considered to have renounced his right to obtain a copy of the sentence. In such case, with due observance of particular law, the dispositive part of the sentence may be communicated to the same party.

Art. 259—A valid definitive sentence cannot be retracted, even if the judges unanimously consent to this.

Art. 260—§ 1. If an error found its way into the text of the sentence in transcribing the dispositive part or in relating the facts or the petitions of the parties, or if those things required by art. 253, § 4 are omitted, the sentence can be corrected or completed by the tribunal which issued it, either at the request of a party or *ex officio*, but the defender of the bond and the parties must always be heard first, and a decree must be added at the end of the sentence (cf. c. 1616, § 1).

§ 2. But if a party or the defender of the bond does not agree, the incidental question is to be decided by decree (cf. c. 1616, § 2).

Art. 261—The other pronouncements of a judge, besides a sentence, are decrees. These however, if they are not merely procedural, do not have force unless they express the reasons at least summarily, or refer to reasons expressed in another act which has been properly published (cf. c. 1617).

Art. 262—An interlocutory sentence or decree has the force of a definitive sentence if it impedes the trial or puts an end to the trial or a grade of it, at least in reference to a party in the cause (c. 1618).

TITLE XI

The Transmission of the Cause to the Tribunal of Appeal and Its Processing

Art. 263—§ 1. For validity, a tribunal must be collegial in the second or higher grade of trial, in accordance with art. 30, § 4.

§ 2. The same is the case if the cause is processed through the shorter form, in accordance with art. 265.

Art. 264—A sentence which has first declared the nullity of a marriage is to be sent *ex officio* to the tribunal of appeal within twenty days of the publication of the sentence, together with the appeals, if there are any, and the other acts of the trial (can 1682, § 1)

Art. 265—§ 1. If a sentence has been pronounced in favor of the nullity of marriage in the first grade of trial, the tribunal of appeal, having considered the observations of the defender of the bond of the same court of appeal and also of the parties, if they have any, is by a decree either to confirm the sentence by an abbreviated procedure or to admit the cause to an ordinary examination in a new grade of trial (cf. c. 1682, § 2).

§ 2. Once the time limits established by law have passed and the judicial acts have been received, a college of judges is to be named as soon as possible and the *praeses* or *ponens* by his decree is to send the acts to the defender of the bond for an opinion and is to advise the parties that, if they wish, they are to propose their observations to the tribunal of appeal.

§ 3. All the acts are to be available to the judges before the college issues the decree mentioned in § 1.

§ 4. For validity, the decree by which an affirmative sentence is confirmed by the abbreviated procedure must express the reasons at least summarily and must respond to the observations of the defender of the bond and, as the case may be, of the parties (cf. c. 1617).

§ 5. Even in a decree by which a cause is admitted to an ordinary examination the reasons are to be expressed summarily, indicating what further instruction is required, if that is the case.

§ 6. If a sentence issued in the first grade of trial declared a marriage null on the basis of several grounds of nullity, that sentence can be confirmed by the abbreviated procedure on several grounds or on one only.

Art. 266—A cause is always to be processed through an ordinary examination in the second or higher grade of trial, whenever it is a matter of a negative sentence against which an appeal has been filed or an affirmative sentence which has been issued in the second or higher grade.

Art. 267—§ 1. If a cause is to be handled in the second or higher grade of trial through an ordinary examination, it is to be processed in the same way as in first instance, with appropriate adaptations (cf. c. 1640).

§ 2. Unless the proofs are to be completed, after the citations have been carried out and the formulation of the doubt has been set, the tribunal is to proceed as soon as possible to the discussion of the cause and to the sentence (cf. c. 1640).

§ 3. New proofs, however, are to be admitted only in accordance with art. 239 (cf. c. 1639, § 2).

Art. 268—§ 1. If in the grade of appeal a new ground of nullity is proposed, the tribunal can, as if in first instance, admit it, with due observance of artt. 114-125, 135-137, and make a judgment concerning it (cf. c. 1683).

§ 2. For validity, however, the hearing of that new ground in the second or higher instance is reserved to a tribunal of the third or higher grade of trial.

§ 3. If a sentence in favor of the nullity of marriage on the basis of that new ground is given as if in first instance, the competent tribunal is to proceed in accordance with art. 265, § 1.

TITLE XII

The Challenge of the Sentence

Chapter I: A complaint of nullity against the sentence

Art. 269—If the tribunal of appeal sees that the oral contentious process was employed in the lower grade of trial, it is to declare the nullity of the sentence and remit the cause to the tribunal which issued the sentence (cf. c. 1669).

Art. 270—In accordance with canon 1620, a sentence is affected by the defect of irremediable nullity if:

1° it was issued by a judge who was absolutely incompetent;
2° it was issued by one who lacked the power of judging in the tribunal which issued the sentence;
3° the judge issued the sentence impelled by force or grave fear;
4° the trial was carried out without the judicial petition mentioned in art. 114, or was not instituted against any respondent party;
5° it was issued between parties, at least one of whom lacked personal standing in the trial;
6° someone acted in the name of another without a legitimate mandate;
7° the right of defense was denied to one or both of the parties;
8° the controversy was not decided even in part.

Art. 271—A complaint of the nullity described in art. 270 can be proposed in perpetuity by way of an exception, but by way of an action it can be proposed within ten years from the day of the publication of the sentence (cf. c. 1621).

Art. 272—A sentence is affected by the defect of remediable nullity only if:

1° it is issued by an illegitimate number of judges, contrary to the rule of art. 30;
2° it does not contain the motives, that is, the reasons for which the decision was made;
3° it lacks the signatures required by law;
4° it does not bear the indication of the day, month, year and place in which it was issued;
5° it is based on a null judicial act, whose nullity has not been sanated;
6° it is issued against a party who was legitimately absent in accordance with art. 139, § 2 (cf. c. 1622).

Art. 273—A complaint of nullity in the cases mentioned in art. 272 can be proposed within three months from the notice of the publication of the sentence; once this term has elapsed the sentence is considered to have been sanated *ipso iure* (cf. c. 1623).

Art. 274—§ 1. The judge who issued a sentence is to hear the complaint of nullity proposed by way of an action; but if the party fears that the judge, who issued the sentence being challenged by a complaint of nullity, is overly concerned about the matter, and thus considers him suspect, he can demand that another judge be appointed in his place, in accordance with art. 69, § 1 (cf. c. 1624).

§ 2. If the complaint of nullity concerns sentences issued in two or more grades of trial, the judge who issued the last sentence is to hear the matter.

§ 3. A complaint of nullity can also be proposed together with an appeal, within the time limit established for appealing, or together with a petition for a new examination of the same cause, mentioned in art. 290 (cf. c. 1625).

Art. 275—The judge before whom a cause is pending is to hear a complaint of nullity proposed by way of an exception or *ex officio* in accordance with art. 77, § 1.

Art. 276—§ 1. Not only the parties who consider themselves aggrieved can propose a complaint of nullity, but also the defender of the bond and the promoter of justice, whenever he had taken part in the cause or is taking part in it by virtue of a decree of the judge (cf. c. 1626, § 1).

§ 2. The judge himself can retract or amend a sentence issued by himself, within the time limit for acting set by art. 273, unless in the meantime an appeal together with a complaint of nullity has been filed or the nullity of the sentence has been sanated by the passage of the time limit mentioned in art. 273 (cf. c. 1626, § 2).

Art. 277—§ 1. Causes of complaint of nullity proposed by way of an action can be handled following the rules for the oral contentious process, while causes of complaint of nullity proposed by way of an exception or *ex officio* in accordance with art. 77, § 1 are to be handled according to artt. 217-225 and 227 concerning incidental causes (cf. c. 1627).

§ 2. It pertains, however, to a collegial tribunal to hear the nullity of a decision issued by a collegial tribunal.

§ 3. Appeal is possible from a decision concerning a complaint of nullity.

Art. 278—If a sentence has been declared null by the tribunal of appeal, the cause is remitted to the tribunal *a quo* so that it may proceed in accordance with the law.

Chapter II: The appeal

Art. 279—§ 1. A party who considers himself aggrieved by a sentence, the defender of the bond, and likewise the promoter of justice if he had taken part in the trial, have the right to appeal from the sentence to the higher judge, without prejudice to the requirement of art. 280 (cf. c. 1628).

§ 2. Without prejudice to the requirement of art. 264, the defender of the bond is bound by office to appeal, if he considers the sentence which first declared the nullity of the marriage to be insufficiently founded.

Art. 280—§ 1. There is no appeal given:

1° from a sentence of the Supreme Pontiff himself or of the Apostolic Signatura;

2° from a sentence affected by the defect of nullity, unless it is filed together with a complaint of nullity, in accordance with art. 274, § 3;

3° from a sentence which has passed into *res iudicata*;

4° from a decree of the judge or from an interlocutory sentence which do not have the force of a definitive sentence, unless it is filed together with an appeal from a definitive sentence;

5° from a sentence or from a decree in a cause which the law provides is to be decided *expeditissime* (c. 1629).

§ 2. The prescription given in § 1, no. 3, does not concern a sentence by which the principal cause of nullity of marriage has been decided (cf. c. 1643).

Art. 281—§ 1. An appeal must be filed before the judge by whom (*a quo*) the sentence was issued, within the peremptory time limit of fifteen canonical days from notice of the publication of the sentence (c. 1630, § 1).

§ 2. It is sufficient that the appellant party signify to the judge *a quo* that he is filing an appeal.

§ 3. If this is done orally, the notary is to consign this to writing in the presence of the appellant himself (c. 1630, § 2).

§ 4. But if the appeal is filed when only the dispositive part of the sentence has been made known to the parties before the sentence is published, in accordance with art. 257, § 1, then art. 285, § 1 is to be observed.

Art. 282—If a question arises concerning the legitimacy of the appeal, the tribunal of appeal is to hear it *expeditissime* following the rules for the oral contentious process (cf. c. 1631).

Art. 283—§ 1. If it is not indicated in the appeal to which tribunal it is directed, it is presumed to have been made to the tribunal of appeal mentioned in art. 25 (cf. c. 1632, § 1).

§ 2. If one party appeals to the Roman Rota but the other party to another tribunal of appeal, the Roman Rota is to hear the cause, without prejudice to art. 18 (cf. c. 1632, § 2).

§ 3. When an appeal to the Roman Rota has been filed, the tribunal *a quo* must send the acts to it. But if the acts already have been sent to the other tribunal of appeal, the tribunal *a quo* is to inform it immediately of the matter, lest it begin to treat the cause, and so that it sends the acts to the Roman Rota.

§ 4. However, before the time limits set by the law have expired, no tribunal of appeal can make a cause its own, lest the parties be deprived of their right of appealing to the Roman Rota.

Art. 284—§ 1. An appeal is to be pursued before the judge to whom (*ad quem*) it has been directed within a month of its filing, unless the judge *a quo* has granted the party a longer time for pursuing it (c. 1633).

§ 2. The appellant can call upon the assistance of the tribunal *a quo* to send to the tribunal *ad quod* the act pursuing the appeal.

Art. 285—§ 1. In order to pursue an appeal, it is required and it is sufficient that the party calls upon the assistance of the higher judge to emend the challenged decision, attaching a copy of this sentence and indicating the reasons for the appeal (c. 1634, § 1).

§ 2. But if the party cannot obtain a copy of the challenged sentence within the canonical time period, the time limits do not run in the meantime and the obstacle is to be made known to the appellate judge, who is to oblige the judge *a quo* to carry out his duty as soon as possible (c. 1634, § 2).

§ 3. Meanwhile the judge *a quo* must send the acts in accordance with art. 90 to the appellate judge (cf. c. 1634, § 3).

Art. 286—When the time limits concerning appeals, before both the judge *a quo* and the judge *ad quem*, have expired without any action, the appeal is considered to have been abandoned (c. 1635).

Art. 287—The appellant can renounce the appeal, with the effects described in art. 151 (cf. c. 1636).

Art. 288—§ 1. An appeal filed by the petitioning party benefits the respondent party as well, and vice versa (cf. c. 1637, § 1).

§ 2. If an appeal is filed by one party regarding one ground of the sentence, the other party, even if the time limits for the appeal have expired, can appeal incidentally concerning other grounds of nullity within the peremptory time limit of fifteen days from the day when the principal appeal had been communicated to him (cf. c. 1637, § 3).

§ 3. Unless it is otherwise evident, an appeal is presumed to be made against all the grounds of a sentence (c. 1637, § 4).

Art. 289—§ 1. Causes of the nullity of marriage never become *res iudicata* (cf. c. 1643).

§ 2. However, a matrimonial cause which has been judged by one tribunal can never be judged again by the same or another tribunal of the same grade, without prejudice to art. 9, § 2.

§ 3. This provision applies only if it is a matter of the same cause, that is, concerning the same marriage and the same ground of nullity.

Chapter III: A petition for a new examination of the same cause after two conforming decisions

Art. 290—§ 1. If a double conforming sentence in a cause of the nullity of marriage has been passed, there is no possibility for an appeal, but the sentence can be challenged at any time before a tribunal of third or higher instance, as long as new and grave proofs or arguments have been brought forward within the peremptory time limit of thirty days from the time the challenge was proposed (cf. c. 1644, § 1).

§ 2. This provision is to be followed also if a sentence which declared the nullity of marriage has been confirmed not by another sentence but by decree (cf. c. 1684, § 2).

Art. 291—§ 1. Two sentences or decisions are said to be formally conforming if they have been issued between the same parties, concerning the nullity of the same marriage, and on the basis of the same ground of nullity and the same reasoning of law and of fact (cf. c. 1641, no. 1).

§ 2. Decisions are considered to be equivalently or substantially conforming when, even though they specify and determine the ground of nullity by different names, they are still rooted in the same facts rendering the marriage null and the same proofs.

§ 3. Without prejudice to art. 136 and without prejudice to the right of defense, the tribunal of appeal which issued the second decision is to decide about the equivalent or substantial conformity, or else a higher tribunal.

Art. 292—§ 1. It is not required that the new arguments or proofs, mentioned in art. 290, § 1, be most grave, much less that they be decisive, that is, those which peremptorily demand a contrary decision, but it is enough that they render this probable.

§ 2. However mere objections or critical observations about the sentence are not sufficient.

Art. 293—§ 1. Within a month of the exhibition of the new proofs and arguments, the tribunal of appeal, having heard the defender of the bond and having informed the other party, must decide by decree whether the new proposition of the cause must be admitted or not (cf. c. 1644, § 1).

§ 2. If the new proposition of the cause is admitted, the tribunal is to proceed in accordance with art. 267.

Art. 294—A petition for obtaining a new proposition of the cause does not suspend the execution of a double conforming decision, unless the tribunal of appeal, holding that the petition is probably founded and that irreparable damage could arise from the execution, orders the suspension (cf. c. 1644, § 2).

TITLE XIII

The Documentary Process

Art. 295—When a petition proposed in accordance with artt. 114-117 has been received, the Judicial Vicar or a judge designated by him, having omitted the solemnities of the ordinary process but with the parties having been cited and with the defender of the bond having taken part, can declare the nullity of the marriage by a sentence if, from a document which is subject to no contradiction or exception, there is established with certainty the existence of a diriment impediment or of the defect of legitimate form, as long as with equal certainty it is clear that a dispensation was not granted, or the lack of a valid mandate of a proxy (cf. c. 1686).

Art. 296—§ 1. The competent Judicial Vicar is determined in accordance with art. 10.

§ 2. The Judicial Vicar or the designated judge first of all is to see whether all those things are present which in accordance with art. 295 are required in order for the cause to be able to be decided through the documentary process. But if he judges or prudently doubts whether all those things are present, the ordinary process must be followed.

Art. 297—§ 1. Since, however, the existence of the impediment of impotence or a defect of legitimate form can only rarely be established through a document not subject to contradiction or exception, the Judicial Vicar or judge is to carry out a preliminary investigation in these cases, lest a cause be admitted lightly and with temerity to the documentary process.

§ 2. But in regard to parties who attempted marriage before a civil official or non-Catholic minister while they were bound to canonical form according to c. 1117, art. 5, § 3 is to be observed.

Art. 298—§ 1. Against the declaration mentioned in art. 295, the defender of the bond, if he prudently thinks that the defects indicated in that same article or the lack of dispensation are not certain, must appeal to the judge of second instance, to whom the acts are to be sent and who is to be advised in writing that it is a matter of the documentary process (cf. c. 1687, § 1).

§ 2. A party who feels aggrieved retains the right to appeal (c. 1687, § 2).

Art. 299—The judge of the second instance, with the intervention of the defender of the bond and having heard the parties, is to decide, in the same manner indicated in art. 295, whether the sentence is to be confirmed or rather that the cause must be handled through the ordinary process of law; in the latter case, he is to remit the cause to the tribunal of first instance (cf. c. 1688).

TITLE XIV

The Recording of the Nullity of the Marriage and Those Things Which Are to Precede the Celebration of a New Marriage

Art. 300—§ 1. As soon as a sentence in favor of the nullity of marriage has been made executable in accordance with art. 301, the Judicial Vicar is to communicate it to the Ordinary of the place in which the marriage was celebrated. The Ordinary, however, must see that mention of the declaration of the nullity of the marriage and of any *vetita* that may have been imposed is made in the marriage and baptismal registers (cf. c. 1685).

§ 2. But if the Ordinary has it for certain that the decision is null, he is to remit the matter to the tribunal, without prejudice to art. 274, § 2, and with the parties having been informed (cf. c. 1654, § 2).

Art. 301—§ 1. After a sentence which has first declared the nullity of marriage has been confirmed in a grade of appeal either by sentence or by decree, those whose marriage has been declared null can contract new marriages as soon as the decree or the second sentence has been communicated to them, unless this has been prohibited by a *vetitum* added to the sentence or decree itself or imposed by the Ordinary of the place, without prejudice to art. 294 (cf. c. 1684, § 1).

§ 2. The same is the case after a marriage has been declared null in a documentary process by a sentence which has not been appealed.

§ 3. However, those things which must precede the celebration of marriage in accordance with c. 1066-1071 are to be observed.

TITLE XV

Judicial Expenses and Gratuitous Legal Assistance

Art. 302—The parties are bound to contribute to paying the judicial expenses according to their ability.

Art. 303—§ 1. The Diocesan Bishop, in regard to a diocesan tribunal, or the *coetus* of Bishops or the Bishop designated by them, in regard to an interdiocesan tribunal, is to set norms:

1° concerning judicial expenses to be paid or reimbursed;
2° concerning the honoraria of procurators, advocates, experts and interpreters, as well as the recompense of witnesses;
3° concerning the granting of gratuitous legal assistance or the reduction of expenses;
4° concerning the reparation of damages if they were inflicted on the other party;
5° concerning the deposit or security to be offered in regard to expenses to be paid or damages to be repaired (cf. c. 1649, § 1).

§ 2. In setting these norms, the Bishop is to keep in mind the particular nature of matrimonial causes, which demands that, inasmuch as this can be done, both spouses take part in a process of nullity (cf. art. 95, § 1).

Art. 304—§ 1. It pertains to the college to determine, in the definitive sentence, whether the expenses are to be paid by the petitioner alone or also by the other party, and to set the proportion of payments between one party and the other. Account is to be taken, however, of the poverty of the parties in terms of the payment of expenses to be decided, with due observance of the norms mentioned in art. 303 (cf. c. 1611, no. 4).

§ 2. No separate appeal is allowed against the decision regarding expenses, honoraria, and damages but a party can have recourse within fifteen days to the same college, which can change the amount charged (cf. c. 1649, § 2).

Art. 305—Those who are completely unable to bear the judicial expenses have a right to obtain an exemption from them; those who can pay them in part, have the right to a reduction of the same expenses.

Art. 306—§ 1. In setting the norms mentioned in art. 303, § 1, no. 3, it is advisable that the Bishop keep the following in mind:

1° one who wishes to obtain an exemption from judicial expenses or their reduction and gratuitous legal assistance, must give the Judicial Vicar or *praeses* a *libellus*, with proofs or documents attached, by which he demonstrates what is his economic condition;

2° the cause however, must enjoy a presumed *bonum ius*, especially if it is a matter of an incidental question which he has proposed;

3° before the granting of gratuitous legal assistance or a reduction of the expenses, the Judicial Vicar or the *praeses*, if he considers it appropriate, is to request the votum of the promoter of justice and the defender of the bond, having first sent them the libellus and documents;

4° the total or partial exemption from expenses is presumed to perdure in higher instance, unless the *praeses* for a just cause revokes it.

Art. 307—§ 1. If the *praeses* thinks that gratuitous legal assistance is to be granted, he is to request the Judicial Vicar to designate an advocate who will provide the gratuitous legal assistance.

§ 2. An advocate designated to provide gratuitous legal assistance cannot withdraw from this function unless for a reason approved by the judge.

§ 3. If the advocate does not fulfill his duty with due diligence, he is to be called to do so, whether *ex officio* or at the insistence of the party or the defender of the bond or the promoter of justice, if he is taking part in the cause.

Art. 308—The Bishop Moderator is to see that neither by the manner of acting of the ministers of the tribunal nor by excessive expenses are the faithful kept away from the ministry of the tribunal with grave harm to souls, whose salvation must always remain the supreme law in the Church.

This Instruction, prepared by this Pontifical Council by mandate of the Supreme Pontiff John Paul II granted *pro hac vice* on the fourth of February, 2003, with the close cooperation of the Congregation for the Doctrine of the Faith, the Congregation for Divine Worship and the Discipline of the Sacraments, the Supreme Tribunal of the Apostolic Signatura and the Tribunal of the Roman Rota, was approved by the same Roman Pontiff on the eighth of November, 2004, who ordered that it be observed by those to whom it pertains immediately from the day of its publication.

Given in Rome at the Pontifical Council for Legislative Texts, on the twenty-fifth day of January, 2005, the Feast of the Conversion of St. Paul.

Julián Cardinal Herranz
President

Bruno Bertagna
Secretary

Notes

1   Second Vatican Council, Past. Const. *Gaudium et Spes*, no. 48d.

2   Second Vatican Council, Past. Const. *Gaudium et Spes*, chap. I, nos. 47-52.

3   Second Vatican Council, Past. Const. *Gaudium et Spes*, no. 48b.

4   Second Vatican Council, Past. Const. *Gaudium et Spes*, no. 48a.

5   John Paul II, Alloc. to the Auditors of the Roman Rota, Jan. 27, 1997, in AAS 89 (1997) 487.

6   St. Augustine, *De Bono Coniugii*, 4, 4, in CSEL 41, 191.

7   John Paul II, Alloc. to the Auditors of the Roman Rota, Jan. 27, 1997, in AAS 89 (1997) 488 (cf. John Paul II, Alloc. to the Auditors of the Roman Rota, Jan. 28, 2002, in AAS 94 [2002] 340- 346).

8   Cf. Pius XII, Alloc. to the Auditors of the Roman Rota, Oct. 3, 1941, in AAS 33 (1941) 423.

9   Cf. especially John Paul II, Alloc. to the Auditors of the Roman Rota, Feb. 5, 1987, in AAS 79 (1997) 1453-1459, and Jan. 25, 1988, in AAS 80 (1997) 1178-1185.

10   John Paul II, Apost. Const. *Sacrae Disciplinae Leges*, Jan. 25, 1983, in AAS 75/2 (1983) VIII and XI.

11   Paul VI, Motu Proprio *Causas Matrimoniales*, Mar. 28, 1971, in AAS 63 (1971) 442.

12   Cf. AAS 28 (1936) 313-361.

13   Cf. John Paul II, Alloc. to the Auditors of the Roman Rota, Jan. 22, 1996, in AAS 88 (1996) 774-775, and Jan. 17, 1998, in AAS 90 (1998) 783-785.

14   AAS 28 (1936) 314.

15   Cf. Pont. Comm. for the Auth. Interp. of the CIC, Resp., June 26, 1984, in AAS 76 (1984) 747.

16   Cf. Pont. Comm. for the Auth. Interpr. of the CIC, Resp., Feb. 28, 1986, in AAS 78 (1986) 1323.

17   Cf. Pont. Comm. for the Auth. Interpr. of the CIC, Resp., Apr. 29, 1986, in AAS 78 (1986) 1324.

18 Cf. Norms of the Tribunal of the Roman Rota, Apr. 18, 1994, art. 70, in *AAS* 86 (1994) 528.

19 Cf. Cong. for the Doctrine of the Faith, *Professio fidei et iusiurandum fidelitatis in suscipiendo officio nomine Ecclesiae exercendo una cum nota doctrinali adnexa*, June 29, 1998, in *AAS* 90 (1998) 542-551.

20 Cf. Cong. for the Sacraments, Circular Letter, Dec. 20, 1986, no. 7.

21 Cf. Cong. for the Sacraments, Circular Letter, Dec. 20, 1986, no. 23b.

22 Cf. Cong. for the Sacraments, Circular Letter, Dec. 20, 1986, no. 7.

23 Cf. Pius XII, Alloc. to the Auditors of the Roman Rota, Oct. 2, 1944, in *AAS* 36 (1944) 281-290.

24 Cf. John Paul II, Alloc. to the Auditors of the Roman Rota, Feb. 5, 1987, in *AAS* 79 (1987) 1453-1459 and Jan. 25, 1988, in *AAS* 80 (1988) 1178-1185.

25 Cf. John Paul II, Alloc. to the Auditors of the Roman Rota, Jan. 22, 1996, no. 4, in *AAS* 88 (1996) 773-777.

CHAPTER VII

Speeches by
Cardinal Tarcisio Bertone

PAPAL LEGATE TO THE
SIXTH WORLD MEETING OF FAMILIES
(MEXICO CITY, JANUARY 14-18, 2009)

Address to the Bishops of the
Mexican Episcopal Conference*

January 16, 2009

Your Excellency, President of the Mexican Bishops' Conference,
Your Eminences, the Cardinals,
My dear brother Bishops,

1. I am happy to be here with you on this day, and I am also grateful for the warm welcome given to me as legate of His Holiness Benedict XVI for the Sixth World Meeting of Families. I thank Bishop Carlos Aguiar Retes, Bishop of Texcoco and president of the Mexican Bishops' Conference, for the kind and thoughtful words of welcome that he has addressed to me in the name of you all. Allow me, above all, to pass on the Successor of Peter's affectionate greeting, as well as his spiritual presence with you. My own presence here is at the Pope's express desire, since, finding it impossible to make this trip he had longed for, he decided to make himself present through me, his closest

---

* This text is an unofficial translation of the Spanish in the Italian compendium.

collaborator as Secretary of State. His Holiness well knows the strength and vitality of the Church in Mexico, the dedication and commitment of all its members, pastors and faithful alike, to the Gospel's cause, as well as its faithfulness and fervent love for the Blessed Virgin and its unity with the Roman Pontiff. Likewise, the Bishop of Rome wishes to encourage you so that, in the midst of the present difficulties, you will not falter in your task of proclaiming the good news of salvation, Jesus Christ Our Savior, to all men. For this reason he accompanies the sons and daughters of this blessed Mexican land, land of Christ and Mary, with his heart at every moment.

2. Dear brothers, in the last meeting of the plenary assembly of the Conference of Mexican Bishops last November, you reflected amply, together with a hundred eighteen laymen coming from many Mexican dioceses, on the need to spearhead a new prominence of the laity (cf. *Message of the Bishops of Mexico to the People of God*, November 13, 2008, no. 3). Indeed, the Second Vatican Council emphasized the specific and absolutely necessary role of the baptized in the saving mission of the Church. As living members of the one Body of Christ, "they are called upon, as living members, to expend all their energy for the growth of the Church and its continuous sanctification" (*Lumen Gentium*, no. 33). There is no doubt that the times are ripe for lay people to assume fully their proper vocation in the Church and in society. Moreover, present circumstances and the general world situation are calling for a more intense, widespread secular apostolate, full of zeal and love for God. But in what does a specifically lay apostolate specific consist? Where does it develop, and by what means is it accomplished? In the last pastoral letter of the Mexican Episcopate, you clearly expressed that "the lay faithful fulfill their Christian vocation principally in secular tasks" (Pastoral Letter *From Encounter with Jesus Christ to Solidarity with All*, 270). You follow the doctrine established by Vatican II on this point, where it affirmed that the baptized "exercise the apostolate in fact by their activity directed to the evangelization and sanctification of men and to the penetrating and perfecting of the temporal order through the spirit of the Gospel. In this way, their temporal activity openly bears witness to Christ and promotes the salvation of men" (*Apostolicam Actuositatem*, no. 2).

3. The witness of lay people is especially relevant and decisive in the political and cultural arenas, by virtue of its transcendence when it comes to molding society according to the spirit of Christ. They must be encouraged and offered all the help necessary to get involved in the influential positions in their country, with integrity and with a true spirit of service. A Christian who is fully aware of his or her vocation as a child of God cannot avoid the charity-filled, respectful effort to make the fertile values of the Gospel

enlighten all levels of society. In this way faithful lay people fulfill their duty as citizens with renewed effort and breadth of vision, since their Christian vocation does not separate them from the world; on the contrary, it moves them to take part in the building up of civil society, contributing in this way to the common good of the whole nation to which they belong by right.

4. I would also like to mention, given its importance, an area of top priority for the Church's apostolate, most especially of the lay apostolate: marriage and the family. Christian spouses are called to give special witness to the sanctity of matrimony, as well as to its importance for society. They are the ones who can best show others the beauty of God's plan for human love, matrimony and the family. Founded on the marriage between a man and a woman, the family is the foundational structure of human society. In the communion of life and love that is marriage, both the sexual difference between man and woman and the call of love that God has placed in our hearts find their *raison d'être*. In fact, God created man *out of* love and *for* love (cf. John Paul II, Apostolic Exhortation *Familiaris Consortio*, no. 11). The bond of spousal self-giving, made of tenderness, respect and responsible surrender, is the natural place for human life to be conceived and to find the protection and welcome that its dignity requires. For this reason, working for the good of marriage and of the family means fighting for the good of the human being and of society. Striving to form a nation's juridical structure so that it will respect the identity of this natural institution, which lies at the basis of its very social structure, is of prime importance. Nevertheless, it is not enough to count on good laws; it is also necessary to work hard on a vast endeavor of education and formation that will help everyone—young people especially—discover and value the beauty and importance of marriage and the family. I am fully convinced, dear brothers, that the celebration of the Sixth World Meeting of Families will be a unique, providential occasion to give further encouragement to family-oriented pastoring in your diocesan communities, empowering and multiplying the numerous pastoral initiatives that are already showing abundant results.

5. In order to fulfill this demanding mission, the faithful need to rely on an intense spiritual life and a solid formation, based above all on an attentive, meditated hearing of the Word of God. All of us in the Church need that intimate contact with the Lord in Scripture. This is why the Pope, in the concluding Mass of the last Synod of Bishops, said that "the Church's principal task, at the start of this new millennium, is above all to nourish herself on the Word of God, in order to make new evangelization, the proclamation in our day, more effective" (Benedict XVI, Homily, October 26, 2008). In fact, evangelizing does not just consist in communicating points of

doctrinal content, but in offering the proposal of an encounter with Christ. An encounter with Jesus, the Savior, who, by touching the mind and heart with the light of his truth and strength of his love, can both quench the deep thirst for God that so many of our brothers have, and bring them in turn to living the Gospel with all of its consequences. In the end, it means offering hope to all, the great hope which is God himself and that stands higher than all other human hopes, giving them a definitive basis (cf. Benedict XVI, *Spe Salvi*, no. 31). The Holy Father urges you that, in these moments when your beloved country is experiencing a difficult situation, you do not cease holding up Christ as the true motive for hope. By going to our Lord and putting his teachings into practice, as the Virgin Mary indicated at the Wedding of Cana (cf. Jn 2:5), Mexico will be able to overcome all obstacles and build a more just, freer tomorrow for all, where an end is put to the blights on society that keep a stranglehold on its development, and especially where the dignity of the human person from conception to natural death will be respected.

6. Dear brother bishops, following the outline of the final document of the Fifth General Latin American and Caribbean Bishops' Conference celebrated in Aparecida, may you desire to know, follow, and surrender yourselves to Christ, so that, as fearless missionaries, you may be able to help others know him. In this vast effort of evangelization, priests play a very important role. They are your first and closest collaborators and, carrying the weight and heat of the day on their shoulders (cf. Mt 20:12), they are deserving of all the care and attention of their bishops. I would like to remind you here of the words addressed by the Pope to the Italian Bishops' Conference: "In fact, it is an essential duty for us Bishops to be constantly close to our priests who participate in the apostolic ministry that the Lord entrusts to us through the Sacrament of Orders. . . . The closer we are to our priests, the greater will be the affection and trust they feel for us, they will excuse our personal limitations, they will welcome our words and will feel solidarity with us in the joys and difficulties of the ministry" (*Address to the Members of the Italian Bishops' Conference*, May 18, 2006). The Pontiff carries all the Mexican priests in his heart and asks you to pass along his recognition and gratitude for their generous dedication, encouraging them to continue carrying out their work with tireless, constant faithfulness, despite often finding themselves in the midst of trials and difficulties.

7. Dear brothers, I wish to thank you one again for your kindnesses and for the welcome you have shown me, as well as to reiterate the Holy Father's special, spiritual closeness and constant concern for you, dear shepherds of the Church in Mexico, for the bishops emeriti, for the priests, seminarians, religious and lay people, and for the whole, beloved Mexican people. May

the Most Blessed Virgin Mary, Our Lady of Guadalupe, Patroness of the Americas, sustain and guide them in their beautiful and demanding pastoral ministry. Thank you so much, and may God bless you.

THEOLOGICAL-PASTORAL CONGRESS
Discourse of Cardinal Tarcisio Bertone

Papal Legate at the Sixth World Meeting of Families "The family, teacher of human and Christian values"

January 16, 2009

Your Eminences,
Dear Brothers in the Episcopate,
Esteemed Brothers and Sisters in the Lord,

I am glad to be able to conclude this Theological-Pastoral Congress in the context of the *Sixth World Meeting of Families*, whose theme proposed by Pope Benedict XVI, "The family, teacher of human and Christian values," has been analyzed.

I greet Cardinal Ennio Antonelli, President of the Pontifical Council for the Family, Cardinal Norberto Rivera Carrera, Archbishop of Mexico City, and also the Cardinals, Bishops, priests, religious and families who have come from various parts of the world.

As Papal Legate, I wish to be the spokesman who delivers the message that the family is the hope and good news for society and for the Church. Human history and the history of humanity's salvation flow through the family. Among the many paths the Church takes to save and serve man, "the family is the first and the most important."[1] The family is not only the axis of man's personal life but also the most important environment and appropriate context in which to live.

The purpose of my discourse is to draw attention to the fact that the family is the most appropriate institution for the transmission of these two values, justice and peace. They are special because in them converge both the individual and social dimensions of the human person that have been thoroughly examined in the past few days.

I shall proceed in this way: after a brief analysis of the current situation, I shall endeavor to show how and why the family is the principle realization of a person's sociability. Secondly, I will analyze the reciprocal relations between society and the family, demonstrating how it is only in this appropriate context that the dynamism of the value of justice and authentic peace are possible. I shall conclude by affirming that only a family founded on a monogamous and indissoluble marriage can faithfully transmit these values.

1. Present historical context

Does the family have anything to offer at the beginning of the third millennium? Could one dispense with the family or is it a permanent reality with an innate value? History shows that the family's contribution to society and to the Church is both considerable and good. It makes possible the very life of society, as well as the incarnation of the Body of Christ throughout the centuries. Historically speaking, when the person, marriage or family is damaged, the whole of created reality is affected. The specificity of the present situation stems from the globalization of problems that in one way or another concern all the continents. We are witnessing numerous conflicts that are threatening to destabilize entire regions. In addition the recent and profound economic crisis is having a strong impact throughout the world.

If what I have just said is worrying, the individualistic and nihilistic diagnosis which is expressed in an exacerbated anthropological pessimism is even more serious. All this is perceptible in vast areas of our planet where widespread malaise and lack of confidence are being felt by society and shown by statistics. It is impossible to overlook the great demographic winter that is gravely threatening entire societies, the lack of meaning in the lives of so many young victims of alcohol and drugs and the extreme violence and exploitation to which we see women and children subjected today, the trafficking of organs and sex that destroys the human person and the neglect of so many sick and elderly people who are deprived of any assistance with which to face the last years of their lives. The crisis of the educational system in many nations that are incapable of transmitting integral knowledge and the political and economic instability that burdens many of the developing countries also deserve mention.

In the whole of this description there is a common denominator: injustice, the lack or absence of rights. Human rights, which derive from the personal nature of being, in both the individual and social aspects of the person, have been trampled upon, diminished or even eliminated. Exasperated individualism creates a replica of the selfishness which, as in the story of Vulcan, is capable of devouring its own children. Hence relativism, hedonism and utilitarianism, with their various expressions and combinations, have generated among other things a commercialization of the whole of Creation and of the human person, its center and its summit (cf. *Gaudium et Spes*, no. 12).

Against this backdrop there are two alternatives: either the deterioration of the situation throughout the planet, reaching limits as yet unknown, or its resolution by applying an appropriate remedy. The latter must be prepared with a healthy anthropology, one that appropriately revives the relations that have deteriorated in every sphere. Only justice imbued with love will be capable of restoring dignity to the person and to the whole of Creation. In this way the civilization of love that was the great passion of the Servant of God Pope Paul VI may become reality. Moreover the family alone, a community of life and love, is in a condition to regenerate society through justice and peace because in the family love presides over all things. In love, the family finds its origins and its purpose. And this family love is what can best teach values. Love by its very nature propagates itself. Therefore the family is like a nursery garden in which seeds of justice and peace are cultivated which will transform, perhaps with difficulty, the mass of all Creation. It is consequently clear that the best investment for governments will be to help, protect and support the family, since it is the institution without which society cannot survive. That so many families can be seen to carry out faithfully the task entrusted to them despite the existing adversities is also a cause of hope. Ever more services are being established in favor of the family. It should be remembered above all that fidelity to its mission has a multiplying effect; the truth about the family, proclaimed and lived, has a constant resonance in the human heart. For this reason let us once again say to families, to every family: "Family, become what you "are."[2]

Family and society

The family as the context and fullest expression of the person is not the product of one epoch but rather a patrimony of all ages and civilizations. The family is far more than a legal, social or financial unit, because to speak of the family is to speak of life of the transmission of values, of education, of solidarity, of stability, of the future and ultimately, of love.[3] The family is a wise institution of the Creator in which the original vocation of the person to interpersonal communion is realized through the sincere gift of self.

The family is the first and original cell of society. In it both the man and the woman live with full meaning their differentiation and complementarity from which the first interpersonal relationship is born. In this sense marriage is the foundation of natural society. This society is called to fulfill itself by generating children: the spousal communion is at the origin of the family.

The family is the original cell of society because in it the person is affirmed for the first time as a person, for himself and freely. He is called to play a role in society similar to that of the cell in the organism. The ethical quality of society is linked to the family. It develops ethically to the extent that it lets itself be modeled by all that constitutes the good of the family.

Not all forms of coexistence serve and contribute to achieving authentic sociability. Necessarily the family must be a family; it is worth noting that its history should develop as a community of life and love in which each of its members is appreciated in his uniqueness: as husband or wife, father or mother, son or daughter, brother or sister. In this way personal dignity will be fully respected, given that interpersonal relations are lived freely, that is, out of love. This is not achieved merely by living together. The family must be a home in which there is "heartfelt acceptance, encounter and dialogue, disinterested availability, generous service and deep solidarity."[4] Thus the family becomes the context in which the true sense of freedom, justice and love can be formed. This must take place: in freedom since only on the basis of freedom is it possible to form responsible people; on the basis of justice, since only in this way is the dignity of others respected; and on the basis of love, since respect for others is ultimately perfected when each one is loved for him or herself.

The family therefore has a specific social function outside the family environment that consists in acting and participating in social life, as a family and because it is a family. However, to contribute to the good of the person to humanization and to society's good it is necessary for the family to respect the overall scale of values that make it a community of life and love. In turn, society must always include among its fundamental tasks the achievement of the common good, which could be described thus: "The common good does not consist in the simple sum of the particular goods of each subject of a social entity. Belonging to everyone and to each person, it is and remains common, because it is indivisible and because only together is it possible to attain it, increase it and safeguard its effectiveness, with regard also to the future."[5]

For its part, the *Catechism of the Catholic Church*, proposing anew the definition of *Gaudium et spes* (no. 26), summarizes the common good in three purposes or properties as follows:

"First, the common good presupposes respect for the person as such . . . the fundamental and inalienable rights of the human person . . . ," and "the conditions for the exercise of the natural freedoms indispensable for the development of the human vocation.

"Second, the common good requires the social well-being and development of the group itself. Development is the epitome of all social duties. Certainly, it is the proper function of authority to arbitrate, in the name of the common good, between various particular interests; but it should make accessible to each what is needed to lead a truly human life: food, clothing, health, work, education and culture. . . .

"Finally, the common good requires peace, that is, the stability and security of a just order. It presupposes that authority should ensure by morally acceptable means the security of society and its members."[6]

Dynamism of justice and peace

We said earlier that justice and peace are fundamental elements of the common good that society must promote and that the family can provide or establish, since it is in the family that the gifts of justice and peace are offered which at the same time constitute the family's proper task. Let us pause for a moment to further consider both values and their relationship to each other.[7]

Peace is one of the values transmitted in both Testaments. It is far more than the absence of war. Peace represents the fullness of life (cf. Mal 2:5). It is an effect of God's Blessing upon his people (cf. Nm 6:26); it produces fruitfulness and well-being (cf. Is 48:18-19) and deep happiness (cf. Prv 12:20). At the same time, peace is the goal of social coexistence as appears in an extraordinary way in the messianic vision of peace described in the Book of the Prophet Isaiah (cf. 2:2-5). In the New Testament, Jesus says explicitly: "Blessed are the peacemakers, for they shall be called sons of God" (Mt 5:9). He not only rejects violence (cf. Mt 26:52; Lk 9:54-55), but goes further, saying: "Love your enemies, do good to those who hate you, bless those who curse you, pray for those who abuse you" (Lk 6:27-28).

Together with the light that comes from Scripture, the history of thought shows us that the culture of peace presupposes order. The definition of St. Augustine and Boethius, taken up by St. Thomas Aquinas, defines peace as tranquility that is born from order.[8] In turn, order presupposes impartiality. St. Thomas defines order as the arrangement of things in conformity with a reference point. Therefore the "reference point" of the order from which peace stems is justice.

Justice, the condition for peace

Justice is a fundamental value of human life. In addition it is an indispensable reality of human coexistence. Justice must be bound to the structure of each person independently of his time, his age or culture. Together with good and truth, justice constitutes the trilogy of the great values and human realities. On the contrary, injustice is related to evil and falsehood. Therefore, the fullness of the human being and the improvement of society are in relation to good, truth and justice. Social coexistence thus loses its meaning if evil, error and injustice prevail. Justice refers us directly to *ius* (right), and in fact one can speak of justice only if rights exist. For this reason, justice consists in giving to each one his right, what he is due.

The triple distinction between commutative, legal and distributive justice covers all aspects of the person, because it includes his rights as well as his duties as an individual, and at the same time demands and safeguards the rights and duties that derive from his radical sociability, an essential constitutive element of the person. In this regard, justice has been the aspiration and duty of every epoch. Plato wrote: "And is not the creation of justice the institution of a natural order and government of one by another in the parts of the soul, and the creation of injustice the production of a state of things at variance with the natural order?"[9]

For its part, Christian tradition supports the undeniable religious dimension of the concepts of *justice* and *just* with regard to the human being's conduct before God, and points out the relationship of justice with the social order.

In this context, we can ask ourselves: is there a biblical doctrine that postulates the value of justice in society? The answer is yes. A wealth of testimonies in both the Old and New Testaments ingrain the precept of fulfilling the duties of justice in social coexistence. Jesus' message contemplates various aspects of the proper coexistence among people, especially in the Synoptics. As the Congregation for the Doctrine of the Faith said in one of its documents, "In the Old Testament, the prophets . . . keep affirming with particular vigor the requirements of justice and solidarity and the need to pronounce a very severe judgments on the rich who oppress the poor. . . . Faithfulness to the Covenant cannot be conceived of without the practice of justice. Justice as regards God and justice as regards mankind are inseparable. . . . These requirements are found once again the New Testament. They are even more radicalized as can be shown in the discourse on the Beatitudes."[10]

In our day, the word "justice" is one of the most frequently used terms in social and political life. In many cases it is the "key" or "joker" of political, economic and social declarations in numerous national and international forums. The continuous use and abuse of it by certain ideologies has endowed it with various meanings.

Despite the clarity of the definition of justice, "its own proper" meaning must be correctly interpreted and defended in each case as a primary subject. If this does not happen, justice will be subjected to the arbitration of the powerful of the moment. Indeed it could happen that justice, which should pave the way to peace, might lose its true meaning and actually provoke extreme violence.

Injustice always spawns violence. At the present time social, economic and political injustice is giving rise to many wars, tensions and conflicts. In the face of war, peace, the fruit of justice and solidarity, should be presented. "Surmounting every type of imperialism and determination to preserve their own hegemony, the stronger and richer nations must have a sense of moral responsibility for the other nations, so that a real international system may be established which will rest on the foundation of the equality of all peoples and on the necessary respect for their legitimate differences. The economically weaker countries, or those still at subsistence level, must be enabled, with the assistance of other peoples and of the international community, to make a contribution of their own to the common good with their treasures of humanity and culture, which otherwise would be lost forever."[11]

However, peace is also achieved on the basis of the small things in ordinary life and in each person's own environment. We Christians must travel all of the earth's paths, scattering peace and joy with our words and actions. No other reality than the family is capable of perseveringly building day after day the peace that results from the manifestation of the inner order of families and also of peoples.

Family: A paradigmatic incarnation between justice and charity

The family is not an accessory and extrinsic structure to the human person. On the contrary, it is the privileged context for the development and growth of the person's personality, in conformity with the needs of the person's constitutive social dimension. "The family, founded on love and enlivened by it, is the place where every person is called to experience, appropriate and participate in that love without which man could not live, and his whole life would be deprived of meaning."[12] Hence the value of love, together with that of freedom and justice, has a central place in the family's role in society. In the Christian proposal, charity holds supremacy. Charity includes and incarnates all the virtues since it consists in participation in the life of Christ, the perfect man.

Although it is certain that some differences exist with regard to their specific aim, charity and justice can and must be integrated. To reach this end, and if it is hoped that both virtues complement each other for the resolution of social problems, they must correspond with the following theses:

a)   There is no love without justice: charity has the character of an "end," whereas justice functions as the "means." Therefore, since it is impossible to reach an end without the use of means, likewise charity will be lacking in social coexistence if justice (the means) is absent in social life. In observing so many forms of social injustice, we can only conclude that we are still very far from achieving charity.

b)   There is no justice if love is lacking: the very doctrine of relations between means and end confirm this thesis, since there is no sense in striving to adopt means (justice) that have no end (charity) in view.

c)   The practice of justice is an ongoing condition for charity: a state of justice facilitates permanent charitable relations between individual persons and, on the contrary, injustice is a constant source of conflict.

It is therefore particularly appropriate to combine the practice of justice and charity, which are as it were "the sublime laws of the social order."[13] In this regard, John Paul II writes: "Justice alone is not enough. . . . Historical experience . . . has led to the formulation of the saying: *summum ius, summa iniuria.*[14]

Family: School of justice, love, peace

Various sociological statistics show that the family in addition to being the most appreciated institution (84-97 percent)[15] and a reference point for people makes a vital contribution to social cohesion. In fact, relations established within families (paternal-filial, fraternal, intergenerational)[16] foster the social responsibility of the family group.

How does the family achieve social cohesion? Various sociological indicators[17] show that the family obtains social cohesion by means of its fertility that assures the continuation of the generations, and that in it one's identity is grasped (I am a child because I have a father, I am a father because I have a child) which consolidates the "rooting of identity" as an element that shapes the personality.

On the other hand, due to the free giving that dominates its nature and dynamism, the family can pass on moral values and offer integral assistance because it is a *spiritual womb*. In these conditions, the family is enabled to carry out its proper role (the principle of subsidiarity) which consists in being the educator of the new generations. Other entities must not arrogate to themselves the roles of others. The family, on the other hand, due to its vocation of permanence in time, is the context in which the essential values of the person which are not only technical but also and fundamentally spiritual are developed, molded and transmitted.

In fact, the complementarity of parents and the stable commitment of spouses make possible the task of integral education that demands constancy, generosity and lasting dedication. This educational process is never completed, which is why the family reference is indispensable for forging a mature personality that contributes to society the values passed on to it in the family. As Marguerite Dubois has said so beautifully, "children do not grow under their parents but beside them. Not in their shadow but in their light."

The family is the school of justice and peace because it educates in and for the truth,[18] in and for freedom, in and for social life. The genuinely educative action of the family consists in "fitting the roots of truth to the wings of freedom." It is in this circle among truth and freedom that the values of dialogue, the *sequela*, responsibility, exigency, discipline, respect, sacrifice and balance can be transmitted. Is society convinced that these and other values for building a just and peaceful society are lacking? This then is the oxygenated lifeblood that the family can bring to society. The social capital that the family contributes is of indisputable value, since it enables a full use of the individual and social dimensions that every human being possesses. Hence common sense and logic are every day increasingly committed to strengthening the family as the true source of justice and peace.

The family is called to be a protagonist of peace, over and above the threats and problems to coexistence and interpersonal and international relations that are surfacing today in so many forms. The family is the context in which every person is helped to attain the full maturity that will enable him to build a society of harmony, solidarity and peace.[19] In fact, in healthy family life certain essential elements are experienced: justice and love between brothers and sisters, the parent's role of authority, affectionate service to the weakest, to the elder and to the sick, mutual help in life's necessities, the willingness to welcome others and if necessary, to forgive them. For this reason the family is *"the first and indispensable teacher of peace."*[20] Experience shows adequately that the values nurtured in the family are a very significant element in the moral development of the social relations of which the fabric of society is woven. The stability of peoples depends on the unity, fidelity and fertility of the family as the foundation of society.

Members of a family must be conscientious of their central role in the cause of peace through education in human values within the family, and through each of its member's participation in the life of society outside the family. Moreover recognizing the right of families to be supported in this role, the State must see that laws are oriented to promoting them, helping them to carry out their tasks. "In the face of increasing pressure nowadays to consider as legally equivalent to the union of spouses forms of union which, by their very nature or their intentional lack of permanence are in no way capable of expressing the meaning and ensuring the good of the family, it is the duty of the State to encourage and protect the authentic institution of the family, respecting its natural structure and its innate and inalienable rights. *"Among these, the fundamental one is the right of parents* to decide, freely and responsibly, on the basis of their moral and religious convictions and with a properly formed conscience, *when to have a child,* and then to educate that child in accordance with those convictions."[21] Supporting families in the various contexts in which their life develops makes an objective contribution to building peace. And "whoever, even unknowingly, circumvents the institution of the family undermines peace in the entire community, national and international, since he weakens what is in effect the primary agency of peace."[22]

Although the disintegration of the family is a threat to peace and a sign of society's moral and economic underdevelopment, its health instead is largely measured by the importance given to conditions that foster the identity and mission of families. It is impossible to ignore the fact that aid to the family contributes to the harmony of society and the nation and also encourages peace among people and in the world. To protect and defend the rights of families as a treasure is the task of all, and in the first place of families, as the protagonists of their own mission. However, it is also the duty of other institutions and, in particular, of the Church and the State. The future of society, the future of humanity passes through the family.

Conclusion

We can now summarize the answer to the question: "What does the family contribute to society?" as follows:

1. *The family is a guarantee of society's future.* In it the fundamental good of human life is transmitted and suitable conditions for the integral education of children are found. The family offers the treasure of procreation and makes a crucial contribution to ensuring that children become good citizens.

2. *The family transmits the cultural heritage.* It is in the bosom of the family that culture is passed on "as a specific way of man's 'existing' and 'being.'"[23] The integration of each individual in his national community language, customs, traditions is begun in the family, assuring the subsistence of the people to which each one belongs. In the family history, through dialogue with the parents and grandparents, an especially important dialogue between generations is recognized; it produces a living memory that forges personal identity.

3. *The family contributes far more to society than the sum of each one of its members would* because the common good is fostered in it. Therefore, in its absence, society would not receive this "extra" proper to the family. As we have pointed out, the common familial good does not consist only in what is good for each one of its members but in what is good for the whole, thereby nourishing development and social cohesion.

4. *The family, in addition to guaranteeing stability, is advantageous for administration.* In fact, as well as providing people for economic production, it is a factor of social cohesion that often acts as a "supportive base" in the face of various adverse situations. The family in our time has become the nucleus of stability for its members with problems of unemployment, illness, dependence or marginalization, alleviating the tragic effects these problems cause. The family today is the primary nucleus of solidarity in society, which can accomplish what it is difficult for the public administration to do.

5. *The family is the first champion of human rights*, since both these and the family's mission are directed toward the person.

6. *The family and society are interdependent* with regard to what affects society.[24] Thus we can say:

   a) *The family personalizes society.* In the family people are valued for their own dignity, emotional ties are established and the development and personal maturation of children is encouraged by the presence and influence of different and complementary models of the father and mother.

   b) *The family socializes the person.* In it the criteria, values and rules for social coexistence are learned which are essential for the development and well-being of its members and for building society: freedom, respect, sacrifice, generosity and solidarity.

In the past few days we have contemplated the Holy Family in Bethlehem and in Nazareth. The Holy Family is called to be a memorial and a prophecy for all the families in the world. The Word of God lived in the Holy Family and through the family has passed on to us a large part of his life, which is a light for every person to know the immensity of what he is called to do: to build already on this earth "a kingdom of truth and life, a kingdom of holiness and grace, a kingdom of justice, love and peace."[25] From the heart of Mexico, this is the gift and task entrusted to all the world's families. May the motherly intercession of Our Lady of Guadalupe help us in this.

Many thanks.

Notes

1   John Paul II, Letter to Families *Gratissimam Sane*, February 2, 1994, no. 2.

2   John Paul II, Apostolic Exhortation *Familiaris Consortio*, no. 17.

3   "In that it is, and ought always to become, a communion and community of persons, the family finds in love the source and the constant impetus for welcoming, respecting and promoting each one of its members in his or her lofty dignity as a person, that is, as a living image of God" (Ibid., no. 22).

4   Ibid., no. 43.

5   Pontifical Council for Justice and Peace, *Compendium of the Social Doctrine of the Church*, no. 164.

6   *Catechism of the Catholic Church*, cf. nos. 1907-1909.

7   Cf. *Compendium of the Social Doctrine of the Church*, nos. 489-493.

8   *Summa Theologiae*, II-II, q. 29, a. 1.

9   Plato, *The Republic*, IV, 18 44 d.

10 Instruction on Certain Aspects of the "Theology of Liberation," August 6, 1984, IV, 6-7.

11 John Paul II, Encyclical Letter *Sollicitudo Rei Socialis*, no. 39.

12 John Paul II, *Address to the Pastoral Theological Congress of the Second World Meeting of Families*, Rio de Janeiro, October 3, 1997, no. 3 in *L'Osservatore Romano* English edition, October 15, 1997, 4; cf. John Paul II, Apostolic Exhortation *Familiaris Consortio*, no. 18.

13 John XXIII, Encyclical Letter *Mater et Magistra*, no. 39. Cf. St. Thomas Aquinas, *Contra gentiles*, 3, 130; Pius XI, Encyclical Letter *Quadragesimo Anno*, no. 137; John Paul II, Encyclical Letter *Dives in Misericordia*, no. 12.

14 "By itself justice is not enough. Indeed, it can even betray itself, unless it is open to that deeper power which is love," John Paul II, *Message for the World Day of Peace 2004*, no. 10.

15 Cf. P.P. Donati (edited by), *Ri-conoscere la Famiglia: quale valore aggiunto per la persona e la società?*, Edizioni S. Paolo, Cinisello Balsamo 2007, 63-173.

16 Cf. Pontifical Council for the Family, XVIII Plenary Assembly: *"I nonni: la loro testimonianza e presenza nella famiglia."* Familia et Vita, Year XIV, no. 4/2008.

17 Cf. E. Herltfelter, *I Congreso de Educación Católica para el siglo XXI*, ed' Instituto de Política Familiar, Valencia 2008.

18 "Wherever and whenever men and women are enlightened by the splendor of truth, they naturally set out on the path of peace," (Benedict XVI, *Message for the World Day of Peace 2006*, no. 3).

19 "Respect for the person promotes peace and . . . in building peace, the foundations are laid for an authentic integral humanism. In this way a serene future is prepared for coming generations." (Benedict XVI, *Message for the World Day of Peace 2007*, no. 1)

20 Cf. Benedict XVI, *Message for the World Day of Peace 2008*, no. 3.

21 John Paul II, *Message for the World Day of Peace 2004*, no. 5.

22 Benedict XVI, *Message for the World Peace Day 2008*, no. 5.

23 Cf. John Paul II, *Address to UNESCO*, June 2, 1980, no. 6.

24 "What is the state of public morality which will ensure the family, and above all the parents, the moral authority necessary for this purpose? What type of instruction? What forms of legislation sustain this authority or, on the contrary, weaken it or destroy it? The causes of success and failure in the formation of man by his family always lie both *within* the fundamental creative environment of culture which the family is, and also at a higher level, that of the competence of the State and the organs, on which these causes depend" (Ibid., no. 12).

25 Roman Missal, *Preface for the Mass of Christ the King*.

Meeting with the President of Mexico*

January 17, 2009

Mr. President,

I greatly thank you for the your kind words to me and for the deference you have shown me as the pontifical legate for the Sixth World Meeting of Families, which this blessed Mexican land welcomes with the graciousness that characterizes its noble peoples and the spirit of hospitality that sets them apart.

First of all, I would like to pass along to you the greetings and heartfelt affection of His Holiness Benedict XVI for you, for your Government, and for all of this country's citizens, so close to the Successor of Peter's heart.

I am overwhelmed with joy to be in this remarkable nation, where the Gospel message has matured into the ripe fruits of culture, beautiful traditions, an illustrious witness of faith and Christian charity, unbreakable fidelity to the Apostolic See, and a deeply rooted devotion to the Virgin Mary, Our Lady of Guadalupe, who desired to give special displays of her predilection for this people and all of the Americas by establishing her house on Tepeyac, where she is venerated fervently by her sons and daughters who honor her as both Mother and Queen.

The current situation presents some challenges for Mexico as well as for other countries: regarding education, immigration, poverty, violence, drug trafficking, corruption, and other social blights. The Church values and supports all steps taken to improve living conditions for the Mexican people. Faithful to its vocation of service and moved by values that are born of the Gospel, the Church only aspires to offer its own contribution to everything that might promote solidarity, social justice, and the harmony of the whole people. With all due respect for pluralism, Catholics work diligently for the common good, knowing that society will have a future as long as the inviolable principles written in the human heart are guaranteed. These are not the results of some self-interested, changeable consensus, since they are essential to the human being. The first of these is the right to life, which no person gives to oneself, but is a gift from God the Creator that has to be cared for by any means from conception to natural death. The Church is tireless in proclaiming this great truth, just as it does for the right to religious liberty, the source and measure of all other basic rights. A State, then, shows itself to

---

*   This text is an unofficial translation of the Spanish in the Italian compendium.

be fully democratic not just by guaranteeing freedom of worship, but when its citizens can practice their religion publicly and privately with full freedom.

Reiterating my great gratitude for your kindness, Mr. President, I assure you of my constant remembrance of you in prayer, asking God, through the intercession of the Most Holy Virgin, *la Morenita* of Tepeyac, heavenly protector of this great nation, that she will grant Your Excellency, your family, and all Mexicans, abundant fruits of peace and brotherhood to build a present marked by serene, productive human communion, as well as a future rich in hope.

Meditation During the Rosary*

January 17, 2009

My dear brothers and sisters,
Friends,

"Blessed be the God and Father of our Lord Jesus Christ, who has blessed us in Christ with every spiritual blessing in the heavens" (Eph 1:3). Seeing so many families gathered in Christ's name, contemplating the ardor of your hearts and energy of your faith, one cannot but give heartfelt thanks to God the Father for the incomparable gift of the family. Thank you all for coming, for being here closely united by the bonds of faith and love so as to form the great family of God's children. Thank you to the families who have traveled from so many places, some with sacrifices and hardships, to the volunteers and families of Mexico who have opened their homes to welcome those coming from outside this beautiful country. The points of origin are diverse, but faith and love for Christ unites everyone in one accord and in one and the same desire to work for the common good of all homes. May God fill your lives and projects with peace and joy.

I warmly welcome Cardinal Ennio Antonelli, President of the Pontifical Council for the family, Cardinal Norberto Rivera Carrera, Archbishop Primate of Mexico, all the cardinals, archbishops and bishops here present, and in a special way the president and members of the Mexican Bishops' Conference, the authorities that accompany us, the priests, religious men and women, and all of you, dear brothers and sisters in the Lord.

---

*   This text is an unofficial translation of the Spanish in the Italian compendium.

It is with great joy and hope that we have gathered this afternoon to celebrate the gift and mystery of the family, and to listen to the varied testimonies
that support our Christian life. His Holiness Benedict XVI convoked this
Sixth World Meeting to proclaim that the family is called to educate the new
generations in the human and Christian values that guide their life according
to the model of Christ and forge in them a rich, harmonious personality (cf.
Letter to Cardinal Alfonso López Trujillo for the Upcoming Sixth World
Meeting of Families, October 1, 2007). The Pope holds all the world's families very present and prays for them. He entrusts to God the faithful love of
spouses, their witness in the presence of their sons and daughters, the affection and respect of children and adolescents toward their parents and elders.
And we, from here, show our devotion to the Holy Father.

We are now preparing to pray the Holy Rosary together, a prayer particularly linked to the family. We will meditate on the Joyful Mysteries, which
eloquently reflect the values of home life. The Annunciation moves us to
contemplate within the Virgin Mary, betrothed to Joseph, a sensitivity that
never closes itself off to life, but rather opens itself with a spotless purity of
heart. The Visitation shows us Our Lady's great charity, as she hurries on her
way to assist her cousin Elizabeth. In the moving encounter between the two
women, the jubilation of a shared life and the love of God, shines forth. It is
reflected in the leap of joy before God's concealed presence, recognized by the
baby in Elizabeth's womb. The Nativity of Our Lord Jesus Christ allows us to
fix our gaze on the Word made flesh in Mary's womb, and there to delight in
Joseph's attention and delicate watchfulness and the Virgin's loving dedication to caring for the Child God. The Presentation of Jesus in the Temple of
Jerusalem shows us the Holy Family fully integrated into the religious traditions of their people, where they live and pass on their many values. Finally,
considering the Child lost and then found in the Temple shows us the Family
of Nazareth celebrating Passover in Jerusalem; from there we can contemplate Jesus' human growth in his family, and we are privileged to admire the
surprising familiarity Jesus has with his Father's house. This opens us to the
deeper mystery it carries: the communion of the Trinity, source of all family love.

In this "little house of Tepeyac," desired by Our Lady of Guadalupe "to
show all of her love within it," we lift our prayer for God to continue watching over the families of the world so that at all times be they will be "the
school of faith, the training-ground for human and civil values, the hearth
in which human life is born and is generously and responsibly welcomed"
(Benedict XVI, Speech at the Inaugural Session of the Groundwork for the
Fifth General Conference of the Latin-American and Caribbean Bishops,
Aparecida, May 13, 2007, no. 5). We wish to once again place all Christian

homes under the faithful guardianship of St. Joseph, her most chaste spouse. Let us all direct our gaze to the Home of Nazareth, for we will find there a school where we can learn to renew our Christian and family life. May Our Lady of Guadalupe be always at your side and guide your steps along the path shown us by her Son Jesus Christ, Our Lord.

Many thanks.

Homily During the Closing Mass[*]

January 18, 2009

Dear brothers and sisters in the Lord:

1. "To all the beloved of God in Rome, called to be holy. Grace to you and peace from God our Father and the Lord Jesus Christ" (Rom 1:7).

With these words of St. Paul the Apostle, whose birth two thousand years ago the Church is celebrating, this year, I want to pass on to you all the affection and spiritual closeness of His Holiness, Benedict XVI, whom it is my honor to represent as papal legate to this sixth World Meeting of Families.

With particular sentiments of fraternal communion in the Lord, I greet Cardinal Ennio Antonelli, president of the Pontifical Council for the Family, and express sincere gratitude to him and his colleagues for the tactful and efficient diligence with which they organized this initiative which has brought together in this beautiful country families from around the world. I also wish to recall Cardinal Alfonso López Trujillo, who involved himself so zealously in the previous World Meetings of Families and who also began the preparations for this present meeting. We commend him to the mercy of God.

In the name of the Holy Father I also greet with affection and gratitude Cardinal Norberto Rivera Carrera, Archbishop Primate of Mexico, for the painstaking attention he, along with his diocesan community, has attended to the details of the celebration of this World Meeting. Nor could I forget to mention with gratitude the intensive work carried out by the Organizing Committee of this great gathering, led by Bishop Jonás Guerrero Corona, auxiliary Bishop of Mexico, and the contribution of the numerous volunteers who collaborated generously, and likewise the love shown by the many families of the City who opened their homes and their hearts to other families who came from afar to take part in this wonderful ecclesial event.

---

[*]   This text is an unofficial translation of the Spanish in the Italian compendium.

I greet with affection the Cardinals, my brothers in the episcopacy, and the delegations coming from many parts of the world, thus bearing witness to the commitment with which the particular Churches are working to promote pastoral care of families in different parts of the world. I offer my cordial and respectful greeting to the civil authorities present at this Eucharist, who are highlighting the vital importance of the family for society's present and for its future.

Equally noteworthy are the enthusiasm and conviction with which the priests, religious men and women and other pastoral are dedicating themselves to promotion of the family and to the apostolate with families and for them. Very special thanks to the families here at this grand liturgical assembly, gathered around the Lord and under the maternal gaze of our Lady of Guadalupe. In a moment, the married couples present here will renew their marital covenant and the blessing of the Lord will descend upon them to revitalize the sacramental grace of matrimony.

2. The readings that have been proclaimed present us with the Word of God that enlightens us and engages us. The first, taken from the book of Proverbs, speaks about the advice of a father to his young son. It is very fitting for this sixth World Meeting of Families, which has as its theme *The Family, Forming Human and Christian Values*.

These fatherly lessons dealing with proper conduct, ethics and human values are the fruit of experience, reflection and good sense. They contain concrete advice for avoiding vices and practicing virtue. The brief text we have heard confines itself to situations like drunkenness, gluttony, laziness and lack of respect for elderly parents. With regard to these, the sacred author says specifically, "Do not join with wine bibbers, nor with those who glut themselves on meat. For drunkards and gluttons come to poverty, and lazing about clothes one in rags. Listen to your father who begot you, do not despise your mother when she is old" (Prv 23:20-22). In the context of the book of Proverbs, however, the panorama is far broader, addressing pride, arrogance, anger, revenge, oppressing the poor—especially widows and orphans—prostitution, adultery, lying and deceit.

In contrast, the virtues are praised. The text just proclaimed insistently calls for being wise, upright, just, honest and committed to goodness. "Hear, my son, and be wise, and guide your heart in the right way. . . . Buy truth and do not sell: wisdom, instruction, understanding!" (Prv 23:19, 23). In this regard too, the advice refers to many other virtues as well: humility, self-control, patience, loyalty, marital fidelity, friendship, forgiveness of enemies, industriousness, sobriety, defense of the poor, generosity and hospitality.

The principle that governs and underpins ethical conduct is the fear of the Lord: "The beginning of wisdom is fear of the LORD" (Prv 9:10); that is, an authentic relationship with God, built on respect, worship, obedience and trust. Something similar is also stated in the Scripture passage we have heard: "Do not let your heart envy sinners, but only those who always fear the LORD; For you will surely have a future, and your hope will not be cut off" (Prv 23:17-18).

The fear of the Lord motivates us to renounce sin and to do his will as concrete moral norms express it. And, according to the book of Proverbs, since God only desires our good, obeying him even shows the way to succeed in this world; that is, to have health, long life, well-being, a close family, descendants and social respectability.

The responsorial Psalm we sang explores this same teaching: "Blessed are all who fear the LORD, and who walk in his ways. What your hands provide you will enjoy; you will be blessed and prosper: Your wife will be like a fruitful vine . . . , Your children like young olive plants" (Ps 128:1-3). According to the Wisdom books of the Old Testament, fear of the Lord, ethical values and moral norms belong to the logic and dynamic of a life which tends toward fulfillment. Acceptance of them means following the way that leads toward our proper growth as human beings, being faithful to God and faithful to ourselves.

These values and norms are known through experience and reflection, which is to say through reason, and, at the same time, since they are contained in the inspired text, they are also the Word of God. It makes sense that certain truths accessible to all, even to non-believers, are confirmed by biblical revelation, since reason, darkened by instincts and prejudices, often does not judge correctly. As St. Augustine says, "there hath been written also in tables that which in their hearts they read not." (*Exposition on the Book of Psalms*, Psalm 58, no. 1). Right reason and faith are allies. Authentically human values also Christian because, as the Apostle Paul exhorts, "Finally, brothers, whatever is true, whatever is honorable, whatever is just, whatever is pure, whatever is lovely, whatever is gracious, if there is any excellence and if there is anything worthy of praise, think about these things" (Phil 4:8).

Jesus' disciples also respect the content and depth proper to human values and activity but the Christian message raises these things to a new and higher meaning and integrates them into the filial relationship with God the Father and into the dynamism of faith, hope and charity. The center of the Christian moral task is the person of Jesus Christ, dialogue and communion with him, and through him, with the Father in the Holy Spirit. In this new relationship with the divine persons the practice of human values and moral norms is made perfect and takes on new motivation and energy, the capacity for sacrifice through following the Crucified One, joy and confidence in the company of the Risen One.

The Christian family makes the person of the Lord Jesus the center of its attention, welcoming him into the home, uniting in prayer around him, seeking to share his teaching, his feelings, his desires and doing his will. Faith in his presence transforms all the family's relationships and activities, uplifts human values and creates an atmosphere of communion and joy. It is at the same time a human and a divine atmosphere, such as the text of the Epistle to the Colossians which we heard in the second reading describes with emotion and enthusiasm: "Put on then, as God's chosen ones, holy and beloved, heart-felt compassion, kindness, humility, gentleness, and patience. . . . as the Lord has forgiven you, so must you also do. And over all these put on love, that is, the bond of perfection. And let the peace of Christ control your hearts. . . . Let the word of Christ dwell in you richly. . . . And whatever you do, in word or in deed, do everything in the name of the Lord Jesus, giving thanks to God the Father through him. Wives, be subordinate to your husbands. . . . Husbands, love your wives. . . . Children, obey your parents in everything. . . . Fathers, do not provoke your children, so they may not become discouraged" (Col 3:12-21).

Here it is: "the family forming human and Christian values." Here many virtues are practiced, united and ennobled by charity; everyday words and deeds are animated by the Spirit of Jesus and directed by attention to his Word. The roles of spouses, parents and children are maintained but they all vie with each other in reciprocal love and service.

All the members of the family are addressed because all of them must participate in the development of human and Christian values. But we cannot forget the particular responsibility that belongs to parents. Their attitude toward their children should resemble that of Mary and Joseph when they found Jesus in the Temple after he had gone missing, as we heard the Gospel narrate.

Mary and Joseph look for him with indescribable concern: "Son, why have you done this to us? Your father and I have been looking for you with great anxiety" (Lk 2:48). They love their son passionately, with all their being.

And so, dear fathers and mothers, love your children and make them feel loved and appreciated, respected and understood. The sense of being loved calls forth gratitude and trust in others, in oneself and in the love of the Heavenly Father; it is a call to respond to love with love.

Mary and Joseph live in intimacy with Jesus but his person and his behavior are a mystery even to them. "He said to them, 'Why were you looking for me? Did you not know that I must be in my Father's house?' But they did not understand what he said to them" (Lk 2:49-50). Mary and Joseph intuit that Jesus does not belong to them; He lives for his true Father who is God and puts himself completely at the disposal of the mysterious divine plan. Even though they do not understand, they accompany him with respectful love and serve him with great solicitude.

Dear fathers and mothers, you too must respect the personality and the vocation of your children. To raise them means to help them develop their hidden potential and to support them in fully becoming themselves according to the plan God has for their lives. Care for them like a gift that has been entrusted to you without becoming possessive. A famous poet writes, "Your children are not your children. They are the sons and daughters of Life's longing for itself. They come through you but not from you. And though they are with you yet they belong not to you. You may give them your love but not your thoughts, for they have their own thoughts. You may house their bodies but not their souls, for their souls dwell in the house of tomorrow, which you cannot visit, not even in your dreams" (K. Gibran, *The Prophet*).

A good educational relationship includes tenderness and affection along with reason and authority. Both parents—father and mother—need to be close to their children and cultivate dialogue with them. Dear fathers and mothers, be generous with your children without being permissive; be demanding without being hard; be clear with them and do not contradict each other; know how to say yes or no at the appropriate time. Be consistent and give them good example. In this way you will be able to help your children to mature into a personality that is balanced, constructive, creative, solid and reliable, able to face the traps and trials which life will never lack.

Forming human and Christian values requires a family that is founded on a monogamous marriage open to life; it requires a close and stable family. Despite human weakness, husbands and wives who try with God's grace to grow ever more consistent in living out their love as a total gift of each one's life to the other build their house upon rock (cfr. Mt 7:24-25); they make their family a living Gospel; they build up the Church and civil society; they reflect in history the presence and the beauty of God who is a unity of three persons: Father, Son and Holy Spirit.

May the Most Holy Virgin, Our Lady of Guadalupe, obtain this grace for Christian families so that all the families of the world may also benefit from it. Oh Mary, Mother of the Beautiful Love, Mother of Hope, Help of Christians, accept this humble supplications and bestow on all the families of the world what they need to grow in holiness, to be salt of the earth and light of the world, to be sanctuaries of life and love, of welcome and forgiveness, of human values and Christian virtues. Amen.

APPENDIX

Interventions of
Cardinal Ennio Antonelli

PRESIDENT OF THE
PONTIFICAL COUNCIL FOR THE FAMILY

Theological-Pastoral Congress of the
Sixth World Meeting of Families*

January 14-16, 2009

Conclusions

1. We are about to conclude our Theological-Pastoral Congress. It will be a high-profile conclusion because of the conference presented by the Papal Legate, Cardinal Tarcisio Bertone, whom we have welcomed with affection and joy. By welcoming the Papal Legate, we renew our devotion to the Holy Father, Benedict XVI who sent him as his personal representative.

Benedict XVI is exercising his universal ministry in the most appropriate way to respond to the spiritual and cultural needs of our time. Perhaps his ministry could be summed up in a simple phrase: Teacher of truth and love and, consequently, teacher of authentic freedom. Teacher of truth for the clarity of his teachings in the light of faith and reason; teacher of charity for his first encyclical *Deus Caritas Est*, and for his extraordinary gentleness and

---

* This text is an unofficial translation of the Spanish in the Italian compendium.

kindness; teacher of authentic freedom because authentic freedom is realized by searching for truth and clinging to what is good.

2. With a sense of profound devotion for the Holy Father, in a moment we will listen to his personal representative, Cardinal Tarcisio Bertone. But before I yield the floor to him, I myself would like to reprise briefly the general theme of the Meeting: "The Family Forming Human and Christian Values," a theme that has been studied in the Congress from various perspectives (biblical, theological, psychological, social, economic, media, juridical, political and pastoral), offering abundant material for the work of the conclusions committee, for the work of the members and consultors of the Pontifical Council for the Family and for the work of the editors of the proceedings and of the periodical *Family and Life*.

For my part I would like to underscore a principal element that has been very present in the work of this Theological-Pastoral Congress and is also present in my heart as an orientation for the future work that will have to be accomplished in the Dicastery that the Holy Father has called me to oversee. I want to invite you to focus your attention on the family as a subject in the Church and in civil society and, as such, as a precious, or rather an indispensable, resource.

3. The family, a subject in the Church, a subject of evangelization. A secularized world like ours can only be evangelized if, as the Aparecida Document exhorts forcefully, all Christians rediscover their vocation to be "disciples and missionaries" as were the Christians of the first centuries who evangelized the pagan world.

At that time everyone, laity included, felt an urgent and compelling interior need to share their faith with others. The Gospel spread spontaneously from person to person, from wife to husband and vice versa, from parents to children and vice versa, from slave to master and vice versa. It spread rapidly from one house to another, from one environment to the next, from one city to another.

An equally lively missionary consciousness needs to be rediscovered in Christians and in Christian families today. It is urgent that we promote the personal and family apostolate, the most penetrating and the most widespread and which is the best prerequisite for the apostolate by associations and parishes.

The family is an ecclesial subject, both disciple and missionary in its own proper way: domestic prayer, listening to God's word together in the Holy Scriptures, reciprocal and interchangeable dialogue and edification, handing on the faith from parents to children, witness in their own environment, faithful participation in the Sunday Eucharist, involvement in the children's catechesis and in the various parish activities of a charitable, cultural and recreational nature, meeting with families and networks of family solidarity, being present to families in difficulty, and taking in abandoned children.

The Church for its part must be attentive in developing different levels of pastoral care not just "for families" but also "with families." The family is a crossroads and a resource for all pastoral activities. The Aparecida Document reminds us, "Inasmuch as the family is the value most cherished by our peoples, we believe that concern for it should be undertaken as one of the thrusts running through all of the Church's evangelizing activity. In every diocese there must be an 'intense and vigorous' family ministry" (Aparecida Concluding Document, no. 435).

4. The family as a subject in civil society. According to what was said in one of the reports of this Congress (Donati, *La familia y las virtudes sociales*, 6, 1), experience attests and sociological studies confirm that the conjugal relationship and the parent-child relationship are socially fruitful when they remain connected to each other; on the contrary, they create problems for society when they are divided from each other. The "unhealthy" family produces insecurity, mistrust, conflict, tensions, lower birth rates, an incomplete education devoid of content; it produces despair and a lack of well-being for the young and loneliness, poverty, and injustice for those who are weakest. It contributes to the breakdown of society.

A healthy family, on the other hand, produces many benefits: the procreation of children, better education, satisfaction for all its members, self-confidence and confidence in others, solidarity, loyalty, justice, concern for children, the disabled, the infirm and the elderly, industriousness and cooperation. Through domestic work it contributes to the good of the nation. It acts as a social buffer in difficult times. It passes on the cultural, ethical and religious heritage of the nation. It is a powerful factor for the cohesion and development of society.

A political agenda that seeks to promote the common good must give adequate legal and economic support to the family based on marriage. A few rights of the family that deserve special attention and diligent commitment may be recalled by way of example: access to decent housing, opportunity for well-compensated work, a balance between work time and time for the family, incentives for birth where these is a population decline, freedom of education and the possibility of school choice, fairness in the tax burden and in the distribution of wealth. In a more general way, what is desirable is not just a political program for families but also with families. This means dialogue with the associations that represent families and identify the potential implications for family life in the laws, government programs and administrative procedures.

5. The family, a subject in the Church and in civil society. Here is a path that invites us on a journey, a destination of great promise. To value the family as a precious resource for evangelization and for socialization. To unleash its great potential for the development of human and Christian values.

International Study Seminar
"The Christian Family, Subject of Evangelization"*

September 10-11, 2009

Expression of Thanks

A very enthusiastic "thank you" to the participants, translators, members of the Pontifical Council for the Family and to the religious house that is hosting us.

Thanks above all to God for the splendid experiences of evangelization that he is constantly bringing about in the Church and which we have also glimpsed in this seminar.

I congratulate you for the richness of the presentations made here and for the atmosphere of fraternity and joy in which we have carried out our work.

My summary is an attempt to gather together the many valuable insights that have emerged in a way that strikes a balance according to the typically Catholic criterion of "both . . . and" (*"Et . . . Et"*).

1. Evangelization: The Vocation of the Church, of All Christians and of All Christian Families

"[The People of God] is sent forth into the whole world as the light of the world and the salt of the earth." (Vatican II, *Lumen Gentium*, no. 9) (cfr. 1 Pt 2:9).

"The Church, sent by Christ to reveal and to communicate the love of God to all men and nations" (Vatican II, *Ad Gentes*, no, 10). Understood in this way, evangelization implies both announcing and handing on the love and presence of God through Christ in the Spirit.

"Evangelizing is in fact the grace and vocation proper to the Church, her deepest identity" (Paul VI, *Evangelii Nuntiandi*, no. 14).

---

*   This text is an unofficial translation of the Italian.

Evangelization defines the identity of the Church not only in what she does but first of all what she is.

The Church is communion and mission. "Communion represents both the source and the fruit of mission: communion gives rise to mission and mission is accomplished in communion" (John Paul II, *Christifideles Laici*, no. 32). This dynamic is suggested by Jesus Himself in His priestly prayer: "I pray not only for them, but also for those who will believe in me through their word, so that they may all be one, as you, Father, are in me and I in you, that they also may be in us, that the world may believe that you sent me" (Jn 17:20-21).

Communion in Christ tends to spread out dynamically. "The Lord is always calling us to come out of ourselves and to share with others the goods we possess, starting with the most precious gift of all—our faith" (John Paul II, *Redemptoris Missio*, no. 49).

On account of this intrinsic dynamic of communion, mission involves every member of the Church. "*Missionary activity is a matter for all Christians*, for all dioceses and parishes, Church institutions and associations" (John Paul II, *Redemptoris Missio*, no. 2). Thus, it is also a matter for all Christian families.

"The Christian family is called upon to take part actively and responsibly in the mission of the Church in a way that is original and specific, by placing itself, in what it is and what it does as an 'intimate community of life and love,' at the service of the Church and of society" (John Paul II, *Familiaris Consortio*, no. 50). Prior to any specific activities, the family evangelizes through its ordinary life.

2. Good News and New Life

All Christians are called to evangelize through prayer, lived witness and, when the occasion presents itself, by proclaiming the Good News (cfr. Vatican II, *Apostolicam Actuositatem*, no. 6; Paul VI, *Evangelii Nuntiandi*, no. 22). In order to evangelize effectively and meaningfully, they must be more than just baptized, more than just practicing (Sunday Mass); they must seriously work at converting themselves to a new life according to the Spirit. Only then do they become the light of the world, the salt of the earth, the city on a mountaintop, leaven in the dough, and credible sign of Christ's love and presence in the world.

The true Christian lives in a conscious relationship with Christ, as His disciple, brother, friend and coworker. He encounters Christ through hearing the word, in the sacraments, (especially in the Eucharist) and in prayer. He admits his sinfulness before Christ, ready to resume the journey in humility and trust. He receives from Christ the joy of being loved, firm hope for eternal life, the perception of a higher meaning and value of persons and of the authentic human facts that are destined to be fulfilled in God, the criteria to discern the true good, the strength to live according to the logic of love as gift and communion, in order to put into practice the new commandment "As I have loved you, so should you love one another" (see Jn 15:12), to shoulder other people's burdens as they grow both as human beings and as Christians, bearing the weight of their limitations and their sins just as Jesus carried the weight of the whole human race all the way to the Cross.

In an analogous way, if a family is to be Christian, it is not enough to be a good family; they need to live out their relationship with Christ in faith. And if they are to be evangelizers in a credible way, it is not enough that the family be made up of baptized persons, or even practicing persons; the family's life must be directed by the Gospel and animated by the Holy Spirit and not conform itself to the mentality of this world. In the family, the grace of the Sacrament of Matrimony must be able to express itself so as to partake of Christ's spousal love and to make constant progress in achieving the family's vocation to be an image of the communion of the divine persons of the Trinity.

The plan of the Pontifical Council for the Family to collect, discern and circulate a few important experiences of ministry to families and family life is sustained by the hope that the experiences given as examples will have fruitful repercussions in many parishes and families. The intention was to intervene in support of practicing families so they might be spiritually reinforced and become ever more courageous and credible subjects of evangelization. In a world that is as secularized and indifferent to religion as ours is today, evangelization has a good chance for success only by reawakening the missionary responsibility of practicing Christians and their families. The family can evangelize at home, in the neighborhood, at school, in the parish, in organizations and even in the *"missio ad gentes"* (world missions, Latin). We turn to practicing families not to stop there but rather through them to reach the greatest possible number of other persons and families, according to the criterion "the few for the many." Conversely, to begin from a minimal outreach addressed without distinction to everyone runs the risk of remaining insipid and without evangelizers. In this way, everyone ends up impoverished.

3. The Plan for the 2010 Meeting

Evangelization includes both pastoral activities specific to the ecclesial community (catechesis, liturgical celebrations, works of charity) and the manifold human relationships and activities carried out in a manner consistent with the Gospel in every personal and social setting. Christian families as subjects of evangelization are always involved in the second and often in the first as well because witness is expected of everyone while properly pastoral work is expected only of some.

In preparation for the meeting in Rome in 2010, on *"The Christian Family Subject of Evangelization,"* the Pontifical Council for the Family will ask the Episcopal Conferences (and also ecclesial organizations) to identify a few of the more relevant experiences in which families play the leading role. Selections from these will be presented at the meeting, whether in the general assembly or in the sharing groups.

The meeting will take place over three days and will include presentations of a general nature on theology, anthropology and family spirituality and on the socio-cultural situation with its challenges and opportunities for the family. The exchange of ideas will take place in discussions in the main hall and in the working groups. The media (especially the internet) will be used in the attempt to provide ample communication. At the end, the more prominent suggestions and positions will be gathered together.

4. Participants in the Meeting

Invitations will be sent to bishops, priests, deacons, religious, families involved in pastoral ministry to families, experts and representatives of Church organizations.

The valuable work carried out in this Study Seminar bodes well for the success of the meeting for which it is a sort of foretaste.

STUDY SESSION OF THE PLENARY ASSEMBLY
"THE RIGHTS OF CHILDHOOD"

The Right of Children to Have a Family*

Rome, February 9-10, 2010

Notes

Foreword

1. The "International Convention on the Rights of the Child" (November 20, 1989) recognizes that minors have important rights with regard to adoption, health care, education, protection for the disabled, protection against

---

*   This text is an unofficial translation of the Italian.

violence, against abandonment, against sexual exploitation and exploitation in the workplace.

2. The civil conscience should condemn without hesitation or ambiguity the very frequent violations of the rights of minors that continue to be committed in the world: slaughters in war, the employment of child soldiers, trafficking for organ transplants, pharmaceutical experiments, physical violence, kidnapping, poor or insufficient nutrition, the lack of health care, discrimination against the disabled, denial of education, exploitation in labor, and coercion to beg, rob, sell drugs or engage in prostitution, pedophilia, sexual abuse, pornography, arranged early marriages, sexual mutilation, exploitation of images for commercial purposes, denial of due justice.

3. In its preamble, the Convention recognizes that a child has a right to protection and to special care "before as well as after birth." Abortion radically contradicts the value of the person and of life, which is the foundation of this affirmation.

4. It is not enough simply to condemn violations of rights; what is needed is vigilance and action to prevent them.

5. Nowadays dangerous ideologies influence the interpretation of the 1989 Convention, leading toward the adoption of meanings in several points that stand in contrast to the original values that inspired it.

Clarifications

6. The right of children to have a family is contained in the Preamble to the Convention, where it states that the family "as the fundamental group of society and the natural environment for the growth and well-being of all its members and particularly children, should be afforded the necessary protection and assistance so that it can fully assume its responsibilities within the community" and it recognizes that "the child, for the full and harmonious development of his or her personality, should grow up in a family environment."

7. The rights of children are inseparable from the rights of the family.

8. A child has the right to have a father and a mother in order to be able to relate from the earliest stages of infancy with two persons of different sexes who love each other and love the child, and thus to be able to form a clear and solid identity, a defined personality.

9. The child has a right to grow up with a father and a mother, to be loved and brought up by them.

10. The child has a right to help in acquiring self-esteem, trust, security, a sense of reality and of limits, psychic harmony and ongoing maturity.

11. In the case of adoption, the child has a right to be entrusted to a couple comprising a man and a woman, united in marriage, so as to give a sufficient guarantee of harmony and stability.

12. It is one thing to be father and mother and another thing to act as father and mother and quite another thing again to serve some procreative function.

13. The unity and psychosomatic coherence of the child are a good that must be cared for and developed through a proper upbringing.

14. Raising children in a way that intentionally seeks to form a homosexual or uncertain or confused personality is unacceptable.

15. It is one thing to teach the necessary respect for all persons and another thing to suggest to children and adolescents that homosexuality is an ideal alternative.

16. The dignity and fundamental human rights of homosexual persons must be respected.

17. Not every desire is a right.

18. Objective goods, not desires, should be the foundation of law.

19. Only a couple composed of a man and a woman united in marriage and open to children is a matter of public interest and relevance.

20. The desire to institutionalize a form of affection simply because a feeling is involved, is like desiring to institutionalize a relationship between friends.

21. Treating different things in the same way is an injustice.

22. It is one thing to provide for the needs and rights of individuals and another to institutionalize the relationship between homosexuals.

23. It is paradoxical to extol pluralism and cultural diversity while at the same time downplaying basic human differences—the sexual difference between

men and women and the generational difference between parents and children—in the name of equality and non-discrimination.

24. Love creates unity in respect for otherness, harmonizing and giving value to differences, beginning with differences of gender and generations.

25. It is a sad contradiction when each of the parents loves their children and at the same time inflicts profound and intense suffering on them by not loving the other spouse, leading even to separation and divorce.

26. Destabilizing marriage and the family increases individualism and conflict, damages the balance and human growth of children, compromises cohesion, development and society's future.

27. According to God's plan, man and woman, united in indissoluble marriage and open to children, form a living image of the one God in three persons, sharing and reflecting the beauty of creative love. Therefore, adultery, divorce, homosexuality and all sexual relations outside of marriage are opposed to the true good of persons and the Word of God (cfr. Mt 5:27, 31-32; 15:19; 19:3-9; Mk 7:21; 10:2-12; Lk 16:18; Rom 1:24-32; 1 Cor 6:9, 15-20; 7:10; Gal 5:19; Ti 4:3-8).

Meeting with the Commissions for the Family of the Catholic Dioceses of the Middle East*

Beirut, February 13, 2010

Speech

Because of globalization, religious pluralism is spreading all over the world. In Lebanon, however, for historical, cultural, social and political reasons, it has specific characteristics.

For Christians, there is a danger of religious relativism and religious indifference. There is a risk of reducing religion to ethics, overlooking the profession of faith, membership in Christ and in his Church and the liturgy, as if these were unimportant traditions and formalities.

---

*   This text is an unofficial translation of the Italian.

It is necessary to encourage an appropriate education to develop a Christian identity that is at once strong and open.

It is understandable that a Muslim, free of fanaticism and not conditioned by political interests and open to western modernity, might reduce religion to ethics (respect for one's neighbor, justice, loyalty, sincerity, trust, collaboration), minimizing the difference that distinguish religions from each other. It is understandable that he might consider Christianity to be no more than a teaching and Jesus no more than a teacher of human values and ethical principles, thus relativizing his person, the ecclesial community he founded, the sacraments and the truths of the faith.

Christianity contains an ethic but it is not reducible to an ethic.

Christianity is essentially a living, person to person relationship with Jesus Christ, the Son of God, made man, crucified and risen, the Lord and Savior, living and always present in the life of each of us and in the history of the Church and of humanity throughout the ages "Behold, I am with you always, until the end of the age" (Mt 28:20).

More than his teaching, what is decisive is the person of Jesus himself and therefore the personal relationship one has with him as his disciples, friends, brothers and coworkers. "Whoever remains in me and I in him will bear much fruit, because without me you can do nothing" (Jn 15:5). "Whoever loves father or mother more than me is not worthy of me" (Mt 10:37). "If anyone does not love the Lord, let him be accursed" (1 Cor 16:22). Christians do not set themselves above believers of other religions, but they consider Christ to be unique and incomparable, worthy of being loved more than every other person and everything.

Christian ethics confirms and takes up the Ten Commandments and thus ensures that fundamental human values are safeguarded. It takes up and goes beyond the Ten Commandments through the logic of love, understood as self-gift and communion.

"Do not kill" deals with more than not killing. Life must be respected and served by encouraging its holistic development (physical, spiritual, social). The true good of others is to be desired with the same seriousness as one's own good: "Do to others whatever you would have them do to you" (Mt 7:12). Justice and graciousness are to be practiced as the opportunity arises, even with sacrifice, even to the point of forgiving enemies.

"Do not commit adultery" does not mean simply avoiding sexual activity outside of marriage, but rather integrating sexuality, the psychosomatic energy of relationship, positively in a love that is understood as desire and as self-gift, as mutual acceptance, collaboration, and a plan for life lived together.

"Do not steal" does not involve simply avoiding appropriating another's goods unjustly; it is also about using one's own economic goods according to the logic of love at the service of others in an ordered way (one's own family, the poor, the Church, society).

"Do not lie" means not only not deceiving others but also communicating the truth with sincerity and trust ("Yes, yes, no, no" Mt 5:37), communicating the truth, spiritual values, the faith and the Gospel with respect for persons.

Christian ethics is an ethics of a love understood not as mere sentiment but as a concrete commitment to the true good "living the truth in love" (Eph 4:15). Truth and love are inseparable.

Christian ethics is necessary in order to resemble Christ, to receive the Holy Spirit, to participate in the life of the Son of God as brothers, coworkers and heirs with him. They are necessary for becoming one with Christ, living with him and like him.

For the Christian, ethics is first a gift received and then a duty to fulfill. The love we experience is communicated to us by the Lord Jesus through the communication of the Holy Spirit. It is grace that enables us to keep the commandments and go beyond them. Our merits are God's gifts, which we accept and which dispose us receive still other gifts.

We must rely on grace and not on our own powers as if we were self-sufficient. We can have trust, even if we do not succeed in observing fully the demands of Christian ethics, so long as we admit humbly that we are sinners, sincerely desire conversion, pray to obtain the necessary grace and do in the meanwhile the good that we are capable of doing.

The sacraments are not just religious practices and traditional social rituals. They are acts of Christ, desired by him to communicate and make visible the gift of the Holy Spirit and divine grace.

According to the Gospel, Jesus taught that religious customs and rituals without love are useless, hypocritical behavior. Nevertheless, he never taught that we can do without religious rituals. It is true that he qualified and abolished some religious institutions but it is also true that he created new ones (for example, Baptism and the Eucharist).

The Eucharist is the center of Christian life. Christ makes his Paschal Sacrifice present under the sign of bread given to eat and wine offered as drink. He gives himself to us with all the love with which he died for us on the Cross, the love with which he continues to love the Church. The Eucharist introduces us into the nuptial covenant of Christ the Bridegroom with his bride the Church. We are called to become one with Him and to share his saving love for all men and for everything that is authentically human. We are called to continue to become the Church, his bride and his body in history. Wanting to be a Christian without Sunday Mass is like wanting to be a Christian without Jesus Christ.

The Church is the body of Christ crucified and risen in this world, the realization and visible expression of his presence. The Church is a sacrament, the invisible made visible both on the level of the Universal Church and on the level of particular Churches. Seeing the Church only in a sociological perspective is completely inadequate and runs the risk of easily leading to error. We cannot redefine the Church and we cannot do without it because it is the spiritual and visible extension of Christ. To belong to Christ is to belong to his Church as well. We must consider the Church our truer and larger family.

Not everything in the Church is the Church. Within the Church the errors and sins committed by Christians cloud and deface her but these errors and sins are not of the Church. On the contrary, they are anti-ecclesial and, therefore, reconciliation with God passed through reconciliation with the Church through the sacrament of Penance or confession. A great medieval Pope, Gregory VII, said that there are spider webs in the temple but the spider webs are not the temple. The Church must constantly be purified and reformed (*semper reformanda*; Latin: always in need of reformation), but in and of itself the Church is not sinful but rather holy and sanctifying.

We are the Church in the measure to which we become one with Christ, both spiritually and visibly; in the measure to which we accept the truth of the faith and profess it; in the measure to which we accept the charity of Christ, live it and make it manifest in love for each other and for all. We are the Church to a greater or lesser degree according to God's gifts and our acceptance of them, from the great saints to the sinners who still remain part of the Church through partial bonds of communion.

Christian identity is a nuptial covenant with Christ, an impassioned identification with him, a joyful and grateful belonging to him and to the Church, more powerful and more important than belonging to a culture, a nation or a political society.

Christian identity is open because Christ is the Savior of all men and of everything that is authentically human. To become one with him in love means also desiring the temporal and eternal good of all, Christians and non-Christians alike.

Thus the Christian is prepared to recognize the truth and good to be found in other people whatever religion or culture they may belong to. A Christian is ready to dialogue, to collaborate, to build friendships and even to accept interreligious marriages.

At the same time, the Christian desires to evangelize all men, to share his faith and his experience of Christ, to pass on and show the love of Christ, professing his own faith and offering it to others with respect and love as if to say to each person: I am happy to be a Christian and I would be even happier if you were one too (1 Jn 1:1, 3-4: "What we have heard, what we have seen with our eyes, what we looked upon and touched with our hands concerns the Word of life . . . what we have seen and heard we proclaim now to you, so that you too may have fellowship with us; for our fellowship is with the Father and with his Son, Jesus Christ. We are writing this so that our joy may be complete").

Evangelization is an offer, respectful of other people's freedom, joined with an appreciation of their values and their tradition. This is how it differs from proselytism, which is animated by a spirit of conquest, of power, of superiority and at times of disdain for others, their convictions and their way of life.

Dialogue is a good thing but evangelization is a greater good. Interreligious marriage is a good thing but sacramental marriage is something better.

As Christ's grace, sacramental marriage is a greater gift than natural marriage. Still the gift can be received and lived out to a greater or lesser extent and can even be betrayed and ruined.

As Christ's grace, sacramental marriage is first of all spousal communion with him and then reciprocal communion between the partners and an openness to children, to the Church and to society. It is a particular actualization and manifestation of the nuptial covenant of Christ with the Church. Christians should ordinarily prefer it to interreligious marriage.

Interreligious marriage is also a great good, a natural human value, a gift of God the creator. It too is under the beneficent influence of Christ the Savior and his redeeming grace, which is extended in various ways to all men and to all human realities. This marriage offers opportunities for personal growth and makes it possible to build a true communion of life and love, to contribute to the dialogue among religions and to peace. An interreligious couple that succeeds can be better in certain ways than a Christian couple that is not compatible.

Still, interreligious marriage is essentially inferior to the sacrament of Matrimony since the latter is a more perfect gift of God, the offer of a deeper communion with Christ and the Church, a more brilliant reflection of the divine Trinity. Moreover, interreligious marriage presents specific difficulties for the relationship between the spouses, the upbringing of the children, relations with the families of origin and concrete membership in the respective religious communities. For this reason, the Church reserves to itself the granting of dispensations for validity and grants them very prudently.

Conjugal love is more than an emotion and reciprocal sexual gratification. It rather consists in the couple living out the truth according to God's plan which corresponds to the authentic good of the persons (a gift that is reciprocal, total, forever and open to children). It is a plan for a shared life toward which all one's energies must be focused and for which commitment is required and even sacrifice. Otherwise, we are not dealing with love but rather with the convergence of mutual selfishness and exploitation. Particularly needed is the courage to forgive in order to conquer evil with good.

In interreligious marriage the Christian partner fully respects the religious freedom of the other and does not proselytize. Still, he or she remains faithful to Christ, living intensely his or her personal relationship with him and not hiding it. He or she rather seeks to make the love and presence of Christ present and manifest to the other partner and the children.

Educating people with a strong and open Christian identity to be able to live out interreligious marriage and to live peacefully in a pluralistic society becomes a very delicate, long and difficult journey. Doctrinal clarity is needed along with a practical exercise of life, attentive discernment and frequent confirmations.

Training to live as Christians in a situation of religious pluralism in society and occasionally in the family must begin with children and adolescents and proceed to young people and engaged couples, continuing with the partners after the marriage, especially couples who have chosen interreligious marriage. In this regard, there needs to be intelligent and conscientious collaboration among parishes, associations, schools, universities and the media.

The main objective of Christian education is always a personal relationship with Jesus Christ, the Savior of all men and of everything human. A conscious and passionate relationship with him safeguards against religious confusion and indifference as well as closed-minded sectarianism. Christ does not destroy human values but renews them all since by bringing himself, he has brought everything new (Irenaeus of Lyons, *Adversus Haereses*, IV, 34, 1). Being a Christian is no cause for boasting but rather for joy and gratitude; it is not a reason to consider oneself better than others but rather to be more humble and more responsible.

International Congress "The Christian Family, Subject of Evangelization"*

Rome, November 25-27, 2010

Conclusions

1. *First and foremost, thanks.* To the Lord for the manifold gifts and experiences that he brings about in the Church. To all of you who have taken an active part in the Congress, with attention, mutual respect and joy. To the speakers who introduced the three days with papers rich in thought and

---

*   This text is an unofficial translation of the Italian.

pastoral experience. To all who offered their testimony with brevity, insight and passion. To my colleagues at the Pontifical Council for the Family whose supported the work as it progressed with punctual dedication and discretion.

2. The Congress centered around the *narration of experiences* and for this reason turned out to be quite unique. There was no discussion, just listening in an atmosphere of great fraternity. Everyone expressed wonder and satisfaction for the variety, the beauty, the fertility and the breadth of the experiences. Everyone has drawn from them reasons for encouragement, for inspiration and above all for praising God.

3. What emerged out of the testimonies was *the primacy of spirituality*. The first day was specifically dedicated to spirituality and it animated all the stories told on the other two days.

a.   Concrete spirituality, *sacramental in a general sense*, inasmuch as every reality (person or thing, event or situation, activity or suffering, place or time) is inhabited by God and takes its full and final meaning from him. What is offered to us is his gift and the possibility of goodness.

b.   Spirituality that is *sacramental in the specific sense*, inasmuch as every marriage, even of non-Christians, is constituted by God as a primordial sacrament, the living image of him and of his love, and inasmuch as the marriage of Christians is raised by Jesus Christ to a sacrament of the new covenant, a participation in His love for the Church. Conjugal love, a synthesis of *eros* and *agape* (desire and gift), to the degree in which it is authentic and conforms to the divine plan, contains and reveals the presence of God, explaining and in a sense makes visible in the world the God who is himself love, the perfect union of three persons (Father, Son and Holy Spirit). Thus, it is necessary to cooperate with the grace of the Holy Spirit and gradually build a beautiful relationship as a couple through trusting and sincere dialogue, the sharing of thoughts and feelings, a respectful and affectionate acceptance of the other, a commitment to the other's good even when it involves sacrifice, forgiveness for hurts inflicted by the other, and sexual encounter where bodies and interior worlds co-penetrate in a reciprocal gift and acceptance. While it responds to the fundamental need to be loved and to love that God the Creator placed in us, the covenant of love between Christian spouses is also a living sacrament of the spousal love of Christ for the Church, to the degree that it is lived out with the support of the Holy Spirit given by Christ the Savior to build up the Church.

c. *Christocentric* spirituality. For Christians, the spiritual life, which is ordinary life animated and given direction by the Holy Spirit, is essentially a personal, living relationship with the person of Jesus himself, crucified, risen and always close to us. From him comes light for the intelligence, strength for the will, love for friends and enemies, joy and consolation in favorable and in painful circumstances, the Gospel written and lived, witnessed and announced. It is the Lord Jesus who makes a "little Church" of the Christian family because he dwells in it "For where two or three are gathered together in my name, there am I in the midst of them" (Mt 18:20). It is he who loves through those who love each other; it is he who gives himself in the reciprocal self-gift of spouses and in their common self-gift to their children. And the greater the human love between spouses and for their children and for everyone, the more intense is his presence. In the good and beautiful atmosphere that reigns in the family, something of him and of his live becomes tangible and visible. The conjugal act itself, to the degree that it is an expression of authentic love, takes on a sacramental dimension, since it is God's gift and a foretaste of eternal intimacy with him; it becomes an encounter with the infinite Mystery, mediated by the mystery of the human persons and their encounter.

d. *Centrality of the Eucharist.* During the Congress this was constantly emphasized—and it could hardly have been otherwise—because it derives directly from the centrality of Christ. The Eucharist is the nuptial covenant and the foretaste of the eternal wedding banquet of Christ with the Church, the sacramental representation of the total self-gift by which Christ the Bridegroom gives life to his bride, the Church, and joins himself to her. Christian marriage finds its indispensable support in the Church because the Lord Jesus constantly shares his spousal love afresh with the married couple and enables them to love each other as he loves the Church, even to love with his own love for the Church. That is why there is no Christian family without attendance at Mass, at least on Sundays. As for the request for a video to help present the feasts of the liturgical year for children in a family context, it seems appropriate for the Pontifical Council for the Family simply to encourage its production by the Episcopal Conferences.

e. *Family prayer.* Its importance was made clear by so many testimonies. And rightly so, since "prayer is not everything but everything begins with prayer." The forms suggested were quite varied: Liturgy of the Hours, family shrines, gathering in every room of the house, etc. It is beautiful to see that pride of place is given to prayerful listening to the

Word of God in order to live it and that people are trying to create a family style. The Pontifical Council for the Family can stimulate the bishops and Episcopal Conferences to offer appropriate aids for domestic prayer as well.

4. *The education of children.* I can only summarize two points out of the many beautiful things that were said.

a. The greatest gift that parents can give their children is to show them that they really love each other. *The reciprocal love between parents* is even more important than the love of each of them for the children. It is through this reciprocal love above all that children learn how to love.

b. *Family catechesis* in cooperation with the parish: handing on the faith to children joyfully even by means of games; preparation for First Holy Communion; catechesis for adolescents after Confirmation. Evangelization is not a one-way street but rather reciprocal between parents and children, between older and younger siblings, between grandparents and grandchildren.

5. It emerged clearly from a great number of testimonies that the family's participation in a *small community of families* is considered practically necessary in a cultural and social context of individualism and privatization such as exists today. Couples need to see other couples who love each other; they need to become part of a network of spirituality, friendship, socializing, mutual help (valuable especially where raising children is concerned). Such small communities (for example, periodic neighborhood gatherings, participation in groups, workshops, movements and associations) should in turn participate in the life of the parish, forming it as a community of communities. In response to the objection of too many responsibilities, you have said that by making a common commitment for others, the family becomes more united, it grows and is strengthened, since it is in giving that we receive. In response to the fear expressed for the risk of cultivating exclusive elites, it was shown that the solution lies in being open to evangelization (the few at the service of the many to bring and show the love of Christ to everyone), while restricting ourselves to bringing a bare minimum to everyone equally ends up impoverishing and hurting everyone. Pastoral practice needs to balance holiness and mercy together in imitation of Jesus, the Holy One of God and the friend of sinners.

6. One happy fact confirmed at this Congress has been the fraternal collaboration of *ecclesial movements* and their involvement in territorial pastoral

ministry at the diocesan and parochial levels in accordance with the request made by John Paul II in 1998. I hope that this practice of ecclesial communion will develop even further as a result of this Congress.

7. Regarding *preparation for marriage*, there were insistent requests in various speeches that it be truly serious, not just theoretical but also practical, as an exercise in Christian living and as a discovery of the meaning and beauty of Christian marriage. In this regard, the Pontifical Commission for the Family is preparing the *Vademecum* requested by the Holy Father, which will probably offer different formats according to the needs and the availability of the engaged couples and the pastoral resources of each ecclesial community, taking into account the extreme diversity of formats used until now (from a single day to two years of preparation). It will consider not only the "short term" and "immediate" formation of engaged couples but also the education of children, adolescents and young adults in the authentic love into which sexuality must be integrated.

8. The need for *mentoring after marriage* was also made very clear in the Congress. This is to be accomplished especially through gatherings and small communities of families in addition to personalized relationships (visits, conversations, consultations, etc.). The Pontifical Council for the Family will study the possibility of extending the *Vademecum* beyond the wedding.

9. The problem of being close to *Christians in irregular* and sometimes humanly irresolvable *situations* (for example, divorced and remarried persons) was also raised. We need to give them signs of friendship so that they feel loved by the Church and by God. But they need to be told clearly that their cohabitation is objectively contrary to the Gospel and the teaching of the Magisterium and that their visible communion with the Church is incomplete and so they cannot be admitted to Eucharistic communion or receive sacramental absolution. Still they must be invited to active participation in the life of the Church (Sunday Mass, catechetical, charitable, cultural, recreational and social activities). Above all they must be accompanied so that they can find the mercy of God by "other ways" than the ordinary way of the sacraments (cfr. John Paul II, *Reconciliatio et Poenitentia*, no. 34): humility so as not to delude themselves with the pretext of determining in conscience what is good and what is evil (something quite different than recognizing good and evil); persevering prayer in order to make progress in knowing and doing God's will; commitment to begin to do immediately the good they can do even with sacrifice (education of children, labor, works of charity, etc.); reflection, in order to grow in understanding the meaning and value of the moral norms and the teaching of the Church on marriage; and trust in divine mercy, which can

free us from evil and lead us to salvation. Present these suggestions as ways on which to travel and not as stopping points in which to get comfortable with presumptuous and deceptive security.

10. Regarding evangelization through *involvement in society* I will restrict myself to recalling three settings:

    a.   Reciprocal aid among families in the realm of education of children.

    b.   Charitable work in the style typical of families who do not merely give something or offer some service but tend to share their everyday life (hospitality, foster care, adoption).

    c.   Cultural and political activity for a society that is more family-friendly, combating the statist mentality (derived from socialism, Marx, Engels) and the individualist mentality (derived from liberalism) that are converging today to fuel privatization and the break-up of the family.

        The speakers have emphasized how these three settings are important for family associations involved in civic life.

11. Finally the speakers have enabled us to recognize how valid experiences of evangelization spread rapidly. So we can hope that the new process of communication encouraged and supported by the Pontifical Council for the Family will be fruitful and contribute to the growth of a mindset of encounter with others and a practice of communion in pastoral activity. This Congress was intended to be the official inauguration of that process which will be continued over time. I think we are off to a good start. Thank you.

Twentieth Plenary Assembly of the Pontifical Council for the Family[*]

Rome, November 29-December 1, 2011

Conclusions

1. Thanks to all of you who have taken part in the work of this assembly with attention, diligence and fraternal congeniality. Special thanks to the speakers at the conferences and round tables.

---

[*]   This text is an unofficial translation of the Italian.

I think we now know much more about the impact of *Familiaris Consortio* in Church and civic circles and the situation of the family in the world today.

Regarding the effects of *Familiaris Consortio* in the pastoral sphere, the speakers have emphasized: the publication of the national directory of pastoral ministry to families in many countries, the establishment of pastoral commissions at the diocesan and parochial levels, the creation of Orientation Centers for Families and other services for families, the development of numerous Family Movements of spirituality and the apostolate, the rising number of married couples involved in evangelization and in pastoral ministry to families, at times with more enthusiasm than the priests themselves (the annual 16 percent increase of Catholics in Asia is said to be mostly due to these couples). It appears that this gradual and continual pastoral ministry of families that was proposed in *Familiaris Consortio* is taking shape in many countries: long-term, short-term and immediate preparation for marriage, communal formation after marriage (meetings, groups, little communities, spiritual retreats) and individual formation (counseling, home visits, etc.).

Regarding the effects of *Familiaris Consortio* in the civil sphere, the compelling experiences of family associations, forums, focus groups, raising awareness through the internet, the many congresses, conventions and days have been recalled. The importance of statistical data to influence public opinion was also emphasized, even if the large media outlets are staging a conspiracy of silence regarding sociological research that supports respect for human life and the conventional family.

As regards the crisis of the family in the world, three general tendencies were noted which have been spread practically everywhere despite the different value ascribed to the family in the various cultures: a decline in marriages and marriages being solemnized at a later age; increases in divorce, cohabitation, single parent families as a matter of choice, choosing to be single, homosexual relationships and cohabitation; a decline in births and, consequently, an aging population and the future of whole peoples at risk; an increase in abortions, artificial procreation and births outside of marriage.

A number of causes were suggested as explanations for such a situation: the reliability of contraception which allows sexual relations to be easily separated from procreation and love; the search for personal self-actualization through work and careers, individualism; the culture of science; subjectivism and relativism in ethics; and the secular mentality that marginalizes God from people's lives.

Many have said that the crisis must not be suffered with resignation but opposed with trust, decisiveness, intelligence and a spirit of initiative. With work, it is possible to obtain good results. The facts bear this out: the bountiful fruits produced by *Familiaris Consortio*; the positive attitude of many young people toward the family and life; the success of important political and social initiatives (for example, in the USA, thirty-one states have blocked so-called homosexual marriage in their legal systems; in Mexico, eighteen states have done the same thing against abortion; in the European Union the proposal to recognize the right to abortion was rejected; in Honduras, civil marriage in City Hall—a prerequisite for religious marriage in that country—was granted free of cost on certain days).

Some meaningful guidelines for pastoral and civic engagement emerged from of the work of the Plenary Assembly.

First of all, we need to be aware that the passage from a Church of tradition to a Church of conversion is underway: a personal encounter with Jesus Christ and a conscious choice of faith; a living relationship and an earnest engagement with the Lord; spirituality understood as the joy of being loved by him and the desire to love even to the point of sacrifice; missionary responsibility for evangelization and a commitment to the advancement of humanity. Even if evil seems to have the upper hand in the world, we need to maintain a firm truest because the Lord loves the world and wants to save it; only he knows the people's hearts and measures their responsibility. Even when it appears that the Church is becoming a minority among many peoples, we must firmly believe that the People of God still constitutes the strongest seed for unity, hope and salvation even when it is reduced to a "small flock, [it] is nonetheless a lasting and sure seed of unity, hope and salvation for the whole human race. Established by Christ as a communion of life, charity and truth, it is also used by Him as an instrument for the redemption of all, and is sent forth into the whole world as the light of the world and the salt of the earth (Lumen Gentium, no. 9); her mission remains universal and her cooperation with Christ the Savior continues to be effective for the eternal salvation and the historical development of all men, both Christian and non-Christian.

From this perspective the priority for pastoral ministry is to promote a "pedagogy of holiness" understood as a high standard of ordinary Christian life and as a missionary responsibility as John Paul II indicated at the conclusion of the great jubilee of 2000 (cfr. Novo Millennio Ineunte, no. 31).

In this regard, the ecclesial movements and new communities constitute a sign of the times, a gift of the Holy Spirit for our time, "creative minorities" for the new evangelization.

A core group of exemplary families needs to be cultivated in the parishes, not as elitist, closed and self-serving groups but as little communities that can be the yeast in the dough, according to the criterion "the few for the many." Such families radiate the Gospel by their witness and spread it by their conversation, their proclamation and their actions. Some of them, with specific training, could become pastoral agents to help lead the main events of pastoral care to families: long-term, proximate and immediate preparation for married life, formation for couples after marriage, initiatives to attract non-practicing and non-believing persons, and pastoral support for wounded families.

On the civil side, there is a need to stimulate and increase the cultural and political action of Christian laypeople; it is up to them, rather than to pastors, to stand at the forefront in promoting families and defending human life. It is a matter of spreading and improving the many good things that are already being done: Family Associations, the Forum of Associations, Focus Groups, an internet presence, congresses, conventions, special days, education in the schools, the use of surveys and statistical data to raise public awareness, the engagement of Catholic universities in pursuing anthropological, philosophical, psychological, biological, sociological and legal studies on today's hot button issues and publishing the results. A staunch defense is particularly urgent for: the right of health care workers to conscientious objection to abortion and euthanasia; the right to freedom of thought regarding an ethical judgment about homosexual behavior; the right of children to a normal family and to the protection that only parents in the stable union of marriage can ensure; the right of the family, based on the marriage of one man and one woman, not to be equated with other forms of cohabitation; the right of parents to freedom of education and, consequently, to a choice of schools and educational programs; the right to fair taxation for families with children.

3. Putting together a few and proposals made over these days, the Pontifical Council for the Family is taking on a few specific commitments.

The members and consultors will promote awareness in their own countries of *Familiaris Consortio* and of preparations for the VII World Meeting in Milan. They will send a report to Rome three times a year with news of events, information about experiences and best practices and documents.

Together with the Archdiocese of Milan, the dicastery will assume responsibility for organizing the World Meeting of 2012 and will begin to prepare for the 2015 Meeting, presenting to the Holy Father some suggestions for host cities and some proposals for topics. The dicastery will move ahead with the preparation of the *Vademecum* for Christian marriage. It will take advantage of the *ad limina* visits and other opportunities to solicit episcopal conferences regarding the following possible initiatives: a revision of the Directory for the pastoral care of the family, editing a catechism for families as *Familiaris Consortio* suggested; production of a video on the liturgical year to explain the feast days to children in a family setting; offering aids for prayer at home; formation of the clergy in pastoral care to families; formation of couples willing to commit themselves to serve as pastoral agents; formation of married couples in responsible procreation and the use of natural methods to regulate births.

In addition, the dicastery will take charge of organizing a congress of marital spirituality by 2013, also in light of the center of spirituality for families that will shortly be constructed in Nazareth.

There is no new evangelization without the Christian family: this was the strong assertion of Pope Benedict XVI in his address to the Assembly. This statement has reechoed among us repeatedly in the course of our work. I am pleased to make it the last word of my remarks.

INDEX

INDEX

A

Aachen, Germany, International Charlemagne Prize awarded to, 56

Abadamloora, Lucas, 267

abandoned children, 474, 584–85

abortion. *See also* culture of life; embryos; fetuses; *entries at* pro-life; right to life

in Africa, 585–86

agencies promoting, 378, 586

chemical, 170, 262

Christian response to those involved in, 187–89, 378–79, 434

conscientious objection to, 652 note 57

as defined in *Code of Canon Law*, 651 note 46

in Europe, 28–29

Guatemala, constitutional protection of life in, 74

interception and contragestation, 262, 638–39

Italian pro-life movement, address of Benedict XVI to members of, 433–35

in Kenya, 102

as maternal health care, 476

pharmacists and, 371–72

post-abortion syndrome, 181–83

procured, 652–55

reduction of embryos as, 637

to save life of mother, 654

social and pastoral initiatives combating, 527, 553–54

"therapeutic," 182, 654

vaccines derived from cells of aborted fetuses, 681–87

Vatican Radio interview with Benedict XVI on, 285–86

Abraham, 77, 149, 152, 473–74, 617

abuse

of alcohol, 13, 518, 586, 791, 806

of children, 75–76, 422–23, 584–85

domestic abuse of women, 411

of drugs, 13, 35, 43, 80, 89, 107, 108, 260, 262, 273, 362, 371, 420, 518, 583, 586, 595, 791, 802, 817

sexual abuse of children, 422–23, 585

sexual violence against women, 476

World Conference of Women Parliamentarians for the Protection of Children and Young Persons, 87–88

Ad Gentes, 339, 591, 813

Adam, 183, 195, 252–53, 614, 666, 670

adoption

by homosexuals, 146

by infertile couples, 633

adultery, 233, 252, 318, 500, 617, 665, 806, 819, 820

advertising, 57

advocates, 741–44

Aemilia, St., 135

Aetatis Novae, 112, 309, 310

G

H

J

O

W